FINDING EARLY CONNECTICUT VITAL RECORDS: THE BARBOUR INDEX AND BEYOND

Finding Early Connecticut Vital Records: The Barbour Index and Beyond

Linda MacLachlan

CLEARFIELD

Printed for Clearfield Company by
Genealogical Publishing Company
2019

ISBN 978-0-8063-5895-6

Linda MacLachlan
Springfield, Virginia 22151
BarbourIndex143@gmail.com
www.ConnecticutGenealogists.com
Facebook page: Barbour Index

CONTENTS

ILLUSTRATIONS

*Cover and Frontispiece reprinted with the permission of the Connecticut State Library

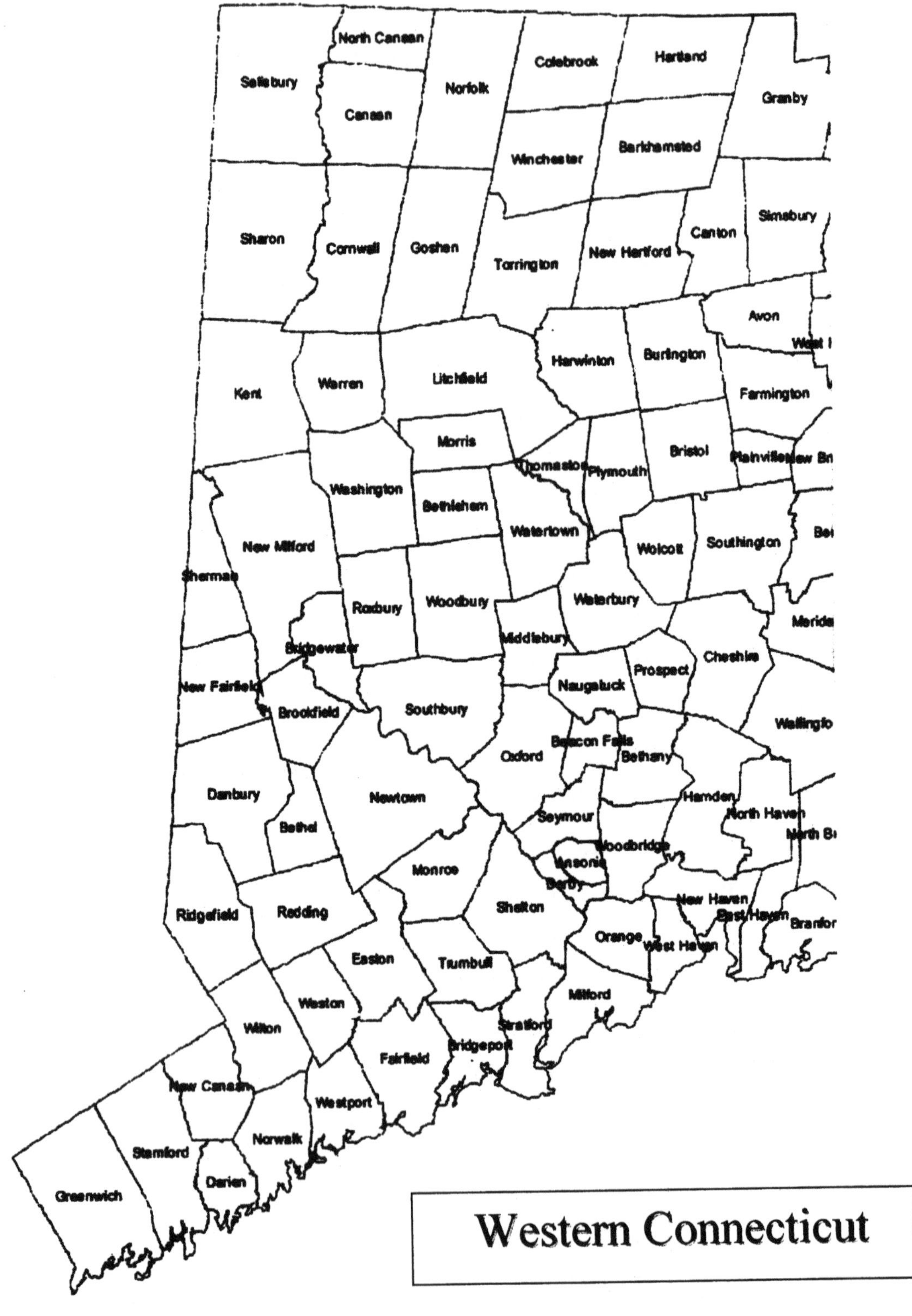

Western Connecticut

Eastern Connecticut

FINDING EARLY CONNECTICUT VITAL RECORDS:

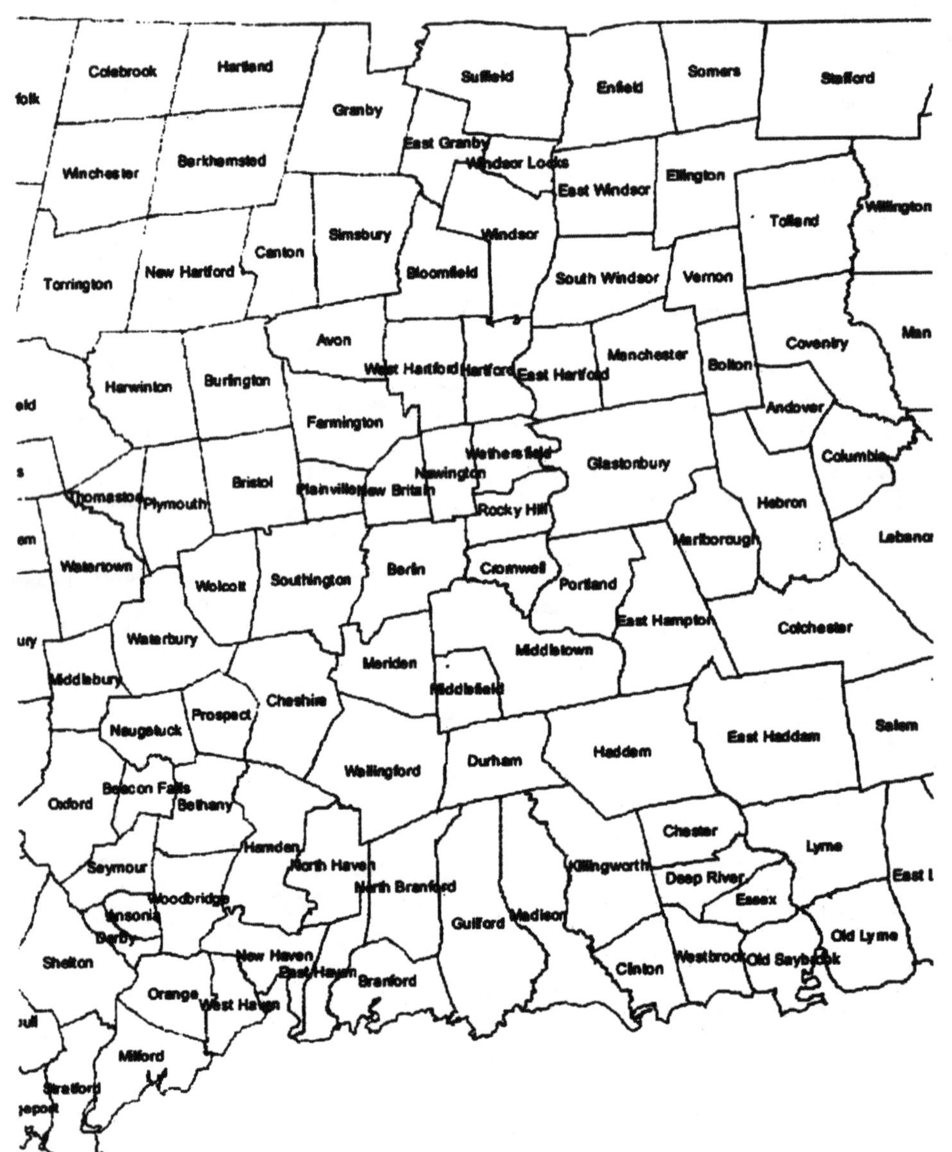

Connecticut River Valley

ACKNOWLEDGEMENTS

I would like to thank all the staff of the Connecticut State Library for their patient support and assistance to all patrons, and especially Mel Smith and Jeanne Sherman for their suggestions and encouragement.

For more than a decade my Family History Center, New England Study Group and Family History Writing group colleagues, have provided help without which this book would never have been completed. Thank you for your guidance, your use of the editor's red pen...

And special thanks go to David Lisbeth and Sassy Mohan for their technical assistance and to my family for their patience.

David Lisbeth dlisbeth@liberty.edu

INTRODUCTION

How to Use This Book

Every genealogist's search for pre-Civil War Connecticut vital records should begin with the Barbour Index created by Lucius B. Barbour, Connecticut Examiner of Public Records from 1922 to 1934.[1] Resist the temptation to settle for the version of the "Barbour Collection of Connecticut Town Records" posted on *Ancestry.com.* As of 2019, it includes Barbour's vital records from only 118 of the 149 Connecticut towns collecting them between 1640 and 1850.[2] The 55 volume Barbour Collection published by the Genealogical Publishing Company (GPC edition) which *Ancestry.com* is imaging includes nineteen additional towns for a total of 137.[3] The source the GPC edition actually copied is now online at two websites.[4] The Barbour Index is not only the source of all these records but also includes six additional towns and abstractions of many private record compilations at the Connecticut State Library (CSL).[5]

---

1 See *https://libguides.ctstatelibrary.org/hg/genealogyindexes/Barbour.* All websites cited herein were accessible on August 1, 2019.

2 Connecticut Town Marriage/Birth/Death Records, pre 1870 (Barbour Collection) [database on-line] Provo UT: Ancestry.com Operations Inc, 2006. The 118 towns from these volumes which are imaged online in 2019 are Andover, Ashford, Avon, Barkhamsted, Berlin, Bethany, Bethlehem, Bloomfield, Bozrah, Branford, Bridgeport, Bristol, Brookfield, Brooklyn, Burlington, Canaan, Canterbury, Canton, Cheshire, Chester, Clinton, Colchester, Colebrook, Columbia, Cornwall, Danbury, Darien, Derby, Durham, East Haddam, East Hampton, East Hartford, East Haven, East Lyme, East Windsor, Eastford, Ellington, Fairfield, Farmington, Franklin, Glastonbury, Goshen, Granby, Greenwich, Griswold, Groton, Guilford, Haddam, Hamden, Hampton, Hartford, Hartland, Harwinton, Hebron, Huntington, Kent, Killingly, Killingworth, Lebanon, Ledyard, Lisbon, Litchfield, Lyme, Madison, Manchester, Marlborough, Meriden, Middlebury, Middletown, Milford, Monroe, Montville, Naugatuck, New London, New Milford, Newtown, Norfolk, North Branford, North Haven, North Stonington, Norwalk, Orange, Oxford, Plainfield, Plymouth, Pomfret, Preston, Saybrook, Sharon, Somers, South Windsor, Southbury, Southington, Stafford, Stamford, Sterling, Stonington, Stratford, Thompson, Tolland, Torrington, Union, Voluntown, Warren, Washington, Waterbury, Waterford, Watertown, Westbrook, Weston, Westport, Willington, Wilton, Winchester, Windham, Wolcott, Woodbury, and Woodstock (1847–1866 records only). The website claims these images contain 590,009 entries. See discussion at note. 49 below.

3 Lorraine Cook White, general editor, *Barbour Collection of Connecticut Town Vital Records,* 55 vols. (Baltimore, Genealogical Publishing Company (GPC): 1995 *et seq.*). These 55 volumes include all the digitized images referenced in note 1 above plus Chaplin, New Canaan, New Hartford, Norwich (1847–1851 records only), Portland, Prospect, Redding, Ridgefield, Rocky Hill, Roxbury, Salem, Salisbury, Sherman, Simsbury, Suffield, Wallingford, Wethersfield, Windsor, and Woodbridge. .

4 GPC copies Barbour's own typescript volumes from CSL or New England Historic Genealogical Society (NEHGS), which are on Family History Library (FHL) of Salt Lake City (SLC)'s microfilms (films) 2,967 through 2,983. They are imaged online at NEHGS' *AmericanAncestors.org.* and *FamilySearch .org.* See further discussion at p. 11 below

5 Lucius Barnes Barbour, "Barbour Collection of Connecticut Vital Records prior to 1850" (card file, n.d., Connecticut State Library (CSL), Hartford). See also, FHL films 2,887 through 2,966 and 2,984). This index includes everything in GPC's 55 volumes plus the towns of Bolton, Coventry, Enfield, Vernon, Mansfield, and New Haven, the 1659–1848 records of Norwich, the 1690–1848 records of Woodstock, and many other original compilations of Connecticut vital records possessed by CSL. This resource includes well over a million entries. See discussion at pp. 3-5 below and "Barbour Collection," *https://libguides.ctstatelibrary.org/hg/genealogyindexes/Barbour.*

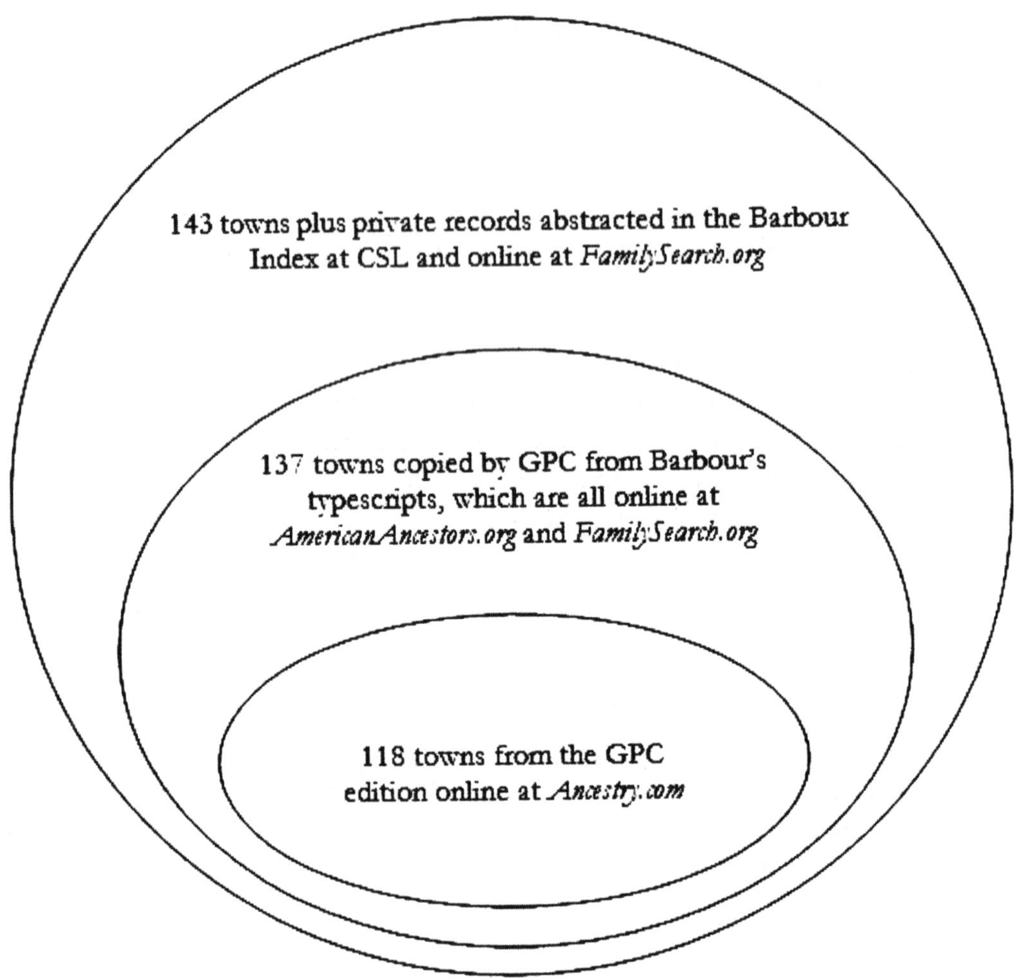

Figure 1: Diagram of towns included in various Barbour Collections

This book goes beyond the Barbour Index by adding six more towns to create a bibliography for all 149 Connecticut towns incorporated by 1850. It also provides:

1. Full source citations to virtually all the sources Barbour abstracted, **highlighting those noticeably incomplete or inaccurate.**
2. Hundreds of town vital records books, manuscripts and articles not abstracted by Barbour (**all highlighted in bold face**);
3. Thousands of additional sources for early births, deaths and marriages in Connecticut.[6]

You can find family records in the Barbour Index without knowing the town that created them[7] or how the surname is spelled or misspelled in that record.[8] If you find your record, your next step should be to verify it by examining the original source cited herein.[9]

---

[6] See discussion at p. 15 below.

[7] In Connecticut a newly incorporated town's first clerk frequently began by recording vital statistics reported by the town's founding families without regard to where those events actually occurred.

[8] Barbour indexed all spellings of a surname under its most common spelling, noting similar surnames not included in the grouping. See e.g., photograph at p. 10 below.

Whether or not the Barbour Index identifies the record you seek, this book will direct you to additional print and microfilmed sources,[10] including six more towns not in the Barbour Index which were also collecting vital records by 1850:[11]

1. Look under your town's **VITAL RECORDS** for citations to vital records **missed** or **misreported** by Barbour.[12]
2. Find citations to your town's **CHURCH RECORDS**.
3. Find citations to the best of your town's **CEMETERY TRANSCRIPTIONS**.
4. Check out **OTHER NOTEWORTHY SOURCES** listed under your town and those listed at the end of this introduction as **STATEWIDE AND COUNTY-WIDE COMPILATIONS**.[13]

What is the Barbour Index?

The original Barbour Index features a set of alphabetized slips in file drawers at CSL in Hartford [14] — one for each Connecticut birth or death and two for each marriage to about 1850. For this project Lucius B. Barbour commissioned knowledgeable agents to go to 135 Connecticut towns and abstract all the birth, marriage, and death records in what they judged to be all the earliest extant town records.

For two additional towns (Norwich and Woodstock) abstractions were commissioned only for more recent vital records not covered by published books abstracting their earlier records,[15] but slips were prepared for the Barbour Index covering both the newly abstracted records and the vital records in the publications. For the other six towns (Bolton, Coventry, Enfield, Mansfield, New Haven, and Vernon) the original vital records were not abstracted all. Instead a recent publication of each town's records was abstracted and indexed.[16] Thus, slips for the records of Bolton, Coventry, Enfield,

---

[9] The GPC edition and *Ancestry.com*, specifies Barbour citation of the page where each record is to be found, but not the book in which that page may be found. The full source citation for virtually all of Barbour's abstraction are published in this book.

[10] A town clerk's vital record may be official but it derives from another source which may be more accurately or fully reported elsewhere.

[11] The additional towns are Cromwell, Easton, New Britain, New Fairfield, Seymour , and Trumbull, Connecticut.

[12] Over 300 collections of omitted vital records are cited herein, 81% of which have been filmed by FHL and 89% of which are at CSL.

[13] See discussion at pp. 17–21 below.

[14] Lucius Barnes Barbour, "Barbour Collection of Connecticut Vital Records prior to 1850" (card file, n.d., CSL, Hartford). See also, FHL films 2,887 through 2,966 and 2,984.

[15] Society of Colonial Wars in the State of Connecticut (SCWC), *Vital Records of Norwich, 1659–1848* (Hartford: Society of Colonial Wars in Connecticut, 1913); Woodstock, *Vital Records of Woodstock 1686–1854* (Hartford: Case, Lockwood & Brainard, 1914).

[16] These books are Connecticut Historical Society (CHS), *Vital Records of Bolton to 1854 and Vernon to 1852* (Hartford: CHS, 1909); Susan W. Dimock, *Births, Marriages, Baptisms, and Deaths: From the Records of the Town and Churches in Coventry, Connecticut, 1711–1844* (New York: Baker & Taylor Company, 1897); Francis Olcott Allen, *History of Enfield, Connecticut: Compiled From All the Public Records of the Town Known to Exist, Covering From the Beginning to 1850, Together with the Graveyard Inscriptions and those Hartford, Northampton and Springfield Records Which Refer to the People of Enfield,* 3 vols. (Lancaster, PA: Wickersham Printing, 1900); Susan W. Dimock, *Births, Baptisms, Marriages and Deaths From the Records of the Town and Churches in Mansfield, Connecticut, 1703–1850* (New York: Baker & Taylor Company, 1898); and Order of the Founders and

Figure 2: Barbour Index at the Connecticut State Library[17]

Mansfield, New Haven, and Vernon — and for the earlier records of Norwich and Woodstock — were interfiled with those from Barbour's 137 abstractions to create what he envisaged as a slip index covering all of the early state vital records. These slips from eight published or partly published town record compilations were not all that Barbour added to the Barbour Index at CSL. He also abstracted and interfiled vital records from many typescripts at CSL compiling vital statistics. These slips cite "private records" as their source and are referenced in Appendix A as well as under applicable town(s).[18]

Patriots of America (OFPA), *Vital Records of New Haven, 1649–1850*, 2 vols. (Hartford: Connecticut Society of the OFPA, 1917–1924).

17 CSL has long employed the term "Barbour Collection" as including both Barbour's statewide index and his town volumes. Given the online dissemination of the information by Town and the GPCF's erroneous claim that Barbour's index is copied from his volumes, (rather than vice versa) it seems appropriate to highlight the index by its own name.

18 These compilations include "N. Coventry Private Records," "Durham Deaths Private Records 1791–1805," "Granby Private Records [of Mrs. A.C. Green]," and "Records of Andrew Griswold, J.P., Lyme, 1784–1810," "Middletown Christ Church Private Records [of] Rev. Samuel F. Jarvis," "New Haven Private Records [by Rev. Jarvis]," "Suffield Private Records [from the] Kent Library," "Woodstock Private Records [from the] Brown Diary, See Figure 4 below at page 10 for an example. Thousand of slips abstracting private records from Wethersfield, New Haven, Madison, Rocky Hill,

The information in each of Barbour's 137 abstractions — but not in the eight similarly indexed books or the private records at CSL for which slips were created and interfiled[19] — was retyped by Barbour's staff in alphabetical order and bound into individual volumes also available at the CSL.[20] These typescripts are the source of the widely available GPC edition of Barbour's work discussed below under "Accessing the Barbour Index." The Barbour Index, however, is clearly more extensive and primary than the Barbour Collection of vital records by town.

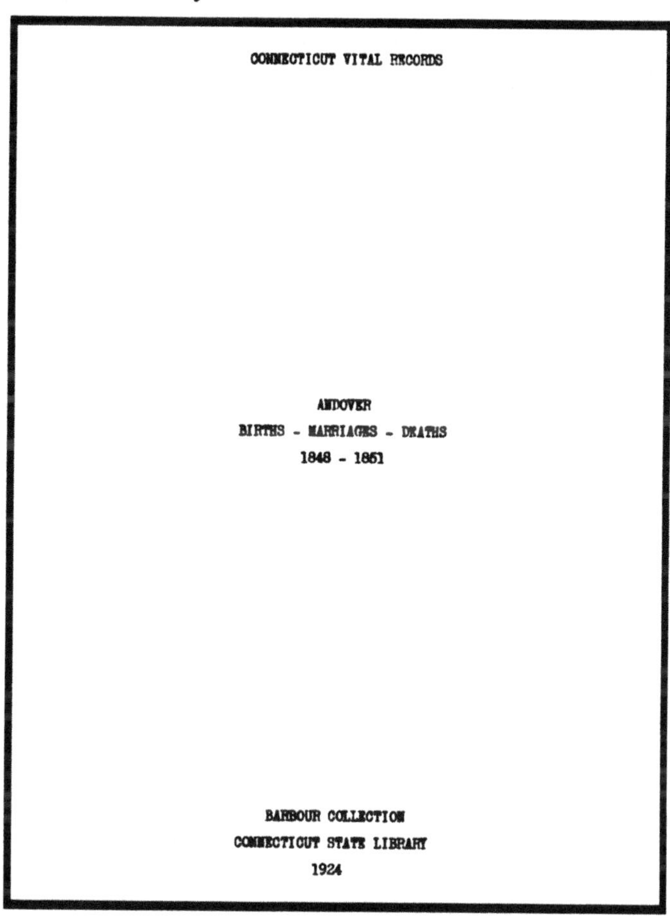

CONNECTICUT VITAL RECORDS

ANDOVER
BIRTHS - MARRIAGES - DEATHS
1848 - 1851

BARBOUR COLLECTION
CONNECTICUT STATE LIBRARY
1924

Figure 3: First title page of typescript Barbour Collection at CSL[21]

Montville, Brooklyn, Wallingford, North Stonington, East Guilford, Bridgewater and Hebron also remain in separate file drawers at CSL, See Appendix C. Harlan R. Jessup, "The Barbour Collection – What's In It and What's Not," footnote 2, online article at *American Ancestors,org.*

19 For Brooklyn, Clinton, Ellington, Preston and Woodstock private record collections at CSL were appended to Barbour's typescript volumes and indexed as "public records."

20 Lucius Barnes Barbour, "Barbour Collection of Connecticut Vital Records prior to 1850," (bound typescripts) 137 vols. (CSL, Hartford: 1909–1929). These 139 volumes (Hartford and Middletown occupy two volumes each), with their all-important introductions, are available on 27 rolls of microfilm, (FHL films 2,967–2,983). These introductions contradict the introductions written by GPC for its 55 volumes, which incorrectly identify the town lists as Barbour's original sources. Very few typographical errors were made retyping all of Barbour's slips. All of Barbour's typescripts may be viewed at NEHGS or online at *AmericanAncestors.org* and *FamilySearch.org*.

21 Lucius B. Barbour: *Connecticut Vital Records: Andover 1848–1851* (Hartford: CSL, 1924)) title page (FHL film 2,967).

Completeness.

How completely does the Barbour Index (or the 143-town combination of town volumes plus the eight additional books) cover all extant pre-1850 Connecticut vital records? While Barbour identifies a date range in each of the 137 town volumes created at his direction, the date range provided herein for each town is the actual date range of all the records abstracted in that town. Several town abstractions stop short of 1850.[22] In the Colebrook volume, for example, the records stop in 1837, and appear quite incomplete after Barbour's specified end date of 1810. Many town vital records books are not consecutive and/or coextensive for marriages, births and deaths so any date range may conceal some gaps in the town records.[23]

In addition, most of Barbour's abstractions appear to begin later than the town's incorporation date, and often this discrepancy is significant. For example, Betty Jean Morrison, in her useful reference, *Connecting to Connecticut*,[24] reports vital records of some towns as beginning earlier than Barbour has specified.[25] The online catalog of the Family History Library (FHL)[26] describes the vital records of many of the towns they have filmed as beginning earlier than the dates Barbour indicated.[27]

Another problem with the completeness of the Barbour Index is that there appear to have been more than 143 Connecticut towns collecting vital records by 1850. The online catalog of the New England Historic Genealogical Society (NEHGS)[28] suggests there were 160 towns eligible to be indexed by Barbour, but perhaps they were referring to the number of towns when Barbour's project commenced.[29] Eight towns not in Barbour are

---

22 See, e.g., Bloomfield, Colebrook, Coventry, Griswold, Hartland, Stratford, and Woodbridge.

23 For example, Connecticut marriage records are regulated much earlier and more closely than other vital records. For a transcription of all pre-1850 Connecticut vital records statutes see Connecticut Historical Society's (CHS) *Vital Records of Bolton to 1854 and Vernon to 1852* (Hartford: CHS, 1909) pp. ix–xvii.

24 Betty Jean Morrison, *Connecting to Connecticut* (East Hartford: Connecticut Society of Genealogists (CSG), 1995).

25 Towns which Morrison reports with vital records predating Barbour's abstraction include: Bolton, Bozrah, Chatham/East Hampton, Cheshire, Derby, East Hartford, East Windsor, Ellington, Enfield, Harwinton, Killingly, Killingworth, Lyme, Madison, New Hartford, New Milford, Newtown, Norwalk, Plainfield, Salem, Saybrook, Simsbury, Sterling, Suffield, Westbrook, Winchester, Windsor, Wolcott, and Woodstock.

26 See *FamilySearch.org*'s "Catalog."

27 Towns which FHL catalogs as having vital records predating Barbour include: Bloomfield, Bolton, Canterbury, Canton, Chatham/East Hampton, Clinton, Darien, East Haddam, East Hartford, East Windsor, Ellington, Enfield, Franklin, Glastonbury, Griswold, Groton, Haddam, Huntington, Killingly, Killingworth, Lisbon, Litchfield, Madison, Mansfield, Meriden, Middlebury, Middletown, Montville, New Canaan, New Hartford, New Milford, Norfolk, North Branford, North Haven, North Stonington, Orange, Oxford, Plainfield, Plymouth, Pomfret, Portland, Preston, Prospect, Redding, Ridgefield, Rocky Hill, Salem, Salisbury, Sharon, Sherman, Simsbury, Southbury, South Windsor, Stafford, Sterling, Suffield, Thompson, Tolland, Union, Vernon, Warren, Washington, Waterbury, Waterford, Watertown, Weston, Wolcott, and Woodstock.

28 See *AmericanAncestors.org*'s Library and Special Collections.

29 Quoting from the NEHGS online catalog description of their 14 linear feet of Barbour's manuscripts: "Typescript transcription of vital records for 137 of 160 towns in Connecticut copied from 1918 to 1928. Each town is bound in one volume except for Hartford and Middletown which are in two

listed as separate entities in the 1850 census.[30] Of these, only Connecticut officially recognized only New Britain, New Fairfield, Seymour and Trumbull by 1850.[31]

Many unincorporated or later-incorporated places not listed in the Barbour Index have pre-1851 church records and/or other transcriptions or compilations listed under their place name in FHL's catalog.[32] Of those, however, FHL catalogs only Cromwell, New Britain, Seymour and Trumbull as having vital records transcribed by their own town clerk by 1850. The New Fairfield vital records were destroyed by fire in 1868[33] and nonexistent at the time of Barbour's abstractions. Easton was only recently found to possess pre-1850 vital records.[34]

This book includes 149 towns: Barbour's 143 plus Cromwell, Easton, New Britain, New Fairfield, Seymour and Trumbull — towns Barbour presumably would have abstracted had he known of pre-1850 vital records there. Vital records substitutes and equivalents listed by FHL for the other Connecticut places populated but unincorporated in 1850 are included in this book within the bibliographies for their respective parent towns.[35]

The FHL catalog also lists a surprising number of microfilms of early Connecticut vital records from at least 96 towns which the Barbour Index does not abstract, most

---

volumes. Each volume is an alphabetical list of vital events for that town. The listings start at or near the founding of the town and come down to the present stopping between 1846 and 1868, and four cases between 1810 and 1840. Eighteen towns in the Barbour Index had prior publications of their vital records: Bolton, Coventry, East Granby, Granby*, Lyme*, Mansfield, Middlebury*, New Haven, Norwich, Salisbury*, Saybrook, Seymour, Simsbury*, Suffield*, Vernon, Windham*, and Woodstock. The eight marked with an asterisk (*) are also in Barbour Volumes. Norwich and Woodstock have continuations transcribed as volumes."

30 The 1850 census reports: East Bridgeport (population 168), Easton (population 1,432), Essex (population 994), Mystic Groton (population 89 sailors on a ship in port), New Britain (population 2,992), New Fairfield (population 897), Seymour (population 1,677), and Trumbull (population 1,309).

31 Connecticut Secretary of State, "*Connecticut Towns In the Order of Their Establishment; With the Origin of Their Names*," online at *https://portal.ct.gov/SOTS/Register-Manual/Section-VII/Connecticut-Towns-in-the-Order-of-their-Establishment.*

32 Thus records cataloged under Abington, Ansonia, Bashan, Beacon Falls, Bethel, Bridgewater, Canton Center, Centerbrook, Centerville, Cos Cob, Danielson, East Berlin, East Glastonbury, East Granby, East Hartland, East Norwalk, East Windsor, East Woodstock, Ellsworth, Essex, Fair Haven, Falls Village, Fitchville, Forestville, Gilead, Glenville, Greenfield Hill, Greens Farms, Groton Heights, Hadlyme, Hanover, Higganum, High Ridge, Jewett City, Kensington, Leesville, Lime Rock, Mianus, Middlefield, Middle Haddam, Montowese, Moodus, Morris, Mount Carmel, Mystic, New Cambridge, Newington. Niantic, Noank, Noroton, North Canaan, Northford, North Granby, North Grosvenordale, North Guilford, North Madison, Old Lyme, Old Mystic, Old Saybrook, Oneco, Plainville, Ponset, Poquetanuck, Poquonock Putnam, Redding , Ridgebury, Riverside, Rockville, Saugatuck, Scotland, Sound Beach, South Britain, South Glastonbury, South Killingly, South Norwalk, Southport, Sprague, Spring Hill, Stafford Springs, Stanwich, Stony Creek, Stratfield, Tariffville, Terryville, Thomaston, Unionville, Versailles, West Hartford, West Hartland, West Haven, , West Woodstock, Windsor Locks, and Winsted, for example, are herein treated as part of their respective parent towns.

33 Morrison, *Connecting to Connecticut*, 186.

34 Harlan R. Jessup, "Easton, Connecticut Marriages, 1845–1854," *CA*, 50:137–41 (Feb 2008).

35 See "List of Connecticut Towns and Counties Including Year Established," online at *https://ctstatelibrary.org/cttowns/counties.*

frequently those reported by school district beginning in 1848.[36] Every town clerk's office also includes early record books which FHL chose not to film. For example, FHL did not typically film town meeting records in Connecticut, and the earliest such books occasionally included early vital records. Other types of unfilmed vital records which some town clerks retained include (1) the actual marriage reports by ministers (sometimes including signed parental permissions for under-age participants) from which marriages were officially recorded, and (2) justice of the peace records, including the marriages they performed. The author has found both of these types of records in Hebron,[37] and would appreciate news of their continued existence in other Connecticut towns.

Finally thousands of additional slips of both vital records and private records were created in Barbour's format which were never interfiled in the Barbour Index or recorded in his typescript volumes. They are mainly abstractions for Brooklyn, East Guilford, Madison, Montville, New Haven, North Stonington, Rocky Hill, Wallingford, and Wethersfield. They remain unpublished in any form and viewable only in the file room at CSL, but their sources are identified herein. See applicable towns and Appendix B below.

Accuracy

Another issue which must be addressed for the Barbour Index is its accuracy. Each introduction to one of Barbour's 137 town volumes includes this statement, or one quite similar to it:[38]

> The manuscript copy [i.e., Barbour-commissioned abstraction], now in the possession of the Connecticut State Library, has not been compared with the original, and doubtless errors exist. It is hoped that as errors or omissions are found notes will be entered in this volume and on the slips which are included in the General Index of Connecticut Vital Records also in the possession of the Connecticut State Library.

---

36 Connecticut towns for which the FHL catalogs volumes of pre-1850 vital records which are not indexed by Barbour include Ashford, Berlin, Bethlehem, Bloomfield, Branford, Bridgeport, Bristol, Canaan, Canterbury, Chaplin (cat), Chester, Colchester (JP), Colebrook, Columbia, Cornwall, Coventry, Cromwell, Danbury, Darien, Derby, Durham, East Haddam, East Hampton, East Haven, Enfield, Fairfield, Farmington, Glastonbury, Granby, Greenwich, Griswold, Groton, Guilford, Haddam, Hartford, Hartland, Harwinton, Hebron, Huntington, Killingly, Killingworth, Lebanon, Ledyard, Lyme, Manchester, Marlborough, Meriden, Middlebury, Middletown, Milford, Monroe, Montville, New Britain, New Hartford, New London, Newtown, North Branford, North Stonington, Norwalk, Orange, Oxford, Pomfret, Preston, Redding, Ridgefield, Rocky Hill, Roxbury, Salisbury, Saybrook, Seymour, Sharon, Simsbury, Southbury, Southington, Stafford, Stamford, Stonington, Stratford, Suffield, Tolland, Torrington, Trumbull, Union, Wallingford, Washington, Waterbury, Watertown, Weston, Westport, Willington, Winchester, Windsor, Wolcott, Woodbury, and Woodstock.

37 See Linda MacLachlan, *New Copies of Old Records from Hebron, Connecticut, 1708–1875* (Westminster, MD: Heritage Books, 2011).

38 Lucius B. Barbour, *Connecticut Vital Records: Barkhamsted 1779–1854* (Hartford: CSL, 1927) unnumbered page after title page (FHL film 2,967). Digital image online at *AmericanAncestors.org* and *FamilySearch.org*.

The significance of this warning varies considerably from one town to the next. A few towns (such as Andover, Avon, East Windsor and Westbrook) seem to have been abstracted from photocopies of the town's vital records book[s]. At least 46 towns scattered their early vital records throughout several books of town meetings and/or land records.[39] In other towns several different (often private) sources covering overlapping periods of time were consolidated creating duplicate entries.[40] A few others (such as Cheshire, Derby, Saybrook, and Simsbury) had a preexisting compilation of the town's vital records, which was indexed without being checked against the original records.

The particular problems (and derivativeness of the sources Barbour relied upon) are detailed below town by town. Barbour's recommendation that researchers check the original records he cites, rather than simply rely upon the generally unchecked Barbour Index is also difficult to comply with for another reason. Many of the sources Barbour cites are not in the FHL catalog or otherwise available to outside of Connecticut.[41]

Accessing the Barbour Index

Barbour's slip index to the vital records of 143 Connecticut towns may be viewed at CSL. As Barbour stated above at note 38, various handwritten additions and corrections appear, in fact, to have been made to the slips on file at CSL. Microfilms of these slips[42] are available at the FHL and online at *FamilySearch.org*. They are the preferred starting point for research because they are more complete than other publications, because they are generally one step closer to the original source, and because one can search virtually the entire state at once there, regardless of the Connecticut town that generated the record sought or the spelling of the surname/

[39] Towns entering vital records in land record books include Avon, Berlin, Branford, Bristol, Burlington, Canaan, Colchester, Colebrook, Cornwall, Derby, East Haddam, Fairfield, Farmington, Glastonbury, Greenwich, Groton, Haddam, Hampton, Hartford, Harwinton, Kent, Killingworth, Lyme, Middletown, New London, New Milford, Newtown Norwalk, Ridgefield, Salisbury, Saybrook, Sharon, Sherman, Simsbury, Southington, Stamford, Stonington, Stratford, Suffield, Union, Wallingford, Waterbury, Weston, Wethersfield, Windsor, and Woodbury.

[40] These include the abstractions for Clinton, Colchester, Durham, East Haven, Hartford, Hebron, Milford, Montville, Salisbury, Sharon, Stamford, Waterbury, and Windsor.

[41] Connecticut towns in which Barbour abstracts sources which do not appear to be published or filmed anywhere include Ashford, Berlin, Bozrah, Branford, Brooklyn, Burlington, Cheshire, Chester, Clinton, Colchester, Columbia, Derby, East Haven, East Lyme, Ellington, Enfield, Fairfield, Franklin, Goshen, Greenwich, Groton, Hamden, Hartford, Hebron, Lyme, Manchester, Milford, Monroe, New Hartford, New London, Newtown, Norwalk, Oxford, Roxbury, Salisbury, Saybrook, Simsbury, Somers, Stamford, Stonington, Suffield, Voluntown, Wallingford, Washington, and Woodbridge. Towns with other sources of pre-1900 records unknown to both FHL and Barbour include Ashford, Barkhamsted, Berlin, Bozrah, Brookfield, Brooklyn, Burlington, Canaan, Canterbury, Cheshire, Colchester, Coventry, Danbury, Durham, East Haddam, Easton, Fairfield, Farmington, Goshen, Greenwich, Guilford, Haddam, Hamden, Hampton, Hartford, Hartland, Harwinton, Hebron, Huntington, Kent, Killingly, Killingworth, Lebanon, Litchfield, Lyme, Madison, Mansfield, Marlborough, Middlebury, Milford, New Canaan, New Haven, Newtown, North Branford, North Stonington, Norwalk, Oxford, Pomfret, Preston, Redding, Ridgefield, Rocky Hill, Salem, Salisbury, Saybrook, Seymour, Sherman, Somers, Southbury, Stafford, Sterling, Stonington, Stratford, Suffield, Thompson, Tolland, Trumbull, Union, Wallingford, Watertown, Weston, Wethersfield, Willington, Windsor, and Woodbury,

[42] FHL films 2,887–2,966 and 2,984 reflect these records as they were in 1949.

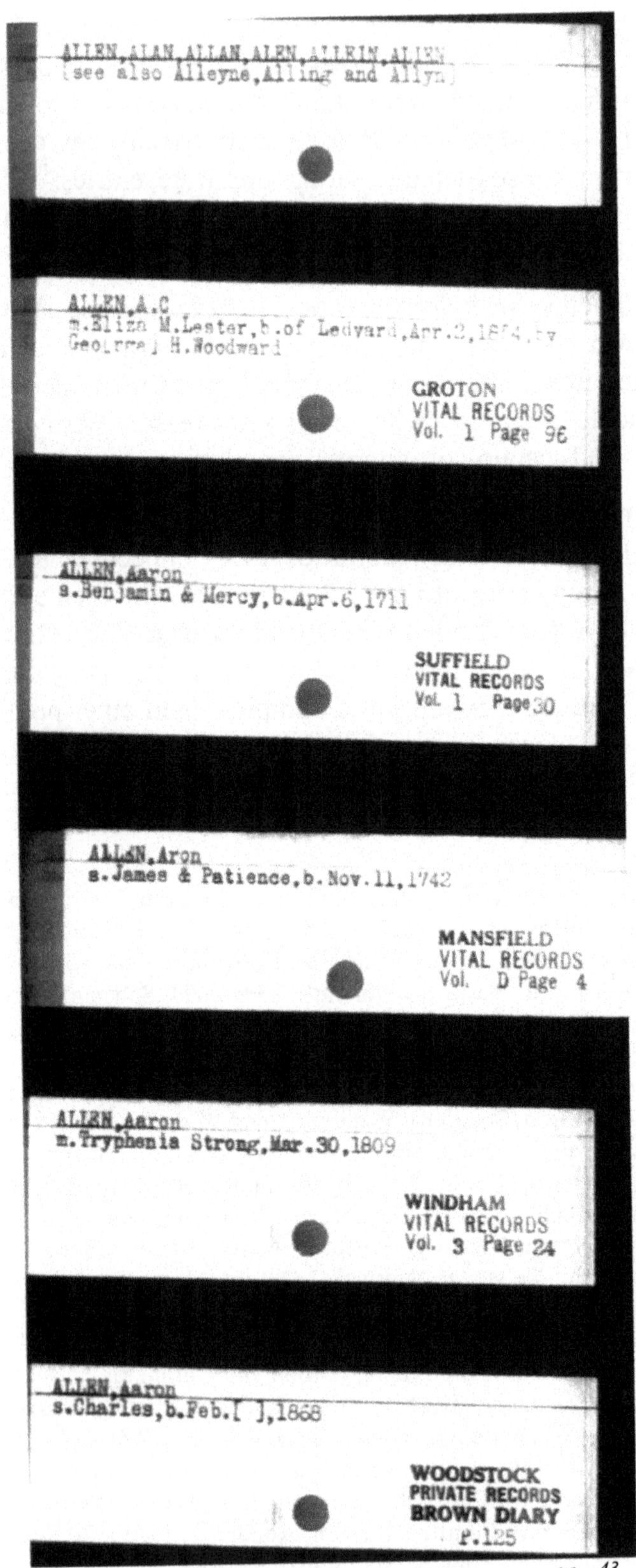

ALLEN,ALAN,ALLAN,ALEN,ALLEIN,ALIEN
(see also Alleyne,Alling and Allyn)

ALLEN,A.C
m.Eliza M.Lester,b.of Ledyard,Apr.2,18[illegible],[illegible]
Geo[rge] H.Woodward
GROTON
VITAL RECORDS
Vol. 1 Page 96

ALLEN,Aaron
s.Benjamin & Mercy,b.Apr.6,1711
SUFFIELD
VITAL RECORDS
Vol. 1 Page 30

ALLEN,Aron
s.James & Patience,b.Nov.11,1742
MANSFIELD
VITAL RECORDS
Vol. D Page 4

ALLEN,Aaron
m.Tryphenia Strong,Mar.30,1809
WINDHAM
VITAL RECORDS
Vol. 3 Page 24

ALLEN,Aaron
s.Charles,b.Feb.[ ],1868
WOODSTOCK
PRIVATE RECORDS
BROWN DIARY
P.125

Figure 4: Barbour Index on FHL microfilm[43]

[43] Barbour collection: Connecticut vital records prior to 1850, General index All–Andr, (FHL film 2,888).

Digital images of virtually all of the Barbour Index are online at *FamilySearch.org*.[44] The FHL films of the Barbour Index also exclude any additions and corrections made to CSL file slips after 14 December 1949. Barbour's 137 typescript volumes may be viewed at *AmericanAncestors.org*, *FamilySearch.org*, CSL, FHL, NEHGS, or on FHL microfilm.[45] GPC has republished these 137 individual volumes as 55 paperbacks, now available in genealogy libraries across the nation.[46]

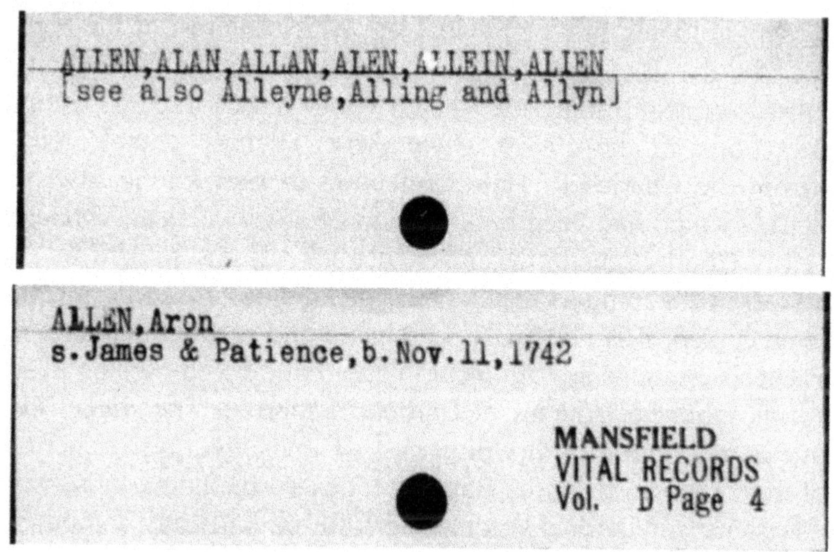

Figures 5–6: Digital images of Barbour Index microfilm online[47]

The typescripts of various towns are transcribed on free websites.[48] From these 55 volumes, 118 towns with a total of 528,009 births, marriages and deaths are now digitized online at *Ancestry.com* — about half of the more than one million slips in CSL's Barbour Index.[49] The GPC edition accurately transcribes the town volumes except for its failure to replicate most of the 137 date ranges on Barbour's original title pages and virtually all of the 137 introductory pages where Barbour describes his sources and warns of his failure to check the accuracy of his work, as described above. As a copy of the

---

[44] This microfilming is not quite complete. For example, FHL film 2,938 is labeled NOS–OW, but the corresponding CSL file drawer also contains ten slips for the OYSTERBANKS family. These slips are included in Barbour's Weston volume and in the *Ricker Compilation*.

[45] FHL films 2,967–2,983.

[46] White, Lorraine Cook (Gen Ed.) *Barbour Collection of Connecticut Town Vital Records* GPC), 55 vols. (Baltimore: GPC, 1995 *et seq.*). White's introduction in these volumes incorrectly states that the Barbour Index was copied from the original typescript source of.these books, rather than vice versa as Barbour states in his prefaces, which White largely omits.

[47] Lucius B. Barbour, Connecticut vital records prior to 1850, General index, file drawer labeled All–Andr, (FHL film 2888). *FamilySearch.org*, digital film #008272218, images 100 and 103.

[48] The hyperlinks to transcriptions of 27 of Barbour's Volumes may be found on *Ray's Place for New England History and Genealogy* at *www.rays-place.com/town/index.htm*. An even larger number are indexed at *www.newhorizonsgenealogicalservices.com*.

[49] The digitized images posted on *Ancestry.com*, as of 2018, do not include GPC's publications for the towns of Chaplin, New Canaan, New Hartford, Norwich, Portland, Prospect, Redding, Ridgefield, Rocky Hill, Roxbury, Salem, Salisbury, Sherman, Simsbury, Suffield, Wallingford, Wethersfield, Windsor, or Woodbridge. See also *https://www.familysearch.org/wiki/en/Barbour_Collection*.

entire Barbour Index, however, even the whole set is incomplete because it omits both (1) the hundreds of thousands of birth, death, and marriage slips only in the 143-town Barbour Index[50] and (2) the many smaller private records compilations which Barbour also abstracted and interfiled into the Barbour Index.

A compact disc titled *The Ricker Compilation of Vital Records of Early Connecticut*, (*Ricker Compilation*)[51] and published in 2006, claims to have abstracted not only Barbour's 137 town volumes and the books from which the rest of the slips identified as "public records" in the Barbour Index were abstracted, but also many other early Connecticut birth, baptism, marriage, death, and burial record compilations. The additional abstractions in the *Ricker Compilation* include church records, the few transcriptions from the Charles R. Hale Collection of Gravestone Inscriptions at CSL (Hale Collection),[52] which had been published in *The Connecticut Nutmegger* (*CN*) and other lists of early Connecticut births, marriages and deaths said to be found at CSL. While the usefulness of a compact disc which consolidates 1.2 million Connecticut vital records cannot be denied, it is not easily searchable and seems to contain many errors.[53] Furthermore Ricker's citations are too incomplete to allow comparison of the text on her compact disc with either her sources or Barbour's sources. The *Ricker Compilation* is, however, unique in its portability. It will permit a Connecticut researcher to gain at least an overview of the vital records in the Barbour Index — including those which are not in any version of Barbour's individual volumes — from virtually any computer anywhere.[54]

---

50 *Ancestry.com* and *AmericanAncestors.org* seek to replicate this aspect of the Barbour Index by creating online databases for all eight of the books that Barbour abstracted only in his state-wide Index. But *Ancestry.com* completely misses 19 of Barbour's 137 volumes at the time this book is published. See note 49. *AmericanAncestors.org* misses only the CSL's later additions and corrections. See note 5 and pages 3 to 5 above and Appendix A.

51 Jacquelyn Ladd Ricker, *The Ricker Compilation of Vital Records of Early Connecticut: Based on the Barbour Collection of Connecticut Town Vital Records and Other Statistical Sources* CD-ROM (Baltimore: GPC, 2006).

52 The Hale Collection transcribes early gravestones in 2,269 Connecticut cemeteries in order of their physical proximity. The state-wide card file at the CSL is arranged in alphabetical order (which obliterates family plots) but is available through FHL films 3,076–3,336) and at NEHGS as Films H35–3374). See CSL's online finding guide, "An Introduction to The Charles R. Hale Collection. The Ricker Compilation seems to incorporate less than 500 of Hale's 2,269 Connecticut cemeteries.

53 Comparing the first page of data on this compact disc with the first 44 slips in the Barbour Index, it appears that none of Ricker's "VR" citations includes the volume and page cited by Barbour and/or the GPC edition. But for this omission, 35 of Ricker's first 44 "VR" entries match Barbour's. Of the other nine, one misspells the surname in a way not recognized by Barbour, even as an alternate spelling, two omit the residence stated for the groom and/or bride; two fail to accurately describe the source of all or part of the record; one misstates the name and title of the person who performed the marriage; one adds a state to a groom's city of residence when it is not stated in Barbour; two omit the brackets Barbour placed around presumed letters; and one misspells the bride's first name. It has not been determined what discrepancies may or may not be present on the balance of the compact disc.

54 If, however, a researcher has ready access to the internet, the versions of the Barbour collection on *AmericanAncestors.org* and *FamilySearch.org* are more accurate and well-sourced and therefore a preferable abstraction for the towns they include.

For example; this is a birth record from page 50 of Hebron's First Book of Vital Records:[55]

January 13 1748/9 Leah daughter to Benjamin Bissell was born.

This is Barbour's abstraction of this birth (alphabetized under "BISSELL, BESEL, BESSEL, BEYSELL, BISEL, BISSALL, BISSEL, BISSILL, BISSET, BIZELL, BYSSEL) in the Barbour Index[56]

BISSELL, Leah
d. Benjamin, b. Jan 13 1748/9

HEBRON
VITAL RECORDS
Vol. 1 Page 50

This is how Barbour's typist erroneously replicated this record in his Hebron volume under "BISSELL, BISEL:"[57]

Leah, d. Benjamin, b. Jan. 13, 1749/9 [sic] 1 50

This is how GPC printed this information in its Hebron volume under "BISSELL, BISEL:"[58]

Leah, d. Benjamin, b. Jan 13 1749/9 [sic] [Book] 1 [Page] 50

And this is how it looks in the *Ricker Compilation* under "BISSELL: BIZELL; BISSIL; BASSEL:"[59]

Leah, d. Benjamin, b. Jan 13 1748/9 — Hebron VR

While Ricker's version is, in fact, accurate (except for her omission of a proper citation and alternate surname spellings), it is unclear how she obtained the correct information, when the source she claims to have copied was, in fact, inaccurate.[60] Thus, for both

---

55 See Hebron Town Clerk, First Book of Vital Records (Hebron Town Hall: ca. 1700–1750) (FHL film 1,376,165, item 2) 50; see also Samuel J. Hendee, Town Clerk, First Book of Records of Births, Marriages and Deaths, Town of Hebron, (Hebron Town Hall: 1849 re-copy) 11.

56 Barbour, "Barbour Collection," (Barbour Index) card file, alphabetical entry for Leah Bissell, Hebron, 1748/9. (FHL film 2,894, Bi–Bo).

57 Barbour, *Connecticut Vital Records: Hebron: 1708–1854* (Hartford: CSL, 1922) Leah Bissell, born 1749/9 [sic]. (FHL film 2,972, item 3).

58 Dorothy Wear, *Barbour Collection of Connecticut Town Vital Records: Hartland 176F1–1848, Harwinton 1737–1854, Hebron 1708–1854,* vol. 18 (Baltimore: GPC, 1999) 123.

59 *Ricker Compilation*, 1433, 1444.

60 Ricker states in her introduction that: "In most cases the town records identified by the letters "VR" were copied from the Barbour Collection of Connecticut Vital Records in the [CSL}. Town records not included in the Barbour Collection were copied from the separately published records of Bolton, Vernon, Coventry, Enfield, Mansfield, New Haven, and much of Norwich and Woodstock. *Ibid.*. p. 2. It would therefore appear that Ricker's transcription is from Barbour's Volumes because only they exclude the six plus towns previously published as books. (If Ricker had copied the original 143-town Barbour Index, she would have had no need to copy the six plus books of the previously published towns as well.) If Ricker faithfully copied the Hebron Volume, however, her transcription of this particular record should have incorporated the same typographical error as in the other copies. It is,

completeness and accuracy, no modern alternative is yet equal to the original Barbour Index. The Barbour Index is, however, only the beginning of a search for Connecticut births, deaths and marriages

Going beyond the Barbour Index

Diligent genealogists should go beyond the Barbour Index in three different ways:

1. Vital records in the Barbour Index should be verified by comparison with the original source he relied upon;
2. Vital records not in the Barbour Index may be in other sources cited herein; and
3. Other evidence for vital statistics may be found in church and cemetery records, and town compilations and other publications, cited herein

This book is a town-by-town review of Barbour's actual sources for the information on his slips for each of the 143 towns in the Barbour Index along with the FHL film numbers for derivative and original sources which have been microfilmed and other source information for those which have not. These reviews also note **(in bold face)** discrepancies[61] and other town records which Barbour did not abstract.

Later sections list other sources for town birth, marriage, and death information, such as church records, cemetery transcriptions, and other available print sources including secondary compilations of town vital statistics from multiple sources. This guide also includes equivalent information for six other pre-1851 Connecticut towns which Barbour did not index: Cromwell, Easton, New Britain, New Fairfield, Seymour, and Trumbull.

Many of the vital records substitutes cited below and not relied upon by Barbour, quote the applicable catalog description of the record's contents and have not been personally examined to determine accuracy of the catalog description or whether that record might be identical to another differently described.[62] It is hoped that readers who discover discrepancies will correct the record at *www.Connecticut Genealogists.com.*

To use this guide, look for an ancestor's hometown. If the town is not listed, it was keeping records by 1850. Consult a general reference to determine which Connecticut town(s) your ancestor's hometown was part of before 1850.[63]

---

therefore, unclear how Ricker came to the correct determination that Leah Bissell was born in 1748/9 and not 1749/50.

61 While it remains to the individual researcher to evaluate the accuracy of the abstraction commissioned by Barbour, the author has noted some problems of accuracy and/or completeness evident upon a cursory comparison. Barbour did not provide standard citations for his sources and some are unrecognizable today. It is estimated that the Barbour Index now comprises over one million slip entries for vital records in some 439 trays at the CSL. See CSL, *Barbour Collection of Connecticut Vital Records*, online guide at *www.cslib.org/barbour.htm;* Harlan R. Jessup, "Barbour Collection – What's in It and What's Not," digitized article online at *https://www.americanancestors.org/browse/articles?searchby=author&subquery=Harlan%20R.%20Jessup&id=46*

62 In general FHL microfilm citations follow the catalog description so that researchers may more easily identify them. Where, however, the FHL has microfilmed a Daughters of the American Revution Genealogical Records Committee (DAR GRC) Report, the report is cited in the form preferred by the DAR, with the FHL film number appended as a parenthetical.

For each of the 137 towns with a typescript volume, its bibliography below is preceded by a transcription of Barbour's own report of his sources for that town's records — the introductory page in each of Barbour's town volumes which was inexcusably omitted from the GPC edition now most frequently relied upon.[64] This guide reports under **VITAL RECORDS** the actual date range of the records abstracted. It also notes any significantly broader dates[65] listed in the FHL catalog or Morrison's *Connecting to Connecticut*, which might imply that additional vital records exist.

The section then describes where one may find the original records Barbour intended to index, including the FHL catalog's report of film numbers and descriptions. **Sources of town vital records NOT abstracted by Barbour and publications about such records are highlighted**. The paragraph closes with citations to other print or exclusively electronic publications or manuscripts containing that town's vital records.[66] If any other pre-1850 vital records or marriage records of a local justice of the peace are cataloged by CSL in the manuscript collection of the Connecticut State Archives (CSA} from that town, that collection is also cited in this paragraph.[67]

CHURCH RECORDS are generally more original sources for births, deaths, and marriages than vital records. Ministers not only presided over baptisms and burials but informed the town clerk of marriages to enter in the town's official records. This second section begins by detailing all town and neighborhood church records[68] listed in the FHL catalog as

---

63 See. e.g., Arthur H. Hughes, *Connecticut Place Names* [Hartford: Connecticut Historical Society, 1976); Michael J. Leclerc, *Genealogist's Handbook for New England Research* (Leclerc, *Genealogist's Handbook)*, 5th ed. (Boston: NEGHS, 2012).

64 See discussion at note 46 above. Digital images of all Barbour's town prefaces are now available online at *FamilySearch.org* and *AmericanAncestors.org*.

65 Many of these anomalies may be the result of the subdivision of towns, or of a misdescription by FHL catalogers, Morrison and/or Barbour. One cannot be sure without further research, however, which discrepancies indicate vital records missed by Barbour.

66 Articles which discuss problems of the Barbour Collection generally (as opposed to the problems with an individual town's vital records) are excluded from further citation. They include: Harlan R. Jessup, "Some Additions and Corrections to Connecticut's Barbour Collection," *Connecticut Ancestry*, 48:47–8 (Aug 2005); Linda MacLachlan's "A Caution for Users of the Barbour Index," CN, 40:407–10 (Dec 2007); Harlan R Jessup, "Chronology of Vital Records Statutes in Connecticut with Some Omissions from the Barbour Collection," *Connecticut Ancestry*, vol. 60, no. 2, (Sept 2017).

67 Many original town vital records are at CSA and generally unfilmed by FHL. They include Avon, Bozrah, Brooklyn, Colchester, Coventry, Deep River, Durham, Fairfield, Farmington, Franklin, Hampton, Hartford, Hartland, Lebanon, Litchfield, Lyme, Manchester, Mansfield, North Canaan, North Stonington, Norwalk, Plainfield, Preston, Redding, Rocky Hill, Roxbury, Salem, Salisbury, Somers, Southbury, Stamford, Union, Willington, Windsor, and Woodbridge. Towns with generally unfilmed early church records include Bristol, Burlington, Canterbury, East Haddam, East Hartford, Ledyard, New London, North Haven, Plymouth, Voluntown, Winchester, and Windham. See Jeannie Sherman, compiler. *Connecticut Town Guides*. Hartford: Connecticut State Library, 2016, digital images, CT State Library *(http://worldcat.org/oclc/965800280/viewonline)*. All the church records collected by the CSL may be found at *http://cslib.cdmhost.com/digital/collection/p128501coll2 /id/250191/rec/20*. The quarter of these records most likely to contain vital statistics have been indexed by CSL. See *https://libguides.ctstatelibrary.org/hg/genealogyindexes/church*.All church records at CSL are listed at *http://cslib.cdmhost.com/digital/collection/p128501coll2/id/250191/rec/20*

68 These Connecticut towns have lost some or all of their pre-1800 church records: Andover, Bethany, Bristol, Canterbury (Westminster), Canton Center, Coventry, East Granby, East Haddam (Hadlyme),

containing baptisms, burials, and/or marriages along with the date ranges of each and the FHL microfilm number(s). It continues with other church records in the microfilm and manuscript Archives of the Episcopal Diocese of Connecticut, in Hartford,[69] in the vast and (frequently not indexed) collection of the CSL,[70] and in the huge collection of Genealogical Record Committee (GRC) Reports at the DAR. If pre-1850 church records are cataloged by CSL in the manuscript collection acquired by the CSA from that town, that collection is cited here as well. Abstractions of Bailey's *Early Connecticut Marriages* by town are not included,

A third section titled **CEMETERY TRANSCRIPTIONS** begins by describing the number of town cemeteries with all headstones transcribed in the 1930s by Charles R. Hale,[71] and the FHL film number for the 167 then-recognized towns which he transcribed and indexed.[72] The Hale Collection is a critical source for genealogists because (1) ninety years ago these headstones were significantly more readable than they are at present and (2) the original books by Hale list graves in order of physical proximity to each other, implying family relationships.[73] Other available print copies of cemetery records are also cited, including some which predate the Hale Collection and may therefore even more accurately report what was originally engraved on a headstone. Websites such as *FindaGrave.com*, *BillionGraces.com*, *Internment.com*, *USGenWeb.com*'s Tombstone Transcription Project, *Godfrey.org*'s Connecticut Cemetery Inscription Project, and the "Cemetery Transcriptions from the NEHGS Manuscript Collections" database at *AmericanAncestors.org*.[74] are recommended for their photographs but not further discussed herein.

A fourth section, titled **OTHER NOTEWORTHY SOURCES,** includes Lucius Barbour's personal compilations of town records as described below, compilations of divorce records, and bible records, as well as compilations containing Connecticut vital records

---

East Lyme, Ellington, Glastonbury, Goshen, Greenwich, Harwinton, Hebron, North Guilford, Litchfield, Lyme (Hanmburgh), Marlborough, Monroe, Plymouth, Ridgefield, Sherman, Somers, South Manchester, Stamford, Tolland, Torringford, Watertown, and West Haven. Frederic W. Bailey, editor, *Early Connecticut Marriages as Found on Ancient Church Records Prior to 1800* (New Haven: Price, Lee & Adkins, 1890).

69 Abstracted from Robert G. Carroon, "The Parochial Records of the Episcopal Church in the Archives of the Diocese of Connecticut," *CN*, 23:30–38, 216–27, 408–19, and 613–25 (Jun 1990–Mar 1991).

70 See CSL *Church Record Index*, www.cslib.org/church.htm, (downloaded 1 Jan 2010).

71 Charles R. Hale, Charles R. Hale Collection of Gravestone Inscriptions and Newspaper Notices (Hale Collection) (state-wide card file & bound typescripts by town) 360 rolls (also incorporating newspaper death and marriage notices). FHL films 3076–3375

72 Hale Collection (bound typescripts, 167 vols. CSL, Hartford, 1930s), available through FHL on 56 rolls: FHL films 3319–3374.

73 Online sources which alphabetize inscriptions lose the relationship implication of proximity.

74 At present, this database contains more than 1650 cemeteries and burial grounds covering all of the New England states, New York, New Jersey, and Eastern Canada

found at NEHGS, CSL, or abstracted in local histories or the *Ricker Compilation.*[75] Some of these sources appear duplicative and may or may not be identical.[76]

Unique Connecticut State Library Collections

State Archives, Connecticut State Library. Many Connecticut towns have archived bound and/or boxed collections of official records now available through CSL. The vital records so archived are cited with other vital records sources under **VITAL RECORDS** for each pre-1850 Connecticut town, both those abstracted by Barbour and those which are not. See "Vital Records Held by the Connecticut State Archives," online at *https://libguides.ctstatelibrary.org/hg/vitalrecords/archives.*

Personal and Family Vital Records. CSL has collected or transcribed pre-1900 original manuscripts compiled by individuals in their capacities as justices of the peace, ministers, tradesmen, or church sextons found in diaries, day books, or account books or copied from newspapers. Many of the transcriptions are shelved beside the Barbour Collection, abstracted in or near to the Barbour Index, in an old card catalog and/or digitized online at *http://cslib.cdmhost.com/digital/collection/p15019coll14.* See note 18 and Appendices A through C.

Barbour's Personal Collection. Over 40 years ago Lucius B. Barbour's own collection of New England records were donated to the State of Connecticut.[77] These 28 cubic feet of manuscripts include nearly two hundred handwritten volumes collecting Connecticut church, vital, probate, cemetery, and family records. This little known archive has never been reproduced in any form but has been catalogd by CSL as 182 manuscripts in a 27 page Finding Aid viewable online.[78]

These manuscripts presage the *Barbour Collection of Connecticut Town Vital Records* but were obviously unknown to the genealogists whom Barbour later engaged to index all the pre-1850 vital records in Connecticut. They include many vital statistics omitted from the published *Barbour Collection* and correlate many of the individual statistics which are separated listed in the Barbour Index.

This personal record collection includes never-microfilmed manuscripts in Barbour's own neat hand, including bound compilations of vital, church, probate, cemetery and "early family" records for many Connecticut towns and organized collections of genealogical records for dozens of important Connecticut surnames[79] These compilations are generally listed in a town's final paragraph because the manuscripts often integrate vital statistics from more than one source where Barbour has himself determined that the

---

[75] Each Ricker citation, most of which omits the author and other vital information, is reproduced as given on the compact disc.

[76] Readers who discover sources in need of combination, addition or correction are encouraged to contact the author.

[77] Connecticut State Library (CSL), "RG 074:36, Lucius B Barbour Genealogical Collection Inventory," Finding Aid, 2009, CSL, Hartford CT.

[78] See *http://www.cslib.org/archives/Finding_Aids/RG074_036.html*

[79] While most of Barbour's manuscripts collect records of a town, some collect records on a surname, such as Barber, Barnes, Bliss, Brewster, Bulkeley, Burt, Case, Clark, Colton, Cooley, Dart, Day, Drake, Ely, Fitch, Hart, Hilliard, Hitchcock, Howlett, Jordon, Marsh, Scarborough, Shaller, Smith, and Stibbins [sic].

records all pertain to the same individual. His statewide compilations from this collection are listed below.

Statewide resources. These vital records compilations are not listed by town below because they include records from most Connecticut towns. Except for Barbour's manuscripts, they are generally available online:

- Lucius B. Barbour's Genealogical notes from Connecticut family bible records, 1742–1872, 1 vol., (manuscript 105 in Box 12) CSL Record Group 074.36, Hartford.
- Lucius B. Barbour, Birth and marriage records of some Connecticut people, 1748–1800, (manuscript 108 in Box 21) CSL Record Group 074.36, Hartford.
- Lucius B. Barbour, Connecticut genealogical data, 1737–1902, 5 volumes, (manuscript 118 in Box 21 & 22) CSL Record Group 074.36, Hartford.
- Lucius B. Barbour's Card index, 1800–1900, I box, Abstract of vital records arranged by surname, (manuscript 119 in Box 22) CSL Record Group 074.36, Hartford.
- Lucius B. Barbour's Abstracts of marriage notices taken from Connecticut newspapers, 1800–1835, 2 vols., (manuscript 126 in Box 22) CSL Record Group 074.36, Hartford.
- Lucius B. Barbour's Marriage notices from Connecticut newspapers, A–E, 1810–1833, 1 vol., (manuscript 128 in Box 22 CSL Record Group 074.36, Hartford.
- Lucius B. Barbour's Deaths from Connecticut newspapers, A–C, 1810–1833, 1 vol., (manuscript 155 in Box 24) CSL Record Group 074.36, Hartford.
- Lucius B. Barbour's Cemetery inscriptions from Connecticut cemeteries, 1676– 1910, 1 vol., (manuscript 165 in Box 24) CSL Record Group 074.36, Hartford.
- Lucius B. Barbour's Connecticut deaths, 1 vol., (manuscript 166 in Box 24 CSL Record Group 074.36, Hartford.
- Lucius B. Barbour's Marriage and death notices from the Christian Secretary published by Philemon Canfield for the Connecticut Baptist Convention, 1824–1827, 4 vols., (manuscript 164 in Box 24) CSL Record Group 074.36, Hartford.
- John Elliot Bowman's "Some Connecticut Marriages: 1820–1837, Items from the Norwich Courier, and other Connecticut newspapers," (typescript at NEHGS)
- "Ye Names & Ages of All Ye Old Folks in Every Hamlet, City, and Town in Ye State of Connecticut Now Living, (New Haven: by author, Price, Lee & Co. [printers]. Frederick H. Nash, 1884.)
- Frederic W. Bailey's *Early Connecticut Marriages as Found in Ancient Church Records to 1800* (New Haven: Bureau of American Ancestry, 1896–1906).
- NEHGS' "Connecticut Gravestone Inscriptions," *NEHGR*, 405–6 (Oct 1904);
- CSA, Vital Records: Birth, death, marriage information on Connecticut residents, mostly pre-1900. (Reports, files from town clerks; indexes, abstracts, cemetery records, headstone inscriptions; and abstracts of newspaper marriage and death notices) CSA RG 072.
- Bowman Collection: "Connecticut Deaths 1792–1833" 14 vols. 1928–1933 from NEHGS' Special Collections. See Appendix A.
- Connecticut deaths seemingly taken from the February 25, 1860 issue of the Columbian Register newspaper, published in New Haven, Connecticut) See Appendix A
- William A. Eardeley's "Connecticut Cemeteries 1673–1911" (Brooklyn: s.n., 1914–1918) (NEHGS microfilm 104)

- William A. Eardeley's Births, marriages & deaths: records copied from 25 family bibles, typescript (Hartford: CSL, 1913).CSL digital collection
- Allison Franks and Marilyn Labbe's *Over 1,000 18th & 19th Century Intentions & Marriages Recorded in Massachusetts* (Danielson, CT: Killingly Historical Society)
- Lucius B. Barbour's "Genealogical Data from Connecticut Cemeteries," NEHGR, 86:372–91 (Oct 1932).
- Harlan R. Jessup, "Some Additions and Corrections to Connecticut's Barbour Collection," *Connecticut Ancestry* (hereafter "*CA*"), 48:47–8 (Aug 2005)
- Harlan R. Jessup's "Chronology of Vital Records Statutes in Connecticut with Some Omissions from the Barbour Collection," November 2017 *CA*, Vol. 60, No. 2
- Northampton [MA] Gazette, newspaper clippings, 1830 (an alphabetical surname arranged listing of CT marriage and death notices taken from clippings of the Northampton Gazette newspaper during the year 1830. The issues and current location of the original newspaper clippings used to create this listing is unknown) 1946, CSL digital collection online.
- Bowman Collection: a card index to Connecticut vital records in Massachusetts, 1800–1900, (FHL films 2,884–2,885).

Countywide Resources:

Fairfield County:

- E.J. Cable's "Accounts of Cemetery Monument Inscriptions Cemeteries in Fairfield and Litchfield Counties, 1836–63," CSL, See Appendix A.
- "Daniel Sanford Account Book," Fairfield Co. CSL; See Appendix A.
- Harlan R. Jessup's "Vital Records of Fairfield County Towns to 1900 with a Focus on 1847–1852," *CA*, Vol. 53, No. 4 (May 2011);
- Harlan R Jessup's "Vital Records by School District for Fairfield County Towns, *CA*, 55m No. 3, pp. ___ (Feb 2013);
- Connecticut. Superior Court (Fairfield County), "Divorce Papers, ,1720–1799" (originals in the Connecticut State Archives) (FHL films 1,673,219 and 1,673,220)
- Helen S. Ullmann's "Some Fairfield County, Connecticut, Anglican Church Records," *NEHGR*, 153:110–21 (Jan 1999);
- Betsey B. Butts' "A Further Note on 'Some Fairfield County, Connecticut, Anglican Church Records," *NEHGR*, 156:418–9 (Oct 2001)
- Patricia L. Haslam's "Deaths Untimely: Fairfield County, Connecticut, Superior Court Inquests 1715–1793," *NEHGR*, 144:39–48 (Jan 1990)
- Mrs. Alexander H. Lane's "Connecticut marriages, Fairfield County record book, 1692–1832," Genealogical Society of PA, vol. VIII, 1923. p. 164 *et seq.*
- Lester Card's "Marriages and Deaths (Not Taken From Cemetery or Tombstone Records), 1790–1855 Fairfield County, Connecticut" (typescript at NYGBS, 1934)

Hartford County:

- Barbara B. Ferris & Grace Louise Knox's *Connecticut Divorces: Superior Court Records for the Counties of Litchfield 1752–1892 and Hartford1740–1849* (Bowie MD, Heritage Books 1989)

- Lucius B, Barbour's Genealogical notes compiled from Hartford, Connecticut district probate records. 1751–1800, 1 volume. Arranged by town, (manuscript 77 in Box 21) CSL Record Group 074.36, Hartford
- Lucius B, Barbour's Notes from probate records, Hartford District. 1635–1750, 1 volume. (manuscript 81 in Box 10) CSL Record Group 074.36, Hartford
- Lucius B, Barbour's Notes from probate records, Hartford District. 1635–1750, 1 volume. (manuscript 81 in Box 10) CSL Record Group 074.36, Hartford

Litchfield County:
- "Rev. Thomas Davies Record, 1761–1766," CSL. See Appendix A.
- E. J. Cable's "Accounts of Cemetery Monument Inscriptions Cemeteries in Fairfield and Litchfield Counties, 1836–63," CSL. See Appendix A.
- Barbara B. Ferris & Grace Louise Knox's *Connecticut Divorces: Superior Court Records for the Counties of Litchfield 1752–1892 and Hartford 1740–1849* (Bowie MD, Heritage Books 1989)
- "DAR, First Resistance Chapter (Great Barrington MA) "Tombstone Inscriptions on Some Back Roads in Litchfield County, CT" (Mss A 6098), R. Stanton Avery Special Collections, NEHGS;
- Genealogical Notes on Families of Litchfield, Connecticut," (2 oversize volumes, negative photostat) CSA, Hartford.
- Joyce Mackenzie Cropsey's *Register of Revolutionary Soldiers and Patriots Buried in Litchfield County* (Canaan NH: Phoenix Publishing, 1976);

New Haven County:
- "Middlebrook's Almanac, 1835– 1836," CSL, See Appendix A.
- "Deaths and Marriages, 1824–1883 CSL. See Appendix A.
- Connecticut. Superior Court (New Haven County) "Divorce papers, 17121899," originals at CSA (FHL film 1,672,069, item 2 through 1,672,075).
- Connecticut. Superior Court (New Haven County) "Divorce papers, no appearance files, 1808–1865," (withdrawn and discontinued divorces cases) A–Salter (FHL film 1,673,026, item 2) and Schoen–Z (FHL film 1,673,027).
- James S. Hedden's SAR, "Roster of Graves of, or Monuments to, Patriots of 1775–1783, and of Soldiers of Colonial Wars In and Adjacent to New Haven County, Connecticut" (typescript photocopy at FHL) (FHL film 1,421,668)
- Connecticut DAR's "Roster of Graves of or Monuments to Patriots of 1775–1783 in and adjacent to New Haven Co., Connecticut," CT DAR GRC Report, ser. 1, vol. 41:27 (1934) (retyped in 199

New London County:
- "Ralph Hurlbutt's Record as Justice of the Peace of New London County, Connecticut," 1807–1837 (FHL film 5,356), CSL, See Appendix A.
- "Records of Nehemiah Waterman, J.P., New London County, 1712–1801," CSL. *Personal and Family Vital Records,* See Appendix A.
- "Grace Louise Knox & Barbara B. Ferris' *Connecticut Divorces Superior Court Records for the Counties of New London, Tolland, & Windham,1719–1910* (Bowie, MD, Heritage Books 1987)

- Ross Gordon Graves' New London County Cemeteries Inscriptions (originals at CSL) (FHL film 1,029,520)
- "New London County, Connecticut Cemeteries, 1646–1850" (originally published in *NEHGR*) (Arvada CO: Ancestor Publishers, [199_]) (FHL fiche 6,334,355 or 6,334,417)
- Edwin R. Ledogar's Vital Statistics of Eastern CT, Western RI & So. Central MA, 1988–1996, vols. 1–4 (Obituaries taken from the Norwich Bulletin) (Danielson, CT: Killingly Historical Society)
- Richard B. Marrin's Abstracts [of vital records] from the New London Gazette: covering southeastern Connecticut (Westminster, MD: Heritage Books, c2007–2008.

Tolland County:

- Connecticut DAR's "Newspaper Obituaries of Tolland Co., Connecticut," CT DAR GRC Report, ser. 2, vol. 33:40 (1997)
- Jan Harris' "Tolland County Divorce Index," online at *http://sites.rootsweb.com/~cttollan/vitalrecords/divorce.htm*
- Grace Louise Knox & Barbara B. Ferris's *Connecticut Divorces Superior Court Records for the Counties of New London, Tolland, & Windham, 1719–1910* (Bowie MD: Heritage Books, 1987)

Windham County:

- Richard M. Bayles's *History of Windham County, Connecticut* (New York: W.W. Preston, 1889),
- Elizabeth Prather Ellsberry's "Cemetery Records of Windham County, Connecticut" (photocopy at FHL) (FHL film 874,014)
- Marcella Houle Pasay's *Family Secrets: 18th & 19th Century Birth Records Found in the Windham County, Ct., County Court Records & Files, at the CT State Library Archives, Hartford* (Bowie MD: Heritage Books, c2000);
- Grace Louise Knox & Barbara B. Ferris' *Connecticut Divorces Superior Court Records for the Counties of New London, Tolland, & Windham, 1719–1910* (Bowie MD: Heritage Books, 1987)
- Robert Charpentier, Lucile McDonald, Janice Burkhart, and Paul P. Delisle's *Marriages recorded in the town of Blackstone, Massachusetts 1845–1900.* (includes many Windham County people) (Pawtucket, RI: American-French Genealogical Society, 1994.)
- NEHGS' Vital records of Montgomery, Massachusetts, to the year 1850 (includes many Windham County people) (Boston: NEHGS, 1902)

FINDING AID FOR 149 EARLY CONNECTICUT TOWNS

ANDOVER

Barbour's typescript volume for Andover,[80] unlike the GPC edition,[81] begins:

> This volume contains a list alphabetically arranged of births and marriages of the town of Andover from its incorporation to about 1851 and deaths to about 1881. This list was taken from a set of cards based on a photostatic copy of the Andover Vital Records made in 1924. The entire record of the town prior to 1881 is found in one volume, which is unpaged. The page numbers in this alphabetical list are those of the photostatic copy, now in the possession of the Connecticut State Library.
>
> The cards, upon which this list is based,[82] have not been compared with the original and doubtless errors exist. It is hoped that as errors or omissions are found notes will be entered in this volume and on the cards which are included in the General Index of Connecticut Vital Records also in the possession of the Connecticut State Library.
>
> Hartford, Conn., April 1924[83]

VITAL RECORDS: Barbour's Andover volume includes vital records as early as 1847 and as late as 1881. Barbour's Andover abstraction refer to Andover's Records of Births, Marriages, and Deaths, vol. 1, 1847–1881, Andover Town Hall, (FHL film 1,376,167).

CHURCH RECORDS: First Congregational Church's Church Records, 1747–1932 (includes deaths 1819–1828 & 1829–1964, baptisms 1818–1826 & 1829–1870, and marriages 1819–1825 & 1829–1848) (originals at CSL) (FHL film 3,670).

CEMETERY INSCRIPTIONS: The Charles R. Hale Collection of Cemeteries by Locality at CSL (Hale Collection) identifies burials in order of physical proximity at five named cemeteries in Andover.[84] Compare with Daniel Hearn's 1979 copy of 115 pre-1800 gravestones in two Andover cemeteries.[85] See also,

---

80 See How to Use This Book, note 3, above.

81 Lorraine Cook White, *Barbour Collection of Connecticut Town Vital Records: Andover, 1848–1879, Ashford, 1710–1851, Avon, 1830–1851*, vol. 1, (Baltimore: GPC, 1994) digital images on *Ancestry.com*.

82 Now part of the Barbour Index and interfiled with similar slips from other towns in the Connecticut State Library (CSL) and on FHL films 2,887 *et seq*. See Introduction above, pp. 1–3.

83 Lucius B. Barbour, *Connecticut Vital Records: Andover, 1848–1879*, (Hartford: CSL, 1924) page after title page (FHL film 2,967). Digital images on *AmericanAncestors.org* and *FamilySearch.org*.

84 Charles R. Hale, "Headstone Inscriptions of the Town of Andover," bound typescript. 1930s. CSL, Hartford, (FHL film 3,319).

- Theodore A. Bingham's "Inscriptions from the Townsend Cemetery Andover, Tolland Co., Conn." (Mss A 3283and Mss C 5207), RSASC, NEHGS;
- Charles R. Hale's Cemetery inscriptions, records of veterans, and other miscellaneous records from the Connecticut State Library (contains a company militia roll from Hebron, 1776, cemetery inscriptions from Hebron, Andover, and Turnerville, manuscript, CSL, Hartford (FHL film 1,029,520, item 8);
- Susan W. Dimock's "Old Cemetery, Andover, Connecticut" *CT DAR GRC Report*, ser. 1, vol. 4:1 (1914) (retyped in 1997) (FHL film 844,454);
- DAR Abigail Wolcott Ellsworth Chapter's "New Andover Cemetery, Andover, Connecticut," *CT DAR GRC Report*, ser. 1, vol. 90:1 (1942) (FHL film 844,451);
- DAR Abigail Wolcott Ellsworth Chapter's "Old Cemetery at Andover Center, Andover, Connecticut," *CT DAR GRC Report*, ser. 1, vol. 90:4 (1942) (FHL film 844,451);
- DAR Abigail Wolcott Ellsworth Chapter's "Townsend Cemetery, Andover, Connecticut," *CT DAR GRC Report*, ser. 1, vol. 103:1 (1946) (FHL film 844,452);
- Connecticut DAR's "Cemeteries in Andover, Tolland Co., Connecticut," *CT DAR GRC Report*, ser. 1, vol. 133:25 (1956, 1984).

OTHER NOTEWORTHY SOURCES: Philip D. Brass' *History of Andover, Connecticut* (Andover: Andover Historical Society, 1991).

ASHFORD

Barbour's typescript volume for Ashford,[86] unlike the GPC edition,[87] begins:

> This volume contains a list alphabetically arranged of all the vital records of the town of Ashford from its incorporation to about 1850. This list was taken from a set of cards[88] based on a copy of the Ashford Vital Records made in 1911 by Lucius B. Barbour, of Hartford, Conn., who transcribed the first four volumes, and James N. Arnold, of Providence, R.I., who copied Volumes 5 and 6 and "Ye Old Paper Book", herein referred to as "Vol. A". The first four original volumes, although formerly torn and tattered, have been silked, rebound and permanently deposited in the Connecticut State Library. The badly worn condition of these four books resulted in the loss of many names and dates. An attempt has been made in this alphabetical list to supply some of the missing information from the original indexes but no positive assurance of the accuracy of such additions can be given. Both copies above re-

85 Daniel Hearn, "Connecticut gravestones, early to 1800," (Records are arranged by town, and within each town by cemetery) manuscript (FHL film 1,477,476, item 1).

86 See How to Use This Book, note 3, above.

87 White, *Barbour Collection: Andover –Avon*, vol. 1, digital images at *Ancestry.com*.

88 Now part of the Barbour Index and interfiled with similar slips from other towns in CSL and on FHL films 2,887 *et seq*. See Introduction above, pp. 1–3.

> ferred to, now in the possession of the Connecticut State Library, has not been compared with the original and doubtless errors exist. It is hoped that as errors or omissions are found notes will be entered in this volume and on the cards which are included in the General Index of Connecticut Vital Records also in the possession of the Connecticut State Library.
>
> Hartford, Conn., March 1921[89]

- **VITAL RECORDS.** Ashford's volume claims to cover the years 1710 to 1851, but it includes records as early as 1675 and as late as 1854. The main source of Ashford vital records listed in the FHL catalog seems to be a microfilm of the Barbour's 1921 transcription. Barbour abstracted seven Ashford volumes:
- 1–4: The rebound "first four original volumes" are archived at CSL, unfilmed by FHL.[90] A photocopy was said to be available in Ashford in 1930, along with the original indexes Barbour relied upon for re-adding "many names and dates" lost over the years.[91]
- "5:" apparently includes births, marriages and deaths on pages 2–135, covering at least the years 1820 to 1848. This volume appears to have been with the Ashford town clerk in 1936 when he reported having "7 volumes of Vital Records 1717–1936."[92] By 1945, when the Genealogical Society of Utah came to Ashford to microfilm, the only volume in Ashford identifiable as a "Book 5" of as Vital Records was apparently the one photographed below, "Records of Vital Statistics, Book 5," the contents of which were identical to Barbour's Book six, below. This was the only vital record book still reported in Ashford by 1975; however, the only original vital record book reported in Ashford was one CSL originally numbered as five but has now renumbered as six."[93] The source and whereabouts of Barbour's abstraction 5 is presently unknown.
- "6:" Ashford Vital Records, vol. 6, 1770–1884" (photostat in CSL archives) is the same as Ashford "Records of Vital Statistics" vol. 5 [sic], 1770–1884, (manuscript contains records of marriages 1770–1851, births 1771–1851, and deaths 1775–1884, (FHL film 1,376,249, item 2 CSL renumbered the title page of its copy when it was rebound in 1930, but the copy in Ashford is still numbered "5". See photographs below. **Some of Barbour's abstractions from this book do not accurately cite its pages and some are omitted or appear only in his abstraction.**
- "A" or "Ye Old Paper Book:" The original seventh volume abstracted by Barbour may no longer exist. It was copied in 1870 by Ashford Clerk John Byers in what he titled "Proprietor Records 1705–1770," (manuscript includes births 1670–1737, marriages 1710–1730 and deaths 1698–1730), repository unspecified (FHL film 3,676).[94]

---

89 Lucius B. Barbour, *Connecticut Vital Records: Ashford, 1710–1851* (Hartford,: CSL, 1921) page after title page (FHL film 2,967). Digital images at *AmericanAncestors.org* and *FamilySearch,org.*

90 Email from Mel E. Smith, Librarian II, History & Genealogy Unit, CSL, 5 Mar 2010.

91 Email from Sherri L. Mutch, Ashford Town Clerk, 7 May 2018.

92 See Connecticut Public Records Examiner, *Biennial Report (1936),* 11;

93 See CSL, *First 200 Years*, and Figures 2 and 3 below.

94 As noted in its microfilmed introduction, this transcription of the "Old Paper Book" was created by Ashford Town Clerk John Byers in 1770, and notes specific locations in the original record where material was then missing. It includes twenty pre-1710 birth records and one 1698 death record

ASHFORD, CONNECTICUT

VITAL STATISTICS

VOLUME V

Marriages 1770-1851;

Births 1771-1851; Deaths 1775-1884;

Registration of Dogs 1855-1871.

Hartford
Connecticut State Library
1930

Figures 7 & 8: Ashford's "Book 5" as microfilmed at Ashford by FHL

---

predating the earliest settlers' arrival at Ashford, and — except for the Fuller death record — appropriately recorded in the correct town's vital records. Two of these early birth records diverge from the information both in Barbour's Ashford Volume and in the vital records of Woburn, Massachusetts, where they actually occurred: (1) Nathaniel Walker is listed as born September 20 1707, instead of September 23rd, and (2) James Walker, born at Woburn 4 August 1709, is misnamed as Benjamin. Additionally the page numbers Barbour assigns to the records he abstracted from this book (which his list refers to as Vol. A) do not correspond to the pages containing those records in this transcription by Byer. Because of these discrepancies, and because the vital records on this film do not include the Parry birth records reported by Labbe in a version of "The Old Paper Book" presently in the Ashford Town Hall (see text above), it seems fair to conclude that **this transcription of the "Old Paper Book" was not consulted by Barbour in creating the Barbour Index**.

- Another copy was discovered by Marilyn Labbe in the town hall. She has cross-checked it against Barbour's abstraction and reported **all differences between these two copies of what may be a lost original.** [95]

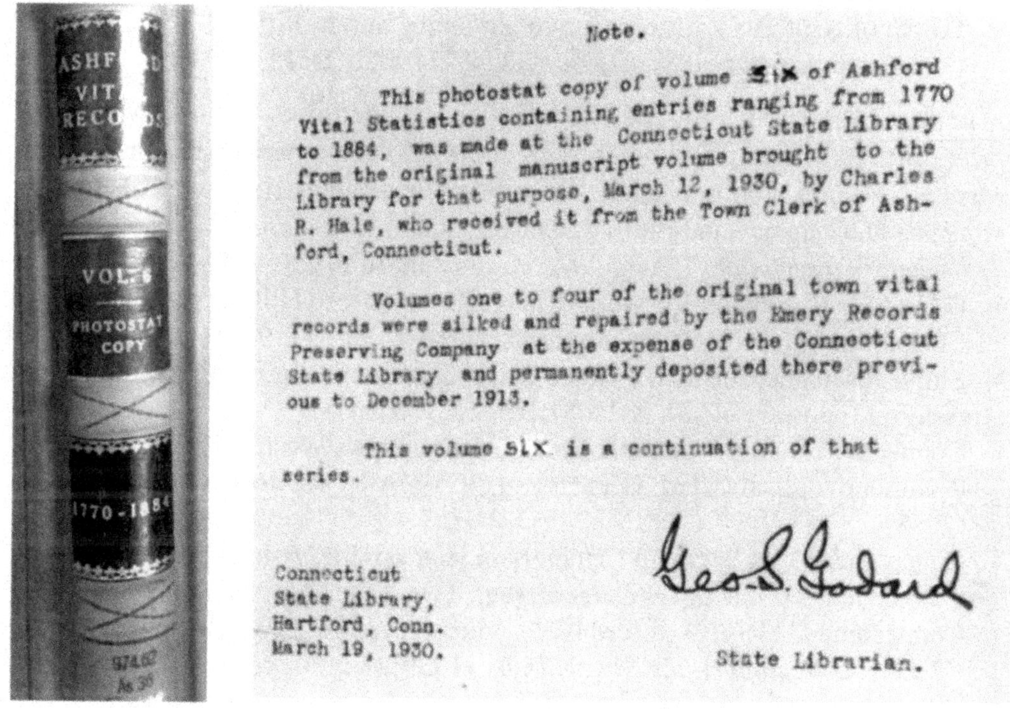

Note.

This photostat copy of volume six of Ashford Vital Statistics containing entries ranging from 1770 to 1884, was made at the Connecticut State Library from the original manuscript volume brought to the Library for that purpose, March 12, 1930, by Charles R. Hale, who received it from the Town Clerk of Ashford, Connecticut.

Volumes one to four of the original town vital records were silked and repaired by the Emery Records Preserving Company at the expense of the Connecticut State Library and permanently deposited there previous to December 1913.

This volume six is a continuation of that series.

Connecticut
State Library,
Hartford, Conn.
March 19, 1930.

Geo. S. Godard
State Librarian.

Figures 9 & 10: Ashford's rebound "Book 6" and Note at CSA

See also,

- **Ashford's Records of births, marriages, and deaths, 1675–1849, (manuscript of births, marriages, and deaths grouped by family and copied from the early books of Ashford town records with a few records from other sources) (FHL film 1,376,249, item 1).**
- **Ashford Vital Records, circa 1845–1905, originals in CSA RG 072.002, Box 1 & 2.**
- **Marilyn Labbe's "Corrections and Additions to the Vital Records of Ashford, Connecticut, and Brooklyn, Connecticut,"** ***CN,*** **44:55–59 (November 2001).**

CHURCH RECORDS:

- Church of Christ's Church Records, 1718–1834 (includes baptisms, deaths and marriages) (photocopy in CSL) (FHL film 1,007,920, item 3);
- Fourth Baptist Church's Church Records, 1795–1850 (includes baptisms) photocopy in CSL (FHL film 1,007,920, item 4);
- Second Baptist Church at Westford's Records 1780–1831 (FHL film 1,007,920, item 5);
- Westford Congregational Church of Ashford's Church Records, 1768–1937 (includes baptisms 1768–1848, marriages 1768–1783, and deaths 1827–1850) originals at CSL (FHL film 6,268);

---

[95] **"Corrections and Additions to the Vital Records of Ashford, Connecticut, and Brooklyn, Connecticut,"** ***CN,*** **31:375—76 (December 1998).**

- Baptist Church of Christ at West Ashford's Church Records, 1765–1863 (includes annotated list of church members 1781–1823) originals at CSL (FHL film 3,692).
- Ministerial Conference of the [Baptist] Ashford Association's Church records, 1846–1903 (FHL film 3,691);
- "Town of Ashford, Westford Congregational Church, 1768–1937," *CN*, 21:19, 209, 411, 436, 601, 643 (1988), 22:69, 177, 247 (1989), 23:78 (1990).

CEMETERY INSCRIPTIONS: The Hale Collection identifies burials in order of physical proximity at 14 named cemeteries in Ashford.[96] Compare with Daniel Hearn's 1979 copy of 150 pre-1800 gravestones in six Ashford cemeteries.[97] See also,

- Grace O. Chapman and Emily J. Chism's *Ashford, Windham County Connecticut Cemetery Inscriptions* (Salem MA: Higginson Book Co., 1998);
- DAR Abigail Wolcott Ellsworth Chapter's "Westford Hill Cemetery, Ashford, Connecticut," *CT DAR GRC Report*, ser. 1, vol. 90:19 (1942) (FHL film 844,451);
- Emily Josephine Chism and Grace Olive Chapman's "Inscriptions in the North Ashford Cemetery" (Mss A 2408), RSASC, NEHGS;
- Connecticut DAR's "Inscriptions from Cemetery at Westford Village (formerly Richmondville), Ashford, Connecticut," CT DAR GRC Report, ser. 1, vol. 67:45 (1938);
- Connecticut DAR's "Small Cemetery in Warrenville, Ashford, Windham Co., Connecticut," *CT DAR GRC Report*, ser. 1, vol. 74:37 (1939);
- Connecticut DAR's "Westford Hill Cemetery, Ashford, Windham Co., Connecticut," *CT DAR GRC Report*, ser. 1, vol. 74:41 (1939).

OTHER NOTEWORTHY SOURCES:

- Lucius B. Barbour's Genealogical notes compiled from Ashford church records: admissions, baptisms, marriages, and deaths, 1760–1817, (manuscript 1 in Box 1) CSL Record Group 074.36, Hartford;
- Connecticut DAR's "Families in or near Westford Congregational Church that Had Children Baptized there & those Born and Baptized Elsewhere Are Included as far as I Am Sure of them," CT DAR GRC Report, ser. 1, vol. 74:63 (1939);
- William Storrs' *Ashford CT Marriages, 1791–1824 and Burial Records, 1829–1841* (manuscript) (Danielson, KHGS, n.d.).

AVON

Barbour's typescript volume for Avon,[98] unlike the GPC edition,[99] begins:

```
     The vital records of Avon, prior to
1851 are found scattered through Volumes
1, 2, and 4 of Land Records.
     This alphabetical list was taken from
a set of cards based on a Photostat copy of
```

96 Charles R. Hale, "Cemetery Inscriptions of Ashford, Connecticut," bound typescript, 1930s, CSL, Hartford, FHL film 3,319.

97 Daniel Hearn, "Connecticut gravestones, early to 1800," manuscript (FHL film 1,477,476, item 3).

98 See How to Use This Book, note 3, above.

99 White, *Barbour Collection: Andover–Avon*, vol. 1, digital images at *Ancestry.com*.

```
the Avon Vital Records made in 1916 in the
State Library. Reference to these entries
is indicated by the abbreviation "LR" and
the number of the volume.
     The cards on which this list is based,[100]
have not been compared with the original and
doubtless errors exist. It is hoped that as
errors or omissions are found notes will be
entered in this volume and on the cards which
are included in the General Index of Connec-
ticut Vital Records also in the possession of
the Connecticut State Library.
                      Hartford, Conn., August 1927[101]
```

VITAL RECORDS: Avon's volume includes vital records as early as 1830 and as late as 1852. Barbour abstracted three Avon "books:"

- "LR1" and "LR2" are Avon's Land Records, vols. 1–2 1830–1851 (vols. 1–2 include records of marriages, 1830–1850). Avon Town Hall, (FHL film 3,672).
- "LR4" is Avon's Land records vols. 3–4 1839–1867 (vol. 4 includes records of births, marriages and deaths, 1847–1851), Avon Town Hall, (FHL film 3,673).

See also,

- **Original Avon vital records in the Connecticut State Archives (CSA) "Town of Avon Records," 1830–1880 (includes marriage certificates 1830–52 and some births, marriages and deaths by school district, 1848–51) original manuscripts in RG 072.002, Box 2 (town hall has photostats);[102]**
- **Avon Vital Records, 1850-1884 (typescript) FHL film 3,662, item 1).**

CHURCH RECORDS:

- Congregational Church's Church Records, 1798–1921 (includes baptisms 1820–1842 & 1841–1904, deaths 1820–1841, and marriages 1819–1840) microfilm of originals in CSL (FHL film 1,007,921 or 3,674);
- "Avon Congregational Church (Originally Third Church of Farmington) 1798–1921," *CN*, 23:80, 263, 452 708 (1990–91);
- West Avon Congregational Church Records, 1751–1941 original records at CSL (FHL film 1,007,922).

CEMETERY INSCRIPTIONS: The Hale Collection identifies burials in order of physical proximity at five named cemeteries in Avon.[103] Compare with Daniel Hearn's 1978 copy of 49 pre-1800 gravestones in three Avon cemeteries.[104] See also,

---

[100] Now part of the Barbour Index and interfiled with similar slips from other towns in CSL and on FHL films 2,887 *et seq*. See Introduction above, pp. 1–3.

[101] Lucius B. Barbour, *Connecticut Vital Records: Avon, 1830–1851* (Hartford: CSL, 1927) page after title page.(FHL film 2,967). Digital images at *AmericanAncestors.org* and *FamilySearch,org*

[102] Connecticut Historical Records Survey. 1987. *Inventory of the town and city archives of Connecticut, no. 2, Hartford County, vol. I, Avon, Berlin, Bloomfield*. Genealogy and Local History. Ann Arbor, Michigan: University Microfilms International, p. 89.

[103] Charles R. Hale, "Headstone Inscriptions of the Town of Avon," bound typescript, 1930s, CSL, Hartford, FHL film 3,319.

- DAR Abigail Wolcott Ellsworth Chapter's "Congregational Churchyard, Avon, Hartford Co., Connecticut," *CT DAR GRC Report*, ser. 1, vol. 90:34 (1942) (FHL film 844,451);
- DAR Abigail Wolcott Ellsworth Chapter's "Greenwood Cemetery, Avon, Connecticut," *CT DAR GRC Report*, ser. 1, vol. 90:44 (1942) (FHL film 844,451);
- DAR Abigail Wolcott Ellsworth Chapter's "West Avon Cemetery, Avon, Hartford Co., Connecticut," *CT DAR GRC Report*, ser. 1, vol. 90:57 (1942) (FHL film 844,451);
- Connecticut DAR's "Church records of West Avon, Connecticut, Baptisms, 1750–1775," *CT DAR GRC Report*, ser. 1, vol. 106:75 (1946) FHL film 844,451);
- "Cider Brook Cemetery, Avon, Connecticut, copied 1931," *CT DAR GRC Report*, ser. 1, vol. 28:1 (1932–3)
- Avon vital records, 1850–1884 (includes some sextons' returns, 1881–1884).typescript at CSL (FHL film 3,662, item 1).

OTHER NOTEWORTHY SOURCES: Mary Frances L. MacKie's *Avon, Connecticut, an historical story* (Canaan, NH: Phoenix Publishing Co., c1988).

BARKHAMSTED

Barbour's typescript volume for Barkhamsted,[105] unlike the GPC edition,[106] begins:

> The vital records of Barkhamsted, prior to 1854, are found in one volume. To these have been added a record of deaths from 1854- to 1867.
>
> This alphabetical list was taken from a set of cards[107] based on a manuscript copy of the Barkhamsted Vital Records made in 1914. Reference to the record of deaths is indicated in red by the pagination of the manuscript copy.
>
> The manuscript copy, now in the possession of the Connecticut State Library, has not been compared with the original and doubtless errors exist. It is hoped that as errors or omissions are found notes will be entered in this volume and on the cards which are included in the General Index of Connecticut Vital Records also in the possession of the Connecticut State Library.
>
> Hartford, Conn., June 1927[108]

---

104 Daniel Hearn, "Connecticut gravestones, early to 1800," manuscript (FHL film 1,477,476, item 4).

105 See How to Use This Book, note 3, above.

106 Lorraine Cook White, *Barbour Collection of Connecticut Town Vital Records: Barkhamsted, 1779–1854, Berlin, 1785–1850, Bethany, 1832–1853, Bethlehem, 1787–1851, Bloomfield, 1835–1853, Bozrah, 1786–1850*, vol. 2, (Baltimore: GPC, 1995) digital image at *Ancestry.com*.

107 Now part of the Barbour Index and interfiled with similar slips from other towns in CSL and on FHL films 2,887 *et seq*. See Introduction above, pp. 1–3.

108 Lucius B. Barbour, *Connecticut Vital Records: Barkhamsted, 1779–1854* (Hartford: CSL, 1927) page after title page (FHL film 2,967). Digital images at *AmericanAncestors.org* and *FamilySearch,org*

VITAL RECORDS: Barkhamsted's volume includes vital records as early as 1742 and as late as 1874. Barbour's abstraction is from Barkhamsted's Vital Statistics, vol. 1, 1742–1912, Barkhamsted Town Hall, (FHL film 1,451,545, item 1).

CHURCH RECORDS:

- First Congregational Church's Church Records, 1781–1914 (includes baptisms 1781–1834 & 1839–1907, deaths 1786–1829 & 1839–1866, and marriages 1787–1833 & 1839–1849) microfilm of originals in CSL (FHL film 1,007,923 or 3,765);
- St. Paul's Church at Riverton's Church Records, 1828–1937 (includes baptisms 1830–1843, marriages 1830–1843, and funerals 1830–1851) (microfilm of originals in CSL) (FHL film 3,766);
- Pleasant Valley Methodist Episcopal Church's Church Records, 1850–1952 (includes marriages, baptisms, and deaths) microfilm of originals at CSL (FHL film 3,764)
- First Congregational Church at Winsted's Church records, 1784–1927 (baptisms 1801–1843, marriages 1806–1841, deaths 1806–1842) originals in CSL (FHL film 6,070);
- "Congregational Church Records, Barkhamsted, Connecticut" typescript in Pittsfield Mass., (FHL film 234,578);
- Rollin H. Cooke's *Barkhamsted, Connecticut [Congregational Church]* (Membership, 1781– 1838; Baptisms, 1781–1834; Deaths, 1786–1829; Marriages, 1787–1833); FHL Digital images of photocopy of original published: [S.l : s.n.]. pp. 250–306;
- Baptisms (1810–43), marriages (1830–43) & burials (1830–51) at St. Paul's [Episcopal] Church at Riverton, formerly the Episcopal Society of the Union Church in Hitchcocksville, Episcopal Diocese, Hartford (ED film 3,766).

CEMETERY INSCRIPTIONS: The Hale Collection identifies burials in order of physical proximity at eight named cemeteries in Barkhamsted.[109] Compare with Daniel Hearn's 1978 copy of eight pre-1800 gravestones in one Barkhamsted cemetery.[110]
See also,

- DAR Abigail Wolcott Ellsworth Chapter's "Center Cemetery, Barkhamsted, Connecticut," *CT DAR GRC Report*, ser. 1, vol. 92:1 (1943) (FHL film 844,451);
- DAR Abigail Wolcott Ellsworth Chapter's "Center Cemetery, Barkhamsted, Connecticut, Soldiers Monument, Soldiers of the Revolution," *CT DAR GRC Report*, ser. 1, vol. 92:18 (1943) (FHL film 844,451);
- DAR Abigail Wolcott Ellsworth Chapter's "Hollow Cemetery, Barkhamsted, Connecticut," *CT DAR GRC Report*, ser. 1, vol. 92:21 (1943) (FHL film 844,451);
- DAR Abigail Wolcott Ellsworth Chapter's "Old Riverton Cemetery, Barkhamsted, Connecticut," *CT DAR GRC Report*, ser. 1, vol. 92:23 (1943) (FHL film 844,451);
- DAR Abigail Wolcott Ellsworth Chapter's "Weed Cemetery, Barkhamsted, Connecticut," *CT DAR GRC Report*, ser. 1, vol. 92:24 (1943) (FHL film 844,451);
- DAR Abigail Wolcott Ellsworth Chapter's "Phelps Farm Cemetery, Barkhamsted, Connecticut," *CT DAR GRC Report*, ser. 1, vol. 92:24 (1943) (FHL film 844,451);
- DAR Abigail Wolcott Ellsworth Chapter's "Riverside Cemetery, Barkhamsted, Connecticut," *CT DAR GRC Report*, ser. 1, vol. 92:25 (1943) (FHL film 844,451);

---

[109] Charles R. Hale, "Headstone Inscriptions of Barkhamsted," bound typescript, 1930s, CSL, Hartford, FHL film 3,319.

[110] Daniel Hearn, "Connecticut gravestones, early to 1800," manuscript (FHL film 1,477,476, item 5).

- DAR Abigail Wolcott Ellsworth Chapter's "Riverview Cemetery, Barkhamsted, Connecticut," *CT DAR GRC Report*, ser. 1, vol. 92:28 (1943) (FHL film 844,451);
- Riverside Cemetery of Pleasant Valley, Conn., *Riverside Cemetery, Pleasant Valley, Litchfield County, Connecticut* (Hartford: Hartford Printing Co., E. Geer Sons, 1903).

OTHER NOTEWORTHY SOURCES:

- Lucius B, Barbour's Genealogical notes compiled from church records of Barkhamsted, Conn. 1769–1818, 1 volume. 1:2. (manuscript 2 in Box 1) CSL Record Group 074.36, Hartford;
- William Wallace Lee's *Barkhamsted, Conn., and its centennial, 1879: to which is added a historical appendix, containing copies of old letters, antiquarian, names of soldiers of the Revolution, 1812, 1846 and 1861, civil officers, and other matter interesting to the people of the town* (Ann Arbor, MI: University Microfilms, 1987) (FHL fiche 6,062,293).

BERLIN

Barbour's typescript volume for Berlin,[111] unlike the GPC edition, [112] begins:

> This volume contains a list alphabetically arranged of all the vital records of the town of Berlin from its incorporation to about 1850 The entire record for this town prior to 1850 is found scattered through Volumes 1, 4, 9 and 12 of Land Records and a Book of marriages from 1820 to 1851. Reference to entries found in the Land Records is indicated by the abbreviation "LR" and the volume number.
>
> This list was taken from a set of cards[113] based on a copy of the Berlin Vital Records made in 1916 by James N. Arnold, of Providence, R.I. The Arnold Copy, now in the possession of the Connecticut State Library, has not been compared with the o-riginal and doubtless errors exist. It is hoped that as errors or omissions are found notes will be entered in this volume and on the cards which are included in the General Index of Connecticut Vital Records also in the possession of the Connecticut State Library.
>
> Hartford, Conn., November 1927[114]

VITAL RECORDS: Berlin's volume includes vital records as early as 1754 and as late as 1850. Barbour abstracted five Berlin "books:"

---

111 See How to Use This Book, note 3, above.

112 White, *Barbour Collection: Barkhamsted- Bozrah*, vol. 2, digital image at *Ancestry.com*.

113 Now part of the Barbour Index and interfiled with similar slips from other towns in CSL and on FHL films 2,887 *et seq*. See Introduction above, pp. 1–3.

114 Lucius B. Barbour, *Connecticut Vital Records: Berlin, 1785–1850* (Hartford: CSL, 1927) page after title page (FHL film 2,967). Digital images at *AmericanAncestors.org* and *FamilySearch,org*

- "LR1" is Berlin's Land Records, vols. 1–2 1785–1824, (Vol. 1 includes births, deaths and marriages) Berlin & New Britain Town Halls, (FHL film 3,728);
- "LR4" is Berlin's Land Records, vol. 3–4 1791–1809, Berlin & New Britain Town Halls, (FHL film 3,730);
- "LR9" is Berlin's Land Records, vols. 8–9, 1809–1817, Berlin & New Britain Town Halls,(FHL film 3,732);
- "LR12" is Berlin's Land Records, vols. 12–13, 1818–1823. Berlin & New Britain Town Halls, (FHL film 3.734);
- "1," which Barbour describes as a Book of Marriages, apparently includes pages 1–139, and covers births and marriage certificates 1820 to 1850, but does not appear to be filmed by FHL or possessed by CSL or the Town Clerk's office.[115]

The FHL offers additional early Berlin records not abstracted by Barbour:

- **Berlin's Land Records, vols. 10–11 (said to include births, deaths and marriages 1815–1825) Berlin & New Britain Town Halls (FHL film 3,733);**
- **Berlin's Records of Births, Marriages & Deaths, vol. 1 1849 *et seq*. (includes a brief return of Civil War soldiers, with the names & ages of their family members) Berlin Town Hall (FHL film 1,317,271).**

CSL reports that when "town was separated in 19=850[,] New Britain took all the original records to that date including 34 volumes of Berlin records 1783–1850 plus 1 volume of Berlin marriages 1820–1850."[116]

CHURCH RECORDS:

- Kensington Congregational Church's "Church Records, 1709–1889" (includes marriages 1756–1888; baptisms 1756–1889; and deaths 1779–1889) originals in CS) (FHL film 3,744);
- Worthington Ecclesiastical Society's "Church Records, 1772–1928" (includes vital records 1775–1779) originals at CSL (FHL film 3,746);
- Congregational Church's "Church Records, 1775–1922," (includes deaths 1811–1844; baptisms 1814–1831, and marriages 1835–1844] originals in CSL (FHL film 3,745 or 1,007,923);
- Methodist Church's "Church Records, 1829–1895" (includes infant baptisms 1837–1867) originals in CSL (FHL film 3,747;
- St. Gabriel's Church of East Berlin's Parish register, 1895–1941 (Contains historical notes, records of families, baptisms 1895–1940, confirmations, communicants, marriages 1896–1939, burials 1895–1941) originals in Episcopal Diocese archives, Hartford (FHL film 1,513,663, item 3) (includes records from the Cemetery of the Congregational Church Yard in Bethel).

CEMETERY INSCRIPTIONS: The Hale Collection identifies burials in order of physical proximity at 13 named cemeteries in what was then Berlin.[117] Compare with Daniel Hearn's 1978 copy of 84 pre-1800 gravestones in three Berlin cemeteries.[118] See also,

---

[115] CSL, *Connecticut Town Records of the First Two Hundred Years, 1620–1820* (Hartford: CSL, 1975); email from Town Clerk Kate Wall, 3 May 2018.

[116] CSL, "Berlin" (6/4/82 note by J.C.) *CT Vital Records.*

[117] Charles R. Hale, "Headstone Inscriptions of the Town of Berlin," bound typescript, 1930s, CSL, Hartford, FHL film 3,320.

- Edward Sweetser Tillotson's *Wethersfield Inscriptions: A Complete Record of the Inscriptions in the Five Burial Places in the Ancient Town of Wethersfield, Including the Towns of Rocky Hill, Newington and Beckley Quarter (in Berlin), also a Portion of the Inscriptions in the Oldest Cemetery in Glastonbury* (Reprint. orig. pub. Hartford: William F.J. Boardman, 1899) (FHL film 908,332, item 1)
- Lucius B. Barbour's *Genealogical Data from Berlin Cemeteries* (1932/1997 copy at NEHGS)
- Connecticut DAR's "Beckley Cemetery" *CT DAR GRC Report*, ser. 1, vol. 18:1 (1930–31);
- DAR Abigail Wolcott Ellsworth Chapter's "Ledge Cemetery, Kensington, (Berlin), Connecticut," *CT DAR GRC Report*, ser. 1, vol. 90: 71 (1942) (FHL film 844,451);
- Connecticut DAR's "East Berlin Cemetery, Wilcox Cemetery, Berlin, Connecticut," *CT DAR GRC Report*, ser. 1, vol. 96:3 (1943) (FHL film 844,452);
- Connecticut DAR's "Blue Hills Cemetery, Stockings Corner, Berlin, Connecticut," *CT DAR GRC Report*, ser. 1, vol. 96:13 (1943) (FHL film 844,452);
- Connecticut DAR's "Maple Cemetery, Berlin, Connecticut," *CT DAR GRC Report*, ser. 1, vol. 96:27 (1943) (FHL film 844,452);
- Connecticut DAR's "Bridge Cemetery, Worthington (or Denison Cemetery, Barbors Col), Berlin, Connecticut," *CT DAR GRC Report*, ser. 1, vol. 96:40 (1943) (FHL film 844,452);
- Connecticut DAR's "Christian Lane Cemetery, Berlin, Connecticut," *CT DAR GRC Report*, ser. 1, vol. 96:52 (1943) (FHL film 844,452);
- Connecticut DAR's "Old Cemetery, Hall's Corner, Berlin, Connecticut," *CT DAR GRC Report*, ser. 1, vol. 96:59 (1943) (FHL film 844,452);
- Connecticut DAR's "The Maple Cemetery, Berlin, Connecticut, taken from "History of Berlin, Connecticut" by Catharine M. North," *CT DAR GRC Report*, ser. 1, vol. 133:11 (1956, 1984);
- Connecticut DAR's "Old Cemetery, Spruce Brook Road, Mt. Lamentation, Berlin, Connecticut," *CT DAR GRC Report*, ser. 1, vol. 96:60 (1943) (FHL film 844,452);
- Connecticut DAR's "West Lane Cemetery, Berlin, Connecticut," *CT DAR GRC Report*, ser. 1, vol. 96:61 (1943) (FHL film 844,452);
- Connecticut DAR's "Wilcox Cemetery, East Berlin, Connecticut, taken from book at Peck's Library, Kensington, Connecticut," *CT DAR GRC Report*, ser. 1, vol. 133:12 (1956, 1984);
- Connecticut DAR's "Fairview Cemetery, North Cemetery, Old Cemetery, Quaker Cemetery all located in West Hartford, Connecticut, Wilcox Cemetery, East Berlin, Connecticut, taken from book at Peck's Library, Kensington, Connecticut," *CT DAR GRC Report*, ser. 1, vol. 133:12 (1956, 1984).
- Connecticut DAR's "Starting of Christian Lane Cemetery, taken from "History of Berlin, Connecticut" by Catharine M. North, 1916," *CT DAR GRC Report*, ser. 1, vol. 133:10 (1956, 1984);
- Connecticut DAR's "List of Berlin, Connecticut Cemeteries," *CT DAR GRC Report*, ser. 1, vol. 133:9 (1956, 1984);

---

[118] Daniel Hearn, "Connecticut gravestones, early to 1800," manuscript (FHL film 1,477,476, item 6).

OTHER NOTEWORTHY SOURCES:

- Diary of Oren Lee of Berlin & Granby, 1809–1841, CSL; see Appendix A;
- David Nelson Camp's *History of New Britain: with sketches of Farmington and Berlin, Connecticut, 1640–1889* (New Britain: William B. Thomson & Co., c1889);
- Catharine M. North and Adolph Burnett Benson's *History of Berlin, Connecticut* (New Haven: Tuttle, Morehouse & Taylor, 1916).

BETHANY

Barbour's typescript volume Bethany,[119] for unlike the GPC edition,[120] begins:

> This volume contains a list alphabetically arranged of all the vital records of the town of Bethany from its incorporation to about 1853. The entire record of this town prior to 1853 is found in one volume.
>
> This list was taken from a set of cards[121] based on a copy of the Bethany in Vital Records made in 1916 by James N. Arnold, of Providence, R.I. The Arnold Copy, now in the possession of the Connecticut State Library, has not been compared with the original and doubtless errors exist. It is hoped that as errors or omissions are found notes will be entered in this volume and on the cards which are included in the General Index of Connecticut Vital Records also in the possession of the Connecticut State Library.
>
> Hartford, Connecticut, December 1924[122]

VITAL RECORDS: Bethany's volume actually abstracts only marriage certifications, from the town's establishment in 1832 to 1853 from Bethany's Records of births, marriages, and deaths, vol. 1, 1832–1853 (FHL film 1,420,662, item 2). Barbour abstracts no Bethany birth or death records.

Although no additional pre-1852 vital records appear at FHL, CSL or the Bethany town hall, do not assume that this abstraction includes all extant pre 1853 Bethany records. Morrison, suggests that more early Bethany records may be found in Woodbridge, New Haven or Milford.[123]

CHURCH RECORDS:

- "New Cambridge Church Records, 1747–1800" (deaths in Bethany, 1788–1793) manuscript at NYGHS (FHL film 4,948 or 1,405,497);

---

119 See How to Use This Book, note 3, above.

120 White, *Barbour Collection: Barkhamsted–Bozrah*, vol. 2, digital image at *Ancestry.com*.

121 Now part of the Barbour Index and interfiled with similar slips from other towns in CSL and on FHL films 2887 *et seq*. See Introduction above, pp. 1–3.

122 Lucius B. Barbour, *Connecticut Vital Records: Bethany, 1832–1853* (Hartford: CSL, 1924) page after title page (FHL film 2,967. Digital images at *AmericanAncestors.org* and *FamilySearch,org.*

123 Morrison, *Connecting to Connecticut*, 14.

- Christ Church's Church Records, 1799–1948, (includes baptisms 1813–1834 & 1836–1880, marriages 1813–1833 & 1836–1896, and burials 1813–1836 & 1836–1894) originals in CSL (FHL film 1,007,924 or 3,817);
- Baptisms (1813–14) marriages (1813–35) & burials 1813–35 & 1836–94) at Christ Church, Episcopal Diocese, Hartford (ED Film 1,007,924);
- R. Manning Chipman's "Select Records of the Congregational Church of Bethany, Conn., 1814–1845" (includes baptisms) manuscript at NEHGS);
- Congregational Church's Congregational Church Papers, 1788–1920 (CSL film #448);
- Congregational Church's Church records, 1762–1920. (includes certificates of withdrawal and correspondence. Also includes certificates from the Bethany Congregational Church to other bodies 1791–1820) (FHL film 1,007,925, item 4).

CEMETERY INSCRIPTIONS: The Hale Collection identifies burials in order of physical proximity at six named cemeteries in what was then the town of Bethany.[124] Compare with Daniel Hearn's 1976 copy of 39 pre-1800 gravestones in two Bethany cemeteries.[125] The Hale Collection also identifies people in order of physical proximity buried at two named cemeteries in what was then the town of Beacon Falls.[126] See also,

- Connecticut DAR's "Bethany Congregational Cemetery on Amity Road, Bethany, Connecticut," *CT DAR GRC Report*, ser. 1, vol. 41:48 (1934) (retyped in 1997);
- Connecticut DAR's "Episcopal Cemetery, Bethany Center, Connecticut," *CT DAR GRC Report*, ser. 1, vol. 41:48 (1934) (retyped in 1997);
- Connecticut DAR's "Carrington Cemetery, Bethany, Connecticut," *CT DAR GRC Report*, ser. 1, vol. 41:48 (1934) (retyped in 1997);
- Connecticut DAR's "Sperry Cemetery, Bethany, Connecticut," *CT DAR GRC Report*, ser. 1, vol. 41:48 (1934) (retyped in 1997);
- Connecticut DAR, "Pines Bridge Cemetery, Beacon Falls, Connecticut," *CT DAR GRC Report*, ser. 1, vol. 41:53;
- Connecticut DAR's "Pines Bridge Cemetery, Beacon Falls, New Haven Co., Connecticut," *CT DAR GRC Report*, ser. 1, vol. 58:169 (1936) (FHL film 844,453);
- Connecticut DAR's "Revolutionary War Soldiers Graves in Pines Bridge Cemetery, Beacon Falls, New Haven Co., Connecticut," *CT DAR GRC Report*, ser. 1, vol. 58:198 (1936) (FHL film 844,453).

OTHER NOTEWORTHY SOURCES:

- W. C. Sharpe's *Bethany Sketches and Records, pt. 2* (Seymour CT: W.C. Sharpe, 1913) (FHL film 1,033,988, item 6);
- Eliza J. Lines' *Bethany and its hills: glimpses of the town of Bethany as it was before the railroads and the fire fiend robbed it of its glory,* (Washington, D.C.: Library of Congress Photoduplication Service, 1987) (FHL film 1,491,098).

---

124 Charles R. Hale, "Headstone Inscriptions of the Town of Bethany," bound typescript, 1930s, CSL, Hartford, FHL film 3,320.

125 Daniel Hearn, "Connecticut gravestones, early to 1800," manuscript (FHL film 1,477,476, item 7).

126 Charles R. Hale, "Headstone Inscriptions of the Town of Beacon Falls," bound typescript, 1930s, CSL, Hartford, FHL film 3,320.

- Wallace Hamilton's "Two Private Connecticut Mortuary Lists," *TAG*, 26:42 (1950)
- "Woodbridge, Inhabitants of Amity & Bethany," 1780; *TAG* 11:192 (1935);

BETHLEHEM

Barbour's typescript volume for Bethlehem,[127] unlike the GPC edition,[128] begins:

> This volume contains a list alphabetically arranged of all the vital records of the town of Bethlehem from its incorporation to about 1851. The entire record of this town prior to 1851 is found in one volume. This list was taken from a set of cards[129] based on a copy of the Bethlehem Vital Records made in 1916 by James N. Arnold, of Providence, R.I. The Arnold Copy, now in the possession of the Connecticut State Library, has not been compared with the original and doubtless errors exist. It is hoped that as errors or omissions are found notes will be entered in this volume and on the cards which are included in the General Index of Connecticut Vital Records also in the possession of the Connecticut State Library.
>
> Hartford, Conn., October 1926[130]

VITAL RECORDS: Bethlehem's volume includes vital records as early as 1752 and as late as 1852 from Bethlehem's Record of Marriages, Births and Deaths, (marriages. births and deaths, 1761–1857) Bethlehem Town Hall, (FHL film 1,522,005, item 1). See also,

- **Bethlehem's "Lists and vital statistics, 1787–1794" (includes some records of births, marriages, and deaths, 1764–1794, Bethlehem Town Hall (FHL film 1,522,005, item 2);**
- **Bethlehem's Records of Births, Marriages and Deaths, 1847–1948, Bethlehem Town Hall, (FHL film 1,522,005, items 4–5);**
- **George M. Kassan and Elizabeth Kassan Hayes' "Memorandum of Deaths in Bethlehem, 1845–1902" (original in town hall) (FHL film 1,522,005, item 3);**
- **Donald Lines Jacobus' "Bethlehem (Conn.) Vital Records (reports two more marriages & one death)," *NEHGR*, 77:158 (Apr 1923).**

CHURCH RECORDS:

- Methodist Church's Church records, 1859–1924, originals at CSL (FHL film 3,804).

---

127 See How to Use This Book, note 3, above.

128 White, *Barbour Collection: Barkhamsted–Bozrah*, vol. 2, digital image at *Ancestry.com*.

129 Now part of the Barbour Index and interfiled with similar slips from other towns in CSL and on FHL films 2,887 *et seq*. See Introduction above, pp. 1–3.

130 Lucius B. Barbour, *Connecticut Vital Records, Bethlehem, 1787–1851* (Hartford: CSL, 1926) page after title page (FHL film 2 967). Digital images at *AmericanAncestors.org.*and *FamilySearch.org.*

- Congregational Church's "Church Records, 1738–1850" (including baptisms 1740–1792 & 1816–1848, marriages 1740–1798 & 1800–1812, and deaths 1741–1798 & 1799–1850) originals in CSL (FHL film 3,803);
- Christ Church's "Church Records, 1807–1905" (includes baptisms 1835–1836 & 1835–1899, & 1838–1840, funerals 1835 & 1837–1841, marriages 1836–1837 & 1839–1900, and burials 1837–1899) originals at CSL (FHL film 3,802);
- Baptisms (1835–6, 1838–40, 1835–99), burials (1835, 1837, 1838–41, 1839–1900) & marriages (1836–7 & 1839–1900) at Christ Church, Episcopal Diocese, Hartford (ED Film 3,802);
- Watertown & Bethlehem Methodist Episcopal Society Records, 1820–1826 (CSL #974.62 W352m) (FHL film 6,092).

CEMETERY INSCRIPTIONS: The Hale Collection identifies burials in order of physical proximity at five named cemeteries in Bethlehem.[131] Compare with Daniel Hearn's 1976 copy of 40 pre-1800 gravestones in two Bethlehem cemeteries.[132] See also,

- Lucius B, Barbour's Bethlehem Cemetery Inscriptions, 2 volumes, CSL film #167.
- Charles R. Hale and Mary H. Babin's "Headstone Inscriptions, Town of Bethlehem, Connecticut," 1934 typescript photocopy at FHL.

OTHER NOTEWORTHY SOURCES:

- William Cothren's *History of ancient Woodbury, Connecticut, from the first Indian deed in 1659 to 1854: including the present towns of Washington, Southbury, Bethlehem, Roxbury, and a part of Oxford and Middlebury* (vol. 3 contains vital records, including those for ancient Stratford) (Baltimore: GPC, 1997)
- Old Bethlem Historical Society, *Bethlehem, a primer of local history, from the beginning to 1876: with addendum* [Bethlehem: Old Bethlem Historical Society, c1976) (FHL fiche 6,087,534).

BLOOMFIELD

Barbour's individual volume for Bloomfield,[133] unlike the GPC edition,[134] begins:

> This volume contains a list alphabetically arranged of all the vital records of the town of Bloomfield from its incorporation to about 1853. The entire record of this town prior to 1853, is found in one volume.
> This list was taken from a set of cards[135] based on a copy of the Bloomfield Vital Records made in 1916 by James N. Arnold, of Providence, R.I. The Arnold Copy has not been compared with the original and doubtless errors exist. It is

131 Charles R. Hale, "Headstone Inscriptions of the Town of Bethlehem," bound typescript, 1930s, CSL, Hartford, FHL film 3,320.

132 Daniel Hearn, "Connecticut gravestones, early to 1800," manuscript (FHL film 1,477,476, item 9).

133 See How to Use This Book, note 3, above.

134 White, *Barbour Collection: Barkhamsted–Bozrah*, vol. 2, digital image at *Ancestry.com*.

135 Now part of the Barbour Index and interfiled with similar slips from other towns in CSL and on FHL films 2887 *et seq*. See Introduction above, pp. 1-3.

```
hoped that as errors or omissions are found notes
will be entered in this volume and on the cards
which are included in the General Index of Connec-
ticut Vital Records also in the possession of the
Connecticut State Library.
                          Hartford, Conn., June 1928[136]
```

VITAL RECORDS: Bloomfield's volume includes vital records as early as 1831 and as late as 1853. Barbour abstracted Bloomfield's Records of Births, Marriages, and Deaths, 1835–1911 Bloomfield Town Hall, (FHL film 1,314,449, last part of item 1)

FHL film 1,314,449 also includes two record sets not abstracted by Barbour:

- **Item 1 begins with Mary B. Bishop's inscriptions from St. Andrews Cemetery (1932 typescript annotated with additional family history);**
- **Item 2 is cataloged by FHL as "Bloomfield's' Index to Vital Statistics, 1738–1938," a start date preceding Bloomfield's founding by nearly a century! It is undetermined whether the original records thus indexed may be in Bloomfield and/or one of its parent towns, Farmington, Hartford, Simsbury, and/or Windsor.**

CHURCH RECORDS:

- Mary K. Talcott's "Records of the Church in Wintonbury Parish (Now Bloomfield), Conn.," *NEHGR*, 71:74–88, 153–66, 271–83, 295–310 (Jan Apr Jul Oct 1917), 72:29–51, 87–107, 166–85 (Jan Apr Jul 1918);
- Congregational Church's "Church Records, 1738–1918" (includes baptisms 1738–1790 & 1792–1862, marriages 1738–1787 & 1792–1863, deaths 1791–1837 & 1845–1866) (originals in CSL) (FHL film 3.752);
- St. Andrew's Church's "Church Records, 1743–1936" (includes baptisms 1763–1800, marriages 1763–1798, and burials 1763–1769) (originals in CSL) (FHL film 3,751);
- Baptisms (1763–1800), burials (1763–96) & marriages (1763–98) at St. Andrew's Church, Episcopal Diocese, Hartford (ED Film 3,751);
- Mary K. Talcott's "Records of the Church in Wintonbury Parish (now Bloomfield), Conn.," *NEHGR*, 71:74–88, 153–66, 271–83, 295–310 (Jan Apr Jul Oct 1917), 72:29–51, 87–107, 166–85 (Jan Apr Jul 1918);
- Blue Hills Baptist Church Records, 1810–1899, (FHL film 4584 , CSL film #223);
- Methodist Episcopal Church Papers, 1833–1836 (CSL film #448) (FHL film 1,007,925, items 5–6);
- "Connecticut Church Records: [partial] Index, Bloomfield Cong. Church, 1738–1924" [1958 manuscript at NEHGS);
- Documents Relating to St. Andrew's Church, Simsbury (now in Bloomfield) and St. Ann's Church, Granby, Conn., 1744–1785, photostatic copies, CSL, Hartford, (FHL film 1,007,925, item 7);
- Albert C. Bates's *Records of Rev. Roger Viets, Rector of St. Andrews, Simsbury, Conn.*, (Hartford: Case, Lockwood & Brainard, 1893) (FHL film 924,061, item 4).

[136] Lucius B. Barbour, *Connecticut Vital Records: Bloomfield, 1835–1853* (Hartford; CSL, 1928) page after title page (FHL film 2,967). Digital images at *AmericanAncestors.org* and *FamilySearch,org*.

CEMETERY INSCRIPTIONS: The Hale Collection identifies burials in order of physical proximity at 11 named cemeteries in Bloomfield.[137] Compare with Daniel Hearn's 1978 copy of 149 pre-1800 gravestones in two Bloomfield cemeteries.[138]

See also,

- DAR's Genealogical Collection (North Bloomfield and Manchester: Cemetery Records) (bound typescript) DAR, Washington, D.C. (FHL film 844,456);
- Mary B. Bishop's "Copy of the Inscriptions on the Tombstones in St. Andrew's Cemetery, North Bloomfield, Connecticut," *CT DAR GRC Report*, ser. 1, vol. 37:1 (1932) (FHL film 844,456);
- DAR Abigail Wolcott Ellsworth Chapter's "New Latimer Hill Cemetery, Bloomfield, Connecticut," *CT DAR GRC Report*, ser. 1, vol. 91:1 (1943) (FHL film 844,451);
- DAR Abigail Wolcott Ellsworth Chapter's "St. Andrews Cemetery, Bloomfield, Connecticut," *CT DAR GRC Report*, ser. 1, vol. 90:6 (1942) (FHL film 844451);
- DAR Abigail Wolcott Ellsworth Chapter's "Wintonbury Cemetery, Bloomfield, Connecticut," *CT DAR GRC Report*, ser. 1, vol. 90:24a (1942).

OTHER NOTEWORTHY SOURCES:

- Lucius B. Barbour's Notes compiled from church records of Wintonbury, Conn. 1735–1840, 1 volume. Abstract of vital records. Arranged alphabetically. (manuscript 69 in Box 8) CSL Record Group 074.36, Hartford;
- Lucius B. Barbour's Genealogical notes compiled from Stebbins family record of Simsbury and inscriptions from St. Andrews Cemetery, Bloomfield, Conn. 1719–1827, 1 volume, (manuscript 49 in Box 6) CSL Record Group 074.36, Hartford;
- Lucius B. Barbour's Some Inscriptions in Ancient Windsor, Conn., circa 1915; 1 volume (Windsor Cemetery; Poquonock Cemetery, Windsor; Wintonbury Cemetery, Bloomfield; East Windsor Cemetery.) (manuscript 65 in Box 8) CSL Record Group 074.36, Hartford;
- Wintonbury Historical Society. *From Wintonbury to Bloomfield: Bloomfield sketches, a collection of papers on the history of the Town of Bloomfield, Connecticut, formerly known as Wintonbury* (Bloomfield: Wintonbury Historical Society, c1983);
- Frederick C. Bidwell's *Over Tunxis trails: commemorating Connecticut's tercentenary 1635–1935, establishment of Wintonbury Parish 1735, incorporation of the town of Bloomfield May 29, 1835* ([S.l.]: F.C. Bidwell, [1935?]);
- Henry R. Stiles's *History of Ancient Windsor, Connecticut: Including East Windsor, South Windsor, and Ellington Prior to 1788, the Date of their Separation from the Old Town, and Windsor, Bloomfield, and Windsor Locks to the Present Time; also the Genealogies and Genealogical Notes of Those Families Which Settled Within the Limits of Ancient Windsor, Connecticut Prior to 1800*, vol. 2 (Albany NY: J. Munsell, 1863) (FHL film 417.935).

137 Charles R. Hale, "Headstone Inscriptions of the Town of Bloomfield," bound typescript, 1930s, CSL, Hartford, FHL film 3,320 & 3,321.

138 Daniel Hearn, "Connecticut gravestones, early to 1800," manuscript (FHL film 1,477,476, item 10).

BOLTON

VITAL RECORDS: Morrison states that Bolton birth, marriage and death records begin in 1720,[139] and the FHL catalogs vital records as early as 1704. Barbour published no individual volume[140] for Bolton. He abstracted the slips in the Barbour Index[141] from CHS' *Vital Records of Bolton to 1854 and Vernon to 1852* (Hartford: CHS, 1909) (images at *AmericanAncestors.org*). CHS abstracted its records from four volumes of Bolton vital records,[142] which are filmed by FHL as Bolton's Records of Births, Marriages, and Deaths, 1799–1880, (including records of births 1704–1880, marriages 1722–1880, deaths 1708–1880), Bolton Town Hall, (FHL film 1,376,044, items 1–3):

- CHS' "Town Records, Volume 1" is from what FHL filmed as item1 (ca. 1704–1771);
- CHS' "Third Book of Records" is from what FHL filmed as item 2 (ca. 1777–1849);
- CHS' "Record of Marriages" is from what FHL filmed as the first part of item 3 (1847–1852);
- CHS' "Record of Births and Deaths" is from what FHL filmed as the second part of what FHL filmed as item 3 (1848–1867).

Bolton possesses several other volumes of town vital record not abstracted by Barbour.[143]

CHURCH RECORDS:

- Bolton Church's "Church Records, 1725–1812" (include baptisms, marriages, and deaths) originals in the CSL (FHL film 1,007,926);
- Congregational Church's "Church Records, 1725–1922" (includes baptisms, marriages, and burials) originals in CSL (FHL film 3,720);
- Mary K. Talcott's "A Copy of the Records of the Rev. Thomas White, the First Pastor Of Bolton, Conn.," *NEHGR*, 52:180–5, 307–11, 408–21, (Apr–Oct 1898), 53:447–50 (Oct 1899), 54:80–6, 253–60 (Jan, Jul 1900) 55:34–9 282–8 (Jan, Jul 1901) 56:162–7, 347–56 (Apr, Oct 1902);
- First Ecclesiastical Society's "Dissenters' certificates 1793–1847," (CSL, film #449, Hartford) (FHL film 1,007,926, item 2).

CEMETERY INSCRIPTIONS: The Hale Collection identifies burials in order of physical proximity at two named cemeteries in Bolton.[144] Compare with Daniel Hearn's 1979 copy of 133 pre-1800 gravestones in two Bolton cemeteries.[145] See also,

- Lucius B. Barbour's "Inscriptions from Gravestones at Bolton, Conn.," *NEHGR*, 83:93–106, 156–64 (Jan, Apr 1929);

---

139 Morrison, *Connecting to Connecticut*, 22.

140 See How to Use This Book, note 3, above.

141 The Barbour Index may be viewed only at CSL and on FHL films 2887 *et seq*. See Introduction above, pp. 1–3

142 CHS, *Vital Records of Bolton to 1854 and Vernon to 1852 (*Hartford: CHS, 1909) pp. 1–153.

143 In 1936 Bolton reported "6 volumes of Vital Statistics 1707–1936. *Biennial Report of the Examiner* for *Public Records* for the Period Ended June 30, 1936 (Hartford, State of CT, 1936, p. 13).

144 Charles R. Hale, "Headstone Inscriptions of the Town of Bolton," bound typescript, 1930s, CSL, Hartford, FHL film 3,322.

145 Daniel Hearn, "Connecticut gravestones, early to 1800," manuscript (FHL film 1,477,476, item 12).

- Susan W. Dimock's "Quarryville Cemetery, lying between North Coventry and Bolton, Connecticut," *CT DAR GRC Report*, ser. 1, vol. 5:124 (1914).

OTHER NOTEWORTHY SOURCES: Lucius B. Barbour's "Genealogical notes compiled from records of Bolton and Vernon, Conn. 1724–1860," 2 volumes. Abstract of vital records, arranged alphabetically. (manuscript 3 in Box 1) CSL Record Group 074.36, Hartford.

BOZRAH

Barbour's typescript volume for Bozrah,[146] unlike the GPC edition,[147] begins:

> This volume contains a list alphabetically arranged of all the vital records of the town of Bozrah from its incorporation to about 1850. This list was taken from a set of cards[148] based on a copy of the Bozrah Vital Records made in 1910 by James N. Arnold, of Providence, R.I. The records here indexed are taken from the first three volumes of vital records. All births, marriages and deaths in the first two volumes have been indexed but in Volume 3 the deaths only. The record of deaths in chronological arrangement ends with an entry bearing the date of December 18, 1871. The Arnold Copy, now in the possession of the Connecticut State Library, has not been compared with the original and doubtless errors exist. It is hoped that as errors or omissions are found notes will be entered in this volume and on the cards which are included in the General Index of Connecticut Vital Records also in the possession of the Connecticut State Library.
>
> Hartford, Conn., November, 1919.[149]

VITAL RECORDS: Bozrah's volume includes vital records as early as 1743 and as late as 1871. Barbour abstracted three Bozrah "books:"

- "1" abstracts "Bozrah First Book of Records of Marriages, Births & Deaths, 1755–1861, Bozrah Town Hall, (FHL film 1,312,386).
- "2"abstracts ten pages of births marriages, and deaths. Books "2" and "3" apparently remain unfilmed at the Bozrah town hall.,[150]

See also, "Bozrah Vital Records *circa* 1852–1905" at CSL (CSA RG 072.002, Box 3) (includes pre-1850 birthdates on death certificates).

---

146 See How to Use This Book, note 3, above.

147 White, *Barbour Collection: Barkhamsted–Bozrah*, vol. 2, digital image at *Ancestry.com*.

148 Now part of the Barbour Index and interfiled with similar slips from other towns in CSL and on FHL films 2,887 *et seq*. See Introduction above, pp. 1–3.

149 Lucius B. Barbour, *Connecticut Vital Records, Bozrah, 1786–1850* (Hartford: CSL, 1919) page after title page.(FHL film 2,967). Digital images at *AmericanAncestors.org* and *FamilySearch,org*.

150 The Bozrah town clerk describes her entire pre-1900 inventory of vital records as "1 Book Vital Records 1785 to 1850, 1 Book Birth Vol. 1 & 2 1846 to 1949, 1 Book Marriages Vol. 1 & 2 1852 to 1946, [and] 1 Book Deaths Vol. 1 & 2 1872 to 1949." email from Bozrah Town Clerk Lynne A. Skinner, 3 May 2018.

CHURCH RECORDS:

- Bozrahville Congregational Church's "Church Records, 1737–1890" (includes marriages 1835–1839 and records of the Ecclesiastical Society and Congregational Church formerly New Concord Society in Norwich for years 1737–1845.) (manuscript at CSL) (FHL film 3,727);
- New Concord Society's Church records, 1832–1851 originals at CSL:(FHL film 1,007,926, item 3);
- First Congregational Church's "Records of baptisms, marriages, deaths and church admissions of the Fifth [i.e. First] Church, of Norwich, Connecticut, from 1730 [i.e. 1739] to 1824 kept by Joseph Murdock, pastor of the church," typescript by Jennie Tefft Gallup; NEHGS Mss A 5587;
- "Records of Baptisms, marriages, deaths, and church admissions of the First Church of Norwich, Conn. from 1739 to 1829," (acquired by CSL 1929)..

CEMETERY INSCRIPTIONS: The Hale Collection identifies burials in order of physical proximity at nine named cemeteries in Bozrah Township.[151] Compare with Daniel Hearn's 1982 copy of 84 pre-1800 gravestones in three Bozrah cemeteries.[152] See also,

- Elizabeth Prather Ellsberry's "Cemetery Records of New London County, Connecticut" *(*typescript photocopy at FHL) (FHL film 874,014);
- DAR Abigail Wolcott Ellsworth Chapter's "Bozrah Street Cemetery, Bozrah, Connecticut," *CT DAR GRC Report*, ser. 1, vol. 90: 80 (1942) (FHL film 844,451);
- DAR Abigail Wolcott Ellsworth Chapter's "Bulkley-Gardner Cemetery, Bozrah, Connecticut," *CT DAR GRC Report*, ser. 1, vol. 90: 84 (1942) (FHL film 844,451);
- DAR Abigail Wolcott Ellsworth Chapter's "Church Cemetery, Bozrah, Connecticut," *CT DAR GRC Report*, ser. 1, vol. 90: 87 (1942) (FHL film 844,451);
- DAR Abigail Wolcott Ellsworth Chapter's "Smith Cemetery, Bozrah, Connecticut," *CT DAR GRC Report*, ser. 1, vol. 90: 87 (1942) (FHL film 844,451)
- DAR Abigail Wolcott Ellsworth Chapter's "Stark Cemetery, Bozrah, Connecticut," *CT DAR GRC Report*, ser. 1, vol. 90: 87 (1942) (FHL film 844,451)
- DAR Abigail Wolcott Ellsworth Chapter's "Hough-Harris Family Yard, Bozrah, Connecticut," *CT DAR GRC Report*, ser. 1, vol. 90: 88 (1942) (FHL film 844,451);
- DAR Abigail Wolcott Ellsworth Chapter's "Bailey-Wightman Yard, Bashan Hill, Bozrah, Connecticut," *CT DAR GRC Report*, ser. 1, vol. 90: 90 (1942) (FHL film 844,451);
- DAR Abigail Wolcott Ellsworth Chapter's "Johnson Cemetery, Fitchville, Bozrah, Connecticut," *CT DAR GRC Report*, ser. 1, vol. 90: 91 (1942) (FHL film 844,451)
- Bozrah Headstones: Bailey-Wightman, Gardiner, Hough-Harris, Johnson, Old Leffingwell, Parker, Cemeteries, *CN*, 19:423, 615 (1985).

OTHER NOTEWORTHY SOURCES: Lucius B. Barbour's Genealogical notes compiled from church records of New Concord and Norwich Fourth Society, Bozrah, Conn. 1739–1813, 1 volume. Abstract of vital records. (manuscript 4 in Box 1) CSL Record Group 074.36, Hartford.

---

151 Charles R. Hale, "Headstone Inscriptions of the Town of Bozrah," bound typescript, 1930s, CSL, Hartford, FHL film 3 322).

152 Daniel Hearn, "Connecticut gravestones, early to 1800," manuscript (FHL film 1,477,476, item 11).

BRANFORD

Barbour's typescript volume for Branford,[153] unlike the GPC edition,[154] begins:

> The vital records of Branford prior to 1850 are found scattered through the first two volumes of Land Records and a book of Town Records and Meetings dated 1697-1788. The entries in these have been alphabetically arranged and listed. Reference to the Land Records is indicated herein by the numbers 1 and 2, to the book of Town Records by the number 3, to the Town Meetings by "TM3". In the Town Records' Volume, referred to as Vol. 3", there appears to be duplicate pagination from 255 through 315.
>
> This list was taken from a set of cards[155] based on a copy of the Branford Vital Records made in 1914 by Miss Ethel L. Scofield, of New Haven, Conn. The Scofield Copy, now in the possession of the Connecticut State Library, has not been compared with the original and doubtless errors exist. It is hoped that as errors or omissions are found notes will be entered in this volume and on the cards which are included in the General Index of Connecticut Vital Records also in the possession of the Connecticut State Library.
>
> Hartford, Conn., September 1924.[156]

VITAL RECORDS: Branford's volume includes vital records as early as 1649 and as late as 1854. Barbour abstracted four Branford "books:"

- "1" refers to Branford's Land records, vols. 1–2, 1645–1680, (Volume 1 includes births, marriages and deaths) Branford Town Hall, (FHL film 3,699);
- "2" refers to Branford's Land records, vols. 1–2, 1680–1710, (Volume 2 includes 3 death and births at pp. 343–47) Branford Town Hall, (FHL film 3,699);
- "3" abstracts vital records for the years 1701–1854 on pages 29–284) and seems to be one of two unfilmed town records book in Branford in 1975;[157]
- "TM3" abstracts vital records for the years 1835–1853 on its pages 160–304 and is apparently unfilmed and available for comparison only at the Town Clerk's office.

No Branford vital records between 1710 and 1850 appear to have been cataloged by FHL, not even the 1820 to 1850 volume of marriage certificates or the 1848 to 1852

---

153 See How to Use This Book, note 3, above.

154 Lorraine Cook White, *Barbour Collection of Connecticut Town Vital Records: Branford, 1644–1850, Bridgeport, 1821–1854*, vol. 3, (Baltimore: GPC, 1995) digital image at *Ancestry.com*.

155 Now part of the Barbour Index and interfiled with similar slips from other towns in CSL and on FHL films 2,887 *et seq*. See Introduction above, pp. 1–3.

156 Lucius B. Barbour, *Connecticut Vital Records: Branford, 1644–1850* (Hartford: CSL, 1924) page after title page (FHL film 2,967). Digital images at *AmericanAncestors.org* and *FamilySearch,or*.

157 In 1975 the Branford town clerk possessed a 465 page book of Town Records 1691–1788 and a 452 page book of Town Records 1786–1849. CSL, *First 200 Years*.

records by school district all towns were required to create.[158] In 1936, however, Branford actually possessed "10 volumes of vital records 1649–1936" and "6 volumes of Town Proceedings 1644–1936."[159] **The town clerk's book shelf (below) shows a useful "Index of BMD, 1644–1850," which may fill gaps in the records Barbour abstracted.**

Figures 11 &12 Photographs by Branford Town Clerk and Registrar of Vital Statistics

The FHL also catalogs under Branford vital records: **Charles M. Taintor, Micaiell Taintor, and Michaell Taintor's *Abstracts from the Records of Colchester: With Some Transcripts from the Recording of Michaell Taintor of "Brainford," Conn.* (Washington DC, LoC, (Photoduplication Service, 1969) (FHL film 1,685,393).**

CHURCH RECORDS:

- Wayne E. Jacobson and Anna E. Symonds' *One Hundred: a History of the Church of Christ, Congregational, Stony Creek, Connecticut, 1877–1977* (North Haven: John Henry Copy and Printing Center, 1978).
- Trinity Church's "Church Records, 1784–1889' (includes baptisms 1785–1825 & 1829–1895, marriages 1808-1894, and burials 1785–1895) photocopy at CSL (FHL film 3,713);
- "Baptisms Copied from Branford Church Records: Kept by Rev. Samuel Russell Commencing 1688–1786" typescript at NYGB) (FHL film 3,696);
- First Congregational Church's "Church Records, 1687–1899" (includes baptisms, marriages, burials, and deaths) originals at CSL (FHL film 3,712);
- Baptisms (1785–1825, 1829–95), burials (1785–1895) & marriages (1808–94) at Trinity Church, Episcopal Diocese, Hartford (ED Film 3,713);
- Branford Church Records, 1688–1706, *TAG* , 9:31 (1933);

---

158 See statutes transcribed in CHS' *Vital Records of Bolton to 1854 and Vernon to 1852* (Hartford: CHS, 1909) pp. ix–xii.

159 *Biennial Report of the Examiner* for *Public Records* for the Period Ended June 30, 1936 (Hartford, State of CT, 1936, p. 14).

CEMETERY INSCRIPTIONS: The Hale Collection identifies burials in order of physical proximity at 10 named cemeteries in Branford.[160] Compare with Daniel Hearn's 1978 copy of 120 pre-1800 gravestones in one Branford cemetery.[161] See also,

- Lucius B. Barbour's Genealogical Data from Branford Cemeteries (1932/1997 copy at NEHGS);
- Genealogical data from Connecticut cemeteries: Branford, (Salem, MA: Higginson Book Co., 1997) digital images at *FamilySearch.org*;
- Edwin A. Hill, "Branford, Conn., Gravestone Inscriptions," NEHGR, 61:143–50 (Apr 1907);
- Glenn Griswold and Charles D. Townsend's Branford, Connecticut Various Cemetery Records: Damascus Cemetery, Mill Plain Cemetery, Stony Creek Cemetery, Bare Plain Cemetery, North Branford (Sarasota FL: Aceto Bookmen, 1994);
- Connecticut DAR's "Branford Cemetery, Branford, Connecticut," CT DAR GRC Report, ser. 1, vol. 41:46 (1934) (retyped in 1997);
- Connecticut DAR's "Damascus Cemetery, Branford, Connecticut," CT DAR GRC Report, ser. 1, vol. 41:46 (1934) (retyped in 1997);
- DAR Mary Clap Wooster Chapter's "Inscriptions from Damascus Cemetery, Branford, New Haven Co., Connecticut," CT DAR GRC Report, ser. 1, vol. 72:1 (1939) (FHL film 844,454);
- DAR Mary Clap Wooster Chapter's "Stony Creek Cemetery, Branford, New Haven Co., Connecticut," CT DAR GRC Report, ser. 1, vol. 72:12 (1939) (FHL film 844,454);
- DAR Mary Clap Wooster Chapter's "Mill Plain Cemetery, Branford, New Haven Co., Connecticut," CT DAR GRC Report, ser. 1, vol. 72:19 (1939) (FHL film 844,454);
- Branford Headstones, Old Branford, Damascus, & Mill Plain Cemeteries, CN 17:217, 395 (1984);
- Edwin A. Hill's "Branford, Conn., Gravestone Inscriptions," NEHGR, 61:143–50 (Apr 1907).

OTHER NOTEWORTHY SOURCES:

- Edward R. Lambert's *History of the Colony of New Haven: Before and After the Union with Connecticut: Containing a Particular Description of the Towns Which Composed that Government, viz., New Haven, Milford, Guilford, Branford, Stamford, & Southold, L.I* " (New Haven: Hitchcock & Stafford, 1838
- Branford Town Records (exerpts); *TAG* 12:112 (1936).
- Lucius B, Barbour, Abstract of Branford, Conn. vital statistics, 1658–1786, 1920, 1 volume (2 copies). Abstract of church vital records. Arranged alphabetically . (manuscript 5 in Box 1) CSL Record Group 074.36, Hartford;
- Charles M. Taintor's "Early Records of Brainford, Now Branford Ct." *NEHGR*, 3:153–6 (Apr 1846);
- John C. Carr's *Old Branford* ([S.l.]: Branford Historical Society, 1985)

---

160 Charles R. Hale, "Headstone Inscriptions of the Town of Branford," bound typescript, 1930s, CSL, Hartford, FHL film 3,322).

161 Daniel Hearn, "Connecticut gravestones, early to 1800," manuscript (FHL film 1,477,476, item 13).

BRIDGEPORT

Barbour's typescript volume[162] for Bridgeport (unlike the GPC edition[163]) begins:

> This volume contains a list alphabetically arranged of marriage records of the town of Bridgeport from its incorporation to about 1854. This list was taken from a set of cards[164] based on a copy of the Bridgeport Vital Records made in 1915 by James N. Arnold, of Providence, R.I. The entire record for this town prior to 1854 is found in one volume.
>
> The Arnold Copy, now in the possession of the Connecticut State Library, has not been compared with the original and doubtless errors exist. It is hoped that as errors or omissions are found notes will be entered in this volume and on the cards which are included in the General Index of Connecticut Vital Records also in the possession of the Connecticut State Library.
>
> Hartford, Conn., September, 1925.[165]

VITAL RECORDS: Bridgeport's volume includes only marriages as early as 1821 and as late as 1862. Barbour's abstraction is of Bridgeport's Records of Marriages, vols. 1–2, 1831–1870, Bridgeport Town Hall, (FHL film 1,428,469). Barbour missed other pre-1862 vital records, possessed by the Bridgeport Town Clerk:

- **Records of Births in the Town of Bridgeport, 1847–1854, Bridgeport Town Hall (FHL film 1,428,299, items 1–2);**
- **Births in the Town of Bridgeport, 1850–1899, Bridgeport Town Hall (FHL film 1,428,299, items 3–4);**
- **Records of Deaths in the Town of Bridgeport, 1853–1904, Bridgeport Town Hall (FHL film 1,428,471);**
- **Two volumes of "Church Records."** [166]

Also cataloged by FHL under Bridgeport vital records is **Lucy Beardsley Canning and Stratfield Society's "Vital Records, 1805–1838" (includes baptisms and marriages) (typescript at CSL) (FHL film 1,008,323, item 3).**

CHURCH RECORDS:

- United Congregational Church's "Church Records, 1695–1911" (includes baptisms (1695–1807,1805–1828 & 1830–1871), marriages 1716–1838 & 1839–1840), and deaths 1732–1838) typescript at CSL (FHL film 3,830 and 3,3833) (originally the Stratfield church set off from Stratford and Fairfield);

---

162 See How to Use This Book, note 3, above.

163 White, *Barbour Collection: Branford–Bridgeport,* vol. 3, digital image at *Ancestry.com*.

164 Now part of the Barbour Index and interfiled with similar slips from other towns in CSL and on FHL films 2,887 *et seq*. See Introduction above, pp. 1–3.

165 Lucius B. Barbour, *Connecticut Vital Records: Bridgeport, 1821–185*, (Hartford: CSL, 1925) page after title page (FHL film 2,967). Digital images at *AmericanAncestors.org* and *FamilySearch,org.*

166 See *Biennial Report* (1936), 15.

- St. John's Church's "Church Records, 1784–1863" (includes baptisms, burials, and marriages) typescript at CSL (FHL film 1,008,323, items 1–2);
- Lucy Beardsley Canning's "[United Congregational] Church Records 1805–1838" (includes baptisms 1805–1828 and marriages 1806–1838) typescript at CS) (FHL film 3,832);
- Church of the Nativity's "Church Records, 1858–1952" (includes baptisms 1858–1951 and burials 1861–1951) originals at CSL (FHL film 1,007,928);
- Congregational Church of Southport's *The Southport Congregational Church: Southport, Connecticut, March 7, 1843–November 30, 1915, an Historical Sketch, Together With the Confession, the Covenant, the Bylaws and Lists of the Pastors, Deacons, Members, and Baptized Children* (New York: Private. print., 1915) (FHL fiche 6,071,137);
- Baptisms (1785–1862), burials (1786–1862) & marriages (1785–1862) at St. John's Church, Episcopal Diocese, Hartford (ED Film 1,008,323);
- Lemuel B. Hull's "Record of Marriages, Baptisms, Admission to the Communion and Funerals, 1822–1835, " manuscript at NEHGS);
- Connecticut DAR's "Baptisms in the Church at Stratfield, the Stratfield Society Now Called the United Congregational Church, 1805–1807," *CT DAR GRC Report*, ser. 1, vol. 40:54 (1934) (retyped) (FHL film 844,460);
- Connecticut DAR's "Marriages in the Church at Stratfield, the Stratfield Society Now Called the United Congregational Church, 1806–1838," *CT DAR GRC Report*, ser. 1, vol. 40:58 (1934) (retyped) (FHL film 844,460);
- Connecticut DAR's "Baptisms in the Church at Stratfield, The Stratfield Society, now called the United Congregational Church, 1807–1828," *CT DAR GRC Report*, ser. 1, vol. 40:71 (1934) (retyped) (FHL film 844,460);
- DAR Mary Silliman Chapter's "Alphabetical Listing of Baptisms, 1784–1825, in Bridgeport (Stratfield), Fairfield, Weston, Easton, Greenfield and surrounding areas (the entire record of baptisms by the Rev. Philo Shelton taken from photostat records in possession of St. John's Episcopal Church, Bridgeport, Connecticut," *CT DAR GRC Report*, ser. 1, vol. 127:1 (1957).

CEMETERY INSCRIPTIONS: The Hale Collection identifies burials in order of physical proximity at seven named cemeteries Bridgeport.[167] Compare with Daniel Hearn's 1975 copy of 223 pre-1800 gravestones in two Bridgeport cemeteries.[168] See also, Connecticut DAR's "Mountain Grove Cemetery, Bridgeport, Connecticut," *CT DAR GRC Report*, ser. 1, vol. 47:20 (1935).

OTHER NOTEWORTHY SOURCES:

- Connecticut DAR's "Asahel Gray Bible & List of Deaths from Bridgeport, Connecticut newspaper of 1887" *CT DAR GRC Report*, ser. 1, vol. 186:26 (1983);
- Samuel Orcutt and Fairfield County Historical Society's *History of the old town of Stratford and the city of Bridgeport, Connecticut.* 2 vols.(New Haven: Tuttle, Morehouse & Taylor, 1886);

---

167 Charles R. Hale, "Headstone Inscriptions of the Town of Bridgeport, Connecticut," bound typescript, 1930s, CSL, Hartford, FHL film 3 322–24.

168 Daniel Hearn, "Connecticut gravestones, early to 1800," manuscript (FHL film 1,477,476, item 14).

- George C. Waldo's *History of Bridgeport and vicinity,* 2 vols. (New York, NY: S. J. Clarke Pub. Co., 1917);
- "[Bridgeport] Marriage Notices," *CN*, 6:611, 624 (1973).

BRISTOL

Barbour's typescript volume for Bristol,[169] unlike the GPC edition,[170] begins:

> The vital records of Bristol, prior to 1854, are found scattered through Volumes 1 and 4 of the Town Records and Volumes 1, 2, and 3 of Vital Records.
>
> This alphabetical list was taken from a set of cards[171] based on a manuscript copy made in 1914 by Louis H. von Sahler, of Southington, Conn. Reference to entries found in the Town Records is indicated by the abbreviation "TR" and the number of the volume. The von Sahler Copy, now in the possession of the Connecticut State Library, has not been compared with the original and doubtless errors exist. It is hoped that as errors or omissions are found notes will be entered in this volume and on the cards which are included in the General Index of Connecticut Vital Records also in the possession of the Connecticut State Library.
>
> Hartford, Conn., August 1927.[172]

VITAL RECORDS: Bristol's volume includes vital records as early as 1753 and as late as 1854. Barbour abstracted five Bristol "books:"

- "TR1" refers to Bristol's Land Records, vols. 1–2, 1785–1817, Bristol Town Hall, (FHL films 3,777);
- 'TR4" refers to Bristol's Land Records, vols. 3–4, 1790–1826, Bristol Town Hall (FHL films 3,778);
- "1" refers to Bristol Town Clerk's Records of Births, Marriages, and Deaths, 1791–1903. (vol. 1. marriages, 1820–1841, Bristol Town Hall (FHL film 1,316,018, items 1–3);
- "2" refers to Bristol Town Clerk's, Records of Births, Marriages, and Deaths, 1791–1903. (vol. 2. births and deaths, 1791–1847) Bristol Town Hall (FHL film 1,316,018, item 2);

---

169 See How to Use This Book, note 3, above.

170 Lorraine Cook White, *Barbour Collection of Connecticut Town Vital Records: Bristol, 1785–1854, Brookfield, 1788–1850, Brooklyn, 1786–1850, Burlington, 1806–1852*, vol. 4, (Baltimore: GPC, 1996) digital image at *Ancestry.com*.

171 Now part of the Barbour Index and interfiled with similar slips from other towns in CSL and on FHL films 2,887, *et seq*. See Introduction above, pp. 1–3.

172 Lucius B. Barbour, *Connecticut Vital Records: Bristol, 1785–1854* (Hartford: CSL, 1927) page after title page.(FHL film 2,967). Digital images at *AmericanAncestors.org* and *FamilySearch,org.*

- "3" refers to Bristol Town Clerk's, Records of Births, Marriages, and Deaths, 1791–1903. (vol. 3, marriages, 1841–1854) Bristol Town Hall (FHL film 1,316,018, item 3).

Barbour does not abstract **Bristol's Records of Births, Marriages, and Deaths, vol. 4 (births, deaths, marriages, 1847–1871) Bristol Town Hall (FHL film 1,316,018, item 3).**

The FHL also catalogs under Bristol vital records: **Silas R. Gridley's "Vital Records" (includes births, deaths and marriages 1700's to late 1800's) (typescript at an unspecified location in Bristol) (FHL film 3,788).**

CHURCH RECORDS:

- First Congregational Church's "Church Records, 1742–1897" (includes baptisms, marriages, and deaths) typescript at CSL (FHL films 3,791–2 and 1,008,324);
- Trinity Church's "Church Records, 1834–1949" (includes baptisms 1836–1863, burials 1837–1858, and marriages 1836–1884) originals at CSL (FHL film 3,794);
- "New Cambridge Church Records, 1747–1800" (deaths in Bethany, 1788–1793) manuscript at NYGHS (FHL film 4,948 or 1,405,497);
- K.A. Pritchard's "Record of Baptisms in the Mission of "New Cambridge," Connecticut — 1747 to 1800," (1897 transcription at NEHGS from Alanson Welton's original manuscript now in the Bristol Public Library& NEHGS) (FHL film 3,054);
- Baptisms (1813–14) marriages (1813–35) & burials 1813–35 & 1836–94) at Christ Church, Episcopal Diocese, Hartford (ED Film 1,007,924);
- St. John's Church of Forestville's, Church records, 1887–1959 (includes records of baptisms 1887–1959, confirmations, communicants, marriages 1887–1946), burials 1887–1953) originals in Episcopal Diocese archives, Hartford (FHL film 1,513,663, item 4).
- Prospect Methodist Episcopal Church's "Church Records, 1849–1916" (includes baptisms 1849–1868) (typescript at CSL) (FHL films 3,793);
- Plymouth Episcopal Church in New Cambridge Records, 1744–1877 originals at CSL (FHL film 5,411, 1,008,324, items 2 & 3 and 1,011,960, items 2–4);
- Baptisms (1836–63), burials (1837–58) & marriages (1836–66) at Trinity Church (ED Film 3,794);
- St. Matthew's Episcopal Church (Bristol, Connecticut)'s *Miscellaneous church records* (contains baptismal record of St. Matthew's Episcopal Church in the parish of New Cambridge, now Bristol, Conn., 1747–1800; index, New Cambridge; Southington, Conn., Baptist Church records;) (FHL film 3,054, item 4).
- Rev. Welton's Episcopal Church in New Cambridge Records, 1747–1829 (in St. Matthew's Church Records) (1868 copy) (CSL film #453)
- Prospect Methodist Episcopal Church Records, 1849–1916 (CSL film #138)
- Farmington Seventh Day Baptist Society Book, 1780–1820 (CSL film #658)
- Farmington Seventh Day Baptist Society Book, 1796–1821 (CSL film #659)
- Connecticut DAR's "Baptisms in New Cambridge Church, now Bristol, Connecticut, 1747–1800," *CT DAR GRC Report*, ser. 1, vol. 80:32 (1941.

CEMETERY INSCRIPTIONS: The Hale Collection identifies buried in order of physical proximity at 11 named cemeteries in Bristol.[173] Compare with Daniel Hearn's 1978 copy of 101 pre-1800 gravestones in two Bristol cemeteries.[174]
See also,

- *Genealogical data from Connecticut Cemeteries: Bristol* (originally published: 1932) (Salem MA: Higginson Book Co., 1997)
- Connecticut DAR's "Inscriptions, Old North Cemetery, Bristol, Connecticut," *CT DAR GRC Report*, ser. 1, vol. 58:92 (1936) (FHL film 844,453)
- Connecticut DAR, "South Cemetery, Bristol, Hartford Co., Connecticut," CT *DAR GRC Report*, ser. 1, vol. 67:42 (1938)
- Connecticut DAR's "New or West Cemetery, Bristol, Connecticut (Atkins Family)," *CT DAR GRC Report*, ser. 1, vol. 69:76 (1938); Connecticut DAR, "Old Cemetery, Bristol, Connecticut (Atkins Family)," *CT DAR GRC Report*, ser. 1, vol. 69:78 (1938)
- Connecticut DAR's "South Yard, Downs Street, Bristol, Connecticut," *CT DAR GRC Report*, ser. 1, vol. 96:66 (1943) (FHL film 844,452)
- *In the Olden Time New Cambridge (Which Includes Forestville)* (Hartford: City Printing Co., 1907) (inscriptions from Old Episcopal Cemetery in Bristol).

OTHER NOTEWORTHY SOURCES:

- "Peck Account Book, CSL; see Appendix A;
- Eddy N. Smith's George Benton Smith, Allena J. Dates, G.W.F. Blanchfield, *Bristol, Connecticut: "in the olden time, New Cambridge", which includes Forestville,* (Hartford: City Printing Company, 1907)
- George Hull, Dorothy A. Manchester's *Epic of Bristol, 1785–1960: 175th anniversary* (S.l. : s.n., 1960?]
- Bruce Clouette, Matthew Roth's *Bristol Connecticut: a bicentennial history, 1785–1985,* (Canaan, NH: Phoenix Pub., c1984)
- Epaphroditus Peck's *History of Bristol* (Evansville, Ind: Unigraphic, 1932).

BROOKFIELD

Barbour's typescript volume for Brookfield,[175] unlike the GPC edition,[176] begins:

> This volume contains a list alphabetically arranged of all the vital records of the town of Brookfield from its incorporation to about 1852. The entire record of the town prior to 1852 is found in one volume.
>
> This list was taken from a set of cards[177] based on a copy of the Brookfield Vital Records made in 1915 by Mrs. Julia E. O. Brush, of Danbury, Conn-

[173] Charles R. Hale, "Headstone Inscriptions of the Town of Bristol, Connecticut," bound typescript, 1930s, CSL, Hartford, FHL film 3,324–5.

[174] Daniel Hearn, "Connecticut gravestones, early to 1800," manuscript (FHL film 1,477,476, item 16).

[175] See How to Use This Book, note 3, above.

[176] White, *Barbour Collection: Bristol–Burlington,* vol. 4, digital image at *Ancestry.com*.

[177] Now part of the Barbour Index and interfiled with similar slips from other towns in CSL and on FHL films 2,887 *et seq*. See Introduction above, pp. 1–3.

```
ecticut. The Brush copy, now in the possession of
the Connecticut State Library, has not been com-
pared with the original and doubtless errors exist.
It is hoped that as errors or omissions are found
notes will be entered in this volume and on the
cards which are included in the General Index of
Connecticut Vital Records also in the possession of
the Connecticut State Library.
                Hartford, Conn., May. 1926[178]
```

VITAL RECORDS: Brookfield's volume includes vital records as early as 1764 and as late as 1852. Barbour's abstraction is from Brookfield's Records of Births, Marriages, and Deaths, 1764–1853, Brookfield Town Hall, (FHL film 1,435,600, item 1). **Additional records for 1847 on were not abstracted by Barbour. See Harlan R. Jessup's "Vital Records of 1847–1848, School District Returns from Brookfield, Easton, and New Canaan, CT," 1847–1850," *CA*, 54:1:12–27 (Aug 2011)**

CHURCH RECORDS:

- St. Paul's Church's 'Church Records, 1707–1930" (includes baptisms 1838–1855 & 1829–1908, deaths 1834–1910 & 1829–1908, and marriages 1829–1906) originals at CSL (FHL film 3,842);
- Robert A. Locke and Harlan R. Jessup's "Brookfield, Connecticut Congregational Church Marriages and Deaths," *CA*, 48: 170–4 (May 2006); – Vol. 48, No. 3 Feb 2006
- Harlan R. Jessup's "More Brookfield, CT, Church Records, *CA*, Vol. 49, No. 3 (Feb 2007);
- Congregational Church Records, 1755–1830 (CSL #454)
- St. Paul's Episcopal Society Church Records, 1789–1853 (CSL film # 141) (FHL film 1,008,325, items 1–2);
- Baptisms (1838–55), burials (1838–52), marriages (1839–51 &1829–1906), annotated list of births (1791–1908), annotated list of parishioners for death or removal (1829–1908), and deaths (1829–1908) at St. Paul's Church, Episcopal Diocese, Hartford (ED Films 3,842–3);
- Lemuel B. Hull's "A Record of Marriages, Baptisms, Admission to the Communion and Funerals, 1822–1835" (manuscript at NEHGS).

CEMETERY INSCRIPTIONS: The Hale Collection identifies burials in order of physical proximity at five named cemeteries in Brookfield Township.[179] Compare with Daniel Hearn's 1976 copy of 24 pre-1800 gravestones in two Brookfield cemeteries.[180] See also,

- Marilyn Whittlesey, Carol Gurski, and Jack Scully, *The Cemeteries of Brookfield, Connecticut: Including Gallows Hill Cemetery – New Milford, CT, Land's End Cemetery – Hawleyville, CT, Wood Creek Cemetery, New Fairfield, CT: 1745–2003* (Brookfield: Historic Cemeteries of Brookfield Assn., [2003);

---

178 Barbour, Connecticut Vital Records: Brookfield,1788–1852, CSL, Hartford,: page preceding p. 1. FHL film 2,967. Digital images at *AmericanAncestors.org* and *FamilySearch,org*

179 Charles R. Hale, "Headstone Inscriptions of the Town of Brookfield, Connecticut," bound typescript, 1930s, CSL, Hartford, FHL film 3,324.

180 Daniel Hearn, "Connecticut gravestones, early to 1800," manuscript (FHL film 1,477,476, item 17).

- Marilyn Whittlesey and Jack Scully's Handbook of Cemeteries, Brookfield, Connecticut (Including Portions of New Milford and Newtown) 1745–1985 ([S.I.]: Old South Cemetery Assn., 1988);
- DAR Abigail Wolcott Ellsworth Chapter's "Cemetery Inscriptions, Brookfield, Connecticut," *CT DAR GRC Report*, ser. 1, vol. 90: 111 (1942) (FHL film 844,451);
- George S. Hoyt's *Record of soldiers buried in Danbury, Brookfield, New Fairfield and Ridgefield*, Photostat copy (Hartford: CSL, 1929) CSL digital collection online.

OTHER NOTEWORTHY SOURCES:

- Emily C Hawley's *Historical sketch of the First Congregational Church of Brookfield, Connecticut, and of the town of Brookfield: written for the one hundred and fiftieth anniversary of the church* [S.I.; s.n., 1907?] (FHL film 1,598,337, item 5).
- Barbara P. Todd's *Newbury to Brookfield, 1700 to 1789*, (Brookfield, Connecticut: Bicentennial Commission, c1976).

BROOKLYN

Barbour's typescript volume[181] for Brooklyn unlike the GPC edition,[182] begins:

> This volume contains a list alphabetically arranged of all the vital records of the town of Brooklyn from its incorporation to about 1850. The entire record of the town prior to 1850 is contained in four volumes. This list was taken from a set of cards[183] based on a copy of Volumes 1 and 2 of the Brooklyn Vital Records made in 1911 by James N. Arnold, of Providence, R.I., and a photostat copy of Volumes 3 and 4. From page 21 to page 40 in the first volume there is a list of freemen. The names have been alphabetically arranged with the date of admission abbreviated "adm.fr." and made an appendix to this list. Admission as freemen or electors usually occurred soon after the twenty-first birthday.
>
> The Arnold Copy of Volumes 1 and 2, now in the possession of the Connecticut State Library, has not been compared with the original and doubtless errors exist. It is hoped that as errors or omissions are found notes will be entered in this volume and on the cards which are included in the General Index of Connecticut Vital Records also in the possession of the Connecticut State Library.
>
> Hartford, Conn., August, 1921.[184]

---

181 See How to Use This Book, note 3, above.

182 White, *Barbour Collection: Bristol–Burlington,* vol. 4, digital image at *Ancestry.com*.

183 Now part of the Barbour Index and interfiled with similar slips from other towns in CSL and on FHL films 2,887 *et seq*. See Introduction above, pp. 1–3.

184 Lucius B. Barbour, *Connecticut Vital Records: Brooklyn, 1786–1850* (Hartford,: CSL, 1921) page after title page (FHL film 2,967). Digital imagse at *AmericanAncestors.org* and *FamilySearch,org.*

VITAL RECORDS: Brooklyn's volume includes vital records as early as 1737 and as late as 1854. As for Barbour abstracted four Brooklyn "books" ," including two apparently unavailable either on microfilm or in print:

- "1"refers to Brooklyn's Records of Births, Marriages, and Deaths, 1770–1839, CSL (FHL film 1,378,051, item 1);
- "2" refers to Brooklyn's Records of Births, Marriages, and Deaths, 1797–1857, CSL (FHL film 1,378,051, item 2);
- "3" refers to part of Brooklyn's vol. 1a, ten pages of marriages 1802–1828. It is unfilmed at Brooklyn Town Hall with a photostat at CSA. and should not be confused with later records which are indexed by the town and filmed by FHL as vol. 3;
- "4" refers to Brooklyn Marriages, 1820–1846. It is unfilmed at Brooklyn Town Hall, indexed by town clerk as part of vol. 1a with a photostat at CSA; and not to be confused with the much later records which are indexed by the town and filmed by FHL as vol. 4.

See also:

- **Brooklyn's "Book 2" (1848–1852) in CSA with oversized books in RG 62;**
- **Some 560–570 Brooklyn private record slips in Drawer 380 at CSLnot interfiled in Barbour Index. They are See Appendix B;**
- **Brooklyn Vital Records, 1782–1867 (mainly deaths) (CSL 974.62 B 794 vi);**
- **Marilyn Labbe's "Corrections and Additions to the Vital Records of Ashford, Connecticut, and Brooklyn, Connecticut,"** ***CN,*** **44:55–59 (November 2001).**

CHURCH RECORDS:

- First Congregational Church's "Church Records, 1731–1913" (includes baptisms 1822–1891, marriages 1823–1899, burials and deaths 1889–1913) typescript in CSL (FHL film 3,811);
- First Trinitarian Church's "Church Records, 1734–1897" (includes baptisms 1735–1891, marriages 1736–1823, and deaths 1771–1873); typescript in CSL (FHL film 3,810);
- Trinity Church's "Church Records, 1771–1866" (includes marriages 1772–1866, baptisms 1772–1866, and burials 1772–1866) typescript in CSL (FHL film 3,813);[185]
- First Baptist Church's "Church Records, 1828–1934" (includes deaths and baptisms) (typescript in CSL) (FHL film 3,812);
- Mary Bugbee Bishop's "Brooklyn, Connecticut, First Congregational Church Baptisms, 1735–1799" (typescript in CSL) (FHL film 1,008,325, item 3);
- "Congregational Church Record of Marriages, 1767 to 1781 including Brooklyn, Windham County, Conn." manuscript at NEHGS; Congregational Church Papers, 1734–1926 (CSL film #454);
- Baptisms (1772–1866), marriages (1772–1866) & burials (1772–1866) at Trinity Church, Episcopal Diocese, Hartford (ED Film 0003,813);
- Connecticut DAR's "Old Trinity Church, Brooklyn, Connecticut," *CT DAR GRC Report*, ser. 1, vol. 21:1 (1929);
- DAR Abigail Wolcott Ellsworth Chapter's "West Cemetery, Brooklyn, Connecticut," *CT DAR GRC Report*, ser. 1, vol. 90: 114 (1942) (FHL film 844,451).

---

[185] A book titled "Trinity Church Records" is in the town clerk's office. *Biennial Report (1936),* 17.

CEMETERY INSCRIPTIONS: The Hale Collection identifies burials in order of physical proximity at eight named cemeteries in Brooklyn Township.[186] Compare with Daniel Hearn's 1979 copy of 147 pre-1800 gravestones in three Brooklyn cemeteries.[187] See also, Lemuel B. Hull's "Record of Marriages, Baptisms, Admission to the Communion and Funerals, 1822–1835" (manuscript at NEHGS).

OTHER NOTEWORTHY SOURCES:

- Lucius B. Barbour's Abstract of Brooklyn probate records. 1786–1900, 1 volume. Abstract of probate records. Arranged alphabetically (manuscript 73 in Box 8) CSL Record Group 074.36, Hartford;
- Lucius B. Barbour's Genealogical notes compiled from the Mortlake Church, Brooklyn, Conn. 1734–1824, 1 volume. Abstract of church vital records. Arranged alphabetically. (manuscript six in Box 1) CSL Record Group 074.36, Hartford.

BURLINGTON

Barbour's typescript volume for Burlington,[188] unlike the GPC edition,[189] begins:

> The vital records of Burlington, prior to 1852, are found scattered through Volume 1 of Land Records and Volumes 1 and 7 [sic] of Vital Records.
>
> This alphabetical list was taken from a set of cards[190] based on a manuscript copy made in 1916 by James N. Arnold, of Providence, R.I. Reference to entries found in the Land Records is indicated by the abbreviation "LR" and the number of the volume.
>
> The Arnold Copy, now in the possession of the Connecticut State Library, has not been compared with the original and doubtless errors exist. It is hoped that as errors or omissions are found notes will be entered in this volume and on the cards which are included in the General Index of Connecticut Vital Records also in the possession of the Connecticut State Library.
>
> Hartford, Conn., July 1927.[191]

VITAL RECORDS: Burlington's volume includes vital records as early as 1777 and as late as 1852. Barbour abstracted three Burlington "books:"

---

186 Charles R. Hale, "Headstone Inscriptions of the Town of Brooklyn, Connecticut," bound typescript, 1930s, CSL, Hartford, FHL film 3,325.

187 Daniel Hearn, "Connecticut gravestones, early to 1800," manuscript (FHL film 1,477,476, item 18).

188 See How to Use This Book, note 3, above.

189 White, *Barbour Collection: Bristol–Burlington,* vol. 4, digital image at *Ancestry.com.*

190 Now part of the Barbour Index and interfiled with similar slips from other towns in CSL and on FHL films 2,887 *et seq*. See Introduction above, pp. 1–3.

191 Lucius B. Barbour, *Connecticut Vital Records: Burlington, 1806–1852* (Hartford: CSL, 1927) page after title page (FHL film 2967). Digitized online at *AmericanAncestors.org* and *FamilySearch.org.*

- "LR1" is Burlington's Land Records, vol. 1, 1806–1817, Burlington Town Hall, (FHL film 3,768);
- "1" is Burlington's "Moral Society Records" a volume said by CSL to be at the Burlington Town Hall, citing the Director of the Local History Room at the Burlington Public Library in March 2013;[192]
- "7" is abstracted from Burlington's Land Records, vol. 7, 1823–1881, Burlington Town Hall, (FHL film 3,771), not vital records, as Barbour states in his preface.

CHURCH RECORDS:

- Congregational Church Records, 1775–1950 (includes 1800–95 baptisms, 1829–87 marriages, 1829–92 deaths) (CSL 974.62 B922c r)
- Leonard Alderman's "Record of the Returns Made by Sextons of Cemeteries, 1915" (1915 typescript at FHL);
- Farmington Seventh Day Baptist Book, 1780–1820 (CSL film #658);
- Farmington Seventh Day Baptist Book, 1796–1821 (CSL film #659);
- Members of First Ecclesiastical Society of Burlington, 1833–1897 (look-ups available through *RootsWeb.com*'s Burlington page).

CEMETERY INSCRIPTIONS: The Hale Collection identifies burials in order of physical proximity at six named cemeteries in Burlington Township.[193] Compare with Daniel Hearn's 1978 copy of 10 pre-1800 gravestones in two Burlington cemeteries.[194] See also,

- Lucius B. Barbour's Burlington Cemetery Epitaphs (Salem MA: Higginson, 1997) (at NEHGS);
- DAR Abigail Wolcott Ellsworth Chapter's "Old Cemetery, Burlington Hill, Burlington, Connecticut," *CT DAR GRC Report*, ser. 1, vol. 95:3 (1943) (FHL film 844,452)
- Connecticut DAR's "Data of Revolutionary Soldiers of Canton & vicinity, Dyer Center Cemetery, Simsbury, Old Center Cemetery, Harwinton, Canton Center Cemetery & Burlington," *CT DAR GRC Report*, ser. 1, vol. 54:63 (1936) (FHL film 845,612);
- Connecticut DAR's "Inscription in Burlington Cemetery, Burlington, Connecticut to Katherine Cole Gaylord," *CT DAR GRC Report*, ser. 1, vol. 58:91 (1936) (FHL film 844,453);
- Leonard Alderman's Record of the returns made by sextons of cemeteries, 1915, (n.s., 19--) FHL digital image of typescript;
- DAR Abigail Wolcott Ellsworth Chapter's "Case Cemetery, Burlington, Connecticut," *CT DAR GRC Report*, ser. 1, vol. 95:16 (1943) (FHL film 844,452);
- Abigail Wolcott Ellsworth Chapter, DAR, "Old Baptist Cemetery, Burlington, Connecticut," *CT DAR GRC Report*, ser. 1, vol. 95:14 (1943) (FHL film 844,452);
- DAR Abigail Wolcott Ellsworth Chapter's "Milford Street Cemetery, Burlington, Connecticut," *CT DAR GRC Report*, ser. 1, vol. 95:21 (1943) (FHL film 844,452).

---

192 See note by CSL staff in vertical file for Burlington town clerk's office.

193 Charles R. Hale, "Headstone Inscriptions of the Town of Burlington, Connecticut," bound typescript, 1930s, CSL, Hartford, FHL film 3 325.

194 Daniel Hearn, "Connecticut gravestones, early to 1800," manuscript (FHL film 1477476, Item 19).

OTHER NOTEWORTHY SOURCES:

- Lucius B. Barbour's Southington, Burlington, Goshen, New Hartford, Conn. marriages. 1732–1850, 1 volume. (manuscript 138 in Box 23) CSL Record Group 074.36, Hartford.
- Leonard Alderman's *Obituaries of Burlington People* ([S.I.: s.n.], 1992) (FHL fiche 6,104,930).

CANAAN

Barbour's typescript volume for Canaan,[195] unlike the GPC edition,[196] begins:

> The vital records of Canaan, prior to 1852, are found scattered through Volumes 1 and 2 of Land Records and Book A of Births, Marriages and Deaths.
>
> This alphabetical list was taken from a set of cards[197] based on a manuscript copy of the Canaan Vital Records made in 1915 by James N. Arnold, of Providence, R.I. Reference to entries found in the Land Records is indicated by the abbreviation "LR" and the number of the volume, and to the book of vital records by the abbreviation "A".
>
> The Arnold Copy, now in the possession of the Connecticut State Library, has not been compared with the original and doubtless errors exist. It is hoped that as errors or omissions are found notes will be entered in this volume and on the cards which are included in the General Index of Connecticut Vital Records also in the possession of the Connecticut State Library.
>
> Hartford, Conn., February 1927.[198]

VITAL RECORDS: Canaan's volume includes vital records as early as 1737 and as late as 1876. Barbour abstracted three Canaan "books:"

- "LR1" is Canaan's Land Records, vol. 1 1740–1811 & Proprietors Records 1737–1825, Canaan Town Hall, (FHL film 3,936);
- "LR2" is Canaan's Land Records, vols. 2–3 1749–1780, Canaan Town Hall, (FHL film 3,937) (not cataloged as including vital records);

---

195 See How to Use This Book, note 3, above.

196 Lorraine Cook White, *Barbour Collection of Connecticut Town Vital Records: Canaan, 1739–1852, Canterbury, 1703–1850*, vol. 5, (Baltimore: GPC, 1996).digital image at *Ancestry.com*.

197 Now part of the Barbour Index and interfiled with similar slips from other towns in CSL and on FHL films 2887 *et seq*. See Introduction above, pp. 1–3.

198 Lucius B. Barbour, *Connecticut Vital Records: Canaan, 1739–1852* (Hartford: CSL, 1927) page after title page (FHL film 2,968). Digital images at *AmericanAncestors.org* and *FamilySearch,org.*

- "A" is Canaan's Town Records, vol. A, 1744–1898, (contains records of births, marriages, and deaths, arranged principally by families) Canaan Town Hall, (FHL film 1,503,196, item 1).

There are additional vital records within Barbour's Canaan time span:

- **Canaan Births, Marriages, and Deaths, 1847–1948. (Volume 1 includes records of burials, 1852–1876. Volume 2 includes a record of the Dean family of Canaan, 1800–1877.) Canaan Town Hall. (FHL film 1,503,196, items 2–3);**
- **Esther S. Dunning and B.J. Granger's "A record of deaths in the town of Canaan or North Canaan, 1739–1875," (original manuscript in Town Hall) (FHL film original records in the Town Hall);**
- **North Canaan Vital Records circa 1845–1905, CSL (CSA RG 070.002, Box 13) (includes pre-1850 birthdates on death certificates);**
- **Connecticut DAR's "Canaan, Connecticut Vital Records,"** ***CT DAR GRC Report*****, ser. 1, vol. 13:1 (1926).**

CHURCH RECORDS:

- "Church records of South and East Canaan, Connecticut, 1769–1870" typescript in Pittsfield, Mass. (FHL film 234,581);
- First Ecclesiastical Society and Congregational Church's "Church records, 1741–1852" originals at CSL (includes baptisms 1752–1800 &1804–1838, marriages 1773–1797 & 1804–1837, and deaths 1804–1838) (FHL film 3,948);
- Second Church of Christ at East Canaan's "Church records, 1767–1942" (includes marriages 1770–1852 & 1816–1834, baptisms 1770–1869 & 1816–1834, and deaths 1770–1850 & 1816–1834) originals at CSL (FHL film 3,946);
- Christ Church's "Parish registers, 1846–1977" (includes baptisms 1847–1976, marriages 1847–1976, and burials 1846–1977) original records in CSL and archives of the Episcopal Diocese, Hartford (FHL film 3,947, item 2);
- Second Church of Christ of North Canaan's, "Church records, 1767–1942" (includes marriages, baptisms, deaths) originals at CSL (FHL film 1,011,948);
- Baptisms (1847–93), burials (1846–93) & marriages (1847–93) at Christ Church, Episcopal Diocese, Hartford (ED Film 3,757);
- Norfolk, Canaan, New Marlborough Baptist Society Records, 1819–1875 (CD film #455)
- Church of Christ's *Church records, 1752–1817*, originals at CSL (FHL film 3,947, item 1).

CEMETERY INSCRIPTIONS: The Hale Collection identifies burials in order of physical proximity at 12 named cemeteries in what was then Canaan Township.[199] Compare with Daniel Hearn's 1978 copy of 146 pre-1800 gravestones in three Canaan cemeteries.[200] The Hale Collection also identifies people in order of physical proximity buried at 10 named cemeteries in what was then North Canaan Township and one just over the state line in Berkshire, Massachusetts.[201] See also,

199 Charles R. Hale, "Headstone Inscriptions of the Town of Canaan, Connecticut," bound typescript, 1930s, CSL, Hartford, FHL film 3,326.

200 Daniel Hearn, "Connecticut gravestones, early to 1800," manuscript (FHL film 1,477,476, item 20).

201 Charles R. Hale, "Headstone Inscriptions of the Town of North Canaan, Connecticut," bound typescript, 1930s, CSL, Hartford, FHL film 3 354.

- "Headstone Inscriptions of the Town of North Canaan, Connecticut" (bound manuscript at CSL) (FHL film 3,354).
- Esther S. Dunning and B.J. Granger's "Record of Deaths in the Town of Canaan or North Canaan, 1739–1875" (originals in North Canaan Town Hall) (FHL film 1,503,194);
- DAR Abigail Wolcott Ellsworth Chapter's "Adam Family Yard, Canaan, Connecticut," *CT DAR GRC Report*, ser. 1, vol. 93:1 (1943) (FHL film 844,451);
- DAR Abigail Wolcott Ellsworth Chapter's "Barrocks Cemetery, Barrock Mountian, Canaan, Connecticut, including Dean Family," *CT DAR GRC Report*, ser. 1, vol. 93:4 (1943) (FHL film 844,451);
- DAR Abigail Wolcott Ellsworth Chapter's "Canaan Valley Cemetery, Canaan, Connecticut," *CT DAR GRC Report*, ser. 1, vol. 93:6 (1943) (FHL film 844,451);
- DAR Abigail Wolcott Ellsworth Chapter's "Hadsall Cemetery, Canaan, Connecticut," *CT DAR GRC Report*, ser. 1, vol. 93:14 (1943) (FHL film 844,451);
- DAR Abigail Wolcott Ellsworth Chapter's "Munson Yard, Canaan, Connecticut," *CT DAR GRC Report*, ser. 1, vol. 93:15 (1943) (FHL film 844,451); ;
- DAR Abigail Wolcott Ellsworth Chapter's "Phelps Yard, Canaan, Connecticut," *CT DAR GRC Report*, ser. 1, vol. 93:16 (1943) (FHL film 844,451);
- DAR Abigail Wolcott Ellsworth Chapter's "Root Yard, Canaan, Connecticut," *CT DAR GRC Report*, ser. 1, vol. 93:17 (1943) (FHL film 844,451);
- DAR Abigail Wolcott Ellsworth Chapter's "Steven's Yard, Canaan, Connecticut," *CT DAR GRC Report*, ser. 1, vol. 93:18 (1943) (FHL film 844,451);
- DAR Abigail Wolcott Ellsworth Chapter's "Mountain Cemetery, Canaan, Connecticut," *CT DAR GRC Report*, ser. 1, vol. 93:21 (1943) (FHL film 844,451);
- DAR Abigail Wolcott Ellsworth Chapter's "East Canaan Churchyard, East Canaan, Connecticut," *CT DAR GRC Report*, ser. 1, vol. 93:26 (1943) (FHL film 844,451);
- DAR Abigail Wolcott Ellsworth Chapter's "Hillside Cemetery, East Canaan, Connecticut," *CT DAR GRC Report*, ser. 1, vol. 93:28 (1943) (844,451);
- DAR Abigail Wolcott Ellsworth Chapter's "Grassy Hill Cemetery, Falls Village, Canaan, Connecticut," *CT DAR GRC Report*, ser. 1, vol. 93:33 (1943) (FHL film 844,451);
- DAR Abigail Wolcott Ellsworth Chapter's "Old Canaan Cemetery, North Canaan, Connecticut," *CT DAR GRC Report*, ser. 1, vol. 93:48 (1943) (FHL film 844,451);
- DAR Abigail Wolcott Ellsworth Chapter's "Brooks Family Yard, Canaan Valley, Canaan, Connecticut," *CT DAR GRC Report*, ser. 1, vol. 93:77 (1943) (FHL film 844,451);
- DAR Abigail Wolcott Ellsworth Chapter's "Huntsville Cemetery, South Canaan, Connecticut," *CT DAR GRC Report*, ser. 1, vol. 93:72 (1943) (FHL film 844,451);
- DAR Abigail Wolcott Ellsworth Chapter's "Sand Hill Cemetery, South Canaan, Connecticut," *CT DAR GRC Report*, ser. 1, vol. 93:74 (1943) (FHL film 844,451);
- Connecticut DAR's "Some Inscriptions on the Graves of Soldiers of the American Revolution in Canaan Parish" *CT DAR GRC Report*, ser. 1, vol. 182:134 (1980)

OTHER NOTEWORTHY SOURCES:

- Edward D. Fales' *The Story of Falls Village, the great falls and the iron country, 1720 to 1972* (Falls Village: National Iron Bank, c1972)).
- Mrs. E.M. Davis' "Corrections of Printed Sources [of Canaan]," *TAG*, 8o:31 (1955);

- Canaan Marriages in Poughkeepsie NY Newspapers, *CN*, 6:623, 627 (1973);

CANTERBURY

Barbour's typescript volume for Canterbury,[202] unlike GPC edition,[203] begins:

> This volume contains a list alphabetically arranged of all the vital records of the town of Canterbury from its incorporation to about 1850. This list was taken from a set of cards[204] Based on a copy of the Canterbury Vital Records made in 1910 by James N. Arnold, of Providence, R.I. The entire record of the town prior to 1850 is found in two volumes. The Arnold Copy now in the possession of the Connecticut State Library, has not been compared with the original and doubtless errors exist. It is hoped that as errors or omissions are found notes will be entered in this volume and on the cards which are included in the General Index of Connecticut Vital Records also in the possession of the Connecticut State Library.
>
> Hartford, Conn., October, 1920.[205]

VITAL RECORDS: Canterbury's volume includes vital records as early as 1698 and as late as 1854. Barbour abstracted two Canterbury "books:"

- "1" refers to Canterbury's Births, Marriages, Deaths, vols. 1 1696–1844, Canterbury Town Hall, (FHL film 1,378,163, item 1); and
- "2" refers to Canterbury's Births, Marriages, Deaths vols. 2–4 1820–1907, Canterbury Town Hall, (FHL film 1,378,164).

See also,

- **Canterbury's "Vital Records kept by town clerk 1851–1922) not transcribed by Arnold [Barbour], CSL photostat of manuscript. CSL, *CT Vital Records;***
- **Canterbury's Births, Marriages, Deaths, vols. 1-A, Canterbury Town Hall, (FHL film 1,378,163, item 2), grouping most of records in volume 1 (and perhaps others) by surname.**

CHURCH RECORDS:

- AC Bates' *Records of the Congregational Church in Canterbury, Connecticut, 1711–1844.* (Hartford Connecticut: CHS and the Society of Mayflower Descendants in the State of Connecticut, (1932);
- Mrs. J.L. Raymond and Congregational Church of Westminster's "Admissions, Baptisms, Marriages 1770–1850" photocopy at CSL (FHL film 3,983, item 4);

---

202 See How to Use This Book, note 3, above.

203 White, *Barbour Collection: Canaan–Canterbury,* vol. 5, digital image at *Ancestry.com*.

204 Now part of the Barbour Index and interfiled with similar slips from other towns in CSL and on FHL films 2,887 *et seq*. See Introduction above, pp. 1–3.

205 Lucius B. Barbour, *Connecticut Vital Records: Canterbury, 1703–1850* (Hartford: CSL, 1920) page after title page (FHL film 2,968). Digital images at *AmericanAncestors.org and FamilySearch.org.*

- First Congregational Church, *Historical notices of the First Congregational Church in Canterbury, Conn: with catalogs of its officers and members* (Northampton, MA: Hopkins, Bridgman & Co., 1853);
- Mrs. J.L. Raymond and First Congregational Church's "Admissions, Baptisms, Marriages 1711–1821" (CSL #90.) (FHL film 3,983, item 3);
- Westminster Ecclesiastical Society's "Church Records 1770–1900" (includes baptisms, marriages, and deaths) (originals at CSL) (FHL film 1,008,327 or 3,983, items 1–2);
- Congregational Church's "Records of the Congregational Church in Canterbury, Connecticut, 1711–1844" (Hartford: CHS and Society of Mayflower Descendants SMD), 1932) (FHL fiche 6,062,300);
- St. Thomas Church Records, 1818–1827 & 1818–1829 (CSL film #455), FHL film 1,008,326, items 2–3;
- *Historical notices of the First Congregational Church in Canterbury, conn., with catalogues of its officers and members* (Northampton MA: Hopkins, Bridgeman & Co., 1853) (database at *AmericanAncestors.org*);
- Separate Church Papers, 1748–1784 (CSL film #455), (FHL film 1,008,326, item 4).

CEMETERY INSCRIPTIONS: The Hale Collection identifies burials in order of physical proximity at 22 named cemeteries in Canterbury Township.[206] Compare with Daniel Hearn's 1979 copy of 206 pre-1800 gravestones in six Canterbury cemeteries.[207] See also,

- Josephine J. Hetrick and Alfred Johnson's "Inscriptions in the Carey Cemetery, Canterbury, Conn.," *NEHGR*, 70:43–51, 153–61 (Jan– Apr 1916);
- Alfred Johnson's "Inscriptions in the Cleveland Cemetery, Canterbury, Conn.," *NEHGR*, 70:342–7 (Oct 1916);
- Sarah Francis Dorrance's "Inscriptions from the Cleveland Cemetery, Canterbury, Conn." (1923 manuscript at NEHGS).

OTHER NOTEWORTHY SOURCES:

- "Soldiers from Canterbury, Ct. [1754, reports deaths]," *NEHGR*, 34:407–8 (October, 1880);
- Connecticut DAR, "Abstracts from Canterbury, Connecticut Revolutionary Records, 1774–1784," *CT DAR GRC Report*, ser. 1, vol. 153:20 (1966).

CANTON

Barbour's typescript volume for Canton,[208] unlike the GPC edition,[209] begins:

```
    This volume contains a list alphabetical-
ly arranged of all the vital records now extant
of the town of Canton from its incorporation to
```

[206] Charles R. Hale, "Headstone Inscriptions of the Town of Canterbury, Connecticut," bound typescript, 1930s, CSL, Hartford, FHL film 3,326.

[207] Daniel Hearn, "Connecticut gravestones, early to 1800," manuscript (FHL film 1,477,476, item 21).

[208] See How to Use This Book, note 3, above.

[209] Lorraine Cook White, *Barbour Collection of Connecticut Town Vital Records: Canton, 1806-1853, Chaplin, 1822-1851, Chatham, 1767-1854, Cheshire, 1780-1840, Chester, 1836-1852, Diary of Aaron G. Hurd-Clinton, 1809-1878*, vol. 6, (Baltimore: GPC, 1996) digital image at *Ancestry.com*.

about 1853. A fire on February 6, 1838, destroyed all records prior to that date. The record is found in one volume.

This list was taken from a set of cards based on a copy of the Canton Vital Records made in 1916 by James N. Arnold, of Providence, R.I. The Arnold Copy now in the possession of the Connecticut State Library, has not been compared with the original and doubtless errors exist. It is hoped that as errors or omissions are found notes will be entered in this volume and on the cards which are included in the General Index of Connecticut Vital Records also in the possession of the Connecticut State Library.

Hartford, Conn., February, 1928.[210]

VITAL RECORDS: Canton's volume includes vital records as early as 1789 and as late as 1877. Barbour abstracted Canton's Records of Births, Marriages, and Deaths, 1788–1923, (includes records of birth, marriage, death (arranged by family) 1788–1877, marriage records 1838–1853, reports of births, marriages, deaths from the school district committee 1847–1869, and record of births, marriages, deaths 1852–1870) Canton Town Hall, (FHL film 1,314,187).

CHURCH RECORDS:

- Congregational Church of Canton Center's, *Church Records, 1785–1953* (includes baptisms, marriages and deaths 1795–1827 & 1826–1851) (originals at CSL) (FHL film 4,001);
- Canton Center Congregational Church Sunday School Records, 1840–1874 (CSL film #434);
- Canton Church of Christ Papers, 1831–1871 (CSL film #457).

CEMETERY INSCRIPTIONS: The Hale Collection identifies burials in order of physical proximity at eight named cemeteries in Canton Township.[211] Compare with Daniel Hearn's 1978 copy of 206 pre-1800 gravestones in two Canton cemeteries.[212] See also,

- Lucius B. Barbour's "Inscriptions from Gravestones at Canton, Conn.," *NEHGR*, 81:275–92, 404–19 (Jul Oct 1927);
- Lucius B. Barbour's "Canton, Conn. Epitaphs" (Mss A 2784), RSASC, NEHGS);
- Connecticut DAR's "Data of Revolutionary Soldiers of Canton & vicinity, Dyer Center Cemetery, Simsbury, Old Center Cemetery, Harwinton, Canton Center Cemetery & Burlington," *CT DAR GRC Report*, ser. 1, vol. 54:63 (1936) (Also on FHL film 845,612);
- DAR Abigail Wolcott Ellsworth Chapter's "Canton Center Cemetery, Canton, Connecticut," *CT DAR GRC Report*, ser. 1, vol. 90:60 (1942) (FHL film 844,451);

---

210 Lucius B. Barbour, *Connecticut Vital Records: Canton, 1806–1853* (Hartford: CSL 1928) page after title page (FHL film 2,968). Digital images at *AmericanAncestors.org* and *FamilySearch.org*.

211 Charles R. Hale, "Headstone Inscriptions of the Town of Canton, Connecticut," bound typescript, 1930s, CSL, Hartford, FHL film 3,326.

212 Daniel Hearn, "Connecticut gravestones, early to 1800," manuscript (FHL film 1,477,476, item 22).

- DAR Abigail Wolcott Ellsworth Chapter's "Canton Street Cemetery, Canton, Connecticut," *CT DAR GRC Report*, ser. 1, vol. 90:68 (1942) (FHL film 844,451);
- Canton, Connecticut, sexton's returns (1946 typescript) CSL digital collection (An alphabetical surname arranged listing of burial entries taken from an unknown source of burials in the Southwest Cemetery Canton, Connecticut in October and November 1915. Most of these burials were reinterments of bodies from the St. John's Cemetery and the Old Canton Southwest Graveyard, which were to be flooded due to the construction of the Nepaug Reservoir)
- Connecticut DAR's "Old Nepaug Cemetery, between Torrington & Canton, Connecticut: Cowles, Kellogg, Merrill (Merrell), & Beckwith Families," *CT DAR GRC Report*, ser. 2, vol. 9:51 (1991);
- DAR Abigail Wolcott Ellsworth Chapter's "Dyer Cemetery, Canton, Connecticut," *CT DAR GRC Report*, ser. 1, vol. 90:78 (1942) (FHL film 844,451);
- DAR Abigail Wolcott Ellsworth Chapter's "South West Cemetery, Canton, Connecticut," *CT DAR GRC Report*, ser. 1, vol. 90:89 (1942) (FHL film 844,451);

OTHER NOTEWORTHY SOURCES:

- Connecticut DAR's "Obituaries of Canton People, Canton, Hartford Co., Connecticut from The Hartford Courant, 1996," *CT DAR GRC Report*, ser. 2, vol. 29:66 (1997);
- Abiel Brown's *Genealogical History with Short Sketches and Family Records of the Early Settlers of West Simsbury, Now Canton, Conn.* (Hartford: Case, Tiffany & Co.,1856, repr. NY, 1899) (images at *AmericanAncestors.org*);
- Noah Amherst Phelps's *History of Simsbury, Granby and Canton from 1642 to 1845,* FHL Microreproduction of original published: Hartford: Press of Case, Tiffany and Burnham, 1845);
- *Genealogical records, Canton, Connecticut, 1740–1850*, typescript in Pittsfield, MA, (FHL film 234,578 item 2);

CHAPLIN

Barbour's typescript volume for Chaplin,[213] unlike the GPC edition,[214] begins:

> This volume contains a list alphabetically arranged of all the vital records of the town of Chaplin from its incorporation to about 1851. This list was taken from a set of cards[215] based on a copy of the Canton Vital Records made in 1911 by James N. Arnold, of Providence, R.I. The entire record for this town prior to 1851 is found in two volumes. The second volume is unpaged and the pagination given is counted from the first on which a record appears. The Arnold Copy now in the possession of the Connecticut State Library, has not been compared with the original and doubt-

---

[213] See How to Use This Book, note 3, above.

[214] White, *Barbour Collection: Canton–Clinton,* vol. 6.

[215] Now part of the Barbour Index and interfiled with similar slips from other towns in CSL and on FHL films 2,887 *et seq*. See Introduction above, pp. 1-3.

```
less errors exist. It is hoped that as errors or
omissions are found notes will be entered in this
volume and on the cards which are included in the
General Index of Connecticut Vital Records also in the
possession of the Connecticut State Library.
                Hartford, Conn., October, 1920.[216]
```

VITAL RECORDS: Chaplin's volume actually abstracts vital records as early as 1792 and as late as 1851. Barbour abstracted Chaplin two "books" from Chaplin's Records of Births and Deaths, 1792–1851 & Records of Marriages, 1821–1854, (includes records of births and deaths organized by family, 1792– 1849; marriage returns, 1821–1854; and reports of births, marriages, and deaths, 1847–1851) Chaplin Town Hall (FHL film 1,378,032, items 2–3):

- "1" refers to FHL item 3 (Marriages 1822–1854 and Birth & Deaths 1848–1851);
- "2" refers to FHL item 2 (Births & Deaths 1797–1853);

The other pre-1852 item on this microfilm was not abstracted by Barbour: **M.A. Chapman's "List of Deaths Which Have Occurred in the Town of Chaplin Since Its Incorporation, July 4, 1822–1906," Chaplin Town Hall, (FHL film 1,378,032, item 1).**

CHURCH RECORDS:

- Congregational Church & Ecclesiastical Society Records, 1809–1906 (FHL film 3,866);
- E. Geer's "Brief Historical Sketch of the Church of Christ in Chaplin" (1840 manuscript) (CSL film #457).

CEMETERY INSCRIPTIONS: The Hale Collection identifies burials in graves at eight named sites in Chaplin Township.[217] Compare with Daniel Hearn's 1979 copy of 26 pre-1800 gravestones in two Chaplin cemeteries.[218] See also,

- Connecticut DAR's "Cemeteries in Chaplin, Windham Co., Connecticut," *CT DAR GRC Report*, ser. 1, vol. 140:23 (1959);
- Connecticut DAR's "Cemeteries in Chaplin, Windham Co., Connecticut," *CT DAR GRC Report*, ser. 1, vol. 140:23 (1959);
- Connecticut DAR's "Old Chewink Cemetery, Chaplin, Windham Co., Connecticut," *CT DAR GRC Report*, ser. 1, vol. 140:26 (1959);
- Connecticut DAR's "Back Cemetery, Chaplin, Windham Co., Connecticut," *CT DAR GRC Report*, ser. 1, vol. 140:27 (1959);
- Connecticut DAR's "Chester Grave, Chaplin, Windham Co., Connecticut," *CT DAR GRC Report*, ser. 1, vol. 140:28 (1959).

OTHER NOTEWORTHY SOURCES: See state and county resources above, pages 18–21.

CHATHAM – see EAST HAMPTON

---

216 Lucius B. Barbour, *Connecticut Vital Records: Chaplin,1822–1857*, (Hartford: CSL, 1920) page after title page (FHL film 2,968). Digital images at *AmericanAncestors.org* and *FamilySearch.org*.

217 Charles R. Hale, "Headstone Inscriptions of the Town of Chaplin, Connecticut," bound typescript, 1930s, CSL, Hartford, FHL film 3326.

218 Daniel Hearn, "Connecticut gravestones, early to 1800," manuscript (FHL film 1,477,476, item 23).

CHESHIRE

Barbour's typescript volume for Cheshire,[219] unlike the GPC edition,[220] begins:

> This volume contains a list alphabetically arranged of all the vital records of the town of Cheshire from its incorporation to about 1840.
>
> This list was taken from a set of cards[221] based on the town records of Cheshire, tombstone records and such church records as do not appear on the town records as printed in "The History of Cheshire, Connecticut", compiled by Joseph Perkins Beach and published in 1912 by Lady Fenwick Chapter of the Daughters of the American Revolution.
>
> It is hoped that as errors or omissions are found notes will be entered in this volume and on the cards which are included in the General Index of Connecticut Vital Records also in the possession of the Connecticut State Library.
>
> Hartford, Conn., February, 1925.[222]

VITAL RECORDS: Cheshire's volume includes vital records as early as 1737 and as late as 1861. *It* is abstracted from a book: Joseph Perkins Beach and Nettie C. Smith's *History of Cheshire, Connecticut, from 1694–1840: including Prospect, which, as Columbia Parish, was a part of Cheshire until 1829* (Cheshire: Lady Fenwich Chapter, D.A.R., 1912) (FHL fiche 6,005,762). The authors *describe the specific groups of* records Barbour chose to paginate from the *History of Cheshire* as:

- "Town Records," pp. 446–499
- "Congregational Church Records (not found in Town Records)" pp. 499–501
- "From Episcopal Church Records (not found in Town Records)" p. 501
- "Matrimonial Records as given by Andrew Hull, Esq. of the Town of Cheshire," pp. 501–502
- "Tombstone Records," pp. 592–513
- "Deaths not in Tombstone List," pp. 513–518
- "Records of Burials from Episcopal Church," pp. 518–521.

The "Town Records" and the "Deaths not in Tombstone List," are abstracted from Cheshire's Town Records, vol. 1–3 (p.1–59) 1765–1853, (includes births, marriages, deaths through 1853) Cheshire Town Hall, (FHL film 1,412,759); and Cheshire's Town records, vol. 3 (p.59–end)–4 1826–1884, Cheshire Town Hall, (FHL film 1,412,760, item 1), but Barbour's citations are to the pagination of *The History of*

---

219 See How to Use This Book, note 3, above.

220 White, *Barbour Collection: Canton–Clinton,* vol. 6, digital image at *Ancestry.com*.

221 Now part of the Barbour Index and interfiled with similar slips from other towns in CSL and on FHL films 2887 *et seq*. See Introduction above, pp. 1–3.

222 Lucius B. Barbour, *Connecticut Vital Records: Cheshire, 1780–1840* (Hartford: CSL, 1925) page after title page (FHL film 2,968). Digital images at *AmericanAncestors.org* and *FamilySearch.org.*

Cheshire, and not to the clerk's original pagination. The original entries from which the book's Congregational and Episcopal marriages and burials are abstracted should be found in the church records cited below. The original entries from which the book's marriage records of Andrew Hull, Justice of the Peace, were copied may be in an unfilmed manuscript of his records in the town clerk's office..

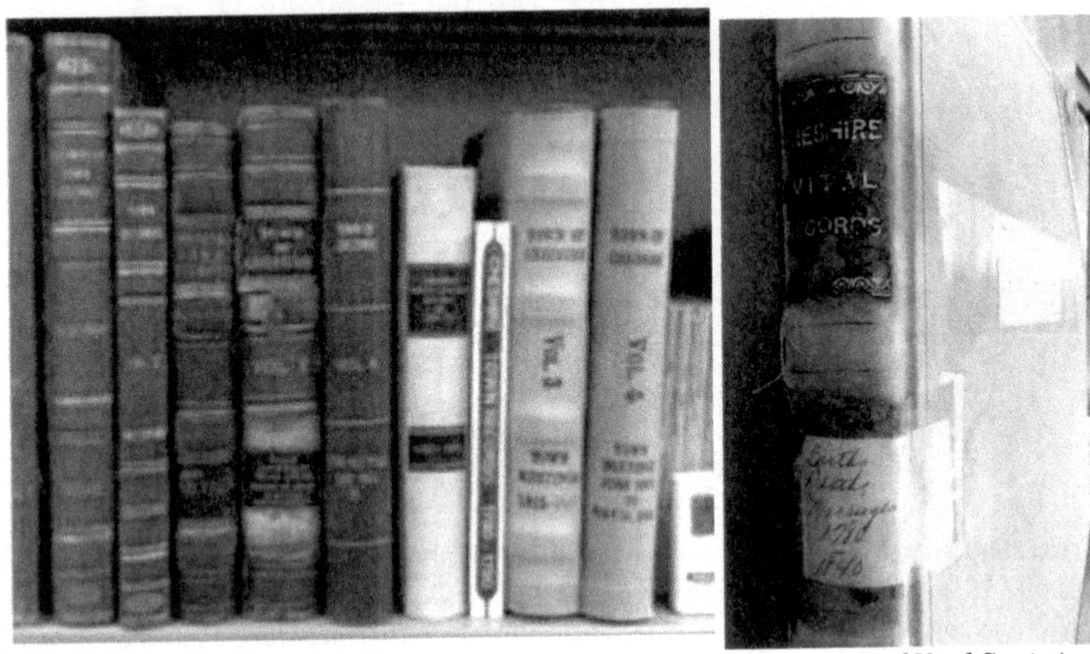

Figures 13& 14: Photographs by Cheshire Town Clerk and Registrar of Vital Statistics

Additional vital records through 1861 may be found in:
Cheshire's Records of Births, Marriages, and Deaths, 1849-1857, Cheshire Town Hall (FHL film 1,412,760, item 3);
Cheshire's Records of Births, Marriages, and Deaths, 1852-1866, Cheshire Town Hall (FHL film 1,412,760, item 2).

CHURCH RECORDS:

- Congregational Church of Cheshire's "Church Records, 1724–1917" (includes baptisms, burials, marriages (1733–1734, 1767–1813 & 1813–1854), and deaths (1813–1852, with other 1767–1858 vital records in Volume 8) (manuscript at CSL) (FHL films 3,998–9).
- St. Peter's Church of Cheshire's "Church Records, 1797–1923" (includes baptisms 1829–1851, marriages 1828–1850, and burials 1828–1851) (manuscript at CSL) (FHL film 4,000);
- Baptisms (1829–51), marriages (1828–50) & burials (1828–51) at St. Peter's Church, Episcopal Diocese, Hartford (ED Film 0004,000).

CEMETERY INSCRIPTIONS: The Hale Collection identifies burials in order of physical proximity at six named cemeteries in Cheshire Township.[223] Compare with Daniel

[223] Charles R. Hale, "Headstone Inscriptions of the Town of Cheshire, Connecticut," bound typescript, 1930s, CSL, Hartford, FHL film 3,326–7.

Hearn's 1976 copy of 184 pre-1800 gravestones in two Cheshire cemeteries.[224] See also,

- Connecticut DAR, "Hillside Avenue Cemetery, Cheshire, Connecticut," *CT DAR GRC Report*, ser. 1, vol. 41:56 (1934) (retyped in 1997);
- Connecticut DAR, "Revolutionary Soldiers' Burials in Hammonassett Cemetery, Madison; Cheshire, North Haven, Waterbury, Wallingford, North Haven, all Connecticut, & Bloomfield, New Jersey," *CT DAR GRC Report*, ser. 1, vol. 133:22 (1956, 1984).

OTHER NOTEWORTHY SOURCES:

- Lucius B. Barbour, Cheshire, Conn. marriages. 1775–1848, 1 volume. (manuscript 124 in Box 21) CSL Record Group 074.36, Hartford;.
- Joseph Perkins Beach, Nettie C Smith, Daughters of the American Revolution. Lady Fenwick Chapter *History of Cheshire, Connecticut, from 1694–1840 : including Prospect, which, as Columbia Parish, was a part of Cheshire until 1829,* (Cheshire: Lady Fenwich Chapter, D.A.R., 1912).

CHESTER

Barbour's typescript volume for Chester,[225] unlike the GPC edition,[226] begins:

> This volume contains a list alphabetically arranged of all the vital records of the town of Chester from its incorporation to about 1852. This list was taken from a set of cards[227] based on a copy of the Chester Vital Records made in 1913 by James N. Arnold, of Providence, R.I. The entire record of the town prior to 1852 is found in one volume.
>
> The Arnold Copy now in the possession of the Connecticut State Library, has not been compared with the original and doubtless errors exist. It is hoped that as errors or omissions are found notes will be entered in this volume and on the cards which are included in the General Index of Connecticut Vital Records also in the possession of the Connecticut State Library.
>
> Hartford, Conn., December, 1923.[228]

VITAL RECORDS: Chester's volume includes at least 35 pages of vital records as early as 1836 and as late as 1869. No Chester vital records before 1847 seem to be cataloged as

224 Daniel Hearn, "Connecticut gravestones, early to 1800," manuscript (FHL film 1,477,476, item 24).

225 See How to Use This Book, note 3, above.

226 White, *Barbour Collection: Canton–Clinton,* vol. 6, digital image at *Ancestry.com*.

227 Now part of the Barbour Index and interfiled with similar slips from other towns in CSL and on FHL films 2,887 *et seq*. See Introduction above, pp. 1–3.

228 Lucius B. Barbour, *Connecticut Vital Records: Chester, 1836–1852,* (Hartford: CSL, 1923) page after title page (FHL film 2,968). Digital images at *AmericanAncestors.org* and *FamilySearch.org.*

such by the FHL. The book Barbour abstracted with Chester vital records as early as 1836, is available only in the Chester Town Clerk's office.[229] **Barbour did not abstract Chester's Records of births, marriages, and deaths, 1847–1917, Chester Town Hall, (FHL film 1,378,292).**
See also, Elizabeth Bull Plimpton's Vital Records of Saybrook Colony, 1635–1860: Including the Towns of Chester, Deep River, Essex, Old Saybrook, and Westbrook, Connecticut (S.i.: Connecticut Valley Shore Research Group, c1985).

CHURCH RECORDS:

- Frederick L'Hommedieu's "Saybrook, Connecticut, Church Records, Frederick L'Hommedieu Copy: Old Saybrook Congregational Church 1736–1782, Centerbrook Congregational Church 1759–1832, Chester Congregational Church 1759–1835" (manuscript at CSL) (FHL film 5,554 or 1,008,328)
- Congregational Church's "Church Records, 1741–1929" (includes baptisms 1782–1838 & 1835–1870, marriages 1759–1836 & 1835–1870, and deaths 1786–1836 & 1836–1871) (manuscript at CSL) (FHL film 3,919)
- Baptisms (1829–51), marriages (1828–50) & burials (1828–51) at St. Peter's Church, Episcopal Diocese, Hartford (ED Film 0004,000)

CEMETERY INSCRIPTIONS: The Hale Collection identifies burials in graves at five named sites in Chester Township.[230] Compare with Daniel Hearn's 1978 copy of 53 pre-1800 gravestones in one Chester cemetery.[231] See also, Lucius B. Barbour's "Chester, Conn. Epitaphs" (Mss A 2783), RSASC, NEHGS).

OTHER NOTEWORTHY SOURCES: *Supplement to the Deep River new era, a.k.a. Chester, a brief history of its past,* (Deep River: [s.n.], 1899).

CLINTON

Barbour's typescript volume for Clinton,[232] unlike the GPC edition,[233] begins:

> This volume contains a list alphabetically arranged of all the vital records of the town of Clinton from its incorporation to about 1854. This list was taken from a set of cards[234] based on copy of the Clinton Vital Records made in 1914 by James N. Arnold, of Providence, R.I. The entire record of the town prior to 1854 is found in one volume.
>
> The Arnold Copy now in the possession of the Connecticut State Library, has not been com-

---

229 Email from Chester Town Clerk Debra Germini Calamari , 15 May 2018.

230 Charles R. Hale, "Headstone Inscriptions of the Town of Chester, Connecticut," bound typescript, 1930s, CSL, Hartford, FHL film 3,327.

231 Daniel Hearn, "Connecticut gravestones, early to 1800," manuscript (FHL film 1,477,476, item 25).

232 See How To Use This Book, note 3, above.

233 White, *Barbour Collection: Canto –Clinton,* vol. 6, digital image at *Ancestry.com*.

234 Now part of the Barbour Index and interfiled with similar slips from other towns in CSL and on FHL films 2,887 *et seq*. See Introduction above, pp. 1–3.

> pared with the original and doubtless errors exist. It is hoped that as errors or omissions are found notes will be entered in this volume and on the cards which are included in the General Index of Connecticut Vital Records also in the possession of the Connecticut State Library.
>
> This volume also contains a second alphabet, beginning on page 28, which is a list of the entries contained in a book of mortality from 1809 and covering a period of nearly seventy years, chronicled by the late Aaron G. Hurd, of Clinton.
>
> The cards, on which this alphabetical list was based and which are now included in the General Index of Connecticut Vital Records, were made from A copy of the Hurd Diary furnished by Frederick L'Hommedieu, late of Deep River.
>
> Hartford, Conn., January, 1924.[235]

VITAL RECORDS. Clinton's volume includes vital records as early as 1833 and as late as 1854. The paginated entries are abstracted from Clinton's "Records of Births, Marriages, and Deaths, 1801–1854," Clinton Town Hall, (FHL film 1,378,439, item 1). The subsequent unpaginated entries are abstracted from Aaron G. Hurd's *List of deaths in Clinton, Conn.: from January 1, 1809, to January 1, 1878*, typescript at CSL (New Haven: Henry W. Vail 1878?).

CHURCH RECORDS:

- Methodist Episcopal Church's "Church Records, 1829–1936" (includes baptisms 1858–1873 and marriages 1858–1873) (manuscript at CSL) (FHL film 3,924);
- First Ecclesiastical Society's Janece Streig, Congressional Church, of Clinton. Used to be on *RootsWeb.com;* at *http://freepages.genealogy.rootsweb.com/~jdevlin /ct/1st_soc_clinton _ct.htm*. Perhaps it was preserved by the *Wayback Machine,* at *https://web.archive.org/ web/20080515000000*/http://freepages.genealogy.rootsweb.com/*

CEMETERY INSCRIPTIONS: The Hale Collection identifies burials in order of physical proximity at four named cemeteries in Clinton Township.[236] Compare with Daniel Hearn's 1978 copy of 135 pre-1800 gravestones in one Clinton cemetery.[237] See also,

- Lucius B. Barbour's *Clinton: All Gravestones in the Town Copied July 1931* (Salem MA: Higginson, 1997) (at NEHGS);
- Connecticut DAR's "Clinton Cemetery, Clinton, Connecticut," *CT DAR GRC Report*, ser. 1, vol. 41:51 (1934) (retyped in 1997);
- Connecticut DAR's "Tombstone Inscriptions, Clinton, Connecticut," *CT DAR GRC Report*, ser. 1, vol. 182:50 (1980).

---

235 Lucius B. Barbour, *Connecticut Vital Records: Clinton, 1838–1854*, (Hartford,: CSL, 1924) page after title [age (FHL film 2,968). Digital images at *AmericanAncestors.org* and *FamilySearch.org.*

236 Charles R. Hale, "Headstone Inscriptions of the Town of Clinton, Connecticut," bound typescript, 1930s, CSL, Hartford, FHL film 3,327).

237 Daniel Hearn, "Connecticut gravestones, early to 1800," manuscript (FHL film 1.477.476, item 26).

OTHER NOTEWORTHY SOURCES:

- Connecticut DAR's "Early Generations of Original Landowners of Clinton, Connecticut," *CT DAR GRC Report*, ser. 2, vol. 29:4 (1997)
- Henry Pierce's *Colonial Killingworth: a history of Clinton and Killingworth,* (Clinton: Clinton Historical Society, 1976)

COLCHESTER

Barbour's typescript volume for Colchester,[238] unlike the GPC edition,[239] begins:

> The vital records of Colchester prior to 1853 are contained in three volumes of births, marriages and deaths. In the first of these other events are recorded, but in volumes two and three there are only vital records and personal items. As in the case of many towns, the earliest vital records appear scattered through the land records and also the earliest book of Town meetings. The prefixes "L" and "TM" in the volume column of the following list indicate in which series each entry is found.
>
> In 1864 the records of Colchester as kept by Michael Taintor were printed in book form and this Book contains certain entries which are not found elsewhere. Such of these items as do not appear elsewhere are included in the list below with the prefix "TPR" in the volume column.
>
> The list following is an alphabetical arrangement of all the vital records of the town of Colchester from its incorporation to about 1853. It was compiled from a set of cards[240] based on a copy made from the records in 1912 by James N. Arnold, of Providence, R.I. The Arnold Copy now in the possession of the Connecticut State Library, has not been compared with the original and doubtless errors exist. It is hoped that as errors or omissions are found notes will be entered in this volume and on the cards which are included in the General Index of Connecticut Vital Records also in the possession of the Connecticut State Library.
>
> Hartford, Conn., February, 1923.[241]

---

238 See How to Use This Book, note 4, above.

239 Lorraine Cook White, *Barbour Collection of Connecticut Town Vital Records: Colchester, 1699-1850, Colebrook, 1779-1810, Columbia, 1804-1854, Cornwall, 1740-1854*, vol. 7, (Baltimore: GPC, 1996) digital image at *Ancestry.com*.

240 Now part of the Barbour Index and interfiled with similar slips from other towns in CSL and on FHL films 2,887, *et seq*. See Introduction above, pp. 3–5.

241 Lucius B. Barbour, *Connecticut Vital Records: Colchester, 1699–1850,* (Hartford; CSL, 1923) page after title page (FHL film 2,968). Digital image at *AmericanAncestors.org* and *FamilySearch.org*.

VITAL RECORDS: Colchester's volume includes vital records as early as 1697 and as late as 1856. Barbour abstracted seven Colchester "books:"

- "1" to "3" refers to Colchester's "Records of Births, Marriages, Deaths vols. 1–3 1712–1865," Colchester Town Hall (FHL film 1,312,155);
- "L-1" refers to Colchester's "Deeds, vols. 1–2 1703–1728" (Includes births, deaths and marriages in volumes 1 and 2 Colchester Town Hall, (FHL film 3,889);[242]
- "L-3" refers to "Deeds, vols. 3–4 1728–1749" (Includes births, deaths and marriages in volume 3.) original at CSA (FHL film 3,890);
- "TM1" refers to pages 193–199 of vital records for the years 1697–1729, but is unfilmed by FHL. It may be viewed today, only at CSA, as the first volume of Colchester Town Meeting Records, 4 vols, 1697–1729 (CSL 974.62 C671, CSA, Hartford. Most of its entries, however, duplicate L-1 to L-3;
- "TPR" refers to Charles M. Taintor's *Abstracts from the records of Colchester: with some transcripts from the recording of Michaell Taintor of "Brainford," Conn.*, (Washington [District of Columbia]: Library of Congress, Photoduplication Service, 1989) (original published: Hartford: Case, Lockwood and Co., 1864) (reprint Heritage Books 1980).

See also,

- **Colchester Meeting Town Records, 4 vols., 1697–1729 (CSL 974.62 C671, CSA, Hartford;**
- **"Ralph Hurlbutt's Record as Justice of the Peace of New London County, Connecticut" (includes marriages 1807–1837) (typescript at CSL) (FHL film 5,356).[243]**

CHURCH RECORDS:

- First Congregational Church, "Church Records, 1702–1937" (includes baptisms (1732–1774, 1792–1891), deaths 1732–1774 & 1792–1813, and marriages 1732–1783) (photocopies and originals at CSL) (FHL film 3,910);
- First Congregational Society, "Baptisms, Marriages, and Deaths 1732–1783," (originals at CSL) (FHL film 1,008,330, items 3–11);
- Second Congregational Church, "Church Records, 1729–1811' (includes baptisms 1742–1761 & 1764–1796; marriages 1755–1761 & 1764–1796, and deaths 1765–1804) (photocopy at CSL) (FHL film 3,911);
- Nathaniel Goodwin and Lena J. Barnard's "First Congregational Society (Colchester, Connecticut): Births, Marriages, Baptisms and Deaths 1732–1783" (manuscript at CSL) (FHL film 1,008,330, item 12);
- First Society of Colchester's "Church Records, 1729–1876" (includes baptisms, marriages and deaths) (original records at CSL) (FHL film 1,008,331, item 1);
- Colchester Methodist Episcopal Church and Hebron Methodist Episcopal Church's "Church Records, 1843–1908" (includes baptisms 1843–1902) (originals in the Boston University School of Theology Library, hereafter "BUSTL") (FHL film 1,508,822);
- Baptist Church's Church minutes, 1835–1953, photocopy at CSL, (FHL film 3,909).

---

242 Volume 2 entries (1713-1721).are mislabeled "vol. 1" by Barbour, but cite correct volume 2 page numbers.

243 "Town of Colchester Records," 1742-1883 (1.5 cubic feet of Court and Justice of the Peace and probate records and tax records) CSA, Hartford.

- Second Church of Christ's 'Church Records, 1729–1876" (includes baptisms, marriages and deaths) (originals at CSL) (FHL film 1,008,331, items 4–6);
- First Baptist Church, Church records, 1780–1939, originals and photocopies at CSL, (FHL film 3,912);
- Third Baptist Church of Christ's Church records, 1809–1875, (originals at CSL) (FHL film 3,915);
- Westchester Ecclesiastical Society's Church records, 1728–1835, photocopies at CSL, (FHL film 3,913);
- Nathaniel Goodwin and Lena J. Barnard's "Second (Third) Congregational Society (Colchester, Connecticut: Births, Marriages, Baptisms, and Deaths 1741–1840" (manuscript at CSL) (FHL film 1,008,331, item 7).

CEMETERY INSCRIPTIONS: The Hale Collection identifies burials in order of physical proximity at 21 named cemeteries in Colchester Township.[244] Compare with Daniel Hearn's 1979 copy of 302 pre-1800 gravestones in four Colchester cemeteries.[245] See also,

- Frank E. Randall's "Memoranda of All the Inscriptions In the Old Burying Ground at Colchester, Conn." *NEHGR*, 42:78–83, 155–9, 269–71, 387–0 (Jan Apr Jul Oct 1888), 43:44–7, 188–91, 253–6, 358–64 (1889) (FHL fiche 6062304);
- Lucius B. Barbour's "Colchester Genealogical Data From Connecticut Cemeteries" (1934 manuscript at NEHGS Library);
- Abigail Wolcott Ellsworth Chapter, DAR, "Brown Family Yard, Marvin Farm, Colchester, Connecticut," *CT DAR GRC Report*, ser. 1, vol. 90:92 (1942) (FHL film 844,451);
- DAR Abigail Wolcott Ellsworth Chapter's "Crouch, Knowles, Wells Family Burial Plot, Colchester, Connecticut," *CT DAR GRC Report*, ser. 1, vol. 90:93 (1942) (FHL film 844,451);
- DAR Abigail Wolcott Ellsworth Chapter's "Linwood Cemetery, Colchester, Connecticut," *CT DAR GRC Report*, ser. 1, vol. 90:94 (1942) (FHL film 844,451);
- Lucius B. Barbours "Colchester, Conn. Epitaphs" (Mss A 6041), RSASC, NEHGS;
- DAR Abigail Wolcott Ellsworth Chapter's "Ponemah Cemetery, Colchester, Connecticut," *CT DAR GRC Report*, ser. 1, vol. 90:104 (1942) (FHL film 844,451);
- DAR Abigail Wolcott Ellsworth Chapter's "Scott Hill Cemetery, Colchester, Connecticut," *CT DAR GRC Report*, ser. 1, vol. 90:107 (1942) (FHL film 844,451);
- DAR Abigail Wolcott Ellsworth Chapter's "Westchester Center Cemetery, Colchester, Connecticut," *CT DAR GRC Report*, ser. 1, vol. 90:109 (1942) (FHL film 844,451);
- Connecticut DAR's "Headstone Inscriptions, Wells Cemetery, Colchester, Connecticut," *CT DAR GRC Report*, ser. 1, vol. 175:31 (1975);
- Connecticut DAR's "Headstone Inscriptions, Chestnut Hill Cemetery, Colchester, Connecticut," *CT DAR GRC Report*, ser. 1, vol. 175:32 (1975);
- Connecticut DAR's "Headstone Inscriptions, Scott Hill Cemetery, Colchester, Connecticut," *CT DAR GRC Report*, ser. 1, vol. 175:33 (1975);

---

244 Charles R. Hale, "Headstone Inscriptions of the Town of Colchester, Connecticut," bound typescript, 1930s, CSL, Hartford, FHL film 3,327).

245 Daniel Hearn, "Connecticut gravestones, early to 1800," manuscript (FHL film 1,477,476, item 27).

- Connecticut DAR's "Headstone Inscriptions, Palmer Cemetery, Colchester, Connecticut," *CT DAR GRC Report*, ser. 1, vol. 175:34 (1975).

OTHER NOTEWORTHY SOURCES:

- "Notes Taken from the Diary of Elisha Niles, 1764–1850;" see Appendix A;
- Connecticut DAR's "Genealogical data taken from Bible of Alfred B. Pierce, cabinetmaker & undertaker of Colchester, Connecticut, also Worthington, Dolbeare Families," *CT DAR GRC Report*, ser. 1, vol. 152:6 (1966);
- Lillian Kruger Brooks' *Life Flows Along Like a River: A History of Haddam Neck.* (East Hampton? Conn.] Haddam Neck Genealogical Group, 1972) (includes vital records of the people of Haddam, East Haddam, Higganum, Hadlyme, Middletown, East Hampton, Haddam Neck, Moodus, Chatham, and Colchester.

COLEBROOK

Barbour's typescript volume for Colebrook,[246] unlike the GPC edition,[247] begins:

> The vital records of Colebrook, prior to 1810, are found in one volume, with the exception of a few marriage records, after 1783, which are found in an unpaged Justice Record.
>
> This alphabetical list was taken from a set of cards[248] based on a manuscript copy of the Colebrook Vital Records made in 1914. Reference to the unpaged Justice Record is indicated by the pagination of the manuscript copy.
>
> The manuscript copy, now in the possession of the Connecticut State Library, has not been compared with the original and doubtless errors exist. It is hoped that as errors or omissions are found notes will be entered in this volume and on the cards which are included in the General Index of Connecticut Vital Records also in the possession of the Connecticut State Library.
>
> Hartford, Conn., April, 1927.[249]

VITAL RECORDS: Colebrook's volume includes vital records as early as 1744 and as late as 1835, Barbour's abstraction refers to Colebrook's Town Records, 1744–1835, (includes births, marriages, deaths) Colebrook Town Hall, (FHL film 1,503,206, item 1). Colebrook's Justice Records are interspersed with the above in Barbour's volume and identifiable only by the Justice's name. They are from Elijah Rockwell's "Justice

246 See How to Use This Book, note 4, above..

247 White, *Barbour Collection: Colchester–Cornwall,* vol. 7, digital image at *Ancestry.com*.

248 Now part of the Barbour Index and interfiled with similar slips from other towns in CSL and on FHL films 2,887 *et seq*. See Introduction above, pp. 3–5.

249 Lucius B. Barbour, *Connecticut Vital Records: Colebrook, 1779–1810,* (Hartford: CSL, page after title page (FHL film 2,968). Digital images at *AmericanAncestors.org* and *FamilySearch.org*.

trials 1783–1818" (contains records of Elijah Rockwell, JP, including marriage index) manuscript at Colebrook Town Hall (FHL 1,503,206 item 2).

Other early Colebrook vital records are not abstracted by Barbour:

- **Colebrook's Births, Marriages, and Deaths, 1846–1852, Colebrook Town Hall, (FHL film 1,503,206, item 4);**
- **Colebrook's "Index to marriages recorded in book 6, land and town records of Colebrook, Conn., 1820–1851," Colebrook Town Hall, (FHL film 1,503,206, item 3);**
- **Colebrook's Land Records, vols. 6 1811–1842, Colebrook Town Hall, (FHL film 3,927) (additional marriages 1826–1851on pp. 320–372).**

CHURCH RECORDS:

- Congregational Church's "Church Records, 1783–1939" (includes baptisms 1821–1861 &1796–1801 in vols. 1 and 2, and a family register 1795–1902 in vol. 7) (manuscript at CSL) (FHL film 3,932);
- West Branch Baptist Church's "Church records, 1799–1879," (originals at CSL) (FHL film 1,008,331, item 8);
- South Baptist Church's "Church Records, 1848–1940" (includes baptisms) (manuscript at CSL) (FHL film 1,008,331, item 11);
- Union Church Society of Colebrook River and Colebrook River Burying Ground Assn.'s Church records, 1815–1849, typescript at CSL, (FHL film 3,932, item 1).

CEMETERY INSCRIPTIONS: The Hale Collection identifies burials in order of physical proximity at 10 named cemeteries in Colebrook Township.[250] Compare with Daniel Hearn's 1978 copy of 12 pre-1800 gravestones in one Colbrook cemetery.[251]

See also,

- DAR Abigail Wolcott Ellsworth Chapter's "Beech Hill Burying Ground, Colebrook, Connecticut," *CT DAR GRC Report*, ser. 1, vol. 92:34 (1943) (FHL film 844,451);
- DAR Abigail Wolcott Ellsworth Chapter's "Cobb Cemetery, Colebrook, Connecticut," *CT DAR GRC Report*, ser. 1, vol. 92:37 (1943) (FHL film 844,451);
- DAR Abigail Wolcott Ellsworth Chapter's "Colebrook Center Cemetery, Colebrook, Connecticut," *CT DAR GRC Report*, ser. 1, vol. 92:38 (1943) (FHL film 844,451);
- DAR Abigail Wolcott Ellsworth Chapter's "Colebrook River Cemetery, Colebrook, Connecticut," *CT DAR GRC Report*, ser. 1, vol. 92:44 (1943) (FHL film 844,451);
- DAR Abigail Wolcott Ellsworth Chapter's "Spencer Family Yard (Whitford), Colebrook, Connecticut," *CT DAR GRC Report*, ser. 1, vol. 92:77 (1943) (FHL film 844,451);
- DAR Abigail Wolcott Ellsworth Chapter's "Hemlock Hill Cemetery, Colebrook, Connecticut," *CT DAR GRC Report*, ser. 1, vol. 92:50 (1943) (FHL film 844,451);
- DAR Abigail Wolcott Ellsworth Chapter's "North or Baptist Cemetery, Colebrook, Connecticut," *CT DAR GRC Report*, ser. 1, vol. 92:53 (1943) (FHL film 844,451);
- DAR Abigail Wolcott Ellsworth Chapter's "Old or South Cemetery, Colebrook, Connecticut," *CT DAR GRC Report*, ser. 1, vol. 92:61 (1943) (FHL film 844,451);

---

250 Charles R. Hale, "Headstone Inscriptions of the Town of Colebrook, Connecticut," bound typescript, 1930s, CSL, Hartford, FHL film 3,327.

251 Daniel Hearn, "Connecticut gravestones, early to 1800," manuscript (FHL film 1,477,476, item 28).

- DAR Abigail Wolcott Ellsworth Chapter's "Colebrook River Cemetery, Colebrook, Connecticut," *CT DAR GRC Report*, ser. 1, vol. 92:44 (1943) (FHL film 844,451).

OTHER NOTEWORTHY SOURCES:

- Connecticut DAR's "Abstracts from Colbrook [sic], Connecticut Revolutionary Records, 1774–1784," *CT DAR GRC Report*, ser. 1, vol. 153:29 (1966);
- Payne Kenyon Kilbourne's "Genealogical notes on families of Litchfield, Connecticut," (2 oversize volumes, negative photostat) CSA, Hartford.

COLUMBIA

Barbour's typescript volume for Columbia,[252] (unlike the GPC edition,[253] begins:

> This volume contains a list alphabetically arranged of all the vital records of the town of Columbia from its incorporation to about 1852. This list was taken from a set of cards[254] based on a copy of the Columbia Vital Records made in 1912 by James N. Arnold, of Providence, R.I. The entire record of the town prior to 1852 is contained in one volume.
>
> The original book has no page numbers and so the pagination of the Arnold Copy has been used in this list.
>
> The Arnold Copy, now in the possession of the Connecticut State Library, has not been compared with the original and doubtless errors exist. It is hoped that as errors or omissions are found notes will be entered in this volume and on the cards which are included in the General Index of Connecticut Vital Records also in the possession of the Connecticut State Library.
>
> Hartford, Conn., November, 1922.[255]

VITAL RECORDS. Columbia's volume includes vital records as early as 1768 and as late as 1854. Barbour's appears to have abstracted the town clerk's "Town Record Volume 1 – (1804–1854(?) – all handwritten entries, includes vitals, meetings, notices…. (very hard to read)."[256] This book is *not* identical to what FHL filmed as **"Town Records, vol. 1, 1768–1868," (contains records of marriages, 1768–1854 & some records of births and deaths 1783–1842) Columbia Town Hall, (FHL film 3,870).** The FHL microfilm contains some of the same vital records as Barbour abstracted, but on different pages. More importantly, **the early book filmed by the FHL contains many early vital records not abstracted by Barbour at all** – and vice versa.

---

252 See How to Use This Book, above, note 4.

253 White, *Barbour Collection: Colchester–Cornwall,* vol. 7, digital image at *Ancestry.com*.

254 Now part of the Barbour Index and interfiled with similar slips from other towns in CSL and on FHL films 2,887 *et seq*. See Introduction above, pp. 3–5.

255 Lucius B. Barbour, Connecticut Vital Records: Columbia, 1804–1852, CSL, Hartford, page preceding p. 1, FHL film 2,968. Digital images at *AmericanAncestors.org* and *FamilySearch.org.*

256 Email to author from Columbia Town Clerk Robin M. Kendrick, 22 Aug 2018.

In addition, Barbour abstracted no part of **"Records of Births, Marriages, and Deaths, 1847–1900" Columbia Town Hall, (FHL film 1,376,168, item 2),**

CHURCH RECORDS:

- Congregational Church (Northwest or Crank Society)'s "Church Records, 1722–1917" (includes baptisms, marriages, and deaths) (manuscript at CSL) (FHL film 3,871);
- Congregational Church's "Vital Records kept fy Rev. Frederick Denison Avery, 1848–1907" (manuscript at CSL) (FHL film 1,008,332).

CEMETERY INSCRIPTIONS: The Hale Collection identifies burials in order of physical proximity at five named cemeteries in Columbia Township.[257] Compare with Daniel Hearn's 1979 copy of 142 pre-1800 gravestones in one Columbia cemetery.[258] See also,

- Louis M. Dewey's "Inscriptions from Old Cemeteries in Connecticut," *NEHGR*, 60:370–3 (Oct 1906);
- Lucius B. Barbour's Columbia, Conn. Epitaphs (Mss A 6040), RSASC, NEHGS;
- Susan W. Dimock's "Inscriptions from the Old Cemetery in Columbia, Connecticut" *CT DAR GRC Report*, ser. 1, vol. 4:26 (1914) (Retyped in 1997) FHL film 844,454).

OTHER NOTEWORTHY SOURCES:

- Lucius B. Barbour's "Genealogical notes compiled from church records of Lebanon Crank and Lebanon Second Society, Columbia, Conn. 1720–1836," 1 volume. Abstract of church vital records. (manuscript 7 in Box 1) CSL Record Group 074.36, Hartford;
- Connecticut DAR's "Roll of Capt. James Pineo's Company, Columbia, Connecticut," *CT DAR GRC Report*, ser. 1, vol. 88:82 (1942);
- Joseph Perkins Beach's *History of Cheshire, Connecticut from 1694 to 1840: Including Prospect, Which, as Columbia Parish, Was a Part of Cheshire Until 1829* (Cheshire: Lady Fenwick Chapter, DAR, 1912);
- "Deaths—Columbia, Conn. Bill of Mortality, 1814–1869". CSL; see Appendix A;
- DAR Abigail Wolcott Ellsworth Chapter's "Old Cemetery, Columbia, Connecticut," *CT DAR GRC Report*, ser. 1, vol. 103:6 (1946) FHL film 844452;
- Connecticut DAR's "Cemeteries in Columbia, Tolland Co., Connecticut," *CT DAR GRC Report*, ser. 1, vol. 133:26 (1956, 1984);
- "Abstracts from the Columbian Register, 1813–1815," *TAG*, 35:228 (1959);
- "Town of Columbia Records," 1805–1940 (18 cubic feet of tax, election, financial and school records for the town of Columbia) CSA, Hartford.

CORNWALL

Barbour's typescript volume for Cornwall,[259] unlike the GPC edition,[260] begins:

```
    The vital records of Cornwall prior to 1854,
are found scattered through Volumes 3 and 4 of
Land Records and Volumes 1, 2 and 3 of Vital Re-
```

257 Charles R. Hale, "Headstone Inscriptions of the Town of Columbia, Connecticut," bound typescript, 1930s, CSL, Hartford, FHL film 3,327.

258 Daniel Hearn, "Connecticut gravestones, early to 1800," manuscript (FHL film 1,477,476, item 29).

259 See How to Use This Book, note 4, above.

260 White, *Barbour Collection: Colchester–Cornwall,* vol. 7, digital image at *Ancestry.com*.

cords.

This alphabetical list was taken from a set of cards[261] based on a manuscript copy of the Cornwall Vital Records made in 1915 by James N. Arnold, of Providence, R.I. Reference to the entries found in the Land Records is indicated by the abbreviation "LR" and the number of the volume.

In "A History of Cornwall, Connecticut", published in 1926 by Edward C. Starr, B.D., there are many vital records of Cornwall, and although the Arnold Copy has not been checked in its entirety with this printed record, a few marked differences have been noted herein.

The Arnold Copy, now in the possession of the Connecticut State Library, has not been compared with the original and doubtless errors exist. It is hoped that as errors or omissions are found notes will be entered in this volume and on the cards which are included in the General Index of Connecticut Vital Records also in the possession of the Connecticut State Library.

Hartford, Conn., February, 1927[262]

VITAL RECORDS: Cornwall's volume includes vital records as early as 1732 and as late as 1853. The applicable FHL catalog entry for these records does not clearly specify the date range covered. Barbour's abstraction also relied upon a widely available book. Barbour abstracted but then **modified** five Cornwall "books:"

- "LR3" and "LR4" refer to Cornwall's Land Records, vol. 3–5 1768–1789, Cornwall Town Hall, (FHL film 3,959) (not cataloged by FHL as including vital records);
- "1" through "3" refer to Cornwall's Records of Births, Marriages, and Deaths in the Town of Cornwall, 1732–1933," (includes some records of delayed registration of births and corrections to birth records") Cornwall Town Hall, (FHL film 1,516,243).

There is no way to readily determine which abstractions were altered to match **data in Edward C. Starr's *A History of Cornwall, Connecticut: A Typical New England Town*** (New Haven: Tuttle, Morehouse & Taylor Co., 1926) (FHL film 1,320,817, item 3); 2nd ed., (Torrington: Rainbow Press, 1982).

See also, Theodore S. Gold's *Historical Records of the Town of Cornwall, Litchfield County, Connecticut* (Hartford: Case, Lockwood & Brainard Co., 1877).

CHURCH RECORDS:

- First Methodist Episcopal Church's "Church Records, 1839–1898" (includes births, marriages and deaths) (manuscript at CSL) (FHL film 3,967);

---

261 Now part of the Barbour Index and interfiled with similar slips from other towns in CSL and on FHL films 2,887 *et seq*. See Introduction above, pp. 3–5.

262 Lucius B. Barbour, *Connecticut Vital Records: Cornwall, 1740–1854*, (Hartford: CSL,1927) page after title page (FHL film 2,968)(. Digital images at *AmericanAncestors.org* and *FamilySearch.org*.

- E.C. Starr's "Cornwall, Conn., [Church Records]," *NEHGR*, 51:70 (Jan 1897);
- Connecticut DAR's "Manual of the Second Congregational Church, Cornwall, Connecticut and Membership Roll from its Formation in 1782," *CT DAR GRC Report*, ser. 1, vol. 40:21 (1934) (retyped) (FHL film 844,460);
- First Congregational Church's "Church Records, 1755–1892" (includes baptisms, deaths, and marriages) (manuscript at CSL) (FHL film 3,966);
- Connecticut DAR's "Roll of Members, First Church of Christ, Cornwall, Connecticut," *CT DAR GRC Report*, ser. 1, vol. 40:1 (1934) (retyped) (FHL film 844,460);
- Cornwall Hollow Baptist Church, Records, 1843–1935 (manuscript at CSL) (FHL 3,968);
- "Cornwall CT Church Records" *NEHGR*, vol. 51 (1897).

CEMETERY INSCRIPTIONS: The Hale Collection identifies burials in order of physical proximity at 11 named cemeteries in Cornwall Township.[263] Compare with Daniel Hearn's 1978 copy of 84 pre-1800 gravestones in three Cornwall cemeteries.[264]
See also,

- Ellen Paul's "Inscriptions from St. Bridget Catholic Cemetery in Cornwall, Conn., 1817–2001" (manuscript at NEHGS);DAR Abigail Wolcott Ellsworth Chapter's "
- Wilcox Family Yard, Near Canaan Line, Cornwall, Connecticut," *CT DAR GRC Report*, ser. 1, vol. 93:77 (1943) (FHL film 844,451);
- DAR Abigail Wolcott Ellsworth Chapter's "Cornwall Bridge Cemetery, Cornwall, Connecticut," *CT DAR GRC Report*, ser. 1, vol. 93:78 (1943) (FHL film 844,451);
- DAR Abigail Wolcott Ellsworth Chapter's "Cornwall Center Cemetery, Cornwall, Connecticut," *CT DAR GRC Report*, ser. 1, vol. 93:88 (1943) (FHL film 844,451);
- DAR Abigail Wolcott Ellsworth Chapter's "Cornwall Hollow Cemetery, Cornwall, Connecticut," *CT DAR GRC Report*, ser. 1, vol. 93:110 (1943) (FHL film 844,451);
- DAR Abigail Wolcott Ellsworth Chapter's "North Cornwall Cemetery, Cornwall, Connecticut," *CT DAR GRC Report*, ser. 1, vol. 93:115 (1943) (FHL film 844,451);
- DAR Abigail Wolcott Ellsworth Chapter's "Old Sedgwick Yard, Cornwall Hollow, Cornwall, Connecticut," *CT DAR GRC Report*, ser. 1, vol. 93:119 (1943) (FHL film 844,451);
- DAR Abigail Wolcott Ellsworth Chapter's "South or East Cemetery (near Warren Line) Cornwall, Connecticut," *CT DAR GRC Report*, ser. 1, vol. 93:121 (1943) (FHL film 844,451).

OTHER NOTEWORTHY SOURCES:

- Harriet Lydia Clark and Andrew Miles Clark Pikosky's *History of East Cornwall area* (Torrington: Rainbow Press, c1977) (FHL film 1,698,292, item 4);
- Harriet Lydia Clark's *Supplement of the History of East Cornwall* (Torrington: Rainbow Press, c1980 (FHL film 1,698,292, item 5).
- "E.S. Millard's Account Book, 1811–53." CSL; see Appendix A;

---

263 Charles R. Hale, "Headstone Inscriptions of the Town of Cornwall, Connecticut," bound typescript, 1930s, CSL, Hartford, FHL film 3,328.

264 Daniel Hearn, "Connecticut gravestones, early to 1800," manuscript (FHL film 1,477,476, Item 30).

COVENTRY

VITAL RECORDS: Barbour published no Coventry volume.[265] He simply included Coventry vital records slips labeled "D" in his statewide Index.[266] His abstraction copies Susan W. Dimock's *Births, Marriages, Baptisms, and Deaths: From the Records of the Town and Churches in Coventry, Connecticut, 1711–1844* (New York: Baker & Taylor Company, 1897) (images at *AmericanAncestors.org*). Dimock generally abstracts Coventry's Town Records, 1692–1853, (includes births, marriages, and deaths) Coventry Town Hall (FHL films 1,376,123, item 2–3 and 1,376,124, item 4). She does not cite the pages abstracted and her **work contains many errors and omissions.**

The Barbour Index also abstracts and interfiles "Record of Deaths, North Coventry, 1826–1869." See also,

- **Coventry's Miscellaneous Town Records, 1692–1840, (includes freemen, births 1692–1810, marriages 1712–1784, and deaths 1712–1840) 2 vols., CSL, Hartford (FHL film 3,861);**
- **Coventry Vital Records, circa 1845–1905, CSL (CSA RG 072:002, Box 18) (includes pre-1850 birthdates on death certificates);**
- **Edith M. Washburn_'s "Index to vital statistics, 17-- to 1936," (1936 manuscript) an index to vital statistics in the town record books, vols. 1–7 (FHL film 1,376,123, item 1) ;**
- **Jan (Wilson) Ramos' "Missing 1770–1800 Coventry Records ("does not include all inhabitants at that time") transcribed on *GenWeb* by 28 Mar 2000, but now absent, CSL's *CT Vital Records* gives inoperative web address from the year 2000. Perhaps it was preserved by the *Wayback Machine,* at *https://web.archive.org/web /2018*/www.usgenweb.org***
- **DAR Abigail Wolcott Ellsworth Chapter's "Birth Records taken from Town Records of Coventry, Connecticut, 1711–1840," *CT DAR GRC Report*, ser. 2, vol. 10:1 (1991);**
- **DAR Abigail Wolcott Ellsworth Chapter's "Marriage Records taken from Town Records of Coventry, Connecticut, 1711–1840," *CT DAR GRC Report*, ser. 2, vol. 12:8 (1991);**
- **DAR Abigail Wolcott Ellsworth Chapter's "Death Records taken from Records of Coventry, Connecticut, 1711–1840," *CT DAR GRC Report*, ser. 2, vol. 12:48 (1991);**

CHURCH RECORDS:

- Second Congregational Church at North Coventry's "Church Records, 1740–1910" (includes deaths 1801–1829 and baptisms 1819–1828) (originals at CSL) (FHL film 3,862);
- Connecticut DAR's "Death Records from Second Church, in North Parish, called North Coventry, Connecticut, 1801 to 1842," *CT DAR GRC Report*, ser. 2, vol. 14:35 (1992).

---

[265] See How to Use This Book, note 4, above.

[266] Now part of the Barbour Index and interfiled with similar slips from other towns in CSL and on FHL films 2,887 *et seq*. See Introduction above, pp. 3–5.

- First Congregational Church at South Coventry's "Church Records, 1740–1936," (includes baptisms 1776–1795, 1795–1844, & 1845–1859, bill of mortality 1763–1796, marriages 1796–1843, deaths 1796–1844 & 1845–1859, and infant baptisms 1849–1867) (originals at CSL) (FHL film 3,863);
- First Church of Christ's "Church Records" (includes records of baptisms, marriages, deaths) (originals at CSL) (FHL film 1,008,334);
- Connecticut DAR's "Baptism Records from First Church, Coventry, Connecticut, 1776–1844," *CT DAR GRC Report*, ser. 2, vol. 5:1 (1990);
- Connecticut DAR's "Death Records from First Church, Coventry, Connecticut, 1763–1844," *CT DAR GRC Report*, ser. 2, vol. 5:36 (1990);
- Connecticut DAR's "Marriage Records from First Church, Coventry, Connecticut, 1714–1843," *CT DAR GRC Report*, ser. 2, vol. 5:73 (1990);
- DAR Abigail Wolcott Ellsworth Chapter's "Baptism records from Second Church, North Coventry, Connecticut, 1819–1843," *CT DAR GRC Report*, ser. 2, vol. 12:1 (1991);

CEMETERY INSCRIPTIONS: The Hale Collection identifies burials in order of physical proximity at 12 named cemeteries in Coventry Township.[267] Compare with Daniel Hearn's 1979 copy of 259 pre-1800 gravestones in three Coventry cemeteries.[268] See also,

- Lucius B. Barbour's "Coventry, Conn. Epitaphs" (Mss A 2785), RSASC, NEHGS;
- Susan W. Dimock's "Old Cemetery at North Coventry sometimes called "Strong" Cemetery," *CT DAR GRC Report*, ser. 1, vol. 5:1 (1914); Susan W. Dimock, "Inscriptions from the Oldest Part of the Cemetery in South Coventry, Connecticut," *CT DAR GRC Report*, ser. 1, vol. 5:33 (1914);
- Susan W. Dimock's "Old Cemetery at the Foot of Silver Street," *CT DAR GRC Report*, ser. 1, vol. 5:98 (1914);
- DAR Abigail Wolcott Ellsworth Chapter's "North Cemetery, North Coventry, Connecticut," *CT DAR GRC Report*, ser. 1, vol. 103:30 (1946) (FHL film 844,452);
- DAR Abigail Wolcott Ellsworth Chapter's "South Cemetery, North Coventry, Connecticut," *CT DAR GRC Report*, ser. 1, vol. 103:43 (1946)) (FHL film 844,452);
- DAR Abigail Wolcott Ellsworth Chapter's "Nathan Hale Cemetery, South Coventry, Connecticut," *CT DAR GRC Report*, ser. 1, vol. 103:55 (1946)) (FHL film 844,452);
- Connecticut DAR's "Cemeteries in Coventry, Tolland Co., Connecticut," *CT DAR GRC Report*, ser. 1, vol. 133:27 (1956, 1984);

OTHER NOTEWORTHY SOURCES:

- Coventry Historical Society's Collection of up to 100 account books, 1773 –1974, See *http://archives.library.wcsu.edu/cao/ctcovhs/accounts.xml?q=the#idp494590544;*
- "Genealogical Notes on the Carpenter & Gurley Families of Coventry;" CSL; see Appendix A;
- Mrs. William Minor, Ruth Amelia Higgins Cassedy, and William H. Minor's Coventry in retrospect: 250 years, [Coventry: Quarter Millennium Celebration, General Committee, 1962];

---

267 Charles R. Hale, "Headstone Inscriptions of the Town of Coventry, Connecticut," bound typescript, 1930s, CSL, Hartford, FHL film 3,328.

268 Daniel Hearn, "Connecticut gravestones, early to 1800," manuscript (FHL film 1,477,476, item 31).

- Connecticut DAR's "Abstracts from Coventry, Connecticut Revolutionary Records, 1774–1784," *CT DAR GRC Report*, ser. 1, vol. 153:33 (1966);
- Winifred L. Holman's "Corrections of Coventry (Conn.) Records; *TAG*, 14:144 (1938).

CROMWELL

VITAL RECORDS: Cromwell was formally established in 1851,[269] but began keeping vital records in 1850. This town was not abstracted in the Barbour Index[270] or in any other version of the Barbour Collection of Connecticut vital records. **But see "Cromwell Vital Records, 1850–1855" (includes births, marriages, and deaths Sep 1850–1851) (originals in Cromwell Town Hall) (FHL film 1,378,209, item 1).**

CHURCH RECORDS:

- First Congregational Church's "Church Records, 1715–1875" (includes baptisms (1715–1736, 1738–1809 & 1809–1874), marriages 1738–1809 & 1809–1874, and deaths 1738–1809 &1809–1875) (originals at CSL) (FHL film 4,004);
- Second Baptist Church in Middletown (Cromwell)'s *Church records, 1802–1920,* originals at CSL (FHL film 4,003);
- First Congregational Church (Cromwell's *Sabbath School records 1843–1845* (FHL film 1,008,338, item 1).

CEMETERY INSCRIPTIONS: The Hale Collection identifies people in order of physical proximity buried at four named cemeteries in Cromwell Township.[271] Compare with Daniel Hearn's 1978 copy of 260 pre-1800 gravestones in one Cromwell cemetery.[272] See also, Lucius B. Barbour's "Cromwell, Conn. Epitaphs" (Mss A 6039), RSASC, NEHGS.

OTHER NOTEWORTHY SOURCES:

- M.S. Dudley's *History of Cromwell: a sketch* (Middletown: Constitution Office, 1880);
- Ranney Memorial and Historical Association's *Founders, fathers, and patriots of Middletown upper houses, since 1851 Cromwell, Conn.* (Cromwell: Ranney Memorial and Historical Assn., 1908);
- Charles Collard Adams' *Middletown upper houses: a history of the north society of Middletown, Connecticut, from 1650 to 1800, with genealogical and biographical chapters on early families and a full genealogy of the Ranney family* (New York: Grafton Press, 1908.

DANBURY

Barbour's typescript volume for Danbury,[273] unlike the GPC edition[274] begins:

---

269 LeClerc, Genealogist's Handbook, 24.

270 See Introduction, pp. 3–5, above.

271 Charles R. Hale, "Headstone Inscriptions of the Town of Cromwell, Connecticut," bound typescript, 1930s, CSL, Hartford, FHL film 3,328.

272 Daniel Hearn, "Connecticut gravestones, early to 1800," manuscript (FHL film 1,477,476, Item 32)t

273 See How to Use This Book, note 4, above.

Although the town of Danbury was settled in 1685, the only vital records extant begin about 1777. On April 27, 1777 the town was burned by the British and in the conflagration the town, church and family records were consumed. Only the Probate Records, which had been removed to New Fairfield, were saved.

The grouping of the entries in the volumes now in existence indicates that they were compiled from family records collected after the destruction of the originals.

The vital records of Danbury, prior to 1848, are found scattered through Volumes 1 and 2 of Town Records and a "Record of Marriages 1820-1848". In this alphabetical list reference to the first Book of Town Records is indicated by "Vol.1", to the second book by "Vol.2", and to the Record of Marriages by "Vol.3".

This list was taken from a set of cards[275] based on a copy of the Danbury Vital Records made in 1915 by Mrs. Julia E.C. Brush, of Danbury, Connecticut. The Brush Copy, now in the possession of the Connecticut State Library, has not been compared with the original and doubtless errors exist. It is hoped that as errors or omissions are found notes will be entered in this volume and on the cards which are included in the General Index of Connecticut Vital Records also in the possession of the Connecticut State Library.

Hartford, Conn., May, 1926.[276]

VITAL RECORDS: Danbury's volume includes vital records as early as the 1730s (plus one 1707 birth) and as late as 1851. Barbour abstracted three Danbury "books:"

- "1" refers to Danbury Births, Marriages, and Deaths, 1711–1841 (Records are arranged in family groups) Danbury Town Hall (FHL film 1,435,525, items 1–2);
- "2" abstracts births, marriages and deaths from 1806 to 1827 from pages numbered 61 through 180 of a town records book unfilmed by FHL and stlll in the Danbury Town Hall.[277]
- "3" refers to Danbury Marriage Returns, 1820–1852, Danbury Town Hall (FHL film 1,435,525, item 3).

Barbour did not abstract these records:

---

274 Lorraine Cook White, *Barbour Collection of Connecticut Town Vital Records: Danbury, 1685-1847, Darien, 1820-1851, Derby, 1655-1852*, vol. 8, (Baltimore: GPC, 1997) digital image at *Ancestry.com*.

275 Now part of the Barbour Index and interfiled with similar slips from other towns in CSL and on –FHL films 2887 *et seq*. See Introduction above, pp. 3–5.

276 Lucius B. Barbour, *Connecticut Vital Records: Danbury, 1685–1847*, (Hartford, CSL, 1926) page after title page (FHL film 2,969). Digital images at *AmericanAncestors.org* and *FamilySearch.org*.

277 CSL, *CT Town Records of the First 200 Years, 1620–1820* (Hartford: CSL, 1975).

- **Danbury's Records of Births, Marriages, and Deaths, vol. 1, 1820–1870, Danbury Town Hall (FHL film 1,435,525, item 4);** and
- **Danbury's Births in the Town of Danbury not timely reported, 1847–1910, Danbury Town Hall (FHL film 1,435,526)**

CHURCH RECORDS:

- First Congregational Church of Bethel's "Church records, 1759–1917" (includes baptisms, marriages, deaths, and funerals,) (originals in the First Congregational Church) (FHL film 2,130,327);
- First Congregational Church's "Church Records, 1754–1930" (includes baptisms 1770–1776, 1786–1796, & 1786–1834; marriages 1770–1776, 1786–1797, & 1786–1805; and deaths 1772–1776, 1787–1797, & 1789–1905) (photocopy at CSL) (FHL film 4,035);
- St. Thomas' Church of Bethel's, "Church records, 1847–1903" (includes baptisms 1847–1903, marriages 1847–1903, and burials 1860–1903) (originals at CSL) (FHL film 3,844);
- St. James Episcopal Church's "Church Records, 1784–1923" (includes baptisms (1812–1839, 1839–1843 & 1848–1885), marriages (1812–1838, 1839–1843 & 1848–1894), and burials (1813–1839, 1839–1844 & 1847–1894)) (originals at CSL) (FHL films 4,039–40);
- First Baptist Church's Church records, 1787–1942, originals at CSL, (FHL film 1,008,335, item 1);
- First Methodist Episcopal Church's Church records, 1811–1915, originals at CSL (FHL film 1.008.335. items 2–10);
- Kings Street Christian Church's Records, 1830–1914, copies at CSL (FHL film 4,038),
- Samuel Camp's *Church records of Ridgebury, Connecticut, 1769–1812: conti. by someone to 1857* (Des Moines, IA: s.n., 1947?);
- Baptisms (1812–39 & 1848–85), marriages (1812–38 & 1848–94) and burials (1813–39 & 1848–94) at St. James' Church, Episcopal Diocese, Hartford (ED Films 0004.039–40);
- Baptisms & marriages 1847–1903 at St. Thomas Church of Bethel, Episcopal Diocese, Hartford (ED Film 0003844);
- Lester Card's "Danbury Methodist Episcopal Church, Conn.: church records, 1848–1851," NEHGS Research Library, Mss A 6105 (transcription, 1942);
- Harlan R. Jessup's "Ministerial Records of the Rev. Lemuel B. Hull of Connecticut: Christ Church, Redding and St. James Church, Danbury," 1822–1835," *CA*, 50:50–55 (Aug 2007).

CEMETERY INSCRIPTIONS: The Hale Collection identifies burials in order of physical proximity at 21 named cemeteries in what was then Danbury Township.[278] Compare with Daniel Hearn's 1975 copy of 104 pre-1800 gravestones in seven Danbury cemeteries.[279]The Hale Collection also identifies people in order of physical proximity

---

278 Charles R. Hale, "Headstone Inscriptions of the Town of Danbury, Connecticut," bound typescript, 1930s, CSL, Hartford, FHL film 3,328-9).

279 Daniel Hearn, "Connecticut gravestones, early to 1800," manuscript (FHL film 1,477,476, item 33).

buried at seven named cemeteries in what was then Bethel Township.[280] Compare with Daniel Hearn's 1975 copy of 43 pre-1800 gravestones in one Bethel cemetery.[281] See also,

- "Cemetery records of Bethel and Fairfield, Connecticut" (typescript at NYGBS).(FHL film 4,197, items 1–2);
- Israel H. Wilson's "Inscriptions from the Cemetery on Main St. Bethel, Conn." (1891 manuscript at NEHGS);
- Lemuel B. Hull's "Record of Marriages, Baptisms, Admission to the Communion and Funerals, 1822–1835" (manuscript at NEHGS);
- Robert Young's *Inscriptions from the Cemeteries of Danbury, Connecticut* (Danbury: Danbury Museum and Historical Society, c2005);
- George S. Hoyt, *Record of soldiers buried in Danbury, Brookfield, New Fairfield and Ridgefield*, Photostat copy (Hartford: CSL, 1929) CSL digital collection online.
- Alice Hubbard (Breed) Benton, "Florida Genealogical Collection," *1932*: [vol. 2] (includes records from the Cemetery of the Congregational Church Yard, Bethel, Connecticut, 1759 to 1890) (typescript at DAR) (FHL film 850,401, item 2);
- Josephine C. Frost's "Cemetery Inscriptions From Danbury and New Fairfield, Conn." (typescript in the NYGBS) (FHL film 4,005) (Mss A 2426), RSASC, NEHGS;

OTHER NOTEWORTHY SOURCES: James Montgomery Bailey and Susan Benedict Hill's *History of Danbury, Conn. 1684–1896* (New York?: 1896).

DARIEN

Barbour's typescript volume for Darien,[282] unlike the GPC edition,[283] begins:

> The vital records of Darien from the formation of the town to about 1851 are found in one volume.[284]
>
> This alphabetical list was taken from a set of cards[285] based on a manuscript copy made in 1914 by James N. Arnold, of Providence, R.I. The Arnold Copy, now in the possession of the Connecticut State Library, has not been compared with the original and doubtless errors exist. It is hoped that as errors or omissions are found notes will be entered in this volume and on the cards which are included in the General Index of Connecticut Vital Records

280 Charles R. Hale, "Headstone Inscriptions of the Town of Bethel, Connecticut," bound typescript, 1930s, CSL, Hartford, FHL film 3,320).

281 Daniel Hearn, "Connecticut gravestones, early to 1800," manuscript (FHL film 1,477,476, item 8).

282 See How to Use This Book, note 4, above.

283 White, *Barbour Collection: Danbury–Derby*, vol. 8, digital image at *Ancestry.com*.

284 Darien Town Clerk, Town Records, 1765–1873, (Contains family records of birth, marriage, and death, 1765–1841) Town Hall, Darien, FHL film 1,434,227.

285 Now part of the Barbour Index and interfiled with similar slips from other towns in CSL and on FHL films 2,887 *et seq*. See Introduction above, pp. 3–5.

```
also in the possession of the Connecticut
State Library.
                    Hartford, Conn., November, 1925.[286]
```

VITAL RECORDS: Darien's volume includes vital records as early as 1820 and as late as 1852, but FHL catalogs vital records as early as 1765. Barbour abstracted one Darien "book:" Darien's Marriage Certificates, vol. 1, 1820–1851, Darien Town Hall (FHL film 1,434,227, item 2).[287]

Other early Darien vital records omitted by Barbour include:

- **Darien's Town Records, 1765–1873, (family records of birth, marriage, and death, 1765–1841) Darien Town Hall (FHL film 1,434,227, item 1). See Harlan R. Jessup's "Darien Vital Records, Book I: Another Barbour Omission,"** ***Connecticut Ancestry*****, 44:55–9 (November 2001);**
- **Darien's Records of Births, Marriages and Deaths, vols. 1–3, 1847–1909, Darien Town Hall (FHL film 1,434,227, items 3–5 See Harlan R. Jessup, "Births, Marriages and Deaths for Darien, CT, 1847–1852,** ***CA*****, 55: #1 (May 2012).**

CHURCH RECORDS:

- Spencer P. Mead's "Abstract of Church Records of the Town of Darien, County of Fairfield and State of Connecticut, From the Earliest Records Extant to 1850" (includes baptisms, marriages and burials from the Congregational Church, 1734–1850) (1920 typescript) (FHL film 899,936 or 926,469 or 4,041);
- First Congregational Church's "Church Records, 1739–1938" (includes baptisms, marriages and deaths) (originals at CSL) (FHL film 1,008,338 or 250,328);
- Methodist Episcopal Church's New York East Conference. Stamford Charge. *Quarterly Conference Records 1864–1916*, Originals at CSL (FHL film 1,013,278, items 2–3).

CEMETERY INSCRIPTIONS: The Hale Collection identifies burials in order of physical proximity at 27 named cemeteries in Darien Township.[288] Compare with Daniel Hearn's 1976 copy of 42 pre-1800 gravestones in four Darien cemeteries.[289]

See also,

- H. D. Byrnes and William J. Banks' *Headstone Inscriptions of Darien, Connecticut* (typescript at CSL) (FHL film 250,329, item 1);
- Lester Card's "Moses Mather Cemetery: A List of Stones in the Old Cemetery at Brookside, Rowayton" (typescript at CSL) (FHL film 250,329, item 2);
- "Rural Cemeteries, New Canaan, Connecticut, 1757–1907" (includes Cemetery of Gracie Street, Darien) (typescript at FHL);
- *Rural cemeteries, New Canaan, Connecticut, 1757–1907, (*Reed-Weed Cemetery, Gracie Street – Cemetery of Gracie Street, Darien);
- *Bates-Middlesex Graveyard Association, Darien, Connecticut,* [S.l.: s.n., 1988?]

---

[286] Lucius B. Barbour, *Connecticut Vital Records: Darien, 1820–1851*, (Hartford: CSL,1925) page after title page (FHL film 2,969). Digital images at *AmericanAncestors.org.* and *FamilySearch.org.*

[287] Darien, Town Records, 1765-1873, (Contains family records of birth, marriage, and death, 1765-1841) Town Hall, Darien, FHL film 1,434,227.

[288] Charles R. Hale, "Headstone Inscriptions of the Town of Darien, Connecticut," bound typescript, 1930s, CSL, Hartford, FHL film 3,329-30.

[289] Daniel Hearn, "Connecticut gravestones, early to 1800," manuscript (FHL film 1,477,476, item 36).

- Doris W. Hollander's "Spring Grove Cemetery (S.l.: Middlesex Genealogical Society, 199-);
- Malcolm P. Hunt's "Transcript of Inscriptions on Headstones in Old Rowayton [sic] Cemetery Rowayton" (typescript at CSL) (FHL film 250,329, item 2 [sic]);
- Baptisms (1812–39 & 1848–85), marriages (1812–38 & 1848–94) & burials (1813–39 & 1848–94) at St. James' Church, Episcopal Diocese, Hartford (ED Films 0004,039–40);
- Francis F. Spies' *Connecticut Epitaphs,* 4 vols: (East Lyme, CT, Waterford, CT, Sound Beach (Potomac Ave, 1st Congregational Church yard, near Adams Corners), Stamford, Noroton in Darien Township, Mianus (Lyon Farm, Bonnell farm), CosCob, Montville, Chesterfield (near church, Martenus Farm, by Congregational meeting house, on Warren farm, & Great Hill Burial Ground), and Yonkers, NY New Canaan, CT, East Port Chester, CT, Greenwich, CT, Port Chester, NY and Rye, NY) (manuscript at NEHGS);
- Spencer P. Mead's "Abstract of Church Records of the Town of Darien, County of Fairfield, and State of Connecticut, from the Earliest Records Extant to 1850" (1920 manuscript at NEHGS).

OTHER NOTEWORTHY SOURCES: E. B. Huntington's *History of Stamford, Connecticut : from its settlement in 1641, to the present time, including Darien, which was one of its parishes until 1820,* (Stamford: E.B. Huntington, 1868) (FHL film 928,516, item 1).

DEEP RIVER: see SAYBROOK

DERBY

Barbour's typescript volume for Derby,[290] unlike the GPC edition,[291] begins:

> The vital records of Derby prior to 1852, are found scattered through the first seven volumes of Land Records, the first book of Town Meetings and Volume 1 of Births, Marriages and Deaths.
>
> This alphabetical list was taken from a set of cards[292] based on the publication in 1901 of volumes 1 and 2 of Land records under the title "Town Records of Derby, Connecticut, 1655-1710", by the Sarah Riggs Humphreys chapter, Daughters of the American Revolution,[293] and a manuscript copy of the later vital

---

290 See How to Use This Book, note 4, above.

291 White, *Barbour Collection: Danbury–Derby*, vol. 8, digital image at *Ancestry.com*.

292 Now part of the Barbour Index and interfiled with similar slips from other towns in CSL and on FHL films 2,887 *et seq*. See Introduction above, pp. 1–3.

293 Nancy O. Phillips and DAR Sarah Riggs Humphreys Chapter's *Town Records of Derby, Connecticut, 1655–1710* (Derby, CT, DAR: 1901) FHL film 928,514, item 1. According to Phillips, she has not transcribed the Derby land records at all, She explains that the bulk of her transcription was "Book 2 from both covers – the 'First Part' being the Acts of the Town, which filled 161 pages. For the 'Second Part' the book was reversed and paged from the end (being 131 pages) and at first was devoted to items 'abstracted out of Court Records' then followed by various town matters, marriages, births, deaths, deeds, earmarks for cattle, etc." See "Note of Explanation," an unnumbered page preceeding her table of contents.

> records made in 1914 by Miss Ethel L. Scofield, of New Haven, Conn. Reference to the printed book is indicated by the original pagination and volume numbers of the Land Records, to Volumes 3, 4, 5, 6, and 7 of Land Records by the volume number and the abbreviation "LR" and to the book of Town Meetings by the abbreviation "TM".
>
> The Scofield Copy, now in the possession of the Connecticut State Library, has not been compared with the original and doubtless errors exist. It is hoped that as errors or omissions are found notes will be entered in this volume and on the cards which are included in the General Index of Connecticut Vital Records also in the possession of the Connecticut State Library.
>
> Hartford, Conn., August, 1925[294]

VITAL RECORDS: Derby's volume includes vital records as early as 1641 and as late as 1852. Barbour abstracted ten Derby "books," including four apparently available only at the town hall:

- "1" refers to Derby's Marriages, Deaths 1783–1874, vol. 1 (1831–1851) Derby Town Hall (FHL film 1,420,815, item 3). This film (**and often the Barbour volume**) are missing births and deaths (as well as the clerk's marriage entries not in certification format) which are indexed in **Derby's Indexes to Vital Statistics 1783–1923, Derby Town Hall (FHL film 1,420,815, item 1);**
- "2" refers to "Book 2, First Part" and Book 2, Second Part" of the DAR's *Town Records of Derby, Connecticut, 1655–1710*, pp. 420–451), but paginates the records as they are found in volume 2 of the original Derby Land Records (FHL film 4,058, item 2);[295]
- "3" refers to one 1709 marriage transcribed from the DAR's "Record Belonging to the Third Book," *Town Records of Derby, Connecticut, 1655–1710*, a volume microfilmed by FHL as the last part of FHL film 4,058, item 2);
- "LR3" refers to from Derby's Land Records, vol. 3, 1690–1733 (includes births, marriages and deaths) Derby Town Hall (FHL film 4,058, item 3);
- "LR4" and "LR5" refer to Derby's Land Records, vols. 4–5 1733–1771, (includes births, marriages and deaths) Derby Town Hall (FHL film 4,059);
- "LR6" and "LR7" refer to Derby's Land Records, vols. 6–7 1751–1765, (only Volumes 1 through 5 include births, marriages and deaths, according to the FHL catalog) Derby Town Hall (FHL film 4,060);
- "TM1" refers to vital records covering the years 1764– 1802 on pages 40 through 367 of an unfilmed Town Meetings book that remains in the Derby Town Hall; [296]

---

[294] Lucius B. Barbour, *Connecticut Vital Records: Derby, 1655–1852*, (Hartford: CSL, 1925) page after title page. (FHL film 2,969). Digital images at *AmericanAncestors.org.* and *FamilySearch.org.*

[295] To be precise, Barbour's abstractions citing Book 2, page one is equivalent to Phillips' book, page 41, and to the Derby Town Clerk's Land Records, vols. 1 and 2 1667–1710, (Volumes 1 and 2 include births, marriages and deaths according to FHL) Derby Town Hall, FHL film 4,058 Item 2, Digital GS 8199597, Image 43.

[296] CSL, *CT Town Records of the First 200 Years, 1620–1820* (Hartford: CSL, 1975).

- "D B" abstracts records from page 9 of volume A1 (1655–1675) of the town records. This unfilmed 40 page pamphlet in the town hall is transcribed as the "Derby and Paggasett Records" chapter (pp. 1–40) in the DAR's *Town Records of Derby, Connecticut, 1655–1710*;
- "A1" refers to Buckley records Barbour abstracted from page 152 of an unspecified source, which is *not* the town clerk's volume A1.

The FHL also catalogs under Derby vital records:

- **"Miscellaneous Church Records" (contains Derby town burials; Derby town poor; index; obstetrical record of Dr. Josiah Colburn, Orange, Derby, Ansonia 1824–1848) NHCHS, New Haven, (FHL film 3,054).**
- **Derby's Births, Marriages, Deaths, vol. 1 (1848–1852) Derby Town Hall (FHL film 1,420,815, item 3, interspersed with the older records Barbour labels "1");**
- **Derby's Births, Marriages, Deaths, vol. 2 (1852–1862) Derby Town Hall (FHL film 1,420,815, item 4);**

CHURCH RECORDS:

- St. Matthew's Episcopal Church (Bristol, Connecticut); Baptist Church (Southington, Connecticut); Guilford Episcopal Church (Guilford, Connecticut)'s *Miscellaneous church records* (contains Derby town burials; Derby town poor; index; obstetrical record of Dr. Josiah Colburn, Orange, Derby, Ansonia 1824–1848; index.) (FHL film 3,054, item 4).
- Methodist Episcopal Church's "Church Records, 1828–1935" (includes births & baptisms 1830–1843 & 1851–1869, and marriages 1832–1833 & 1841–1868) (originals at CSL) (FHL film 4,075);
- Christ Church of Ansonia's, Records 1834–1941) copy at CSL (FHL film 3,693, item 1);
- First Congregational Church of Ansonia's Records 1850–194, copy at CSL (FHL film 1,007,920, item 2);
- St. James' Church's "Church Records, 1740–1929" (includes baptisms, marriages, and burials) (originals at CSL) (FHL films 1,008,339–40);
- St. Matthew's Episcopal Church, Baptist Church, Guilford Episcopal Church, Ansonia Christ Church Records, 1834–1941, CSL #974.62 An842ec r (film #114);
- Baptisms (1740, 1748–1805,1822–41 & 1841–70), marriages (1822–42, & 1841–69) & burials (1841–70) at St. James' Church, Episcopal Diocese, Hartford (ED Film 1,008,339 and/or 1,008.340);
- Baptisms (1844–62), marriages (1844–62) & burials (1843–62) at Christ Church in Ansonia (ED Film 0003.693);
- Donald Lines Jacobus' "Records of St. James's Church, Derby, Conn., 1740–1796," *NEHGR*, 75:130–54, 170–4 (Apr–Jul 1921);

CEMETERY INSCRIPTIONS: The Hale Collection identifies burials in order of physical proximity at five named cemeteries in what was then Derby Township.[297] Compare with Daniel Hearn's 1976 copy of 109 pre-1800 gravestones in one Derby cemetery.[298]

---

297 Charles R. Hale, "Headstone Inscriptions of the Town of Derby, Connecticut," bound typescript, 1930s, CSL, Hartford, FHL film 3,329-30.

298 Daniel Hearn, "Connecticut gravestones, early to 1800," manuscript (FHL film 1,477,476, item 38).

The Hale Collection also identifies people in order of physical proximity buried at six named cemeteries in what was then Ansonia Township.[299] Compare with Daniel Hearn's 1976 copy of 26 pre-1800 gravestones in one Ansonia cemetery.[300] See also,

- Paul R. Keroack's "St. Mary's (New and Old) Cemeteries, Ansonia, CT: Headstone Inscriptions listing Immigrants' Birthplaces," *CA* 53:2:92–96 (Feb 2012);
- W.C. Sharpe and James S. Hedden's "Roster of Graves of, or Monuments to, Patriots of 1775–1783, and of Soldiers of Colonial Wars in and Adjacent to New Haven County, Connecticut" (photocopy at FHL) (SAR FHL film 1,421,668);
- Arthur Walker, Frank F. O'Brien, and George Donahue's "Headstone Inscriptions, Mt. St. Peter's Cemetery, Derby, Connecticut" (1934 photocopy at FHL);
- Arthur Walker, Frank F. O'Brien, and George Donahue's "Headstone Inscriptions, Oak Cliff Cemetery, Derby, Connecticut" (1934 photocopy at FHL);
- *Inscriptions from Gravestones, Derby, Connecticut: with Additions & Corrections* (Salem MA: Higginson, 1987);
- Anne Bryant Bassett's "Derby Uptown Burying Ground Derby, Connecticut" (Mss A 6106), RSASCs, NEHGS; and Ann E. Bassett, "Inscriptions from Gravestones in the Uptown Burying Ground, Derby, Conn.," *NEHGR*, 84:134–42 (Apr 1930);
- DAR's Genealogical Collection (Ansonia: inscriptions in the Elm Street Cemetery) (Bound typescript) DAR, Washington, D.C. (FHL film 844,454).

OTHER NOTEWORTHY SOURCES:

- *Illustrated review of the Naugatuck Valley : embracing Ansonia, Derby, Birmingham, Shelton and Seymour, a record of the development of these centers, their progress in commerce manufacturing and political life, with sketches of their leading official, business and professional men* (New York: Sovereign Publishing and Engraving, 1890) (FHL fiche 6,071,068).
- Rev. Samuel Orcutt's *History of the Old Town of Derby, Connecticut, 1642–1880 with Biographies and Genealogies* (Springfield, Mass.: Springfield Printing Co., 1880);

DURHAM

Barbour's typescript volume for Durham,[301] unlike the GPC edition,[302] begins:

> In "The History of Durham", compiled by William Chauncey Fowler, L.D, and published by the town in 1866, all the vital records prior to 1866 and the church records of Rev. Nathaniel Chauncey, Rev. Elizur Goodrich and

---

299 Charles R. Hale, "Cemetery inscriptions of Ansonia," bound typescript, 1930s, CSL, Hartford, FHL film 3,319.

300 Daniel Hearn, "Connecticut gravestones, early to 1800," manuscript (FHL film 1,477,476, item 2).

301 See How to Use This Book, note 4, above..

302 Lorraine Cook White, *Barbour Collection of Connecticut Town Vital Records: Durham, 1708-1852, Eastford, 1847–1851, East Haddam, 1743–1857*, vol. 9, (Baltimore: GPC, 1997) digital image at *Ancestry.com*.

Rev. David Smith[303] have been published without an index.

In this alphabetical list, based on a set of cards,[304] only the births, marriages, deaths and baptisms found in the printed history are included. Where it was possible the baptism has been added to the birth entry.

The published volume, a copy of which is in the Connecticut State Library, has not been compared with the original records and doubtless errors exist. It is hoped that as errors or omissions are found notes will be entered in this volume and on the cards which are included in the General Index of Connecticut Vital Records also in the possession of the Connecticut State Library.

Hartford, Conn., November, 1923.[305]

VITAL RECORDS: Durham's volume includes vital records as early as 1671 and as late as 1869. Barbour abstracted and cited William Chauncey Fowler's *History of Durham*[306] and not the original sources Fowler claimed to have abstracted. Barbour's pages:

- 252–298 refer to "Nathaniel Chauncey's Baptisms" 1711–1755 from Fowler's book;
- 305–334 refer to "Elizur Goodrich's Baptisms" 1735–1783 from Fowler's book;
- 334–339 refer to "Rev. David Smith's Records" 1804–1828 from Fowler's book;
- 339–350 refer to "Proprietors' Record" ca. 1706–1730 from Fowler's book;
- 350–443 refer to "Town Records ca. 1743–1860" from Fowler's book;

These same entries are almost all scattered through the NYGBS typescript, which also contains some discrepancies with Foster and a few entries he did not replicate: *Records of Churches and Cemeteries of Connecticut: Town Records of Durham, Hartford and Enfield, Conn.,* (includes church and town records of Durham) typescript at NYGBS, New York, FHL film 2,798 item 2, Digital GS 7833427, images 27–40. Thorough research requires comparison of both with the original sources they rely upon, but the "Town Records" or "Proprietors Records" described by Fowler do not match the Durham town clerk's descriptions.[307]

---

303 Contrary to Barbour's implication, Foster's abstraction of Rev. Smith's church admissions records on pp. 335–339, are not copied into the Barbour collection even in the rare case (such as the death of Asahel Strong in 1862) when they report vital statistics.

304 Now part of the Barbour Index and interfiled with similar slips from other towns in CSL and on FHL films 2,887 *et seq*. See Introduction above, pp. 3–5.

305 Lucius B. Barbour, *Connecticut Vital Records: Durham, 1708–1852*, (Hartford, CSL, 1923) page after title page (FHL film 2,969). Digital images at *AmericanAncestors.org.* and *FamilySearch.org.*

306 William Chauncey Fowler, *The History of Durham* (includes proprietors' and town records of births, marriages, and deaths: p. 339–443) (Hartford: Wiley, Waterman & Eaton, 1866; reprint Durham: s.n., 1970) FHL film 908,331 or 1,398,795, item 1

307 **In 1975 the Durham Town Clerk Marjorie Hatch reported possession of a 200 page book of "Town Records 1730–1769," "Vital Statistics, 1741–1804," a 320 page book of "Town Meetings, 1769–1835," and various folios collectively called "Grand Lists, 1791–1835."** CSL, *CT Town Records of the First 200 Years, 1620–1820* (Hartford: CSL, 1975).

Diana Ross McCain, under a grant from the Connecticut Humanities Council, January–February 1998: found these [pre 1852] Records of Historical Interest in Durham Town Clerk's Office:[308]

- ***Records of the Births, Marriages, & Deaths in the Town of Durham from 1723 to ca. 1772*** **(a few dates as late as 1813) (included in volume of Town Meeting Records from 1730 to 1769);**
- ***Family Records of Miles Merwin & Phebe Camp, m. November 27. 1784, and their children.*** **In Account book of Miles Merwin, "Bought January ye 11th AD 1796."(entries primarily from 1796–1834 with a few more to 1849);**
- ***Deaths in Durham, 1794–1912, CSL*** **manuscript, volume kept chronologically, "gift of Mary Newton;"**
- ***Deaths in Durham from 1800 to ca. 1906.*** **One manuscript volume, inscribed P.W. Smith, Durham, Conn.," and Mrs. D.S. Smith, Durham, Conn.," (attached note says "Francis Earle Korn brought this in for safe-keeping (My impression is that it was found in the Historical Society Material. Perhaps begun by the Rev. Davis Smith?)** ***M[arge] H[atch]");***
- ***Births, deaths, marriages, 1847–1947, Durham, Conn., 1 volume.*** **(FHL film 1,398,795, item 2**
- **(In back of book of** ***Names of Electors admitted since the year1882–1883):***
  - ***Record of births, marriages & deaths in the town of for the year preceding the first Monday of August, 1848, Marriages 1848, Deaths 1848***
  - ***Record of births, marriages & deaths in the town of Durham for the year ending August 8, 1849***
  - ***Record of births, marriages & deaths in the town of Durham for the year ending July 31, 1850***
  - ***Record of births, marriages & deaths in the town of Durham for the year ending July 31, 1851***

The Barbour Index abstracts and interfiles "Durham Deaths 1791–1805" from CSA, but CSA also possesses:

- **Durham Deaths, 1746–1908;**
- **Calla Hickox Burr's collection of Durham Vital Records, 1785–1835.**

See also, Durham's 'Records of Connecticut churches and cemeteries" (contains church and town records of Durham, 1712–1864) (FHL film 2,798, item 2).

CHURCH RECORDS:

- Congregational Church's "Church Records, 1756–1938" (includes deaths 1800–1831, baptisms 1832–1853; marriages and deaths 1832–1857.) (originals and manuscripts at CSL) (FHL film 4,054);
- Church of the Epiphany's "Church Records, 1850–1940" (includes baptisms 1850–1940, marriages 1864–1940, and burials 1850–1940) (originals at CSL) (FHL film 4,055);

[308] *CT Vital Records — Additions, Comments, Corrections, Questions on Originals — Not All Towns* Included (Hartford, CSL Reference Desk, various dates) unpaginated in alpha order by town)

- Baptisms (1833–1842 & 1833–1862), marriages 1833–43 & 1833–62) & burials (1833–43 & 1833–62) at St. Stephen's Church, Episcopal Diocese, Hartford (ED Film 0004,113 & manuscript).

CEMETERY INSCRIPTIONS: The Hale Collection identifies burials in order of physical proximity at four named cemeteries in Durham Township.[309] Compare with Daniel Hearn's 1978 copy of 393 pre-1800 gravestones in two Durham cemeteries.[310] See also,

- Lucius B. Barbour's "Durham, Conn. Epitaphs" (Mss A 6044), RSASC, NEHGS);
- Alice Hubbard Breed Benton's "Cemetery at Durham, Connecticut" (typescript) (FHL film 165,997);
- Alice Hubbard Breed Benton's Cemetery Records" (typescript at DAR) (FHL film 850,401);
- Sneath, Anna Sheldon Camp's Tombstone records in ye olde cemetary [i.e. cemetery] at Durham Connecticut," Salt Lake City, Utah: Digitized by FHL, 2006;
- Records of churches and cemeteries of Connecticut: town records of Durham, Hartford and Enfield, Conn., Microfilm of typescript in the NYGBS, New York, (FHL film 2,798, item 2).

OTHER NOTEWORTHY SOURCES:

- "Durham Deaths 1746 – 1908" CSL; See Appendix A;
- Lucius B. Barbour's Genealogical notes complied from church records of Durham, Conn., 1699–1820. I volume. Abstract of vital records. (manuscript 12 in Box 1) CSL Record Group 074.36, Hartford.

EAST HADDAM

Barbour's typescript volume for East Haddam,[311] unlike the GPC edition.[312] begins:

> This volume contains a list alphabetically arranged of all the vital records of the town of East Haddam from its incorporation to about 1857. The early vital statistics are found scattered through the first eight volumes of Land Records and four volumes of Vital Records. Reference to entries found in the Land records is indicated in this list by the number of the land record volume and the abbreviation "LR".
>
> This list was taken from a set of cards[313] based on a copy of the East Haddam Vital Records made in 1913 by James N. Arnold, of Providence, R.I., and Irene H. Mix, of Hartford, Conn.

---

309 Charles R. Hale, "Headstone Inscriptions of the Town of Durham, Connecticut," bound typescript, 1930s, CSL, Hartford, FHL film 3,330.

310 Daniel Hearn, "Connecticut gravestones, early to 1800," manuscript (FHL film 1,477,476, item 39).

311 See How to Use This Book, note 4, above.

312 White, *Barbour Collection: Durham–East Haddam*, vol. 9, digital image at *Ancestry.com*.

313 Now part of the Barbour Index and interfiled with similar slips from other towns in CSL and on FHL films 2,887 *et seq*. See Introduction above, pp. 3–5.

> The Arnold-Mix Copy, now in the possession of the Connecticut State Library, has not been compared with the original and doubtless errors exist. It is hoped that as errors or omissions are found notes will be entered in this volume and on the cards which are included in the General Index of Connecticut Vital Records also in the possession of the Connecticut State Library.
>
> Hartford, Conn., April, 1923.[314]

VITAL RECORDS: East Haddam's volume includes vital records as early as 1689 and as late as 1868. The East Haddam volume actually contains records as early as 1689 and as late as 1868. Barbour implies eleven East Haddam "books" were abstracted:

- "1:" Barbour abstracts no records citing volume 1 as their source. The East Haddam clerk has labeled it as an index to all the vital records in the Land Records books as "Vital Statistics volume 1." According to the FHL, volume 1 of its set of four matched Vital Statistics volumes is a compilation of all the births, marriages, and deaths originally recorded in vols. 1–8 of East Haddam's land records (FHL film 1,398,799);
- "2" refers to some **but not all** of the records in the East Haddam Town Clerk's Vital Statistics, vol. 2 (FHL film 1,398,798, item 1);
- "3" refers to some **but not all** of the records in the East Haddam Town Clerk's Vital Statistics, vol. 3 (FHL film 1,398,798, item 3), and on different pages than Barbour cites;
- "4" refers to some **but not all** of the records in the East Haddam Town Clerk's Vital Statistics, vol. 4 (FHL film 1,398,798, item 2);
- "LR1" refers to East Haddam's Land Records, vol. 1 1704–1912 (Volume 1 includes town and vital records, 1687–1761) East Haddam Town Hall (FHL film 4,096);
- "LR2" and "LR3 refer to East Haddam's Land Records, vols. 2–3 1725–1749, East Haddam Town Hall (FHL film 4,097);
- "LR4" and "LR5" refer to East Haddam's Land Records, vols. 4–5 1750–1763 East Haddam Town Hall (FHL film 4,098);
- "LR6" to "LR8" refer to East Haddam's Land Records, vols. 6–8 1758–1784 East Haddam Town Hall (FHL film 4,099).

See also:

- **East Haddam's Vital statistics vol. 1 1687–1789, (Volume 1 is a copy of births, marriages, and deaths originally recorded in vols. 1–8 of the land records. It is arranged alphabetically by surname.) East Haddam Town Hall, (FHL film 1,480,163);**
- **D.W. Patterson's "First Book of East Haddam Land Records (which includes births, deaths & marriages)," *NEHGR*, 11:273–9 (Jul 1857);**
- **D. Williams Patterson's "East Haddam, Ct. Records (BMD in 2nd book of land records)," *NEHGR*, 12:4–7 (Oct 1858) 13:125–31 (Apr 1859).**

CHURCH RECORDS:

- Millington Congregational Church's Records 1733–1931 (FHL film 4,115);

---

[314] Lucius B. Barbour, *Connecticut Vital Records: East Haddam, 1743–1857*, (Hartford, CSL, 1923) page after title page (FHL film 2,969). Digital images at *AmericanAncestors.org.* and *FamilySearch.org.*

- First Congregational Church and Ecclesiastical Society's "Church Records, 1702–1927" (includes baptisms 1704–1816 & 1816–1856, marriages (1702, 1751–1822, 1816–1856 & 1872–1891), and deaths 1785–1915) (originals at CSL) (FHL film 4,112);
- Second Congregational Church and Ecclesiastical Society's "Church Records, 1733–1931" (includes baptisms 1745–1768, marriages 1745–1776, and deaths 1745–1895) (originals at CSL) (FHL film 4,115);
- St. Stephen's Church's "Church Records, 1791–1933" (includes baptisms 1833–1842 & 1833–1862, marriages 1833–1843 & 1833–1862, and burials 1833–1843 & 1833–1862) (originals at CSL) (FHL film 4,113);
- John Luther Kiborn's First Congregational Church Records, 1704–1891 , bound copy shelved at CSL;
- Gertrude A. Barber's "Record of the First Congregational Church at East Haddam, Connecticut" (includes baptisms 1704–1802) (typescript.) (FHL film 547,537) (images at *AmericanAncestors.org*);
- Karl P. Stofko's "Vital Statistics Records From the Records of the First Church of Christ, Congregational in East Haddam, Connecticut, 1704–1850" (1980–1981 typescript at FHL);
- "Records of the First Congregational Church at East Haddam, Connecticut, 1704–1802" from H. M. Shelden, Bridgehampton, L. I., to Mrs. Annie A. Hopkins, typescript in Pittsfield, MA & NEHGS (FHL film 234,579, item 2);
- DAR's Genealogical Collection, (East Haddam: records of the First Congregational Church) (bound typescript) DAR, Washington, D.C. (FHL film 844,458);
- Baptisms (1829–51), marriages (1828–50) & burials (1828–51) at St. Peter's Church, Episcopal Diocese, Hartford (ED Film 0004,000);
- Moodus Methodist Church, Records, 1940–1913, copy at CSL (FHL film 4,114);
- M.O. LeBrun's "Hadlyme Church Book of Records, 1742–1854" (includes vital records) (manuscript at NEHGS);
- Marriage records of the Congregational Church, Middle Haddam, Connecticut, 1740–1824, originals at NYGBS (FHL film 4,786).

CEMETERY INSCRIPTIONS: The Hale Collection identifies burials in order of physical proximity at 21 named cemeteries in East Haddam Township.[315] Compare with Daniel Hearn's 1979 copy of 176 pre-1800 gravestones in seven East Haddam cemeteries.[316] See also,

- "Cemetery Inscriptions, Bashan, Connecticut" (typescript at NYGBS) (FHL film 3,695);
- Leesville cemetery inscriptions, manuscript in the NYGBS (FHL film 2,798, item 4).
- Mary Virginia Wakeman's " Inscriptions on the Old Grave Markers in All of the Burying Grounds in East Haddam, and Seven of Those in Lyme: Being All of the Legible Records of People Born Previous To, or During the Year 1800, With a Few Later Ones" (1947 photocopy at FHL) (original 1907 manuscript at East Haddam: Rathbun Memorial Library);

---

315 Charles R. Hale, "Headstone Inscriptions of the Town of East Haddam, Connecticut," bound typescript, 1930s, CSL, Hartford, FHL film 3,331.

316 Daniel Hearn, "Connecticut gravestones, early to 1800," manuscript (FHL film 1,477,476, item 42).

- *Moodus Cemetery* (manuscript in NYGBS) (FHL film 4,853 or 1,405,496);
- Karl P. Stofko's "Inscriptions of Monuments, Markers, Tombs & Footstones, First Church Cemetery, Town Street, East Haddam, Connecticut" (1972 photocopy at FHL);
- Francis H. Parker's *Bashan Cemetery* (photocopy at FHL) (original in possession of Mary G. Dean, East Haddam);
- Francis H. Parker's "Eight Mile River Burying Yard" (photocopy at FHL) (original in possession of Mary G. Dean);
- Francis H. Parker's "Foxtown Burying Ground" (photocopy at FHL) (original in possession of Mary G. Dean);
- Long Pond Yard: also Known as North East Dist., Ackley Dist., Shaw's Lake, Newton's Pond, Hayward's Pond, and Perhaps Other Names" (manuscript in NYGBS) (FHL film 4,852, item 2 or 1,405,496, item 7);
- "Hungerford Yard, Hadlyme, East Haddam" (manuscript in NYGBS) (FHL film 2,798, item 6);
- "Millington Green," (manuscript in NYGBS) (FHL film 4,852, item 1 or 1,405,496, item 12);
- "North Plain: Eight Mile River, Three Bridge" (manuscript in NYGBS) (FHL film 2,798, item 5 or 1,405,496, item 19);
- 'River View Cemetery, East Haddam: also Known as the Landing Graveyard" (manuscript in NYGBS) (FHL film 4,429 or 1,405,496, item 1);
- "Record of Inscriptions Found on Gravestones in the Town of East Haddam Dated Prior to A.D. 1850" (6 vols.) (Cove Cemetery, Leesville yard, Moodus yard, Bashan yard, Cone yard, Goodspeeds Church yard, Warner yard, Hungerford yard, Wicket Lane yard, Congregational Churchyard, Mt. Panassus yard, Hadlyme Churchyard, Three Bridge Cemetery, Tatar Hill yard, Cheser yard, Millington Cemetery, Ackley Cemetery, Foxtown Cemetery) (manuscript at NEHGSD;
- Williams Patterson's "Births, Marriages, and Deaths, East Haddam, Conn., 1711–1757" (Mss C 2014), RSASC, NEHGS);
- "Inscriptions from Gravestones at East Haddam, Conn.," *NEHGR*, 80:415–46 (Oct 1926), 81:46–62, 263–71 (Jan Jul 1927).

OTHER NOTEWORTHY SOURCES:

- Lucius B. Barbour's Early Families of East Haddam, 1662–1894. I volume. Abstract of record. (manuscript 109 in Box 13) CSL Record Group 074.36, Hartford;
- Lillian Kruger Brooks' *Life Flows Along Like a River: History of Haddam Neck.* (East Hampton, Conn.] Haddam Neck Genealogical Group, 1972) (includes vital records of the people of Haddam, East Haddam, Higganum, Hadlyme, Middletown, East Hampton, Haddam Neck, Moodus, Chatham, and Colchester).

EAST HAMPTON/CHATHAM

Barbour's typescript volume for East Hampton,[317] unlike the GPC edition,[318] begins:

```
This volume contains a list alphabetically
arranged of all the vital records of the town of
```

[317] See How to Use This Book, note 4, above.
[318] White, *Barbour Collection: Canton–Clinton,* vol. 6, digital image at *Ancestry.com*.

> East Hampton from its incorporation to about 1854. The town was incorporated under the name of Chatham and was so known until 1915 when its name was changed by legislative act to East Hampton.
>
> This list was taken from a set of cards[319] based on a copy of the Chatham Vital Records made in 1912 by James N. Arnold, of Providence, R.I. The entire record for the town prior to 1854 is contained in one volume.
>
> The Arnold Copy, now in the possession of the Connecticut State Library, has not been compared with the original and doubtless errors exist. It is hoped that as errors or omissions are found notes will be entered in this volume and on the cards which are included in the General Index of Connecticut Vital Records also in the possession of the Connecticut State Library.
>
> Hartford, Conn., January, 1923.[320]

VITAL RECORDS: East Hampton was established in 1767, but part of Chatham until 1915.[321] East Hampton's volume includes vital records as early as 1746 and as late as 1854. Barbour abstracted East Hampton's Vital Statistics vol. 1 1731–1884, East Hampton Town Hall, (FHL film 1,480,162 or 1,378,211).
Barbour does not refer to the **Chatham Town Clerk's Marriage Records, 1822–1851, East Hampton Town Hall, (FHL film 1,313,571, item 4).**

CHURCH RECORDS:

- Congregational Church's "Church Records, 1748–1930" (includes baptisms (1778–1807, 1792–1828, 1828–1831, & 1839–1866), deaths (1778–1790, 1792–1827, 1829–1831, 1838–1865, & 1852–1865), and marriages (1779–1790, 1792–1827, 1828–1832, & 1852–1865)) (originals at CSL) (FHL film 4,193);
- "Marriage Records of the Congregational Church, Middle Haddam, Connecticut, 1740–1824," manuscript, NYGBS, New York City, NY (FHL film 4,786);
- Baptisms (1802–91), marriages (1827–28 & 1840–1910) & burials (1789–1907) at Christ Church, Episcopal Diocese, Hartford (ED Film 0,004,192).
- Christ Church at Middle Haddam's "Church Records, 1794–1912" (includes baptisms 1795–1828, marriages 1795–1828, and deaths 1794–1828 in vol. 1, and more baptisms, marriages, and burials in vol. 3) (originals at CSL) (FHL film 4,192);
- Haddam Neck Congregational Church's "Church Records, 1740–1944" (includes baptisms, deaths, and marriages) (originals at CSL) (FHL film 4,194);
- H. M. Shelden's Bridgehampton, L. I. to Mrs. Annie A. Hopkins, "Congregational Church records, Middle Haddam, Connecticut, 1740–1800," typescript, Pittsfield MA (FHL film 234,579, item 2);

---

319 Now part of the Barbour Index and interfiled with similar slips from other towns in CSL and on FHL films 2,887 *et seq*. See Introduction above, pp. 3–5.

320 Lucius B. Barbour, *Connecticut Vital Records Chatham, 1767–1854*, (Hartford, CSL, 1923) page after title page (FHL film 2,969). Digital images at *AmericanAncestors.org.* and *FamilySearch.org.*

321 Morrison, *Connecting to Connecticut*, 79.

CEMETERY INSCRIPTIONS: The Hale Collection identifies burials in order of physical proximity at 13 named cemeteries in East Hampton Township.[322] Compare with Daniel Hearn's 1978 copy of 33 pre-1800 gravestones in seven East Hampton cemeteries.[323] See also,

- Lucius B. Barbour's "East Hampton, Conn. Epitaphs" (Mss A 6045), RSASC, NEHGS);
- "Inscriptions from Gravestones at East Haddam, Conn.," *NEHGR*, vol. 80:415 (1926).

OTHER NOTEWORTHY SOURCES:

- Lucius B. Barbour's East Hampton, Conn. marriages, 1733–1850.1 volume.. (manuscript 129 in Box 22) CSL Record Group 074.36, Hartford;
- George S. Hubbard's "Historical Sketch of the Second Congregational Church, Middle Haddam" (1890 mss) (CSL film #471);
- Lillian Kruger Brooks' *Life Flows Along Like a River: A History of Haddam Neck.* (East Hampton? Conn.] Haddam Neck Genealogical Group, 1972) (includes vital records of the people of Haddam, East Haddam, Higganum, Hadlyme, Middletown, East Hampton, Haddam Neck, Moodus, Chatham, and Colchester).
- "Notes Taken from the Diary of Elisha Niles, 1764–1850," CSL; see Appendix A.

EAST HARTFORD

Barbour's typescript volume for East Hartford,[324] unlike the GPC edition,[325] begins:

> This volume contains a list alphabetically arranged of all the vital records of the town of East Hartford from its incorporation to about 1853. The Entire record of this town, prior to 1853, is found In Volume 1 of Vital Records and Volume 2 of Town Records. Reference to the book of Town records is indicated by the abbreviation "TR2".
>
> This list was taken from a set of cards[326] based on a copy of the East Hartford Vital Records made in 1917 by James Lahy, formerly of Hartford, Conn. The manuscript copy has not been compared with the originals and doubtless errors exist. It is hoped that as errors or omissions are found notes will be entered in this volume and on the cards which are included in the General Index of Connecticut Vital Records also in the possession of the Connecticut State Library.
>
> Hartford, Conn., October, 1928.[327]

---

[322] Charles R. Hale, "Headstone Inscriptions of the Town of East Hampton, Connecticut," bound typescript, 1930s, CSL, Hartford, FHL film 3,331.

[323] Daniel Hearn, "Connecticut gravestones, early to 1800," manuscript (FHL film 1,477,476, item 43).

[324] See How to Use This Book, note 4, above..

[325] Christina Bailey, *Barbour Collection of Connecticut Town Vital Records: East Hartford, 1783–1853, East Haven, 1700–1852, East Lyme, 1839–1853*, vol. 10, (Baltimore: GPC, 1997).) images at *Ancestry.com*.

[326] Now part of the Barbour Index and interfiled with similar slips from other towns in CSL and on FHL films 2,887 *et seq*. See Introduction above, pp. 3–5.

VITAL RECORDS: East Hartford's volume includes vital records as early as 1751 and as late as 1853. Barbour abstracted two East Hartford "books:"

- "1" refers to East Hartford's Records of births, marriages, and deaths, 1739–1876, Town Hall, East Hartford, FHL film 1,312,794, item 2;
- "TR2" refers to "Volume 2 of Town Records," (including vital records 1774–1800). It was not filmed by FHL, but can be accessed at the town hall. All of the records abstracted from it appear to be duplicated in the other book Barbour abstracted.

CHURCH RECORDS:

- First Congregational Church and Ecclesiastical Society's "Church Records, 1699–1912" (includes marriages 1816–1820 & 1830–1831, and baptisms 1748–1833 & 1830–1876) (originals at CSL) (FHL film 4,130);
- Joseph O. Goodwin's "Baptisms and Births From Records of First Congregational Church 1747–1848 (East Hartford, Connecticut) and Deaths from Cemeteries" (manuscript at CSL) (FHL film 1,008,343);
- St. John's Church and Grace Church's "Church Records, 1854–1956" (includes baptisms, deaths and marriages). (originals at CSL) FHL film 1,008,344);
- W. Herbert Wood's "Records of the Rev, Samuel Woodbridge, East Hartford, Connecticut 1723–1895 " (typescript at CSL & NEHGS, 1933).

CEMETERY INSCRIPTIONS: The Hale Collection identifies burials in order of physical proximity at eight named cemeteries in East Hartford Township.[328] Compare with Daniel Hearn's 1979 copy of 386 pre-1800 gravestones in three East Hartford cemeteries. See also,

- DAR's Genealogical Collection, (Hartford, West Hartford, East Hartford, and Manchester: annotated list of soldiers of the American Revolution buried in the cemeteries of ancient Hartford) (manuscript) DAR, Washington DC (FHL film 844,455);
- Lucius Barnes Barbour's "Inscriptions From Gravestones At New Hartford, Conn.," *NEHGR*, vol. 80:375.

OTHER NOTEWORTHY SOURCES:

- "Private records of Rev. Samuel Woodbridge of East Hartford, 1723–1805." CSL, see Appendix A.
- Lucius B. Barbour's Genealogical notes complied from church records of East Hartford, Conn., 1748–1800. I volume (1255 p.). Abstract of baptisms. (manuscript 16 in Box 2) CSL Record Group 074.36, Hartford.
- Lucius B. Barbour's Genealogical notes compiled from East Hartford and Glastonbury probate records, 1800–1830. I volume. Abstract of record. (manuscript 75 in Box 7) CSL Record Group 074.36, Hartford.
- Lucius B. Barbour's East Hartford, Conn. marriages, 1733–1853.1 volume.. (manuscript 130 in Box 22) CSL Record Group 074.36, Hartford.

---

327 Lucius B. Barbour, *Connecticut Vital Records, East Hartford, 1783–1853*, (Hartford, CSL, 1928) page after title page (FHL film 2,969). Digital images at *AmericanAncestors.org.* and *FamilySearch.org.*

328 Charles R. Hale, "Headstone Inscriptions of the Town of East Hartford, Connecticut," bound typescript, 1930s, CSL, Hartford, FHL film 3,331.

EAST HAVEN

Barbour's typescript volume[329] for East Haven (unlike the GPC edition,[330] begins:

> The vital records of East Haven prior to 1852 are found in the first four volumes of Town Meetings. Reference to entries therein is indicated in this book by the abbreviation "TM" with the volume number following.
>
> This alphabetical list was taken from a set of cards[331] based on a copy of the East Haven Vital Records made in 1914 by Miss Ethel L. Scofield, of New Haven, Conn. To this copy has been added the death and marriage records found in Rev. Stephen Dodd's "East Havan Register" reference to which is indicated in this book by the abbreviation "DR".
>
> The Scofield Copy, now in the possession of the Connecticut State Library, has not been compared with the original and doubtless errors exist. It is hoped that as errors or omissions are found notes will be entered in this volume and on the cards which are included in the General Index of Connecticut Vital Records also in the possession of the Connecticut State Library.
>
> Hartford, Conn., October, 1924.[332]

VITAL RECORDS: East Haven's volume includes vital records as early as 1650 and as late as 1852, mostly from Town Meeting record books which remain unfilmed in the East Haven town clerk's office:[333]

- "TM1" refers to includes 1700–1733 vital records between pages 30 and 284.
- "TM2" refers to 1736–1805 vital records between pages 21 and 290.
- "TM3" refers to 1798–1840 vital records between pages 11 and 328.
- "TM4" refers to udes 1842–1852 vital records between pages 207 and 218.
- "DR" refers to death and marriage records from Stephen Dodd's *East Haven Register: in three parts. Part I. containing a history of the town of East Haven, from its first settlement in 1644, to the year 1800 ... Part II. Containing an account of the names, marriages and births of the families ... to the year 1800 ... Part. III. Containing an account of the deaths ... from the year 1647 to ... 1823,* (New Haven: A.H. Maltby, 1824).

---

[329] See How to Use This Book, note 4, above.

[330] Bailey, *Barbour Collection: East Hartford–East Lyme,* vol. 10. digital image at *Ancestry.com*.

[331] Now part of the Barbour Index and interfiled with similar slips from other towns in CSL and on FHL films 2,887 *et seq*. See Introduction above, pp. 3–5.

[332] Lucius B. Barbour, *Connecticut Vital Records: East Haven, 1700–1852,* (Hartford: CSL, 1924) page after title page (FHL film 2,969). Digital images at *AmericanAncestors.org.* and *FamilySearch.org.*

[333] East Haven's town clerk possessed "6 volumes of town proceedings 1659–1936" in 1936. *Biennial Report of the Examiner of Public Records* (Hartford, State of CT, 1936).

Dodd's *East Haven Register* also reports East Haven births to 1800, which Barbour did not abstract.

CHURCH RECORDS:

- First Congregational Church's "Church Records, 1755–1905" (including baptisms 1775–1849, marriages 1755–1849 and deaths 1773–1849) (manuscript at CSL) (FHL film 4,084); (also called the Old Stone Church);
- Christ Church's Records 1788–1889 (CSL #474) (FHL film 1,008,699 reportedly includes only 1846–1870).

CEMETERY INSCRIPTIONS: The Hale Collection identifies burials in order of physical proximity at nine named cemeteries in East Haven Township.[334] Compare with Daniel Hearn's 1976 copy of 160 pre-1800 gravestones in one East Haven cemetery.[335] See also,

- "Inscriptions From Gravestones At East Lyme, Conn.," *NEHGR*, vol. 79:66.
- "Cemetery Records of East Haven, Connecticut" (originals at NYGBS) (FHL film 4,077 or 1,405,497);
- DAR's Genealogical Collection (East Haven: cemetery inscriptions) (Bound typescript) DAR, Washington, D.C. (FHL film 844,454);

OTHER NOTEWORTHY SOURCES: See state and county resources above, pages 18–21.

EAST LYME

Barbour's typescript volume for East Lyme,[336] unlike the GPC edition,[337] begins:

> This volume contains a list alphabetically arranged of all the vital records of the town of East Lyme from its incorporation to about 1853.
>
> This list was taken a set of cards[338] based on a copy of the East Lyme Vital Records made in 1917 by the Town Clerk, Mr. Ernest C. Russell, of Niantic, Conn. The entire record of the town prior to 1853, is found in one volume.
>
> The Russell Copy, now in the possession of the Connecticut State Library, has not been compared with the original and doubtless errors exist. It is hoped that as errors or omissions are found notes will be entered in this volume and on the cards which are included in the General Index of Connecticut Vital Records also in the possession of the Connecticut State Library.
>
> Hartford, Conn., October, 1924.[339]

334 Charles R. Hale, "Headstone Inscriptions of the Town of East Haven, Connecticut," bound typescript, 1930s, CSL, Hartford, (FHL film 3,332).

335 Daniel Hearn, "Connecticut gravestones, early to 1800," manuscript (FHL film 1,477,476, item 45).

336 See How to Use This Book, note 4, above.

337 Bailey, *Barbour Collection: East Hartford–East Lyme,* vol. 10, digital image at *Ancestry.com.*

338 Now part of the Barbour Index and interfiled with similar slips from other towns in CSL and on FHL films 2 887 *et seq*. See Introduction above, pp. 3–5

VITAL RECORDS: Barbour's East Lyme volume includes vital records as early as 1784 and as late as 1853. Barbour abstracted the East Lyme Town Clerk's Record of Births, Marriages, and Deaths, 1784–1943, East Lyme Town Hall, (FHL film 1,312,385). **This book is not the original record for East Lyme because the earliest records in the book begin at page 150, out of chronological order. Could there be another at the town hall?**

CHURCH RECORDS:

- First Baptist Church and Flanders Baptist and Community Church's "Church Records, 1752–1952" (includes deaths and baptisms); (manuscript at CSL) (FHL film 1,008,700 or 4,095);
- First Congregational Church at Niantic's, "Church Records, 1719–1914" (includes baptisms, deaths and marriages) (originals at CSL) (FHL film 4,094);
- Herman W. Smith's "Copy of a Part of the Records of the First Congregational Church of East Lyme, Niantic, Conn., 1828–1923" (typescript at CSL) (FHL film 1,008,701);
- Niantic Community Church has records from 1719 on its premises.[340]

CEMETERY INSCRIPTIONS: The Hale Collection identifies people in order of physical proximity buried at 25 named cemeteries in East Lyme Township.[341] Compare with Daniel Hearn's 1979 copy of 78 pre-1800 gravestones in three East Lyme cemeteries.[342] See also,

- "Inscriptions From Gravestones at Old Lyme, Lyme and East Lyme" (reproduced from *NEHGR*) (Salem, MA: Higginson, 199-);
- "Record of Inscriptions Found on Gravestones in the Town of East Lyme Dated Prior to A.D. 1850" (3 vols.) (Old Stone Church yard, Old Stone Church yard, Union Cemetery, Banty yard, Old Roger yard, Pest yard, Cutter yard & Fosdick stones, Huntley yard, Crocker yard, Powers yard, Flanders churchyard & Taber stones) (manuscript at NEHGS);
- Francis F. Spies' "Connecticut Epitaphs" (4 vols.: East Lyme CT (1st Churchyard, Flanders, & Golden Spur), Waterford, CT, Sound Beach (Potomac Ave, 1st Congregational Church yard, near Adams Corners); Stamford (St Andrew's Churchyard, North Street, Mill River yard, Richmond Hill Ave); Noroton in Darien Township, Mianus (Lyon Farm, Bonnell farm), CosCob, Montville, Chesterfield (near church, Martenus Farm, by Congregational meeting house, on Warren farm, & Great Hill Burial Ground); and Yonkers, NY, New Canaan CT, East Port, Chester CT, Greenwich CT, Port Chester, NY, and Rye, NY). (manuscript at NEHGS).

OTHER NOTEWORTHY SOURCES: See state and county resources above, pages 18–21.

---

339 Lucius B. Barbour, *Connecticut Vital Records: East Lyme, 1839–1853*, (Hartford, CSL, 1924) page after title page FHL film 2,969) Digital images at *AmericanAncestors.org.* and *FamilySearch.org.*

340 Morrison, *Connecting to Connecticut*, 87.

341 Charles R. Hale, "Headstone Inscriptions of the Town of East Lyme, Connecticut," bound typescript, 1930s, CSL, Hartford, (FHL film 3,332).

342 Daniel Hearn, "Connecticut gravestones, early to 1800," manuscript (FHL film 1,477,476, item 46).

EAST WINDSOR

Barbour's typescript volume for East Windsor,[343] unlike the GPC edition,[344] begins:

> This volume contains a list alphabetically arranged of all the vital records of the town of East Windsor from its incorporation to about 1860. The records prior to 1860, are found in one volume.
>
> This list was taken a set of cards[345] based on a photostat copy of the East Windsor Vital Records made in 1914 which is now in the possession of the Connecticut State Library. It is hoped that as errors or omissions are found corrections will be entered in this volume and on the cards which are included in the General Index of Connecticut Vital Records also in the possession of the Connecticut State Library.
>
> Hartford, Conn., March, 1925[346]

VITAL RECORDS: The East Windsor volume includes vital records as early as 1757 and as late as 1860. Barbour abstracted East Windsor's Records of Births, Marriages, and Deaths, 1758–1945, East Windsor Town Hall (FHL film 1,317,066).

CHURCH RECORDS:

- St. John's Parish's "Church Records, 1802–1926" (includes baptisms 1803–1862, marriages 1806–1861, and burials 1822–1862); (originals at CSL) (FHL film 4,184);
- First Congregational Church's "Church Records, 1803–1932" (includes baptisms 1850–1932) (originals and photocopies at CSL) (FHL film 4,181 Items 3–4);
- Methodist Episcopal Church at Warehouse Point's "Church Records, 1830–1912" (includes marriages, baptisms, etc.) (originals at CSL) (FHL film 4,180);
- Broad Brook Congregational Church's "Church Records, 1851–1907" (includes baptisms 1854–1906 & marriages 1855–1859) (photocopies at CSL) (FHL film 4,181, items 1–2);
- Grace Episcopal Church at Broad Brook's "Church Records, 1845–1909" (includes baptisms 1857–1909) (originals at CSL) (FHL film 4,185);
- Baptisms (1803–62), marriages (1806–61) & burials (1822–62) at St. John's Church, Episcopal Diocese, Hartford (ED Film 4,184 & manuscript);
- St. John's Church at Warehouse Point's Church records, 1796–1915, originals at CSL (FHL film 1,008,702–3).

---

343 See How to Use This Book, note 4, above.

344 Lorraine Cook White, *Barbour Collection of Connecticut Town Vital Records: East Windsor, 1768–1860, Ellington Part I – Vital records 1786-1850, Ellington Part II – Marriage Records 1820–1853*, vol. 11, (Baltimore: GPC, 1998) al image at *Ancestry.com*.

345 Now part of the Barbour Index and interfiled with similar slips from other towns in CSL and on FHL films 2,887 *et seq*. See Introduction above, pp. 3–5

346 Lucius B. Barbour, *Connecticut Vital Records: East Windsor, 1768–1860*, (Hartford: CSL, 1925) page after title page (FHL film 2,969). Digital images at *AmericanAncestors.org*.and *FamilySearch.org*.

- Katherine B. Drake and First Congregational Church's "Church Records 1722–1838" (includes miscellaneous baptisms, marriages, deaths and burials) (manuscript at CSL) (FHL film 1,008,702);
- Mary Janette Elmore's "Church Records of the First Church of Christ in East Windsor, Connecticut, 1695–1853" (manuscript at CSL) (FHL film 4,183);
- Albert C. Bates, Ransom Warner, and Roger Viets' *Records of Rev. Ransom Warner, 1823–1854, Rector of St. Andrew's Simsbury and Bloomfield, St. Peter's Granby, St. John's East Windsor, Connecticut: also Additional Records, 1777–1778, of Rev. Roger Viets, Rector of St. Andrews, Simsbury* (Hartford: [s.n.], 1923) (FHL fiche 6,005,264);

CEMETERY INSCRIPTIONS: The Hale Collection identifies people in order of physical proximity buried at 25 named cemeteries in East Windsor Township.[347] Compare with Daniel Hearn's 1978 copy of 171 pre-1800 gravestones in four East Windsor cemeteries.[348] See also,

- "Cemetery Records of East Windsor, Connecticut" (typescript at the NYGBS) (FHL film 4430);
- "Cemetery Records, East Windsor, Connecticut, 1730–1805" (typescript in Pittsfield MA) (FHL film 234,578);
- Lucius B. Barbour's "East Windsor, Conn. Epitaphs" (Mss A 2787), RSASC, NEHGS);
- Lucius B. Barbour's Some Inscriptions in Ancient Windsor, Conn., circa 1915; 1 volume (Windsor Cemetery; Poquonock Cemetery, Windsor; Wintonbury Cemetery, Bloomfield; East Windsor Cemetery.) (manuscript 65 in Box 8) CSL Record Group 074.36, Hartford.

OTHER NOTEWORTHY SOURCES:

- "Allen family births, 1771–1811,"CSL; see Appendix A;
- "Humphrey Davis Pension Record," CSL; see Appendix A;
- Lucius B. Barbour's East Windsor, Conn., Marriages 1820–1850; 1 volume (manuscript 131 in Box 23) CSL Record Group 074.36, Hartford;
- Lucius B. Barbour's Abstracts of probate records from East Windsor, Conn., 1782–1800; 1 volume (manuscript 76 in Box ?) CSL Record Group 074.36, Hartford;
- Lucius B. Barbour's East Windsor, Conn., Marriages 1820–1850; 1 volume (manuscript 131 in Box 23) CSL Record Group 074.36, Hartford;
- Henry R. Stiles' *History of Ancient Windsor, Connecticut: Including East Windsor, South Windsor, and Ellington Prior to 1788, the Date of Their Separation From the Old Town; and Windsor, Bloomfield, and Windsor Locks to the Present Time; also the Genealogies and Genealogical Notes of Those Families Which Settled Within the Limits of Ancient Windsor, Connecticut Prior to 1800*, vol. 2 (Albany, NY: J. Munsell, 1863) (FHL film 417,935).

---

[347] Charles R. Hale, "Headstone Inscriptions of the Town of East Windsor, Connecticut," bound typescript, 1930s, CSL, Hartford, (FHL film 3,332).

[348] Daniel Hearn, "Connecticut gravestones, early to 1800," manuscript (FHL film 1,477,476, item 44).

EASTFORD

Barbour's typescript volume for Eastford,[349] unlike the GPC edition,[350] begins:

> This volume contains a list alphabetically arranged of all the vital records of the town of Eastford from its incorporation to about 1851. This list was taken a set of cards[351] based on a copy of the Eastford Vital Records made in 1911 by James N. Arnold, of Providence, R.I. The entire record for this town prior to 1851 is found in two volumes. The Arnold Copy, now in the possession of the Connecticut State Library, has not been compared with the original and doubtless errors exist. It is hoped that as errors or omissions are found notes will be entered in this volume and on the cards which are included in the General Index of Connecticut Vital Records also in the possession of the Connecticut State Library.
> Hartford, Conn., December, 1920.[352]

VITAL RECORDS: The Eastford volume includes vital records as early as 1843 and as late as 1861. Barbour abstracted two 'books" from Eastford's Records of Births, Marriages, and Deaths, vols. 1–4, 1847–1915, Eastford Town Hall (FHL film 1,378,042):

- "1"refers to vol. 2–B, "Eastford Marriages 1852[sic]–1880"[353] (FHL film 1,378,042, item 1
- "2" refers to vol. 1 "Births, Marriages, Deaths 1847–1852" (FHL film 1,378,042, item 3)

CHURCH RECORDS:

- Lester Card's "Church of Christ: Church Records 1778–1803" (includes marriages performed by Rev. Andrew Judson) (typescript at CSL) (FHL film 1,008,341);
- Congregational Church's "Church Records, 1777–1941" (includes baptisms 1779–1868) (originals at CSL) (FHL film 4,187);
- Andrew Judson's Private (Congregational Church) records 1780–1803 (copies at CSL) (FHL film 1,008,341);
- Eastford Methodist Episcopal Church's "Church Records, 1834–1916" (originals in BUSTL) (FHL film 1,508,864);
- Claude W. Barlow, "Eastford, Conn. Congregational Church Baptisms and Communicants" (Mss A 6108), RSASCs, NEHGS;

---

349 See How to Use This Book, note 4, above.

350 White, *Barbour Collection: Durham East Haddam,* vol. 9, digital image at *Ancestry.com*.

351 Now part of the Barbour Index and interfiled with similar slips from other towns in CSL and on FHL films 2,887 *et seq*. See Introduction above, pp. 3–5.

352 Lucius B. Barbour, *Connecticut Vital Records: Eastford, 1847–1851*, (Hartford, CSL, 1920), page after title page (FHL film 2,969). Digital images at *AmericanAncestors.org* and *FamilySearch.org*.

353 These marriage records actually begin in 1847and include the bride's and groom's birthdates. The volume also includes a few birth records as early as 1843.

- Baptist Church's Records 1850–1938 (copies at CSL) (FHL film 4,188)
- John P. Trowbridge's "Eastford, Conn., Church Records," *NEHGR*, 62:84–90, 63:89 (1909)

CEMETERY INSCRIPTIONS: The Hale Collection identifies people in order of physical proximity buried at 13 named sites in Eastford Township.[354] Compare with Daniel Hearn's 1979 copy of 79 pre-1800 gravestones in one Eastford cemetery. [355]
See also,

- Grace Olive Chapman's "Latham-Bullard Cemetery Phoenixville, Eastford, Connecticut" (Mss A 6109), RSASCs, NEHGS;
- Grace Olive Chapman's "Spaulding-Snow Cemetery Eastford, Windham County, Connecticut" (Mss A 6110), RSASCs, NEHGS;
- Grace Olive Chapman's "Eastford, Conn., General Lyon Cemetery Inscriptions" (Mss A 2314), RSASC, NEHGS;
- Emily Josephine Chism's "Eastford, Connecticut Old Cemetery Inscriptions" (Mss A 6107), RSASCs, NEHGS;
- Emily Josephine Chism and Grace Olive Chapman's "Inscriptions in the North Ashford Cemetery" (Mss A 2408), RSASC, NEHGS;
- Grace Olive Chapman's "Latham-Bullard Cemetery Phoenixville, Eastford, Connecticut" (Mss A 6109), RSASCs, NEHGS;
- DAR's Genealogical Collection (cemetery inscriptions Eastford Village and Westford:) (Bound typescript) DAR, Washington, D.C. (FHL film 844,454).

OTHER NOTEWORTHY SOURCES: Lucius B. Barbour's Genealogical notes complied from church records of Eastford, Conn., 1770–1804. 1 volume, abstract of vital records. (manuscript 14 in Box 2) CSL Record Group 074.36, Hartford.

EASTON

VITAL RECORDS: This town is not abstracted in any version of the Barbour Collection. In 1845 Easton separated from Weston, Connecticut and began keeping its own land records.[356] Harlan R. Jessup reports that the Easton town clerk also possesses:

- ***Town Clerk Edward Hill's Record Book of Marriages in the Town of Easton since its First Organization,* Easton Town Hall, 1854;**[357]
- ***"Births, Marriages, Deaths, 1852–54* (probably FHL film 1,319,938) and**
- ***"Births, Marriages, Deaths,* (1845–1876)."**[358]

CHURCH RECORDS:

- Christ Church's Records 1784–1898 (copies at CSL) (FHL film 4,187).

---

354 Charles R. Hale, "Headstone Inscriptions of the Town of Eastford, Connecticut," bound typescript, 1930s, CSL, Hartford, FHL film 3,330.

355 Daniel Hearn, "Connecticut gravestones, early to 1800," manuscript (FHL film 1,477,476, item 40).

356 Easton, Land Records, vol. 1, 1845–1860, Easton Town Hall, FHL film 4,189, item 2.

357 1845–1854 vital records transcribed by **Harlan R. Jessup, "Easton, Connecticut Marriages, 1845–1854," *CA*, 50:137–41 (Feb 2008).**

358 Jessup reports that this book was made in the early 20th century and is full of transcription errors and omissions. *Ibid.*, 137.

- Ecclesiastical Society and Congregational Church's "Church records, 1762–1930" (includes baptisms 1764–1926; marriages 1763–1905; deaths 1764–1929) (originals at CSL) (FHL film 4191);

CEMETERY INSCRIPTIONS: The Hale Collection identifies people in order of physical proximity buried at six named sites in Easton Township.[359] Compare with Daniel Hearn's 1975 copy of 46 pre-1800 gravestones in two Easton cemeteries.[360] See also,

- Francis F. Spies' *Easton, Fairfield Co., Conn. Inscriptions From the Graveyards With Genealogical Notes and Index* (1934/1997 copy at NEHGS);
- Marshall C. Nye's "Easton, Connecticut Cemeteries," (typescript photocopy at FHL).

OTHER NOTEWORTHY SOURCES: Calista K. Cleary's "Little Egypt, Black History in Three New England Towns" (includes inscriptions from the Wheeler-Baldwin Cemetery/Den Cemetery in Easton) (1989 manuscript at FHL).

ELLINGTON

Barbour's typescript volume for Ellington,[361] unlike the GPC edition.[362] begins:

> Part I
>
> This volume contains a list alphabetically arranged of all the vital records of the town of Ellington from its incorporation to about 1850. The entire record for this town prior to 1851 is found in one volume. This list was taken a set of cards[363] based on a copy of the Ellington Vital Records made in 1911. A few entries in a copy made in 1916 by James N. Arnold, of Providence, R.I. vary from the 1911 copy and these differences have been noted in this list with an interrogation mark following each. Both copies are now in the possession of the Connecticut State Library and neither has been compared with the original. Doubtless errors exist and it is hoped that as errors or omissions are found notes will be entered in this volume and on the cards which are included in the General Index of Connecticut Vital Records also in the possession of the Connecticut State Library.
>
> Hartford, Conn., November, 1922.[364]

---

[359] Charles R. Hale, "Headstone Inscriptions of the Town of Easton, Connecticut," bound typescript, 1930s, CSL, Hartford, FHL film 3,332.

[360] Daniel Hearn, "Connecticut gravestones, early to 1800," manuscript (FHL film 1,477,476, item 47).

[361] See How to Use This Book, note 4, above.

[362] White, *Barbour Collection: East Windsor Ellington*, vol. 11, Digital image at *Ancestry.com*.

[363] Now part of the Barbour Index and interfiled with similar slips from other towns in CSL and on FHL films 2.887 *et seq*. See Introduction above, pp. 3–5.

[364] Lucius B. Barbour, *Connecticut Vital Records: Ellington, 1786–1850* and *Marriages 1820–1853*, (Hartford: CSL, 1922 & 1949) page after title page (FHL film 2,969). Digital images at *FamilySearch.org*

```
                    Part II
     This volume contains a list alphabetically
arranged of MARRIAGES from the town of Ellington,
1820-1853, which were taken from a set of cards[365]
based on a microfilm copy made in 1949 by Mr.
Lloyd S. Hughes, of the Genealogical Society,
Salt Lake City, Utah. This volume is known as
"Vol. M". The original records are in possession
of the Town Clerk of Ellington.
                   Hartford, Conn. April, 1949[366]
```

VITAL RECORDS: The Ellington volume and supplement actually include vital records as early as 1732 and as late as 1852 in Part I and a separately indexed Book of Marriages 1820–1852 in Part II. The single volume Barbour originally abstracted as Part I is Town Clerk Miles H. Aborn's Ellington Births, Marriages, and Deaths, 1786–1850, Ellington Town Hall (FHL film 1,319,920, item 3). According to the FHL catalog, it is a March 1898 copy of the original town record, which is Ellington's Records of Births, Marriages, and Deaths, 1754–1856, (contains records of births 1754–1847, marriages 1761–1819, and deaths 1758–1856), manuscript at Ellington Town Hall (FHL film 1,319,920, item 2).

The marriages in Part II of Barbour's Ellington volume are abstracted only in CSL's Barbour Collection. NEHGS' online volume includes digital images of the original typescript: Ellington's Records of Marriages, from 1820 to 1853, manuscript at Ellington Town Hall, (FHL film 4,156).

CHURCH RECORDS:

- Congregational Church's "Church Records, 1785–1941" (includes baptisms 1800–1900 & deaths 1850–1900) (originals at CSL) (FHL film 4,157);
- Congregational Church's catalog of its members since 1799 (CSL, 974.62 qE156c).

CEMETERY INSCRIPTIONS: The Hale Collection identifies people in order of physical proximity buried at ten named sites in Ellington Township.[367] Compare with Daniel Hearn's 1979 copy of 167 pre-1800 gravestones in two Ellington cemeteries.[368]

See also,

- Lucius B. Barbour's "Ellington, Conn. Epitaphs" (1931 manuscript at NEHGS);
- Claude W. Barlow's "Inscriptions from the Crystal Lake Cemetery, Ellington, Conn." (Mss A 6113), RSASCs, NEHGS;
- DAR Sabra Trumbull Chapter's Crystal Lake Cemetery, Dimmock's Crossing, Ellington (CSL 974.62 qE 156 c);
- Mary Kimball, Sabra Trumbull DAR Chapter's Ellington Cemetery, (CSL 974.82 qE156c);

---

[365] Now part of the Barbour Index and interfiled with similar slips from other towns in CSL and on FHL films 2,887 *et seq*. See Introduction above, pp. 3–5.

[366] *AmericanAncestors.org* lacks the 1949 portion of this typescript. Instead it presents a handwritten version,

[367] Charles R. Hale, "Headstone Inscriptions of the Town of Ellington, Connecticut," bound typescript, 1930s, CSL, Hartford, FHL film 3,332.

[368] Daniel Hearn, "Connecticut gravestones, early to 1800," manuscript (FHL film 1,477,476, item 49).

- Mary Kimball, Sabra Trumbull DAR Chapter's McKinley Cemetery, (CSL, 974.62 qE156c).

OTHER NOTEWORTHY SOURCES: Henry R. Stiles' *The History of Ancient Windsor, Connecticut: Including East Windsor, South Windsor, and Ellington Prior to 1788, the Date of their Separation from the Old Town; and Windsor, Bloomfield, and Windsor Locks to the Present Time; also the Genealogies and Genealogical Notes of Those Families Which Settled Within the Limits of Ancient Windsor, Connecticut Prior to 1800*, vol. 2 (Albany, NY: J. Munsell, 1863) (FHL film 417,935).

ENFIELD

VITAL RECORDS: Barbour made no individual Enfield volume.[369] He abstracted the slips in his statewide index[370] from Francis Olcott Allen's *History of Enfield, Connecticut: Compiled From All the Public Records of the Town Known to Exist, Covering From the Beginning to 1850, Together with the Graveyard Inscriptions and Those Hartford, Northampton and Springfield Records Which Refer to the People of Enfield,* vols. 2 & 3 (Lancaster, PA: Wickersham Printing, 1900) (FHL film 1,321,486). Volume 2 contains about 150 pages of vital records on pages 1758 through 1904; volume 3 contains over 50 more, plus many, additions and corrections to both volumes. Barbour's work is secondary to Allen, who cites his sources: Enfield's Town Records, 1682–1851, Enfield Town Hall, (FHL film 1,317,124, items 1–4) and Enfield's "Record of Births, Marriages, Deaths, 1848–1851," Enfield Town Hall (FHL film 1,317,125, item 4):[371]

- Allen's pages 1585 to 1737 transcribe 1682 to 1848 births;
- Allen's pages 1585 to 1737 transcribe 1847 to 1849 births ;
- Allen's pages 1755 to 1764 transcribe 1725 to 1749/50 intentions of marriage;
- Allen's pages 1765 to 1851 transcribe 1682 to 1849 marriages;
- Allen's pages 1852 to 1860 transcribe 1847 to 1849 marriages;
- Allen's pages 1861 to 1896 transcribe 1682 to 1849 deaths;
- Allen's pages 1897 to 1904 transcribe 1847 to 1849 deaths;
- Allen's pages 2175 to 2214 transcribe 1730 to 1750 town records from Somers;
- Allen's pages 2615 to 2632 transcribe 1847 to 1849 additional 1785–1849 death records from a private Record Book created by Abigail, Asahel, and Jabez Parsons, present whereabouts unknown;
- Allen's pages lxxxiv to lxxxix contains additions and correction to his volumes 2 and 3.

See also, William & John Pynchon, "Vital Records, Massachusetts and Connecticut" (contains births, marriages, and deaths (1638–1696) of towns including Suffield and Enfield) original at Pynchon Memorial Building, Springfield, MA (FHL film 14,766).

---

369 See How to Use This Book, note 4, above.

370 The Barbour Index may be viewed only at CSL and on FHL films 2,887 *et seq*. See Introduction above, pp. 3–5.

371 Barbour calls the latter "book 5" while citing Allen's volume 2 pagination.

CHURCH RECORDS:

- First Congregational Church's "Church Records, 1770–1907" (includes baptisms 1783–1855, marriages 1816–1851, and deaths 1808–1851) (originals at CSL) (FHL film 4,145);
- First Presbyterian Church at Thompsonville's "Church Records, 1839–1972" (includes marriages 1839–1866, baptisms 1839–1866 & deaths 1839–1856) (originals at CSL) (FHL film 1,008,704);
- St. Andrew's Church at Thompsonville's "Church Records, 1844–1920" (includes baptisms 1844–1879, marriages 1851–1879, and burials 1849–1873) (originals at CSL) (FHL film 4,146);
- DAR's Genealogical Collection, (Enfield: records of First Congregational Church) (bound typescript) DAR, Washington, D.C. (FHL film 844,460);
- Allen's *History of Enfield, Connecticut* (FHL film 1,321,486) transcribes 1st Ecclesiastical Society Church Records (infant and adult baptisms, marriages, and deaths including Shakers and Thompsonville) at pages1339–1524.

CEMETERY INSCRIPTIONS: The Hale Collection identifies people in order of physical proximity buried at nine named sites in Enfield Township.[372] Compare with Daniel Hearn's 1978 copy of 227 pre-1800 gravestones in two Enfield cemeteries.[373]
See also,

- Allen's *History of Enfield, Connecticut* (FHL film 1,321,486) transcribes Enfield grave yard inscriptions at pages 2310 to 2453;
- "Records of Churches and Cemeteries of Connecticut: Town Records of Durham, Hartford and Enfield, Conn." (typescript in NYGBS) (FHL film 2798);
- DAR (Florida) GRC, "Bible and Cemetery Records" (includes Enfield) (original typescript at the DAR Library) (FHL film 850,400);
- James Allen Kibbe's *Additional Record of Deaths in Enfield 1785–1849*, (Hartford: CSL, n.d.) (FHL film 481,068);
- James Allen Kibbe's "Graveyard Inscriptions – Enfield," in Francis Olcott Allen, *The History of Enfield, Connecticut,* Vol. 3;
- "Burials of the United Society of Believers (Shakers), Enfield, CT." *CN*, 31:365 (December 1998) and in the *Ricker Compilation*;
- Lucius B. Barbour's "Enfield, Conn. Epitaphs" (Mss A 6115), RSASCs, NEHGS);
- Louis M. Dewey's "Inscriptions from Old Cemeteries in Connecticut," *NEHGR*, 60:305–8 (Jul 1906).

OTHER NOTEWORTHY SOURCES:

- Lucius B. Barbour's "Genealogical notes compiled from town and church records of Enfield, Conn. 1724–1860," 2 volumes. Abstract of vital records. Arranged alphabetically. (manuscript 18 in Box 2) CSL Record Group 074.36, Hartford;
- William and John Pynchon, and J. Walter Bassett's *Index to Hampshire Records of Births, Marriages and Deaths, 1638–1696, Privately Kept by William and John*

---

372 Charles R. Hale, "Headstone Inscriptions of the Town of Enfield, Connecticut," bound typescript, 1930s, CSL, Hartford, FHL film 3,333.

373 Daniel Hearn, "Connecticut gravestones, early to 1800," manuscript (FHL film 1,477,476, item 50).

Pynchon: Brookfield, Enfield, Hadley, Hatfield, Northampton, Springfield, Suffield, and Westfield (Hartford, CSL, 1957) (FHL film 1,033,996).

FAIRFIELD

Barbour's typescript volume for Fairfield,[374] unlike the GPC edition,[375] begins:

> The vital records of Fairfield, prior to 1850, are found scattered through three volumes of Land Records and a volume of Vital Records and a Book of Marriages.
>
> This alphabetical list was taken from a set of cards[376] based on a manuscript copy made in 1914 by James N. Arnold, of Providence, R.I., Reference to entries found in the Land records is indicated by the abbreviation "LR" and the letter or number of the volume, to the book of Vital Records by "Vol.1" and to the Book of Marriages by "Vol.1-M".
>
> The Arnold Copy, now in the possession of the Connecticut State Library, has not been compared with the original and doubtless errors exist. It is hoped that as errors or omissions are found notes will be entered in this volume and on the cards which are included in the General Index of Connecticut Vital Records also in the possession of the Connecticut State Library.
>
> Hartford, Conn., October, 1925.[377]

VITAL RECORDS: The earliest record in Barbour's Fairfield volume is actually dated 1661. Barbour's designations for the land record books he abstracted (LR-A2, LR-2, LR-B, and LR-A) do not correspond with FHL's designations: Vol. A1– 2 (1649–1713, FHL film 4,273) and vols. 3–4 (1713–1732, FHL film 4,274). Barbour abstracted five, not six, Fairfield "books:"

- "LR-A" and "LR-A2" both equate to a volume the town clerk labels A part 2, which is the middle part of what FHL catalogs as the Fairfield Town Clerk's "Land Records, volumes. A1, 2, (volumes 1 and 2 include births, marriages, deaths) Fairfield Town Hall (FHL film 4,273);

[374] See How to Use This Book, note 4, above.

[375] Nancy E. Schott, *Barbour Collection of Connecticut Town Vital Records: Fairfield 1639–1850, Farmington 1645–1850*, vol. 12, (Baltimore: GPC, 1998). Digital image at *Ancestry.com*.

[376] Now part of the Barbour Index and interfiled with similar slips from other towns in CSL and on FHL films 2,887 *et seq*. See Introduction above, pp. 3–5.

[377] Lucius B. Barbour, *Connecticut Vital Records: Fairfield, 1639–1850*, (Hartford, CSL, 1925) page after title page (FHL film 2,970). Digital images at *AmericanAncestors.org*.and *FamilySearch.org*.

- "LR-2" refers to Fairfield's Land Records volume 2 and the last part of what FHL catalogs as Fairfield's "Land Records, volumes. A1, 2, (volumes 1 and 2 include births, marriages, deaths)" Fairfield Town Hall (FHL film 4,273);
- "LR-B" refers to two unfilmed volumes CSA calls "Fairfield Town Records B, 1661–1826" (CSL 974.62 fF 15 to).Barbour does not cite individual pages in these books and **excludes some records**;
- "1" refers to an unfilmed volume CSA calls "Fairfield, Family Book, 1696–1855" (some dates 1628–1880) (CSL 974.62 fF 15 fa);
- "1-M" refers to Fairfield's Record of Marriages, 1820–1853 Fairfield Town Hall, FHL film 1,434,093, item 1.

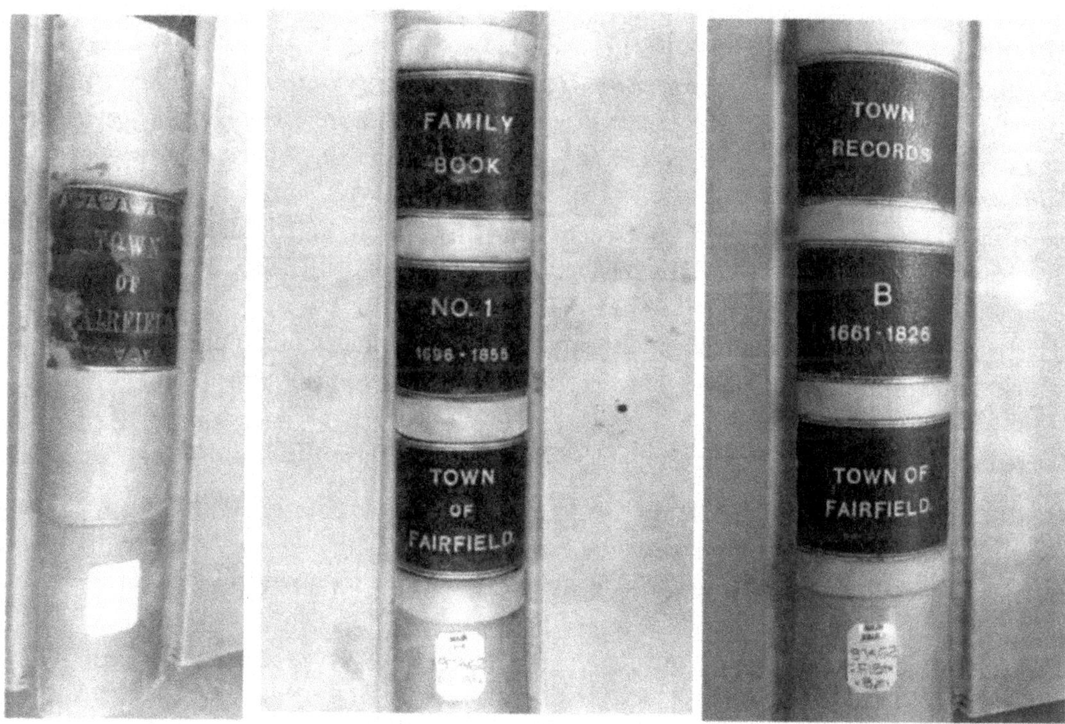

Figures 15, 16, & 17: Three Fairfield Record Books in the State Archives

Additional Fairfield vital records are:

- **Land Records volume A, part 1 contains many 1649–1694 births, marriages, and deaths not abstracted by Barbour. See the first part of what FHL catalogs as Fairfield's "Land Records, volumes. A1, 2, (volumes 1 and 2 include births, marriages, deaths) Fairfield Town Hall, FHL film 4,273);**
- **Fairfield Town Records, 5 vols., 1649–1826, CSA (CSL 974.62 fF15to).**
- **Fairfield's Reports of Births, Marriages, and Deaths in the School Districts, 1847–1850, Fairfield Town Hall, (FHL film 1,434,093, item 2) contains detailed mid-19th century records not in the Barbour Index;**

The catalog also lists as vital records: **Edwin Stanley Welles'** ***Births, Marriages and Deaths Returned from Hartford, Windsor and Fairfield and Entered in the Early Land Records of the Colony of Connecticut: Volumes I and II of Land records and***

***No. D of Colonial Deeds* (Hartford: Case, Lockwood & Brainard, 1898) (FHL film 823,816 or 847,591) (images at *AmericanAncesrtors.org*).**

CHURCH RECORDS:

- Ecclesiastical Society and Congregational Church of Easton's "Church Records, 1762–1930" (includes baptisms 1764–1926; marriages 1763–1905; deaths 1764–1929) (originals at CSL) (FHL film 4,191);
- Greenfield Hill Church's "Church Records, 1668–1881" (includes births, deaths, baptisms, marriages, etc.) (originals at CSL) (FHL film 4,199);
- First Congregational Church's "Church Records, 1694–1806" (includes baptisms and marriages) (originals at CSL) (FHL film 4,201);
- Stratfield Baptist Church's "Church Records, 1751–1938" (includes deaths 1767) (originals at CSL) (FHL film 4,200);
- William H. Holman's *Southport Congregational Church, Southport, Connecticut, March 7, 1843–November 30, 1915 : an historical sketch, together with the confession, the covenant, the by-laws and lists of the pastors, deacons, members, and baptized children* (New York: Gillis Press, 1915);
- Mary K. Talcott's "Records of the Greenfield Hill Church, Fairfield, Conn.," *NEHGR*, 68:169–77, 286–300, 375–9 (Apr Jul Oct 1914), 69:39–50, 127–36, 230–42, 364–79 (Jan Apr Jul Oct 1915) 70:33–43 (Jan 1915).
- Barbara Dempsey's "Greens Farms Congregational Church, Fairfield/Westport, Records beginning 1715 [through 1822]," *CA*, Vol. 58, No. 4 (August 2015) through Vol. 61, No. 4; (May 2019).
- Marriages (1845 & 1847) & burials (1848) at Christ Church (ED Film 4,146);

CEMETERY INSCRIPTIONS: The Hale Collection identifies people in order of physical proximity buried at 12 named sites in Fairfield Township.[378] Compare with Daniel Hearn's 1975 copy of 331 pre-1800 gravestones in two Fairfield cemeteries.[379] See also,

- "Cemetery Records of Bethel and Fairfield, Connecticut" (typescript at NYGBS) (FHL film 4,197);
- Kate E. Perry and Wm. A. Beers' *The Old Burying Ground of Fairfield, Conn.: A Memorial of Many of the Early Settlers in Fairfield, and an Exhaustive and Faithful Transcript of the Inscriptions and Epitaphs on the 583 Tombstones Found in the Oldest Burying Ground Now Within the Limits of Fairfield* (Hartford: American Publishing Co., 1882) (FHL film 924,072);
- K.E. Perry's *Old Burying Ground of Fairfield: Memorial of Many Early Settlers & Transcript of the Inscriptions & Epitaphs on the Tombstones* (1882/1988 copy at NEHGS);
- Francis F. Spies's *Fairfield, Fairfield Co., Conn. Inscriptions from the Graveyards Arranged With Notes and Index* (1934/1997 copy at NEHGS).

---

378 Charles R. Hale, "Headstone Inscriptions of the Town of Fairfield, Connecticut," bound typescript, 1930s, CSL, Hartford, FHL film 3 333–4.

379 Daniel Hearn, "Connecticut gravestones, early to 1800," manuscript (FHL film 1,477,476, item 52).

OTHER NOTEWORTHY SOURCES:

- "Daniel Sanford Account Book," Fairfield Co. CSL; see Appendix A;
- Cable, E.J., "Accounts of Cemetery Monument Inscriptions of E. J. and A. Cable for Cemeteries in Fairfield and Litchfield Counties, 1836–63;" original volume at CSL; see Appendix A;
- Charlotte Alvord Lacey and Fairfield Historical Society's *Historical story of Southport, Connecticut* (Fairfield: Fairfield Publishing Company, 1927);
- Donald Lines Jacobus' *History and Genealogy of the Families of Old Fairfield*. 2 vols. (New Haven: The Tuttle, Morehouse & Taylor Company, 1930–1932).

FARMINGTON

Barbour's typescript volume for Farmington,[380] unlike the GPC edition,[381] begins:

> The vital records of Farmington, prior to 1850, are found scattered through volumes 1, 2, 3, 4, 5, 6, 7, 8, 9, 10, 11, 12, 14, 15, 16, 17, 21, 22, 29, 32, 35, 40, 41, 42, and 47 of Land Records.
>
> This alphabetical list was taken from a set of cards[382] based on a manuscript copy made in 1915 by James N. Arnold, of Providence, R. I. Reference to entries found in the Land Records is indicated by the abbreviation "LR" and the number of the volume.
>
> The genealogical notes on the Miller family by Elbert H.T. Miller, of Scottsville, N.Y., which are entered on pages 333-338 of volume 2 of Farmington Land Records, have not been included in this index. These notes have been copied and indexed in a volume now in the possession of the Connecticut State Library.
>
> The Arnold Copy, now in the Connecticut State Library, has not been compared with the original and doubtless errors exist. It is hoped that as errors or omissions are found notes will be entered in this volume and on the cards which are included in the General Index of Connecticut Vital Records also in the possess-ion of the Connecticut State Library.
>
> Hartford, Conn., September, 1927.[383]

---

380 See How to Use This Book, note 4, above.

381 Schott, *Barbour Collection: Fairfield, Farmington*, vol. 12, Digital image at *Ancestry.com*.

382 Now part of the Barbour Index and interfiled with similar slips from other towns in CSL and on FHL films 2887 *et seq*. See Introduction above, pp. 3–5.

383 Lucius B. Barbour, *Connecticut Vital Records: Farmington, 1645–1850*, (Hartford: CSL, 1927) page after title page (FHL film 2.970). Digital images at *AmericanAncestors.org*.

VITAL RECORDS: The Farmington volume includes vital records as early as 1643 and as late as 1850. Barbour abstracted 24 "books" of Farmington's Land Records: vol. 1–13 1645–1769, vols. 17–18 1769–1772, vols. 21–22 1775–1779, vols. 29–32 1791–1801 vols. 39–42 1815–1829, vols. 47–48 1833–1845, Farmington Town Hall.[384]

- "LR1" and "LR2" refer to FHL film 4,215 (1643–1769);
- "LR3" refers to FHL film 4,216 (1712–1722);
- "LR4" refers to FHL film 1,577,517 (1721–1733);
- "LR5" refers to FHL film 4,217 (1722–1737);
- "LR6" and "LR7" refer to FHL film 4,218 (1736–1750);
- "LR8" and "LR9" refer to FHL film 4,219 (1750–1756);
- "LR10" and "LR11" refer to FHL film 4,220 (1754–1768);
- "LR14," "LR15," and "LR16" refer to FHL film 4,222 (1763–1769);
- "LR17" refers to FHL film 4,223 (1769–1772)'
- "LR21" and "LR22" refer to FHL film 4,225 (1775–1779);
- "LR29" refers to FHL film 4,229 (1791–1794);
- "LR32" refers to FHL film 4,230 (1797–1801);
- "LR35" refers to FHL film 4,232 (1804–1815);
- "LR40" refers to FHL film 4,234 (1817–1820);
- "LR41" and "LR42" refer to FHL film 4,235 (1820–1829);
- "LR47" refers to FHL film 4,238 (1833–1840).

See also, Farmington's Birth, Marriage, and Death Records of Farmington, 1643–1850 (A record of vital statistics from vols. 1–47 of the Farmington land records. Records are arranged with separate sections for births, marriages and deaths. Within each section records are arranged by the original volume and page number) Farmington, (FHL film 1,315,116, Items 3–4).

More pre-Civil War Farmington vital records may be found in:

- **Farmington's Record of Births, Marriages, and Deaths in the Town of Farmington, vol. *1 1847–1868,* Farmington Town Hall, (FHL film 1,315,115. item 2);**
- **Farmington Vital Records, 1823–1896, Listed From the Original Certificates (typescript) CSL, Hartford, 1931) (FHL film 3,662, item 4);**
- **Plainville's Records of births, marriages, deaths in the town of Plainville, 1869–1914 (contains a few marriage records of Farmington, 1824–1833) Plainville Town Hall, (FHL film 1,318,029);**
- **Farmington Vital Records circa 1845–1905, CSA (CSL RG 072.002, Boxes 4–7, index in Box 4) (includes typescript "Farmington Vital Records 1823–1897," with a few pre-1850 entries not in Barbour).**

CHURCH RECORDS:

- Farmington Seventh Day Baptist Church Book, 1780–1820 (originals at 7th day Baptist Historical Society, (CSL film # 658 by Princeton University);

---

384 *CSL, Vital Records*, Note: "Barbour Index has citations to land records that post-date the event recorded. For example, — Catherine Selden b. May 30, 1797 is in LR47 WY. LR47 =1833-1848, but record does appear in the place the index indicated, i.e., between the names indexed w through y. Mar 19 2013 (JS).

- "The Farmington Cemetery, Maine Street, Farmington, Conn." (typescript at FHL);
- Farmington Seventh Day Baptist Church Book, 1796–1821 (originals at 7th day Baptist Historical Society, (CSL film # 659 by Princeton University);
- Congregational Church of Plainville's, "Church Records, 1839–1942" (includes deaths 1846–1869) (originals at CSL) (FHL film 5462); First Congregational Church, "Church Records, 1652–1938" (includes baptisms (1653–1711, 1758–1794, & 1787–1883), births & baptisms 1661–1668, marriages (1752–1785, 1795–1820, & 1825–1855), and deaths 1760–1783 & 1796–1877, (originals at CSL) (FHL film 4,241);
- Christ Church at Unionville's, "Church Records, 1845–1883" (includes baptisms, marriages, and burials) (originals at CSL) (FHL film 1008707);
- Charles R. Weldon's *Notes From the Plainville Congregational Church Records, Volumes I, II, III, IV, V, 1837–1917* (includes baptisms and deaths) (S.l.: s.n., 2000?) (FHL film 1,573,511);
- Christ Church's "Church Records, 1846–1883" (includes marriages 1847) (originals at CSL) (FHL film 4,244);
- Julius Gay's "Church Records of Farmington, Connecticut." *NEHGR*, 38:275–9, 410–14 (Jul Oct 1884), 39:48–52, 118–21, 241–5, 338–41 (Jan Apr Jul Oct 1885), 40:31–4, 155–8, 358–62 (Jan Apr Oct 1886) 359–62;
- Charles R. Weldon's *Plainville [Connecticut] Congregational Church Records: Baptisms 1852–1939, Death Records 1840–1870, List of Men who Died in the Civil War, List of Burials in the Old Burying Grounds on East Street* (Connecticut?: self-published, 200-?) (FHL film 1,573,699);
- Plainville Congregational Church's Records 1839–1942, originals at CSL (FHL film 5,462);
- Nathaniel Goodwin's "Church Records of Farmington in Connecticut." *NEHGR*, 11:323–9 (Oct 1857) 12:34–9, 147–51, 327–31 (Jan Apr Oct 1858), 13:57–61 (Jan 1859].

CEMETERY INSCRIPTIONS: The Hale Collection identifies people in order of physical proximity buried at five named sites in what was then Farmington Township.[385] Compare with Daniel Hearn's 1978 copy of 223 pre-1800 gravestones in one Farmington cemetery.[386] The Hale Collection identifies people in order of physical proximity buried at three named sites in what was then Plainville Township.[387] Compare with Daniel Hearn's 1987 copy of 23 pre-1800 gravestones in one Plainville cemetery.[388] See also,

- Charles Weldon's "List of Burials in the Old Burying Ground on East Street in Plainville, CT," (1916 compilation) *CN,* March 2001 and *Ricker Compilation*;
- Lucius B. Barbour's "Genealogical Data From Connecticut Cemeteries, Plainville (Formerly a Part Of Farmington: All Gravestone Records From The Old or East And New or West Cemeteries" (1932 typescript at NEHGS).

---

385 Charles R. Hale, "Headstone Inscriptions of the Town of Farmington, Connecticut," bound typescript, 1930s, CSL, Hartford, FHL film 3,334).

386 Daniel Hearn, "Connecticut gravestones, early to 1800," manuscript (FHL film 1,477,476, item 53).

387 Charles R. Hale, "Headstone Inscriptions of the Town of Farmington, Connecticut," bound typescript, 1930s, CSL, Hartford, FHL film 3,358

388 Daniel Hearn, "Connecticut gravestones, early to 1800," manuscript (FHL film 1,477,477, item 27).

OTHER NOTEWORTHY SOURCES:

- "Amasa Woodford's Account Book,_Farmington, CSL; see Appendix A;
- Julius Gay's Farmington Papers (1929/1997 copy at NEHGS);
- Daniel Wadsworth, and Edwin Stanley Welles' R*ecord of deaths found in the diary, 1737–1747, of the Rev. Daniel Wadsworth, seventh pastor of the First church of Christ in Hartford, Conn.* [Hartford, Conn.]: [E.S. Welles] 1900);
- Henry Allen Castle's History of Plainville, Connecticut, 1640–1918 (Chester: Pequot Press, 1972).

FRANKLIN

Barbour's typescript volume for Franklin,[389] unlike the GPC edition,[390] begins:

> The earliest record of vital statistics of Franklin that has been in use in the Town Clerk's office for many years, certainly during the term of office of the late Samuel G. Hartshorn, is not the record of original entry but an excellent, though not verbatim, copy of it. This volume contains all, or practically all, that was in the original volume and many later entries and additional information. The original volume was found practically discarded in the attic of the Town Clerk's office by the Examiner of Public Records and has been donated to the State Library by the town.
>
> In the alphabetical list below the original volume is referred to as "Vol.1" and the copy as "Vol.2". However, only such entries from Vol. 2 have been taken which do not appear in Vol. 1, or which show a variation from the entry recorded in Vol. 1, in which case both entries appear.
>
> This list was taken a set of cards[391] based on the original book and a copy of the record now in Franklin made in 1910 by James N. Arnold, of Providence, R.I. The Arnold Copy, now in the possession of the Connecticut State Library and neither has been compared with the original and doubtless errors exist. It is hoped that as errors or omissions are found notes will be entered in this volume and on the cards which are included in the General Index of Connecticut Vital Records also in the possession of the Connecticut State Library.
>
> Hartford, Conn., December, 1919.[392]

VITAL RECORDS: The Franklin volume includes vital records as early as 1678 and as late as 1862. Barbour abstracted two Franklin books:

---

389 See How to Use This Book, note 4, above.

390 Lorraine Cook White, *Barbour Collection of Connecticut Town Vital Records: Franklin 1786–1850, Glastonbury 1690–1854*, vol. 13, (Baltimore: GPC, 1999). Digital images at *Ancestry.com*

391 Now part of the Barbour Index and interfiled with similar slips from other towns in CSL and on FHL films 2,887 *et seq*. See Introduction above, pp. 3–5.

392 Lucius B. Barbour, *Connecticut Vital Records: Franklin, 1786–1850*, (Hartford: CSL,1919) page after title page (FHL film 2,970), Digital images at *AmericanAncestors.org* and *FamilySearch.org*.

- "1" refers to "Franklin Book of Marriages, Births & Deaths, 1760–1848," CSA (CSL 974.62 ff 85v).
- "2" refers to Franklin Births, Marriages, Deaths, 1786–1964 (contains records arranged chronologically and also by family group) (FHL film 1,311,444).

CHURCH RECORDS:

- Congregational Church's "Church Records, 1718–1934" (includes baptisms, marriages, and deaths) (photocopy at CSL) (FHL film 4206);
- Pautipaug Hill Congregational Church, "Death Records, 1763–1802" (photocopy at CSL) (FHL film 1,008,707);
- Hanover Congregational Church of Sprague's, "Church Records, 1761–1915" (includes marriages, baptisms, some births, and deaths) (originals at CSL) (FHL film 5,821);
- SMD in the State of Connecticut's *Records of the Congregational Church, Franklin, Connecticut, 1718–1860: and a Record of Deaths in Norwich Eighth Society, 1763, 1778, 1782, 1784–1802* (Hartford: SMD in Connecticut and the Society of the Founders of Norwich, Connecticut, 1938) (FHL film 908,841);
- DAR's Genealogical Collection, (Norwich: records of Second Congregational Church; records of the Second Church (West Farms) now Franklin, 1718–1852) (bound typescript) DAR, Washington, D.C. (FHL film 844,459).

CEMETERY INSCRIPTIONS: The Hale Collection identifies people in order of physical proximity buried at five named sites in what was then Franklin Township.[393] Compare with Daniel Hearn's 1982 copy of 252 pre-1800 gravestones in two Franklin cemeteries.[394] The Hale Collection identifies people in order of physical proximity buried at five named sites in what was then Sprague Township.[395] Compare with Daniel Hearn's 1982 copy of 68 pre-1800 gravestones in two Sprague cemeteries.[396]

See also, Lucius B. Barbour's "Genealogical Data from Connecticut cemeteries: Sprague, Connecticut. Headstone records from the Old and New Cemeteries, Hanover, Lovett Cemetery, near Versailles" (see also Lisbon) (1932 typescript at NEHGS);

OTHER NOTEWORTHY SOURCES:

- Lucius B. Barbour's "Genealogical notes compiled from church records of West Farms and Second Society of Norwich, Franklin, Conn. 1724–1860," 2 volumes. Abstract of vital records. Arranged alphabetically. (manuscript 18 in Box 3) CSL Record Group 074.36, Hartford;
- Lucius B. Barbour's "Genealogical notes compiled from records of the church in Hanover, the Eighth Society of Norwich, organized 1768, incorp. 1761, Sprague, Conn., 1768–1832," 1 vol. Abstract of vital records. Arranged alphabetically. (manuscript 53 in Box 7) CSL Record Group 074.36, Hartford.;
- "Joseph B. Ayer's School Records., CSL, see Appendix A.

---

393 Charles R. Hale, "Headstone Inscriptions of the Town of Franklin, Connecticut," bound typescript, 1930s, CSL, Hartford, FHL film 3,334.

394 Daniel Hearn, "Connecticut gravestones, early to 1800," manuscript (FHL film 1,477,476, item 54).

395 Charles R. Hale, "Headstone Inscriptions of the Town of Sprague, Connecticut," bound typescript, 1930s, CSL, Hartford, FHL film 3,363.

396 Daniel Hearn, "Connecticut gravestones, early to 1800," manuscript (FHL film 1,477,477, item 50).

GLASTONBURY

Barbour's typescript volume for Glastonbury,[397] unlike the GPC edition,[398] begins:

> This volume contains a list alphabetically arranged of all the vital records of the town of Glastonbury from its incorporation to about 1854. The entire record for this town prior to 1854 is found in three volumes.
>
> The genealogical notes on the Miller family by Elbert H.T. Miller, of Scottsville, N.Y., which are entered on pages 231-360 of volume 2, have not been included in this alphabetical list. These notes have been copied and indexed in a volume, now in the Connecticut State Library.
>
> This list was taken a set of cards[399] based on a copy of the Glastonbury Vital Records made in 1916 by James N. Arnold, of Providence, R.I. The Arnold Copy, now in the possession of the Connecticut State Library, has not been compared with the original and doubtless errors exist. It is hoped that as errors or omissions are found notes will be entered in this volume and on the cards which are included in the General Index of Connecticut Vital Records also in the possession of the Connecticut State Library.
>
> Hartford, Conn., November, 1927.[400]

VITAL RECORDS: The Glastonbury volume includes vital records as early as 1680 and as late as 1854. Barbour abstracted three Glastonbury "books" from the town clerk's Births, Marriages, Deaths, vol. 1–5, 1680–1887, (FHL film 1316154, items 2–6):

- "1" refers to Glastonbury's Births, Deaths and Marriages 1704–1773 vol. 1 (FHL film 1,316,154, item 2);
- "2" refers to Glastonbury's Births, Deaths and Marriages 1770–1866 vol. 2 (FHL film 1,316,154, item 3);
- "3" refers to is Glastonbury's Births, Deaths and Marriages 1820–1856 vol. 3 (FHL film 1,316,154, item 4).

The town clerk's office includes these vital records not abstracted by Barbour:

- **Glastonbury Births, Deaths and Marriages 1820–1856 vol. 4 (FHL film 1,316,154, item 5);**
- **Glastonbury, Land Records, vols. 1–3 1690–1737 ("Volume 2 includes some records of births, marriages and deaths") Town Hall, Glastonbury, (FHL film 4,377).**

---

397 See How to Use This Book, note 4, above.

398 White, *Barbour Collection: Franklin–Glastonbury*, vol. 13, digital images at *Ancestry.com*.

399 Now part of the Barbour Index and interfiled with similar slips from other towns in CSL and on FHL films 2,887 *et seq*. See Introduction above, pp. 3–5.

400 Lucius B. Barbour, *Connecticut Vital Records; Glastonbury, 1690–1854*, (Hartford: CSL, 1927) page after title page (FHL film 2,970), Digital images at *AmericanAncestors.org.and FamilySearch,org.*

CHURCH RECORDS:

- South Glastonbury Methodist Episcopal Church's "Church Records, 1831–1905" (includes baptisms (1831–1842, 1869–1879), marriages (1873–1884) (originals at BUSTL) (FHL film 1,508,864);
- Congregational Church of South Glastonbury's, "Church records, 1836–1950" (includes 1837–1854, deaths 1851– 1853) (originals at CSL) (FHL film 5,816);
- Buckingham Congregational Church's "Church Records, 1731–1899" (includes marriages 1760–1819 & 1769–1858) (originals at CSL) (FHL films 1,008,708 & 4,394);
- First Congregational Church's "Church Records, 1731–1924" (includes baptisms 1797–1858, marriages 1797–1868, and deaths 1807–1868) (originals at CSL) (FHL film 4,393);
- East Glastonbury Methodist Church's "Church Records, 1795–1911" (includes South Glastonbury 1837–1839, East Glastonbury 1839, Wausuck 1838) (originals at CSL) (FHL film 4,395);
- St. Luke's Church in South Glastonbury's "Church Records, 1806–1921" (includes baptisms 1831–1857, marriages 1831–1855, and burials 1831–1855) (originals at CSL) (FHL film 4,396);
- Baptisms (1831–57), marriages (1831–55) & burials (1831–55) at St. Luke's Church, Episcopal Diocese, Hartford (ED Film 4,396);
- Mary K. Talcott's "Records of the Church in Eastbury, Conn.," *NEHGR*, 60:376–83 (Oct 1906) 61:84–91, 190–7, 293–9, 387–93 (Jan–Oct 1907) 62:83–91, 192–7, 295–300, 375–81 (Jan–Oct 1908) 67–73 (Jan 1909).

CEMETERY INSCRIPTIONS: The Hale Collection identifies people in order of physical proximity buried at 13 or 14 named sites in Glastonbury Township.[401] Compare with Daniel Hearn's 1978 copy of 487 pre-1800 gravestones in five Glastonbury cemeteries.[402] See also,

- Lucius B. Barbour's "Inscriptions from Gravestones at Glastonbury, Conn.," *NEHGR*, 85:57–69, 159–75, 305–21, 401–17 (Jan–Oct 1931) 86:46–69, 157–74, 314–24 (Jan–Jul 1932);
- John Spaulding's "Eastbury Cemetery, Glastonbury, Hartford County, Dewey & Barbour, "Inscriptions From Gravestones in Glastonbury" (copy at NEHGS);
- Lucius B. Barbour's Cemetery inscriptions copied from Wethersfield, Old Saybrook, Newington, Rocky Hill, and Glastonbury cemeteries, (1721–1903) 1 vol. (manuscript 158 in Box 23) CSL Record Group 074.36, Hartford;
- Louis M. Dewey's "Inscriptions from Old Cemeteries in Connecticut," *NEHGR*, 60:370–3 (Oct 1906).

OTHER NOTEWORTHY SOURCES:

- "Letters of Gideon Hale, Jr., 1798–1816," CSL; See Appendix A;

---

401 Charles R. Hale, "Headstone Inscriptions of the Town of Glastonbury, Connecticut," bound typescript, 1930s, CSL, Hartford, FHL film 3,334). Hale names these Green, St. James, Old Church, Still Hill, St. Augustine, Wassau, Nipsic, Eastbury, Buckingham, Tom & John Hill, Graveyard, Single Grave (Elijah Miller), & Hollister.

402 Daniel Hearn, "Connecticut gravestones, early to 1800," manuscript (FHL film 1,477,476, item 55).

- Lucius B. Barbour's Genealogical notes complied from church records of Glastonbury, Conn., 1770–1848. I volume. Abstract of vital records. (manuscript 13 in Box 2) CSL Record Group 074.36, Hartford;
- Sherman W. Adams' *History of Ancient Wethersfield, Connecticut: Comprising the Present Towns of Wethersfield, Rocky Hill, and Newington: and of Glastonbury prior to its Incorporation in 1693, from Date of Earliest Settlement Until the Present Time* (New York: Grafton Press, 1904);
- Lucius B. Barbour's Glastonbury, Conn., Marriages 1772–1799; 1 volume (manuscript 132 in Box 23) CSL Record Group 074.36, Hartford;
- Lucius B. Barbour's Genealogical notes compiled from East Hartford and Glastonbury probate records, 1800–1830. 1 volume. Abstract of record. (manuscript 75 in Box 7) CSL Record Group 074.36, Hartford;
- "Miscellaneous Records of East Glastonbury, Connecticut" (typescript at NYGBS) (FHL film 5,468 or 1,405,497).

GOSHEN

Barbour's typescript volume for Goshen,[403] unlike the GPC edition,[404] begins:

> The vital records of Goshen prior to 1854, is found in Volumes 1 and 2 of the Vital Records and a "Book of Marriages". town of Glastonbury from its incorporation to about 1854. The entire record for this town prior to 1854 is found in three volumes.
>
> This alphabetical list was taken a set of cards[405] based on a manuscript copy of the Goshen Vital Records made in 1915 by James N. Arnold, of Providence, R.I. Reference to the entries found in the "Book of Marriages" is indicated by the abbreviation "M".
>
> In "A History of the Town of Goshen, Connecticut", published in 1897 by Rev. A.G. Hibbard, A,M., there are many vital records of Goshen, and although the Arnold Copy has not been checked in its entirety with this printed record, a few marked differences have been noted herein.
>
> The Arnold Copy, now in the possession of the Connecticut State Library, has not been compared with the original and doubtless errors exist. It is hoped that as errors or omissions are found notes will be entered in this volume and on the cards which are included in the General Index of Connec-

---

403 See How to Use This Book, note 4, above.

404 Christina Bailey and Lorraine Cook White, *Barbour Collection of Connecticut Town Vital Records: Goshen 1739–1854, Granby 1786–1850, Greenwich 1640–1848*, vol. 14, (Baltimore: GPC, 1999). Digital image at *Ancestry.com*.

405 Now part of the Barbour Index and interfiled with similar slips from other towns in CSL and on FHL films 2887 *et seq*. See Introduction above, pp. 3–5.

```
ticut Vital Records also in the possession of the
Connecticut State Library.
                Hartford, Conn., January, 1927.[406]
```

VITAL RECORDS: The Goshen volume includes vital records as early as 1715 and as late as 1854. None of the three "books" of Goshen vital records which Barbour abstracted appear to have been microfilmed by the FHL:

- "1" refers to Goshen Town Records, vol. 1 (1716 to 1829) which remains shelved and unfilmed at the Goshen Town Clerk's office.
- "2" refers to is a Book of Births and Deaths 1805 to 1831 which remains shelved and unfilmed at the Goshen Town Clerk's office.
- "M" refers to a Book of Marriages 1820 to 1854 which remains shelved and unfilmed at the Goshen Town Clerk's office.
- "Marked differences" are based upon Rev. A.G. Hibbard's *1897 A History of the Town of Goshen, Connecticut* (Hartford Case, Lockwood & Brainard, 1897) (FHL film 908,331), but Barbour does not note where he has taken Hibbard's word over that of the town clerk.

Figure 18: Photograph by Goshen Town Clerk and Registrar of Vital Statistics

CHURCH RECORDS:

- First Church of Christ's Congregational Church records, 1791–1855 (includes deaths 1812–1851, births 1834–1835, marriages 1811–1854, and baptisms 1810–1851) (typescript and originals at CSL) (FHL film 4,427);
- North Congregational Church's Records 1828–1850) (CSL 974.62 G6942 cn rc).
- West Goshen Methodist Church's Records 1832–1910 (originals at CSL) (FHL film 1,008,709, items 7–9 or 4,428, item 1).

---

406 Lucius B. Barbour, *Connecticut Vital Records: Goshen, 1739–1854*, (Hartford, CSL, page after title page. (FHL film 2,970), Digital images at *AmericanAncestors.org* and *FamilySearch.org.*

- North Goshen Methodist Episcopal Church's Records, 1840–1940) (FHL film 4,428, items 2–3).
- Lawrence P. Hall's *Glimpses of Goshen: Old Churches, Burying Grounds* ([S.l., s.n.], c1978) (FHL film 1,033,653);

CEMETERY INSCRIPTIONS: The Hale Collection identifies people in order of physical proximity buried at 12 or 13 named sites in Goshen Township.[407] Compare with Daniel Hearn's 1978 copy of 58 pre-1800 gravestones in four Goshen cemeteries.[408] See also,

- Mary E. Brooks and Harry W. Flieg's *God's Acre: Old Middle Street Burying-Ground 1745–1905 in Goshen, Connecticut* (S.l.: privately printed, 199-?);
- Mabel Ingalls, "Inscriptions in the East Street Burying Ground, Goshen, Conn., Sept. 11, 1893" (1741 manuscript) (FHL film 1,003,287).

OTHER NOTEWORTHY SOURCES:

- Family Register of Lydia Smith. 1761–1855, CSL; see Appendix A;
- Family register by Lydia Smith, 1756–1871, (An alphabetical surname arranged listing of births, marriages, and deaths of the Moses Smith family of Goshen, Connecticut taken from a family register created and drawn by his wife, Lydia Brown Smith in February 1821). CSL digital collection online;
- Lucius B. Barbour's Southington, Burlington, Goshen, New Hartford, Conn. marriages. 1732–1850, 1 volume. (manuscript 138 in Box 23) CSL Record Group 074.36, Hartford;
- "A genealogical record of Benjamin Oviatt: who emigrated from Goshen, Litchfield County, Connecticut to Hudson, Summit County, Ohio in 1901 and his descendants," CSL digital collection online;
- Goshen Family History," *NEHGR*, 39:79 (Jan 1885).

GRANBY

Barbour's typescript volume for Granby,[409] unlike the GPC edition,[410] begins:

> This volume contains a list alphabetically arranged of all the vital records of the town of Granby from its incorporation to about 1850. The entire record for this town prior to 1850 is found in Volumes 1 and 2 of Town Meetings and Volume 1 of Births, Marriages and Deaths. Reference to entries in the Town Meetings is indicated by the abbreviation "TM" and the volume number

407 Charles R. Hale, "Headstone Inscriptions of the Town of Goshen, Connecticut," bound typescript, 1930s, CSL, Hartford, FHL film 3,334). Hale names these Center, West Goshen, West Side, Esat Street, Private (3 different locations), Beach, Old, Middle Street, & Hall Meadow.

408 Daniel Hearn, "Connecticut gravestones, early to 1800," manuscript (FHL film 1,477,476, item 56).

409 See How to Use This Book, note 4, above.

410 Bailey and White, *Barbour Collection: Goshen–Greenwich*, vol. 14. Digital images at *Ancestry.com*.

> This list was taken a set of cards[411] based on a copy of the Granby Vital Records made in 1927 by Percy Hulbert, of Hockanum, Conn. The Hulbert Copy, now in the possession of the Connecticut State Library, has not been compared with the original and doubtless errors exist. It is hoped that as errors or omissions are found notes will be entered in this volume and on the cards which are included in the General Index of Connecticut Vital Records also in the possession of the Connecticut State Library.
>
> Hartford, Conn., December, 1927.[412]

VITAL RECORDS: The Granby volume includes vital records as early as 1642 and as late as 1850. The three "books" abstracted by Barbour are:

- "TM1" and "TM2" refer to Granby's Town meetings, volumes 1 and 2, 1786–1853 (Vol. 1 includes an index to births, marriages, and deaths; Vol. 1 also includes records of marriages 1820–1822, and family registers of birth, marriage, and death, 1758–1816. Vol. 2 includes a few death records of the Weed family, 1812–1829) Granby Town Hall (FHL film 1,317,454, items 1–2).
- "1" refers to Granby's Vital statistics, 1829–1855 (contains records of marriages 1829–1854; and reports of births, deaths, and marriages in the town of Granby 1848–1851) Granby Town Hall (FHL film 1,317,454. item 3).

The Barbour Index also abstracts Mrs. A. C. Green's mortality list 1874–1887."See Appendix A. See also,

- **Mark Williams and Carol Laun's *Granby Town Records, 1786–1853* (Granby: Salmon Brook Historical Society, c1986) (FHL film 1,597,896, item 12);**
- **Albert Carlos Bates' *Sundry Vital Records of and Pertaining to the Present Town of East Granby, Connecticut, 1737–1886* (Hartford: s.n., 1947) (FHL film 908,340) (images at *AmericanAncestore.org*).**

CHURCH RECORDS:

- Albert Carlos Bates' *Records of the Congregational Church in Turkey Hills, now the town of East Granby, Connecticut, 1776–1858,* (Hartford, CT: Albert Carlos Bates, 1907);
- First Congregational Church's "Church Records, 1739–1919" (includes baptisms 1836–1858, marriages and deaths 1839–1844, baptisms 1794–1871, and marriages 1843–1849) (originals at CSL) (FHL film 4,413);
- West Granby Methodist Church's "Church Records, 1844–1939" (includes baptisms 1849–1891) (manuscript in CSL) (FHL film 4,414, items 2–4);
- First Universalist Church's Records 1832–1912 (copies at CSL) (FHL film 4,412);
- St. Andrews Church, Records 1743–1936 (originals at CSL) (FHL film 3,751

---

[411] Now part of the Barbour Index and interfiled with similar slips from other towns in CSL and on FHL films 2,887 *et seq*. See Introduction above, pp. 3–5.

[412] Lucius B. Barbour, *Connecticut Vital Records: Granby, 1786–1850*, (Hartford, CSL, 1927) page after title page (FHL film 2,970), Digital images at *AmericanAncestors.org* and *FamilySearch.org*.

- Albert C. Bates, Ransom Warner, and Roger Viets' *Records of Rev. Ransom Warner, 1823–1854, Rector of St. Andrew's Simsbury and Bloomfield, St. Peter's Granby, St. John's East Windsor, Connecticut: also Additional Records, 1777–1778, of Rev. Roger Viets, Rector of St. Andrews, Simsbury* (Hartford: [s.n.], 1923) (FHL fiche 6,005,264);
- Turkey Hills Society's "Church Records, 1766–1842" (includes brief notations of baptisms and deaths) (originals at CSL) (FHL film 1,008,341);
- "Church Records. Turkey Hills, Connecticut, 1776–1860" (Includes births, baptisms, marriages, deaths) (typescript in Pittsfield MA) (FHL film 234,579);
- "Turkey Hills, Conn., Church Records, 1776–1858" (includes records of births, baptisms, marriages, and deaths) (manuscript at NYGBS) (FHL film 5,837 or 1,419,455);
- Albert Carlos Bates' *Records of the Second School Society in Granby, now the town of East Granby, Connecticut, 1796–1855* (Hartford: self, nd);
- "Church Records, North Granby, Connecticut, 1794–1843" (includes baptisms, marriages and deaths) (typescript in Pittsfield, MA) (FHL film 234,579, item 5);
- Rollin H. Cooke's North Granby, Connecticut, church records (Baptisms, 1794–1844; Marriages, 1794–1845; Deaths, 1797–1843) Manuscript digitally imaged at *FamilySearch,org*;
- Documents Relating to St. Andrew's Church, Simsbury (Now in Bloomfield) and St. Ann's Church, Granby, Conn., 1744–1785, Photostats at CSL, (FHL film 1,007,925 item 7).

CEMETERY INSCRIPTIONS: The Hale Collection identifies people in order of physical proximity buried at 12 named sites in what was then Granby Township.[413] Compare with Daniel Hearn's 1975 copy of 331 pre-1800 gravestones in two Granby cemeteries.[414] The Hale Collection identifies people in order of physical proximity buried at about seven named sites in what was then East Granby Township.[415] Compare with Daniel Hearn's 1978 copy of 112 pre-1800 gravestones in one East Granby cemeteries.[416]

- Carol Laun's *Beneath These Stones: More Granby, Connecticut Cemeteries: Fourteen Granby Cemeteries, Two East Granby Cemeteries, Granby Vital Records, Private Journals* (Granby: Salmon Brook Historical Society, 2003);
- West Granby Burial Ground Records; 1810–1906 originals at CSL (FHL film 4,414);
- "Granby, Connecticut, West Granby Burying Ground Records, 1810–1908: Two Diagrams; List of Names, With Date, Cause of Death, Age, and Number of Lot" (manuscript in CSL) (FHL film 4,414, item 1);
- Carol A. Laun's *Burials in the Granby Center Cemetery, Granby, Connecticut, 1740–1997* (S.i.: Granby Cemetery, c1998) (FHL film 1,425,144);

---

413 Charles R. Hale, "Headstone Inscriptions of the Town of Granby, Connecticut," bound typescript, 1930s, CSL, Hartford, FHL film 3335. Hale names these Granby Street, West Granby, Baptist, Lee, Merriman, Old Town Farm, Cossett, Day, Holcomb, Cooley, Osborn, & Pratt.

414 Daniel Hearn, "Connecticut gravestones, early to 1800," manuscript (FHL film 1,477,476, item 57).

415 Charles R. Hale, "Headstone Inscriptions of the Town of East Granby, Connecticut," bound typescript, 1930s, CSL, Hartford (FHL film 3,331). Hale names these Esat Granby, Elmwood, Copper Hill, Holcomb, Small Pox, Veits, & Prisoners.

416 Daniel Hearn, "Connecticut gravestones, early to 1800," manuscript (FHL film 1,477,476, item 41).

- Lucius B. Barbour's "East Granby, Conn. Epitaphs" (Mss A 6042), RSASC, NEGHS);
- Lucius B. Barbour's "Granby, **Connecticut** Epitaphs" (Mss A 6119), RSASCs, NEHGS);
- George S. Godard's "Granby (Conn.) Cemetery Inscriptions," *NEHGR*, 70:91–2 (1916).

OTHER NOTEWORTHY SOURCES:

- "Francis Case Account book, 1799–1845," CSL; see Appendix A;
- "Account book, 1821–1828, of Thompson & Dibble," CSL; see Appendix A;
- "Oren Lee Diary 1809–1841," CSL; see Appendix A;
- "Bate's Turkey Hill, 1852–3," CSL; see Appendix A;
- Lucius B. Barbour's Genealogical notes complied from Turkey Hills church records, East Granby, Conn., 1643–1848. I volume. Abstract of vital records. (manuscript 15 in Box 2) CSL Record Group 074.36, Hartford;
- Mary Jane Springman and Betty Finnell Guinan's East Granby Historical Committee *East Granby, the Evolution of a Connecticut town* (Canaan, NH: Phoenix Pub., c1983)
- Noah A. Phelps' *History of Simsbury, Granby and Canton: From 1642 to 1845* (Hartford: Case, Tiffany and Burnham, 1845);
- Elmer I. Shepard's "Elmer I. Shepard Collection: Vermont, Connecticut, and miscellaneous United States marriages and intentions, ca. 1760–1880," (original abstracted Hartford & Granby records at Berkshire Anthenaeum, Pittsfield MA).(FHL film 1,684,454).

GREENWICH

Barbour's typescript volume for Greenwich,[417] unlike the GPC edition,[418] begins:

> The vital records of Greenwich, prior to 1848, are found scattered through the first volume of Land Records, a "Book of Early Records, 1640-1754", the "Common Place Book, 1671-1754" and volume 1 of Vital Records.
>
> In this alphabetical list, which was taken from a set of cards[419] based on a manuscript copy made in 1915 by James N. Arnold, of Providence, R.I., reference to the Land Record volume is indicated by the abbreviation "LR", to the Book of Early Records by "ER" and to the Common Place Book by "CP".
>
> The Arnold Copy, now in the possession of the Connecticut State Library, has not been compared with the original and doubtless errors exist. It is hoped that as errors or omissions are found notes will be entered in this volume and on the cards which are included in the General Index of

417 See How to Use This Book, note 4, above.

418 Bailey and White, *Barbour Collection: Goshen–Greenwich*, vol. 14. Digital images at *Ancestry.com*.

419 Now part of the Barbour Index and interfiled with similar slips from other towns in CSL and on FHL films 2,887 *et seq*. See Introduction above, pp. 3–5.

```
Connecticut Vital Records also in the possession
of the Connecticut State Library.
               Hartford, Conn., February, 1926.
```
[420]

VITAL RECORDS: The Greenwich volume includes vital records as early as 1677 and as late as 1848. Barbour abstracted four Greenwich "books:":

- "1" refers to Greenwich's Town Records, 1700–1848 (includes births, marriages, deaths, approximately 1700–1848) Greenwich Town Hall, (FHL film 185,372, items 1–2);
- "LR1" refers to Greenwich's Land Records, vols. 1–2 1640–1724 (Volume 1 includes births, marriages and deaths found at the end of the volume). Greenwich Town Hall, (FHL film 4,313);
- "ER" refers to an unfilmed "Book of Early Records" 1640 to 1765 in the Greenwich Town Hall (virtually duplicates "1" and/or "LR1.");[421]"
- "CP:" is an unfilmed "Common Place Book" 1671 to 1759 in the Greenwich Town Hall.[422]

Barbour did not abstract:

- **Greenwich's Births, marriages, deaths vol. 1–2 (p.1–191) 1847–1892, Greenwich Town Hall, (FHL film 1,434,365);**
- **Greenwich's "Town Records copy 1640–1705," (CS974.62 fG85).[423]**

See also,

- **Harlan R. Jessup's "Vital Records for Greenwich, CT, 1847–1852," and "Births, Greenwich, CT," CA, 55: #2 (Nov. 2012);**
- **Harlan R. Jessup's "Marriages and Deaths for Greenwich, CT, 1847–1852"** ***CA*****, 55: #3 (Feb 2013);**
- **Abstract of Records and Tombstones of the Town of Greenwich, County of Fairfield and State of Connecticut. Mss 895. RSASCs, NEHGS, Boston, MA online database at** ***AmericanAncestors.org*****).**

CHURCH RECORDS:

- First Congregational Church at Old Greenwich's "Church Records, 1785–1936" (includes baptisms 1810–1853) (photocopy at CSL) (FHL film 4,327, items 1–2);

---

420 Lucius B. Barbour,: *Connecticut Vital Records: Greenwich, 1640–1848*,(Hartford: CSL, 1926) page after title page (FHL film 2,970), Digital images at *AmericanAncestors.org.* and *FamilySearch,org.*

421 Called "Proprietors Records 1674" in CSL's *First 200 Years,*

422 Called "Town Records 1671–1754" in CSL's *First 200 Years,*

423 This book's Introduction refers to the Book of Early Records and the Common Place Book: "These records were kept on Foolscap paper stitched together into small books of from ten to twenty or thirty sheets. These books were in the process of time tied together by the stitching threads without apparent reference either to the subjects or chronology of the records & the larger packages were kept loosely in two or more leather covers. No numbers evidently were used for paging the books and no titles appear on the records excepting such as belong to a much later date. One of the books leather covers in which the remains of these records have been kept has on it the letters B & F, but evidently the earlier lettering has been effaced. The other of these covers which now remains has, in a recent hand, the title 'Common place book from 1671 to 1754 with some other writings,' Within both of these covers which are --- --- --- of loose leaves which show no token of their original position." CSL's *CT Vital Records*.

- Church of England's "Church Records, 1742–1746" (includes baptisms & marriages for Norwalk, Ridgefield, Stamford, Greenwich 1742–1746) (originals at CSL) (FHL film 5,815, item 2);
- First Congregational Church's Records 1720–1887 (includes baptisms 1721–1855, deaths 1762–1855 and marriages 1720–1857) originals at CSL (FHL film 4,374 or 1,008,714);
- Abstract of Church Records of the Town of Greenwich, County of Fairfield, and State of Connecticut to 1850 (Mss A 6120. RSASCs, NEHGS, Boston) (online database at *AmericanAncestors.org*);
- Christ Church's "Church Records, 1833–1947" (includes baptisms, marriages, & funerals) (originals at CSL) (FHL film 1,008,712);
- Emanuel Church at Glenville's, "Church Records, 1847–1916" (includes baptisms, marriages, & burials) (originals at CSL) (FHL film 1,008,713);
- Jonathan Murdock's "List of Persons Married by Me, Jonth. Murdock, Since June 8, 1774, the Day in Which I was Installed Pastor of the Church in West Greenwich" (transcribed from Dr. George S. Hobbie's papers) (FHL film 165,998);
- Platt Buffett's "Stanwich Congregational Church Records 1796–1835" (includes baptisms 1796–1833 and marriages 1796–1834) (original at CSL) (FHL film 4,327, item 3);
- Baptisms (1835–87), marriages (1834–87) & burials (1834–87) at Christ Church, Episcopal Diocese, Hartford (ED Film 1,008,712);
- Baptisms (1847–71), marriages (1847) & burials (1847–48) at Emmanuel Church at Glenville, Episcopal Diocese, Hartford (ED Film 1,008,713);
- Spencer P. Mead's "Abstract of Church Records of the Town of Greenwich, County of Fairfield, and State of Connecticut to 1850" (1913 manuscript at NEHGS);
- Abstract of Church Records of the Town of Greenwich, County of Fairfield, and State of Connecticut to 1850. Mss A 6120. RSASCs, NEHGS, Boston.

CEMETERY INSCRIPTIONS: The Hale Collection identifies people in order of physical proximity buried at 62 to 66 cemeteries in Greenwich Township.[424] Compare with Daniel Hearn's 1977 copy of 54 pre–1800 graves in seven Greenwich cemeteries.[425] See also,

- Francis F. Spies' "Connecticut Epitaphs" (4 vols: East Lyme, CT, Waterford, Sound Beach (Potomac Ave, 1st Congregational Church yard, near Adams Corners), Stamford, Noroton in Darien Township; Mianus (Lyon Farm, Bonnell farm), CosCob (old yard, N CosCob), Montville (Uneasville and Chesterfield); Chesterfield (near church, Martenus Farm, by Congregational meeting house, on Warren farm, & Great

---

[424] Charles R. Hale, "Headstone Inscriptions of the Town of Greenwich, Connecticut," bound typescript, 1930s, CSL, Hartford, FHL film 3,335. Hale names these Bonnell, Lyon (3 different locations), Church, Mead (5 different locations), Old (5 different locations), Ferris, June, Close, Putnam, Catholic, Town, Calvary Church, Methodist Church, Knapp, Burying Hill, North Greenwich Congregational Church, Peck (3 different locations), Brown, Old Baptist, Merritt (2 different locations), Anderson, Baptist, Strong, Green, Howe, Radford, Mills, Reynolds (2 different locations), Selleck, Studwell, Union, Davis, 2nd Congregational, Lewis, Old Catholic, Episcopal Church, Ingersoll, Johns, Hitchcock, Old Cos Cob, Timpany, Morrell, Fraser, Kitch, 1 Stone, Pelmer, Adams, & First Congregational Church.

[425] Daniel Hearn, "Connecticut gravestones, early to 1800," manuscript (FHL film 1,477,476, item 58).

Hill Burial Ground), and Yonkers, NY, New Canaan, CT, East Port Chester, CT; Greenwich, CT (Chichahominy); Port Chester, NY, and Rye, NY (manuscript at NEHGS);

- Francis F. Spies' Greenwich Epitaphs: Inscriptions From Gravestones Arranged With Genealogical Notes and a List of Revolutionary Soldiers (1930/1997 copy at NEHGS);
- DAR's Genealogical collection (Greenwich: unmarked graves, 1936 and inscriptions from 52 cemeteries including family plots) (FHL film 844,453);
- DAR's Genealogical Collection (Greenwich: inscriptions copied from graveyards arranged with many genealogical notes and a record of Revolutionary service) (bound typescript) DAR, Washington, D.C. (FHL film 844,454);
- DAR's Genealogical Collection (Greenwich: abstract of records and tombstones) (bound typescript) DAR, Washington, D.C. (FHL film 845,617).

OTHER NOTEWORTHY SOURCES:

- "Greenwich, Conn. marriages, 1785–1791, by Dr. Amos Mead, Justice of Peace," CSL; see Appendix A;
- Daniel M. Mead's *History of the Town of Greenwich, Fairfield County, Conn.: With Many Important Statistics* (New York: Baker & Godwin, 1857).

GRISWOLD

Barbour's typescript volume for Griswold,[426] unlike the GPC edition,[427] begins:

> This volume contains a list alphabetically arranged of all the vital records of the town of Griswold from its incorporation to about 1848. This list was taken a set of cards[428] based on a copy of the Griswold Vital Records made in 1909 by James N. Arnold, of Providence, R.I. The entire record for this town prior to 1848 is found in one volume. The Arnold Copy, now in the possession of the Connecticut State Library, has not been compared with the original and doubtless errors exist. It is hoped that as errors or omissions are found notes will be entered in this volume and on the cards which are included in the General Index of Connecticut Vital Records also in the possession of the Connecticut State Library.
>
> Hartford, Conn., May, 1919.[429]

VITAL RECORDS: The Griswold volume includes vital records as early as 1737 and as late as 1877. Barbour abstracted Griswold's Records of births, marriages, deaths

426 See How to Use This Book, note 4, above..

427 Jerri Lynn Burket, *Barbour Collection of Connecticut Town Vital Records: Griswold 1815–1848, Groton 1704–1853,* vol. 15, (Baltimore: GPC, 1999). Digital image at Ancestry.com.

428 Now part of the Barbour Index and interfiled with similar slips from other towns in CSL and on FHL films 2,887 *et seq*. See Introduction above, pp. 3–5.

429 Lucius B. Barbour, *Connecticut Vital Records Griswold, 1815–1848*, (Hartford, CSL, 1919) page after title page (FHL film 2,970). Digital images at *AmericanAncestors.org* and *FamilySearch.org.*

1737– 1884, Griswold Town Hall (FHL film 1,311,196 Item 5). **Item 6 of this microfilm includes a volume of 1847–1852 vital records by school district not abstracted by Barbour.**

CHURCH RECORDS:

- First Congregational Church's "Church Records, 1720–1887" (includes baptisms 1721–1855, deaths 1762–1855 and marriages 1720–1857) (photocopies and originals at CSL) (FHL film 4,374 or 1,008,714);
- Second Congregational Church at Jewett City's, "Church Records, 1825–1928" (includes baptisms 1825–1861, marriages 1832–1857 and deaths 1832–1861) (photocopies and originals at CSL) (FHL film 4,376 or 1,008,895);
- Methodist Episcopal Church at Jewett City's Records 1844–1930, originals at CSL (FHL film 4,375);
- St. George's Church at Jewett City's Records 1813–1824, originals at CSL (FHL film 1,008,895).

CEMETERY INSCRIPTIONS: The Hale Collection identifies people in order of physical proximity buried at 28 to 30 named sites in Griswold Township.[430] Compare with Daniel Hearn's 1978 copy of 115 pre-1800 gravestones in five Griswold cemeteries.[431]

OTHER NOTEWORTHY SOURCES: Lucius B. Barbour's Genealogical notes complied from church records of Griswold, Conn., 1720–1809. I vol. Church established as Preston Second Society. Abstract of vital records. (manuscript 20 in Box 3) CSL Record Group 074.36, Hartford.

GROTON

Barbour's typescript volume for Groton,[432] unlike the GPC edition,[433] begins:

> This volume contains a list alphabetically arranged of all the vital records of the town of Groton from its incorporation to about 1853. This list was taken a set of cards[434] based on a copy of the Groton Vital Records made in 1912 by James N. Arnold, of Providence, R.I.
>
> The first volume, or the earliest records have been copied in the last part of the Book of Marriages started about 1820, and as the original is not paged the page references in this list are to the copy and the combined volume called "Volume 1". The references

---

430 Charles R. Hale, "Headstone Inscriptions of the Town of Griswold, Connecticut," bound typescript, 1930s CSL, Hartford, FHL film 3336. Hale names these 28: Rixtown, Pachaug, Brown, Geer, Cook, Spy Rock, Kinne, Hopeville, Leonard, Walton, Hatch, Spencer, Jewett City (Lower), High Banks, Phillips, Green, Jewett City Baptist, Clark Saunders, Davis, Billings, Wilcox, St. Thomas, Tadpole, Indian, Hartshorn, Dawley, Reynolds, & Tiffany.

431 Daniel Hearn, "Connecticut gravestones, early to 1800," manuscript (FHL film 1,477,476, item 59).

432 See How to Use This Book, note 4, above.

433 Burket, *Barbour Collection: Griswold–Groton*, vol. 15. Digital images at *Ancestry.com*.

434 Now part of the Barbour Index and interfiled with similar slips from other towns in CSL and on FHL films 2,887 *et seq*. See Introduction above, pp. 3–5.

> to Volume "II" (Roman letters) indicate that the original entries were on loose sheets of Paper and are in the Arnold Copy, the basis of this arrangement.
>
> The Arnold Copy, now in the possession of the Connecticut State Library, has not been compared with original and doubtless errors exist. It is hoped that as errors or omissions are found notes will be entered in this volume and on the cards which form the basis of the General Index of Connecticut Vital Records also in the possession of the Connecticut State Library.
>
> Hartford, Conn., August, 1918.[435]

VITAL RECORDS: The Groton volume includes vital records as early as 1686 and as late as 1868. Barbour abstracted five Groton "books:"

- "1" abstracts Groton's Births, marriages, deaths, vol. 1(p.1–78), 1686–1875, Groton Town Hall, FHL film 1,306,248, item 8 and Births, marriages, deaths, vol. 1 (p.78–end), 1686–1867, (FHL film 1,306,249, item 1);
- "2" abstracts Groton's Births, marriages, deaths, (vol. 2), 1730–1829, Groton Town Hall, (FHL film 1,306,248, item 7);
- "3" abstracts Groton's Births, marriages, deaths, vol. 3, 1802–1860, Groton Town Hall, (FHL film 1,306,249, between items 1 and 2;
- "II" abstracts some loose pages from the town clerk's office not in Groton's vital records index[436] or filmed by FHL;
- "LR2" abstracts Williams family births presumably on an unfilmed flyleaf of Land Records, vol. 2, 1723–1731, viewable at the Groton Town Hall.[437]

Groton vital records not abstracted by Barbour include:

- **Groton's Births, marriages, deaths, vol. 3, 1768–1872, Groton Town Hall, (FHL film 1,306,249, item 2);**
- **Groton's Births, marriages, deaths, vol. 4, 1848–1875, Groton Town Hall, (FHL film 1,306,249, item 3 in FHL catalog but item 2 on film);**
- **Groton's Records of births, marriages, deaths, and earmarks, Groton Town Hall, 1686–1749. (FHL film 1,306,248, item 6);**
- **Groton's Land Records, vol. 1A–1B, 1705–1723 (family records with births and marriages in vol. 1A through 2), Groton Town Hall, (FHL film 4,293–4).**
- **Groton's Birth records, 1825–1904, Groton Town Hall, (FHL film 1,306,244).**

CHURCH RECORDS:

- Groton Congregational Church's original record books1727–1893 at CSL, See Finding Aid at *https://ctstatelibrary.org/RG070_082.html* (include baptisms, marriages, deaths)
- Noank Baptist Church's "Church Records, 1843–1892" (includes deaths & baptisms) (originals at CSL) (FHL film 4,306);

---

435 Lucius B. Barbour, *Connecticut Vital Records: Groton, 1704–1853*, (Hartford: CSL, 1918) page after title page (FHL film 2,971). Digital images at *AmericanAncestors.org* and *FamilySearch.org*.

436 Groton Town Clerk, Indexes to births, marriages, deaths vol. 1–4, Groton Town Hall, 1686–1875, FHL film 1,306,249, item 4.

437 These births are not included in the recent GPC edition. Nor are a couple of additional records about Mary Williams (citing a will), which are inserted by hand in Barbour's volume.

- First Baptist Church at Old Mystic's, "Church Records, 1754–1899" (includes deaths and baptisms) (originals at CSL) (FHL film 4,305 or 1,008,895);
- Mrs. J.L. Raymond's "Congregational Church Records, 1723–1841" (typescript at CSL) (FHL film 4,307);
- Union Baptist Church of Mystic's, "Church Records, 1765–1910" (contains baptisms and deaths) (originals at CSL) (FHL film 1,008,896);
- Mariners Free Church's Records 1828–1858, originals at CSL (FHL film 1,008,895, item 5).

CEMETERY INSCRIPTIONS: The Hale Collection identifies people in order of physical proximity buried at about 37 named sites in Groton Township.[438] Compare with Daniel Hearn's 1980 copy of 225 pre-1800 gravestones in six Groton cemeteries.[439] See also,

- Anne and Susan B. Meech's "Cemetery Inscriptions From Groton, Preston and Stonington, Connecticut" (typescript) (FHL film 4,291);
- Charles R. Hale and Mary H. Babin's *Headstone Inscriptions, Town of Groton, New London County, Connecticut* (Hartford: December 8, 1932);
- Benjamin F. Rathbun's "Noank Cemetery Burials" (1986–1987 manuscript at FHL);
- Frances Manwaring Caulkins and Emily S Gilman, *The Stone Records of Groton* (Norwich: Free Academy Press, c1903) (FHL film 1,697,9250;
- "Cemetery inscriptions from Small Cemeteries in Ledyard, CT" (Mss A 4376), RSASC, NEHGS;
- "Inscriptions, Crary Cemetery, Groton, Conn." (Mss C 3056), RSASC, NEHGS;
- DAR's Genealogical Collection, (Mystic: cemetery inscriptions) (bound typescript) DAR, Washington, D.C. (FHL film 844,455).

OTHER NOTEWORTHY SOURCES:

- Carl C. Cutler's *Mystic: the story of a small New England seaport* [S.i.: Marine Historical Association, 1945)
- Claude M. Chester's *Noank* (Essex: Pequot Press, c1970).
- Lucius B. Barbour's Genealogical notes complied from church records of Groton, Conn., 1727–1811. I vol. First Society. Abstract of vital records. (manuscript 21 in Box 3) CSL Record Group 074.36, Hartford.

GUILFORD

Barbour's typescript volume for Guilford,[440] unlike the GPC edition[441]) begins:

```
            The vital records of Guilford prior to
        1850 are found in two volumes. The entries
```

438 Charles R. Hale, "Headstone Inscriptions of the Town of Groton, Connecticut" (bound typescript, CSL, Hartford, FHL film 3,336. Hale names these Col. Ledyard, Starr, Wood, 2 Graves, Perkins, Knowles, Burrows #1, Turner, Wightman, Smith Lake, Morgan Avery, Burrows #3, Wells, Fish, Niles, St. Patrick's Burrows #2, Packer, Fishtown, old Town House, Crary, Noank Valley, Fish #2, Binks, Park #1, Park #2, Old, Cushman, Palmer, Packer #2, Adams, Crouch, Mitchell, Baley, Smith, Edgecomb, & Bill.

439 Daniel Hearn, "Connecticut gravestones, early to 1800," manuscript (FHL film 1,477,476, item 60).

440 See How to Use This Book, note 4, above.

441 Wilma J. Standifer Moore, *Barbour Collection of Connecticut Town Vital Records: Guilford 1639–1850*, vol. 16, (Baltimore: GPC, 1999). Digital images at *Ancestry.com*.

> from the volume known as "Volume A" were made from a copy of the original.
>
> This alphabetical list was taken from a set of cards[442] based on a copy of the Guilford Vital Records made in 1914 by James N. Arnold, of Providence, R.I. The Arnold Copy, now in the possession of the Connecticut State Library, has not been compared with original and doubtless errors exist. It is hoped that as errors or omissions are found notes will be entered in this volume and on the cards which form the basis of the General Index of Connecticut Vital Records also in the possession of the Connecticut State Library.
>
> Hartford, Conn., June, 1924.[443]

VITAL RECORDS: The Guilford volume includes vital records as early as 1640 and as late s 1849. Barbour abstracted two books from Guilford's Births, Marriages, Deaths 1639–1905, vols. A, 1–2½ 1645–1880, Guilford Town Hall, FHL film 1,428,110:

- "A" refers to Guilford's Vol. A, (FHL film 1,428,110, item 2);
- "2" refers to some **but not all** vital records in Guilford's vol. 2, FHL film 1,428,110, item 4).[444]

The other items on this film but not in the Barbour Index are:

- **Guilford's vol. 1 (with records starting in 1696 not abstracted by Barbour) is FHL film 1,428,110, item 3.[445]**
- **Guilford's vol. 2 ½ (with records starting in 1841 not abstracted by Barbour) is FHL 1,428,110, item 5);**
- **Guilford Vital Records, Volume 3, beginning in 1771 (see loose page filmed at the first page of vol. 2, FHL 1,428,110, item 4) is unfilmed beyond that loose page. Its records, indexed but undated as part of the clerk's item 1, are not in the Barbour Collection, but remain in the Guilford Town Hall.[446]**

See also,

- **East Guilford Private Records slips not interfiled in Barbour Index. See Appendix B;**
- **Record of Mortality, Guilford, 1646–1843 (originals in NHCHS) (FHL film 3,025).**

---

442 Now part of the Barbour Index and interfiled with similar slips from other towns in CSL and on FHL films 2,887 *et seq*. See Introduction above, pp. 3–5.

443 Lucius B. Barbour, *Connecticut Vital Records: Guilford, 1639–1850*, (Hartford: CSL, 1924) page after title page (FHL film 2,971) Digital image at *AmericanAncestors.org* and *FamilySearch.org*.

444 According to the clerk's index, this is not "vol. III, beginning in 1771 as written on the first (loose) page filmed, but volume 2, beginning much earlier. The loose page that is microfilmed as the first page of volume 1 (Item 3) is actually the first page of this vol. 2 (Item 4). See Guilford Town Clerk, Index to Births Marriages, Deaths 1639–1905, vols. A, 1–2 1/2 1645–1880, Guilford Town Hall, (FHL film 1,428,110, item 1).

445 On this film, this volume loose first page identifies the book "Vol. 3," but the town clerk indexes its records as vol. 1. See Guilford Town Clerk, Index to Births, Marriages, Deaths 1639–1905, vols. A, 1–2 1/2 1645–1880, Guilford Town Hall (FHL film 1,428,110). See notes 115 and 116 above.

446 The town clerk had "19 volumes of vital records" in 1936. *Biennial Report (1936),* 31.

- **Donald Lines Jacobus' "Guilford (Conn.) Vital Records,"** ***TAG*****, vols. 15–19 (1938–1942);**
- **Lucius Barnes Barbour and Alvin Bates Palmer's "Record of deaths in Guilford, 1883–1890, kept by Alvan Bates Palmer," (typescript transcription of original records at NEHGS, 1945) (images online at** ***AmericanAncestors.org*****.);**
- **Herbert H. Olding Jr.'s "Old Guilford Marriages," from vol. 1 of the Guilford Vital Records.** ***CN*****, Vol. 8, No. 3, pp. 347–354.**

CHURCH RECORDS:

- First Ecclesiastical Society and Congregational Church's "Church Records, 1717–1921" (baptisms 1800–1835; 1844–1918 & 1843–1920), marriages 1806–1842 & 1844–1869; deaths 1806–1843; and bill of mortality 1843–1858) (originals at CSL) (FHL film 4,370);
- Second Congregational Church at North Guilford's "Church Records, 1720–1859" (includes baptisms (1748–1763, 1748–1764 & 1766–1845), marriages (1748–1764, 1748–1764 & 1767–1820), and deaths (1748–1764, 1724–1827, 1842–1843, 1748–1764 & 1767–1844)) (originals at CSL) (FHL film 4,367);
- Christ Episcopal Church's "Church Records, 1744–1909" (includes baptisms 1807–1909, marriages 1808–1909, and burials 1807–1909) (photocopy at CSL) (FHL film 4,368);
- Christ Church's "Rector's records, 1807–1882" (includes baptisms, burials and marriages) (FHL film 1,008,899);
- Mrs. Henry E. Fowler's "Records of the Fourth Church in Guilford, Conn., 1743–1788," *NEHGR*, 58;299–305, 360–4 (Jul Oct 1904) 59:61–7 (Jan 1905);
- St. John's Church at North Guilford's "Church Records, 1749–1868" (contains baptisms 1749–1860, marriages 1755–1861, and deaths 1751–1860) (originals at CSL) (FHL film 4,366);
- St. Matthew's Episcopal Church's Baptist Church and Guilford Episcopal Church, "Miscellaneous Church Records" (includes Guilford Episcopal Church baptisms 1744–1775) (typescript in NHCHS) (FHL film 3,054);
- Baptisms (1732–1, 1807–1909, 1808–1909, 1807–1834, & 1840–67), marriages (1808–1909, 1808–34, 1834–45, 1845–89), & burials (1807–1909, 1807–35, 1835–41, & 1842–63) at Christ Church (ED Films 4,368 & 1,008,899);
- Baptisms (1749–1869), marriages (1755–1861) & burials (1751–1860) at St. John's Church in North Guilford (ED Film 4,366);
- Guilford Episcopal Church (Guilford, Connecticut)'s *Miscellaneous church records* (contains Ralph D. Smyth manuscript, Guilford Episcopal Church, baptisms 1744–1775, church meetings) FHL film 3,054, item 4.

CEMETERY INSCRIPTIONS: The Hale Collection identifies people in order of physical proximity buried at about 27 named sites in Guilford Township.[447] Compare with Daniel Hearn's 1978 copy of 119 pre-1800 gravestones in four Guilford cemeteries.[448]

---

[447] Charles R. Hale, "Headstone Inscriptions of the Town of Guilford, Connecticut" (bound manuscript at CSL) (FHL film 3,336–7). Hale names these Alderbrook, West Side, St. John's North Guilford, Leete's Island, Nut Plains, Moose Hill, Private (6 different locations), Clapboard Hill, Murray, Foote, Bluff, Green, Frisbie, & Episcopal Church.

See also,

- Glenn E. Griswold's *Connecticut Inscriptions, New Haven County, Guilford, North* Guilford (Sarasota FL: Aceto Bookmen, 1993);
- DAR's Genealogical Collection, (Guilford: inscriptions from gravestones, up to and including the year 1855 Hampton: 58 inscriptions taken from headstones in Grow Cemetery Hartford, West Hartford, East Hartford, and Manchester: annotated list of soldiers of the American Revolution buried in the cemeteries of ancient Hartford Killingly: cemeteries vol. 1–2 Ledyard: cemeteries and burials, including deceased veterans of all wars Manchester: inscriptions from East Cemetery) (manuscript) DAR, Washington DC(FHL film 844,455);
- Lucius B. Barbour's *Genealogical Data From Guilford Cemeteries* (1932/1997 copy at NEHGS).

OTHER NOTEWORTHY SOURCES:

- "Letters by Thomas Burgess, 1709–1868; CSL; see Appendix A;
- "Thomas Fitch's Book, 1815–1874;" CSL, See Appendix A;
- "Guilford Deaths, 1735–1783," CSL, See Appendix A;
- DAR Oneida Chapter's "Volume 6, Bible, Cemetery and Church Records, 1746–1927" (includes births, 1746–1810, undated marriages, Guilford, Ct.) (1928–1929 typescript at Utica Public Library) (FHL film 1,435,718);
- Edwin E. Atwater, *et al.'s History of the Colony of New Haven, With Supplementary History and Personnel of the Towns of Branford, Guilford* (1902/1993 copy at NEHGS);
- Lucius B. Barbour's "Record Of Deaths In Guilford, 1883–1890, Kept By Alvan Bates Palmer" (ca. 1945 manuscript at NEHGS) (digital images online);
- Ralph D. Smith's *History of Guilford, Connecticut: From Its First Settlement in 1639* (Albany, NY: J. Munsell, Printer, 1877);
- Edward R. Lambert's *History of the Colony of New Haven: Before and After the Union with Connecticut: Containing a Particular Description of the Towns Which Composed that Government, viz., New Haven, Milford, Guilford, Branford, Stamford, & Southold, L.I* " (New Haven: Hitchcock & Stafford, 1838).

HADDAM

Barbour's typescript volume for Haddam,[449] unlike the GPC edition,[450] begins:

> The vital records of Haddam prior to 1852 are found in the first nine and the twelfth volumes of Land Records and the first volume of vital records. In this alphabetical list reference to entries found in the Land Records is indicated by the abbreviation "LR"

---

448 Daniel Hearn, "Connecticut gravestones, early to 1800," manuscript (FHL film 1,477,476, item 61).

449 See How to Use This Book, note 4, above.

450 Jan Tilton, *Barbour Collection of Connecticut Town Vital Records: Haddam 1668–1852, Hamden 1786–1854, Hampton 1786–1851*, vol. 17, (Baltimore: GPC, 1999). Digital images at *Ancestry.com*.

> before the volume number. There is no pagination in the third volume of Land Records.
>
> This list was taken from a set of cards[451] based on a copy of the Haddam Vital Records made in 1913 by James N. Arnold, of Providence, R.I. The Arnold Copy, now in the possession of the Connecticut State Library, has not been compared with original and doubtless errors exist. It is hoped that as errors or omissions are found notes will be entered in this volume and on the cards which are included in the General Index of Connecticut Vital Records also in the possession of the Connecticut State Library.
>
> Hartford, Conn., December, 1923.[452]

VITAL RECORDS: The Haddam volume includes vital records as early as 1662 and as late as 1854. Barbour abstracted ten Haddam "books," nine of which are from "LR" records are from Haddam's Land Records, 1668–1857, Haddam Town Hall, (FHL film 4,464 to 4,479, *viz*:

- "LR1" refers to Land Records, vol. 1 (1673–1744), (FHL films 4,464);
- "LR2" refers to Land Records, vol. 2 (1704–1730) (FHL film 4,464);
- "LR3" through "LR4" refer to Land Records, vols. 3–4, 1728–1759 (FHL film 4,465);
- "LR5" through "LR6" refer to Land Records, vol. 5–6 1746–1762 (FHL film 4,466);
- "LR7" through "LR9" refer to Land Records, vol. 7–9 1762–1790 (FHL film 4,467);
- "LR12" through "LR13" refer to Land Records, vol. 12–13 1793–1810 (FHL film 4,469).
- "1" refers to Haddam's Births, Marriages, Deaths (1662–1854) Haddam Town Hall, (FHL film 1,398,664).

See also,

- **Haddam's Births, Marriages, Deaths: "Second Book"1848–1884 (includes records by school district as well as an alphabetization of earlier vital records taken from Books 1 to 12 of the land records), Haddam Town Hall, (FHL film 1,398,664, item 2);**
- **David Hoffman's Marriage Records of Dec. Ezra Brainerd, Justice of Peace, Transcribed from a File at the Haddam Town Clerk's Office, database at *Rootsweb.org.***

CHURCH RECORDS:

- Congregational Church of Higganum's, "Church Records, 1844–1893" (includes baptisms 1844–1892, marriages 1844–1892, and deaths 1844–1892) (originals at CSL) (FHL film 4,619);

---

451 Now part of the Barbour Index and interfiled with similar slips from other towns in CSL and on FHL films 2,887 *et seq*. See Introduction above, pp. 3–5.

452 Lucius B. Barbour, *Connecticut Vital Records: Haddam, 1668–1852,*(Hartford: CSL, 1923) page after title page (FHL film 2,971). Digital images at *AmericanAncestors.org* and *FamilySearch.org.*

- "Marriage Records of the Congregational Church's Middle Haddam, Connecticut, 1740–1824" (originals at CSL) (FHL film 4,786);
- First Congregational Church's "Church Records, 1739–1908" (includes baptisms 1756–1798, & 1804–1869, deaths 1756–1798 & 1804–1872; and marriages 1756–1799 & 1804–1844) (originals at CSL) (FHL film 4,480, items 1–7);
- Methodist Episcopal Church of Middle Haddam's "Church Records, 1810–1887" (includes baptisms 1844, 1847 & 1877; marriages (1847 & 1880–1886), and deaths 1846–1847 & 1887)) (originals in BUSTL) (FHL film 1,508,864);
- "Congregational Church Records, Middle Haddam, Connecticut, 1740–1800: From H. M. Shelden, Bridgehampton, L. I., To Mrs. Annie A. Hopkins" (typescript in Pittsfield MA) (FHL film 234,579);
- Frederick L'Hommedieu's "Haddam Congregational Church Records 1756–1799" (includes baptisms 1756–1798, marriages 1756–1799 and deaths 1756–1798.) (photocopy at CSL) (FHL film 4,480, item 8).

CEMETERY INSCRIPTIONS: The Hale Collection identifies people in order of physical proximity buried at 16 named sites Haddam Township.[453] Compare with Daniel Hearn's 1978 copy of 164 pre-1800 gravestones in five Haddam cemeteries.[454] See also,

- Lucius B. Barbour's Haddam, Conn. Epitaphs: All Gravestones Standing In The Town, Copied June – Oct. 1931 (Salem MA: Higginson Book Co., 1997);
- Leesville [cemetery inscriptions.] (manuscript in NYGBS) (FHL film 2798 or 1405496);
- William C. Knowles' *By-Gone Days in Ponset-Haddam, Middlesex Co.* (1914/1994 copy at NEHGS).

OTHER NOTEWORTHY SOURCES:

- "James Brainerd's Account Book," CSL; see Appendix A;
- "Private records of William & John Pynchon, 1638–1696" CSL; see Appendix A;

HAMDEN

Barbour's typescript volume for Hamden,[455] unlike the GPC edition,[456] begins:

> This volume contains a list alphabetically arranged of all the vital records of the town of Hamden from its incorporation to about 1854. The entire record for this town prior to 1854 is found in one volume.
>
> This list was taken from a set of cards[457] based on a copy of the Hamden Vital Records made

[453] Charles R. Hale, "Headstone Inscriptions of Haddam, Connecticut" (bound typescript, CSL, Hartford (FHL film 3,337). Hale names these Haddam New, Haddam Old, Tylerville, Turkey Hill, Beaver Meadow, Burr District, New Rock Landing, Higganum, Old Rock Landing, Old Ponsett, Emmons, Little City, Daniel Dickinson, & Clark.

[454] Daniel Hearn, "Connecticut gravestones, early to 1800," manuscript (FHL film 1,477,476, item 63).

[455] See How to Use This Book, note 4, above.

[456] Tilton, *Barbour Collection: Haddam–Hampton*, vol. 17. Digital images at *Ancestry.com*.

```
in 1914 by Miss Ethel L. Scofield, of New Haven,
and Miss Irene H. Mix, of Hartford, Conn. This
copy, now in the possession of the Connecticut
State Library, has not been compared with the
original and doubtless errors exist. It is hoped
that as errors or omissions are found notes will
be entered in this volume and on the cards which
are included in the General Index of Connecticut
Vital Records also in the possession of the Conn-
ecticut State Library.
                Hartford, Conn., January, 1925.[458]
```

VITAL RECORDS: The Hamden volume includes vital records as early as 1736 and as late as 1854. The volume Barbour abstracted is Hamden's "First Town Meeting Book: births deaths, marriages v.1, 1786 –1834," unfilmed by FHL at the town hall.[459] FHL catalogs no vital records or town records filmed at Hamden before 1867 that can verify Barbour's abstraction, not even the marriage certificate whose collection was required in 1822 or school district reports each town began in 1847 to 1849.[460]

CHURCH RECORDS:

- Grace Church's "Church Records, 1790–1927" (includes baptisms 1821–1850 & 1821–1926, marriages 1834–1850 & 1834–1927, and burials 1835–1850 & 1835–1927) (originals at CSL) (FHL film 4,616);
- "New Cambridge Church Records, 1747–1800 (New Haven County, Conn.)" (inscriptions of burial ground in northwest corner of Hamden) (handwritten records at NYGHS) (FHL film 4,948 or 1,405,497).
- George Sherwood Dickerman's "Hamden Church Records" (including baptisms (1764–1812, 1791– 1795 & 1795–1824), marriages 1783–1810, deaths 1784–1827 & 1773–1811, and vital records of Hamden, Conn., 1736–1836*)* (typescript in NHCHS) (FHL film 3,054, item 3);
- Whitneyville Congregational Church's "Church Records, 1795–1915" (includes baptisms 1791, 1792–1795 & 1795–1895) (originals at CSL) (FHL film 4,617);
- Baptisms 1766–1812; Marriages 1783–1810; and Deaths 1784–1829) (typescript in NHCHS) (FHL film 3,054, item 3 [sic]);
- Baptisms (1821–50,1821–1926), marriages (1834–50 & 1834–1927) at Grace Church (ED Film 4,616);

---

457 Now part of the Barbour Index and interfiled with similar slips from other towns in CSL and on FHL films 2,887 *et seq*. See Introduction above, pp. 3–5.

458 Lucius B. Barbour, *Connecticut Vital Records: Hamden, 1786–1854*, (Hartford: CSL, 1925) page after title page (FHL film 2,971). Digital images at *AmericanAncestors.org* and *FamilySearch.org*.

459 In 1975 the Hamden Town clerk reported possession of a 272 page volume of Town Records 1786–1854. CSL, *First 200 Years*. See also, CSL's *CT Vital Records*.

460 See CHS, "Laws Related to Births, Marriages, and Deaths from 1649–1854," *Vital Records of Bolton to 1854 and Vernon to 1852* (Hartford: CHS, 1909) pp. ix–xvii.

CEMETERY INSCRIPTIONS: The Hale Collection identifies people in order of physical proximity buried at nine named sites in Hamden Township.[461] Compare with Daniel Hearn's 1977 copy of 94 pre-1800 gravestones in four Hamden cemeteries.[462]
See also,

- George Sherwood Dickerman's *Historical Materials Relating to the Old Mount Carmel Parish of New Haven, Now the Northern Part of Hamden, Conn.*(includes old gravestones) (Ann Arbor, MI: University Microfilms, 1967);
- Alice H. Benton's "Cemetery at Centreville, Conn." (typescript) (FHL film 165,997);
- Mrs. F.H. Benton's "Mt. Carmel Cemetery, Carmel, Conn.: Between Cheshire & New Haven" (typescript) (FHL film 165,997);
- "Gravestone Inscriptions in the Cemetery at Centerville in the Town of Hamden, Conn." (Mss A 2821), RSASC, NEHGS online database.

OTHER NOTEWORTHY SOURCES: See state and county resources above, pages 18–21.

HAMPTON

Barbour's typescript volume for Hampton,[463] unlike the GPC edition,[464] begins:

> The vital records of Hampton prior to 1851 are found in three volumes. In March 1849 Jonathan Clark compiled, in semi-alphabetical form and unpaged, a list of freemen from 1786 to October 1849. This list has been indexed and included with the vital records herein with the date of admission abbreviated "adm.fr." Admission as freemen or electors usually occurred soon after the twenty-first birthday.
>
> This volume contains a list alphabetically arranged of all the Vital Records of the town to about 1851. This list was taken from a set of cards[465] based on a copy of the Hampton Vital Records made in 1913 by James N. Arnold, of Providence, R.I. The Arnold Copy, now in the possession of the Connecticut State Library, has not been compared with original and doubtless errors exist. It is hoped that as errors or omissions are found notes will be entered in this volume and on the cards which form the basis of the General Index of Connec-

---

461 Charles R. Hale, "Headstone Inscriptions of the Town of Hamden, Connecticut" (bound typescript, CSL, Hartford, FHL film 3337. Hale names these State Street, Whittneyville, Hamden Plains, Centerville, St. Mary's St. Carmel, Jewish (2 different locations).

462 Daniel Hearn, "Connecticut gravestones, early to 1800," manuscript (FHL film 1,477,476, item 64).

463 See How to Use This Book, note 4, above.

464 Tilton, *Barbour Collection: Haddam–Hampton*, vol. 17. Digital images at *Ancestry.com*.

465 Now part of the Barbour Index and interfiled with similar slips from other towns in CSL and on FHL films 2,887 *et seq*. See Introduction above, pp. 3–5.

```
ticut Vital Records also in the possession of
the Connecticut State Library.
                Hartford, Conn., December, 1920.[466]
```

VITAL RECORDS: The Hampton volume includes vital records as early as 1736 and as late as 1852. Barbour abstracted three volumes in addition to the "TM" volume[467] from which he abstracted only unpaginated information on admitted freemen:

- "1" refers to Hampton's Town records, vol. A–B, 1786–1856, Hampton Town Hall, FHL film 1,450,841, item 1;
- "2" refers to Hampton's Land Records, vol. A–B, 1786–1794 (Volume A at the Town Hall includes births, marriages and deaths) Hampton Town Hall, (FHL film 4,432);
- "3" refers to Hampton's Records of Births, Marriages, and Deaths, 1838–1901 Hampton Town Hall, FHL film 1,450,841, item 3.

See also,

- **Two volumes the town clerk calls "Windham Family Records 1692–1859;"[468]**
- **Hampton vital records, circa 1845–1905, CSL (CSA RG 070.002, Box 8) (does not include any pre-1850 vital reports by school district).**

CHURCH RECORDS:

- First Congregational Church, "Church Records, 1723–1879" (includes baptisms 1723–1824, deaths 1731–1733, marriages 1734–1789, and deaths 1824–1839) (originals at CSL) (FHL film 4,438 or 1,008,901, items 7–10);
- Hampton Baptist Church's Church records, 1770–1853, originals at CSL (FHL film 1,007,891, items 1–6).
- Baptist Church, Church records, 1770–1853, originals at CSL (FHL film 4,439);

CEMETERY INSCRIPTIONS: The Hale Collection identifies people in order of physical proximity buried at six named sites in Hampton Township.[469] Compare with Daniel Hearn's 1979 copy of 188 pre-1800 gravestones in two Hampton cemeteries.[470]
See also,

- Lucius B. Barbour's "Hampton, Connecticut, Cemetery Inscriptions" (originals in CSL) (FHL film 1,029,520);
- DAR's Genealogical Collection, (Hampton: 58 inscriptions taken from headstones in Grow Cemetery) (manuscript) DAR, Washington DC (FHL film 844,455) .

OTHER NOTEWORTHY SOURCES: Lucius B. Barbour's Genealogical notes complied from church records of Canada Parish and Windham Second Society, Hampton, Conn., 1723–1824. I vol., abstract of vital records. (manuscript 22 in Box 3) CSL Record Group 074.36, Hartford.

---

466 Lucius B. Barbour, *Connecticut Vital Records: Hampton, 1786–1851*, (Hartford: CSL, 1920) page after title page (FHL film 2,971). Digital image at *AmericanAncestors.org* and *FamilySearch.org.*

467 Hampton Town Clerk, Town records, vol. A–B, 1786–1856, Town Hall, Hampton (FHL film 1,450,841, item 2;

468 *Biennial Report (*1936), 32.

469 Charles R. Hale, "Headstone Inscriptions of the Town of Hampton, Connecticut" (bound typescript, CSL, Hartford (FHL film 3,337). Hale names these Hammond or North, South, Litchfield, Grow, Litchfield Incorporated, & Calvin-Burnham.

470 Daniel Hearn, "Connecticut gravestones, early to 1800," manuscript (FHL film 1,477,476, item 65).

HARTFORD

Barbour's typescript volumes for Hartford,[471] unlike the GPC edition,[472] begins:

> This volume contains a list alphabetically arranged of all the vital records of the town of Hartford from its incorporation to about 1855. The entire record for this town prior to 1854 is found scattered through the Book of Distributions and early Land Records. Only scattering items between 1700 and 1786 are extant. That known as Volume 1 of Vital Records begins about 1786 but contains mostly marriages only.
>
> This list was taken from a set of cards[473] based on the Vital Records found in the "Original Distribution of the Lands in Hartford Among the Settlers, 1639", printed in 1912 by the Connecticut Historical Society, a book published in 1898 by E. Stanley Welles entitled "Births Marriages and Deaths-----entered in Volume 1 and 2 of Land Records and No. D. of Colonial Deeds", a copy of the Vital Records found in the Land Records and made by Mr. Frank Farnsworth Starr, of Middletown, Conn., and a photostat copy of Volume 1 of Vital Records, all of which are now in the Connecticut State Library. Reference to entries in the Book of Distributions is indicated by the abbreviation "D" and the originnal pagination; reference to Mr. Welles' book is indicated by the abbreviation "Col." and the folio number; reference to Mr. Starr's copy is indicated by the abbreviation "FFS" and the pagination of Mr. Starr's manuscript. Pages 1 to 39 of this manuscript duplicate entries from the Book of Distributions; pages 39 to 56 are entries found in Vol. 1 of Land Records; pages 56 to 75, entries found in Vol. 2, of Land Records; pages 75 to 83, entries in Vol. 3 of Land Records; pages 83 to 84, entries in Vol. 5, of Land Records; page 84 has one entry found on page 467 of Vol. 11 of Land Records; pages 84 to 87, entries in Vol. 12 of Land Records; page 86 has entries found on page 430 of Vol. 14 of Land Records; pages 86 to 94, entries in Vol. 30 of Land Records; and pages 94 to 98, entries in Vol. 31 of Land Records.
>
> The cards have not been compared with the original records and doubtless errors exist. It is hoped that as errors or omissions are found notes will be entered in this volume and on the cards which are included in the Gen-

---

471 See How to Use This Book, note 4, above.

472 Wilma J. Standifer Moore, *Barbour Collection of Connecticut Town Vital Records: Hartford 1635–1855*, vol. 19, (Baltimore: GPC, 1999). Digital images at *Ancestry.com*.

473 Now part of the Barbour Index and interfiled with similar slips from other towns in CSL and on FHL films 2,887 *et seq*. See Introduction above, pp. 3–5.

```
eral Index of Connecticut Vital Records also in the
possession of the Connecticut State Library.
     This book forms the first part and contain the
alphabet A - K inclusive.
                    Hartford, Conn., January, 1929.[474]
```

VITAL RECORDS: Barbour allows Hartford two volumes[475] and includes vital records as early as 1638 and as late as 1855. Barbour abstracted four Hartford "books:"

- "1" refers to Hartford's Records of Births, Marriages, and Deaths, 1797–1868, (photostat beginning with the year 1666 at CSL)[476] original at Hartford Municipal Building, (FHL film 1,313,828, item 1);
- "D" refers to Albert C. Bates' *Original Distribution of the Lands in Hartford among Settlers, 1639* (A copy, with explanatory notes, of the earliest volume of land records of Hartford. (early records of births, marriages, deaths at pp. 575–625) (CHS, Hartford 1912) (FHL film 897,073, item 1).[477] Previously published in *NEHGR*, volumes 12–13 (1858–59) and corrected in 1912. Almost all of the "D" entries are also supplied by "FFS." CSL has Nathaniel Goodwin's transcription of the records on its microfilm 1559 (FHL film 4,510);
- "FFS" copies vital records in the Hartford land records 1643 through 1848. This manuscript by Mr. Frank Farnsworth Starr of Middletown" is in CSA (CSL 974.62 q H25vi), and not filmed by FHL;
- "Col. 2" refers to Edwin Stanley Welles' *Births, Marriages and Deaths Returned from Hartford, Windsor and Fairfield and Entered in the Early Land Records of the Colony*
- *of Connecticut: Volumes I and II of Land records and No. D of Colonial Deeds* (Hartford: Case, Lockwood & Brainard, 1898) (FHL film 823,816 or 847,591) (images at *AmericanAncestors.org*). Almost all of the "Col.2" records are also recorded in "D" and "FFS."

FHL also catalogs under Hartford vital records:

- **Hartford's Records of Births, Marriages, and Deaths, 1848–1851, Hartford Municipal Building, FHL film 1,313,828, item 2;**
- **Albert C. Bates' *Hartford, Connecticut Land Records, 1639–1688; and Births, Marriages and Deaths, 1644–1730* (originally published in 1969) CD (Bowie MD: Heritage Books, 1989);**
- **Rollin H. Cooke's "Stanley Collection: Death Records, Hartford, Connecticut 1790–1840" typescript, Pittsfield, MA (FHL film 234,579).**

NEHGS offers additional Hartford vital records sources:

- **Lucius M. Boltwood's "Births, Marriages, and Deaths," *NEHGR*, 12:173–6, 196–9, 331–6 (Apr– Oct 1858) 13:48–54, 141–9, 239–45, 343–6 (Jan–Oct 1859), 20:234–73 (Jul 1866) 22:192–6 (Apr 1868), 23:42–7 (Jan 1869);**

---

474 Lucius B. Barbour, *Connecticut Vital Records: Hartford, 1635–1855*, (Hartford: CSL, 1925) page after title page (FHL film 2,971). Digital image at *AmericanAncestors.org* and *FamilySearch.org*

475 *Ibid*, vols. 52 a & b, (FHL film 2,971;

476 See Robert C. Anderson, *Great Migration Newsletter*, vol. 3, no. 4 (Oct.–Dec. 1992) pp. 28–29.

477 The original sources of virtually all these transcriptions are also available through the FHL: Hartford, Proprietors records 1639–1753 (Proprietors records are referred to as "dist." in general index. Proprietors records and deed book 1 include births, marriages, deaths, and ear markings) Hartford Town Hall, (FHL film 4,510); Deeds vol. 1–3, 1678–1732 (FHL film 4,511); Deeds vol. 4–5 1721–1735 (FHL Film 4,512); Proprietors records 1792–1931 film 4,599.

- **R. R. Hinman's "Hartford, Ct. Births, Baptisms, & Marriages 1644 to 1740," (manuscript at NEHGS);**
- **Lucius Manlius Boltwood's "Hartford, Ct. Records, 1664–1855" (bulk: 1726–1855) (manuscript at NEHGS);**
- **Elizabeth Ellery Dana's "Vital Records Kept By William Watson Of Hartford, Conn., 1819–1834," *NEHGR*, vol. 79:150, 80:54.**

CHURCH RECORDS:

- Congregational Church (West Hartford, Connecticut) Congregational Church of West Hartford's "Church Records, 1713–1933" (includes baptisms 1714–1839 & 1840–1873, marriages 1727–1840 & 1841–1875, intentions of marriages or publishments 1758– 1838, deaths 1757–1840 & 1840–1876) (transcripts and originals at CSL) (FHL film 6,261);
- First Congregational Church and Ecclesiastical Society of East Hartford's "Church Records, 1699–1912" (marriages 1816–1820 and 1830–1831, baptisms 1748–1833 & 1830–1876 and deaths 1833–1911) (originals at CSL) (FHL film 4,130);
- *Hartford, CT: Historical Catalog of the First Church, 1633–1885.* Hartford: Published by the church, 1885 (shelved at NEHGS) (FHL film 1,009615);
- Second Congregational Church's "Church Records, 1792–1862, 1912" (includes baptisms) (manuscript) (FHL film 1,010,149 or 4,574);
- Christ Church's "Church Records, 1795–1927" ((includes baptisms, marriages, burials) (original records at CSL) (FHL film 4,587–8 or 1,008,903);
- Blue Hills Baptist Church's "Church Records, 1810–1899" (includes deaths 1811–1839) (originals at CSL) (FHL film 4,584);
- North and Park Congregational Church's "Church Records, 1823–1926" (includes baptisms 1824–1867) (originals at CSL) (FHL film 4,585);
- First Congregational Church's "Church Records, 1684–1930" (includes baptisms, 1818–1866 and marriages, 1818–1867 and transcribed death, cemetery, marriage and baptismal records, 1685–1811) (FHL films 1,009,610 –14);
- First Independent Universalist Church's Church records, 1824–1923 (FHL film 1,009,609, item 2);
- South Baptist Church's Church records, 1834–1928, originals at CSL (FHL films 4,580–1);
- Society of Friends. West Hartford and Society of Friends. Nine Partners Monthly Meeting's Monthly meeting records (1769–1862) original at the Society of Friends Archives in NYC (FHL film 17,306, item 1);
- St. Paul's Church's Church records, 1850–1879, originals at CSL (FHL film 4,593, items 1–2);
- Central Baptist Church's Papers, 1789–1948, originals at CSL (FHL film 1,008,902, item 4);
- First Methodist Church's "Church Records, 1824–1935" (includes baptisms 1825–1908 & 1824–1935, and marriages & deaths 1824–1935) (FHL films 1,009,616–17);
- Fourth Congregational Church's "Church Records, 1832–1953" (includes baptisms 1832–1907) (originals at CSL) (FHL film 4,576);
- St. John's Church's "Church Records, 1841–1925" (includes baptisms, marriages, and burials) (originals at CSL) (FHL film 4,590);

- Nathaniel Goodwin's Second Church, Hartford, Connecticut" (includes baptisms) (manuscript at CSL) (FHL film 1,010,728, item 4);
- Joseph O. Goodwin's Baptisms and Births from Records of First Congregational Church (East Hartford) and Deaths from Cemeteries (manuscript at CSL) (FHL film 1,008,343);
- West Hartford Congregational Church's Church records {1713–1933) originals and transcripts at CSL (FHL film 6,261);
- West Hartford Society of Friends' Monthly meetings 1800–1823, photocopy at CSL (FHL film 6,266);
- West Hartford First Church of Christ Papers (1882–1937) includes newspaper clippings, obituaries, statistics (FHL film 1,014,194, item 1),
- First Ecclesiastical Society of West Hartford's, Records, 1736–1920, (FHL film 1,014,194, item 3);
- Second Ecclesiastical Society's Records, 1767–1920, Originals at CSL (FHL film 1,010,729 or 4,574, items 3–4);
- Baptisms (1848–77), marriages (1848–77) & burials (1848–77) at Christ Church (ED Film 8,903);
- Baptisms (1842–1918), marriages (1842–1918) & burials (1842–1918) at St. John's Church (ED Film 4,590);
- Baptisms (1851–76), marriages (1850–78) & burials (1851–76) at St. Paul's Church (ED Film 4,593);
- First Baptist Church, Records, 1789–1909, photostats at CSL (FHL film 4,579);
- Old North Church. North Sunday School Assisting Committee's Records, 1826–1830, originals at CSL (FHL film 1,010,149, item 3);
- Rockwell Harmon Potter's *Hartford's First Church* (Hartford: The Church, 1932);
- Church of the Redeemer's Pastor's Register (marriages 1846–1851, burials 1849–1852 (CSL 974.62 H25u p);
- Universalists of Connecticut's Hartford County Assn. Records 1832–1948, originals at CSL (FHL film 1,010,150);
- Society of Friends' Quaker Records, 1800–1823, photocopy at CSL) (FHL 6,266).

CEMETERY INSCRIPTIONS: The Hale Collection identifies people in order of physical proximity buried at 40 named sites *in* what was then Hartford Township.[478] Compare with Daniel Hearn's 1977 copy of 347 pre-1800 gravestones in one Hartford buried at cemetery.[479] The Hale Collection also identifies people in order of physical proximity

---

[478] Charles R. Hale, "Headstone Inscriptions of the Town of Hartford, Connecticut" (bound typescript, CSL, Hartford (FHL film 3,337–40). Hale names these Old Burial Ground, Old South, Old North, Spring Grove, Zion Hill, Mt. Pleasant, Beth Israel, Holy Trinity, St. Patrick's Small Pox, Graveyard, Cedar Hill, Branch #326 (Jewish), Cong. Atereth Israel. Cong. Aqudath, Hartford Peddlers Asso., Hevre Mishnaeth, Brith Sholom, Wladimer Wolinsk B.S., Tikrath Zion Camp, St. Joseph's R.C. Cathedral, St. Patrick's Church, Jesish #610, Workman's Circle #184, Hartford Mutual Soc., H.P.L. !162 I.O.B.S., Lodge, 1913, (Name in Jewish), No name on gate (6 different locations), Hartford Workmen's S.B.S., Hartford City Lodge 202 I.O.B.A., Drepfus Lodge 123 I.O.B.S., Cong. A.D.S. Israel, & Jewish.

[479] Daniel Hearn, "Connecticut gravestones, early to 1800," manuscript (FHL film 1,477,476, item 66).

about two named sites in what was then Newington Township.[480] Compare with Daniel Hearn's 1978 copy of 105 pre-1800 gravestones in one Newington cemetery.[481]The Hale Collection also identifies people in order of physical proximity buried at nine or 10 named sites in what was then West Hartford Township.[482] Compare with Daniel Hearn's 1978 copy of 67 pre-1800 gravestones in two West Hartford cemeteries.[483] See also,

- William DeLoss Love's *Colonial History of Hartford, Gathered From Original Records* (1914/1993 copy at NEHGS);
- William Hosley and Shepherd M. Holcombe's *By Their Markers Ye Shall Know Them: A Chronicle of the History and Restorations of Hartford's Ancient Burying Ground* (Hartford: Ancient Burying Ground Assn., c1994);
- DAR's Genealogical Collection, (Hartford, West Hartford, East Hartford, and Manchester: annotated list of soldiers of the American Revolution buried in the cemeteries of ancient Hartford) (manuscript) DAR, Washington DC(FHL film 844,455);
- DAR's Genealogical Collection, (West Hartford: North Cemetery and Old North Cemetery) (bound typescript) DAR, Washington, D.C. (FHL film 844,457);
- Lucius B. Barbour's Burials at Old North Cemetery, Hartford, Conn., 1821–1908. I vol. Incomplete. (manuscript 156 in Box 24) CSL Record Group 074.36, Hartford.
- Edward A. Cohen and Lewis Goldfarb's *Jewish Cemeteries of Hartford, Connecticut* (Bowie MD: Heritage Books, c1995);
- Lucius B. Barbour's Inscriptions from the Ancient Burying Ground in Hartford, copied by C.J. Hardy, 1877 (manuscript 159 in Box 24) CSL Record Group 074.36, Hartford.

OTHER NOTEWORTHY SOURCES:

- Lucius B. Barbour's Genealogical notes complied from church records of Hartford and West Hartford, Conn., 1670–1821. I vol. Abstract of vital records. (manuscript 23 in Box 3) CSL Record Group 074.36, Hartford;
- Lucius B. Barbour's Genealogical notes complied from Hartford, Conn., probate records, circa 1820. I vol. Church estab. as Preston Second Society. Abstract of vital records. (manuscript 78 in Box 9) CSL Record Group 074.36, Hartford;
- Lucius Barnes Barbour's *Families of Early Hartford, Connecticut* (Baltimore MD: Genealogical Pub. Co., 1977) (FHL film 1,421,857);
- Lucius B. Barbour's Genealogical notes complied vital statistics of Hartford, land records from vols. 2, 3, & 5. 1660–1800. 1 vol. (manuscript 24 in Box 4) CSL Record Group 074.36, Hartford;
- "Talcott Memorandum Book, 1697–1786," CSL, See Appendix A;
- Lucius B. Barbour's Genealogical notes on Hartford Families 2 vols.. Abstract of vital records. (manuscript 1111 in Box 15) CSL Record Group 074.36, Hartford;

---

480 Charles R. Hale, "Headstone Inscriptions of the Town of Newington, Connecticut" (bound typescript, CSL, Hartford, FHL film 3,352. Hale names these: Newington & Church Street.

481 Daniel Hearn, "Connecticut gravestones, early to 1800," manuscript (FHL film 1,477,477, item 13).

482 Charles R. Hale, "Headstone Inscriptions of West Hartford, Connecticut" (bound typescript, CSL, Hartford (FHL film 3,370). Hale names these North, Old North, Fairview, Quaker, French Camp Grounds, 2 stones, Nuns (2 different cemeteries) & Jewish.

483 Daniel Hearn, "Connecticut gravestones, early to 1800," manuscript (FHL film 1,477,477, item 73).

- William H. Hall's *West Harford* (Hartford: West Hartford Chamber of Commerce, c1930) (FHL fiche 6,071,108);
- William Smith Porter and Connecticut Historical Society's *Historical notices of* E. Burleson's "Lamentation in Memory of the Distressing Sickness in Hartford;" see Appendix A;
- DAR (Wisconsin) GRC's *Bible and Cemetery Records, 1800–1940* (original submitted to DAR) (FHL film 848,696);
- Elizabeth E. Dana's "Vital Records Kept by William Watson of Hartford, Conn., 1819–1834," *NEHGR*, 79:158–07 (Apr 1925).

HARTLAND

Barbour's typescript volume for Hartland,[484] unlike the GPC edition,[485] begins:

> This volume contains a list alphabetically arranged of all the vital records of the town of Hartland from its 1782 to about 1846. This list was taken a set of cards[486] based on a copy of the Hartland Vital Records made by Lucius B. Barnes of Hartford, Conn. The entire record for this town prior to 1848 is found in one volume. The Barbour copy, now in the possession of the Connecticut State Library, has not been compared with the original and doubtless errors exist. It is hoped that as errors or omissions are found notes will be entered in this volume and on the cards which are included in the General Index of Connecticut Vital Records also in the possession of the Connecticut State Library.
>
> Hartford, Conn., January, 1925[487]

VITAL RECORDS: The Hartland volume includes vital records as early as 1771 and as late as 1851. Barbour abstracted Hartland's Town Records, (1772–1867) Hartland Town Hall, (FHL film 1,317,069, item 1).

See also,

- **Hartland Vital Records, 1840–1905 (typescript) CSL, Hartford, 1931) (FHL film 3,662, item 5);**
- **Hartland vital records circa 1845 [sic]–1905, CSL (CSA RG 070.002, Box 9) (includes certificates as early as 1840 not abstracted by Barbour).**

---

484 See How to Use This Book, note 4, above.

485 Dorothy Wear, *Barbour Collection of Connecticut Town Vital Records: Hartland 1761–1848, Harwinton 1737–1854, Hebron 1708–1854*, vol. 18, (Baltimore: GPC, 1999). Digital images at *Ancestry.com*.

486 Now part of the Barbour Index and interfiled with similar slips from other towns in CSL and on FHL films 2,887 *et seq*. See Introduction above, pp. 3–5.

487 Lucius B. Barbour, *Connecticut Vital Records: Hartland, 1761–1848*, (Hartford: CSL, 1925) page after title page (FHL film 2,972). Digital images at *AmericanAncestors.org* and *FamilySearch.org*.

CHURCH RECORDS:

- Congregational Church of West Hartland's, "Church Records, 1779–1899" (includes baptisms 1780–1832, marriages 1782–1836, deaths 1782–1890) (originals at CSL) (FHL film 6,264, items 1–2);
- First Congregational Church's Second Congregational Church, and East Hartland Congregational Church's "Church Records, 1768–1899" (includes baptisms, marriages, and deaths) (originals and transcripts at the CSL) (FHL film 1,010,730);
- "Copy of Church Records of West Hartland" (includes marriages, baptisms, and deaths for 1782–1901) (transcript at CSL) (FHL film 6,264, item 3);
- First Ecclesiastical Society and Congregational Church at East Hartland Church records, 1768–1931, originals at CSL (FHL film 4,493);
- Correll H. Tiffany's "Church Records and a List of Hartland Revolutionary Soldiers" (includes records of First Congregational Church at East Hartland, 1731–1896, and Second Congregational Church at West Hartland, 1781–1912) (manuscript at CSL) (FHL film 4,494);
- David N. Gaines' Church records of the East Hartland and West Hartland Congregational Churches 1768–1922, originals at CSL (FHL film 4,495);
- Rollin H. Cooke's "Congregational Church Records, East and West Hartland, Connecticut, 1762–1880" (includes minutes, baptisms, and deaths) (typescript in Pittsfield, MA) (FHL film 234,578) (on microfilm at NEHGS);
- Elmer I. Shepard's "Elmer I. Shepard Collection: Massachusetts and Connecticut Church Records, ca. 1750–1880" (originals at Berkshire Anthenaeum, Pittsfield MA) (FHL film 1,684,455).

CEMETERY TRANSCRIPTIONS: The Hale Collection identifies people in order of physical proximity buried at five named sites in Hartland Township.[488] Compare with Daniel Hearn's 1978 copy of 71 pre-1800 gravestones in two Hartland cemeteries.[489]

OTHER NOTEWORTHY SOURCES: Lester Gaines' "Undertaker Records, 1846–1867," CSL, see Appendix A.

HARWINTON

Barbour's typescript volume for Harwinton[490] unlike the GPC edition[491] begins:

> The vital records of Harwinton, prior to 1854, are found scattered through Volumes 1, 2, 3, 4, 7, and 12 of Land Records and a book of Marriages dated 1819-1854.
>
> This alphabetical list was taken from a set of cards[492] based on a manuscript copy of the

488 Charles R. Hale, "Headstone Inscriptions of the Town of Hartland, Connecticut" (bound manuscript at CSL) (FHL film 3340). Hale names these East Hartland, West Hartland, Hartland Hollow, Tiffany Farm, & Family.

489 Daniel Hearn, "Connecticut gravestones, early to 1800," manuscript (FHL film 1477476, Item 67).

490 See How to Use This Book, note 4, above.

491 Wear, *Barbour Collection: Hartland–Hebron*, vol. 18. Digital images at *Ancestry.com*.

> Harwinton Vital Records made in 1916 by James N. Arnold, of Providence, R.I. Reference to the entries found in the Land Records is indicated by the abbreviation "LR" and the number of the volume, and to the book of Marriages by the abbreviation "M".
>
> The Arnold Copy, now in the possession of the Connecticut State Library, has not been compared with the original and doubtless errors exist. It is hoped that as errors or omissions are found notes will be entered in this volume and on the cards which are included in the General Index of Connecticut Vital Records also in the possession of the Connecticut State Library.
>
> Hartford, Conn., May, 1927.[493]

VITAL RECORDS: The Harwinton volume includes vital records as early as 1729 and as late as 1854. Barbour abstracted seven Harwinton "books:"

- "LR1" and "LR2" refer to Harwinton's Land Records, vol. 1–2, 1738–1777 (births 1725–1785, deaths 1725–1792, marriages 1724–1762) Harwinton Town Hall (photostat at CSL) (FHL film 4,498);
- "LR3" and "LR4" refer to Harwinton's Land Records, vol. 3–4, 1775–1804, Harwinton Town Hall (FHL film 4,499);
- "LR7" refers to Harwinton's Land Records, vol. 7, 1805–1821, Harwinton Town Hall (FHL film 4,501, item 1);
- "LR12" refers to Harwinton's Land Records, vol. 12, 1831–1849, Harwinton Town Hall (FHL film 4,503, item 2);
- "M" refers to Harwinton's Record of Births, Marriages, and Deaths, 1819–1930 (contains marriages 1819–1930 and births and deaths 1850–1930) Harwinton Town Hall, (FHL film 1,521,829, item 2).

See also,

- **Harwinton's "Harwinton Family Records, 1725–1899" (originals in Harwinton Town Hall) (FHL film 4,496, item 1 and film 1,521,829, item 1);**
- **Harwinton's Births, Marriages and Deaths 1850–1930 (originals in Harwinton Town Hall) (FHL film 4,496, item 2);**
- **In 1935 the town clerk reported possession of a book of Vital Records (as well as Land Records) beginning in 1737;[494]**
- **In 1975 the town clerk reported that "some vital statistics were in a book of "Town Meetings, 1787–1804."[495]**

---

492 Now part of the Barbour Index and interfiled with similar slips from other towns in CSL and on FHL films 2,887 *et seq*. See Introduction above, pp. 3–5..

493 Lucius B. Barbour, *Connecticut Vital Records: Harwinton, 1737–1854*, (Hartford: CSL, 1927) page after title page (FHL film 2,972) Digital images at *AmericanAncestors.org* and *FamilySearch.org*.

494 *1936 Biennial Report,* 34.

495 CSL, *First 200 Years,*

CHURCH RECORDS: First Congregational Church's "Church Records, 1791–1861" (includes deaths 1791–1861) (typescript at CSL) (FHL film 4,507);

CEMETERY TRANSCRIPTIONS: The Hale Collection identifies people in order of physical proximity buried at six named sites in Harwinton Township.[496] Compare with Daniel Hearn's 1978 copy of 26 pre-1800 gravestones in one Harwinton cemeteries.[497] See also, Charles A. Page, Frank D. Andrews, and Sharon M. Barber, *Tombstone Inscriptions in the Old Burying Ground at Harwinton, Conn.* (Vineland NJ: C.A. Page, 1913).

OTHER NOTEWORTHY SOURCES:

- Lucius B. Barbour's Genealogical notes complied from records of Harwinton, Conn., 1737–1790, 1 vol. Abstract of vital records. (manuscript 26 in Box 3) CSL Record Group 074.36, Hartford;
- Raymond George Bentley's *History of Harwinton: from the time it was settled through the mid 1960s,* (Winsted: Dowd Printing Company, c1970) (FHL film 1,598,271, item 1);
- R. Manning Chipman's *History of Harwinton, Connecticut* (Hartford: Williams, Wiley & Turner, 1860).

HEBRON

Barbour's typescript volume for Hebron[498] unlike the GPC edition,[499] begins:

> This volume contains a list alphabetically arranged of all the vital records of the town of Hebron from its 1782 to about 1854. This list was taken a set of cards[500] based on a copy of the Hebron Vital Records made in 1921 by Mrs. Anne C. Gilbert, of Hebron, Conn. The entire record for this town prior to 1854, is contained in five volumes. References to the fifth volume are indicated by the letter "M" added to the page numbers, but the volume has been referred to as "Volume 4".
>
> The Gilbert copy, now in the possession of the Connecticut State Library, has been compared with the original this alphabetical list has not and doubtless errors exist. It is hoped that as errors or omissions are found notes will be entered in this volume and on the cards which are included in the General Index of Connecticut Vital Records also in the possession of the Connecticut

---

496 Charles R. Hale, "Headstone Inscriptions of the Town of Harwinton, Connecticut" (bound manuscript at CSL) (FHL film 3,340). Hale names these Oldest, South, North, West, East or Jones, & Scoville.

497 Daniel Hearn, "Connecticut gravestones, early to 1800," manuscript (FHL film 1,477,476, item 68).

498 See How to Use This Book, note 4, above.

499 Wear, *Barbour Collection: Hartland–Hebron*, vol. 18. Digital images at *Ancestry.com*.

500 Herein called the Barbour Index; now interfiled with those of other Connecticut towns in CSL and on FHL films 2,887 *et seq*. See Introduction above, pp. 3–5.

```
State Library.
                    Hartford, Conn., December, 1922.
```
[501]

VITAL RECORDS: The Hebron volume includes vital records as early as 1703 and as late as 1854. The five books of vital records abstracted in Barbour are:

- "1"refers to Hebron's Births, marriages, deaths, earmarks, 1684–1801, Hebron Town Hall (FHL film 1,376,165, item 2);
- "2" refers to Hebron's Births, marriages, deaths, 1750–1792, Hebron Town Hall (FHL film 1,376,165, item 4);
- "3" refers to Hebron's Births, marriages, deaths, 1684–1849, Hebron Town Hall (FHL film 1,376,166, item 1);
- "4" refers to "Births – Family Records – Book 4 – 1594–1909," an unfilmed authorless seventeen page manuscript in the Hebron Town Clerk's vault;[502]
- "4" with a page number followed by "M" refers to Hebron's Record of Marriages, 1820–1854 **(page 55 not abstracted)** (FHL film 1,376,166, item 3).

The Hebron Town Clerk's office also includes additional vital records abstracted by Linda MacLachlan in *New Copies of Old Records from Hebron, Connecticut, 1708 –* 1875 (Westminster MD: Heritage Books, 2011):

- **Hebron's "Book 4: Births, Marriages and Deaths, 1847–1954," Hebron Town Hall (FHL film 1,376,166, item 2);**
- **Hebron's Marriage certificates, certifications (and permission slips for under age brides) 1827–1881, 1814–1821, Hebron Town Hall (FHL film 1,376,166, item 6);**
- **Hebron's Index to births, marriages, deaths, books 1 through 4 (includes many unabstracted entries not in books 1–4, including a clerk's record of marriages by Elihu Marvin, J.P., 1735–1812 at pp. 168 – 176.[503] (FHL film 1,376,165, item 3);**
- **An unfilmed, untitled 42 page string-bound leaflet folio of Hebron deaths, 1796–1860;[504]**
- **An unfilmed, untitled notebook collecting vital records of Hebron people from clerks of other towns. [505]**

See also,

---

[501] Lucius B. Barbour, *Connecticut Vital Records Hebron, 1708–1854*, CSL, Hartford, 1922) page after title page (FHL film 2,972). Digital images at *AmericanAncestors.org and FamilySearch.org*.

[502] CSL possesses a photocopy of this manuscript but has not cataloged it to date. Many of the family records it contains are not entered in the Hebron vital records, perhaps because it is unclear which of these Hebron family births actually occurred in Hebron. The earliest birth record included is that of England-born Robert Carver, said to be the immigrant founder of Hebron's Carver families.

[503] The unfilmed original manuscript of Elihu Marvin's records as Hebron JP is in the CSA. All the marriages they report have been abstracted in Linda MacLachlan, "Marriages by Elihu Marvin, J.P., of Hebron, Connecticut, 1785–1812," *NEHGR,* 161:175–80 (Jul 2007).

[504] This record was first reported in Harlan R. Jessup, "Some Additions and Corrections to Connecticut's Barbour Collection," *Connecticut Ancestry*, 48:47–8 (Aug 2005). An uncataloged photocopy is available at the CSL. In 2009, it was loose inside a volume of Minutes of Town Meetings labeled "Vital Statistics, Vol. 3."

[505] Lucius J. Hendee, Town Clerk, First Book of Records, Births, Marriages and Deaths, Town of Hebron (manuscript in the Hebron Town Hall, copied from an old manuscript book also in the town clerk's office, in August 1849, by order of the town, and arranged alphabetically by first letter of surname) (FHL film 1,376,165, item 1).

- **Town Clerk Lucius J. Hendee's "First book of records, births, marriages and deaths, town of Hebron" (1849 copy of records, arranged alphabetically by first letter of surname including page numbers of records in the old book) manuscript in Hebron Town Hall (FHL film 1,376,165, item 1);**
- **Hebron Private Records slips not interfiled in Barbour Index. See Appendix B.**

CHURCH RECORDS:

- "Gilead Church Records 1752–1936" (3 volumes) and "Hebron Church Records 1787–1915 (3 volumes) are with the Hebron town clerk;[506]
- First Congregational Church's Church records, 1787–1915, originals at CSL (FHL film 4,460, items 2–3);
- Methodist Episcopal Church's "Church Records 1809–1845" (includes baptisms, 1809–1845) (original records in BUSTL) (FHL film 1,508,864);
- St. Peter's Church's "Church Records, 1787–1905" (includes baptisms 1824–1864, marriages 1822–1864 and deaths 1822–1865) (photocopy at CSL) (FHL film 4,462);
- St. Peter's Church's Church records, 1809–1888, originals at CSL (FHL film 1,010,732);
- Hebron Registrar of Vital Statistics' St. Peter's Church, Records of births, marriages, deaths in the town of Hebron, 1848–1911 (includes a few records of marriages and burials from the parish register of St. Peters Church in Hebron) (FHL film 1,376,166, items 2 and 1–4).
- Mary Jane Post's Gilead Congregational Church, "Church Records, 1752–1943" (includes baptisms 1752–1878, marriages 1752–1879 and deaths 1761–1883) (originals at CSL) (FHL film 4,460, items 4–5);
- Colchester Methodist Episcopal Church's "Church Records, 1843–1908" (contains baptisms 1843–1902 and marriages 1853–1895) (original records in BUSTL) (FHL film 1,508,822);
- Mary Jane Post's "Abstracts of Church Records 1841–1879" (includes deaths 1845–1879 and marriages 1841–1879) (photocopy at CSL) (FHL film 4,460, item 1);
- Baptisms (1824–64), marriages (1822–64) & burials (1822–65) at St. Peter's Church (ED Film 1,010,732);
- Methodist Society Female Benevolent Association's Register, 1837–1871, originals at CSL (FHL film 1,010, 731, item 4);

CEMETERY TRANSCRIPTIONS: The Hale Collection identifies people in order of physical proximity buried at about nine named sites in Hebron Township.[507] Compare with Daniel Hearn's 1979 copy of 280 pre-1800 gravestones in five Hebron cemeteries.[508] See also,

- Lucius B. Barbour, "Hebron, Connecticut Epitaphs" (inscriptions from the Union, Parker Hill, Stone House, Episcopal Church, Pine Orchard, Lane, Old South West, New South West) (Mss A 6127), RSASCs, NEHGS).

---

[506] *Biennial Report (1936),* 34.

[507] Charles R. Hale, "Headstone Inscriptions of the Town of Hebron, Connecticut" (bound manuscript at CSL) (FHL film 3,340). Hale names these Old, Gilead, Church of England, Jones Street, Burrows Hill, Gott, Summer, Graveyard, & St. Peter's.

[508] Daniel Hearn, "Connecticut gravestones, early to 1800," manuscript (FHL film 1,477,476, item 69).

- Lucius B. Barbour, "Hebron, Connecticut Epitaphs"(Mss A 6123), RSASCs, NEHGS;

OTHER NOTEWORTHY SOURCES:

- William J. Warner's "Baptisms, Marriages, Deaths, 1752–1876," CSL; see Appendix A;
- Walter E Corbin, Robert J. Dunkle (ed.)'s *Corbin manuscript collection* (vol. 2. Records of Connecticut towns including Gilead, Norwalk, Stafford, Stamford, West Stafford, and Willington,), 3 CD-ROMs (Boston: NEHGS, c2003–c2005);
- "A.R. Bailey's purchase," CSL; see Appendix A;
- "White family records, 1752–1814," CSL; see Appendix A;
- Annie Hutchinson Foote's *In Gilead* (Tolland: Clinton Press, 1970);
- Lila James Roney's "Marriage Records in Hebron, Connecticut, 1752–1797" (manuscript 1928) (FHL film 2,798) and (*New York DAR GRC Report, series 3, vol. 24;* 1927);
- John Sibun's *Our town's heritage 1708–1958, Hebron, Connecticut,* ([S.l.: s.n.], c1975, 1992 printing).

HUNTINGTON (SHELTON)

Barbour's typescript volume for Huntington,[509] unlike the GPC edition,[510] begins:

> This volume contains a list alphabetically arranged of all the vital records of the town of Huntington from its incorporation to about 1850. The town was incorporated under the name of Huntington and was so known until 1919 when its name was changed by legislative act to Shelton.
>
> This list was taken a set of cards[511] based on a copy of the Huntington Vital Records made in 1912 by Miss Irene H. Mix, of Hartford, Conn. The entire record for this town prior to 1850 is found in one volume.
>
> The manuscript copy, now in the possession of the Connecticut State Library, has not been compared with the original and doubtless errors exist. It is hoped that as errors or omissions are found notes will be entered in this volume and on the cards which are included in the General Index of Connecticut Vital Records also in the possession of the Connecticut State Library.
>
> Hartford, Conn., May, 1926.[512]

---

509 See How to Use This Book, note 4, above.

510 Lorraine Cook White, *Barbour Collection of Connecticut Town Vital Records: Huntington 1789–1850, Kent 1739–1852, Killingly 1708–1850*, vol. 20, (Baltimore: GPC, 1999).

511 Now part of the Barbour Index and interfiled with similar slips from other towns in CSL and on FHL films 2,887 *et seq*. See Introduction above, pp. 3–5.

512 Lucius B. Barbour, *Connecticut Vital Records: Huntington 1789–1850*, (Hartford: CSL, 1926) page after title page (FHL film 2,972). Digital images at *AmericanAncestors.org* and *FamilySearch.org*.

VITAL RECORDS: The Huntington volume includes vital records as early as 1749 and as late as 1850. Barbour abstracted Shelton's Births, Marriages, Deaths, vol. 1, 1739–1898, Shelton Town Hall, (FHL film 1,435,632, item 1).

Barbour did not abstract Shelton's Births, Marriages, Deaths, vol. 2, 1848–1873, Shelton Town Hall, FHL film 1,435,632, item 2).

See also, Harlan R. Jessup, "Huntington (Shelton) Marriages, 1820–1827," ***CA*****, 43:143–6 (May 2001).**

CHURCH RECORDS:

- Huntington Congregational Church and Ecclesiastical Society's "Church Records, 1717–1946" (includes baptisms & marriages 1773–1819; deaths, marriages, & baptisms 1818–1844 & 1844–1904) (originals in CSL) (FHL film 5,769);
- "Ripton Parish Record" (includes baptisms 1773–1781) (typescript in NHCHS) (FHL film 3,054;
- "St. Paul's Episcopal Church records, Huntington, Connecticut" (microfilm at NEHGS);
- St. Paul's Church's "Church Records, vol. 1–4, 1755–1907" (includes births 1758–1907, marriages 1758–1878 and burials 1758–1907) (photocopies in CSL) (FHL film 5,765);
- White Hills Baptist Church's Church records, 1838–1932, photocopies at CSL (FHL film 5,768).

CEMETERY TRANSCRIPTIONS: The Hale Collection identifies people in order of physical proximity buried at ten named sites in what was then Shelton Township.[513] Compare with Daniel Hearn's 1976 copy of 121 pre-1800 gravestones in three Shelton cemeteries.[514] See also. Arthur Walker's *Headstone inscriptions Old Coram Cemetery, Shelton, Connecticut* [S.l.: s.n., 2016].

OTHER NOTEWORTHY SOURCES:

- Samuel Orcutt's *History of the Old Town of Stratford and the City of Bridgeport, Connecticut* (New Haven: Press of Tuttle, Morehouse & Taylor 1886);
- Jane de Forest Shelton's *Salt-box house: eighteenth century life in a New England hill town*, (New York: Baker and Taylor, c1901);
- *Illustrated review of the Naugatuck Valley : embracing Ansonia, Derby, Birmingham, Shelton and Seymour, a record of the development of these centers, their progress in commerce manufacturing and political life, with sketches of their leading official, business and professional men* (New York: Sovereign Publishing and Engraving, 1890)(FHL fiche 6,071,068).

KENT

Barbour's typescript volume for Kent,[515] unlike the GPC edition,[516] begins:

---

513 Charles R. Hale, "Headstone Inscriptions of the Town of Shelton, Connecticut" (bound manuscript at CSL) (FHL film 3,361–2). Hale names these Old Coram, Riverview, Riverside, Upper White Hill, Lower White Hill, Long Hill, Lawn, Cong. Sons of Israel, St. Paul's & Old Huntington Center.

514 Daniel Hearn, "Connecticut gravestones, early to 1800," manuscript (FHL film 1,477,477, item 43).

515 See How to Use This Book, note 4, above.

> The vital records of Kent prior to 1852 are found scattered through the first volume of Land Records and Volumes 1, 2 and 3 of Vital Records. In this alphabetical list reference to entries found in the Land Records is indicated by the abbreviation "LR1"
>
> This list was taken from a set of cards[517] based on a copy of the Kent Vital Records made in 1915 by James N. Arnold, of Providence, R.I. The Arnold Copy, now in the possession of the Connecticut State Library, has not been compared with the original and doubtless errors exist. It is hoped that as errors or omissions are found notes will be entered in this volume and on the cards which are included in the General Index of Connecticut Vital Records also in the possession of the Connecticut State Library.
>
> Hartford, Conn., October, 1926.[518]

VITAL RECORDS: The Kent volume includes vital records as early as 1730 and as late as 1854. Barbour abstracted his first three record sets from the Kent Town Clerk's Records of Births, Marriages, and Deaths, 1723–1903 Kent Town Hall, (FHL film 1,516,999, items 1–3):

- "1" is from FHL item 1, 1723–1778;
- "2" is from FHL item 2, 1757–1834;
- "3" is from FHL item 3, 1846–1866 certificates of marriage;
- "LR1" is from Kent's Land Records, vol. 1 (1735–1752) Kent Town Hall, (FHL film 4,643).

Kent's reports by school district of 1847–1852 births, deaths and marriages appear to be at the town hall, though they were neither abstracted by Barbour nor microfilmed by FHL.[519]

CHURCH RECORDS:

- Church of Christ's "Church Records, 1739–1915" (includes baptisms, marriages, births and deaths) (originals and photocopies at CSL) (FHL film 4,654 or 1,010,733, item 1);
- St. Andrew's Church's "Church Records, 1775–1953" (includes baptisms, marriages and burials) (originals in CSL) (FHL film 1,010,733, items 2–11);
- Baptisms (1847–54), marriages (1848–57) & burials (1847–57) at St. Andrew's Church (ED Film 1,010,733).

---

516 White, *Barbour Collection: Huntington–Killingly*, vol. 20. Digital images at *Ancestry.com*.

517 Now part of the Barbour Index and interfiled with similar slips from other towns in CSL and on FHL films 2,887 *et seq*. See Introduction above, pp. 3–5.

518 Lucius B. Barbour, *Connecticut Vital Records: Kent, 1739–1852*, (Hartford: CSL, 1926) page after title page (FHL film 2,972). Digital images at *AmericanAncestors.org* and *FamilySearch.org*.

519 In 1936 Kent possessed "7 volumes of Vital Records 1739–1936" and **"1 volume of old Town School Districts Records."** *Biennial Report (1936)*.

CEMETERY TRANSCRIPTIONS: The Hale Collection identifies people in order of physical proximity buried at about 10 named sites in Kent Township.[520] Compare with Daniel Hearn's 1978 copy of 107 pre-1800 gravestones in two Kent cemeteries.[521] See also, Lawrence Van Alstyne's *Burying Grounds of Sharon, Connecticut, Amenia and North East, New York: Being an Abstract of Inscriptions From Thirty Places of Burial in the Above Named Towns* (includes Kent's Skiff Mountain burying ground) (Amenia NY: Walsh, Griffen & Hoysradt, 1903) (FHL film 17,516 or 908,330).

OTHER NOTEWORTHY SOURCES:

- Kent, Connecticut — Names of Early Residents. (Mss CT KEN 5. 1934). RSASCs, NEHGS, Boston, MA;
- Francis Atwater's *History of Kent, Connecticut: including biographical sketches of many of its present or former inhabitants,* (Meriden: Journal Pub. Co., 1897);
- Mable Seymour and Elizabeth Forgeus' *Lawyer of Kent: Barzillai Slosson and his account books, 1794–1812,* (New Haven: Yale University Press, 1935) FHL film 1,321.058, item 4 or 1,697,313, item 47).

KILLINGLY

Barbour's typescript volume for Killingly, [522] unlike the GPC edition,[523]begins:

> This volume contains a list alphabetically arranged of all the vital records of the town of Killingly from its incorporation to about 1850. This list was taken from a set of cards[524] based on a copy of the Killingly Vital Records made in 1908 by James N. Arnold, of Providence, R.I. The entire record for the town prior to 1850, is contained in two volumes. The duplicate pagination of the first book and the irregular chronological arrangement suggest that it may have been composed of several books bound as one. In this volume the pagination of the book in its present form has been followed. The pagination of the second volume as far as page 56, with the exception of the first three pages which repeat, is duplicated but the duplication is distinguished by the letter "a" after the page number.
>
> The Arnold Copy, now in the possession of the Connecticut State Library, has not been compared with the original and doubtless errors exist.

[520] Charles R. Hale, "Headstone Inscriptions of Kent, Connecticut" (bound manuscript at CSL) (FHL film 3341). Hale names these Congregational, St. Andrews, Good Hill, Skiff Mountain, Indian Reservation, Bull's Bridge, Kent Hollow, & Private (3 different locations).

[521] Daniel Hearn, "Connecticut gravestones, early to 1800," manuscript (FHL film 1,477,476, item 70).

[522] See How to Use This Book, note 4, above.

[523] White, *Barbour Collection: Huntington–Killingly*, vol. 20. Digital images at *Ancestry.com*.

[524] Now part of the Barbour Index and interfiled with similar slips from other towns in CSL and on FHL films 2,887 *et seq*. See Introduction above, pp. 3–5.

> It is hoped that as errors or omissions are found notes will be entered in this volume and on the cards which are included in the General Index of Connecticut Vital Records also in the possession of the Connecticut State Library.
>
> Hartford, Conn., November, 1920.[525]

VITAL RECORDS: The Killingly volume includes vital records as early as 1711 and as late as 1853. In Killingly Barbour abstracted:

- "1" refers to Killingly's Records of Births, Deaths, and Marriages, Book no. 1, 1700–1835 (Records are arranged alphabetically by first letter of surname), Killingly Town Hall (FHL film 1,451,024, item 2);
- "2" refers to Killingly's Births, Marriages, Deaths, vol. 1 (1700–1835), Killingly Town Hall (FHL film1,451,023, item 3 and 1,451,024, item 1);
- "2" with a page number followed by "a" refers to a record from Killingly's Births, Marriages, Deaths, (1848–1853), Killingly Town Hall (FHL film 1,451,024, item 3).

See also,

- **Killingly's Births, Marriages, Deaths, (1849–1881), Killingly Town Hall, (FHL Film 1,451,024, item 4);**
- **Natalie Coolidge, Edwin Leogar, and Melissa Wyatt's *Killingly Vital Records* (Danielson: KHGS, n.d.) said to contain all of Killingly's *Records of Births, Marriages, and Deaths, 1700– 1903 Vols. 1–5, General Index to Births, Marriages, Deaths, to 1905.* (FHL films 1,451,023–25).**

CHURCH RECORDS:

- First Congregational Church in Killingly's Church records, 1790–1858, photocopies at CSL (FHL film 5,814, item 1);
- South Congregational Church at Breakneck Hill (South Killingly)'s "Church Records, 1746–1755" (includes 1746–1755) originals at CSL (FHL film 5,814);
- Danielson Methodist Episcopal Church's "Church Records, 1842–1917" (includes baptisms, 1842–1889) originals in CSL (FHL film 1,010,735 or 4,675);
- First Christian Church's East Putnam Congregational Church, "Church Records, 1715–1904' (includes baptisms 1839–1876, deaths 1839–1904, marriages 1838–1866) originals at CSL (FHL film 5,465);
- First Christian Church's *Record of marriages, funerals, and baptizings*, (original in possession of Norman C. Kennedy, Las Vegas, Nevada. Contains records of marriages 1840–1903, funerals, lists of members, minutes of meetings, baptisms 1859) (FHL film 1,598,063, item 2);
- East Putnam Congregational Church's "Church Records, 1715–1904" (includes baptisms 1839–1876, deaths 1839–1904, marriages 1838–1866) (originals at CSL) (FHL film 5,465);
- Congregational Church of Putnam's, "Church Records, 1848–1933" (includes baptisms 1848–1850; and baptisms, marriages & deaths 1848–1918 & 1848–1928) (photocopies at CSL) (FHL film 5,464);

---

[525] Lucius B. Barbour, *Connecticut Vital Records Killingly, 1708–1850*, (Hartford: CSL,1920) page after title page (FHL film 2,972(. Digital images at *AmericanAncestors.org and FamilySearch.org.*

- Westfield Congregational Church at Danielson's, "Church Records, 1801–1936" (includes marriages, baptisms, deaths) originals at CSL (FHL film 4,673);
- Abington Congregational Church's Records, 1749–1923, copies at CSL (FHL film 3,694);
- Baptist Church's Church records, 1796–1837, photocopies at CSL (FHL film 1,010,738, item 8);
- Ebenezer Loomis and Edwin A. Hill's Record of membership from the foundation of the Church in A.D. 1776, photocopy at CSL (FHL film 1,010, 738, item 9);
- Mrs. J.L. Raymond's Church Records, 1727–1835 (includes records from the Congregational Church of North Stonington for 1727–1827, from the "Breakneck" Congregational Church for 1746– 1754 and the Congregational Church of South Killingly for 1746–1835.) (typescript at CSL) (FHL film 5,080);
- Ellen D. Larned's "Transcript of the Baptisms, Marriages and Deaths for 1711–1829 of the Putnam First or Putnam Heights Congregational Church" (typescript in CSL & NEHGS) (FHL film 5,466) (images online at *AmericanAncestors.org* of data in the *Putnam Patriot,* 18 May 1894);
- "Record of Marriages, Funerals, and Baptizings" (includes marriages 1840–1903, funerals, and baptisms 1859) (original in possession of Norman C. Kennedy, Las Vegas, NV) (FHL film 1,598,063);
- Pasay, M. H.'s *First Congregational Church of Dayville, in Killingly, Ct. 1840–1903: Clerks' records, membership lists, marriages & funerals performed by Reverend George W. Greenslit*. (Danielson: Killingly Historical Society, 1996);
- Marcella Houle Pasay's *South Killingly, CT Congregational Church, 1746–1996* (Danielson: Killingly Historical Society, 1999);
- Edwin R. Ledogar's *Westfield Congregational Church, Danielson, Killingly, Windham Co. CT vital statistics : marriages, baptism, death, 1801–1843* (Dayville: Edwin Richard Ledogar, 1992).

CEMETERY TRANSCRIPTIONS: The Hale Collection identifies people in order of physical proximity buried at about 67 named sites in what was then Killingly Township.[526] Compare with Daniel Hearn's 1979 copy of 96 pre-1800 gravestones in three Killingly cemeteries.[527]The Hale Collection also identifies people in order of physical proximity buried at about 11 named sites in what was then Putnam Township.[528] Compare with Daniel Hearn's 1979 copy of 86 pre-1800 gravestones in one Putnam cemetery.[529]

---

526 Charles R. Hale, "Headstone Inscriptions of the Town of Killingly, Connecticut" (bound manuscript at CSL) (FHL film 3,341). Hale names these Babbitt, Covell, Harrington, Basto-Spencer, Bartlett #2, Adams-Smith, Old Chestnut Hill, Wescott, Durfee, Burgess #1, Mathewson, Alvah Chase, Simmons, Tucker, Bartlett #1, Smith-Mason, Angell, Henry, Chase #1, Aldrich, Sparks, Smith-Aldrich, Fuller, Smith, Slate #1, Fiske, Burgess #2, Hall, Old South Killingly, Young #1, Mashentuck #1, Mashentuck #2, Burlingame, Slater #2, Cleveland, Chase #2, Warren, Brainard, Breakneck, Mitchell, Mathews, Chase-Haines, Whitmore, St. Joseph's Cross rozads, Old Westfield, St. James, Holy Cross, Hutchins Street, Hutchins-Franklin Street, Young #2, & Town Farm.

527 Daniel Hearn, "Connecticut gravestones, early to 1800," manuscript (FHL film 1,477,476, item 71).

528 Charles R. Hale, "Headstone Inscriptions of the Town of Putnam, Connecticut" (bound manuscript at CSL) (FHL film 3,359). Hale names these Grove Street, Putnam Heights, Munyan, Wheelock, Mallbone (colored family), Carpenter-Dresser, Day, Babbitt, Aspinwall, St. Mary's & Malbone.

529 Daniel Hearn, "Connecticut gravestones, early to 1800," manuscript (FHL film 1,477,477, item 33).

See also:

- Edwin R. Ledogar and Leroy Schrump's Tombstone Records of Killingly (Danielson: KHGS, 1993);
- Edwin Richard Ledogar's *Sexton Returns For the Town of Killingly, Connecticut, 1885–1949: Burial Records* (Dayville: self-published, 1993) (FHL film 1,750,731, item 22);
- Lucius B. Barbour's "Connecticut Cemetery Inscriptions," *NEHGR*, vol. 100: 328 (1946);
- Edwin R. Ledogar, Charles Henry, and Leroy Schrump's *Putnam Cemetery Records* (Danielson: KHGS, n.d.).

OTHER NOTEWORTHY SOURCES:

- Lucius B. Barbour's Genealogical notes complied from church records of Killingly, Conn., 1715–1816. I vol. Abstract of probate records. (manuscript 23 in Box 3) CSL Record Group 074.36, Hartford;
- M. H. Pasay's *Killingly, Connecticut, January 1835 – October 1853: And William Rhoades Rawson account book.* (Danielson, CT: Killingly Historical Society, 1996);
- Marcella Houle Pasay's *William Rhoades Rawson Accounte Book, 1835–1853* (Danielson, CT: Killingly Historical Society);
- Lucius B. Barbour's Genealogical notes complied from church records of South Killingly, Conn., 1745–1825. I vol. Abstract of probate records. (manuscript 52 in Box 8) CSL Record Group 074.36, Hartford;
- Marilyn Dunham Labbe and Marcella Houle Pasay's "Marriages & Deaths With Killingly, CT References from Providence, RI Newspapers, 1770–1832," *Killingly Historical Journal* vol. 3, no. 2 (1997);
- Edwin R. Ledogar's Westfield Congregational Church Records, Danielson, CT (Danielson, CT: Killingly Historical Society, Baptismal-Marriages-Death, 1801–1843, Marriages, 1966–1980 (Danielson, CT: Killingly Historical Society);
- Killingly Historical Society, *Killingly Historical Journal*, vols. 5–10 (Danielson: KHGS, 1995) (FHL film 2,444,636, item 1, 2,401,874, item 4);
- Charles Seney & Lawrence Choiniere's Gilman-Valade Funeral Records (Danielson: KHGS, n.d.).

KILLINGWORTH

Barbour's typescript volume for Killingworth, [530] unlike the GPC edition,[531] begins:

> This volume contains a list alphabetically arranged of all the vital records of the town of Killingworth from its incorporation to about 1850. This list was taken from a set

[530] See How To Use This Book, note 4, above.

[531] Marsha Wilson Carbaugh, *Barbour Collection of Connecticut Town Vital Records: Killingworth 1667–1850, Ledyard 1836–1855, Lisbon 1786–1850*, vol. 21, (Baltimore: GPC, 1999). Digital images at *Ancestry.com*.

of cards[532] based on a copy of the Killingworth Vital Records made in 1914 by James N. Arnold, of Providence, R.I. The entire record of the town prior to 1850 is found in three volumes.

The Arnold Copy, now in the possession of the Connecticut State Library, has not been compared with the original and doubtless errors exist. It is hoped that as errors or omissions are found notes will be entered in this volume and on the cards which are included in the General Index of Connecticut Vital Records also in the possession of the Connecticut State Library.

Hartford, Conn., January, 1924.[533]

VITAL RECORDS: The Killingworth volume includes vital records as early as 1667 and as late as 1850:

- "1" abstracts Killingworth's Land Records, vol. 1 (1664–1703) Killingworth Town Hall (FHL film 4,621, item 1);
- "2" abstracts a 1786–1908 transcription (FHL films 1,378,382, item 2 (pp.1–165) and 1,378,453, item 1 (pp. 165 on) of Killingworth's "Land Records and Vital Statistics," vol. 2 (1697–1791) Killingworth Town Hall (FHL film 4,621, item 2);
- "3" abstracts E. Kelsey and Julius Dudley's "Marriages, 1820–1861," from Col. Aaron Eliot and Abraham Pierson's *Killingworth, Connecticut Miscellaneous Town Records, 1663– 1747, Marriages, 1820–1861 Entered by E. Kelsey, Julius Dudley. et al.,* "Killingworth Town Hall (FHL 1,378,382, item 1), pp. 358–418.[534]

Other vital records not abstracted by Barbour include:

- **Col. Aaron Eliot and Abraham Pierson's "Killingworth, Connecticut Miscellaneous Town Records, 1663– 1747,** [except for] Marriages, 1820–1861" **(a 1786–1790 transcription of Killingworth's first book of records and two smaller books with "such corrections and amendments as we should judge necessary") (FHL 1,378,382, item 1), pp. 1–357;**
- **Killingworth's Land Records, vol. 3, 1715–1724 (contains vital records 1708–1771 in digital images 775–777) Killingworth Town Hall (FHL Film 4,621, item 3, digital film 8140655);**
- **Two volumes at the town hall listing vital events in Killingworth which the town clerk calls "Vital Statistics from Church Records of the Congregational Church of Killingworth" and "Killingworth Cemetery Records;"** [535]
- **Killingworth's "Births, Deaths 1847 – 1908; Marriages 1847 – 1906," Town Hall, Killingworth, (FHL film 1,378,453, item 2).**

---

[532] Now part of the Barbour Index and interfiled with similar slips from other towns in CSL and on FHL films 2887 *et seq*. See Introduction above, pp. 3–5.

[533] Lucius B. Barbour, *Connecticut Vital Records: Killingworth, 1667–1850,* (Hartford: CSL, 1924) page after title page (FHL film 2,972). Digital images at *AmericanAncestors.org* and *FamilySearch.org*..

[534] Email from Killingworth Town Clerk Dawn Rees Mooney, CCTC; CSL, *First 200 Years.*

[535] Email from Killingworth Town Clerk Dawn Rees Mooney, CCTC, MCTC.

CHURCH RECORDS:

- First Congregational Church's "Church Records, 1735–1893" (includes baptisms, marriages, marriages by Abraham Pierson, J.P., and deaths) (originals at CSL) (FHL film 4,637);
- Baptisms (1800–82), marriages (1809–83), burials (1874–83), infant baptisms copied from old records (1800–74), & marriages copied from old register (1809–70) at Emmanual Church (ED Films 0004,638, 1,010,738, & original manuscript).
- "Church Records, Killingworth, Middlesex County, Connecticut, 1738–1839" (includes north parish marriages and second parish deaths) (originals at CSL) (FHL film 4,620);
- Emmanuel Church's "Church Records, 1800–1883" (includes baptisms 1800–1882 and marriages 1809–1883) (originals at CSL) (FHL film 4,638);
- Abraham Pierso's "Note Book of Deacon Abraham Pierson, 1787–1802, of Killingworth, Connecticut" (includes deaths, marriages, and baptisms 1787–1802) (originals at CSL) (FHL film 4,639).

CEMETERY TRANSCRIPTIONS: The Hale Collection identifies people in order of physical proximity buried at nine named sites in Killingworth Township.[536] Compare with Daniel Hearn's 1978 copy of 108 pre-1800 gravestones in three Killingworth cemeteries.[537]

OTHER NOTEWORTHY SOURCES: Henry Pierce's Clinton Historical Society *Colonial Killingworth: a history of Clinton and Killingworth*, (Clinton: Clinton Historical Society, 1976).

LEBANON

Barbour's typescript volume for Lebanon ,[538] unlike the GPC edition,[539] begins:

> The early vital records of Lebanon are contained in two volumes. The second volume is in two parts the second half of which appears in a second alphabet beginning on page 194 of this volume but in considered as Volume 3.
>
> This book contains an alphabetical list of these records from the date of the incorporation of the town to about 1854 and was taken from a set of cards[540] based on a copy of the Lebanon Vital Records made in 1912 by James N. Arnold, of Providence, R.I. The Arnold Copy, now in the possession of the Connecticut State Library, has not been com-

536 Charles R. Hale, "Headstone Inscriptions of the Town of Killingworth, Connecticut" (bound manuscript at CSL) (FHL film 3,341). Hale names these Old, Union, South West, Nettleton, South West, Pine Orchard, Stone House, Old South West, & Lane.

537 Daniel Hearn, "Connecticut gravestones, early to 1800," manuscript (FHL film 1,477,476, item 72).

538 See How to Use This Book, note 4, above.

539 Carbaugh, *Barbour Collection: Killingworth–Lisbon*, vol. 21. Digital images at *Ancestry.com*.

540 Now part of the Barbour Index and interfiled with similar slips from other towns in CSL and on FHL films 2,887 *et seq*. See Introduction above, pp. 3–5.

```
pared with original and doubtless errors exist.
It is hoped that as errors or omissions are found
notes will be entered in this volume and on the
cards which are included in the General Index of
Connecticut Vital Records also in the possession
of the Connecticut State Library.
                        Hartford, Conn., April, 1920.[541]
```

VITAL RECORDS: The Lebanon volume includes vital records as early as 1682 and as late as 1882. FHL films Lebanon's Records of Births, Marriages, and Deaths, vols. 1–4, 1700–1854, Lebanon Town Hall, FHL film 1,312,154. Barbour abstracted two volumes:

- "1" refers to volume 1, 1700–1882 original at CSA (CSL 974.62 L49b) (film 1,312,154 item 1).
- "2" refers to volume 2, 1766–1854, Lebanon Town Hall (film 1,312,154, first part of item 2).

Barbour does not abstract volume 3 1848–1854 (FHL film 1,312,154, last part of item 2). See also,

- **Lebanon Town Records, 1699–1840 (originals at CSA (CSL 974.62 L49b);**
- **Walter G Kingsley's Miscellaneous records, 1638–1883 (includes baptisms 1715–1813, deaths 1702–1888, index to marriages 1671–1883 with notes on the Kingsley family 1638–1871 and Juduthan Woodworth family 1794–1864) CSL, Hartford, (FHL Film 4,727).**

CHURCH RECORDS:

- First Congregational Church, "Church Records, 1700–1883" (includes baptisms (1701–1782, 1782–1836 & 1782–179), marriages (1720–1774, 1815–1821 & 1782–1797), and deaths 1782–1840 & 1796–1797) (originals at CSL) (FHL film 4,724 or 1,010,739);
- Exeter Congregational Church's "Church Records, 1709–1920" (includes marriages 1848–1874, baptisms 1813–1912, deaths 1812–1912 and inscriptions 1709–1846) (photocopy at CSL) (FHL film 4,726 items 1–3);
- Goshen Congregational Church's "Church Records, 1728–1895" (includes baptisms 1731–1882, marriages 1731–1860 and deaths 1854–1867) (photocopy at CSL) (FHL film 4,726 items 4–5);
- Orange Baptist Church's Church records, 1818–1881, photocopy at CSL (FHL film 4,725).

CEMETERY TRANSCRIPTIONS: The Hale Collection identifies people in order of physical proximity buried at about 11 named sites in Lebanon Township.[542] Compare with Daniel Hearn's 1979 copy of 393 pre-1800 gravestones in three Lebanon

---

541 Lucius B. Barbour, *Connecticut Vital Records Lebanon, 1700–1854*, (Hartford: CSL, 1920) page after title page (FHL film 2,973). Digital images at *AmericanAncestors.org*.and *FamilySearch.org*.

542 Charles R. Hale, "Headstone Inscriptions of the Town of Lebanon, Connecticut" (bound manuscript at CSL) (FHL film 3,341–2). Hale names these Liberty Hill, Exeter, Lebanon Center, Lebanon Old, New South, Goshen, Geer, Scoville or Buckingham, Segar, Greenman, & Small Pox.

cemeteries.[543] See also, Lucius B. Barbour's "Lebanon, **Connecticut** Epitaphs" (Mss A 6128), RSASCs, NEHGS);

OTHER NOTEWORTHY SOURCES:

- Lucius B. Barbour's Genealogical notes complied from church records of Lebanon, Conn., 1729–1822. I vol. Abstract of vital records. (manuscript 28 in Box 4) CSL Record Group 074.36, Hartford;
- "Sexton's Records, 1733–1937" CSL; see Appendix A;
- "Diary of Rev. John Robinson, 1702–1729," CSL; see Appendix A;
- Lucius B. Barbour's Genealogical notes complied from church records of Lebanon Street and Lebanon First Society, Lebanon, Conn., 1701–1821. Abstract of vital records. (manuscript 29 in Box 4) CSL Record Group 074.36, Hartford;
- Rev. John Robinson, Diary (an alphabetical surname arranged index of marriages, deaths and names mentioned taken from a photostat copy of the record book of Rev. John Robinson, of Duxborough [Duxbury], Massachusetts and Lebanon, Connecticut, covering 1702–1729) 1946 CSL digital collection;
- Robert Charles Anderson's "Genealogy and social history: the early settlement of Lebanon, Connecticut, as a case study" (M.A., University of Massachusetts, 1983);
- George M. Milne's Lebanon: Three Centuries in a Connecticut Hilltop Town (1986/1995 copy at NEHGS);
- Orlo Daniel Hine and Nathaniel H. Morgan's *Early Lebanon: an historical address delivered in Lebanon, Conn., by request, on the national centennial July 4, 1876: with an appendix of historical notes by Nathaniel H. Morgan,* (Hartford: Case, Lockwood & Brainard Co., 1880))FHL film 476,933, item 2);

LEDYARD

Barbour's typescript volume for Ledyard,[544] unlike the GPC edition,[545] begins:

> This volume contains a list alphabetically arranged of all the vital records of the town of Ledyard from its incorporation to about 1855. This list was taken from a set of cards[546] based on a copy of the Ledyard Vital Records made in 1911 by James N. Arnold, of Providence, R.I. The entire record of the town prior to 1855 is found in one volume.
>
> The Arnold Copy, now in the possession of the Connecticut State Library, has not been compared with the original and doubtless errors exist. It is hoped that as errors or omissions are found notes will be entered in this volume and on the cards which are included in the General In-

---

543 Daniel Hearn, "Connecticut gravestones, early to 1800," manuscript (FHL film 1,477,476, item 73).

544 See How to Use This Book, note 4, above.

545 Carbaugh, *Barbour Collection: Killingworth Lisbon*, vol. 21. Digital images at *Ancestry.com*.

546 Now part of the Barbour Index and interfiled with similar slips from other towns in CSL and on FHL films 2887 *et seq*. See Introduction above, pp. 3–5.

```
dex of Connecticut Vital Records also in the pos-
session of the Connecticut State Library.
                    Hartford, Conn., August, 1918.
```
[547]

VITAL RECORDS: The Ledyard volume includes vital records as early as 1836 and as late as 1854. Barbour abstracted Ledyard's Records of Births, Marriages, and Deaths, 1836–1917 (FHL film 1,312,384).

FHL also catalogs as vital records (because it includes a catalog of deaths, 1718–1854): John Avery's *History of the Town of Ledyard, 1650–1900*, (Norwich: Noyes & Davis, 1901) (FHL film 908,332)

The Barbour Index also abstracts "Record of deaths, Watrous Family, 1818–1838," CSL; see Appendix A.

CHURCH RECORDS:

- Second Ecclesiastical Society's "Church Records, 1725–1897" (includes baptisms, marriages, and deaths) (originals at CSL) (FHL film 1,010,740);
- Congregational Church's Records 1810–1956, originals at CSL (FHL film 4,731);
- First Ecclesiastical Society's Records 1837–1889 (CSL 974.62 L512e).

CEMETERY TRANSCRIPTIONS: The Hale Collection identifies people in order of physical proximity buried at about 52 named sites in Ledyard Township.[548] Compare with Daniel Hearn's 1980 copy of 29 pre-1800 gravestones in three Ledyard cemeteries.[549] See also, Irving F. Maynard and Harold F. Bartlett's *Cemeteries and burials in the town of Ledyard: including deceased veterans of all wars*. (Ledyard: [Town of Ledyard] 1964).

OTHER NOTEWORTHY SOURCES: Ellen Geer's "Marriages performed in North Groton, CT, 1773–1814," CSL; see Appendix A.

LISBON

Barbour's typescript volume for Lisbon,[550] (unlike the GPC edition,[551] begins:

```
        This volume contains a list alphabetical-
ly arranged of all the vital records of the
town of Lisbon from its incorporation to about
```

[547] Lucius B. Barbour, *Connecticut Vital Records Ledyard, 1836–1853*, (Hartford: CSL, 1918) page after title page (FHL film 2,973). Digital images at *AmericanAncestors.org* and *FamilySearch.org*.

[548] Charles R. Hale, "Headstone Inscriptions of the Town of Ledyard, Connecticut" (bound manuscript at CSL) (FHL film 3,342). Hale names these Allen, Allyn's Point, B.T. Avery (3 different locations), Fanning, Bill, Brown, Gales Ferry, Bolles, Lamb #1, Gallup, Lamb #2, Center, Maintown, Morgan #1, Morgan #2, Morgan #3, Myers or Williams, Newton, Quakertown #1, Roach, Spicer, Stoddard (2 different locations), Williams #1, Williams #2, Williams, Eldredge, Lee, Geer, Gray, Holdredge, Hallet, Hewitt, Hurlbut, Kate Swamp, Indian (2 different locations), Woodbridge, Lester, Quakertown #2, Bailey, Private, Thomas Main, Rogerene, Lamb, Rose Hill, Single Grave, McGuire, Chapman, & Allyn.

[549] Daniel Hearn, "Connecticut gravestones, early to 1800," manuscript (FHL film 1,477,476, item 74).

[550] See How to Use This Book, note 4, above.

[551] Carbaugh, *Barbour Collection: Killingworth–Lisbon*, vol. 21. Digital images at *Ancestry.com*.

> 1850. This list was taken from a set of cards[552] based on a copy of the Lisbon Vital Records made in 1909 by James N. Arnold, of Providence, R.I. The records here indexed are taken the first three volumes of vital records. Every entry in the first two volumes has been indexed and in Volume 2 all births prior to December 31 1850, all marriages prior to December 31 1850, and all of the deaths. The record of deaths ends with an entry bearing the date of July 29, 1875. The Arnold Copy, now in the possession of the Connecticut State Library, has not been compared with the original and doubtless errors exist. It is hoped that as errors or omissions are found notes will be entered in this volume and on the cards which are included in the General Index of Connecticut Vital Records also in the possession of the Connecticut State Library.
>
> Hartford, Conn., October, 1919.[553]

VITAL RECORDS: The Lisbon volume includes vital records as early as 1762 and as late as 1873. Barbour's three volumes abstract Lisbon's Records of Births, Marriages, Deaths, 1771–1917, Lisbon Town Hall, (FHL film 1,311,198, items 1–2):

- "1" generally abstracts FHL's item 1, but **with omissions and errors;**
- "2"refers to Lisbon's Records of Births, Marriages, Deaths, 1845–1854, Lisbon Town Hall, (FHL film 1,311,198, unnumbered item before item 2);
- "3" refers to Lisbon's Records of Deaths, 1853–1875, Lisbon Town Hall, (FHL film 1,311,198), item 2.

CHURCH RECORDS:

- Newent Congregational Church's "Church Records, 1724–1932" (includes baptisms 1724–1898, marriages 1724–1861 and deaths 1743–1787) (photocopy at CSL) (FHL film 4,706);
- Hanover Congregational Church of Sprague's "Church Records, 1761–1915" (includes marriages, baptisms, some births, and deaths) (originals at CSL) (FHL film 5,821);
- Rev. R Manning Chipman's Newent Congregational Church Papers 1736–1873 (photocopy at CSL) (FHL film 1,010,741, item 2).

CEMETERY TRANSCRIPTIONS: The Hale Collection identifies graves in order of physical proximity buried at about four named sites in what was then Lisbon Township.[554] Compare with Daniel Hearn's 1980 copy of 29 pre-1800 gravestones in three Lisbon cemeteries.[555] The Hale Collection also identifies graves in order of physical proximity

---

552 Now part of the Barbour Index and interfiled with similar slips from other towns in CSL and on FHL films 2,887 *et seq*. See Introduction above, pp. 3–5.

553 Lucius B. Barbour, *Connecticut Vital Records: Lisbon, 1786–1850*, (Hartford: CSL, 1919) page after title page (FHL film 2,973): Digital images at *AmericanAncestors.org* and *FamilySearch.org*.

554 Charles R. Hale, "Headstone Inscriptions of the Town of Lisbon, Connecticut" (bound manuscript at CSL) (FHL film 3,342). Hale names these Ames, Read-Haskell, St. Mary's & Kinsman.

555 Daniel Hearn, "Connecticut gravestones, early to 1800," manuscript (FHL film 1,477,476, item 75).

buried at about four named sites in what was then Sprague Township.[556] Compare with Daniel Hearn's 1982 copy of 68 pre-1800 gravestones in two Sprague cemeteries.[557]

See also,

- Charles R. Hale and Mary H. Babin's "Headstone Inscriptions, Town of Lisbon, Connecticut" (1937 typescript in the Town Hall) (FHL film 1,311,193);
- Lucius B. Barbour's "Genealogical Data From Connecticut Cemeteries Lisbon" (1932 manuscript at NEHGS);
- Lucius B. Barbour's "Genealogical Data From Connecticut Cemeteries: Sprague, Connecticut. Headstone Records from The Old And New Cemeteries. Hanover; Lovett Cemetery, Near Versailles" (See also Lisbon). (1932 manuscript at NEHGS);
- Lucius B. Barbour's "Lisbon, Connecticut Epitaphs" (Mss A 6131), RSASCs, NEHGS);
- Lucius B. Barbour's "Kinsman Cemetery, Versailles, Lisbon, Conn." (Mss A 6132), RSASC, NEHGS.

OTHER NOTEWORTHY SOURCES:

- Henry F. Bishop's *Historical sketch of Lisbon, Conn., from 1786 to 1900,* (New York: H.F. Bishop's c1903) (FHL film 1,710,440);
- R. Manning Chipman's *Papers 1736–1873,* (manuscript ay CSL containing historical and biographical sketches; lists of ministers, physicians, soldiers and voters from Lisbon; catalog of deaths; letters and other miscellaneous papers) (FHL film 1,010,741, item 2).
- Lucius B. Barbour's Genealogical notes complied from church records of Newent and Norwich Third Society, Lisbon, Conn., 1723–1803. I vol. Abstract of vital records. (manuscript 29 in Box 4) CSL Record Group 074.36, Hartford,

LITCHFIELD

Barbour's individual volume for Litchfield,[558] unlike the GPC edition.[559] begins:

> This volume contains a list alphabetically arranged of all the vital records of the town of Litchfield from its incorporation to about 1854.
>
> The entire record of the town prior to 1854 is found in two volumes and Volume 49 of Town Meetings. Reference to entries found in the book of Town Meetings is indicated herein by the abbreviation "M49".
>
> This list was taken from a set of cards[560] based on a copy of the Litchfield Vital Records made in

---

556 Charles R. Hale, "Headstone Inscriptions of the Town of Sprague, Connecticut" (bound manuscript at CSL) (FHL film 3,363). Hale names these Lovetts, New Hanover, St. Mary's & Old Hanover.

557 Daniel Hearn, "Connecticut gravestones, early to 1800," manuscript (FHL film 1,477,477, item 50).

558 See How to Use This Book, note 4, above.

559 Debra F. Wilmes, *Barbour Collection of Connecticut Town Vital Records: Litchfield 1719–1854*, vol. 23, (Baltimore: GPC, 2000). Digital images at *Ancestry.com*.

560 Now part of the Barbour Index and interfiled with similar slips from other towns in CSL and on FHL films 2,887 *et seq*. See Introduction above, pp. 3–5.

> 1916 by James N. Arnold, of Providence, R.I. The Arnold Copy, now in the possession of the Connecticut State Library, has not been compared with the original and doubtless errors exist. In "A" Genealogical Register of the Inhabitants of the Town of Litchfield, Connecticut" published in 1900 by George Catlin Woodruff, the early vital records are arranged by families, and although the Arnold Copy has not been compared in its entirety with this publication, a few marked differences have been noted. It is hoped that as errors or omissions are found notes will be entered in this volume and on the cards which are included in the General Index of Connecticut Vital Records also in the possession of the Connecticut State Library.
>
> Hartford, Conn., December, 1926.[561]

VITAL RECORDS: The Litchfield volume includes vital records as early as 1701 and as late as 1862. Barbour abstracted three Litchfield "books:"

- "1" refers to Litchfield's Town Records, vol. 1 (includes births, marriages, deaths, 1701–1815) Litchfield Town Hall (FHL film 1,516,502, item 1);
- "2" refers to Litchfield's Town Records, vol. 2 (includes births, marriages, deaths, 1780–1843) Litchfield Town Hall (FHL film 1,516,502, item 2);
- "TM49" refers to Litchfield Town Records, vol. 49, containing births, marriages, and deaths 1842–1866) with a partial index.), Litchfield Town Hall (FHL film 1,516,502, item 3);

See also Litchfield Town Records, 1732–1849 (originals at CSA CSL 974.62 fL71 ca).

CHURCH RECORDS:

- First Methodist Episcopal Church's "Church records, 1790–1932" (includes baptisms 1849–1871) (originals at CSL) (FHL film 4,769);
- St. Michael's Parish's "Church Records, 1750–1870" (includes marriages 1757–1848, 1802, 1814–1831, 1836, 1839, 1842—1848, 1832–1837, 1845–1870; burials 1833–1837, 1845–1863, 1865–1870; baptisms 1750–1774, 1811–1827, 1836, 1833–1837, 1845–1857, 1844, 1846–1848; and deaths 1811–1831, 1836, 1844–1848) (originals at CSL) (FHL film 4,773);
- Northfield Congregational Church's "Church Records, 1795–1954" (includes baptisms and marriages) (originals at CSL) (FHL film 1,010,743);
- Church of Christ in Milton's "Church Records, 1779–1898" (includes baptisms 1844–1891, marriages 1844–1858, and deaths 1844–1857) (originals at CSL) (FHL film 4,767);
- Trinity Church at Northfield's "Church Records, 1793–1892" (includes marriages 1840–1880, deaths 1841–1880) (originals at CSL) (FHL film 4,775);
- Church of Christ in South Farms (Morris)'s Church records, 1767–1892 (contains baptisms, marriages, deaths) (FHL film 4,947);

---

[561] Lucius B. Barbour, *Connecticut Vital Records: Litchfield, 1719–1854*, (Hartford: CSL, 1926) page after title page (FHL film 2,973). Digital images at *AmericanAncestors.org* and *FamilySearch.org.*

- First Congregational Church's Records 1768–1927, originals at CSL (FHL film 4,766)
- Trinity Church's "Church Records, 1832–1940" (includes marriages 1833–1856, 1860; baptisms 1832–1866, and deaths & funerals 1832–1866) (originals and photocopies at CSL) (FHL film 4,774);
- St. Paul's Church at Bantam's "Church Records, 1832–1916" (includes baptisms, marriages, and burials) (originals at CSL) (FHL film 4,771 or 1,010,744);
- Church of Christ in South Farms' "Church Records, 1767–1892" (includes baptisms, marriages, deaths) (originals at CSL) (FHL film 4,947 or 1,010,752);
- Almira A. Bissell's "Church records 1799–1866" (includes marriages 1832–1857; baptisms 1832–1851 & 1832–1866; and funerals, burials and deaths 1832–1868 & 1832–1860) (typescript at CSL) (FHL film 4,772);
- Baptisms (1833–37, 1811–27, 1836, 1844, 1846–48), marriages (1757–18, 1832–73, 1845–70, 1802, 1814–31, 1836, 1839, 1842–48) & burials (1833–37,1845–63, 1865–70, 1811–31, 1836, 1844–48) at St. Michael's Church (ED Film 4,473);
- Baptisms (1832–60), marriages (1832–60) & burials (1832–60) at St. Paul's Church at Bantam (ED Film 4,771).

CEMETERY TRANSCRIPTIONS: The Hale Collection identifies graves in order of physical proximity buried at about 11 named sites in what was then Litchfield Township.[562] Compare with Daniel Hearn's 1978 copy of 101 pre-1800 gravestones in five Litchfield cemeteries.[563]The Hale Collection also identifies graves in order of physical proximity buried at three named sites in what was then Morris Township.[564] Compare with Daniel Hearn's 1978 copy of 16 pre-1800 gravestones in two Morris cemeteries.[565] See also,

- Charles Thomas Payne, *Litchfield and Morris Inscriptions: A Record of Inscriptions Upon the Tombstones in the towns of Litchfield and Morris, Ct.* (Litchfield: D.C. Kilbourn, 1905) (FHL film 823,773);
- Cemetery Inscriptions of Litchfield and Morris (Beach Family Burial Ground, Catholic Cemetery, East Burying Ground, Soldier's Lot, West Burying Ground), Godfrey Memorial Library online database.

OTHER NOTEWORTHY SOURCES:

- Alain C. White, *History of the Town of Litchfield, 1720–1920* (1920/1992 copy at NEHGS);
- Payne Kenyon Kilbourne, Genealogical Notes on Families of Litchfield, Conn., 2 vols. in CSA RG 074:021, See Finding Aid at *https://ctstatelibrary.org/RG074_021.html*;
- Payne Kenyon Kilbourne, *Sketches and Chronicles of the Town of Litchfield, Connecticut, Historical, Biographical, and Statistical: Together With a Complete Official Register of the Town* (Hartford: Case, Lockwood and Co., 1859);

---

562 Charles R. Hale, "Headstone Inscriptions of the Town of Litchfield, Connecticut" (bound manuscript at CSL) (FHL film 3,342). Hale names these West, East, Bantam, Northfield, Milton, Headquarters, Stone, Private, Catholic, Beach, & Footville.

563 Daniel Hearn, "Connecticut gravestones, early to 1800," manuscript (FHL film 1,477,476, item 76).

564 Charles R. Hale, "Headstone Inscriptions of the Town of Morris, Connecticut" (bound manuscript at CSL) (FHL film 3,347). Hale names these Morris, Footville, & Town Poor.

565 Daniel Hearn, "Connecticut gravestones, early to 1800," manuscript (FHL film 1,477,477, item 7).

- George C. Woodruff, *Genealogical Register of the Inhabitants of Litchfield From the Settlement, 1720 to the Year 1800* (1900/1997 copy at NEHGS);
- "Records of Deaths, 1767–1789, at South Farms, Now In the Town of Morris, Litchfield, Connecticut" (photocopy at NYGBS) (FHL film 4,676).

LYME

Barbour's typescript volume for Lyme,[566] unlike the GPC edition,[567] begins:

> The early vital records of Lyme are found in the first seven volumes of Land Records and in three volumes of Vital Records. An incomplete summany of the earlier entries appears in the New England Historical and Genealogical register, Vol. 23, p. 425; Vol. 24, p. 30; Vol. 31, p. 211; Vol. 32, p. 82; Vol. 33, p. 438; Vol. 34, p. 37. The records herein cover all of the vital records of Lyme from its incorporation to about 1852.
>
> The following alphabetically arranged list was taken from a set of cards[568] based on a copy of the Lyme Vital Records made in 1912 by James N. Arnold, of Providence, R.I. The Arnold Copy, now in the possession of the Connecticut State Library, has not been compared with original and doubtless errors exist. It is hoped that as errors or omissions are found notes will be entered in this volume and on the cards which are included in the General Index of Connecticut Vital Records also in the possession of the Connecticut State Library.
>
> Hartford, Conn., October, 1919.[569]

VITAL RECORDS: The Lyme volume includes vital records as early as 1664 and as late as 1860. Barbour abstracted ten Lyme "books:"

- "1" refers to Lyme's Records of births, marriages, and deaths, 1743–1812, Lyme Town Hall, Lyme Town Hall (FHL film 1,311,111, start of first section) (film not itemized by FHL);
- "2" refers to Lyme's Records of births, marriages, and deaths, 1789–1832, 1812, Lyme Town Hall, (FHL film 1,311,111, end of first section) (not itemized by FHL);;
- "3" refers to Lyme's Marriages 1835–1854 Lyme Town Hall (FHL film 1,311,111, second section) (film not itemized by FHL);
- "L-1" and "L-2" refer to Lyme's Land Records, vols. 1–2 1664–1749, Lyme Town Hall, (FHL film 4,678);

---

566 See How to Use This Book, note 4, above.

567 Lillian Bentley Karlstrand, *Barbour Collection of Connecticut Town Vital Records: Lyme 1667–1852*, vol. 24, (Baltimore: GPC, 2000). Digital images at *Ancestry.com* and FamilySearch.org.

568 Now part of the Barbour Index and interfiled with similar slips from other towns in CSL and on FHL films 2,887 *et seq*. See Introduction above, pp. 3–5.

569 Lucius B. Barbour, *Connecticut Vital Records: Lyme, 1667–1852*, (Hartford: CSL, 1919) page after title page (FHL film 2,973): Digital images at *AmericanAncestors.org* and *FamilySearch.org.*

- "L-3" and "L-4 refer to Lyme's Land Records, vols. 3–4 1721–1730, Lyme Town Hall, (FHL film 4,679);
- "L-5" and "L-6" refer to Lyme's Clerk's Land Records, vols. 5–6 1731–1739, Lyme Town Hall, (FHL film 4,680);
- "L-7" refers to Lyme's Land Records, vols. 1–7 1737–1749, Lyme Town Hall, (FHL film 4,681).

The Barbour Index also abstracts and interfiles "Marriage Records of Andrew Griswold, J.P., 1784–1810," online at *http://cslib.cdmhost.com/index.php.*See also,

- **Lyme's Records of births, marriages, and deaths, 1847–1856, Lyme Town Hall, (FHL film 1,311,111, third section) (film not itemized by FHL);**
- **"Justice Records 1790–1896" in possession of Lyme town clerk;**[570]
- **Lyme's Town [Land] Records, 1667–1794, (births 1662–1702, marriages 1673–86, deaths 1676–1694) 2 vols. (originals at CSL 974.62 L89 m);**
- **Verne M. Hall and Elizebeth B. Plimpton's *Vital Records of Lyme, Connecticut to the End of the Year 1850* (Lyme: American Revolution Bicentennial Commission of Lyme, c1976);**
- ***"Vital Statistics Lyme Connecticut.* SL LYM 7-4a. RSASC, NEHGS, Boston, MA;**
- **F.W. Clapham's "Births, Marriages and Deaths in Lyme, Conn.," *NEHGR*, vol.23:425, *et seq*;**
- **Maria O. LeBrun's *Lyme Vital Statistics, Book 4* (includes births 1847–1856, marriages 1851–1854, and deaths) (online databases at *AmericanAncestors.org*).**

CHURCH RECORDS:

- First Congregational Church of Old Lyme's "Church Records, 1721–1876" (includes baptisms 1731–1841, marriages 1731–1827 and deaths 1731–1840) (originals at CSL) (FHL films 5,358–9);
- Third or North Society's "Church Records (Excerpts), 1801–1804" (includes baptisms, marriages, and deaths performed in New York by a minister who served Lyme both before and after the time period, 1801–1804) (photocopy of originals at New York State Library) (FHL film 17,128);
- First Ecclesiastical Society's minutes of meetings, certificates of membership and withdrawal, and accounts. CSL (FHL film 1,010,744, items 4–5);
- North Lyme Baptist Church's, Church records, 1810-1903 (some baptisms in the minutes) originals at CSL (FHL film 4,702);
- North Lyme Baptist Church's "Church Records," (includes marriage, 1731–1780) (manuscript in NYGBS) (FHL film 4,677, item 1 or 1,419,455, item 15);
- Baptist Ecclesiastical Society of Hadlyme's Records 1844–1874 (copies at CSL (FHL film 1,010,744. item 3);
- First Baptist Church of Old Lyme's, "Church Records, 1842–1924" (includes deaths 1843–1888, baptisms 1842–1875) (originals at CSL) (FHL film 5,360);
- Hadlyme Ecclesiastical Society and Congregational Church's Church records, 1742–1932, originals at CSL (FHL film 4,700 or 1,010,744, item 1);
- Rev. Joseph Vail, Hadlyme Congregational marriage records ca. 1800–1820 (originals in CSA RG 070);

---

570 *Biennial Report (1936)*, 37.

- M.O. LeBrun's "A Copy of the Ancient Records of the 2d Society in Lyme, Later Known as the 1st Congregational Society in East Lyme, 1719–1859" (1908 manuscript at NEHGS);
- First Congregational Church's "Church Records, 1787–1932" (includes deaths, burials, baptisms and marriages) (originals at CSL) (FHL film 4,701);
- Baptist Ecclesiastical Society of Hadlyme's Church records, 1844–1874, Photostats at CSL (FHL film 1,010,744, item 3);
- M.O. LeBrun's "Church Records [of the] First Church of Christ in Lyme, [Conn., 1731–1867]" (1911 manuscript at NEHGS);
- M.O. LeBrun's "A Book of Records for the Church in the 3d or North Society in Lyme" (1908 manuscript at NEHGS);
- M.O. LeBrun's "Third Church of Lyme, Conn. Records, 1788–1850" [1906 manuscript at NEHGS).

CEMETERY TRANSCRIPTIONS: The Hale Collection identifies graves in order of physical proximity buried at about 24 named sites in what was then Lyme Township.[571] Compare with Daniel Hearn's 1979 copy of 59 pre-1800 gravestones in two Lyme cemeteries.[572]The Hale Collection identifies graves in order of physical proximity buried at about 13 named sites in what was then Old Lyme Township.[573] Compare with Daniel Hearn's 1979 copy of 239 pre-1800 gravestones in three Old Lyme cemeteries.[574] See also,

- Charles R. Hale and Mary H. Babin's "Headstone Inscriptions, Town of Lyme Connecticut" (typescript (dated 1937) in the Lyme Town Hall) (FHL film 1,311,118);
- "Hamburg Church Yard, Town of North Lyme" (manuscript in NYGBS) (FHL film 4,429 or 1,405,496);
- Alice Hubbard Breed Benton's DAR (Florida), "Cemetery Records" (includes Duck River Cemetery of Old Lyme) (typescript carbon copy submitted to DAR) (FHL Film 850,401);
- Alice Hubbard Breed Benton's "Duck River Cemetery, Old Lyme, Conn." (typescript. from Daughters of Founders and Patriots of America, Vol. 4) (FHL film 165,997);
- "Record of Inscriptions Found on Gravestones in the Town of Old Lyme Dated Prior to A.D. 1850" (4 vols: Duck River Cemetery, Layville yard, Peck yard, yard near Black Hall School House, Champion yard, Wait yard, Champion yard No. 2, Meeting House Hill's Griswold yard, yard near Swayneys and Hayens, yard near Episcopal Church, yard near B.W. Chadwick's) (manuscript at NEHGS);

---

571 Charles R. Hale, "Headstone Inscriptions of the Town of Lyme, Connecticut" (bound manuscript at CSL) (FHL film 3342). Hale names these Sterling (2 different locations), Congregational Church, Bill Hill, Marvin, Brockway, Joshuatown, Selden, Gove, Luther, Daniels, Indian Grave, Becket Hill, Gillett, Grassy Hill, Colt, Beebe, Griffin, Sisson, Pleasant View, North Lyme Baptist (moved to Pleasant View), Ely, Lord, & Hall (moved to Grassy Hill).

572 Daniel Hearn, "Connecticut gravestones, early to 1800," manuscript (FHL film 1,477,476, item 77).

573 Charles R. Hale, "Headstone Inscriptions of the Town of Old Lyme, Connecticut" (bound manuscript at CSL) (FHL film 3,357). Hale named these Duck River, Layville, Peck, Black Hall Schoolhouse, Champion #1, Wait, Champion #2, Meeting House Hill, Griswold, Graveyard (2 different locations), & 1 stone (2 different locations.

574 Daniel Hearn, "Connecticut gravestones, early to 1800," manuscript (FHL film 1,477,477, item 23).

- "Inscriptions from Gravestones at Old Lyme, Lyme and East Lyme," *NEHGR,* vol. 77:194, 78:365;
- Mary Virginia Wakeman's "Inscriptions on the Old Grave Markers in All of the Burying Grounds in East Haddam, and Seven of Those in Lyme: Being All of the Legible Records of People Born Previous To, or During the Year 1800, With a Few Later Ones" (1907 typescript, in Rathbun Memorial Library, 1923);
- Elizabeth French's "Inscriptions from the Old Burying Ground, Meeting House Hill, Lyme, Conn.," *NEHGR*, vol. 61:75.

OTHER NOTEWORTHY SOURCES:

- "Lyme (Hamburg) Marriage Certificates, 1834–1853," CSL; see Appendix A;
- Lucius B. Barbour's Early Families of Lyme, 1715–1845. I vol. Abstract of vital records. (manuscript 31 in Box 4) CSL Record Group 074.36, Hartford;
- M.O. LeBrun's "Old Lyme Marriages 1731–1906" (manuscript at NEHGS);
- M.O. LeBrun's "Vital Statistics Taken From First Seven Volumes of Lyme Land Records and From the Regular Volumes of Births, Deaths & Marriages" (3 volume manuscript at NEHGS);
- Maria O. LeBrun's "Lyme Vital Statistics, Book 4" *(births 1847–1856)* RSASC, NEGHS, Boston;
- "Lyme Vital Statistics, Book 4" (deaths) RSASC, NEGHS, Boston;
- *"Vital Statistics Lyme Connecticut" (Marriages, 1851–1854)* NEHGS, RSASC, Boston;
- Bruce P. Stark's *Lyme, Connecticut, from founding to independence,* ([S.l.] : B.P. Stark, c1976);
- George J. Willauer's *Lyme miscellany, 1776–1976,* (Middletown: Wesleyan University Press, c1977);
- Jean Chandler Burr's *Lyme Records, 1667–1730* (Stonington. 1968);
- Old Lyme Bicentennial Commission's *Lyme: a chapter of American genealogy,* (Old Lyme: Old Lyme Bicentennial Comn., 1976).

MADISON

Barbour's typescript volume for Madison,[575] unlike the GPC edition,[576] begins:

> This volume contains a list alphabetically arranged of all the vital records of the town of Madison from its incorporation to about 1850. This list was taken from a set of cards[577] based on a copy of the Madison Vital Records made in 1914 by James N. Arnold, of Providence, R.I. The en-

575 See How to Use This Book, note 4, above.

576 Nancy E. Schott, *Barbour Collection of Connecticut Town Vital Records. Madison 1826–1850, Manchester 1823–1853, Marlborough 1803–1852, Meriden 1806–1853, Middlebury 1807–1850. Monroe 1823–1854, Montville 1786–1850, Naugatuck 1844–1853*, vol. 25, (Baltimore: GPC, 2000). Digital images at *Ancestry.com*.

577 Now part of the Barbour Index and interfiled with similar slips from other towns in CSL and on FHL films 2,887 *et seq*. See Introduction above, pp. 3–5.

tire record of the town prior to 1850, is found in two volumes.

The Arnold Copy, now in the possession of the Connecticut State Library, has not been compared with the original and doubtless errors exist. It is hoped that as errors or omissions are found notes will be entered in this volume and on the cards which are included in the General Index of Connecticut Vital Records also in the possession of the Connecticut State Library.

Hartford, Conn., April, 1924.[578]

VITAL RECORDS: The Madison volume includes vital records as early as 1751 and as late as 1852. Barbour abstracted two Madison "books:"

- "1"refers to Madison's Records of Births, Marriages, and Deaths, 1700–1835, Madison Town Hall, FHL Film 1,420,981, item 1;
- "2" refers to Madison's Records of Births, Marriages, and Deaths, 1835–1921, Madison Town Hall, FHL Film 1,420,981, item 2.

See also,

- **Louise R. Allen's "Madison, Conn. town records," (typescript of original town records, 1718–1890, RSASC, NEHGS, 1935) (images at AmericanAncestoirs.org);**
- **Madison Vital Records slips, 1852-ca. 1863) not interfiled in Barbour Index abstracted from Madison's Records of births, marriages, and deaths, 1852 et seq., (typescript in alpha order) (FHL film 1,420,981, item 3). See Appendix B.**

CHURCH RECORDS:

- First Congregational Church's "Church Records, 1707–1917" (includes baptisms, marriages, and deaths) (originals and photocopies at CSL) (FHL film 4,782);
- North Madison Congregational Church's "Church Records, 1754–1888" (includes marriages, baptisms, and deaths) (originals at CSL) (FHL film 1,010,745);
- Rockland Methodist Episcopal Church's "Church Records, 1833–1906" (typescript at CSL) (FHL film 4,785, item 2);
- Madison Methodist Episcopal Church's "Church Records, 1839–1923" (includes marriages, baptisms, etc.) (typescript at CSL) (FHL film 4,785, item 3);
- Congregational Church of North Madison's "Church Records, 1754–1877" (originals at CSL) (FHL film 5,349);
- Louise R Allen's "Early Church Records of Madison, Conn." (typescript in NYGBS) (FHL film 4,776);
- "Early Church Records of Madison, Conn. *1791–1827,* Mss A 2397. RSASC, NEHGS, Boston, MA (online database at *AmericanAncestors.org*).

CEMETERY TRANSCRIPTIONS: The Hale Collection identifies graves in order of physical proximity buried at about six named sites in Madison Township.[579] Compare with Daniel Hearn's 1978 copy of 151 pre-1800 gravestones in two Madison cemeteries.[580]

---

578 Lucius B. Barbour, *Connecticut Vital Records: Madison, 1826–1850*, (Hartford: CSL,1924) page after title page (FHL film 2,974): Digital images at *AmericanAncestors.org* and *FamilySearch.org*

See also

- Glenn E. Griswold's *New Haven County, Connecticut, Inscriptions, Madison, North Madison* (Bradford: G.E. Griswold, 1936) (FHL film 928,515);
- Lucius B. Barbour's "Madison, **Connecticut** Epitaphs" (Mss A 6133), RSASC, NEHGS) online as "Vital **Records of Madison, Connecticut.**"

OTHER NOTEWORTHY SOURCES:

- B.C. Steiner's *History of the Plantation of Menunkatuck, & the Original Town of Guilford (including Madison)* (Baltimore, MD: B.C. Steiner, 1897),1992 copy at NEHGS);
- Merritt W. Cleaver's *History of North Madison, Connecticut,* ([S.l.]: M.W. Cleaver, c2006);
- Charles Daniel Hubbard's *Old Guilford: including the land now constituting the towns of Guilford and Madison,* ([Guilford?]: Tercentenary Committee of Guilford, Conn., 1939) (FHL fiche 6,071,119).

MANCHESTER

Barbour's typescript volume for Manchester,[581] unlike the GPC edition,[582] begins:

> This volume contains a list alphabetically arranged of all the vital records of the town of Manchester from its incorporation to about 1853. The entire record of this town, prior to 1853, is found in one volume.
>
> This list was taken from a set of cards[583] based on a copy of the Manchester Vital Records made in 1918 by James Lahy, formerly of Hartford. This copy has not been compared with the originals and doubtless errors exist. It is hoped that as errors or omissions are found notes will be entered in this volume and on the cards which are included in the General Index of Connecticut Vital Records also in the possession of the Connecticut State Library.
>
> Hartford, Conn., June, 1928.[584]

VITAL RECORDS: The Manchester volume includes vital records as early as 1823 and as late as 1853, consistent with Manchester's establishment in 1823. The records Barbour abstracted are in an unfilmed volume of Town Meeting Records in the Manchester

---

579 Charles R. Hale, "Headstone Inscriptions of the Town of Madison, Connecticut" (bound manuscript at CSL) (FHL film 3,343). Hale names these Hammonassett. West, Summer Hill, Rockland, West side, & Old.

580 Daniel Hearn, "Connecticut gravestones, early to 1800," manuscript (FHL film 1,477,476, item 78).

581 See How to Use This Book, note 4, above.

582 Schott, *Barbour Collection. Madison–Naugatuck*, vol. 25. Digital images at *Ancestry.com*.

583 Now part of the Barbour Index and interfiled with similar slips from other towns in CSL and on FHL films 2,887 *et seq*. See Introduction above, pp. 3–5.

584 Lucius B. Barbour, *Connecticut Vital Records: Manchester, 1823–1853*, (Hartford: CSL, 1928) page after title page (FHL film 2,974). Digital images at *AmericanAncestors.org* and *FamilySearch.org*.

town hall.[585] The earliest Manchester vital records book cataloged by FHL is **Manchester's "Births, Marriages, Deaths, vol. 1 1847–1854," Manchester Town Hall (FHL Film 1,318,080, item 1) a volume containing only 55 pages, and not abstracted by Barbour**.

CHURCH RECORDS:

- First Congregational Church's "Church Records, 1772–1917" (contains baptisms 1800–1850, marriages 1800–1846, and deaths 1800–1840) (originals in CSL) (FHL film 4,907);
- Second Congregational Church's Records 1833–1906, originals at CSL (FHL film 4,908);
- Methodist Church's "Church Records, 1850–1941" (includes baptisms & marriages, 1850–1879, 1851–1896 and 1851–1941) (originals at CSL) (FHL film 4,910 & 4,785);
- Rockland Methodist Episcopal Church's Records 1833–1906, typescript at CSL (FHL film 4,875, item 2).

CEMETERY TRANSCRIPTIONS: The Hale Collection identifies graves in order of physical proximity buried at about six named sites in Manchester Township.[586] Compare with Daniel Hearn's 1979 copy of 124 pre-1800 gravestones in three Manchester cemeteries.[587]

OTHER NOTEWORTHY SOURCES: Matthias Spiess and Percy W. Bidwell's *History of Manchester* (1924/1997 copy at NEHGS).

MANSFIELD

VITAL RECORDS: Barbour created no individual volume[588] for Mansfield. Barbour abstracted all the Mansfield town records (but not the church records) from Susan W. Dimock's *Births, Baptisms, Marriages and Deaths From the Records of the Town and Churches in Mansfield, Connecticut, 1703–1850* (New York: Baker & Taylor Company, 1898) (FHL film 823,814) (images at *AmericanAncestors.org*). He labeled them all "Mansfield Vital Records, vol. D," with Dimmick's page numbers and interfiled the slips in his statewide Index[589]

The original town vital records Dimock abstracted are in:

- Mansfield's "Records of Births, Marriages, and Deaths, 1686–1901," Mansfield Town Hall, (FHL films 1,376,016–7, which are said to cover the years 1686–1872) and
- Mansfield's Births, Marriages, Deaths vol. 4A 1848–1877 (FHL film 1,450,839, items 2–3).

---

585 Email from Manchester Town Clerk Joseph VOL. Camposeo, 2 Jul 2018.

586 Charles R. Hale, "Headstone Inscriptions of the Town of Manchester, Connecticut" (bound manuscript at CSL) (FHL film 3,343). Hale names these East, West, Northwest, St. James, St. Bridget's & Cheney Association.

587 Daniel Hearn, "Connecticut gravestones, early to 1800," manuscript (FHL film 1,477,476, item 79).

588 See How to Use This Book, note 4, above.

589 Now part of the Barbour Index and interfiled with similar slips from other towns in CSL and on FHL films 2,887 *et seq*. See Introduction above, pp. 3–5.

Dimmock grouped her records by family and did not identify the page on which each record was found. Dimock's abstractions contain **errors and omissions**, but the primary information is unorganized and rather illegible. See also,

- **Mansfield Vital Records circa 1845–1905, CSL (CSA RG 070.002, Box 10) (includes pre 1850 birthdates on death certificates);**
- **"Mansfield, Connecticut Early Vital Records Index 1679 to 1906,"** at *http://free-pages.rootsweb.com/~windhamcoct/genealogy/mansfieldvr/mansfieldindex.html.*

CHURCH RECORDS:

- First Congregational Church's "Church Records, 1710–1927" (includes baptisms, marriages, and deaths) (originals at CSL) (FHL film 1,010,746, items 2–10 or 4882);
- Second Congregational Church's "Church Records, 1737–1867" (includes baptisms, marriages, and deaths 1737–1824 and baptisms and deaths 1744–1867) (originals at CSL) (FHL films 4,883 or 1,010,746, item 11 or12);
- Dimock's *Town and Church* records, above (FHL film 823,814)(images at AmericanAncestors.org)

CEMETERY TRANSCRIPTIONS: The Hale Collection identifies graves in order of physical proximity buried at about thirteen named sites in Mansfield Township.[590] Compare with Daniel Hearn's 1979 copy of 238 pre-1800 gravestones in four Mansfield cemeteries.[591] See also,

- Adelaide B. Crandall's "'Pink' or Gurley Cemetery, Mansfield, Conn." (Mss C 3059), RSASC, NEHGS;
- Edmund F. Slafter's "Inscriptions on Gravestones In North Mansfield, CT,"*NEHGR*, 22:387 (October 1868).

OTHER NOTEWORTHY SOURCES:

- Lucius B. Barbour's Abstract of Mansfield, Conn., Marriages 1712–1849; 1 volume (manuscript 133 in Box 23) CSL Record Group 074.36, Hartford;
- Lucius B. Barbour's Copy of vital records from Mansfield volume "Vital Statistics and earmarks."(manuscript 121 in Box 21) CSL Record Group 074.36, Hartford;
- "Zalmon Storrs marriage records, 1817–1818," CSL: see Appendix A;
- "Sexton Martin Phillips' Account book, 1819–1866," CSL; see Appendix A;
- "Barrow Account Book, 1807–1825," CSL, see Appendix A;
- Mansfield Historical Society's *Chronology of Mansfield, Connecticut, 1702–1972, (*Storrs: Parousia Press, c1974);
- Roberta K. Smith, *Listen to the Echoes: the Early History of Spring Hill, Mansfield, Conn.* (Mansfield: History Workshop of the Mansfield Historical Society, c1983).

---

590 Charles R. Hale, "Headstone Inscriptions of the Town of Mansfield, Connecticut" (bound manuscript at CSL) (FHL film 3,343). Hale names these Old Mansfirld Center, New Mansfield Center, Attwoodville, Mt. Hope, Wormwood Hill, Gurleyville, New Storrs, Old Storrs, Gurley, Spring Hill, Pleasant Valley, Ridges, & Jewish.

591 Daniel Hearn, "Connecticut gravestones, early to 1800," manuscript (FHL film 1,477,476, item 80).

MARLBOROUGH

Barbour's typescript volume for Marlborough,[592] like the GPC edition,[593] begins:

> This volume contains a list alphabetically arranged of all the vital records of the town of Marlborough from its incorporation to about 1853. The entire record of this town, prior to 1853, is found in one volume.
>
> This list was taken from a set of cards[594] based on a copy of the Marlborough Vital Records made in 1912 by Mr. James N. Arnold, of Providence, R.I. The Arnold Copy, now in the possession of the Connecticut State Library, has not been compared with the originals and doubtless errors exist. It is hoped that as errors or omissions are found notes will be entered in this volume and on the cards which are included in the General Index of Connecticut Vital Records also in the possession of the Connecticut State Library.
>
> Hartford, Conn., January, 1925.[595]

VITAL RECORDS: The Marlborough volume includes vital records as early as 1737 and as late as 1851. Barbour abstracted Marlborough's Town Records, 1729–1852, (contains births, marriages, deaths, Marlborough Town Hall, FHL film 1,318,178, item 1. **See also, Marlborough Vital Records circa 1845–1905, CSL (CSA RG 072.002, Box 12) (includes pre-1850 birthdates on death certificates).**

CHURCH RECORDS:

- Congregational Church's "Church Records, 1749–1951" (includes baptisms, marriages, and deaths) (originals at CSL) (FHL film 1,010,747);
- Marlborough Methodist Episcopal Church's "Church Records, 1834–1872" (includes baptisms,1846) (originals in BUSTL) (FHL film 1,508,864);
- Myrtle A. Jones' "Congregational Church Records 1749–1855, with Marlborough Deaths 1718–1900" (includes baptisms 1749–1855, deaths 1718–1900 & 1754–1855) (photocopy at CSL) (FHL film 4,887);
- Myrtle A. Jones' "Marlboro [Conn.] Congregational Church Records, 1749–1855" (manuscript at NEHGS).

CEMETERY TRANSCRIPTIONS: The Hale Collection identifies people in order of physical proximity buried at about four named sites in Marlborough Township.[596] Compare

---

592 See How to Use This Book, note 4, above.

593 Schott, *Barbour Collection. Madison–Naugatuck*, vol. 25. Digital images at *Ancestry.com*.

594 Now part of the Barbour Index and interfiled with similar slips from other towns in CSL and on FHL films 2,887 *et seq*. See Introduction above, pp. 3–5.

595 Lucius B. Barbour, *Connecticut Vital Records: Marlborough, 1803– 1852*, (Hartford: CSL, 1925 (page after title page (FHL film 2,974). Digital images on *AmericanAncestors.org* and *FamilySearch.org*.

596 Charles R. Hale, "Headstone Inscriptions of the Town of Marlborough, Connecticut" (bound manuscript at CSL) (FHL film 3,344). Hale names these Old, New, Fawn Brook, & Jones Hollow,

with Daniel Hearn's 1978 copy of 63 pre-1800 gravestones in two Marlborough cemeteries.[597] See also, Lucius B. Barbour's "Genealogical Data from Connecticut Cemeteries: Marlborough" (1932 manuscript at NEHGS).

OTHER NOTEWORTHY SOURCES: See state and county resources above, pages 18–21.

MERIDEN

Barbour's typescript volume for Meriden,[598] like the GPC edition,[599] begins:

> This volume contains a list alphabetically arranged of all the vital records of the town of Meriden from its incorporation to about 1853. The entire record of the town, prior to 1853, is found in one volume.
>
> This list was taken from a set of cards[600] based on a copy of the Meriden Vital Records made in 1915 by Miss Ethel L. Scofield, of New Haven, Conn. The Scofield Copy, now in the possession of the Connecticut State Library, has not been compared with the original and doubtless errors exist. It is hoped that as errors or omissions are found notes will be entered in this volume and on the cards which are included in the General Index of Connecticut Vital Records also in the possession of the Connecticut State Library.
>
> Hartford, Conn., January, 1925.[601]

VITAL RECORDS: The Meriden volume includes vital records as early as 1762 and as late as 1853. Barbour abstracted Meriden's Town Records, 1729–1852, Meriden Town Hall, FHL film 1,403,297, item 4, pp. 1 through 122.

A second book of 223 pages includes 1848–1953 vital reports by school district not abstracted by Barbour. FHL has microfilmed it as the last half of item 4 of FHL film 1,403,297.

CHURCH RECORDS:

- St. Andrew's Episcopal Church's "Church Records, 1789–1929" (includes vital statistics 1824–1849. & 1850–1875) (originals at CSL) (FHL films 4,899–4,900);
- First Congregational Church's "Church Records, 1729–1937" (includes marriages, baptisms and deaths 1729–1872) (photocopies at CSL) (FHL film 4,898);
- Center Congregational Church, Records 1846–1925, originals at CSL (FHL film 4,897);

---

597 Daniel Hearn, "Connecticut gravestones, early to 1800," manuscript (FHL film 1,477,476, item 81).

598 See How to Use This Book, note 4, above.

599 Schott, *Barbour Collection. Madison–Naugatuck*, vol. 25. Digital images at *Ancestry.com*.

600 Now part of the Barbour Index and interfiled with similar slips from other towns in CSL and on FHL films 2,887 *et seq*. See Introduction above, pp. 3–5.

601 Lucius B. Barbour, *Connecticut Vital Records: Meriden, 1806–1853*, (Hartford: CSL, 1925) page after title page (FHL film 2,974): Digital images at *AmericanAncestors.org* and *FamilySearch.org*

- First Baptist Church's "Church Records, 1786–1852" (includes baptisms 1839–1840 and marriages 1837–1852) (originals at CSL) (FHL film 4,896);
- Albert Henry Wilcox and Margaret H. Wilcox's "Baptisms, Marriages and Deaths from First Congregational Church" (transcripts at CSL) (FHL film 1,010,748);

CEMETERY TRANSCRIPTIONS: The Hale Collection identifies graves in order of physical proximity buried at about 14 named sites in Meriden Township.[602] Compare with Daniel Hearn's 1977 copy of 80 pre-1800 gravestones in one Meriden cemetery.[603]

OTHER NOTEWORTHY SOURCES:

- C.H.S. Davis's *History of Wallingford, From Its Settlement in 1670 to the Present, Including Mereden* [sic] *& Cheshire* (1870/1988 copy at NEHGS);
- C. Bancroft Gillespie's *An Historic Record and Pictorial Description of the Town of Meriden, Connecticut, and Men Who Have Made It: From Earliest Settlement to Close of Its First Century of Incorporation* (Meriden: Journal Pub. Co., 1906).

MIDDLEBURY

Barbour's typescript volume for Middlebury,[604] unlike the GPC edition,[605] begins:

> This volume contains a list alphabetically arranged of all the vital records of the town of Middlebury from its incorporation to about 1850. The records prior to 1850 are found in one volume.
>
> This list was taken from a set of cards[606] based on a copy of the Middlebury Vital Records made in 1915 by Mr. James N. Arnold, of Providence, R.I. The Arnold Copy, now in the possession of the Connecticut State Library, has not been compared with the originnal and doubtless errors exist. It is hoped that as errors or omissions are found notes will be entered in this volume and on the cards which are included in the General Index of Connecticut Vital Records also in the possession of the Connecticut State Library.
>
> Hartford, Conn., March, 1925.[607]

---

602 Charles R. Hale, "Headstone Inscriptions of the Town of Meriden, Connecticut" (bound manuscript at CSL) (FHL film 3,344–5). Hale names these Broad Street (very old), Indian - Buckwheat Hill (oldest), Walnut Grove, St. Laurents, St. Stanislaus, East (old), St. Patrick's Sacred Heart, Hebrew, West (old), Gethsemane, St. Boniface, Workman Circle, & St. Peter & St. Paul.

603 Daniel Hearn, "Connecticut gravestones, early to 1800," manuscript (FHL film 1,477,476, item 82).

604 See How to Use This Book, note 4, above.

605 Schott, *Barbour Collection: Madison–Naugatuck*, vol. 25. Digital images at *Ancestry.com*.

606 Now part of the Barbour Index and interfiled with similar slips from other towns in CSL and on FHL films 2,887 *et seq*. See Introduction above, pp. 3–5.

607 Lucius B. Barbour, *Connecticut Vital Records: Middlebury, 1807–1850*, (Hartford: CSL,1925) page after title page (FHL film 2,974). Digital images on *AmericanAncestors.org* and *FamilySearch,org*.

VITAL RECORDS: The Middlebury volume includes vital records as early as 1755 and as late as 1852. Barbour abstracted Middlebury's Town Records, 1734–1855 (contains records of births 1734–1853, marriages 1755–1853, deaths 1776–1853), Middlebury Town Hall (FHL film 1,412,972).

See also, **Bradford E. Smith's *Middlebury, Connecticut Church and Vital Records, 1775–1900* (Middlebury: Middlebury Historical Society, 1984).**

CHURCH RECORDS:

- Methodist Episcopal Church's "Church Records, 1832–1922" (includes baptisms 1836–1862) (originals at CSL) FHL film 4,916).
- Congregational Church's "Church Records, 1751–1916" (contains marriages 1818–1830, funerals 1818–1844, and baptisms 1818–1846) (originals at CSL) (FHL film 4,915).

CEMETERY TRANSCRIPTIONS: The Hale Collection identifies graves in order of physical proximity buried at about one named sites in Middlebury Township. [608] Compare with Daniel Hearn's 1976 copy of eight pre-1800 gravestones in one Middlebury cemetery.[609] See also,

- Jeffrey Lutz, "Headstone Inscriptions, Town of Middlebury, Conn., July 31, 1987" (1987 photocopy at FHL);
- William Cothren's *History of Ancient Woodbury, Connecticut: From the First Indian Deed in 1659, Including the Present Towns of Washington, Southbury, Bethlehem, Roxbury, and a Part of Oxford and Middlebury* (Woodbury: W. Cothren, 1872–1879) (FHL film 2,055,359 & 6,181).

OTHER NOTEWORTHY SOURCES:

- "Miss M. Hine Book, 1827;" see Appendix A;
- Henry Bronson's *History of Waterbury, Connecticut: Original Township Embracing Present Watertown and Plymouth, and Parts of Oxford, Wolcott, Middlebury, Prospect and Naugatuck, with an Appendix of Biography, Genealogy and Statistics* (Waterbury: Bronson Bros., 1858.

MIDDLETOWN

Barbour's typescript volume for Middletown,[610] unlike the GPC edition,[611] begins:

> The vital records of Middletown prior to 1854 are found in the first two volumes of Land Records and in four volumes of Vital Statistics. The entries in these have been alphabetically arranged and listed. The ab-

---

608 Charles R. Hale, "Headstone Inscriptions of the Town of Middlebury, Connecticut" (bound manuscript at CSL) (FHL film 3,345). Hale names this Middlebury.

609 Daniel Hearn, "Connecticut gravestones, early to 1800," manuscript (FHL film 1,477,477, item 1).

610 See How to Use This Book, note 4, above.

611 Marie Schlumbrecht Crossley, *Barbour Collection of Connecticut Town Vital Records: Middletown—Part I A-J 1651–1854*, vol. 26 (Baltimore: GPC, 2000); Carole Magnuson, *Barbour Collection of Connecticut Town Vital Records: Middletown—Part II K-Z 1651-1854*, vol. 27, (Baltimore: GPC, 2000). Digitized at *Ancestry.com*.

> breviation "LR" indicates that the entry is taken from Land Records.
>
> This list was taken from a set of cards[612] based on a copy of the Middletown Vital Records made in 1918 by James N. Arnold, of Providence, R.I. The Arnold Copy, now in the possession of the Connecticut State Library, has not been compared with the original and doubtless errors exist. It is hoped that as errors or omissions are found notes will be entered in this volume and on the cards which are included in the General Index of Connecticut Vital Records also in the possession of the Connecticut State Library.
>
> Hartford, Conn., November, 1923.[613]

VITAL RECORDS: The Middletown occupies two Barbour volumes and includes vital records as early as 1640 and as late as 1858. Barbour abstracted six Middletown "books:"

- "LR1" and "LR2" refer to Middletown's Land Records, vols. 1 & 2, (1654–1742) Middletown Town Hall, (CSL copies: 974.62 fM58L) (FHL film 4,792);[614]
- "1" refers to Middletown's Records of Births, Marriages, Deaths, vol. 1, 1714–1778, Middletown Municipal Hall, (FHL film 1,513,707, item 2);
- "2" refers to Middletown's Records of Births, Marriages, Deaths, 1738–1820, vol. 2 (p.1–230) FHL film 1,513,707, item 3. and vol. 2 (p.230–end) FHL film 1,513,708, item 1);
- "3" and "4" refer to Middletown's Records of Births, Marriages, Deaths, vols. 3–4 1778–1847 (FHL film 1,513,708, items 2 –3).

The Barbour Index also abstracts vital records from Rev. Samuel F. Jarvis' "Christ Church, Middletown, 1836–1839," CSL; see Appendix A.

Additional pre-1855 records may be found in:

- **Middletown's Records of Births, Marriages, Deaths, Vol. 6 Births 1852–1868 (FHL film 1,513,708, item 5), vol. 7 Marriages 1852–1855 (FHL film 1,513,709, item 3), & Vol. 8 Deaths 1852–1878 (FHL Film 1,513,709, item 4);**
- **Middletown's Records of Births, Marriages, Deaths, Vol. 5 Marriages 1855–1870 (FHL film 1,513,708, item 4) & vol. 8 (part copy) Deaths 1855–1868 FHL film 1,513,709, item 4);**
- **Nettie Barnum Eells' "Data Copied From Original Records at Middletown, Conn." (includes principally material copied from the town vital records, but also**

---

612 Now part of the Barbour Index and interfiled with similar slips from other towns in CSL and on FHL films 2887 *et seq*. See Introduction above, pp. 3–5.

613 Lucius B. Barbour, *Connecticut Vital Records:Middletown, 1651–1854, A–J & I–Z,* (Hartford: CSL, 1923) page after title page (FHL film 2,974). Digital images at *AmericanAncestors.org* and *FamilySearch.org*.

614 The Middletown Town Clerk made his own copy of all the vital records in the first two books of land records in 1859 See Records of Births, Marriages, Deaths, Vol. 0-2 (p.1-230) 1640-1742, Middletown Municipal Hall, FHL film 1,513,707, Item 1.

some material copied from church records, probate records, and cemetery records) (manuscript in NYGBS) (FHL film 4,787 or 1,405,496).

CHURCH RECORDS:

- Congregational Church of Middlefield's, "Church Records, 1744–1940" (includes baptisms 1808–1892, marriages 1845–1887, deaths 1845–1890) (originals at CSL) (FHL film 4,946);
- First Church of Christ's "Church Records, 1668–1871" (marriages and deaths 1762–1815) (originals at CSL) (FHL film 4,848);
- First Church of Christ, Series II Records, 1702–1864 (originals at CSL) (FHL film 1,010,749);
- Rev, Sam Jarvis' Holy Trinity Records 1818–1837, copies at CSL (FHL film 4,841 or 1,010,262);
- Church of the Holy Trinity's "Church Records, 1750–1947" (includes christenings (1750–1760, 1764–1770, 1770–1799 & 1809–1813), marriages (1752–1799, 1809–1813 & 1842–1867), burials 1753–1799 & 1809–1813; Negroes christened 1764–1793; baptised 1809–1813; baptisms 1750–1813, burials 1753–1772; baptisms, burials, and marriages 1829–1845; baptisms and burials 1842–1868) (originals and transcripts at CSL) (FHL film 4,841);
- First Universalist Church's 1846–1911, copies at CSL (FHL 4,849)
- Third Congregational Church at Westfield's, "Church Records, 1773–1929" (includes baptisms (1795–1813, 1817–1843 & 1840–1915) and deaths 1817–1844 & 1841–1894) (originals at CSL) (FHL films 4,850–1);
- South Congregational Church's Church records, 1773–1923, originals at CSL (FHL film 4,850);
- Baptisms (1750–60, 1764–70, 1770–90, 1791–99, 1809–1813, 1750–1813, 1845–68, & 1842–68), marriages (1752–99, 1809–13, 1844–68, & 1842–67), & burials (1753–99, 1809–13, 1753–72. 1813–28, 1842–68, & 1842–68), & Negros christened (1764–78, 1771–90, & 1790–73, baptized 1809–13) at Church of the Holy Trinity (ED Film 4,841).;
- First Baptist Church's "Church Records, 1795–1926" (includes deaths.) (originals at CSL) (FHL film 4,847).

CEMETERY TRANSCRIPTIONS: The Hale Collection identifies graves in order of physical proximity buried at about 19 named sites in what was then Middletown Township.[615] Compare with Daniel Hearn's 1978 copy of 651 pre-1800 gravestones in six Middletown cemeteries.[616]The Hale Collection also identifies graves in order of physical proximity buried at about two named sites in what was then Middlefield Township.[617] Compare with Daniel Hearn's 1978 copy of 110 pre-1800 gravestones in

---

615 Charles R. Hale, "Headstone Inscriptions of the Town of Middletown, Connecticut" (bound manuscript at CSL) (FHL film 3,345-6). Hale names these Indian Hill, Pine Grove, Mortimer, West Street, Miner, New Farm Hill, Old Farm Hill, Maromas, New St. John's Old St. John's Conn. State Hospital, Washington Street, Wesleyan University, Old Highland, New Highland, Jewish, Swedish, New Conn. State Hospital, & McDonough.

616 Daniel Hearn, "Connecticut gravestones, early to 1800," manuscript (FHL film 1,477,477, item 3).

617 Charles R. Hale, "Headstone Inscriptions of the Town of Middlefield, Connecticut" (bound manuscript at CSL) (FHL film 3,345). Hale names these North & Middlefield.

one Middlefield cemetery.[618] See also, Lucius B. Barbour's "Cromwell Genealogical Data From Connecticut Cemeteries" (1933 manuscript at NEHGS);

OTHER NOTEWORTHY SOURCES:

- Lucius B. Barbour's Genealogical notes complied from town records of Middletown, Conn., 1662–1833. I vol. Abstract of vital records. (manuscript 32 in Box 4–5) CSL Record Group 074.36, Hartford;
- Lucius B. Barbour's Genealogical notes complied from early Middletown families. 1 vol. Abstract of early Middletown families, 1652–1753. (manuscript 33 in Box 5) CSL Record Group 074.36, Hartford;
- Lucius B. Barbour's Middletown, Conn., Marriages 1781–1835; 1 volume (manuscript 135 in Box 23) CSL Record Group 074.36, Hartford;
- Thomas Atkins' *History of Middlefield and Long Hill* (includes Middlefield Dead From 22d of May 1761); (Hartford: Case, Lockwood & Brainard Co., 1883).

MILFORD

Barbour's typescript volume for Milford,[619] unlike the GPC edition,[620] begins:

> The vital records of Milford prior to 1850 are found in the one volume. Supplementing the town records are records from four other sources. These have been alphabetically arranged and listed. In this alphabetical list the abbreviation "OL' refers to entries in the Old Long Book, "SM" to the Book of Mortality kept by Samuel Bryan Marshall, "BP" to the Death records kept by Rev. Bezaleel Pineo, "ES" to A Statistical Account of the Township of Milford, by Erastus Scranton, and "LL" to loose leaves found in Volume 1, the reference used for the town book of records.
>
> This list was taken from a set of cards[621] based on a copy of the Milford Vital Records made in 1914 by Mr. James N. Arnold, of Providence, R.I. The Arnold Copy, now in the possession of the Connecticut State Library, has not been compared with the original and doubtless errors exist. It is hoped that as errors or omissions are found notes will be entered in this volume and on the cards which are included in the General Index of Connecticut Vital Records also in the possession of the Connecticut State Library.

---

[618] Daniel Hearn, "Connecticut gravestones, early to 1800," manuscript (FHL film 1,477,477, item 2).

[619] See How to Use This Book, note 4, above.

[620] Jan Tilton, *Barbour Collection of Connecticut Town Vital Records. Milford 1640–1850, New Canaan 1801–1854, New Hartford 1740–1854*, vol. 28, (Baltimore: GPC, 2000). Digital images at *Ancestry.com*.

[621] Now part of the Barbour Index and interfiled with similar slips from other towns in CSL and on FHL films 2,887 *et seq*. See Introduction above, pp. 3–5.

Hartford, Conn., May, 1925[622].

VITAL RECORDS: The Milford volume includes vital records as early as 1635 and as late as 1840. FHL has filmed "Milford Vital Records, Indexes to Births, Marriages, Deaths, 1640–1936," Milford Town Hall, (FHL Film 1,428,120), but not the records indexed therein. Milford has deposited in CSA what CSL calls "Births, Marriages, and Deaths, 1649–1874," 6 vols. (CSL 974.62 M594bi.[623] This collection includes the first five books abstracted by Barbour:

- "1" refers to CSA's vol. 2: "Births, Marriages and Deaths, 1649–1718."
- "OL" refers to the "Old Long Book," a volume of at least 98 pages with vital records 1643–1716. Its records are largely duplicated in "1." This is CSA's vol. 3: "Births, Marriages and Deaths, 1653–1803."
- "SM" refers to Samuel Bryan Marshall's Book of Mortality, at least 65 pages long with deaths 1777–1804. This is CSA's vol. 4: "Deaths, 1776–1805."
- "BP:" Rev. Bezaleel Pineo's Death records are at least 83 pages long which contains deaths 1805–1840. This is CSA's vol. 5: "Deaths, 1799–1840."
- "ES" refers to Abbott, Morris W, and Erastus Scranton. *A Statistical Account of the Township of Milvord* [i.e. Milford]. (Milford: Morris W. Abbott, 1977). This is CSA's vol. 1: "A Statistical Account of the Town of Milford by Erastus Scranton."
- "LL" refers to "loose pages" presumably within the unfilmed volume 1, but perhaps not within its index. There are no "loose pages" in the Milford books at CSA.

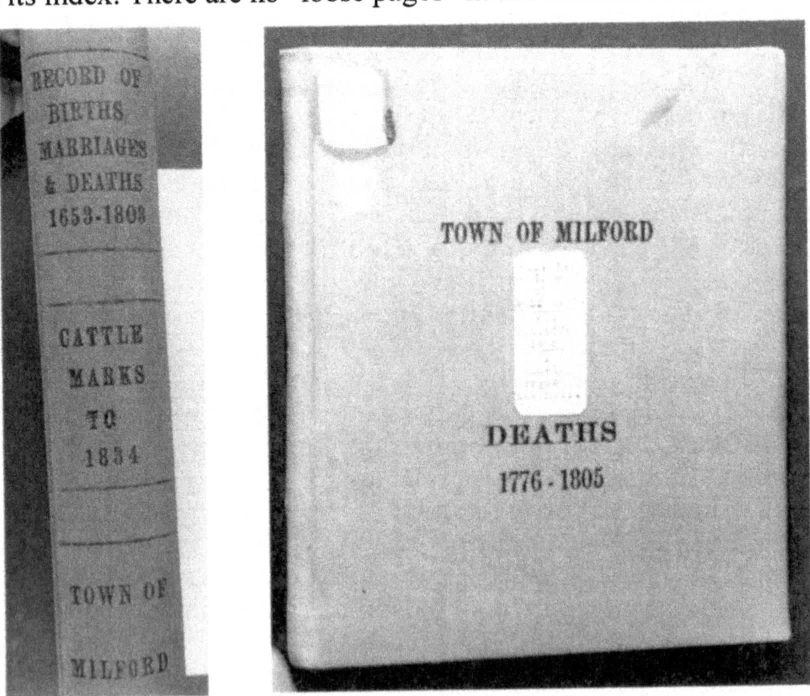

Figures 19 & 20: Two of Milford's six archived books

622 Lucius B. Barbour,: *Connecticut Vital Records Milford, 1640–1850,* (Hartford: CSL, 1925) page after title page (FHL film 2,974). Digital images on *AmericanAncestors.org* and *FamilySearcg.org*.

623 Jeannie Sherman, *Connecticut Town Guides: Milford,* p. 100; CSL online at https://cdm15019.contentdm.oclc.org/digital/api/sibgleitem/image/pdf/p.128501coll2/358841/default.png

The only Milford microfilm cataloged by the FHL as containing vital records is not abstracted by Barbour:

- **Milford's Records of Births, Marriages, and Deaths, vol. 7–8, 1847–1849 & 1852–1867, Milford Town Hall, (FHL film 1,428,120, vols. 7–8).**
- **See also, Milford Births, Marriages, and Deaths, vol. 6, Deaths, 1841–1874. (original with vols. 1 to 5 in CSA).**

CHURCH RECORDS:

- First Church of Christ's "Church Records, 1639–1964," including baptisms, marriages, and deaths (manuscript) (FHL film 1,012,263 or 4,936);
- St. Peter's Church's 'Church Records, 1764–1869'' (vols. 3–4 include baptisms, marriages, and burials,1832–1868) (photocopy of manuscript at CSL) (FHL film 4,938);
- "Baptisms in the First Church of Milford; baptisms and marriages in Milford Second Society Church records," RSASC, NEHGS, Boston, MA. 1932) (images at *AmericanAncestors.org*);
- Second Congregational Church's Records 1747–1926, originals at CSL (FHL film 4,937, items 1–3 and 1,010,750, items 4–6)) database at *AmericanAncestors.org*);
- Mrs. Morris W. Abbott's 'Records of Plymouth Congregational Church, Formerly Second Church, Milford, Conn.: Baptisms, Marriages, Burials, Deaths, 1747–1885' (DAR typescript, 1949) (FHL film 823,816);
- Mrs. Morris W. Abbott's 'Records of St. Peters Episcopal Church, Formerly St. George's Milford, Connecticut, 1832–1868:;
- Baptisms, Confirmations, Communicants, Marriages, Burials' (DAR typescript, 1953) (FHL film 924,067);
- DAR Freelove Baldwin Stow Chapter's 'Baptisms, First Church (Congregational) Records, Milford, Connecticut" (typescript) (FHL film 1,012,263);
- "Baptisms in the First Church of Milford; baptisms and marriages in Milford Second Society Church records." RSASC, NEHGS, Boston, MA. 1932). (FHL films 4,937 & 1,010,750, items 4–6);
- First Ecclesiastical Society's Records, 1760–1830, originals at CSL (FHL film 1,010,750, items 1–3),

CEMETERY TRANSCRIPTIONS: The Hale Collection identifies graves in order of physical proximity buried at about three named sites in Milford Township.[624] Compare with Daniel Hearn's 1975 copy of 405 pre-1800 gravestones in one Milford cemetery.[625] See also,

- Nathan G. Pond's *Inscriptions on Tombstones in Milford, Conn. Erected Prior to 1800: Together With a Few of Aged Persons Who Died After that Date* (Washington DC: LC, Photoduplication Service, 1989) (FHL film 1,685,389).
- Morris W. Abbott and Susan Woodruff Abbott's *Milford Tombstone Inscriptions* (Milford: [s.n.], 1967) (FHL film 897,321);

---

624 Charles R. Hale, "Headstone Inscriptions of the Town of Milford, Connecticut" (bound manuscript at CSL) (FHL film 3,346-7). Hale names these Milford, St. Mary's & New.

625 Daniel Hearn, "Connecticut gravestones, early to 1800," manuscript (FHL film 1,477,477, item 4).

- Morris Woods Abbott and Roland Faucher's *Here Charted Are the Oldest Stones in the Old Milford Cemetery: Newly Done and an Index* (1981 retracing of 1943 manuscript at FHL;

OTHER NOTEWORTHY SOURCES:

- 'Milford Deaths, 1833–1869," CSL; see Appendix A;
- "Milford Deaths 1849–1869," see Appendix A;
- Edward R. Lambert's *History of the Colony of New Haven: Before and After the Union with Connecticut: Containing a Particular Description of the Towns Which Composed that Government, viz., New Haven, Milford, Guilford, Branford, Stamford, & Southold, L.I "* (New Haven: Hitchcock & Stafford, 1838);
- Omar W Platt's "Milford Deaths 1849–1860," (from *Prindle's Almanac* and attributed by Ricker to CSL, 1962);
- Federal Writers' Project's *History of Milford, Connecticut 1639–1939,* (Ann Arbor, MI: University Microfilms, 1897) (FHL fiche 6,062,209);
- Nathan G Pond, Milford families, typescript of NHCHS (FHL film 3,024).
- George Hare Ford's *Historical Sketches of the Town of Milford* (New Haven: Tuttle, Morehouse and Taylor, c1914) (FHL film 1,550,801);
- Susan Woodruff Abbott's *Families of early Milford, Connecticut (*Baltimore, MD: GPC, c1979) (FHL fiche 6,087,946);

MONROE

Barbour's typescript volume for Monroe ,[626] like the GPC edition,[627] begins:

> This volume contains a list alphabetically arranged of all the vital records of the town of Monroe from its incorporation to about 1854. The entire record of the town prior to 1854 if found in one volume.
>
> This list was taken from a set of cards[628] based on a copy of the Monroe Vital Records made in 1917 by Mr. James N. Arnold, of Providence, R.I. The Arnold Copy, now in the possession of the Connecticut State Library, has not been compared with the original and doubtless errors exist. It is hoped that as errors or omissions are found notes will be entered in this volume and on the cards which are included in the General Index of Connecticut Vital Records also in the possession of the Connecticut State Library.
>
> Hartford, Conn., May, 1926.[629]

---

626 See How to Use This Book, note 4, above.

627 Schott, *Barbour Collection. Madison–Naugatuck*, vol. 25. Digital images at *Ancestry.com*.

628 Now part of the Barbour Index and interfiled with similar slips from other towns in CSL and on FHL films 2,887 *et seq*. See Introduction above, pp. 3–5.

629 Lucius B. Barbour, *Connecticut Vital Records: Monroe, 1823–1854*, (Hartford: CSL, 1926) page after title page (FHL film 2,974). Digital images on *AmericanAncestors.org* and *FamilySearch.org*..

VITAL RECORDS: The Monroe volume abstracted by Barbour (1823–1854) remains available only in the Monroe Town Hall.[630] **FHL has, however, filmed Monroe's Reports of Births, Marriages, and Deaths, 1847–1901, Monroe Town Hall (FHL film 1,435,631), which Barbour has not abstracted.**

CHURCH RECORDS:

- Congregational Church records, 1762–1812, (originals at CSL (FHL film 4943);
- St. Peter's Church's Protestant Episcopal Church records (photocopy at CSL) (FHL film 4,944).

CEMETERY TRANSCRIPTIONS: The Charles R. Hale Collection of Cemeteries by Locality at CSL identifies graves buried in graves at about five named sites in Monroe Township.[631] Compare with Daniel Hearn's 1975 copy of 46 pre–1800 gravestones in four Monroe cemeteries.[632]

OTHER NOTEWORTHY SOURCES: See state and county resources above, pages 17–21.

MONTVILLE

Barbour's typescript volume for Montville,[633] like the GPC edition,[634]begins:

> This volume contains a list alphabetically arranged of all the vital records of Montville earlier than 1852.
>
> In 1896 Henry A. Baker, for a number of years Town Clerk of Montville, published his "History of Montville, Connecticut, 1640-1896" and many vital records appear therein. For the past few years the originals, on which this history was probably based, have been lost. In the fall of 1925 a book of records, with the cover and pages 1 and 2 missing, was found and a year later was copied.
>
> This list was taken from a set of cards[635] based on the manuscript copy which is now in the possession of the Connecticut State Library. This copy has not been compared with the original and doubtless errors exist. It is hoped that as errors or omissions are found notes will be entered in this volume and on the cards which are included in the General Index of Connecticut Vital Records also in the possession of the Connecticut State Library.

---

[630] Email from Town Clerk Vida VOL. Stone, 13 Aug 2018.

[631] Charles R. Hale, "Headstone Inscriptions of the Town of Monroe, Connecticut" (bound manuscript at CSL) (FHL film 3,347). Hale names these Elm Street, East Village, Stepney, Walker's Farm, & Center.

[632] Daniel Hearn, "Connecticut gravestones, early to 1800," manuscript (FHL film 1,477,477, item 5).

[633] See How to Use This Book, note 4, above.

[634] Schott, *Barbour Collection. Madison–Naugatuck*, vol. 25. Digital images at *Ancestry.com*.

[635] Now part of the Barbour Index and interfiled with similar slips from other towns in CSL and on FHL films 2,887 *et seq*. See Introduction above, pp. 3–5.

Hartford, Conn., January, 1927.[636]

VITAL RECORDS: The Montville volume includes vital records as early as 1752 and as late as 1850. Barbour abstracted Montville's Records of Births, Marriages, Deaths vol. 1–3 1750–1884 Montville Town Hall, (FHL film 1,311,444, items 5–7).

Hundreds of 1820–1855 Montville vital records slips remain out of Barbour Index in file drawer 392 at CSL. See Appendix B. These slips abstract "Book No. 1, Marriages," a booklet purchased by CSL at a bookstore in 1936, after Barbour's death,. This record is catalogd by FHL "Marriage records, 1820–1855" (originals at CSL) (FHL film 4,863, item 1). with a note that "this volume was kept separate from other vital records found in the town of Montville, Connecticut."

MONTVILLE, CONNECTICUT

MARRIAGE RECORDS

1820 - 1855

Marked:

"Book No. 1, Marriages"

Hartford
Connecticut State Library
1935

Note.

This volume, with leather back and pasteboard sides, measuring 6½ x 8, 179 pages, containing marriage records of the Town of Montville, covering the period 1820-1855, labelled on the inside cover "Book No. 1, Marriages", was secured July 31, 1935 from Tracy's Book Store, Meridian Street, New London, for $ 15.00, the price asked in the letter which called the State Librarian's attention to this volume.

In the Report of the Temporary Examiner of Public Records for 1904, page 112, on which the list of records in the office of the Montville Town Clerk are enumerated, this volume is not mentioned. The only mention of vital statistics records was: "4 volumes 1852 - 1904". Hence, this volume could not have been in the office of the Montville Town Clerk for many years.

It is expected a photostat copy of this volume will be made for the Town of Montville.

Connecticut
State Library,
Hartford, Conn.
August 16, 1935

Geo. S. Godard
State Librarian.

Figures 21–22: Front matter by CSL in rebound Montville marriage records

---

636 Lucius B. Barbour, *Connecticut Vital Records: Montville 1786–1850*, (Hartford: CSL, 1927) page after title page (FHL film 2,974). Digital images on *AmericanAncestors.org* and *FamilySearch.org.*

FHL catalogs two other Montville volumes which Barbour did not abstract:

- **Index of Montville vital records 1744–1937 (FHL 1,311,446);**
- **Henry A. Baker's *History of Montville, Connecticut: formerly the North parish of New London from 1640 to 1896*. (Hartford: Case, Lockwood & Brainard Press, 1896). (FHL film 4,862).**

CHURCH RECORDS:

- Congregational Church's "Church Records, 1722–1909" (includes baptisms 1722–1740, 1784–1825, & 1830–1907 and marriages 1724–1738 & 1784–1791) (photocopy at CSL) (FHL film 4,863, item 2);
- Baptist Church's Church records, 1749–1827, originals at the Western Reserve Historical Society in Cleveland, Ohio (FHL film 960,619, items 1–3).

CEMETERY TRANSCRIPTIONS: The Hale Collection identifies people in order of physical proximity buried at about 42 named sites in Montville Township.[637] Compare with Daniel Hearn's 1981 copy of 108 pre-1800 gravestones in four Montville cemeteries.[638] See also,

- Francis F. Spies' *Connecticut Epitaphs* (4 vols: East Lyme CT, Waterford CT, Sound Beach (Potomac Ave, 1st Congregational Church yard, near Adams Corners); Stamford; Noroton in Darien Township; Mianus (Lyon Farm, Bonnell farm); CosCob, Montville (Uneasville and Chesterfield), Chesterfield (near church, Martenus Farm, by Congregational meeting house, & Great Hill Burial Ground), and Yonkers, NY, New Canaan CT (Yard back of Dr Keeler's & Lakeview Cemetery), East Port Chester CT, Greenwich CT, Port Chester, NY, and Rye, NY (manuscript at NEHGS);
- Lucius B. Barbour's "Montville, Conn. Epitaphs" (Mss A 6180), RSASCs, NEHGS).

OTHER NOTEWORTHY SOURCES:

- Lucius B. Barbour's Genealogical notes complied from church records of Montville, Conn., 1722–1785. I vol. Abstract of vital records. (manuscript 34 in Box 5) CSL Record Group 074.36, Hartford;
- Henry A. Baker's *History of Montville, Connecticut, formerly the North Parish of New London, from 1640–1896* (Hartford: Case, Lockwood and Brainard Company, 1896) (FHL film 4,862 or fiche 6,062,213).

NAUGATUCK

Barbour's typescript volume for Naugatuck, [639] unlike the GPC edition,[640] begins:

```
        This volume contains a list alphabetical-
    ly arranged of all the vital records of the
```

[637] Charles R. Hale, "Headstone Inscriptions of the Town of Montville, Connecticut" (bound manuscript at CSL) (FHL film 3,347). Hale names these Comstock (2 different locations), St. Patrick's Chesterfield, Raymond Hill, Shantock, Maples #1, Maples #2, Parker, Mosler #1, Dolbeare, Smith (2 different locations), Lewis, Rogers (2 different locations), Johnson, Indian, Gay, Fox, Raymond, Miner, Champlin, Chester, Thompson, Mynard, Dobeare, Baker (3 different locations), Chapel, Mosler #2, Jewish, Gilbert, DeWolf, Martenus, Latimer, Removed to Waterford, 1 stone, Chapman, & Street-Conlan.

[638] Daniel Hearn, "Connecticut gravestones, early to 1800," manuscript (FHL film 1,477,477, item 6).

[639] See How to Use This Book, note 4, above.

[640] Schott, *Barbour Collection. Madison–Naugatuck*, vol. 25. Digital images at *Ancestry.com*.

> town of Naugatuck from its incorporation to about 1853. The entire record of the town prior to 1853 if found in one volume.
>
> This list was taken from a set of cards[641] based on a copy of the Naugatuck Vital Records made in 1927 by Percy E. Hulbert, of Hockenum, Conn. The Hulbert Copy, now in the possession of the Connecticut State Library, has not been compared with the original and doubtless errors exist. It is hoped that as errors or omissions are found notes will be entered in this volume and on the cards which are included in the General Index of Connecticut Vital Records also in the possession of the Connecticut State Library.
>
> Hartford, Conn., February, 1928.[642]

VITAL RECORDS: The Naugatuck volume includes vital records as early as 1844 and as late as 1853. Barbour abstracted Naugatuck's Records of Births, Marriages, and Deaths, vols. A–D, 1844–1862, Naugatuck Town Hall, (FHL film 1,412,958, items 1–4).

CHURCH RECORDS:

- Congregational Church's "Church Records, 1781–1901" (includes, baptisms (1785–1831, 1832–1849 & 1850–1901), and deaths (1801–1832, 1832–1838 & 1850–1901), and marriages 1800–1830 & 1850–1900) (originals at CSL) (FHL film 5,185);
- St. Michael's Church's "Church Records, 1786–1886" (includes baptisms, marriages, and burials) (originals at CSL) (FHL film 1,010,753);
- Helen S. Ullmann's *Naugatuck, Connecticut, Congregational Church Records, 1781–1901* (Bowie, MD: Heritage Books, 1987, c1987) (FHL film 1,440,696);
- Infant baptisms (1832–47), baptisms (1832–86), marriages (1832–52, 1852–57, 1832–66) & burials (1832–47, 1847–49, & 1849–57, 1832–86) at St. Michael's Church (ED Film 1,010,753).

CEMETERY TRANSCRIPTIONS: The Hale Collection identifies graves in order of physical proximity buried at about eight named sites in Naugatuck Township.[643] Compare with Daniel Hearn's 1976 copy of 17 pre-1800 gravestones in three Naugatuck cemeteries.[644] See also,

OTHER NOTEWORTHY SOURCES:

- Henry Bronson's *History of Waterbury, Connecticut: Original Township Embracing Present Watertown and Plymouth, and Parts of Oxford, Wolcott, Middlebury, Prospect*

---

641 Now part of the Barbour Index and interfiled with similar slips from other towns in CSL and on FHL films 2,887 *et seq*. See Introduction above, pp. 3–5.

642 Lucius B. Barbour, *Connecticut Vital Records: Naugatuck, 1844–1853*, (Hartford: CSL, 1928) page after title page (FHL film 2,975). Digital images at *AmericanAncestors.org* and *FamilySearch.org*.

643 Charles R. Hale, "Headstone Inscriptions of the Town of Naugatuck, Connecticut" (bound manuscript at CSL) (FHL film 3,347). Hale names these Grove, St. James, Gunntown, Ancient, Hillside, St. Francis, Wooster, & Polish National Catholic.

644 Daniel Hearn, "Connecticut gravestones, early to 1800," manuscript (FHL film 1,477,477, item 8).

and Naugatuck, with an Appendix of Biography, Genealogy and Statistics (Waterbury: Bronson Bros., 1858);

- Constance McLaughlin Green's *History of Naugatuck* (1948/1999 copy at NEHGS).

NEW BRITAIN

VITAL RECORDS: New Britain was incorporated in May 1850 from Berlin.[645] It possesses an Index to Vital Statistics 1850–1905 (New Britain Town Hall) (FHL film 1,451,353, items 2–3 (A–O) and FHL film 1,451,354 (P–Z)). No record book corresponding to this index has been microfilmed by FHL. Morrison suggests the underlying records may be in Farmington or Berlin.[646] **See Linda MacLachlan's "New Britain, Connecticut: Vital Records 1846–1865. " *CN*, vols. 43 to 44 (Births: March 2011, Marriages: June–March 2012), Deaths: March 2012)**

CHURCH RECORDS:

- First Baptist Church's Records 1821–1922, copies at CSL (FHL film 5,350);
- First Church of Christ of New Britain's "Church Records, 1757–1925" (includes baptisms, marriages, deaths) (originals at CSL) (FHL films 1,010,755 and 1,010,756, items 1–2);
- South Congregational Church of New Britain's "Church Records, 1842–1919" (includes baptisms and deaths) (originals at CSL) (FHL film 1,010,757);
- St. Mark's Church of New Britain's "Church Records, 1848–1902" (includes baptisms, marriages, & burials) (originals at CSL) (FHL film 1,010,756, items 4–5);
- James Shepard's *History of Saint Mark's Church, New Britain, Conn., and of Its Predecessor Christ Church, Wethersfield and Berlin : from the First Church of England Service in America to Nineteen Hundred and Seven* (New Britain CT: Tuttle, Morehouse & Taylor Co., 1907) FHL film 1,440,672, item 3.
- Baptisms (1849–73), marriages (1849–73) & burials (1849–73) at St. Mark's Church in New Britain, Episcopal Diocese, Hartford (ED Film 1,010,756);

CEMETERY INSCRIPTIONS: The Hale Collection identifies people in order of physical proximity buried at about 10 named sites in New Britain Township.[647] See also,

- Kenneth and Marcia Witt's *Index to Family Tombstone Locations* (West Palm Beach Fl: K. & M. Witt, [1980?] FHL fiche 6,018,757;
- Connecticut DAR's "Record of Clark Homestead, probably New Britain," *CT* Connecticut DAR, "Old Fairview Cemetery, New Britain, Connecticut," *CT DAR GRC Report*, ser. 1, vol. 47:121 (1935);
- Connecticut DAR's "Graves of Revolutionary War soldiers: Lt. Elijah Francis, Fairview Cemetery, New Britain, CT; Capt. Justus Francis, Fairview Cemetery, New

---

645 *Biennial Report* (1936) 42. Berlin claims that New Britain took "all the old records up to that date." *Ibid.*,12. New Britain does not acknowledge possessing them in 1936 or in 1975. See CSL< *First 200 Years*. In 1936, however, New Britain held "46 volumes of Vital Records 1850-1936" in contrast to Berlin's "5 volumes of Vital Records 1830-1936. *Ibid.*

646 Morrison, *Connecting to Connecticut*, 181.

647 Charles R. Hale, "Headstone Inscriptions of the Town of New Britain, bound typescript, 1930s, CSL, Hartford, FHL film 3,348. Hale names these Fairview, New St. Mary's Old St. Mary's Sacred Heart, Beth Israel, Greek Catholic, & Andrews.

Britain, CT; Ralph Jennings, Milton, CT; Grant Wickwire, Lakeside, Connecticut; Jasper Stannard, Westbrook, CT," *CT DAR GRC Report*, ser. 1, vol. 57:9 (1936).

OTHER NOTEWORTHY SOURCES:

- Lucius B. Barbour's Genealogical notes complied from church records of New Britain, Conn., 1680–1850. I vol. Abstract of vital records. (manuscript 35 in Box 5) CSL Record Group 074.36, Hartford;
- David N. Camp's *History of New Britain, With Sketches of Farmington & Berlin, 1640–1889* (1889/1994 copy at NEHGS) (FHL film 833,382);
- Albert W. Savage, Jr.'s "Town of New Britain Records," 1822–1965 (202 cubic feet of tax, election, school and town welfare records for the town of New Britain) CSA, Hartford;
- William C. Sharpe's *South Britain sketches and records* (Seymour: Record Print, 1898) Digital images on *FamilySearch.org*.

NEW CANAAN

Barbour's typescript volume for New Canaan,[648] unlike the GPC edition,[649] begins:

> This volume contains a list alphabetically arranged of all the vital records of the town of New Canaan from its incorporation to about 1854. The entire record of the town prior to 1854 is found in one volume.
>
> For many years the book of original records was thought to have been lost and it was only recently unearthed by Mr. Edward Rutledge, the Town Clerk of New Canaan. A very copious index in the original volume has been checked with the entries and any variations between it and the text have been noted herein.
>
> This list was taken from a set of cards[650] based on a copy of the Naugatuck Vital Records made in 1926 by Mrs. Julia E.C. Brush, of Danbury, Connecticut. The Brush Copy, now in the possession of the Connecticut State Library, has not been compared with the original and doubtless errors exist. It is hoped that as errors or omissions are found notes will be entered in this volume and on the cards which are included in the General Index of Connecticut Vital Records also in the possession of the Connecticut State Library.
>
> Hartford, Conn., May, 1926.[651]

---

[648] See How to Use This Book, note 4, above.

[649] Tilton, *Barbour Collection: Milford–New Hartford*, vol. 28.

[650] Now part of the Barbour Index and interfiled with similar slips from other towns in CSL and on FHL films 2,887 *et seq*. See Introduction above, pp. 3–5.

[651] Lucius B. Barbour, *Connecticut Vital Records New Canaan, 1807–1854*, (Hartford: CSL, 1926) page after title page (FHL film 2,975). Digital images on *AmericanAncestors.org* and *FamilySearch.org*.

VITAL RECORDS: The New Canaan volume includes vital records as early as 1766 and as late as 1851. Barbour abstracted New Canaan's Records of Births, Marriages, and Deaths, vol. 1–2, 1766–1900, New Canaan Town Hall, (FHL film 1,450,629).

CHURCH RECORDS:

- Congregational Church's "Church Records, 1733–1899" (contains baptisms 1733–1853, marriages 1742–1806, deaths 1773–1808) (originals at CSL) (FHL film 4,960);
- St. Mark's Church's "Church Records, 1835–1913" (includes baptisms, marriages, and burials) (originals at CSL) (FHL film 1,010,758);
- Jay Harris's *Index to Records of the Methodist Episcopal Community Church, Pound Ridge, New York 1833–1983* (Pound Ridge, NY: Community Church, 1991) (FHL film 1,750,737);
- Baptisms (1835–71), marriages (1835–71) & burials (1835–71) at St. Mark's Church (ED Film 1,010,758).

CEMETERY TRANSCRIPTIONS: The Hale Collection identifies graves in order of physical proximity buried at about 28 named sites in New Canaan Township.[652] Compare with Daniel Hearn's 1977 copy of 22 pre-1800 gravestones in three New Canaan cemeteries. [653] See also,

- "Cemeteries In and Near New Canaan, Connecticut" (typescript in NYGBS) (FHL film 4,949 or 1,421,100);
- "Record of burials, Lakeview Cemetery, New Canaan, Connecticut," (manuscript at FHL);
- "Rural Cemeteries, New Canaan, Connecticut], 1757–1907" (typescript at FHL);
- William A. Eardley's Connecticut Cemeteries 1673–1911 (Brooklyn: sn, 1914–1918); (NEHGS microfilm 104);
- Lester Card's "New Canaan, Conn.: Cemetary [sic] Records" (Mss A 2422), RSASC , NEHGS;
- Francis F. Spies' "Connecticut Epitaphs" (4 vols: East Lyme CT, Waterford, CT, Sound Beach (Potomac Ave, 1st Congregational Church yard, near Adams Corners), Noroton in Darien Township, Mianus (Lyon Farm, Bonnell farm); CosCob, Montville, Chesterfield (near church, Martenus Farm, by Congregational meeting house, on Warren farm, & Great Hill Burial Ground), and Yonkers NY, New Canaan CT (Yard back of Dr Keeler's & Lakeview Cemetery), East Port Chester, CT, Greenwich CT, Port Chester NY; and Rye NY) (manuscript at NEHGS);
- Francis F. Spiess' *New Canaan Inscriptions With Genealogical Notes & Revolutionary Service* (1930/1997 copy at NEHGS);
- "Record of Burials, Lakeview Cemetery, New Canaan, Connecticut" (manuscript at FHL);

---

652 Charles R. Hale, "Headstone Inscriptions of the Town of New Canaan, Connecticut" (bound manuscript at CSL) (FHL film 3,349). Hale names these Talmadge Hill, Private Graveyard, Stevens, Wood, Parade Ground, Lakeview, Park Street, Old (moved to Lakeview), Small private yard, Old (moved), Crissey, Young, Crissy, Selleck's Corner, Church Hill, Carter, Valley Road, Hickok, Private yard, Silvermine, White Oak Shade, --issy, --yt, --d, --w Richards, --d Richards, --d Mather, & --ters.

653 Daniel Hearn, "Connecticut gravestones, early to 1800," manuscript (FHL film 1,477,477, item 9).

OTHER NOTEWORTHY SOURCES:

- Vi L. Kemp and Thomas Jay Kemp's *Index to births, engagements, marriages & obituaries, New Canaan advertiser, New Canaan, Connecticut, 1989,* (Darien: Middlesex Genealogical Society, c1990);
- Mary Louise King's *Portrait of New Canaan: the history of a Connecticut town* ([New Canaan: New Canaan Historical Society, c1981);
- New Canaan Historical Society's *Readings in New Canaan history.* (New Canaan: New Canaan Historical Society, 1949);
- Lester Card's "Marriages and Deaths in New York State from New Canaan, Conn. "ERA" 1865–1871" (RSASCs typescript., NEHGS 1941)..

NEW FAIRFIELD

VITAL RECORDS: New Fairfield was settled 1728, incorporated 1740, and had a population of 927 in 1850 census.[654] New Fairfield's vital records were destroyed by fire in 1867.[655] The FHL catalog lists no vital records by the town clerk before 1867 and its vital records are not in the Barbour Collection. The Barbour Index, however, abstracts "Marriages 1741–1791" by Ephriam Hubbell, J.P. See Appendix A.

CHURCH RECORDS:

- New Fairfield South Congregational Church's "Church Records, 1742–1900" (includes births, baptisms, marriages and church communicants 1742–1870) (originals at CSL) (FHL film 5,351, items 1–2);
- "New Fairfield, Conn., Church Records" (Mss A 6179), RSASC, NEHGS;
- Congregational Church of New Fairfield's "Church Records, 1742–1900" (includes baptisms & deaths) (photocopy at CSL) (FHL film 5,351, item 3);
- St. Matthew's Bristol Bristol Episcopal Church's Southington Baptist Church, Guilford Episcopal Church, "Miscellaneous Church Records" (typescript in NHCHS) (FHL film 3,054);
- "Miscellaneous Church Records," including inscriptions from the old burying ground opposite the Town House in New Fairfield; record of marriages, New Fairfield 1746–1791; FHL film 3054 Item 4.

CEMETERY TRANSCRIPTIONS: The Hale Collection identifies people in order of physical proximity buried at about four named sites in New Fairfield Township.[656] Compare with Daniel Hearn's 1977 copy of 22 pre-1800 gravestones in one New Fairfield cemetery.[657] See also,

- Josephine C. Frost's "Cemetery Records of Haviland Hollow and Quaker Hill, Dutchess County, New York" (1909–1912 typescript in possession of NYGBS) (FHL film 17705);

---

[654] Morrison, *Connecting to Connecticut,* 185.

[655] Thomas Jay Kemp, *Connecticut researcher's Handbook*. Detroit MI: Gale Research Co., 1981).

[656] Charles R. Hale, "Headstone Inscriptions of the Town of New Fairfield, Connecticut" (bound manuscript at CSL) (FHL film 3,349). Hale names these New Fairfield, Old, Gerow, & Bails Pond.

[657] Daniel Hearn, "Connecticut gravestones, early to 1800," manuscript (FHL film 1,477,477, item 10).

- Josephine C. Frost's "Cemetery Inscriptions From Danbury and New Fairfield, Conn." (1915 typescript in NYGBS) (FHL film 4005); (Mss A 2426) RSASC, NEHGS;
- George S. Hoyt's *Record of soldiers buried in Danbury, Brookfield, New Fairfield and Ridgefield*, Photostat copy (Hartford: CSL, 1929) CSL digital collection online.

OTHER NOTEWORTHY SOURCES:

- Samuel Willett Comstock's "Congregational Church, New Fairfield, Conn., New Fairfield, Connecticut 1790 U.S. Census" (includes birth and death **records** for 1758–1764, marriage records for 1758–1775, baptisms for 1758–1764; deaths for 1772–1801 & a list of New Fairfield residents listed in the 1790 U.S. census) (manuscript at NEHGS);
- Ephraim Hubbel, Jr.'s "New Fairfield, Connecticut: Index Cards to Marriages, 1746–1791" (card file at CSL) (FHL film 2,883) CSL; see Appendix A;
- Irving Bernard Simon's *Our town: the history of New Fairfield* (New Fairfield: New Fairfield Bicentennial Commission, c1975).

NEW HARTFORD

Barbour's typescript volume for New Hartford,[658] unlike the GPC edition,[659] begins:

> This volume contains a list alphabetically arranged of all the vital records of the town of New Hartford from its incorporation to about 1854. This list was taken from a set of cards[660] based on a copy of the New Hartford Vital Records made in 1916 by James N. Arnold, of Providence, R.I. The entire record of the town prior to 1854 is found in three volumes.
>
> The Arnold Copy, now in the possession of the Connecticut State Library, has not been compared with the original and doubtless errors exist. It is hoped that as errors or omissions are found notes will be entered in this volume and on the cards which are included in the General Index of Connecticut Vital Records also in the possession of the Connecticut State Library.
>
> Hartford, Conn., June, 1927.[661]

VITAL RECORDS: The New Hartford volume includes vital records as early as 1718 and as late as 1853. Barbour abstracted three New Hartford "books:"

- "1" refers to New Hartford's Town Records, 1739–1864 (includes family registers of births, marriages, and deaths 1718–1776) New Hartford Town Hall, (FHL film 1,318,241, item 1 **with some omissions.**

---

658 See How to Use This Book, note 4, above.

659 Tilton, *Barbour Collection: Milford–New Hartford*, vol. 28.

660 Now part of the Barbour Index and interfiled with similar slips from other towns in CSL and on FHL films 2,887 *et seq*. See Introduction above, pp. 3–5.

661 Lucius B. Barbour, *Connecticut Vital Records: New Hartford, 1740–1854*, (Hartford: CSL, 1927) page after title page (FHL film 2,975). Digital images on *AmericanAncestors.org* and *FamikySearch.org*.

- "2" refers to New Hartford's Town Records, 1739–1864 (includes family registers of births, marriages, and deaths 1774–1852) New Hartford Town Hall, (FHL film 1,318,241, item 2.
- "3" appears to be abstracted from marriage certificates, 1820–1854, records not filmed by FHL. New Hartford's Town Clerk denies having such records today.[662]

The volume the New Hartford Town Clerk actually numbered three is not abstracted by Barbour: Report of Births, Marriages, and Deaths, 1847–1851, New Hartford Town Hall, (FHL film 1,318,241, item 3). Additional records for the period 1852–53 are in Records of Births, Marriages, and Deaths, 1852–1921, New Hartford Town Hall, FHL film 1,318,241, item 4.

CHURCH RECORDS:

- Church of Christ's "Church Records, 1739–1877" (includes baptisms; marriages; and deaths) originals at CSL) (FHL film 1,010,759 or 5,167);
- South Ecclesiastical Society's "Records, 1846–1933" (originals in CSL) (FHL film 1,010,760);
- South Congregational Church's "Church Records, 1848–1932" (includes deaths and burials) (originals in CSL) (FHL film 1,010,761);
- St. John's Church at Pine Meadow's "Church Records, 1850–1904" (includes baptisms 1850–1873, marriages 1850– 1871, and burials 1850–1876) (originals at CSL) (FHL film 5,168);
- Baptisms (1850–73), marriages (1850–71) & burials (1850–76) at St. John's Church (ED Film 5,168 and original manuscript).

CEMETERY TRANSCRIPTIONS: The Hale Collection identifies graves in order of physical proximity buried at about eight named sites in New Hartford Township.[663] Compare with Daniel Hearn's 1978 copy of 44 pre-1800 gravestones in one New Hartford cemetery.[664]

OTHER NOTEWORTHY SOURCES:

- Lucius B. Barbour's Genealogical notes complied from church records of New Hartford, Conn., 1697–1827. I vol. Abstract of vital records. (manuscript 36 in Box 5) CSL Record Group 074.36, Hartford;
- Lucius B. Barbour's Southington, Burlington, Goshen, New Hartford, Conn. marriages. 1732–1850, 1 volume. (manuscript 138 in Box 23) CSL Record Group 074.36, Hartford.

NEW HAVEN

VITAL RECORDS: Barbour's abstraction of New Haven vital records extends from 1649 to 1850, but his slips are only in *Barbour Index*. See page 1, above. Barbour's slips are

---

662 Email from Town Clerk Donna LaPlante, 23 Oct 2018. In 1936, however, New Hartford, reported "6 volumes of Vital Records 1739-1936." *Biennial Report* (1936)

663 Charles R. Hale, "Headstone Inscriptions of the Town of New Hartford, Connecticut" (bound manuscript at CSL) (FHL film 3,349-52). Hale named these Town Hill, North Village, Immaculate Conception, Pine Grove, Old Nepaug, Pine Meadow, & Bakerville.

664 Daniel Hearn, "Connecticut gravestones, early to 1800," manuscript (FHL film 1,477,477, item 11).

copied from the OFPA's *Vital Records of New Haven, 1649–1850*, 2 vols. (Hartford: Connecticut Society of the OFPA, 1917–1924) (FHL films 599,303–04) (images at *AmericanAncestors.org*). The original town vital records abstracted by the book are New Haven's "Records of Births, Marriages, and Deaths, 1639–1902; (7 vols. on FHL films 1,405,830 and 1,405,858

- Volume 1, Book I (birth, marriages and deaths 1649–1750) refers to FHL film 1,305,830, items 1–3;
- Volume 1, Book II (birth, marriages and deaths 1753–1790) refers to FHL film 1,305,830, item 4;
- Volume 1, Book III (birth, marriages and deaths 1785–1824) refers to FHL film 1,405,858, item 1;
- Volume 1, Book IV (marriages 1820–1839) refers to FHL film 1,405,858, item 1;
- Volume 2, Book V (deaths 1821–1840) refers to FHL film 1,405,858, item 2;
- Volume 2, Book VI (deaths, 1828–1849) refers to FHL film 1,405,858, item 3;
- Volume 2, Book VII (marriages 1835–1853) refers to FHL film 1,405,858, item 4;

OFPA's Book I contains additional information in brackets that is not on these microfilms. This specified secondary information is taken from "an alphabetically arranged copy of this volume now [i.e., in 1902] in constant use."[665] The location and sources and precise title of that alphabetical copy is presently unknown.

Thousands of New Haven private records slips (1824–1883) remain outside of Barbour Index, in file drawer 393 at CSL. See Appendix B. They are abstracted from a source described as New Haven County records in Appendices A and C.
See also,

- **Donald Lines Jacobus'** ***New Haven, CT: Families of Ancient New Haven.*** **originally published as** ***New Haven Genealogical Magazine.*** **vols. I–VIII. 8 vols. (Rome, NY: Clarence D. Smith, 1923–1932).**
- **"New Haven Book 01 Marriage Record (marriage certifications 1835–1854," New Haven Town Hall (FHL film 5,344, item 3);**
- **New Haven's Records of Births, Marriages, and Deaths, 1846–1860, New Havwn Town Hall (FHL film 1,405,859, items 1–2);**
- ***Religious intelligencer*****, New Haven, Connecticut, 1760-1835, typescript in Pittsfield, MA (FHL film 234,579, items 3–4).**

The Barbour Index also abstracted "New Haven Private Records by Rev. Samuel Jarvis." See Appendix A.

CHURCH RECORDS:

- First Church of Christ and Ecclesiastical Society's "Church Records, 1639–1926" (includes baptisms (1639–1812, 1789–1797, 1798–1805, 1812–1840 & 1841–1896), marriages (1806–1809, 1789–1796 & 1798–1806), and deaths (1730, 1806–1812, 1789–1797 & 1789–1805)) originals at the CSL) (FHL film 5,343);
- Trinity Church's "Church Records, 1767–1939" (includes marriages and burials 1815–1858; and 1848–1894) (transcripts at CSL) (FHL films 5,341—2);

665 OFPA, *Vital Records of New Haven*, vol. 2, p. 1.

- First Baptist Society's Records 1824–1902, copies at CSL (FHL film 5,329);
- Church of Christ in the United Society's "Church Records, 1796–1879" (includes baptisms, marriages and deaths) (originals at CSL) (FHL film 1,011,941, items 7–8);
- First Baptist Church's "Church Records, 1816–1831" (includes parish register 1816–1831 of baptisms) (transcript at CSL) (FHL film 5,331);
- First Congregational Church of Fair Haven's, "Church Records, 1830–1894" (includes baptisms 1836–1888) (photocopy at CSL) (FHL film 5,334);
- Church of the Redeemer's "Church Records, 1838–1933" (includes marriages 1839 and baptisms 1839–1840) (originals at the CSL) (FHL film 5,340);
- Beecher's registers of baptisms, marriages, & burials at Trinity Church (ED Film 5.341);
- Fair Haven Church's "Church Records, 1769–1819" (includes baptisms and marriages) (original records at CSL) (FHL film 1,011,941, items 4–6);
- St. James Church at Fair Haven's, "Church Records, 1843–1925" (includes baptisms, marriages and burials) (originals in CSL) (FHL film 1,011,939);
- St. Paul's Church's "Church Records, 1845–1940" (includes 1845–1856 baptisms, marriages, etc.) (originals at CSL) (FHL film 5,337);
- St. Thomas's Church's *Church Records, 1848–1931* (vol. 7 parish register 1848–1892 includes baptisms, marriages, deaths, etc.) (originals at CSL) (FHL film 5,338–9);
- "Religious Intelligencer, New Haven, Connecticut, 1760–1835" (typescript in Pittsfield, MA) (FHL film 234,579);
- Clara Louise Weed's "Records of the Dwight Place Congregational Church, New Haven, Connecticut, 1838–1865" (includes baptisms) (photocopy in CSL) (FHL film 1,010,761);
- "New Haven, Connecticut, Marriages for 1835–1854" (manuscript at CSL) (FHL film 5,344);
- Christ Church's Protestant Episcopal Records, 1788–1903, includes baptisms, marriages, confirmations, burials (FHL films 6,270 or 1,014,195);
- Baptisms (1845–1896), marriages (1845–1925) & burials (1845–1925) at St. James Church at Fair Haven (ED Film 1,011,939);
- Baptisms (1845–1856), marriages (1846–56) & burials (1847–56) at St. Paul's Church (ED Film 5.337);
- Baptisms (1848–92), marriages (1848–92) & burials (1848–92) at St. Thomas Church (ED Film 5,339);
- Second Baptist Church, Records 1842–1865, copies at CSL (FHL film 5,333);
- Baptisms (1848–94), marriages (1848–94) & burials (1848–94) at Trinity Church (ED Film 5,342);
- Baptisms (1839–50), marriages (1841–50) & burials (1840–50) at Christ Church in West Haven (ED Film 1,014,195);
- Baptisms (1839–52, 1847), marriages (1839–51, 1847) & burials (1839–45, 1847) at St. James the Apostle Church in Westville (ED Original manuscript);

CEMETERY TRANSCRIPTIONS: The Hale Collection identifies graves in order of physical proximity buried at about 11 named sites in what was then New Haven Township.[666] Compare with Daniel Hearn's 1975 copy of 726 pre–1800 gravestones in two New Haven cemeteries.[667] The Hale Collection also identifies graves buried in graves at about four named sites in what was then West Haven Township.[668] Compare with Daniel Hearn's 1975 copy of 132 pre-1800 gravestones in two West Haven cemeteries.[669]

See also,

- DAR GRC's "Bible and Cemetery Records, 1800–1940" (original typescript at the DAR Library in Washington D.C.) (FHL film 848,696);
- B. Edwards' *The Burial Ground at New Haven*, (New Haven: Yale University Photographic Services, 1981) (FHL film 1,685,385);
- Henry H. Townshend's *The Grove Street Cemetery: A Paper Read Before the New Haven Colony Historical Society, October 27, 1947* (New Haven: The Society, 1948) (FHL film 1,550,142);
- Mrs. Frank S. Torrens' "Cemetery Records in the Sparta, Illinois Collection" (includes New Haven (Old Grove Cemetery) (manuscript) (FHL film 897,008);
- Franklin B. Dexter's *Inscriptions on Tombstones in New Haven, Erected Prior to 1800* (New Haven?: s.n., 1882?) (FHL fiche 6,062,243);
- Gold Street Cemetery's "Names From Gold Street Cemetery, Hartford, Connecticut" (typescript.) (FHL film 5,347).

OTHER NOTEWORTHY SOURCES:

- Lucius B. Barbour's Abstract of Genealogical records of New Haven, Conn., 1650–1850. 6 vols. Abstract of vital records. (manuscript 112 in Box 16) CSL Record Group 074.36, Hartford;
- Edward R. Lambert's *History of the Colony of New Haven: Before and After the Union with Connecticut: Containing a Particular Description of the Towns Which Composed that Government, viz., New Haven, Milford, Guilford, Branford, Stamford, & Southold, L.I "* (New Haven: Hitchcock & Stafford, 1838);
- Death Records 1793–1859. CSL; see Appendix A;
- Lucius B. Barbour's New Haven marriages from church records, 1702–1891; 1 volume (manuscript 136 in Box 23) CSL Record Group 074.36, Hartford;
- Edwin E. Atwater, *et.al.'s History of the Colony of New Haven, With Supplementary History and Personnel of the Towns of Branford, Guilford* (1902/1994 copy at NEHGS);
- Curtis Clark Bushnell and J. T. Hathaway's *Historical sketch of old Fair Haven: with additional notes* (New Haven: Press of J.T. Hathaway, 1916) (FHL fiche 6, 062,225);

---

666 Charles R. Hale, "Headstone Inscriptions of the Town of New Haven, Connecticut" (bound manuscript at CSL) (FHL film 3,349-52). Hale named these Grove Street, Evergreen, Mapledale, Fair Haven Union, Cellar of Church, St. Bernard's Westville, Beaverdale, Mishkam Israel, & Order Breth Abraham.

667 Daniel Hearn, "Connecticut gravestones, early to 1800," manuscript (FHL film 1,477,477, item 12).

668 Charles R. Hale, "Headstone Inscriptions of the Town of West Haven, Connecticut" (bound manuscript at CSL) (FHL film 3,370-1). Hale names these Old, Lower, Upper, & New Upper.

669 Daniel Hearn, "Connecticut gravestones, early to 1800," manuscript (FHL film 1,477,477, item 74).

- Doris B. Townshend's *Fair Haven, a journey through time* (New Haven: New Haven Colony Historical Society, c1976);
- Charles J. Hoadley's *Records of the Colony and Jurisdiction of New Haven From May 1653 To the Union* (1858 copy at NEHGS);
- John H. Dickerman's *Colonial history of the parish of Mount Carmel: as read in its geologic formations, records and traditions* (New Haven: Ryder's Printing House, 1904) (FHL film 1,697,530, item 6).

NEW LONDON

Barbour's typescript volume for New London,[670] unlike the GPC edition,[671] begins:

> Official copies of the first three books of Births, Marriages and Deaths of the Town of New London were made by the authority of the Court of Common Council and approved June 1, 1896. These copies of the first two books have furnished the basis for the text of the following list, but the entries from the third and fourth books have been taken from the originals. The New London Vital Records prior to 1852 are contained in these four volumes.
>
> This volume contains a list alphabetically arranged of all the Vital Records of the Town of New London from the earliest records to about 1852. This list was taken from a set of cards[672] based on a copy of the New London Vital Records made in 1911 by James N. Arnold, of Providence, R.I. The Arnold Copy, now in the possession of the Connecticut State Library, has not been compared with the original except for the third and fourth books and doubtless errors exist. It is hoped that as errors or omissions are found notes will be entered in this volume and on the cards which are included in the General Index of Connecticut Vital Records also in the possession of the Connecticut State Library.
>
> Hartford, Conn., September, 1919.[673]

VITAL RECORDS: The New London volume includes vital records as early as 1644 and as late as 1852. There are two versions of the records to 1858: the original records and a clearer 1890 official copy. FHL intermingled their microfilms of the two as the New London's "Births, Marriages, Deaths vol. 1–3A (p.1—244) 1644–1842" (FHL film 1,312,157, items 1–5) and "Births, Marriages, Deaths vol. 3A (p.244–end) 1768–1857,

---

670 See How to Use This Book, note 4, above.

671 Nancy E. Schott, *Barbour Collection of Connecticut Town Vital Records: New London 1646–1854*, vol. 29 (Baltimore: GPC, 2000). Digital images at *Ancestry.com*.

672 Now part of the Barbour Index and interfiled with similar slips from other towns in CSL and on FHL films 2,887 *et seq*. See Introduction above, pp. 3–5.

673 Lucius B. Barbour, *Connecticut Vital Records: New London, 1646–1854,* (Hartford: CSL, 1919) page after title page (FHL film 2,975). Digital images at *AmericanAncestors.org* and *FamilySearch,org*.

vol. 3C (2) 1848– 1861 vol. 2 1862–1878 Births vol. 4(p.1–72) 1847–1858" (FHL film 1,312,158, items 1–3.). Barbour chose to abstract earlier records from the 1890 copy and later records from the original records as follows:

- "1" refers to FHL film 1,312,157, item 1, the 1890 copy of the original volume 1, which was not filmed;
- "2" refers to FHL film 1,312,157, item 4, the 1890 copy of the original volume.2, which is FHL film 1,213,567, item 2;
- "3" (pp. 1–244) refers to FHL film 1,312,157, item 5, the 1890 copy of the original volume.3a, which is FHL film 1,213,567, item 3;
- "3" (pp. 244–end) is not filmed by FHL, but the 1890 copy (which was not abstracted by Barbour is FHL film 1,312,158. item 1;
- "4" [pp. 1—72] refers to FHL film 1,312,158, item 2. (FHL film 1,312,160, item 4 contains same names but different pagination.);
- "4" [pp. 73–end]) refers to FHL film 1,312,158, item 3|;

In other words, the abstractions Barbour labels "2," "3," and "4 [73–end]" may be verified from the originals through FHL microfilms. The original volumes "1" and "4 [1–72]" can accessed only in New London.

FHL has microfilmed several additional early New London record books:

- **New London's Marriages vol. 3B (1) 1820–1852 and Marriages vol. 4A–5A (p.1–196) 1847–1900 (FHL film 1,312,160, items 3–5);**
- **New London's Marriages vol. 5A (p. 196–end) and Deaths vol. 4B 1847–1878 New London Town Hall, (FHL film 1,312,161, item 1 & last part of item 4);**
- **New London's "Land Records, vol. 1A–4 1646–1724," said to include vital records, 1646–1724 *(*originals in New London Town Hall) (FHL film 5,083);**
- **Elwood M. Avery's "Marriage, Birth and Death Records from the Town Records of New London, Connecticut" (photocopy of typescript at FHL).**

CHURCH RECORDS:

- First Congregational Church of New London's *List of All Those Who Have Been Members of the First Congregational Church in New London, Between the Fifth Day of October, 1670, and the First Day of May, 1840* (Sarasota FL: Aceto Bookmen, 1996. Reprint) (Originally published: New London: Ebenezer Williams, 1840);
- First Church of Christ's "Church Records, 1670–1903" (baptisms, marriages and deaths) (FHL films 1,011,943 items 1–6 and 1,011,943, items 7–9);
- St. James Church's "Church Records, 1725–1874" (includes baptisms, marriages and burials, 1804–1909) (photocopy at CSL) (FHL film 5,132);
- First Baptist Church and Society's Church records, 1804–1909, photocopy at CSL (FHL film 5,137);
- Federal Street Methodist Episcopal Church's "Church Records, 1816–1918" (includes marriages and baptisms) (photocopy at CSL) (FHL film 5,136);
- Second Congregational Church's "Church Records, 1725–1874, " (photocopies at CSL) (FHL film 5,135);
- First Church of Christ's Records 1784–1901, copies at CSL (FHL film 1,011,944 or 5,134);

- First Congregational Church's "Church Records, 1670–1916" (includes deaths 1860–1896, marriages 1691–1753 & 1871–1894; and baptisms 1670–1731 & 1739–1767) (photocopy at CSL) (FHL films 5,134 or 1,011,943–4);
- *B*aptisms (1792–1874), marriages (1792–1874) & burials (1792–1874) at St. James Church (ED Film 5,132).

CEMETERY TRANSCRIPTIONS: The Hale Collection identifies graves in order of physical proximity buried at about four named sites in New London Township.[674] Compare with Daniel Hearn's 1977 copy of 328 pre-1800 gravestones in one New London cemetery.[675] See also,

- Edward Prentis' *Ye Ancient Buriall Place of New London, Conn.* (Salem, MA: Higginson, 1990);
- Lucius B. Barbour's *New London, Connecticut Genealogical Data from Connecticut Cemeteries: Second Burial Ground, Third Burial Ground, Cedar Grove Cemetery, Soldiers' Field* (Salem MA: Higginson Book Co., 1998);
- J.R. Bolles and Anna B. Williams' *New London the Rogerenes: Some Hitherto Unpublished Annals Belonging to the Colonial History of Connecticut With Appendix of Rogerene Writings* (1904/1990 copy at NEHGS);
- S. Leroy Blake's First Church of Christ (1900 copy at NEHGS);
- "Genealogical data from Connecticut cemeteries New London," (Mss A 2405), ccf, NEHGS).

OTHER NOTEWORTHY SOURCES:

- Joshua Hempstead's Diary of Joshua Hempstead of New London, Connecticut: covering a period of forty-seven years, from September 1711 to November 1758: containing valuable genealogical data relating to many New London families…, (New London: New London County Historical Society, 1901) (FHL film 2,028, item 4 or 1,036,510, item 5);
- Lucius B. Barbour's Genealogical notes complied from church records of New London, Conn., 1671–1821. 1 vol. Abstract of vital records. (manuscript 37 in Box 5) CSL Record Group 074.36, Hartford;
- Frances Manwaring Caulkins' *History of New London, Connecticut: From the First Survey of the Coast in 1612 to 1852* (New London: F.M. Caulkins, 1852);
- Richard B. Marrin's Abstracts [of vital records from the New London Gazette: covering southeastern Connecticut (Westminster, MD : Heritage Books, c2007–2008);
- Charles Dyer Parkhurst's *Parkhurst Manuscript: Early families of New London and vicinity,* 36 vols., photocopy at CSL (FHL films 5,123–30).

NEW MILFORD

Barbour's typescript volume for New Milford,[676] unlike the GPC edition,[677] begins:

---

674 Charles R. Hale, "Headstone Inscriptions of the Town of New London, Connecticut" (bound manuscript at CSL) (FHL film 3,353). Hale named these Cedar Grove, Ancient Burial, Gardner, & St. Mary's.

675 Daniel Hearn, "Connecticut gravestones, early to 1800," manuscript (FHL film 1,477,477, item 14).

676 See How to Use This Book, note 4, above.

> The vital records of New Milford prior to 1850 are found scattered through Volumes 2, 4, 5, 6, 7, 8, 9, 10, 11, 12, and 13 of Land Records and Volumes 1 and 2 of Vital Records. In this alphabetical list reference to entries found in the Land Records is indicated by the abbreviation "LR" and the volume number.
>
> This list was taken from a set of cards[678] based on a copy of the New Milford Vital Records made in 1915 by Mrs. Julia E.C. Brush, of Danbury, Conn. The Brush Copy, now in the possession of the Connecticut State Library, has not been compared with the original and doubtless errors exist. It is hoped that as errors or omissions are found notes will be entered in this volume and on the cards which are included in the General Index of Connecticut Vital Records also in the possession of the Connecticut State Library.
>
> Hartford, Conn., July, 1926.[679]

VITAL RECORDS: The New Milford volume includes vital records as early as 1699 and as late as 1854. Barbour abstracted 13 New Milford "books:"

- "1"refers to New Milford's "Births, Marriages, Deaths, vol. B 1747–1860" New Milford Town Hall, FHL film 1,516,559, item 2, (& some records not in Vol. B;
- "2" refers to New Milford's "Births, Marriages, Deaths, vol. D 1847–1861" New Milford Town Hall, (FHL film 1,516,559, item 3);
- "LR2" refers to New Milford's Land Records, vol. 1–2 1706–1778 New Milford Town Hall, (FHL film 5,189);
- "LR4" refers to New Milford's Land Records, vol. 3–4 1728–1753, New Milford Town Hall, (FHL film 5,190);
- "LR5" and "LR6" refer to New Milford's Land Records, vol. 5–6 1739–1776, New Milford Town Hall, (FHL film 5,191);
- "LR7" and "LR8" refer to New Milford's Land Records, vol. 7–8 1750–1792, New Milford Town Hall, (FHL film 5,192);
- "LR9" and "LR10" refer to New Milford's Land Records, vol. 9–10 1750–1816, New Milford Town Hall, (FHL film 5,193);
- "LR11" and "LR12" refer to New Milford's Land Records, vol. 11–12 1768–1792, New Milford Town Hall, (FHL film 5,194);
- "LR13" refers to New Milford's Land Records, vol. 13–14 1773–1803, New Milford Town Hall, (FHL film 5,195).

---

[677] Lorraine Cook White, *Barbour Collection of Connecticut Town Vital Records: New Milford 1712–1860, Norfolk 1758–1850, North Stonington 1807–1852*, vol. 30, (Baltimore: GPC, 2000). Digital images at *Ancestry.com*.

[678] Now part of the Barbour Index and interfiled with similar slips from other towns in CSL and on FHL films 2887 *et seq*. See Introduction above, pp. 3–5.

[679] Lucius B. Barbour, *Connecticut Vital Records: New Milford, 1712–1860,* (Hartford: CSL, 1926) page after title page (FHL film 2,975). Digital images at *AmericanAncestors.org* and *FamilySearch.org*.

Note that a few Bridgewater Private Records slips are neither interfiled in the Barbour Index nor otherwise available outside of the CSL file room. See Appendix B.

See also, *Old New Milford, Connecticut records* (includes 1812 deaths) Mss A6183, RSASC, NEHGS manuscript (database at *AmericanAncestors.org*).

CHURCH RECORDS:

- The New Milford Town Clerk also possesses an unspecified "3 volumes of Old Church Records [and] 5 volumes of Church Records;"[680]
- Congregational Church's "Church Records, 1716–1938" (burials, baptisms, and marriages) (originals at CSL) (FHL films 1,011,946, items 1–9 or 5,222);
- Congregational Church of Bridgewater's, "Church Records, 1809–1919" (includes baptisms 1810–1919, marriages 1844–1916, deaths 1834–1919, deaths in Bridgewater 1835–1897) (originals at CSL) (FHL film 3,846);
- St. Mark's Church of Bridgewater's, "Church Records, 1810–1951" (includes baptisms 1844–1858. marriages 1845–1875, burials 1845–1860) (originals at CSL) (FHL film 3,845 or 1,008,323);
- Baptist Church at Northville's Church records, 1814–1939, copies at CSL (FHL film 5,221);
- St. John's Church's "Church Records, 1784–1899" (includes baptisms, marriages, burials) (originals at CSL) (FHL film 1,011,947);
- Baptisms (1827–37, 1844–48, 1849–51, & 1852–99), marriages (1828–37, 1843–48, 1849–51, & 1852–99) and burials (1827–37, 1843–48, & 1849–51) at St. John's Church (ED film 101,947 & original manuscript);
- Baptisms 1844–58, marriages 1845–75, burials, 1845–60 at St. Mark's Church (ED film 3,845).

CEMETERY TRANSCRIPTIONS: The Hale Collection identifies graves in order of physical proximity buried at about 12 named sites in what was then New Milford Township.[681] Compare with Daniel Hearn's 1975 copy of 126 pre-1800 gravestones in five New Milford cemeteries.[682] The Hale Collection also identifies graves buried in graves at about two named sites in what was then Bridgewater Township.[683] Compare with Daniel Hearn's 1976 copy of 21e pre-1800 gravestones in one Bridgewater cemetery.[684] See also, Marilyn Whittlesey and Jack Scully's *Handbook of Cemeteries, Brookfield, Connecticut (Including Portions of New Milford and Newtown), 1745–1985* ([S.l.]: Old South Cemetery Association, 1986);

---

680 *Biennial Report (1936)*, p. 45.

681 Charles R. Hale, "Headstone Inscriptions of the Town of New Milford, Connecticut" (bound manuscript at CSL) (FHL film 3,353-4). Hale named these Center, St. Francis Xaviers, Morningside, Gaylords, Quaker, Rickett District, Lower Merryall, Northville, West Meeting house, Long Mountain, Gallow's Hill, & Private.

682 Daniel Hearn, "Connecticut gravestones, early to 1800," manuscript (FHL film 1,477,477, item 15).

683 Charles R. Hale, "Headstone Inscriptions of the Town of Bridgewater, Connecticut" (bound manuscript at CSL) (FHL film 3,324). Hale names these Center & South.

684 Daniel Hearn, "Connecticut gravestones, early to 1800," manuscript (FHL film 1,477,476,item 15).

OTHER NOTEWORTHY SOURCES:

- *Old New Milford, Conn. Records* (1812 *List of Deaths) 1812*Mss A 6183. RSASCs, NEHGS, Boston, MA;
- Richard Marshall Clarke's *300 Years of Select Genealogy and History of New Milford, Litchfield County, Connecticut: 1707–2007*, CD-ROM, (New Milford: R.M. Clarke, 2007);
- Samuel Orcutt's H*istory of the Towns of New Milford and Bridgewater, Connecticut, 1803–1882* (Hartford: Case, Lockwood and Brainard Co, 1882).

NEWTOWN

Barbour's typescript volume for Newtown,[685] unlike the GPC edition,[686] begins:

> The vital records of Newtown prior to 1852 are found scattered through the Proprietor' Records, Volumes 2, 8, 9, 19 and 20 of Land Records, Volumes 1 and 2 of Vital Records, two books of Marriages and a book of Deaths.
>
> In this alphabetical list reference to entries found in the Proprietors' Records is indicated by the abbreviation "PR", to those found in the Land Records by "LR" and the volume number, to the Book of Marriages, 1822-1848, by "Vol. 3", to the Book of Marriages, 1848-1862, by "Vol.3-B", and to the Book of Deaths, 1844-1870, by "Vol. 4".
>
> This list was taken from a set of cards[687] based on a copy of the Newtown Vital Records made in 1915 by Mr. James N. Arnold, of Providence, R.I. The Arnold Copy, now in the possession of the Connecticut State Library, has not been compared with the original and doubtless errors exist. It is hoped that as errors or omissions are found notes will be entered in this volume and on the cards which are included in the General Index of Connecticut Vital Records also in the possession of the Connecticut State Library.
>
> Hartford, Conn., June, 1926.[688]

VITAL RECORDS: The Newtown volume includes vital records as early as 1686 and as late as 1870. Barbour abstracted 11 Newtown "books:"

---

685 See How to Use This Book, note 4, above.

686 Greater Omaha Genealogical Society (GOGS), *Barbour Collection of Connecticut Town Vital Records: Newtown 1711*–1852, *North Branford 1831–1854, North Haven 1786–1854*, vol. 31 (Baltimore: GPC, 2000). Digital images at *Ancestry.com*.

687 Now part of the Barbour Index and interfiled with similar slips from other towns in CSL and on FHL films 2,887 *et seq*. See Introduction above, pp. 3–5.

688 Lucius B. Barbour, *Connecticut Vital Records: Newtown, 1711–1852*, (Hartford: CSL, 1926) page after title page (FHL film 2,975). Digital images on *AmericanAncestors.org* and *FamilySearch.org*.

- "LR2" refers to Newtown's Land Records, vol. 1–4 1712–1782, (Volume 2 includes births, marriages and family records at end of volume) Newtown Town Hall, (FHL film 4,967);
- "LR8" refers to Newtown's Land Records, vol. 7–8 1756–1770, Newtown Town Hall, (FHL film 4,969);
- "LR10" (no abstractions are from LR9) refers to Newtown's Land Records, vol. 9–10 1721–1772, Newtown Town Hall, (FHL film 4,970), although the records said to be abstracted from the first page of volume 10 actually range from 1781–1801;
- "LR19" & "LR20' refer to Newtown's Land Records, vol. 19–20 1796–1802, Newtown Town Hall, (FHL film 4,975);
- "1" & "2" (**with some omissions**) refer to Newtown's Records of births, marriages, and deaths, 1716–1871 (contains records of births, marriages, and deaths arranged in family groups. Includes also a few records of marriages, 1820–1822; and a bill of mortality, 1797–1847), Newtown Town Hall, (FHL film 1.435.629, items 1–2) (differently itemized at CSL);
- "PR1" refers to an unfilmed book at the town hall titled "Proprietors Records," which includes 1704–1735 vital records;[689]
- "3" refers to Newtown's Marriage record, 1822–1848, Newtown Town Hall, (FHL film 1,435,629, item 4) (differently itemized at CSL);
- "3-B" is refers to Newtown's Report of Births, Marriages and Deaths in the School Districts of Newtown, 1847–1851, Newtown Town Hall, (FHL film 1,435,629, item 6) (differently itemized at CSL);
- "4" refers to Newtown's Bill of Mortality, 1844–1870 (contains date of death, name of deceased, age and cause of death), Newtown Town Hall, (FHL film 1,435,629, item 5) (differently itemized at CSL).

See also

- **Charles H. Peck's "Records of marriages, deaths, and births, 1847–1852" (Includes a bill of mortality for persons whose surnames begin with A and B, 1826–1846) 1875 manuscript (FHL film 1,435,629, item 3);**
- **Gertrude A. Barber's Vital records of Newton, Connecticut about 1740–1817 (copied from the original records in the town clerk's office, date unknown) (FHL film 823,815, item 1);**
- **Town records of Newtown, Connecticut (contains records of births, marriages, and deaths arranged by family, ca. 1700–1875; and record of deaths, 1797–1817) typescript at NYGBS (FHL film 4,961 or 1,421,103, item 5);**
- **Harlan R. Jessup's "Newtown, CT – Bills of Mortality, 1797–1821: A Supplement to the Barbour Index," *CN*, 29:395–407 (December 1996);**
- **Harlan R. Jessup's "Newtown Marriages: 1794–1810, A Recent Discovery, CA, 40:172–3 (May 1998);**
- **"Vital records of Newtown, Connecticut 1701–1891" (Mss A 6182 in the RSASCs at NEHGS) (database at *AmericanAncestors.org*).**

---

689 CSL, *First 200 years.*

CHURCH RECORDS:

- First Congregational Church's "Church Records, 1742–1951" (includes baptisms, marriages, and deaths) (originals at CSL) (FHL film 4991); Trinity Church, *Church Records, 1764–1921* (includes baptisms, marriages, and burials) (originals at CSL) (FHL film 4,991);
- Methodist Episcopal Church's "Church Records, 1805–1932" (includes deaths 1805–1932) (originals at CSL) (FHL film 4,989, item 2);
- Trinity Church, Church records, 1764–1921, originals at CSL (FHL film 4,990, items 1–5);
- DAR. Mary Silliman Chapter (Newtown, Conn.)'s "Church Records of the Congregational Church: Baptisms and Marriages 1800–1875" (typescript at CSL) (FHL film 4,989);
- Baptisms (1819–32, 1831–51), marriages (1818–32, 1831–53) & burials (1831–52) at Trinity Church (ED Film 4,990);
- Lemuel B. Hull's "A Record of Marriages, Baptisms, Admission to the Communion and Funerals, 1822–1835 " (manuscript at NEHGS).

CEMETERY TRANSCRIPTIONS: The Hale Collection identifies graves in order of physical proximity buried at about 15 named sites in Newtown Township.[690] Compare with Daniel Hearn's 1975 copy of 217 pre-1800 gravestones in five Newtown cemeteries.[691] See also,

- Marilyn Whittlesey and Jack Scully's *Handbook of Cemeteries, Brookfield, Connecticut (Including Portions of New Milford and Newtown), 1745–1985* ([S.l.]: Old South Cemetery Association, 1986);
- "Hopewell Cemetery, Newtown, Connecticut: Poverty Hollow Road, Joins Redding Line" (typescript at.FHL).

OTHER NOTEWORTHY SOURCES:

- Jane Eliza Johnson's *Newtown's history and historian Ezra Levan Johnson with additional material* (Newtown: [s.n.], 1917) (FHL film 844,900, item 1);
- John Neville Boyle's *Newtown: 1708–1758 : historical notes and maps* (Newtown: Bee Pub. Co., [1945?]) (digital images at FHL);
- James Hardin George's *Newtown's bicentennial, 1705–1905* (New Haven: Tuttle Morehouse & Taylor Co., 1906). (digital images at FHL).

NORFOLK

Barbour's typescript volume for Norfolk,[692] unlike the GPC edition,[693] begins:

```
The vital records of Norfolk, prior to
```

---

690 Charles R. Hale, "Headstone Inscriptions of the Town of Newtown, Connecticut" (bound manuscript at CSL) (FHL film 3,354). Hale named these Town plot, Village, Lands End, Berkshire, Taunton, Huntingtown, Sandy Hook, Flat Swamp #1, Flat Swamp #2, Bradleyville, Hopewell, Pratt's Old, Botsford, St. Rose's.

691 Daniel Hearn, "Connecticut gravestones, early to 1800," manuscript (FHL film 1,477,477, item 16).

692 See How to Use This Book, note 4, above.

693 White, *Barbour Collection: New Milford–North Stonington*, vol. 30. Digital images at *Ancestry.com*.

> 1850, are found scattered through a book of Town Meetings dated 1758-1776 and Volumes 1 and 2 of Vital Records.
>
> This alphabetical list was taken from a set of cards[694] based on a manuscript copy of the Norfolk Vital Records made in 1916. The entries in the volume of Town Meetings, reference to which is indicated herein by the abbreviation "TM", and those in Volume 1 were copied by Irene H. Mix, of Hartford, Conn. Volume 2 was copied by James N. Arnold, of Providence, R.I.
>
> The manuscript copy, now in the possession of the Connecticut State Library, has not been compared with the original and doubtless errors exist. It is hoped that as errors or omissions are found notes will be entered in this volume and on the cards which are included in the General Index of Connecticut Vital Records also in the possession of the Connecticut State Library.
>
> Hartford, Conn., April, 1927.[695]

VITAL RECORDS: The Norfolk volume includes vital records as early as 1740 and as late as 1850. Barbour abstracted three Norfolk "books:"

- "TM" refers to Norfolk's records of births, marriages, and deaths, 1740–1776, Norfolk Town Hall, (FHL film 1,503,193, item 1);
- "1" refers to Norfolk's Records of births, marriages, and deaths, 1775–1811, Norfolk Town Hall, (FHL film 1,503,193, item 2);
- "2" refers to Norfolk's Records of births, marriages, and deaths, 1789–1947, Norfolk Town Hall, (FHL film 1,503,193, item 3).

CHURCH RECORDS:

- Ammi Ruhamah Robbins' *Baptisms, Marriages, Burials and List of Members Taken From the Church Records of the Reverend Ammi Ruhamah Robbins, First Minister of Norfolk, Connecticut, 1761–1813: In Commemoration of the One Hundred and Fiftieth Anniversary of the Organization of the Church* (Norfolk: printed for Carl and Ellen Battelle Stoeckel, 1910) (FHL film 238,374 or 908,340);
- Church of Christ's "Church Records, 1760–1928" (includes baptisms 1761–1815 & 1814–1816 marriages 1762–1813; deaths 1761–1815 & 1814–1816, and record kept by Joseph Jones, clerk, between the death of Rev. A. R. Robbins and the settlement of Rev. Ralph Emerson) (originals at CSL) (FHL film 5,182);
- "Norfolk, Ct., Church of Christ, 1760–1769" (includes baptisms) (manuscript in NYGBS & NEHGS) (FHL film 4,676 or 1,419,455)
- The Norfolk Town Clerk also possesses "4 volumes of Church Records;"[696]

---

[694] Now part of the Barbour Index and interfiled with similar slips from other towns in CSL and on FHL films 2,887 *et seq*. See Introduction above, pp. 3–5.

[695] Lucius B. Barbour, *Connecticut Vital Records Norfolk, 1758–1850,* (Hartford: CSL, 1927) page after title page (FHL film 2,975). Digital images at *AmericanAncestors.org* and *FamilySearch.org*.

CEMETERY TRANSCRIPTIONS: The Hale Collection identifies graves in order of physical proximity buried at about 10 named sites in Norfolk Township.[697] Compare with Daniel Hearn's 1978 copy of 30 pre-1800 gravestones in two Norfolk cemeteries.[698]

OTHER NOTEWORTHY SOURCES:

- "Heman Swift's Account Book," 1769–1865, CSL; see Appendix A;
- Joseph Eldridge, D.D. and Theron Wilmot Crissey's *History of Norfolk, Litchfield County, Connecticut 1744–1900* (1900);
- Isabella Club's *Norfolk, Connecticut, the first two hundred years, 1758–1958 : the Isabella club papers* ([Norfolk]: Bicentennial Committee of Norfolk, CT [1958])

NORTH BRANFORD

Barbour's typescript volume for North Branford,[699] unlike the GPC edition,[700] begins:

> This volume contains a list alphabetically arranged of all the vital records of the town of North Branford from its incorporation to about 1854. This list was taken from a set of cards[701] based on a copy of the North Branford Vital Records made in 1914 by Miss Ethel L. Scofield, of New Haven, Conn. The entire record of the town prior to 1854 is found in one volume.
>
> The Scofield Copy, now in the possession of the Connecticut State Library, has not been compared with the original and doubtless errors exist. It is hoped that as errors or omissions are found notes will be entered in this volume and on the cards which are included in the General Index of Connecticut Vital Records also in the possession of the Connecticut State Library.
>
> Hartford, Conn., October, 1924.[702]

VITAL RECORDS: The North Branford volume includes vital records as early as 1780 and as late as 1854. Barbour abstracted North Branford's Town Records, vol. 1, 1780–1870 (contains records of marriages 1803–1854, births 1780–1861, deaths 1809–1844), North Branford Town Hall, (FHL film 1,429,924, item 2).

Barbour does not abstract these North Branford vital records:

---

696 *Biennial Report (1936), p. 46.*

697 Charles R. Hale, "Headstone Inscriptions of the Town of Norfolk, Connecticut" (bound manuscript at CSL) (FHL film 3,354). Hale named these Center, St. Mary's Sop. Norfolk, Hinckley, Grantville, Cemetery, Meekertown, Benedict, Graveyard, & New St. Mary's.

698 Daniel Hearn, "Connecticut gravestones, early to 1800," manuscript (FHL film 1,477,477, item 17).

699 See How to Use This Book, note 4, above.

700 GOGS, *Barbour Collection: Newtown–North Haven*, vol. 31. Digital images at *Ancestry.com*.

701 Now part of the Barbour Index and interfiled with similar slips from other towns in CSL and on FHL films 2,887 *et seq*. See Introduction above, pp. 3–5.

702 Lucius B. Barbour, *Connecticut Vital Records: North Branford, 1831–1854*, (Hartford: CSL, 1924) page after title page (FHL film 2,976). Digital images at *AmericanAncestors.org* and *FamilySearch.org*.

- **North Branford's "Records of Births, Marriages, and Deaths, 1847–1908" (FHL film 1,420,924, item 3;**
- **"North Branford Town and Church Records, 1769–1885" (originals in North Branford Town Hall) (FHL film 1,420,924, item 1).**

CHURCH RECORDS:

- St. Andrew's Church at Northford's "Church Records, 1763–1899" (includes baptisms, marriages, and burials) (originals at CSL) (FHL film 5,143);
- Congregational Church of Northford's, "Church Records, 1750–1926" (includes baptisms 1750–1847 & 1847–1925, deaths 1750–1847, and marriages 1750–1846 (originals at CSL) (FHL film 5,354, items 2–4);
- Congregational Church's "Church Records, 1796–1867" (includes marriages (1769–1804, 1809–1825 & 1828–1855); baptisms 1769–1805 & 1809–1858; and deaths 1769–1804 & 1808–1859) (originals at CSL) (FHL film 5,142);
- Zion Church's "Church Records, 1812–1875" (includes baptisms 1812–1866 and deaths 1812–1875) (originals at CSL) (FHL film 5,141);
- Edith M. A. Raymond's "Church Records of the Congregational Church" (includes marriages, deaths and baptisms for 1750–1825) (photocopy at CSL) (FHL film 5,354, item 1);
- Baptisms (1843–58), marriages (1846–56) & burials (1843–55) at St. Andrew's Church (ED Film 5,143);

CEMETERY TRANSCRIPTIONS: The Hale Collection identifies graves in order of physical proximity buried at five named sites in North Branford Township.[703] Compare with Daniel Hearn's 1978 copy of 239 pre-1800 gravestones in two North Branford cemeteries.[704] See also,

- DAR (Florida). GRC's "Bible and Cemetery Records" (original typescript submitted to DAR) (FHL film 850,400);
- Alice Hubbard (Breed) Benton and Florida DAR's "Florida Genealogical Collection, 1932": [vol. 2] (includes cemetery at North Branford and Northford) (typescript submitted to DAR) (FHL film 850,401, item 2);
- Lucius B. Barbour's "Genealogical Data From Connecticut Cemeteries: North Branford, Conn. Old, Congregational, Episcopal, Bare Plain And Northford Cemeteries" (1932 manuscript at NEHGS);
- Charles R. Hale and Mary H. Babin's "Headstone Inscriptions, Town of North Branford, Connecticut" (Hartford: CSL: 1934);
- "Northford [Conn.] Cemetery Inscriptions" [ca. 1748–ca. 1938] (manuscript at NEHGS).

OTHER NOTEWORTHY SOURCES: Herbert C. Miller's *History of North Branford and* Northford (North Branford: Totoket Historical Society, c1982).

---

703 Charles R. Hale, "Headstone Inscriptions of the Town of North Branford, Connecticut" (bound manuscript at CSL) (FHL film 3,354). Hale named these Bare Plain, Episcopal Church, Congregational Church, Old Northford, & New Northford.

704 Daniel Hearn, "Connecticut gravestones, early to 1800," manuscript (FHL film 1,477,477, item 18).

NORTH HAVEN

Barbour's typescript volume for North Haven,[705] unlike the GPC edition,[706] begins:

> This volume contains a list alphabetically arranged of all the vital records of the town of North Haven from its incorporation to about 1854. This list was taken from a set of cards[707] based on a copy of the North Haven Vital Records made in 1914 by James N. Arnold, of Providence, R.I. The entire record of the town prior to 1854 is found in two volumes.
>
> The Arnold Copy, now in the possession of the Connecticut State Library, has not been compared with the original and doubtless errors exist. It is hoped that as errors or omissions are found notes will be entered in this volume and on the cards which are included in the General Index of Connecticut Vital Records also in the possession of the Connecticut State Library.
>
> Hartford, Conn., October, 1924.[708]

VITAL RECORDS: The North Haven volume includes vital records as early as 1766 and as late as 1854. Barbour abstracted two North Haven "books:"

- "1" refers to North Haven's Records of Births, Marriages, and Deaths, 1756–1811, North Haven Town Hall (FHL film 1,428,122, item 1), but **some vital records in this book were not abstracted by Barbour**;[709]
- "2" refers to North Haven's Records of Births, Marriages, and Deaths, 1756–1854, North Haven Town Hall (FHL film 1,428,122, item 2).

CHURCH RECORDS:

- Congregational Church's "Church Records, 1716–1910" (includes baptisms 1760–1826, marriages 1761–1826, and deaths 1761–1832) (photocopies at CSL) (FHL film 5,154);
- St. John's Church's "Church Records, 1759–1858" (includes baptisms, marriages, and deaths) (transcript at CSL) (FHL film 5,153 or1,011,948);
- Baptisms (1759–1858 & 1759–1858), marriages (1843–58 & 1843–58), burials (1846–58 & 1846–58), & deaths (1768–1855 & 1768–1855 at St. John's Church (ED Films 1011948 & 5,153);
- "Record of Baptisms Performed at the Congregational Church in North Haven, CT During the Pastorate of Rev. Benjamin Trumbull 1760–1789." *CN*, Vol. 20, No.4 and in *Ricker Compilation.*

---

[705] See How to Use This Book, note 4, above.

[706] GOGS, *Barbour Collection: Newtown–North Haven*, vol. 31. Digital images at *Ancestry.com*.

[707] Now part of the Barbour Index and interfiled with similar slips from other towns in CSL and on FHL films 2,887 *et seq*. See Introduction above, pp. 3–5.

[708] Lucius B. Barbour, *Connecticut Vital Records: North Haven, 1786–1854*, (Hartford: CSL, 1924) page after title page (FHL film 2976). Digital images at *AmericanAncestors.org* and *FamilySearch.org*.

[709] **The abstraction includes significant errors and omissions.**

CEMETERY TRANSCRIPTIONS: The Hale Collection identifies graves in order of physical proximity buried at about three named sites in North Haven Township.[710] Compare with Daniel Hearn's 1977 copy of 224 pre-1800 gravestones in two North Haven cemeteries.[711] See also,

- DAR (Florida). GRC's "Bible and Cemetery Records" (contains North Haven cemetery records) (original typescript at the DAR Library) (FHL film 850,400);
- Gloria H. Furnival's *On the Green: the Old Center Cemetery in North Haven, Connecticut, 1723–1882* (North Haven: North Haven Historical Society, c2000).

OTHER NOTEWORTHY SOURCES:

- "Marriages in North Haven, CT Performed by Jonathan Dayton JP 1782–1784." *CN*, Vol. 18, No. 4, p. 767 and in *Ricker Compilation*;
- Sheldon B. Thorpe's "List of Marriages Performed by Dr. Benjamin Trumbull at the North Haven Congregational Church 1760–1820," *CN,* Vol. 19, No. 2 and in *Ricker Compilation*;
- Sheldon B. Thorpe's *North Haven Annals: History of the Town From Its Settlement, 1680* (1892/1994 copy at NEHGS);
- DAR (Florida) GRC's *Bible and cemetery records*, includes cemetery records: Enfield, Montowese, New Haven, Northford, North Haven) (FHL film 850,400, item 9);
- Notebook of Abraham Blakeslee, North Haven, Connecticut, photocopy at CSL (FHL film 5,154, item 3).

NORTH STONINGTON

Barbour's typescript volume for North Stonington,[712] unlike the GPC edition,[713] begins:

> This volume contains a list alphabetically arranged of all the vital records of the town of North Stonington from its incorporation to about 1852. This list was taken from a set of cards[714] based on a copy of the North Stonington Vital Records made in 1914 by James N. Arnold, of Providence, R.I. The entire record of the town prior to 1852 is found in one volume. The Arnold Copy, now in the possession of the Connecticut State Library, has not been compared with the original and doubtless errors exist. It is hoped that as errors or omissions are found notes will be entered in this volume and on the cards which are included in the General Index of Connecticut Vital Records also in the possession of the Connecticut State Library.

---

710 Charles R. Hale, "Headstone Inscriptions of the Town of North Haven, Connecticut" (bound manuscript at CSL) (FHL film 3,355). Hale named these Center, Old Center, & Montowese.

711 Daniel Hearn, "Connecticut gravestones, early to 1800," manuscript (FHL film 1,477,477, item 19).

712 See How to Use This Book, note 4, above.

713 White, *Barbour Collection: New Milford–North Stonington*, vol. 30. Digital images at *Ancestry.com*.

714 Now part of the Barbour Index and interfiled with similar slips from other towns in CSL and on FHL films 2,887 *et seq*. See Introduction above, pp. 3–5.

```
Hartford, Conn., March, 1918.[715]
```

VITAL RECORDS: The North Stonington volume includes vital records as early as 1759 and as late as 1852. Barbour abstracted North Stonington's Records of Births, Marriages, and Deaths, 1758–1920, North Stonington Town Hall, (FHL film 1,309,964). See also,

- **North Stonington Vital Records circa 1845–1905, CSL (CSA RG 072.002, Box 14) (includes pre-1850 birthdates on death certificates).**
- **Hundreds of North Stonington Private Records (perhaps all deaths, 1890-1910) slips in Drawer 394 at CSL. See Appendix B. They appear to be abstracted from C.R. Hale's North Stonington Vital Records, 1880-1905: from the North Stonington town clerk (typescript in alpha order) (FHL film 3,662, item 9)**

CHURCH RECORDS:

- Congregational Church's "Church Records, 1720–1887" (includes deaths 1828–1871, baptisms 1727–1875, and marriages 1727–1868) (originals at CSL) (FHL film 5,081);
- North Society's Church records, 1720–1781, originals at CSL (FHL film 1,011,949);
- Mrs. J.L. Reynolds, "Church Records, 1727–1835" (includes baptisms and marriages) (typescript at CSL) (FHL film 5,080);
- Strict Congregational Church's "Church Records, 1746–1822" (includes baptisms and deaths) (originals in CSL) (FHL film 1,011,949);
- First Baptist Church at Pendleton Hill's "Church Records, 1754–1905" (includes baptisms and deaths) (originals at CSL) (FHL film 5,079).

CEMETERY TRANSCRIPTIONS: The Hale Collection identifies graves in order of physical proximity buried at about 95 named sites in North Stonington Township.[716] Compare with Daniel Hearn's 1985 copy of 89 pre-1800 gravestones in four North Stonington cemeteries.[717] See also,

- Charles R. Hale and Mary H. Babin's "Headstone Inscriptions, Town of North Stonington, Connecticut" (1932 typescript in North Stonington Town Hall) (FHL film 1,311,117);
- Anne and Susan B. Meech's "Cemetery Inscriptions From Groton, Preston and Stonington, Connecticut" (typescript) (FHL film 4,291);
- "New England tombstone inscriptions," *Genealogy, Journal of American Ancestry*, 5:17 (March 1915) digital images on *FamilySearch.org*.

---

[715] Lucius B. Barbour, *Connecticut Vital Records: North Stonington, 1807–1852*, (Hartford: CSL, 1918) page after title page (FHL film 2,976). Digital images at *AmericanAncestors.org* and *FamilySearch.org*.

[716] Charles R. Hale, "Headstone Inscriptions of the Town of North Stonington, Connecticut" (bound manuscript at CSL) (FHL film 3,355). Hale named these Browning (2 different locations), Denison (2 different locations), Prentice, Swan, Baldwin, Main (2 different locations), Billings, Eccleston, Field stones (7 different locations), Congdon, Palmer, Wilcox, Holdredge, Lewis, York (3 different locations), Family (4 different locations), Burdick, Maine, Breed or Brown, Crumb, Chapman (3 different locations), Holmes (2 different locations), Coats, Stewart Hill, Hewitt (4 different locations), Children's Wheeler (3 different locations), Woodward, Ayer, Avery, Phelps, Stanton (2 different locations), Edgcomb, Hillard, Indian, Great Plain, Hull, Grant, Munsell, Pitcher, Williams, Crary, Frink, Brown (2 different locations), Brown-Randall, Union, Partlow, Lewis, Miner (2 different locations), Brown, Kenyon, Spalding, Austin, Babcock, -a-, York, Clark, Thompson, Parks, & Randall.

[717] Daniel Hearn, "Connecticut gravestones, early to 1800," manuscript (FHL film 1,477,477, item 20).

- "Wheeler family burials," North Stonington, Connecticut from 1777–1894," *Genealogy, Monthly Magazine of American Ancestry*, 6:32 (February 1916) digital images on *FamilySearch.org*.
- "Cemetery Inscriptions from Small Cemeteries in Ledyard, CT" (Mss A 4376), RSASC, NEHGS.

OTHER NOTEWORTHY SOURCES: See state and county resources above, pages 18–21.

NORWALK

Barbour's typescript volume for Norwalk,[718] unlike the GPC edition,[719] begins:

> The vital records of Norwalk, prior to 1850, are found scattered through Volumes 1, 4, 9, 13, 16, 17, 18 and 19 of Land Records and Volume 1 of Births, Marriages and Deaths.
>
> This alphabetical list was taken from a set of cards[720] based on a manuscript copy made in 1915 by James N. Arnold, of Providence, R.I. Reference to entries found in the Land Records is indicated by the abbreviation "LR", and the number of the volume, and to the book of Vital Records by "Vol.1".
>
> The Arnold Copy, now in the possession of the Connecticut State Library, has not been compared with the original and doubtless errors exist. It is hoped that as errors or omissions are found notes will be entered in this volume and on the cards which are included in the General Index of Connecticut Vital Records also in the possession of the Connecticut State Library.
>
> Hartford, Conn., November, 1925.[721]

VITAL RECORDS: The Norwalk volume includes vital records as early as 1653 and as late as 1848. Barbour abstracted nine "books:"

- "LR1" refers to Norwalk's Land Records, vol. 1–3 1652–1711, Norwalk Town Hall (FHL film 5,001);
- "LR4" refers to Norwalk's Land Records, vol. 4–5 1698–1750, Norwalk Town Hall (FHL film 5,002);
- "LR9" refers to Norwalk's vol. 8–9 1735–1747, Town Hall, Norwalk Town Hall, (FHL film 5,004);

---

718 See How to Use This Book, note 4, above.

719 Debra F. Wilmes, *Barbour Collection of Connecticut Town Vital Records: Norwalk 1651-1850, Norwich 1847-1851*, vol. 32, (Baltimore: GPC, 2000). Digital images at *Ancestry.com*.

720 Now part of the Barbour Index and interfiled with similar slips from other towns in CSL and on FHL films 2,887 *et seq*. See Introduction above, pp. 3–5.

721 Lucius B. Barbour, *Connecticut Vital Records: Norwalk, 1651–1850*, (Hartford: CSL, 1925) page after title page (FHL film 2,976). Digital images at *AmericanAncestors.org and FamilySearch.org.*

- "LR13" refers to Norwalk's vol. 12–13 1762–1776, Norwalk Town Hall, (FHL film 5,006);
- "LR16" and "17" refer to Norwalk's vol. 16–17 1785–1795, Norwalk Town Hall, (FHL film 5,008);
- "LR18" and "19" refer to Norwalk's vol. 18–20 1795–1804, Norwalk Town Hall, (FHL film 5,009);
- "Vol.1" is at least 50 pages long and includes marriages 1821–48 and then births, 1847–48. It remains at the Norwalk town clerk's office, but in **several volumes with many unfilmed records not abstracted by Barbour, especially deaths.**[722]

See also,

- **Burton Collection, Norwalk Marriage Records, 1834–1853 (CSL call no, 974.62 N83m);**
- **Norwalk's Records of Births, Marriages, and Deaths, 1848–1909, Norwalk Town Hall, (FHL film 1,434,202). See Paul Keroack, Barbara Dempsey, Nora Galvin, "Marriages in Norwalk, CT, 1848–1851 with School District,"** ***CA*****, vol. 55, No. 1 (Aug 2012);**
- **Aaron Fancher and Lester Card's "Marriage Records of Aaron Fancher, Justice of the Peace, Poundridge [sic], N.Y., 1838–1871" (1931 typescript at NYGBS) (FHL film 17860);**
- **"Marriage and probate records from Norwalk, Connecticut" (typescript at NYGBS) (FHL film 4,993).**

CHURCH RECORDS:

- Norwalk's *Listing of vital records found in Congregational Church when Wilton was a Parish of Norwalk 1700's Abbott through Wood,* Norwalk Town Hall;[723]
- St. Paul's Church, "Church Records, 1741–1925" (includes baptisms, marriages, and burials) (originals at the CSL) (FHL film 5,019);
- South Norwalk Congregational Church Sunday School, Church records, 1838–1847, originals at CSL (FHL film 5,815, item 1).
- Church of England, "Church Records, 1742–1746" (includes baptisms and marriages) (originals at CSL) (FHL film 5,815, item 2);
- South Norwalk First Methodist Church, Records, 1850–1890, copy at CSL (FHL film 5,815, items 3–4);
- Baptisms (1830–54), marriages (1830–54) & burials (1831–36) at St. Paul's Church (ED Film 5,019);
- Paul Keroack's "Deaths in the First Church of Norwalk, 1807–1851, from the Manual of the First Church, 1851," *CA*, vol. 56, No. 3 (Feb 2014).
- Paul R. Keroack's "Marriages of Norwalk Residents at Greens Farms Congregational Church, *CA*, 54:119 (Feb 2012)

CEMETERY TRANSCRIPTIONS: The Hale Collection identifies people in order of physical proximity buried at about 17 named sites in Norwalk Township.[724] Compare with

---

722 On 12 Sep 2018 Norwalk Town Clerk Rick McQuaid reported these pre 1850 vital records collections in his vault: **Deaths 1848-61 (A-Z), Marriages 1848-61 (A-Z), Marriages 1847-61 (Groom/Bride), Marriages 1820-37, Births 1847-48, and Deaths 1847-48.**

723 Email from Town Clerk Rick McQuaid 12 Sep 2018.

Daniel Hearn's 1975 copy of 227 pre-1800 gravestones in seven Norwalk cemeteries.[725] See also,

- Harold Secor Martin's *Record of Inscriptions and Epitaphs Found on the Monuments and Headstones in East Norwalk Historical Cemetery, the Oldest Cemetery in Norwalk* (East Norwalk: s.n.,1971);
- David H. Van Hoosear's *Complete Copy of the Inscriptions Found on the Monuments, Headstones, etc., in the Oldest Cemetery in Norwalk, Conn., September, 1892: Dedicated to the Memory of Norwalk's First Ancestors* (Bridgeport: Standard Association, 1895) (FHL film 823,677);
- Lester Card's *Cemetery Inscriptions Norwalk, Connecticut* ([S.i.: s.n.], 1933–1934) digital images at *FamilySearch.org*;
- Lester Card's *Norwalk Cemetery* (1945/1997 copy at NEHGS);
- Francis F. Spiess' *Norwalk Inscriptions Copied From Gravestones Arranged With Genealogical Notes & Records of Revolutionary Service* (1931/1997 copy at NEHGS);
- Robert Smith's "Burials in Raymond Cemetery, Norwalk, Connecticut," *CA*, Vol. 52, No. 1 (Aug 2009).

OTHER NOTEWORTHY SOURCES:

- Charles M. Selleck's *Norwalk, Vol.1, With Supplemental Genealogical Register* (1896/1997 copy at NEHGS);
- Mariam Olmstead's "Wilton Parish, 1726–1800: a historical sketch," digital images at *FamilySearch,org*;
- Edwin Hall's *Ancient historical records of Norwalk, Conn.: with a plan of the ancient settlement, and of the town in 1847* (Norwalk: A. Selleck, 1865);
- Paul Keroack's "For Whom the Hearse was Used: Persons Buried by the Norwalk Hearse Association, 1832–1848," *CA*, Vol. 56, No. 3 (Feb 2014);
- Deborah Wing, Ray and Gloria P. Stewart's *Norwalk: being an historical account of that Connecticut town* (Canaan, NH: Phoenix Pub., 1989).
- Walter E Corbin and Robert J. Dunkle's Corbin manuscript collection (vol. 2. Records of Connecticut towns including Gilead, Norwalk, Stafford, Stamford, West Stafford, and Willington,), 3 CD-ROMs (Boston: NEHGS, c2003–c2005);

NORWICH

Barbour's typescript volume for Norwich,[726] unlike the GPC edition,[727] begins:

> Volumes 1 to 7 of the of Norwich Vital Records, covering the period from 1659 to 1848, were printed and published in 1913 by the Society of Colonial

[724] Charles R. Hale, "Headstone Inscriptions of the Town of Norwalk, Connecticut" (bound manuscript at CSL) (FHL film 3.355-6). Hale named these Norwalk, Riverside, St. Mary's Union, Pine Island, East Norwalk, Town House Hill, Hebrew, Silvermine, St. Paul's Church, West Norwalk, Raymond, Gregory, Jewish, New Catholic, Old Five Mile River, & Huguenot.

[725] Daniel Hearn, "Connecticut gravestones, early to 1800," manuscript (FHL film 1.477.477, item 21).

[726] See How to Use This Book, note 4, above.

[727] Wilmes, *Barbour Collection: Norwalk–Norwich*, vol. 32,

> Wars in the State of Connecticut This publication was in two volumes or parts.
>
> The records herewith are all that are contained in what is known as Volume 7 1/2, and cover the period from 1848 to about 1852. Many of the marriage records duplicate entries in the printed volumes as to name and date, although wide variations occur in some of the names. The printed volumes were carefully checked with the original, but Volume 7 1/2 has not been compared, therefore where discrepancies occur the printed volume should be relied upon.
>
> The following alphabetically arranged list was taken from a set of cards[728] based on a copy made in 1910 by James N. Arnold, of Providence, R.I. The Arnold Copy, now in the possession of the Connecticut State Library, has not been compared with the original and doubtless errors exist. It is hoped that as errors or omissions are found notes will be entered in this volume and on the cards which are included in the General Index of Connecticut Vital Records also in the possession of the Connecticut State Library.
>
> Hartford, Conn., December, 1919.[729]

VITAL RECORDS: The Norwich volume includes vital records as early as 1847 and as late as 1851. Barbour abstracted them from Norwich's Births, Marriages, Deaths, Volume 7½ 1847–1869, Norwich Town Hall, FHL film 1,311,436, item 1. Norwich's earlier records are abstracted only in the SCW's *Vital Records of Norwich, 1659–1848* (Hartford: Society of Colonial Wars in Connecticut, 1913) and in the Barbour Index (images at *AmericanAncestors.org*).

The original sources of both Barbour abstractions[730] are the first seven volumes of Norwich's Records of Births, Marriages, and Deaths, 1640–1921,vol, 1–4 (p. 1–65) 1640–1834 (FHL film 1,311,434) and Norwich's Records of Births, Marriages, and Deaths, 1640–1921, vol. 4 (p. 65–end)–7 1770–1861 (FHL film 1,311,435):

- "1" starting in 1640 refer to FHL film 1,311,434, item 5;
- "2" starting in 1739 refers to FHL film 1,311,434, item 6;
- "3" starting in 1768 refers to FHL film 1,311,434, item 7;
- "4" (1–65) (about 1785 on) refers to FHL film 1,311,434, item 8;
- "4" (65–end) refers to FHL film 1,311,435, item 1;
- "5" (ca 1820 on) refers to FHL film 1,311,435, item 2;
- "6" (ca. 1832 on) refers to FHL film 1,311,435, item 3;
- "7" (ca. 1848 on) refers to FHL film 1,311,435, item 4.

---

728 Now part of the Barbour Index and interfiled with similar slips from other towns in CSL and on FHL films 2.887 *et seq*. See Introduction above, pp. 3–5.

729 Lucius B. Barbour, *Connecticut Vital Records: Norwich, 1847–1851, Part III*, (Hartford: CSL, 1919) page after title page. (FHL film 2.976). Digital images at *AmericanAncestors.org* and *FamilySearch.org.*

730 The pagination of the Norwich Vital Records in the Barbour Index is to the original records and not the publication.

CHURCH RECORDS:

- First Congregational Church's "Church Records, 1660–1928" (includes baptisms 1700–1916, marriages 1660–1916, deaths 1660–1892, births 1892–1916, inscriptions 1706–1863) (originals in CSL) (FHL film 5,069);
- First Congregational Church Records 1807–1826, originals at CSL (includes deaths in Norwich First Society and some baptisms) originals at CSL (FHL 1,011,950, items 8–11);
- Christ Church's "Church Records, 1746–1901" (includes funerals, baptisms 1769–1901, marriages 1822–1902, deaths 1844–1858 and burials 1870–1901) (originals at CSL) (FHL film 5,064);
- Christ Church's "Church Records, 1757–1849" (includes headstone and footstone inscriptions; baptisms, and deaths, 1809–1823) (originals in the CSL) (FHL film 1,011,950);
- Second Congregational Church's "Church Records, 1821–1825" (includes marriages 1760–1831, baptisms 1762–1831, and deaths 1814–1831) (originals at CSL) (FHL film 5,070);
- Norwich Methodist Episcopal Church's "Church Records, 1845–1878" (includes baptisms 1847–1874 and marriages 1868–1870) (originals in BUSTL) (FHL film 1,508,864);
- First Universalist Church's Minutes, 1838–1946, originals at CSL (FHL film 5,065);
- Mary Ann Huntington, Bonnie J. Linck's *Deaths in the First Congregational Church of Norwich, Connecticut, 1822, 1826–1846: From the Journals of Mary Ann Huntington* (Granby: B.J. Linck, c1998) (FHL film 1,573,511);
- First Baptist Church's "Church Records, 1800–1924" (includes baptisms and deaths) (photocopy at CSL) (FHL films 5,066–7);
- Fifth Church of Norwich's "Records of the Baptisms, Marriages, Deaths and Church Admissions of the Fifth Church of Norwich, Connecticut, 1739–1824" (includes baptisms, marriages, and deaths) (typescript in NYGBS) (FHL film 5,022);
- Mary Ann Huntington's "Sermon Text Book of Mary Ann Huntington, 1826–1846: Including Deaths in Norwich First Society 1826–1830 and 1832–1846" (originals at CSL) (FHL film 5,071);
- Fourth Congregational Church's "Minutes, 1833–1857" (includes baptisms 1833–1857 and deaths 1833–1857) (originals at CSL) (FHL film 5,068);
- Greenville Congregational Church's Records 1833–1857, copies at CSL)FHL film 5,068);
- Norwich Falls Congregational Church's Records 1827–1842, copies at CSL (FHL film 5,072);
- Hanover Congregational Church's "Church Records, 1761–1915" (includes marriages, baptisms, some births, deaths) (originals at CSL) (FHL film 5,821);
- Baptisms (1789–1857, 1844–57), marriages (1822–55, 1844–57, 1854–56) & burials (1822–54, 1844–58) at Christ Church (ED Film 5,064);
- *Records of Baptisms, Marriages, Deaths and Church Admissions of the Fifth [i.e. First] Church, of Norwich, Connecticut, from 1730 [i.e. 1739] to 1824 Kept by Joseph Murdock, Pastor of the Church,* 1928 typescript NEHGS;

- Baptisms (1850–82), marriages (1850–62) & burials (1850–62) at Grace Church (ED Film 1,011,954);
- Lemuel B. Hull's *Record of Marriages, Baptisms, Admission to the Communion and Funerals, 1822–1835* (manuscript at NEHGS);
- Noah Strong's "Commonplace book of Noah Strong" (Mss A 6843), RSASCs, NEHGS;
- Greenville Congregational Church's Church records 1843–1938 (originals at CSL)FHL Film 1,011,954. item 3;
- Trinity Church's Church records 1850–1905 (originals at CSL) FHL film 1,011,954, items 5–8;
- Norwich Methodist Episcopal Church's Church records, 1845–1878, originals at Boston School of Theology Library (FHL film 1,508,864, item 12);
- Norwich Falls Church's Documentary history of religion, work and worship at Norwich Falls, Connecticut, between the years 1827–1841: with some memoranda of earlier date, originals at CSL (FHL film 1,011,954).

CEMETERY TRANSCRIPTIONS: The Hale Collection identifies people in order of physical proximity buried at about 18 named sites in Norwich Township.[731] Compare with Daniel Hearn's 1978 copy of 397 pre-1800 gravestones in two Norwich cemeteries.[732] See also,

- George S. Porter, *Inscriptions from Gravestones in the Old Burying Ground, Norwich Town, Connecticut* (Norwich: Society of the Founders of Norwich, Conn., 1933) (FHL film 908,330) (1933/1996 copy at NEHGS);
- George S. Porter, *Inscriptions from Gravestones in Christ Church, Norwich, Conn.* (Boston MA: David Clapp & Son, 1906) *NEHGR*, vol. 60:16 (1906);
- *Cemetery Inscriptions, Christ Church, Norwich* (card file in CSL) (FHL film 5,553);
- Paul R. Keroack , "Irish Emigrant Headstone Inscriptions from St. Mary Cemetery, Norwich, CT," *CN*, June 1999 and in *Ricker Compilation*;
- Frances Manwaring Caulkins, *History of Norwich, Connecticut: From Its Possession by the Indians to the Year 1866* (New London?: Friends of the author," 1874);
- Rev. Charles T. Weitzel's "Inscriptions from Gravestones in Norwich Town Burial Ground, 1706–1863" (manuscript in CSL) (FHL film 1,011,950).

OTHER NOTEWORTHY SOURCES:

- Marian K. O'Keefe and Catherine Smith Doroshevich's Society of the Founders of Norwich, Connecticut, *Norwich historic homes & families* (Stonington: Pequot Press, Inc., 1967).
- Robert Nicholas's *The Norwich Courier: marriages and obituaries, Norwich Connecticut* (Olathe, Kansas : Nicholas Pub. Co., c2007–2008);
- *Notes on persons and places in the ancient town of Norwich in Connecticut* (Norwich: Bulletin Print, 1909);

---

731 Charles R. Hale, "Headstone Inscriptions of the Town of Norwich, Connecticut" (bound manuscript at CSL) (FHL film 3,357). Hale named these Maplewood, St. Joseph's St. Mary's Yantic, Sacred Heart, Gifford (Private), Ray-Yarrington (Private), Norwich Town (Oldest), City, Greenville, West Plain, Hamilton, St. Nicholas (Polish), Uncas, Mason, Private, World War, & Greek.

732 Daniel Hearn, "Connecticut gravestones, early to 1800," manuscript (FHL film 1,477,477, item 22).

- "M.A. Huntington, JP, Norwich;" see Appendix A;
- "Cemetery Inscriptions in Christ Church, 1762–1835;" see Appendix A;
- Mary E.Perkins' *Old houses of the ancient town of Norwich, 1660–1800 : with maps, illustrations, portraits and genealogies(*Norwich: Bulletin Co., 1895);

ORANGE

Barbour's typescript volume for Orange,[733] unlike the GPC edition,[734] begins:

> This volume contains a list alphabetically arranged of all the vital records of the town of Orange from its incorporation to about 1850. The entire record of the town prior to 1850 is found in one volume.
>
> This list was taken from a set of cards[735] based on a copy of the Orange Vital Records made in 1914 by Mr. James N. Arnold, of Providence, R.I. The Arnold Copy, now in the possession of the Connecticut State Library, has not been compared with the original and doubtless errors exist. It is hoped that as errors or omissions are found notes will be entered in this volume and on the cards which are included in the General Index of Connecticut Vital Records also in the possession of the Connecticut State Library. Hartford, Conn., January, 1925.[736]

VITAL RECORDS: The Orange volume includes vital records as early as 1822 and as late as 1852. Barbour's abstracted Orange's Records of Births, Marriages, and Deaths, (no vol. number) 1804– 1857, West Haven Town Hall, (FHL film 1.420, 923, item 1).

Barbour did not abstract Orange's Records of Births, Marriages, and Deaths, (no vol. number) 1848– 1857, West Haven Town Hall, (FHL film 1, 420, 923, item 2).

CHURCH RECORDS:

- Congregational Church's "Church Records, 1804–1929" (includes marriages 1805–1896 and deaths 1805–1907) (photocopies and originals at CSL) (FHL film 5,365);
- Christ Church of West Haven's "Church Records, 1788–1903" (includes baptisms, marriages, burials) (originals at ED) (FHL film 1,014,195);
- Baptisms 1839–50, marriages 1841–50, burials 1840–50 at Christ Church (ED film 1,014,195);

---

733 See How to Use This Book, note 4, above.

734 Carole Magnuson, *Barbour Collection of Connecticut Town Vital Records: Orange 1822-1850, Oxford 1798-1850, Plainfield 1699-1852*, vol. 33, (Baltimore: GPC, 2000). Digital images at *Ancestry.com*.

735 Now part of the Barbour Index and interfiled with similar slips from other towns in CSL and on FHL films 2,887 *et seq*. See Introduction above, pp. 3–5..

736 Lucius B. Barbour, *Connecticut Vital Records: Orange, 1822–1850,* (Hartford: CSL, 1925) page after title page (FHL film 2,976). Digital images at *AmericanAncestors.org* and *FamilySearch.org*.

- First Congregational Church of West Haven's "Church Records, 1724-1916" (includes baptisms 1843–1871, baptisms in reports of preparatory and other meetings 1843–1852; and marriages 1843–1844) (originals at CSL) (FHL film 6,269);
- DAR (Florida). GRC's "Bible and Cemetery Records" (original typescript submitted to DAR) (FHL film 850,400);
- St. Matthew's Episcopal Church (Bristol, Connecticut); Baptist Church (Southington, Connecticut); Guilford Episcopal Church (Guilford, Connecticut)'s Miscellaneous church records (contains obstetrical record of Dr. Josiah Colburn, Orange, Derby, Ansonia 1824–1848;). FHL film 3,054, item 4.

CEMETERY TRANSCRIPTIONS: The Hale Collection identifies people in order of physical proximity buried at about two named sites in Orange Township.[737] See also, Alice Hubbard Breed Benton's "Cemetery at Orange, Conn." (typescript.) (FHL film 165,997).

OTHER NOTEWORTHY SOURCES:

- "J. Seymour Pardee records;" see Appendix A;
- Harry I. Thompson and Lucena Stevens Smith's "Aunt Lucena's list: Bill of Mortality in West Haven, From August 1774 When the Bell Was First Tolled" (typescript in West Haven Town Hall) (FHL film 1,420,923);
- Harlan R. Jessup's "Family Records of Orange, Connecticut, 1717 to 1880, by Erastus Scranton, Minister of the North Milford Society," CA, Vol. 49, No. 3 (Feb 2007);
- Harlan R. Jessup's "Corrections to Orange, Connecticut, Family Records: Fenn, Mallett, Smith, and Others," *CA*, Vol. 49, No. 4 (May 2007).

OXFORD

Barbour's typescript volume for Oxford,[738] unlike the GPC edition,[739] begins:

> This volume contains a list alphabetically arranged of all the vital records of the town of Oxford from its incorporation to about 1850. The records prior to 1850 are found in two volumes.
>
> This list was taken from a set of cards[740] based on a copy of the Oxford Vital Records made in 1917 by Mr. James N. Arnold, of Providence, R.I. The Arnold Copy, now in the possession of the Connecticut State Library, has not been compared with the original and doubtless errors exist. It is hoped that as errors or omissions are found notes will be

737 Charles R. Hale, "Headstone Inscriptions of Orange, Connecticut" (bound manuscript at CSL) (FHL film 3,358). Hale named these Orange & Hebrew of Ansonia and Darby.

738 See How to Use This Book, note 4, above.

739 Magnuson, *Barbour Collection: Orange–Plainfield*, vol. 33. Digital images at *Ancestry.com*.

740 Now part of the Barbour Index and interfiled with similar slips from other towns in CSL and n FHL films 2,887 *et seq*. See Introduction above, pp. 3–5.

```
entered in this volume and on the cards which
are included in the General Index of Connecti-
cut Vital Records also in the possession of
the Connecticut State Library.
            Hartford, Conn., March, 1925.[741]
```

VITAL RECORDS: The Oxford volume includes vital records as early as 1756 and as late as 1849. Barbour abstracted two Oxford "books:"

- "1" refers to chronologically arranged marriage certificates, an unfilmed volume called "Record of Marriages, 1818–1850" by the Oxford town clerk;[742]
- "2" refers to Oxford's Records of Births, Marriages, Deaths, vol. 1, 1767–1847, Oxford Town Hall (FHL film 1,420,658) (which appears to be missing several earlier pages).

FHL also catalogs as Oxford vital records:

- **Oxford's Records of Births, Marriages, Deaths, 1847–1908, Oxford Town Hall (FHL film 1,420,659);**
- **William C. Sharpe's *History of Oxford: Part First, Church records, births, marriages, deaths, etc Part Second Sketches and Records* (Seymour: Record Print, 1885).**

CHURCH RECORDS:

- Congregational Church's "Church Records, 1741–1929" (includes baptisms, 1745–1813, marriages 1746–1814, and deaths 1764–1814) (originals at CSL) (FHL film 5,375);
- Christ Church's "Church Records, 1845–1948" (includes baptisms 1845–1856, marriages 1845–1854, and burials 1845–1855) (originals at the CSL) (FHL film 5,376);
- St. Peter's Church's "Church Records, vol. 1–3, 1769–1948" (includes baptisms 1847–1948, marriages 1845–1948, and burials 1845–1948) (originals in CSL) (FHL film 1,011,955 or 5,377).
- Baptisms (1845–56), marriages (1845–54) & burials (1845–55) at Christ Church at Quaker Farms (ED film 5,376);
- Baptisms (1847–1904 & 1847–1904), & marriages (1845–1904 & 1845–1904) at St. Peter's Church (ED films 1,011,955 & 5,377);

CEMETERY TRANSCRIPTIONS: The Hale Collection identifies people in order of physical proximity buried at about seven named sites in Oxford Township.[743] Compare with Daniel Hearn's 1976 copy of 18 pre-1800 gravestones in three Oxford cemeteries.[744]

---

[741] Lucius B. Barbour, *Connecticut Vital Records: Oxford, 1798–1850,(* Hartford: CSL, 1925) page after title page (FHL film 2,976). Digital images at *AmericanAncestors.org* and *FamilySearch.org.*

[742] Email from Oxford Town Clerk Margaret A West-Mainor, 20 June 2018.

[743] Charles R. Hale, "Headstone Inscriptions of the Town of Oxford, Connecticut" (bound manuscript at CSL) (FHL film 3,358). Hale named these Congregational, St. Peter's Southford, Quaker Farms #1, Quaker Farms #2, Riverside, & Jack's Hill.

[744] Daniel Hearn, "Connecticut gravestones, early to 1800," manuscript (FHL film 1,477,477, item 25).

OTHER NOTEWORTHY SOURCES:

- Edward R. Lambert's *History of the Colony of New Haven: Before and After the Union With Connecticut: Containing a Particular Description of the Towns Which Composed that Government, viz., New Haven, Milford, Guilford, Branford, Stamford, & Southold, L.I., With a Notice of the Towns Which Have Been Set Off from "the Original Six"* (New Haven: Hitchcock & Stafford, 1838);
- Henry Bronson's *History of Waterbury, Connecticut: Original Township Embracing Present Watertown and Plymouth, and Parts of Oxford, Wolcott, Middlebury, Prospect and Naugatuck, With an Appendix of Biography, Genealogy and Statistics* (Waterbury: Bronson Bros., 1858);
- William Cothren's *History of ancient Woodbury, Connecticut, from the first Indian deed in 1659 to 1854: including the present towns of Washington, Southbury, Bethlehem, Roxbury, and a part of Oxford and Middlebury* (vol. 3 contains vital records, including those for ancient Stratford) (Baltimore, MD: GPC, 1997).

PLAINFIELD

Barbour's typescript volume for Plainfield,[745] unlike the GPC edition,[746] begins:

> This volume contains a list alphabetically arranged of all the vital records of the town of Plainfield from its incorporation to about 1852. This list was taken from a set of cards[747] based on a copy of the Plainfield Vital Records made in 1909 by Mr. James N. Arnold, of Providence, R.I. The entire record for this town prior to 1852 is found in four volumes. The Arnold Copy, now in the possession of the Connecticut State Library, has not been compared with the original and doubtless errors exist. It is hoped that as errors or omissions are found notes will be entered in this volume and on the cards which are included in the General Index of Connecticut Vital Records also in the possession of the Connecticut State Library.
>
> Hartford, Conn., June, 1920.[748]

VITAL RECORDS: The Plainfield volume includes vital records as early as 1695 and as late as 1854. Barbour abstracted four Plainfield "books:"[749]

- "1" is from Plainfield's Vital Records, Births, Marriages, Deaths: vol. 1, 1694–1747, Plainfield Town Hall, (FHL film 1,378,030, item 2;[750]

---

[745] See How to Use This Book, note 4, above.

[746] C Magnuson, *Barbour Collection: Orange–Plainfield*, vol. 33. Digital images at *Ancestry.com*.

[747] Now part of the Barbour Index and interfiled with similar slips from other towns in CSL and n FHL films 2,887 *et seq*. See Introduction above, pp. 3–5.

[748] Lucius B. Barbour, *Connecticut Vital Records: Plainfield, 1699–1852,* (Hartford: CSL, 1920) page after title page (FHL film 2,977). Digital images at *AmericanAncestors.org* and *FamilySearch.org*.

[749] CSL catalogs the year ranges of these very films as 1: 1694-1745, 2: 1723-1853, 3: 1847-1858, 4: 1853-1867, and 6:1867-1879.

- "2" is Plainfield's Vital Records, Births, Marriages, Deaths: vol. 2 (1st book), 1723–1858, Plainfield Town Hall, (FHL film 1,378,030, item 3;
- "3" is Plainfield's Vital Records, Births, Marriages, Deaths:, vol. 2 (2nd book), 1785–1848, Plainfield Town Hall, (FHL film 1,378,030, item 4;
- "4" abstracts **most of** Plainfield's Vital Records, Births, Marriages, Deaths: vol. 3, B 1847–1851, M 1847–1858, D 1847–1851; Plainfield Town Hall, (FHL film 1,378,030, item 5), but page numbers are double the numbers cited by Barbour.

CHURCH RECORDS:

- First Congregational Church's "Church Records, 1747–1899" (includes baptisms; marriages; and deaths) (originals at CSL) (FHL film 1,011,956 or 5,452);
- Mary Kingsbury Talcott's "Records of the First Congregational Church, Plainfield, Conn.," *NEHGR*, 70:171 *et seq.* (1916);
- Union Baptist Church and Ecclesiastical Society at Moosup's "Church Records, 1792–1931" (includes baptisms 1813–1831 and deaths through 1839) (photocopies at CSL) (FHL film 5,458);
- Packerville Baptist Church's "Church Records, 1828–1928" (deaths 1829–1830 & 1828–1928, and baptisms) (originals at CSL) (FHL film 5,457);
- Central Village Congregational Church's "Church Records,1846–1941" (includes baptisms, marriages and deaths 1846–1941) (photocopies at CSL) (FHL film 5,454);
- Methodist Episcopal Church at Moosup's New England Southern Conference, Church records 1842–1932 1941 (Photocopy at CSL) (FHL film 5,456);
- North Plainfield Ecclesiastical Society's *Church records, 1845–1941,* photocopies at CSL (FHL film 5,453).

CEMETERY TRANSCRIPTIONS: The Hale Collection identifies people in order of physical proximity buried at about 22 named sites in Plainfield Township.[751] Compare with Daniel Hearn's 1979 copy of 214 pre-1800 gravestones in two Plainfield cemeteries.[752] See also,

- Emma Finney Welch's "Gravestone Inscriptions, Plainfield, Connecticut" (1910 manuscript in the Historical Society of Pennsylvania) (FHL film 441,390);
- John Eben Prior's "Inscriptions From Gravestones at Plainfield, Conn.," *NEHGR*, vol. 70:33 (1917).

OTHER NOTEWORTHY SOURCES: John Eben Prior's "Record of Deaths Kept by Manuel Kinne of Plainfield, Conn.," *NEHGR*, vol. 71:133. (1917).

---

750 Plainfield's Town Records, 1699-1748 (CSL call # 974.62 tm) include no vital records.

751 Charles R. Hale, "Headstone Inscriptions of the Town of Plainfield, Connecticut" (bound manuscript at CSL) (FHL film 3,358). Hale named these Bennett, Cornell-Monrow, Randall Farm, North Davis Farm, South Davis Farm. Gallup, One stone near Flat Rock School, Neighborhood lot, Parke, Spalding, Hammett, Small, Hopkins, Rood, Joseph Roode Farm, Union, All Hollows, Evergreen, Old Plainfield, New Plainfield, St. John's & Looke Farm.

752 Daniel Hearn, "Connecticut gravestones, early to 1800," manuscript (FHL film 1,477,477, item 26).

PLYMOUTH

Barbour's typescript volume for Plymouth,[753] unlike the GPC edition,[754] begins:

> This volume contains a list alphabetically arranged of all the vital records of the town of Plainfield from its incorporation to about 1850. This list was taken from a set of cards[755] based on a copy of the Plainfield Vital Records made in 1909 by Mr. James N. Arnold, of Providence, R.I. The entire record of the town prior to 1854 is found in two volumes.
>
> The Arnold Copy, now in the possession of the Connecticut State Library, has not been compared with the original and doubtless errors exist. It is hoped that as errors or omissions are found notes will be entered in this volume and on the cards which are included in the General Index of Connecticut Vital Records also in the possession of the Connecticut State Library.
>
> Hartford, Conn., July, 1927.[756]

VITAL RECORDS: The Plymouth volume includes vital records as early as 1756 and as late as 1852. Barbour abstracted two Plymouth "books:"

- "1" refers to Plymouth's Records of Births, Marriages, and Deaths, 1745–1938 (contains records of marriages, births, and deaths, arranged primarily by family), Plymouth Town Hall, (FHL film 1,521,827, item 1);
- "2" refers to Plymouth's Records of Births, Marriages, and Deaths, 1745–1938 (contains records of freemen, marriages, a few births and deaths), Plymouth Town Hall, (FHL film 1,521,827, item 2).

CHURCH RECORDS:

- St. Matthew's Church's "Church and Cemetery Records 1744–1901" (includes baptisms) (originals and transcripts at CSL) (FHL film 5,411);
- St. Matthew's Church at New Cambridge's Baptisms, *etc.*,1747–1800, originals at CSL (FHL film 5,411);
- First Congregational Church's "Church Records, 1736–1949" (includes baptisms, marriages and deaths) (originals at CSL) (FHL film 1,011,959 or 5,412);
- St. Peter's Church's "Church Records, 1807–1828" (includes baptisms, marriages and funerals) (originals at CSL) (FHL film 1,011,960);
- Congregational Church at Terryville's Papers, 1835–1838, Photostats at CSL (FHL film 1,011, 964, item 2);

---

753 See How to Use This Book, note 4, above.

754 Marie Schlumbrecht Crossley, *Barbour Collection of Connecticut Town Vital Records: Plymouth 1795-1850, Pomfret 1705-1850*, vol. 34, (Baltimore: GPC, 2000). Digital images at *Ancestry.com.*

755 Now part of the Barbour Index and interfiled with similar slips from other towns in CSL and n FHL films 2,887 *et seq*. See Introduction above, pp. 3–5..

756 Lucius B. Barbour, *Connecticut Vital Records: Plymouth, 1745–1850, (*Hartford: CSL, 1927) page after title page (FHL film 2,977). Digital images at *AmericanAncestors.org* and *FamilySearch.org.*

- Baptisms (1789–1857 & 1844–57), marriages (1822–55, 1844–57 & 1854–56) and burials (1822—54 & 1844–58) at Christ Church (ED Film 5,064);
- Congregational Society's Thomaston Church records, 1837–1921, (location of originals unspecified) (FHL film 1,014,185, item 1).
- St. Peter's Church's "Church Records, 1784–1919" (includes baptism 1832, burials 1832, marriages 1837–1865, and burials 1837–1864) (originals at CSL) (FHL film 5,413);

CEMETERY TRANSCRIPTIONS: The Hale Collection identifies people in order of physical proximity buried at about 10 named sites in what was then Plymouth Township.[757] Compare with Daniel Hearn's 1978 copy of 23 pre-1800 gravestones in two Plymouth cemeteries.[758] The Hale Collection also identifies people in order of physical proximity buried at about two named sites in what was then Thomaston Township.[759] Compare with Daniel Hearn's 1978 copy of three pre-1800 gravestones in one Thomaston cemetery.[760] See also, Linda J. Zapatka's *Old Plymouth Burying Ground: Plymouth, Conn.* ([S.l.]: L.J. Zapatka, 2012).

OTHER NOTEWORTHY SOURCES:

- "Sexton records for St. Matthew's Cemetery in East Plymouth 1846–1886;" CSL; see Appendix A;
- Henry Bronson's *History of Waterbury, Connecticut: Original Township Embracing Present Watertown and Plymouth, and Parts of Oxford, Wolcott, Middlebury, Prospect and Naugatuck* (Waterbury: Bronson Bros., 1858);
- Francis Atwater's *History of the town of Plymouth, Connecticut: with an account of the centennial celebration May 14 and 15, 1895; also a sketch of Plymouth, Ohio, settled by local families* (Meriden: Journal Pub. Co., 1895) (FHL film 1,321,003, item 3).

POMFRET

Barbour's typescript volume for Pomfret,[761] unlike the GPC edition,[762] begins:

> This volume contains a list alphabetically arranged of all the vital records of the town of Pomfret from its incorporation to about 1850. This list was taken from a set of cards[763] based on a copy of the Pomfret Vital Records made in 1910 by Mr. James N. Arnold, of Providence, R.I. The en-

---

757 Charles R. Hale, "Headstone Inscriptions of the Town of Plymouth, Connecticut" (bound manuscript at CSL) (FHL film 3,358). Hale names these Old (2 different locations), East Plymouth, Allentown, Hillside, St. Mary's St. John's Greek Catholic, Greek Orthodox, & West.

758 Daniel Hearn, "Connecticut gravestones, early to 1800," manuscript (FHL film 1,477,477, item 28).

759 Charles R. Hale, "Headstone Inscriptions of the Town of Thomston, Connecticut" (bound manuscript at CSL) (FHL film 3,365). Hale names these Hillside & St. Thomas.

760 Daniel Hearn, "Connecticut gravestones, early to 1800," manuscript (FHL film 1,477,477, item 57).

761 See How to Use This Book, note 4, above.

762 Crossley, *Barbour Collections: Plymouth Pomfret*, vol. 34. Digital images at *Ancestry.com*.

763 Now part of the Barbour Index and interfiled with similar slips from other towns in CSL and n FHL films 2,887 *et seq*. See Introduction above, pp. 3–5.

> tire record of the town prior to 1850 is contained in four volumes. In this alphabetical list all marriages and births in the fifth volume have been omitted but all deaths have been indexed, the date of the last one being April 1, 1869. The Arnold Copy, now in the possession of the Connecticut State Library, has not been compared with the original and doubtless errors exist. It is hoped that as errors or omissions are found notes will be entered in this volume and on the cards which are included in the General Index of Connecticut Vital Records also in the possession of the Connecticut State Library.
>
> Hartford, Conn., May, 1921.[764]

VITAL RECORDS: The Pomfret volume includes vital records as early as 1702 and as late as 1869. Barbour abstracted five Pomfret "books:"

- "1" generally abstracts Pomfret's Births, Marriages, Deaths, vol. 1, 1695–1810, Pomfret Town Hall (FHL film 1,376,250, item 1, **but not always.**
- "2" generally abstracts Pomfret's Births, Marriages, Deaths, vol. 2, 1771–1841, Pomfret Town Hall (FHL film 1,376,250, item 2, **but not always.**
- "3" generally abstracts Pomfret's Births, Marriages, Deaths, vol. 3, 1802–1853, Pomfret Town Hall (FHL film 1,376,251, item 2, **but not always.**
- "4 "generally abstracts Pomfret's Births, Marriages, Deaths, vol. 4, 1823–1857, Pomfret Town Hall (FHL film 1,376,251, item 3, **but not always.**
- "5" generally abstracts Pomfret's Births, Marriages, Deaths, vol. 5, 1833–1869, Pomfret Town Hall (FHL film 1,376,251, item 4, **but not always.**

Barbour did not abstract:

- **Most of the events recorded in Pomfret's Births, Marriages, Deaths vol. 1–2 1695–1840, Pomfret Town Hall, (FHL film 1,376,250, Item 3). (BMD 1706–1802 on pages 349 to 657);**
- **Some of those in Pomfret's "Copy of First Records, 1686–1865" (includes early births, marriages and deaths, 1695–1865) (includes the proprietors' records, 1715–1767; town meetings, 1713–1788; early births, marriages and deaths, 1695–1865; some other early miscellaneous town records) manuscript in Pomfret Town Hall (FHL films 1,376,250, item 4 & 1,376,251, item 1);**
- **Any of Marilyn Labbe's "Six Marriages Performed by Lemuel Ingalls, Justice of the Peace, Pomfret,"** ***CN*****, 32:8 (June 1999).**

CHURCH RECORDS:

- Congregational Church of Abington's, "Church Records, 1749–1923" (includes deaths, baptisms, marriages) (originals at CSL) (FHL film 3,694);
- Ellen D. Larned's "Transcript of the Baptisms, Marriages and Deaths for 1711–1829 of the Putnam First or Putnam Heights Congregational Church" (typescript in CSL) (FHL film 5,466);

---

[764] Lucius B. Barbour, *Connecticut Vital Records: Pomfret, 1705–1850,* (Hartford: CSL, 1921) page after title page (FHL film 2,977). Digital images at *AmericanAncestors.org* and *FamilySearch.org.*

- Christ Church's "Church Records, 1826–1889" (includes baptisms, marriages, and burials) (originals at CSL) (FHL film 5,432, items 2–3);
- Baptist Church of Putnam's, Church records, 1847–1941, originals at CSL (FHL film 5,467);
- Abington Ecclesiastical Society's *Church records, 1761–1883*, originals at CSL (FHL films 1,011,965–6);
- Catholic Reformed Christian Church's *Church records, 1792–1798,* originals at CSL (FHL film 5,432, item 1);
- Baptisms (1789–1870), marriages (1789–1870) & abstracts from wills (1789–1837) at Christ Church (ED Film 5,432);
- Lemuel B. Hull's "A Record of Marriages, Baptisms, Admission to the Communion and Funerals, 1822–1835" (manuscript at NEHGS),

CEMETERY TRANSCRIPTIONS: The Hale Collection identifies people in order of physical proximity buried at about 12 named sites in what was then Pomfret Township.[765] Compare with Daniel Hearn's 1979 copy of 237 pre-1800 gravestones in two Pomfret cemeteries.[766] The Hale Collection also identifies people in order of physical proximity buried at about 11 named sites in what was then Putnam Township.[767] Compare with Daniel Hearn's 1979 copy of 86 pre-1800 gravestones in one Putnam cemetery.[768] See also,

- Dorman Hubbard Weaver's "Old Abington Cemetery Stones: Parish Cemetery, Abington Congregational Church" (typescript photocopy at FHL);
- "Tombstone Readings : Old Abbington Cemetery, Pomfret, CT," *Ingalls inquirer* – vol. 1–10 (1984–1993) – vol. 3, no. 3 (Novol. 1986) Digital images: *FamilySearch.org*.
- Marian Chandler Holt's *Monumental Inscriptions From Wappaquian Burial Ground in Pomfret, Copied in 1862* (1913/1997 copy at NEHGS);
- Edwin R. Ledogar and Leroy Schrump's *Tombstone Records of Pomfret* (Danielson: Killingly Historical Society, n.d.);
- George Chandler's "Monumental Inscriptions in Pomfret, Conn.." (NEHGS manuscript);
- "Inscriptions in the Wappaquians Burial Ground, Pomfret. Conn.," *NEHGR*, vol. 73:105 (1919).

OTHER NOTEWORTHY SOURCES:

- Emily Wilder Leavitt's "Marriages at Pomfret, Conn., 1706–1753," *NEHGR*, vol. 67: 371 (1917);
- Margaret M. Weaver's Aspinock Historical Society, *Perspectives of Putnam: a History of Putnam, Connecticut* (Putnam: Wimco Printing, 1980).

---

765 Charles R. Hale, "Headstone Inscriptions of the Town of Pomfret, Connecticut" (bound manuscript at CSL) (FHL film 3,358-9). Hale names these Chandler, Pomfret Street, Episcopal Church, Sabin, New Abbintpn, Old Abbington, Bruce, Dennis, Graveyard (3 diffewrent locations), & Randall-Botham.

766 Daniel Hearn, "Connecticut gravestones, early to 1800," manuscript (FHL film 1,477,477, item 29).

767 Charles R. Hale, "Headstone Inscriptions of the Town of Putnam, Connecticut" (bound manuscript at CSL) (FHL film 3,359-60). Hale names these Grove Street, Putnam Heights, Munyan, Wheelock, Mallbone (colored family), Carpenter-Dresser, Day, Babbitt, Aspinwall, St. Mary's & Malbone.

768 Daniel Hearn, "Connecticut gravestones, early to 1800," manuscript (FHL film 1,477,477, item 33).

- "Pomfret Manufacturing Company death records 1814–1851;" CSL; see Appendix A;

PORTLAND

Barbour's typescript volume for Portland,[769] unlike the GPC edition,[770] begins:

> This volume contains a list alphabetically arranged of all the vital records of the town of Portland from its incorporation to about 1850. This list was taken from a set of cards[771] based on a copy of the Portland Vital Records made in 1912 by Mr. James N.Arnold, of Providence, R.I. The entire record of the town prior to 1850 is found in one volume.
>
> The Arnold Copy, now in the possession of the Connecticut State Library, has not been compared with the original and doubtless errors exist. It is hoped that as errors or omissions are found notes will be entered in this volume and on the cards which are included in the General Index of Connecticut Vital Records also in the possession of the Connecticut State Library.
>
> Hartford, Conn., January, 1923.[772]

VITAL RECORDS: The Portland volume includes vital records as early as 1841 and as late as 1851. Barbour abstracted Portland's Vital Records, vol. 1, Births, Marriages, Deaths 1809–1855, Portland Town Hall, (FHL film 1,378,375, item 1)

CHURCH RECORDS:

- First Congregational Church's "Church Records, 1710–1925" (baptisms 1721–1731, 1731–1811 & 1816–1862; marriages 1767–1815 & 1816–1865; and deaths 1751–1815 & 1816–1865) (originals at CSL) (FHL film 5,398);
- Trinity Church's "Church Records, 1789–1945" (includes baptisms, marriages, and burials) (originals at CSL) (FHL film 1,011,967);
- Baptisms (1789–1857, 1844–57), marriages (1822–55, 1844–57, 1854–56) & burials (1822–54, 1844–58) at Trinity Church in Chatham (ED Film 1,011,967).

CEMETERY TRANSCRIPTIONS: The Hale Collection identifies people in order of physical proximity buried at about six named sites in Portland Township.[773] Compare with

[769] See How to Use This Book, note 4, above.

[770] Wilma J. Standifer Moore, *Barbour Collection of Connecticut Town Vital Records: Portland 1841-1850, Prospect 1827-1853, Redding 1767-1852, Ridgefield 1709-1850*, vol. 36, (Baltimore: GPC, 2000).

[771] Now part of the Barbour Index and interfiled with similar slips from other towns in CSL and n FHL films 2,887 *et seq*. See Introduction above, pp. 3–5..

[772] Lucius B. Barbour, *Connecticut Vital Record: Portland, 1841–1850*,(Hartford: CSL, 1923) page after title page (FHL film 2,977). Digital images at *AmericanAncestors.org* and *FamilySearch.org.*

[773] Charles R. Hale, "Headstone Inscriptions of the Town of Portland, Connecticut" (bound manuscript at CSL) (FHL film 3359). Hale named these Trinity, Center, Swedish, St. Mary's Old, & Phelps.

Daniel Hearn's 1979 copy of 287 pre-1800 gravestones in two Portland cemeteries.[774] See also,

- Lucius B. Barbour's "Portland, Conn. Epitaphs" (Mss A 2790), RSASC, NEHGS;
- Portland Burying Ground Association's *Portland Burying Ground Association and its Cemetery* (Portland: Middlesex County Printery, 1897).

OTHER NOTEWORTHY SOURCES: Portland Historical Society's *History of Portland, Connecticut* ([S.l.]: Portland Historical Society, 1976).

PRESTON

Barbour's typescript volume for Preston,[775] unlike the GPC edition,[776] begins:

> The vital record series of the town of Preston consists of eight volumes and in this book is a list alphabetically arranged of the original entries. In the first four volumes every entry is taken. Volumes 5 and 8 contain in tabulated form the births, deaths and marriages from 1848 to 1867, and the following entries only from these volumes appear: the births prior to December 31, 1850, the marriages prior to December 32 1850, and all the deaths, the last entry being December 22, 1867. Volumes 6 and 7 are a recent compilation of matter gleaned principally from the records of the First Church, the Second Church, the Separatists' Church and the private marriage record of Justice Samuel Mott. These records contain marriages and baptisms and are said to be not recorded in the other volumes of Town records. They have been completely indexed and are listed in a separate alphabet beginning on page 224.
>
> The following list was made from a set of cards[777] based on a copy of the Preston Vital Records made in 1910 by James N. Arnold, of Providence, R.I. The Arnold Copy, now in the possession of the Connecticut State Library, has not been compared with the original and doubtless errors exist. It is hoped that as errors or omissions are found notes will be entered in this volume and on the cards which are included in the General Index of Connecticut Vital Records also in the possession of the Connecticut State Library.
>
> Hartford, Conn., May, 1919.[778]

---

774 Daniel Hearn, "Connecticut gravestones, early to 1800," manuscript (FHL film 1,477,477, item 30).

775 See How to Use This Book, note 4, above.

776 Marsha Wilson Carbaugh, *Barbour Collection of Connecticut Town Vital Records: Preston 1687-1850, Parts I & II*, vol. 35, (Baltimore: GPC, 2000). Digital images at *Ancestry.com*.

777 Now part of the Barbour Index and interfiled with similar slips from other towns in CSL and n FHL films 2,887 *et seq*. See Introduction above, pp. 3–5.

778 Lucius B. Barbour, *Connecticut Vital Records: Preston, 1687–1850,* (Hartford: CSL, 1919) page after title page (FHL film 2,977). Digital images at *AmericanAncestors.org* and *FamilySearch.org*.

VITAL RECORDS: The Preston volume includes vital records as early as 1678 and as late as 1867. Barbour abstracted six Preston "books:"

- "1" refers to from Preston's Records of Births, Marriages, Deaths vol. 1 1672–1790, Preston Town Hall, (FHL Film 1,311,194, item 1);
- "2" refers to Preston's Records of Births, Marriages, Deaths vol. 2 Births, 1721–1844; Marriages, 1722–1835; Deaths, 1737–1848; Preston Town Hall, (FHL Film 1,311,194, item 2);
- "3" refers to Preston's Records of Marriages, vol. 3 (1822–1836), Preston Town Hall, (FHL film 1,311,195, item 1);
- "4" refers to Preston's Records of Marriages, vol. 4 (1837–1854), Preston Town Hall, (FHL film 1,311,195, item 2);
- "5" refers to Preston's Records of Marriages, vol. 5 (1848–1851), Preston Town Hall, (FHL film 1,311,195, item 3);
- "8-C" refers to Preston's Records of Deaths, vol. 5 (1848–1867), Preston Town Hall, (FHL film 1,311,195, item 6.

See also

- **Preston Town Records, 1772–1861 (including marriage certificates 1821–1944) CSA (CSL 974.62 P93 t);**
- **Preston Vital Records, ca 1845, CSL (CSA RG 072.002, Box 15);**
- **Marriages by Samuel Mott, Preston Justice of the Peace, are in Preston's "Records of Early Marriages in Preston from Church & Other Records Not Recorded in Books of Marriages 1725–1814, Vol. VI, Preston Town Hall, FHL film 1,311,195, item 4).**
- **First book of records, Preston, Connecticut (contains 1645–1780 records of birth, marriage, and death, organized by family) (n.d. 145 p. typescript in NYGBS) (FHL Film 5,380, item 3);**
- **Preston, Connecticut, First book of marriages: containing the birth dates of the children born to each couple (a copy of the first volume of vital records of the town, with handwritten notes) (FHL film 1,597,833, item 5);**

CHURCH RECORDS:

- Preston Town Clerk's "Record of Children Born in Preston and Baptized in the First and Second Churches of Preston," Preston Town Hall, FHL film 1,311,195, item 5);
- *First Congregational Church of Preston, Connecticut, 1698–1898: together with statistics of the church taken from church records.* Preston, Conn.: The Society, 1900) (images at *AmericanAncestors.org);*
- First Congregational Church's "Church Records, 1698–1917" (includes baptisms, marriages, and deaths) (originals at CSL) (FHL film 1,011,968 or 5,395);
- St. James Church at Poquetanuck's "Church Records, 1712–1948" (includes baptisms, marriages, and burials) (originals at CSL) (FHL film 1,011,969 or 5,394);
- Long Society of Preston (formerly Norwich East Society)'s Church records, 1757–1938 typescript at CSL (miscellaneous records 1775–1938). (FHL film 5,393);
- "Preston, Connecticut Baptisms, 1674–1755" (manuscript in NYGBS) (FHL film 5,380);
- Preston City Baptist Church's Records 1815–1874 originals at CSL (FHL film 1,011968);

- Baptisms (1839–82), marriages (1840–82) & burials (1840–83) at St. James' Church in Poquetanuck (ED Film 1,011,969);
- H. Gidman and Mary E Morse's *First Congregational Church of Preston, Connecticut, 1698–1898: Together With Statistics of the Church Taken From Church Records.* (Preston: The Society, 1900);
- Baptist Church. Church records, 1815–1874 (originals at CSL) (FHL film 1,011,968, item 6);
- Ruby Parke Anderson's *The Parke scrapbook* {includes records of the Separate Church, Preston, Conn., 1747–1800 by Rev. Paul Park) (Baltimore, Maryland : Port City Press, c1965).

CEMETERY TRANSCRIPTIONS: The Hale Collection identifies people in order of physical proximity buried at about 18 named sites in Preston Township.[779] Compare with Daniel Hearn's 1982 copy of 127 pre-1800 gravestones in three Preston cemeteries.[780] See also,

- Mrs. Sidney Hall's *Cemetery Records of Preston, Connecticut* ([S.l.]: Preston Historical Society, 1967);
- Daniel L. Phillips' "Cook Cemetery Transcriptions" (Mss C 5709), RSASCs, NEHGS;
- Mrs. Sidney Hall, Joyce Steffenson, and David A. Oat's *Cemetery inscriptions in the town of Preston* ([Preston]: Preston Historical Society (Connecticut), [1991?];
- *Cemeteries and burials in the town of Preston* ([S.l.]: Preston Historical Society (Connecticut), 1984);
- Anne Meech and Susan B. Meech's"Cemetery inscriptions from Groton, Preston and Stonington," Connecticut (typescript includes the following cemeteries: Old Plain Cemetery in North Stonington, Wightman Cemetery in Groton Township, and Avery Cemetery, Preston Plains, Preston) (FHL film 4,291);
- "New England tombstone inscriptions," *Genealogy* – vol. 3–5 (1913–1915) – vol. 5, no. 3 (Mar. 1915) = whole no. 71;
- Preston Historical Society's *Cemeteries and burials in the town of Preston : including deceased veterans, (1967);*
- George S. Porter's "Inscriptions from the Long Society Burying Ground, Preston, Conn.," *NEHGR*, vol. 60: 124 (1906).

OTHER NOTEWORTHY SOURCES:

- Marion White Hall's *Preston in review,* (Preston: Preston Historical Society, 1971);
- Marion White Hall's *Preston early homes and families,* (Stonington: Stonington Print. & Pub. Co, 1968).

---

779 Charles R. Hale, "Headstone Inscriptions of the Town of Preston, Connecticut" (bound manuscript at CSL) (FHL film 3359). Hale named these Preston City, Avery, New Poquetaunke, Long Soc., Palmer, Gates, Guile, Old, Davis, Gore, Carey, Brown, Brewster, Jewish, Killam, Bentley, Old Poquetaunke, & Safford.

780 Daniel Hearn, "Connecticut gravestones, early to 1800," manuscript (FHL film 1477477, Item 31).

PROSPECT

Barbour's typescript volume for Prospect,[781] unlike the GPC edition,[782] begins:

> This volume contains a list alphabetically arranged of all the vital records of the town of Prospect from its incorporation to about 1853. The entire record of the town prior to 1853 is found in one volume.
>
> This list was taken from a set of cards[783] based on a copy of the Prospect Vital Records made in 1912 by Mr. James N. Arnold, of Providence, R.I. The Arnold Copy, now in the possession of the Connecticut State Library, has not been compared with the original and doubtless errors exist. It is hoped that as errors or omissions are found notes will be entered in this volume and on the cards which are included in the General Index of Connecticut Vital Records also in the possession of the Connecticut State Library.
>
> Hartford, Conn., December, 1924.[784]

VITAL RECORDS: The Prospect volume includes vital records as early as 1827 and as late as 1852. Barbour abstracted Prospect's Records of Marriages, Births, and Deaths, 1801–1880 (contains records of marriages 1827–1855, 1867–1879; births 1801–1836, 1867–1879; and deaths 1828–1848, 1867–1880), Prospect Town Hall, (FHL film 1,412,971, item 1).

CHURCH RECORDS:

- Congregational Church's "Church Records, 1797–1937" (baptisms 1799–1826 & 1827–1863; deaths 1798–1812 & 1834–1864; and marriages 1837–1864) (originals at CSL) (FHL film 5,461);
- Bristol/Prospect Methodist Episcopal Church's Records 1849–1916, originals at CSL (FHL film 3.793).

CEMETERY TRANSCRIPTIONS: The Hale Collection identifies people in order of physical proximity buried at one named site in Prospect Township.[785] Compare with Daniel Hearn's 1976 copy of three pre-1800 gravestones in one Prospect cemetery.[786]

---

781 See How to Use This Book, note 4, above.

782 Moore, *Barbour Collection: Portland–Ridgefield*, vol. 36.

783 Now part of the Barbour Index and interfiled with similar slips from other towns in CSL and n FHL films 2,887 *et seq*. See Introduction above, pp. 3–5.

784 Lucius B. Barbour, *Connecticut Vital Records: Prospect, 1827–1853* (Hartford: CSL, 1924) page after title page. (FHL film 2,977). Digital images at *AmericanAncestors.org* and *FamilySearch.org.*

785 Charles R. Hale, "Headstone Inscriptions of the Town of Prospect, Connecticut" (bound manuscript at CSL) (FHL film 3,359). Hale named this Prospect Cemetery,

786 Daniel Hearn, "Connecticut gravestones, early to 1800," manuscript (FHL film 1,477,477, item 6).

OTHER NOTEWORTHY SOURCES:

- "Payne, Philemon;s Account Book," 1766–1864, CSL; see Appendix A;
- Henry Bronson's *History of Waterbury, Connecticut: Original Township Embracing Present Watertown and Plymouth, and Parts of Oxford, Wolcott, Middlebury, Prospect and Naugatuck, With an Appendix of Biography, Genealogy and Statistics* (Waterbury: Bronson Bros., 1858);
- Edward R. Lambert's *History of the Colony of New Haven: Before and fter the Union with Connecticut* (New Haven: Hitchcock & Stafford, 1838);
- John R. Guevin's *View from the top: the story of Prospect, Connecticut* (Prospect: Biographical Pub. Co., c1995).

REDDING

Barbour's typescript volume for Redding,[787] for Redding unlike the GPC,[788] begins:

> **The vital records of Redding from the formation of the town to about 1852 are found in one volume.**
>
> **This alphabetical list was taken from a set of cards[789] based on a manuscript copy made in 1915 by Miss Irene H. Mix, of Hartford, Conn. The manuscript copy, now in the possession of the Connecticut State Library, has not been compared with the original and doubtless errors exist. It is hoped that as errors or omissions are found notes will be entered in this volume and on the cards which are included in the General Index of Connecticut Vital Records also in the possession of the Connecticut State Library.**
>
> **Hartford, Conn., March, 1925.**[790]

VITAL RECORDS: Redding volume includes vital records as early as 1729 and as late as 1852. Barbour abstracted Redding's Records of Births, Marriages, & Deaths, vol. 2–3, 1726– 1888 (vol. 2 includes records of enrollment of freemen, 1803–1917), Redding Town Hall, (FHL film 1,435,589).

Barbour did not abstract:

- **Redding Town Records. 1754–1772 contains a few scattered vital records) CSA (CSL 974.62 fR24 tm);**
- **Miscellaneous records of Redding, Connecticut, 1750–1780, typescript at NYGBS (FHL film 4,431, item 2);**

---

787 See How to Use This Book, note 4, above..

788 Moore, *Barbour Collection: Portland –Ridgefield*, vol. 36.

789 Now part of the Barbour Index and interfiled with similar slips from other towns in CSL and n FHL films 2,887 *et seq*. See Introduction above, pp. 3–5.

790 Lucius B. Barbour, *Connecticut Vital Records: Redding, 1767–1852,* (Hartford: CSL, 1925) page after title page (FHL film 2978). Digital images at *AmericanAncestors.org* and *FamilySearcg.org.*

- **Lester Card's "Cemetery, Church and Vital Records of Redding, Connecticut" (typescript at the NYGBS) (FHL film 4431);**
- **Harlan R. Jessup's "Vital Records of 1847–1848, School District Returns from Redding, Sherman and Ridgefield, CT," *CA*, Vol. 54, No. 2 (Nov 2011);**
- **Harlan R. Jessup's "Early Vital Records of Redding, CT, a Recent Discovery," *CA*, Vol. 50, No. 1 (Aug 2007).**

CHURCH RECORDS:

- Congregational Church's "Church Records, 1729–1882" (includes baptisms, marriages, and deaths) (originals at CSL) (FHL film 1,011,970, items 2–6);
- Congregational Church and Ecclesiastical Society's "Church Records, 1729–1882" (includes baptisms 1733–1780 & 1809–1875; deaths 1734–1775 & 1830–1863; and marriages 1734–1780 & 1809–1861) (originals at CSL) (FHL film 5,481, items 1–4);
- Methodist Episcopal Church's "Church Records, 1779–1850" (includes births 1779–1846, baptisms 1790–1850 and marriages 1792–1846) (originals at CSL) (FHL film 5,481);
- Redding Circuit's "Church Records, 1779–1850" (includes births, baptisms and marriages) (original records at CSL) (FHL film 1,011,970, item 8);
- Baptist Society Minutes of meetings, 1784–1798, originals at CSL (FHL film 1,011,970, item 1);
- John N. Nickerson's "Redding, Connecticut Congregational Church, Vital Records, 1731–1860" (1896 manuscript in CSL) (FHL film 1,011,970, item 7);
- John N. Nickerson's "Redding, Connecticut, Methodist Episcopal Church, Redding Center, Vital Records 1747–1855" (manuscript in CSL) (FHL film 1,011,970, item 9);
- Harlan R. Jessup's "Early Records of Redding, Connecticut: Marriages and Burials, Christ Church, Episcopal, Redding, CT, 1814 to 1879," *CA*, Vol. 50, No. 2 (Nov 2007);
- Harlan R. Jessup's "Baptisms of Christ Church, Episcopal, Redding, CT, 1814 to 1878," *CA*, Vol. 50, No. 1 (Aug 2007);
- Lemuel B. Hull's "A Record of Marriages, Baptisms, Admission to the Communion and Funerals, 1822–1835" (manuscript at NEHGS);
- Harlan R. Jessup's "Ministerial Records of the Rev. Lemuel B. Hull of Connecticut: Christ Church, Redding, and St. James Church, Danbury, 1822 to 1835," *CA*, Vol. 50, No. 1 (Aug 2007).

CEMETERY TRANSCRIPTIONS: The Hale Collection identifies people in order of physical proximity buried at about 11 named sites in Redding Township.[791] Compare with Daniel Hearn's 1975 copy of 88 pre-1800 gravestones in four Redding cemeteries.[792]

OTHER NOTEWORTHY SOURCES: Charles Burr Todd's *History of Redding, Connecticut from its first settlement to the present time : with notes on the Adams, Banks, Barlow, Bartlett, Bartram, Bates, Beach, Benedict, Betts, Burr, Burritt, Burton, Chatfield, Couch, Darling, Fairchild, Foster, Gold, Gorham, Gray, Griffin, Hall, Hawley,*

---

[791] Charles R. Hale, "Headstone Inscriptions of the Town of Redding, Connecticut" (bound manuscript at CSL) (FHL film 3,360). Hale named these Old, Wuepawaug, Center, Isaac Hamilton, Christ Church, Hull, Ridge, Sanford, Graveyard, Putnam, & Family.

[792] Daniel Hearn, "Connecticut gravestones, early to 1800," manuscript (FHL film 1,477,477, item 34).

Heron, Hill, Hull, Jackson, Lee, Lyon, Lord, Mallory, Meade, Meeker, Merchant, Morehouse, Perry, Platt, Read, Rogers, Rumsey, Sanford, Smith, Stow, and Strong families (New York: Grafton Press, c1906).

RIDGEFIELD

Barbour's typescript volume for Ridgefield,[793] unlike the GPC edition,[794] begins:

> The vital records of Ridgefield, prior to 1850, are found in the first volume of Land Records and volume 1 of Vital Records.
>
> In this alphabetical list, which was taken from a set of cards[795] based on a manuscript copy made in 1915 by James N. Arnold, of Providence, R.I., reference to the Land Record volume is indicated by the abbreviation "LR", and the book of vital records by "Vol.1".
>
> The Arnold Copy, now in the possession of the Connecticut State Library, has not been compared with the original and doubtless errors exist. It is hoped that as errors or omissions are found notes will be entered in this volume and on the cards which are included in the General Index of Connecticut Vital Records also in the possession of the Connecticut State Library. Library.
>
> Hartford, Conn., April, 1926.[796]

VITAL RECORDS: The Ridgefield volume includes vital records as early as 1700 and as late as 1850. Barbour abstracted two Ridgefield "books:"

- "1" refers to Ridgefield's Records of Births, Marriages, Deaths vol. 2 1762–1852 Ridgefield Town Hall, (FHL film 1,435,730, item 2);
- "LR1" refers to Ridgefield's Land Records, vol. 1–2 1709–1765 (vol. 1 includes births, marriages and deaths 1708–1765) Ridgefield Town Hall, (FHL film 5,496).

Additional sources of Ridgefield vital records include:

- **Marriage records of Aaron Fancher, Justice of the Peace, Poundridge [sic], N.Y., 1838–1871 FHL film 17,860, item 2);**
- **George Lounsbury Rockwell's *History of Ridgefield, Connecticut, Records of Vital Statistics":* p. 451–517) (Ridgefield: Privately printed by author, 1927) (FHL film 1,697,767, item 6);**
- **Harlan R. Jessup's "Vital Records of 1847–1848, School District Returns from Redding, Sherman and Ridgefield, CT," *CA*, Vol. 54, No. 2 (Nov 2011).**

---

793 See How to Use This Book, note 4, above.

794 Moore, *Barbour Collection: Portland–Ridgefield*, vol. 36.

795 Now part of the Barbour Index and interfiled with similar slips from other towns in CSL and n FHL films 2,887 *et seq*. See Introduction above, pp. 3–5.

796 Barbour, *Connecticut Vital Records Ridgefield, 1769–1850,* Hartford: CSL, page preceding p.1 of volume.FHL film 2,978. Digital images at *AmericanAncestors.org* and *FamilySearch.org*.

CHURCH RECORDS:

- Church of England's "Church Records, 1742–1746" (includes baptisms) (originals at CSL) (FHL film 5,815);
- Ridgebury Congregational Church's "Church Records, 1761–1916" (includes marriage, death, and baptism records) (originals and photocopies in CSL) (FHL film 1,011,971, items 1–4);
- Ridgebury Congregational Church's "Church Records, 1761–1931" (vital records in minutes) originals at CSL (FHL film 5,509);
- Samuel Camp's *Church records of Ridgebury, Connecticut, 1769–1812 : conti. by someone to 1857* (Des Moines, IA: s.n., 1947?);
- Aaron Fancher and Lester L. Card's "Marriage Records of Aaron Fancher, Justice of the Peace, Poundridge [sic], N.Y., 1838–1871" (1931 typescript at NYGBS) (FHL film 17,860);
- St. Stephen's Church's "Church Records, 1784–1918" (includes baptisms, marriages, and burials) (originals at CSL) (FHL film 1,011,971, items 5–8);
- Baptisms (1812–78), marriages (1812–89) & funerals (1813–87) at St. Stephen's Church (ED Film 1,011,971);
- First Congregational Church's *Catalog of the members of the First Congregational Church in Ridgefield, Ct : also of those who have died, or received letters of dismission and recommendation to other churches, January 1, 1849*, (New York: S.W. Benedict, 1849) (FHL film 1,751,788, item 75);
- Barbara Smith Buys' Daughters of the American Colonists. Dutchess of York Chapter, *Ridgefield, Connecticut (church) records*, (includes marriages of the Ridgefield, Congregational Church from 1820 through 18620 (Poughkeepsie, NY: Dutchess of York Chapter, D.A.R., 1976);
- Pound Ridge Presbyterian Church's *Church Records, 1822–1899*, (original records at the Presbyterian Historical Society in Philadelphia) (FHL film 525,748, item 3.

CEMETERY TRANSCRIPTIONS: The Hale Collection identifies people in order of physical proximity buried at about 19 named sites in Ridgefield Township.[797] Compare with Daniel Hearn's 1975 copy of 110 pre-1800 gravestones in two Ridgefield cemeteries.[798] See also, George S. Hoyt's *Record of soldiers buried in Danbury, Brookfield, New Fairfield and Ridgefield*, Photostat copy (Hartford: CSL, 1929) CSL digital collection online.

OTHER NOTEWORTHY SOURCES:

- Daniel W. Teller's *History of Ridgefield, Conn: From Its First Settlement to the Present Time* (Danbury: T. Donovan, 1878);
- Glenna M. Welsh's *Proprietors of Ridgefield, Connecticut* (Ridgefield, Connecticut: Caudatowa Press, 1976);

---

797 Charles R. Hale, "Headstone Inscriptions of the Town of Ridgefield, Connecticut" (bound manuscript at CSL) (FHL film 3.340). Hales named these Old Town, Catholic, Branchville, Beers, Davis, Seymour, Gamaliel Smith, Old Florida, Florida, Bennett's Farm, Ridgebury, Town, Mapleshade, Scott's Hurlbutt, Lounsbury, Fair Lawn, Smith, & Old Episcopal Church.

798 Daniel Hearn, "Connecticut gravestones, early to 1800," manuscript (FHL film 1,477,477, item 35).

- Kenneth W. Rockwell's "Genealogies of Early Families of Ridgefield, CT: a Bibliographical Essay," *CA*, Vol. 53, No. 1 (August 2010) and Vol. 53, No. 2 (Nov 2010);
- Keith Marshall Jones' *Farms of Farmingville : a two-century story of twenty-three Ridgefield, Connecticut farmhouses and the people who gave them life,* (Ridgefield: Connecticut Colonel Publishing Company, c2001).

ROCKY HILL

Barbour's typescript volume for Rocky Hill,[799] unlike the GPC edition,[800] begins:

> This volume contains a list alphabetically arranged of all the vital records of the town of Rocky Hill from its incorporation to about 1854. The entire record of the town prior to 1854 is found in one volume.
>
> On Oct. 20, 1879 it was voted "that such portions of the Congregational and Society records from 1765 to 1848 as refer to marriages, baptisms and deaths be copied on the town records by the town clerk for preservation". These records were accordingly copied, but a comparison with the original Church Records, now in the State Library, show many omissions and discrepancies.
>
> This list was taken from a set of cards[801] based on a copy of the Rocky Hill Vital Records made in 1917 by James N. Arnold, of Providence, R.I. The Arnold Copy, now in the possession of the Connecticut State Library, has not been compared with the original and doubtless errors exist. It is hoped that as errors or omissions are found notes will be entered in this volume and on the cards which are included in the General Index of Connecticut Vital Records also in the possession of the Connecticut State Library.
>
> Hartford, Conn., February, 1928.[802]

VITAL RECORDS: The Rocky Hill volume includes vital records as early as 1765 and as late as 1853. Barbour abstracted Rocky Hill's Records of Marriages, Deaths, and Baptisms, 1764–1854, Rocky Hill Town Hall, (FHL film 1,316,153, item 1). He criticizes the church records abstracted from the town clerk's copy at page 60 *et seq.* as unreliable and urged comparison with their source: Rocky Hill Congregational

[799] See How to Use This Book, note 4, above.

[800] Lillian Bentley Karlstrand, *Barbour Collection of Connecticut Town Vital Records: Rocky Hill 1765-1854, Roxbury 1796-1835, Salem 1836-1852, Salisbury 1741-1846*, vol. 37, (Baltimore: GPC, 2000).

[801] Now part of the Barbour Index and interfiled with similar slips from other towns in CSL and n FHL films 2,887 *et seq*. See Introduction above, pp. 3–5.

[802] Lucius B. Barbour, *Connecticut Vital Records: Rocky Hill, 1843–1854,* (Hartford: CSL, 1928) page after title page (FHL film 2,978). Digital images at *AmericanAncestors.org* and *FamilySearch.org.*

Church Records, 1726–1955 (contains baptisms, marriages, deaths) original records in the CSL, Hartford (FHL film 1,012,867, items 2–5).
Barbour failed to abstract **Rocky Hill's Births, Marriages, & Deaths vol. 1 1847–1868, Rocky Hill Town Hall, (FHL film 1,316,153, items 2–3).**
See also,

- **Rocky Hill Vital Records circa 1845–1905, CSL (CSA RG 070.002, Boxes 16A & 16B);**
- **Many Rocky Hill Vital Records slips in Drawer 395, not interfiled in Barbour Index. They may all be abstracted from Rocky Hill Vital Records, 1865–1879 (typescript in Alha order) (FHL film 3,662, item 10). See Appendix B.**

CHURCH RECORDS:

- Congregational Church's "Church Records, 1726–1955" (includes baptisms, marriages, and deaths) (originals in CSL) (FHL film 1,012,867);
- "Rocky Hill Church, 1722–1855" (includes baptisms, marriages, and burials, 1727–1855) (1929 typescript in CSL) (FHL film 5,483).

CEMETERY TRANSCRIPTIONS: The Hale Collection identifies people in order of physical proximity buried at about three named sites in Rocky Hill Township.[803] Compare with Daniel Hearn's 1978 copy of 207 pre-1800 gravestones in one Rocky Hill cemetery.[804] See also,

- Edward Sweetser Tillotson's *Wethersfield Inscriptions: A Complete Record of the Inscriptions in the Five Burial Places in the Ancient Town of Wethersfield, Including the Towns of Rocky Hill, Newington, and Beckley Quarter (in Berlin), also a Portion of the Inscriptions in the Oldest Cemetery in Glastonbury* (Hartford: W.F.J. Boardman, 1899);
- Sherman W. Adams's *The History of Ancient Wethersfield, Connecticut: Comprising the Present Towns of Wethersfield, Rocky Hill, and Newington: and of Glastonbury Prior to Its Incorporation in 1693, from Date of Earliest Settlement Until the Present Time* (New York: Grafton Press, 1904);
- Frances Wells Fox's *1634 to 1934*, (Hartford: Case, Lockwood & Brainard Co., (c.1934)).

OTHER NOTEWORTHY SOURCES:

- Sherman W. Adams and Henry R. Stiles' *History of ancient Wethersfield, Connecticut: comprising the present towns of Wethersfield, Rocky Hill, and Newington; and of Glastonbury prior to its incorporation in 1693, from date of earliest settlement until the present time* (New York: Grafton Press, c1904);
- Frances Wells Fox's *Wethersfield and her daughters: Glastonbury, Rocky Hill, Newington, from 1634 to 1934* (Hartford: Case, Lockwood & Brainard Co., (c.1934));
- Peter J. Revill's *Short History of Rocky Hill, Connecticut: a Connecticut River town* (S.I.: Rocky Hill Historical Society, [1972?]).

---

803 Charles R. Hale, "Headstone Inscriptions of the Town of Rocky Hill, Connecticut" (bound manuscript at CSL) (FHL film 3,360). Hale named these Rocky Hill, Graveyard, & Rose Memorial.

804 Daniel Hearn, "Connecticut gravestones, early to 1800," manuscript (FHL film 1,477,477, item 36).

ROXBURY

Barbour's typescript volume for Roxbury[805] unlike the GPC edition,[806] begins:

> The vital records of Roxbury prior to 1835, are found in a volume known as "Book A, Town Meetings, List of Electors, Estrays, etc."
>
> This alphabetical list, was taken from a set of cards[807] based on a copy of the Roxbury Vital Records made in 1915 by Mr. James N. Arnold, of Providence, R.I., The Arnold Copy, now in the possession of the Connecticut State Library, has not been compared with the original and doubtless errors exist. It is hoped that as errors or omissions are found notes will be entered in this volume and on the cards which are included in the General Index of Connecticut Vital Records also in the possession of the Connecticut State Library.
>
> Hartford, Conn., June, 1926.[808]

VITAL RECORDS: The Roxbury volume includes vital records as early as 1772 and as late as 1839. The "Town Meetings" book Barbour abstracted has not been microfilmed by FHL and is now at CSL cataloged as "Roxbury Town Record Book, 1796–1832." CSA RG 062.120.[809]

However, the FHL does catalog subsequent records that Barbour missed: Roxbury's Report of births, deaths, and marriages, 1847–1851, Town Hall, Roxbury, (FHL film 1,522,004).

CHURCH RECORDS:

- Congregational Church and Ecclesiastical Society's "Church Records, 1742–1930" including baptisms 1797–1863, 1868, and 1873–1876; marriages 1797–1862, deaths 1797–1886 (originals at CSL), (FHL film 5,494);
- Christ Church's "Church Records, 1806–1941," includes baptisms, marriages, and burials (originals at CSL) (FHL film 1,012,868);
- Congregational Church and Ecclesiastical Society's "Church Records, 1742–1930" (includes baptisms 1797–1863, 1868 and 1873–1876, marriages 1797–1862, deaths 1797–1886) (originals at CSL) (FHL film 5,494);
- Christ Church's "Church Records, 1806–1941" (includes baptisms, marriages, and burials) (originals at CSL) (FHL film 1,012,868);

---

805 See How to Use This Book, note 4, above..

806 Karlstrand, *Barbour Collection: Rocky Hill–Salisbury*, vol. 37.

807 Now part of the Barbour Index and interfiled with similar slips from other towns in CSL and n FHL films 2,887 *et seq*. See Introduction above, pp. 3–5.

808 Lucius B. Barbour, *Connecticut Vital Records: Roxbury, 1796–1835,* (Hartford: CSL, 1926) page after title page (FHL film 2,978). Digital images at *AmericanAncestors.org* and *FamilySearch.org.*

809 Jennie Sherman, *Connecticut Town Guides: Roxbury,* 139

- "A Biographical Sketch of the Rev. Thomas Davies A.M., Missionary," printed in 1843 (includes a list of marriages, baptisms, and church dismissals covering several towns in Litchfield County), attributed by Ricker to CSL;
- "Copy of Christ Church in Roxbury, Conn. Records, 1763–1891" (includes baptisms 1763–1766) (manuscript at NEHGS);
- Presbyterian Society's *Subscriptions 1818–1833,* originals at CSL (FHL film 1,012,868, item 8).

CEMETERY TRANSCRIPTIONS: The Hale Collection identifies people in order of physical proximity buried at about five named sites in Roxbury Township.[810] Compare with Daniel Hearn's 1976 copy of 63 pre-1800 gravestones in three Roxbury cemeteries.[811]

OTHER NOTEWORTHY SOURCES: William Cothren's *History of ancient Woodbury, Connecticut, from the first Indian deed in 1659 to 1854: including the present towns of Washington, Southbury, Bethlehem, Roxbury, and a part of Oxford and Middlebury* (vol. 3 contains vital records, including those for ancient Stratford) (Baltimore, MD: GPC, 1997) (FHL film 2,055,359 and 6,181).

SALEM

Barbour's typescript volume for Salem,[812] unlike the GPC edition,[813] begins:

> This volume contains a list alphabetically arranged of all the vital records of the town of Salem from its incorporation to about 1852. This list was taken from a set of cards[814] based on a copy of the Rocky Hill Vital Records made in 1912 by James N. Arnold, of Providence, R.I. The entire record of the town prior to 1852 is found in one volume. The Arnold Copy, now in the possession of the Connecticut State Library, has not been compared with the original and doubtless errors exist. It is hoped that as errors or omissions are found notes will be entered in this volume and on the cards which are included in the General Index of Connecticut Vital Records also in the possession of the Connecticut State Library.
>
> Hartford, Conn., December, 1919.[815]

---

810 Charles R. Hale, "Headstone Inscriptions of the Town of Roxbury, Connecticut" (bound manuscript at CSL) (FHL film 3360). Hales named these Roxbury Center, Old South, Old, North, Beardsley-Leavenworth.

811 Daniel Hearn, "Connecticut gravestones, early to 1800," manuscript (FHL film 1477477, Item 37).

812 See How to Use This Book, note 4, above.

813 Karlstrand, *Barbour Collection: Rocky Hill–Salisbury*, vol. 37.

814 Now part of the Barbour Index and interfiled with similar slips from other towns in CSL and on FHL films 2,887 *et seq*. See Introduction above, pp. 3–5.

815 Lucius B. Barbour, *Connecticut Vital Records: Salem, 1836–1852,* (Hartford: CSL, 1919) page after title page.(FHL film 2,978). Digital images at *AmericanAncestors.org* and *FamilySearch.org.*

VITAL RECORDS: The Salem volume includes vital records as early as 1790 and as late as 1851. Barbour abstracted Salem's Records of Births, Marriages, & Deaths, 1786–1967, Salem Town Hall, (FHL film 1,312,309, items 5–6).
See also, **Salem Vital Records circa 1845–1905, CSL (CSA RG 072.002, Box 16B).**

CHURCH RECORDS: none

CEMETERY TRANSCRIPTIONS: The Hale Collection identifies people in order of physical proximity buried at about 23 named sites in Salem Township.[816] Compare with Daniel Hearn's 1982 copy of eight pre-1800 gravestones in one Salem cemetery.[817] See also,

- Lucius B. Barbour's "Genealogical Data From Connecticut Cemeteries: Salem, All Stones Standing In the Town, Copied August 1931 [and 1932]" (1931–1932 manuscript at NEHGS); see also, *NEHGR*, vol. 89:243.
- "Record of Inscriptions Found on Gravestones in the Town of Salem Dated Prior to A.D. 1850" (manuscript at NEHGS).

OTHER NOTEWORTHY SOURCES: See state and county resources above, pages 17 to 21.

SALISBURY

Barbour's typescript volume for Salisbury,[818] unlike the GPC edition,[819] begins:

> The vital records of Salisbury prior to 1846 are found scattered through Volumes 1 and 2 of Town Meetings, Volume 1 of the Land Records, the "Records of Justice Court 1758-1796" and a book of Vital Records known as Volume 3.
>
> This alphabetical list, was taken from a set of cards[820] based on a manuscript copy made in 1915 by James N. Arnold, of Providence, R.I., Reference to entries found in the volumes of Town Meetings and the book of Vital Records is indicated by the volume number, to those found in the Land Records by the abbreviation "LR" and the volume number and to those in the Justice Court Records by the abbreviation "J.C."
>
> "Historical Collections Relating to the Town of Salisbury", Volume 1 of which was published in 1913 and Volume 2 in 1916 by The Salisbury Association, Inc., contains most of the records of Salisbury, and although the manuscript copy has not been checked in its entirety with the printed history, a few marked differences have been noted herein.

---

816 Charles R. Hale, "Headstone Inscriptions of the Town of Salem, Connecticut" (bound manuscript at CSL) (FHL film 3360). Hale names these Woodbridge, Baptist, Dolebear Place, Lathrop, Old Rathbone, Rathbone, Wesley Brown, Graveyard (2 different locations), Niles, Hillard, Harris, 1 stone (2 different locations), Miner, Raymond, Rogers, Mosswood Glen, Fox, Whittlesey, Fish, Way, & Loomis.

817 Daniel Hearn, "Connecticut gravestones, early to 1800," manuscript (FHL film 1,477,477, item 38).

818 See How to Use This Book, note 4, above..

819 Karlstrand, *Barbour Collection: Rocky Hill–Salisbury*, vol. 37.

820 Now part of the Barbour Index and interfiled with similar slips from other towns in CSL and n FHL films 2,887 *et seq*. See Introduction above, pp. 3–5.

> The manuscript copy, now in the possession of the Connecticut State Library, has not been compared with the original and doubtless errors exist. It is hoped that as errors or omissions are found notes will be entered in this volume and on the cards which are included in the General Index of Connecticut Vital Records also in the possession of the Connecticut State Library.
>
> Hartford, Conn., April, 1927.[821]

VITAL RECORDS: The Salisbury volume includes vital records as early as 1728 and as late as 1848. Barbour abstracted five Salisbury "books:"

- "1" and "2" refer to Salisbury's Records of Births, Deaths, Marriages, & Town Meetings, 1740–1848 (contains vol. 1–2 Births, Deaths, Marriages, 1740–1798), Salisbury Town Hall, (FHL film 1,509,740, items 1–4);
- "3" refers to Salisbury's Records of Births, Deaths, Marriages, & Town Meetings, 1740–1848 (contains vol. 3 Births, Deaths, Marriages, 1769–1848), Town Hall, Salisbury Town Hall, (FHL film 1,509,740, item 5);
- "LR1" refers to Salisbury's Proprietors records 1739–1813 Land records, vol. 1 1741–1750 Salisbury Town Hall, (FHL film 5,511);
- "J.C." refers to a "Justice Court" volume of at least 152 pages still in the town clerk's possession, unfilmed. It contains only one marriage (in 1791)[822] abstracted by Barbour.
- **Unspecified additions and/or corrections were made from the Salisbury Association's *Historical Collections Relating to the Town of Salisbury* (New Haven: Salisbury Assoc., 1916) (images at *AmericanAncestors.org*).**

Barbour did not abstract Salisbury's Records of births, deaths, and marriages, 1847–1905, Salisbury Town Hall, (FHL film 1,509,740, items 6–7) or **Salisbury Vital Records circa 1845–1905, CSL (CSA RG 070.002, Box 19) (pre 1850 birthdates on death certificates).**

FHL also catalogs under Salisbury vital records:

- **Donna Valley Russell's *Salisbury, Connecticut records,* 2 vols. Middletown, MD: Catoctin Press, c1983);**
- **Salisbury Association's *Historical Collections Relating to the Town of Salisbury, Litchfield County Connecticut,* 4 vols. (New Haven: Tuttle, Morehouse & Taylor Co., 1913, 1916) (FHL films 928,514, item 2 and 924,072, item 3) now numbers four volumes of vital records and cemetery inscriptions. This abstraction often differs from Barbour's and its digital images are online at *AmericanAncestors.org;***
- **Notes from minutes of meetings for Freemen of the town of Salisbury, Connecticut, manuscript at NYGBS (FHL films 5,510, items 4–5 or 1,405,497, items 24–25).**

CHURCH RECORDS:

- "Congregational Church Records, Salisbury, Connecticut, 1740–1891" (typescript in Pittsfield, MA) (FHL film 234,579);

---

821 Lucius B. Barbour, *Connecticut Vital Records: Salisbury, 1741–1845,* (Hartford: CSL, 1927) page after title page.(FHL film 2,978). Digital images at *AmericanAncestors.org* and *FamilySearch.org.*

822 Salisbury reports "1 vol of Justice Court Records" in 1936, *Biennial Report* (1936).

- Rollin H. Cooke's Salisbury, Conn. Cong. Church, 1977 manuscript online at FHL;
- Salisbury Congregational Church's "Church Records, 1744–1941" (includes baptisms (1714–1788, 1793–1817 & 1818–1873), deaths (1807–1812, 1752–1890 & 1818–1874), and marriages 1808–1812 & 1818–1873) (originals in CSL) (FHL film 5,526);
- Salisbury's "Congregational Church Records, 1744–1891" (includes marriages 1808–1812, obituaries 1807–1812, and baptisms 1744–1817) (manuscript in NYGBS) (FHL film 5,510, item 1);
- Trinity Church in Lime Rock's, Parish register, 1873–1933, (contains records of families, baptisms 1874–1933, confirmations, communicants, marriages 1876–1926, and burials 1876–19300 original records in the archives of the Episcopal Diocese, Hartford (FHL film 1,513,663, item 70);
- St. John's Church's "Church Records, 1823–1883" (includes births 1824–1862, marriages 1824–1862, and funerals and burials 1823–1862) (photocopies in CSL) (FHL film 5,527);
- Baptisms (1824–62), marriages (1824–62) & burials (1823–62) at St. John's Church (ED Film 5,527).

CEMETERY TRANSCRIPTIONS: The Hale Collection identifies people in order of physical proximity buried at about twelve named sites in Salisbury Township.[823] Compare with Daniel Hearn's 1978 copy of 136 pre-1800 gravestones in four Salisbury cemeteries.[824] See also,

- Malcolm Day Rudd's *Inscriptions at Salisbury Center, Lime Rock, etc.* (Boston: David Clapp, 1898) (FHL Film 1,435,147);
- Donna Valley Russell's *Salisbury, Connecticut records* (Middletown, MD: Catoctin Press, c1983).

OTHER NOTEWORTHY SOURCES:

- "Rev. Crossman's "Special Genealogy File;" see Appendix A;
- Julia Pette's *Rev. Jonathan Lee and his eighteenth century Salisbury Parish: the early history of the town of Salisbury, Connecticut* (Salisbury: Salisbury Association, 1957);
- Malcom Day Rudd and Irvin W Sanford's *Historical sketch of Salisbury, Connecticut* (New York: [s.n.], 1899);
- Willard A. Hanna's *Berkshire-Litchfield legacy: Litchfield, Ancram, Salisbury, Stockbridge, Lenox (*Rutland, VT: C.E. Tuttle, c1984)

SAYBROOK

Barbour's typescript volume for Saybrook (now Deep River),[825] unlike the GPC edition,[826] begins:

---

823 Charles R. Hale, "Headstone Inscriptions of the Town of Salisbury, Connecticut" (bound manuscript at CSL) (FHL film 3 360-1). Hale names these Center, Chapinville, Dutchess Bridge, Mt. Hope, Town Hill, Lime Rock, Salisbury, New, Catholic, Private 3 stones, Private 2 stones, & Family.

824 Daniel Hearn, "Connecticut gravestones, early to 1800," manuscript (FHL film 1,477,477, item 39).

825 See How to Use This Book, note 4, above.

826 Nancy E. Schott, *Barbour Collection of Connecticut Town Vital Records: Saybrook 1735-1850, Sharon 1739-1865*, vol. 38, (Baltimore: GPC, 2000). Digital images at *Ancestry.com*.

> The vital records of Saybrook prior to 1850 are found in the first eight volumes of Land Records and in two volumes of Vital Records. This list includes all items found in these and also some printed in the New England Historical and Genealogical Register, Vol. IV, which were evidently taken from an ancient copy and which do not appear today in the original record. In this alphabetical list usually references to Volumes 1 and 2 before 1750 in date will be found in the Land Records and after 1750 in the Vital Records.
>
> This list was taken from a set of cards[827] based on a copy of the Saybrook Vital Records known as "The L'Hommedieu Copy". Mr. Frederick L'Hommedieu, Town Clerk of Saybrook, late of Deep River, deceased, deposited this in the State Library, but it is not known who made it. On comparison with the original records many inaccuracies were found in the L'Hommedieu Copy and these have been corrected in the alphabetical list so far as possible. It is hoped that if other errors or omissions are found notes will be entered in this volume and on the cards which are included in the General Index of Connecticut Vital Records also in the possession of the Connecticut State Library.
>
> Hartford, Conn., March, 1924.[828]

VITAL RECORDS: The Saybrook volume includes vital records from 1642 through 1859. Barbour abstracted the "L'Hommedieu Copy" of Saybrook's records and then corrected its "many inaccuracies … so far as possible." This copy is available only at CSL but need not be consulted as Barbour's citations are to pagination in the original Saybrook (now Deep River) records. Because, however, Barbour has abstracted only events listed in "The L'Hommedieu Copy," **there are vital statistics in the original town records which Barbour missed. Barbour.**

- "1" abstractions before circa 1750 refer to Saybrook's Land Records, vol. 1 (1648–1760) Deep River Town Hall, (FHL film 5,536, item 1) **but entries are incomplete.** "1" abstractions after circa 1750 refer to "Saybrook Births, Marriages, Deaths, Vol. 1" (family groupings, 1767–1833), which is archived, unfilmed, at CSL;
- "2" abstractions before circa 1750 are from Saybrook's Land Records, vol. 2, (1700–1781) Deep River Town Hall, (FHL film 5,536, item 2);
- "2" abstractions before circa 1750 are from "Saybrook Births, Marriages, Deaths, Vol. 1." (family groupings 1829 to 1850), which is archived, unfilmed, at CSL;
- "3" and "4" are Saybrook's Land Records, vol. 3–4 1719–1735 (volumes 1–4 of the town records include births, marriages, and deaths) (FHL film 5,537, items 1 & 2);

---

827 Now part of the Barbour Index and interfiled with similar slips from other towns in CSL and on FHL films 2,887 *et seq*. See Introduction above, pp. 3–5.

828 Lucius B. Barbour, *Connecticut Vital Records: Saybrook, 1635–1850,* (Hartford, CSL,1924) page after title page (FHL film 2978). Digital images at *AmericanAncestors.org* and *FamilySearcg.org*

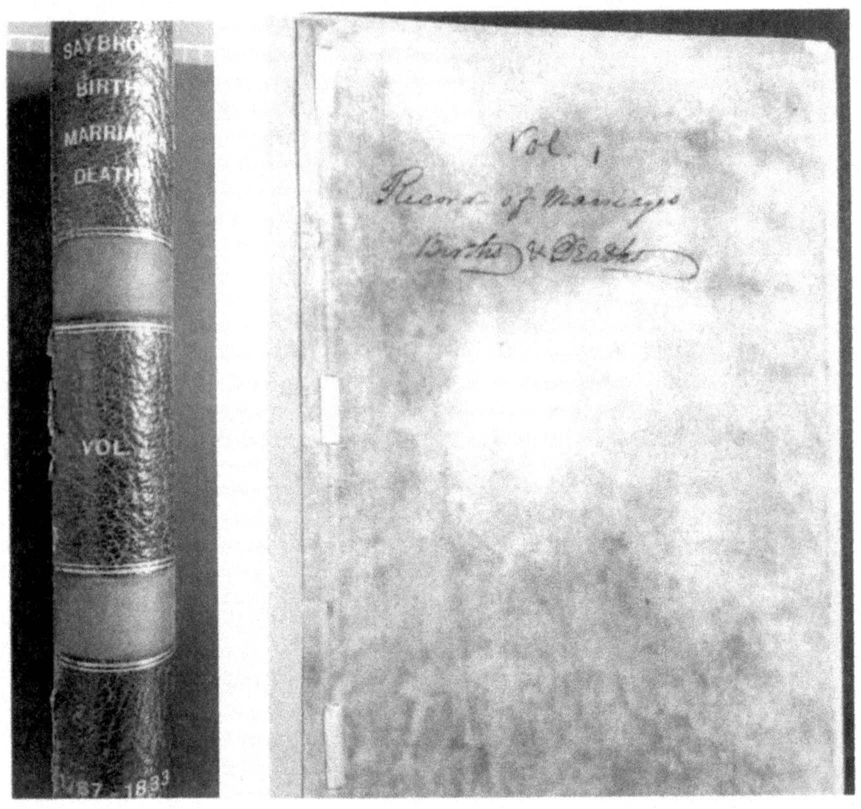

Figures 23 & 24: Saybrook Vital Records, volume 1

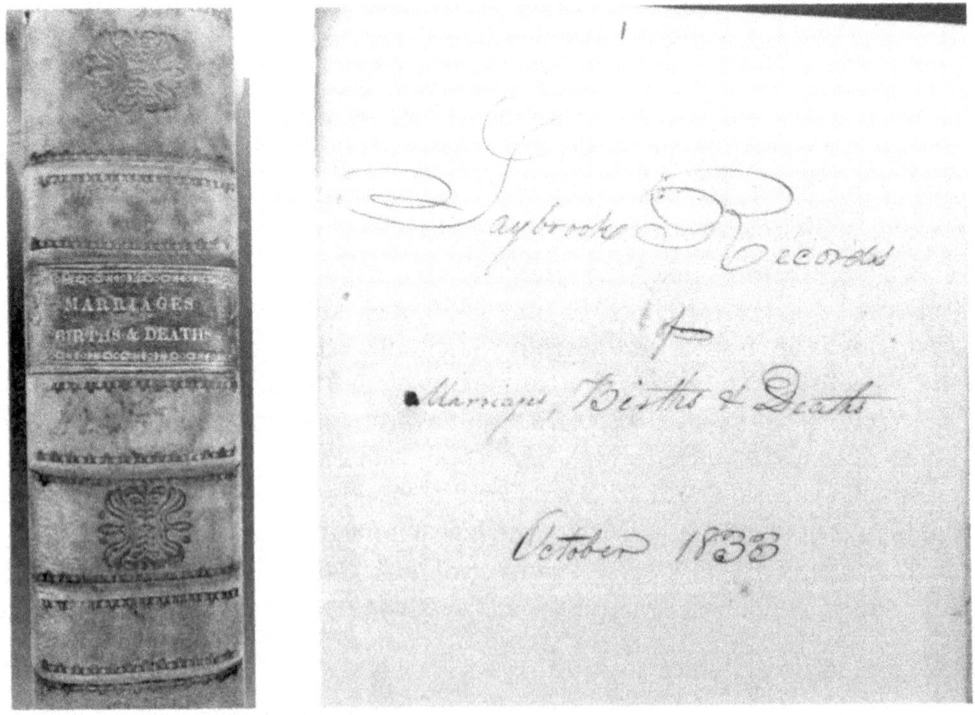

Figures 25 & 26: Saybrook Vital Records, volume 2

- "5" and "6" refer to Saybrook's Land Records, vol. 5–6, 1735–1749 (FHL film 5,538, items 1 & 2), but **entries are incomplete;**
- "7" are Saybrook's Land Records, vol. 7–8, 1748–1775, (FHL film 5,539, item 1), but **entries are incomplete;**
- "Reg-4" refers to "Records of Saybrook, CT." *NEHGR* 4:19 *et seq.* (1850).

The FHL catalogs only one "vital record" for Saybrook (now Deep River): "Town and Miscellaneous Records of Saybrook, Connecticut," (including cemetery records ca. 1641–1860) (FHL film 5,528, item 2).
See also,

- **Deep River's Vital Statistics book "Births, Marriages, Deaths 1847–1884;"[829]**
- **Saybrook's "Marriages, Births, Deaths 1847–1851, archived at CSL as vol. 2 of Saybrook Vital Records, 1757–1930," (CSL 974.62 C83r m1);**
- **CHS' *Vital Records of Saybrook, 1647–1834*, (Hartford: CHS and the Connecticut Society of the OFPA, 1952) (images at *AmericanAncestors.org*;**
- **John Bull's Death records from the John Bull account book, 1814–1831, card file in CSL, (FHL film 5,553, item 1).**
- **Elizabeth Bull Plimpton's *Vital Records of Saybrook Colony, 1635–1860: Including the Towns of Chester, Deep River, Essex, Old Saybrook, and Westbrook, Connecticut* (S.I.: Connecticut Valley Shore Research Group, c1985);**

CHURCH RECORDS:

- St. John's Church of Essex's "Church Records, 1790–1938" (includes baptisms 1797–1881, marriages 1798–1881, burials 1798–1881) (originals at CSL) (FHL film 4,087);
- Centerbrook Congregational Church of Essex's, "Church Records, 1759–1842" (includes baptisms, 1759–1786 and marriages, 1759–1842) (originals at CSL) (FHL film 1,008,705);
- Frederick L'Hommedieu's "Saybrook, Connecticut, Church Records, Frederick L'Hommedieu Copy: Old Saybrook Congregational Church 1736–1782, Centerbrook Congregational Church 1759–1832, Chester Congregational Church 1759–1835" (manuscript in CSL) (FHL film 5,554, item 1 or 1,008,328).
- Centerbrook Ecclesiastical Society and Congregational Church of Essex's, "Church Records, 1722–1931" (includes baptisms 1785–1842 & 1844–1916, marriages 1786–1843 & 1844–1855, deaths by "sea or land" 1786–1843, and deaths 1844–1923) (photocopy at CSL) (FHL film 4,088);
- Congregational Church of Old Saybrook's, "Church Records, 1736–1935" (includes baptisms 1741–1782 & 1783–1935, deaths 1736–1751 & 1783–1875, and marriages 1760–1778 & 1783–1875) (photocopies at CSL) (FHL film 5,379);
- Grace Church of Old Saybrook's, "Church Records, 1815–1948" (includes baptisms, marriages, & burials) (FHL film 5,378);
- First Baptist Church, Records 1810–1921, copy at CSL(FHL film 8,705);
- "Church Records, 1736–1842, Saybrook, Connecticut" (includes baptisms, marriages, and deaths, 1736–1782, copied from the First Congregational Church in Saybrook (now part of Old Saybrook Congregational Church) (manuscript in the Historical Society of Pennsylvania) (FHL film 441,390 or 5,554, item 2);

[829] Email from Deep River Town Clerk Amy M. Winchell, CCTC, 14 Jun 2018.

- Baptisms (1797–1881), marriages (1798–1881) & burials (1798–1881) at St. John's Church in Essex (ED Film 0004087); Baptisms (1825–78), marriages (1825–78) & burials (1815–78) at Grace Church in Old Saybrook (ED Film 5378).

CEMETERY TRANSCRIPTIONS: The Hale Collection identifies people in order of physical proximity buried at about three named sites in what was then Saybrook Township.[830] The Hale Collection also identifies people in order of physical proximity buried at about five named sites in what was then Essex Township.[831] Compare with Daniel Hearn's 1978 copy of 109 pre-1800 gravestones in one Essex cemetery.[832] The Hale Collection also identifies people in order of physical proximity buried at about four named sites in what was then Old Saybrook Township.[833] Compare with Daniel Hearn's 1977 copy of 171 pre-1800 gravestones in two Old Saybrook cemeteries.[834] See also,

- "Inscriptions, Town of Old Saybrook, Conn (includes Saybrook Point, Saybrook Junction, and a new cemetery in Old Saybrook)" (typescript in NYGBS) (FHL film 5528);
- Walter Cox and Edward O. Goullin's "Winthrop Cemetery" (1934 photocopy at FHL);
- Dorothy Kurze and Winthrop Cemetery Association's "Winthrop Cemetery, Sept. 21, 1982" (typescript) (SLC: FHL, 1982);
- Lucius B. Barbour's "Genealogical Data From Connecticut Cemeteries: Saybrook, Connecticut Cemetery At Winthrop, Conn., Town Of Saybrook, Essex Street Cemetery, Deep River, Fountain Hill Cemetery, Deep River" (1907–1932 manuscript at NEHGS).
- *Cemetery Inscriptions of Essex, Connecticut* (typescript at NYGBS) (FHL film 4086);

OTHER NOTEWORTHY SOURCES:

- John Bull Account Book," 1814–1831, CSL; see Appendix A;
- Solomon Purdy Special Genealogy File;" see Appendix A;
- Gilman C. Gates' *Saybrook at the Mouth of the Connecticut: the First One Hundred Years* (Orange: W.H. Lee Co., 1935);
- Thomas A. Stevens' *Founders of Deep River*, Deep River: Deep River Historical Society, [1976?];
- Charles R. Weldon's Newspaper clippings from the Deep River New Era newspaper, Old Saybrook...(Old Saybrook: Weldon, Charles R., 2001–2002) (FHL film 1,391,969, items 2–5);
- Elaine F Staplins' *Founders of Saybrook Colony and their descendants, 1635–1985* (S.i, sn, 1985).

---

830 Charles R. Hale, "Headstone Inscriptions of the Town of Saybrook, Connecticut" (bound manuscript at CSL) (FHL film 3,361). Hale names these Fountain Hill, Winthrop, & Old Cong. Church.

831 Charles R. Hale, "Headstone Inscriptions of the Town of Essex, Connecticut" (bound manuscript at CSL) (FHL film 3,332). Hale names these River View, Prospect Hill, Grove Street, Central Burial Ground, & Graveyard.6

832 Daniel Hearn, "Connecticut gravestones, early to 1800," manuscript (FHL film 1,477,476, item 51).

833 Charles R. Hale, "Headstone Inscriptions of the Town of Old Saybrook, Connecticut" (bound manuscript at CSL) (FHL film 3,357). Hale names these Cypress, Upper, St. John's & River View.

834 Daniel Hearn, "Connecticut gravestones, early to 1800," manuscript (FHL film 1,477,477, item 24).

SEYMOUR

VITAL RECORDS: Seymour was incorporated in 1850, but its clerk began maintaining vital records in March, 1849. Its population was 1,677 in the 1850 census.[835] The town was not abstracted by Barbour and has no individual volume. For its vital records, see,

- **Seymour's "Marriage Returns, 1850–1853" (originals in Town Hall) (FHL film 1,420,660, item 2);**
- **Seymour's "Records of Births, Marriages, and Deaths, 1849–1904" (originals in Seymour Town Hall) (FHL film 1,420,660, item 1);**
- **Linda MacLachlan and Jan Taylor, "Seymour, Connecticut: Another Town Barbour Missed," *CN*, vol. 41. p. 148;**
- **William Carvosso Sharpe's *Vital Statistics of Seymour, Conn.* 1700–1910, 4 vols. (Seymour: Record Print, 1883–1911) (FHL film 928,514) (images online at *AmericanAncestors,org*).**

CHURCH RECORDS:

- Trinity Church's "Church Records, 1797–1853" (includes baptisms 1822–1835 & 1851–1852 , marriages 1822–1836 &1853 , burials 1822–1842, baptisms, marriages, and burials for 1845–1847, and burials 1851–1853) (originals at CSL) (FHL film 5,820);
- Baptisms (1822–35, 1845–47 & 1851–52), marriages (1822–36 & 1845–47) and 5,820).

CEMETERY TRANSCRIPTIONS: The Hale Collection identifies people in order of physical proximity buried at about eight named sites in what was then Seymour Township.[836] Compare with Daniel Hearn's 1976 copy of 23 pre-1800 gravestones in three Seymour cemeteries.[837] The Hale Collection also identifies people in order of physical proximity buried at about two named sites in what was then south Beacon Falls Township.[838]

OTHER NOTEWORTHY SOURCES

- Hollis A. Campbell, William C. Sharpe & Frank G. Bassett's *Seymour, Past and Present* (1902/1995 copy at NEHGS); (FHL film 599,304, item 2);
- *Illustrated review of the Naugatuck Valley : embracing Ansonia, Derby, Birmingham, Shelton and Seymour, a record of the development of these centers, their progress in commerce manufacturing and political life, with sketches of their leading official, business and professional men* (New York: Sovereign Publishing and Engraving, 1890) (FHL fiche 6,071,068);
- W.C. Sharpe's *History of Seymour, With Biographies and Genealogies* (1879/1993 copy at NEHGS).

---

835 1850 U.S Census, Seymour, New Haven, Connecticut, p. 359.

836 Charles R. Hale, "Headstone Inscriptions of the Town of Seymour, Connecticut" (bound manuscript at CSL) (FHL film 3,361). Hale names these Union, Trinity, St. Augustine, Congregational, Methodist, Squqntic, St. Kirylot and St. Meftody, & Great Hill.

837 Daniel Hearn, "Connecticut gravestones, early to 1800," manuscript (FHL film 1,477,477, item 41).

838 Charles R. Hale, "Headstone Inscriptions of the Town of Beacon Falls (bound manuscript at CSL) (FHL film 3,320). Hale names these Pine Bridge & Ribbon Hill.

SHARON

Barbour's typescript volume for Sharon,[839] unlike the GPC edition,[840] begins:

> The vital records of Sharon prior to 1865, are found scattered through Volumes 2, 3, 4, 5, 6, 7, 8, 9, 10, 15, 20, 22 and 27 of the Land Records and Volume 1 of Vital Records.
>
> This alphabetical list, was taken from a set of cards[841] based on a manuscript copy of the Sharon Vital Records made in 1917 by James N. Arnold, of Providence, R.I., Reference to entries found in the Land Records is indicated by the abbreviation "LR" and the number of the volume. In Volume 1 of Vital Records the pagination from 1 to 50 is duplicated, but entries prior to 1852 appear in the first part of the book.
>
> In "A Record of Births, marriages and Deaths in the Town of Sharon", published in 1897 by Lawrence Van Alstyne, there are many of the vital records of Sharon, and although the Arnold Copy has not been checked in its entirety with this printed record, a few marked differences have been noted herein.
>
> The Arnold Copy, now in the possession of the Connecticut State Library, has not been compared with the original and doubtless errors exist. It is hoped that as errors or omissions are found notes will be entered in this volume and on the cards which are included in the General Index of Connecticut Vital Records also in the possession of the Connecticut State Library.
>
> Hartford, Conn., March, 1927.[842]

VITAL RECORDS: The Sharon volume includes vital records as early as 1715 and as late as 1866. Barbour abstracted 15 Sharon "books:"

- "1" refers to Sharon's Records of Births, Marriages, and Deaths, 1848–1851, Sharon Town Hall, (FHL film 1,509,629, item 1);
- "LR2" and "3" refer to Sharon's Land Records, vols. 2–3 1739–1756, Sharon Town Hall, FHL film 5,667;
- "LR4 "and "5" refer to Sharon's Land Records, vols. 4–5 1755–1765, Sharon Town Hall, FHL film 5,668;
- "LR6" and "7" refer to Sharon's Land Records, vols. 6–7 1764–1778. Sharon Town Hall, FHL film 5,669;

---

839 See How to Use This Book, note 4, above.

840 Schott, *Barbour Collection: Saybrook–Sharon*, vol. 38. Digital images at *Ancestry.com*.

841 Now part of the Barbour Index and interfiled with similar slips from other towns in CSL and in FHL films 2,887 *et seq*. See Introduction above, pp. 3–5..

842 Lucius B. Barbour, *Connecticut Vital Records: Sharon, 1739–1865,* (Hartford, CSL, 1927) page after title page (FHL film 2,978). Digital images at *AmericanAncestors.org* and *FamilySearch.org*

- "LR8" and "9" refer to Sharon's Land Records, vols. 8–9 1778–1789, Sharon Town Hall, FHL film 5,670;
- "LR10" refers to Sharon's Land Records, vols. 10–11 1789–1797, Sharon Town Hall, FHL film 5,671;
- "LR12" refers to Sharon's Land Records, vols. 12–13 1796–1806, Sharon Town Hall, FHL film 5,671;
- "LR15" refers to Sharon's Land Records, vols. 14–15 1804–1816, Sharon Town Hall, FHL film 5,673;
- "LR20" refers to Sharon's Land Records, vols. 20–21 1823–1832, Sharon Town Hall, FHL film 5,676;
- "LR22" refers to Sharon's Land Records, vols. 22–23 1832–1846, Sharon Town Hall, FHL film 5,677;
- "LR27" refers to Sharon's Land Records, vols. 26–27 1843–1865, Sharon Town Hall, FHL film 5,679.

Barbour did not abstract **Sharon's Records of births, marriages, and deaths, 1848–1851, originals in Sharon Town Hall (FHL film 1,509,629, item 1).**

See also, **L. Van Alstyne's *Born, Married and Died, in Sharon, Connecticut*: *a record of births, marriages and deaths, in the town of Sharon, Conn. from 1721 to 1879: taken from the ancient land and church records and other authentic sources* (Sharon: Press of Pawling chronicle, 1897) ()FHL film 496,869, item 3 or fiche 6,004,529).**

CHURCH RECORDS:

- First Church of Christ Congregational's "Church Records, 1755–1879" (includes baptisms 1759–1795 &1796–1859, marriages 1758–1831 and 1871, and deaths 1799–1879) (originals at CSL) (FHL film 5,691);
- "Copy of Records of the Church in Ellsworth, Conn." (includes marriages & deaths) (1898 manuscript at NEHGS).
- Christ Church's Church records, 1809–1932, originals at CSL (FHL film 5,692);

CEMETERY TRANSCRIPTIONS: The Hale Collection identifies people in order of physical proximity buried at about 12 named sites in Sharon Township.[843] Compare with Daniel Hearn's 1978 copy of 274 pre-1800 gravestones in two Sharon cemeteries.[844] See also, Lawrence Van Alstyne's *Burying Grounds of Sharon, Connecticut, Amenia and North East, New York: Being an Abstract of Inscriptions From Thirty Places of Burial in the Above Named Towns* (Amenia NY: Walsh, Griffen & Hoysradt, 1903) (FHL film 17,516 or 908,330.

OTHER NOTEWORTHY SOURCES:

- Charles F. Sedgwick's *General History of the Town of Sharon, Litchfield County, Conn.: From Its First Settlement* (Amenia, NY:C. Walsh, Printer and Publisher,1877);

---

843 Charles R. Hale, "Headstone Inscriptions of the Town of Sharon, Connecticut" (bound manuscript at CSL) (FHL film 3,361). Hale names these Sharon Burying Ground, Hillside, Cartwright, Boland District, Pine Swamp, Malcuit Farm, Ticknor's Woods, Amenia union, Ellsworth, St. Bridget's. Moravian, & Catholic.

844 Daniel Hearn, "Connecticut gravestones, early to 1800," manuscript (FHL film 1,477,477, item 42).

- Giles Frederick Goodenough's *Gossip about a country parish of the hills and its people* (Amenia, NY: Times Press], 1900) (FHL film 1,573,587, item 4);
- Poconnuck Historical Society,*Collections, no. 3.* (Lakeville: Lakeville Journal, 1912).

SHELTON: see **HUNTINGTON**

SHERMAN

Barbour's typescript volume for Sherman,[845] unlike the GPC edition,[846] begins:

> The vital records of Salisbury prior to 1850 are found scattered through the first volume of Land Records and a Town Book of Miscellaneous entries known as "Book V" but referred to in this alphabetical list as "Vol.1". Reference to entries found in the Land Records is indicated by the abbreviation "LR" and the volume number.
>
> This list, was taken from a set of cards[847] based on a copy of the Sherman Vital Records made in 1917 by Mr. James N. Arnold, of Providence, R.I., The Arnold Copy, now in the possession of the Connecticut State Library, has not been compared with the original and doubtless errors exist. It is hoped that as errors or omissions are found notes will be entered in this volume and on the cards which are included in the General Index of Connecticut Vital Records also in the possession of the Connecticut State Library.
>
> Hartford, Conn., May, 1926.[848]

VITAL RECORDS: The Sherman volume includes vital records as early as 1800 and as ate as 1854. Barbour abstracted two Sherman "books:"

- "LR1" frequently refers to Sherman's Land Records, vol. 1–2, 1803–1822, Sherman Town Hall, (FHL film 5,557) but **several vital records scattered through this book are abstracted incorrectly or not at all;**
- "1" refers to Sherman's Town Records, vol. 5, 1782–1877 (contains marriages 1820–1864, some family records of births and deaths, report of births, marriages, deaths 1847–1850), Sherman Town Hall, (FHL film 1,435,635, item 1);

See also, Harlan R. Jessup's "Vital Records of 1847–1848, School District Returns from Redding, Sherman and Ridgefield, CT," *CA*, Vol. 54, No. 2 (Nov 2011).

---

845 See How to Use This Book, note 3, above.

846 Lorraine Cook White, *Barbour Collection of Connecticut Town Vital Records: Sherman 1802-1850, Simsbury 1670-1855*, vol. 39, (Baltimore: GPC, 2000).

847 Now part of the Barbour Index and interfiled with similar slips from other towns in CSL and n FHL films 2,887 *et seq*. See Introduction above, pp. 3–5.

848 Lucius B. Barbour, *Connecticut Vital Records: Sherman, 1802–1850,* (Hartford, CSL, 1926) page after title page (FHL film 2,978). Digital images at *AmericanAncestors.org* and *FamilySearch.org*.

CHURCH RECORDS:

- North Congregational Church's "Church Records, 1744–1921" (deaths 1798–1821 & 1822–1881, baptisms 1798–1821 & 1822–1844, and marriages 1797–1821, 1822–1845) (originals at CSL) (FHL film 5,560. items 3–7);
- Sherman Congregational Church's "Church Records, 1786–1949" (includes baptisms 1846–1941, marriages 1846–1866, and deaths 1846–1858) (originals at CSL) (FHL film 5,560, items 1–2).

CEMETERY TRANSCRIPTIONS: The Hale Collection identifies people in order of physical proximity buried at about eight named sites in Sherman Township.[849] Compare with Daniel Hearn's 1977 copy of three pre-1800 gravestones in one Sherman cemetery.[850] See also,

- Josephine C. Frost's "Cemetery Inscriptions from Sherman, Connecticut" (1912 typescript in the NYGBS) (FHL film 5,555);
- Josephine C. Frost's "Cemetery Records of Haviland Hollow and Quaker Hill, Dutchess County, New York" (includes cemeteries in the town of Sherman) (1909–1912 typescript in NYGBS) (FHL film 17,705);
- Wilford Platt's "Cemeteries of Sherman, Connecticut "(1941 manuscript at FHL);
- Josephine C. Frost's "Cemetery inscriptions from Sherman, Connecticut" (1913 typescript at NEHGS).

OTHER NOTEWORTHY SOURCES:

- "Northrop's Private Records; " see Appendix A;
- "Sherman Family Papers;" see Appendix A;
- Allie Hungerford Giddings, *History of Sherman: records and recollections* (Sherman: Sherman Historical Society, 1977).

SIMSBURY

Barbour's typescript volume for Simsbury,[851] unlike the GPC edition,[852] begins:

> This volume contains a list alphabetically arranged of all the vital records of the town of Simsbury from its incorporation to about 1855. The entire record of the town prior to 1855 is found scattered through Volumes 1 and 2 of Land Records and Volumes 2, 3, 4 and 5 of Town Acts. Reference to entries found in the Land Records is indicated by the abbreviation "LR" and to those in the Town Acts of the abbreviation "TM" followed by the Volume number. In the first book of Land Records a duplication of page numbers appears due to the recording having been done with the book reversed, and re-

---

849 Charles R. Hale, "Headstone Inscriptions of the Town of Sherman, Connecticut" (bound manuscript at CSL) (FHL film 3,362). Hale names these Graveyard (2 different locations), North Sherman, Center, Leach, Wanzer, Pepper, & Old Graveyard.

850 Daniel Hearn, "Connecticut gravestones, early to 1800," manuscript (FHL film 1,477,477, item 42).

851 See How to Use This Book, note 4, above.

852 White, *Barbour Collection:: Sherman–Simsbury*, vol. 39..

ference to this portion of the volume is indicated by the abbreviation "LR1-A".

This list was taken from a set of cards[853] based on the printed copy of the Simsbury Vital Records published by Mr. Albert C. Bates, of Hartford, Connecticut, in 1898, and a manuscript copy, made in 1927 by Percy E. Hulbert, of Hockanum, Connecticut, of vital statistics found in Volume 5 of Town Acts. These copies have not been compared with the original and doubtless errors exist. It is hoped that as errors or omissions are found notes will be entered in this volume and on the cards which are included in the General Index of Connecticut Vital Records also in the possession of the Connecticut State Library.

Hartford, Conn., April, 1928.[854]

VITAL RECORDS: The Simsbury volume includes vital records as early as 1670 and as late as 1854. Barbour claims that his abstraction of all but the 5th book of vital records is taken from Albert C. Bates' *Simsbury, Connecticut, Births, Marriages and Deaths* (Hartford: Case, Lockwood & Brainard Co., 1898) (FHL film 896,756 item 10) (images at *AmericanAncestors.org*), but this cannot be true. The book does not cite the page upon which any record may be found, only the volume. Barbour cites the actual page for each record which has been microfilmed by FHL, but the FHL's filming is incomplete:[855] Barbour abstracts eight Simsbury "books:"

- "LR1" refers to a book remaining in Simsbury which was not microfilmed by FHL,.[856]
- "LR1-A" refers to "The Red Book," a book not microfilmed by FHL, which the town now numbers "1½" because it is the earlier of two volumes originally numbered "2." FHL has, however, microfilmed a 1902 unpaginated typescript which claims to have accurately transcribed all "The Red Book's" births, marriages, deaths and baptisms: Simsbury Town Records, vol. 1½ (1680 to 1712) Simsbury Town Hall, (FHL film 5,621, item 2). Barbour's abstraction includes most **but not all** vital records in copies 1 and 1½. **The 1902 typescript includes vital records not abstracted by Barbour.**

---

853 Now part of the Barbour Index and interfiled with similar slips from other towns in CSL and n FHL films 2887 *et seq*. See Introduction above, pp. 3–5.

854 Lucius B. Barbour, *Connecticut Vital Records: Simsbury, 1670–1855,* (Hartford, CSL, 1928) page after title page (FHL film 2979). Digital images at *AmericanAncestors.org* and *FamilySearch.org.*

855 Much of the FHL microfilming (and NEHGS' digitization) is of an official 1900-1902 typed copy of Simsbury's deed books, which insists the label "Red Book" applied to the earlier of two record books numbered "2," and not to a two-part volume one, as Bates claimed. See "Explanation" beginning Simsbury Town Records Copy, vol. 1½ (1680 to 1712) Simsbury Town Hall, (FHL film 5,621, item 2). The fact the original "Second Book of Deeds" also identifies itself as "Small Folio Book) suggests a need to distinguish it from another volume numbered "2." See Simsbury "Second Book of Deeds," (1697-1724) Simsbury Town Hall (FHL film 1,314,486, item 2) (miscataloged by FHL as Simsbury Town Records, vol. 2).

856 Simsbury possesses a Book of Land Records 1670 to 1693, which it keeps "in a tin canister." CSL, *First 200 Years*. It presumably contains these vital records on its 1st 10 pages. FHL has, however, microfilmed an Oct 1900 typed copy with vague references to the original's pagination and no reference to any vital records and is not what Barbour abstracted: Simsbury Town Records Copy, vol. 1 (1666-1696) Simsbury Town Hall, (FHL film 5,621, item 1).

- "LR2" refers to Simsbury's "Second Book of Deeds (a/k/a "Small Folio Book) (1697–1724) Simsbury Town Hall (FHL film 1,314,486, item 2) (miscataloged by FHL as Simsbury Town Records, vol. 2). This book includes some marriages (abstracted by Barbour citing this volume) and deaths (abstracted by Barbour citing LR1-A), but no births). FHL also offers an unpaginated 1902 typed copy titled "Simsbury Town Records, vol. 2 (1704–1713)" Simsbury Town Hall, (FHL film 5,621, item 3);
- "TM1" refers to Simsbury's "Book of Town Acts," vol. 1, 1670–1713 (contains records of births, marriages, deaths), Simsbury Town Hall, (FHL film 1,314,486, item 1;
- "TM2" refers to Simsbury vol. 2, 1693–1718, Simsbury Town Hall, (FHL film 5,621, item 4) (miscataloged by FHL as Simsbury Land Records, vol. 2);
- "TM3" refers to Simsbury's "Book of Town Acts," Book Three," vol. 3 1719–1832 (contains records of births, marriages, deaths), Simsbury Town Hall, (FHL film 1,314,486, item 3);
- "TM4" refers to Simsbury's "Book of Town Acts," Book Four, Town Proceedings, Marriages, Births & Deaths," vol.4, 1719–1758 (contains records of births, marriages, deaths), Simsbury Town Hall, (FHL film 1,314,486, item 4);
- "TM5" refers to Simsbury's Town Records vol. 5 1832–1864 (contains records of births, marriages, deaths), Simsbury Town Hall, FHL film 1,314,487, item 1.

Barbour did not abstract:

- **Simsbury's Town Records Copy, vol. 1 (1666–1696) Simsbury Town Hall, (FHL film 5,621, item 1);**
- **Simsbury's "Records of Births, Marriages, and Deaths, vol. 1–2, 1847–1908" (FHL film 1,314,487, items 2–3);**
- **Ruth C. Duncan's "Record of Marriages Performed at Simsbury, Connecticut, 1784–1810 by Dudley Pettibone, Justice of the Peace" (transcription at FHL from a manuscript in the collection of the Simsbury Historical Society).**
- **Cooke's "Vital Statistics, Simsbury, Connecticut, 1621–1845," (typescript in Pittsfield, Mass.) (FHL film 234,581, item 3);**

CHURCH RECORDS:

- Thomas Dunmore Ayres's *Sense of place : First Church records, Simsbury, Connecticut 1682–1930* (Simsbury: Simsbury Historical Society, c2009);
- Presbyterian Church of Tariffville's, "Church Records, 1844–1852" (includes deaths, baptisms 1844–1852 & marriages 1846–1852) (originals at the Presbyterian Historical Society in Philadelphia) (FHL film 468,364);
- Methodist Church's "Church Records, 1849–1934" (1849–1926 baptisms and marriages) (originals at CSL) (FHL film 5,648);
- Trinity Church at Tariffville's "Church Records, 1849–1953" (includes baptisms, marriages, and burials) (originals at CSL) (FHL film 5,649);
- Methodist Church's "Church Register, 1849–1890, 1926" (Includes baptisms and marriages) (originals in the CSL) (FHL film 1,012,869);
- Samuel Stebbins' "First Church, Simsbury: Records of the Rev. Samuel Stebbins, 1777–1806" (1988 typescript photocopy at FHL);
- Allen McLean's "First Church, Simsbury: Records of the Rev. Allen McLean, 1809–1849" (1988 typescript photocopy at FHL);

- Albert C. Bates and Roger Viets' *Records of Rev. Roger Viets, Rector of St. Andrews, Simsbury, Conn. Parts, 1763–1800: and Missionary From the Society for the Propagation of the Gospel in Foreign Parts, 1763–1800* (Hartford: Case, Lockwood & Brainard, 1893) (FHL film 924,061 or fiche 6,005,264).
- Baptist Church's Church records, 1764, 1772, originals at CSL (FHL film 1,012,869, item 3);
- First Church's *Rev. Dudley Woodbridge: his church record at Simsbury in Conn., 1697–1710,* (Press of the Case, Lockwood & Brainard Co., 1894);
- Simsbury First Church's Records, vol. 1 1682–1929 & vol. 2 1832–1907, CSL (CSA RG 070.076);

CEMETERY TRANSCRIPTIONS: The Hale Collection identifies people in order of physical proximity buried at about five named sites in Simsbury Township.[857] Compare with Daniel Hearn's 1979 copy of 127 pre-1800 gravestones in one Simsbury cemetery.[858] See also,

- *Simsbury Cemetery Gravestone Inscriptions, Simsbury, Connecticut, 1688–2000* (Simsbury: Simsbury Free Library, c2001) ;
- Bill and Pam Case's "Burial Records, "North Burial Place, West Simsbury, Connecticut (1754–1855)" (typescript photocopy at FHL);
- Ruth C. Duncan and Calvin Barber's "Hopmeadow Cemetery: Accounts of the Graves Opened, 1785–1853" (1988 photocopy at FHL);
- Aaron Moses' "Record of the Burials in the North Burying Place in West Simsbury: Copies From a Record Kept by Mr. Thomas Phelps" (typescript photocopy at FHL);
- Lucius B. Barbour's "Genealogical Data From Connecticut Cemeteries: Simsbury, Connecticut. All Gravestone Records In The Town Of Simsbury (Except St. Barnard's Roman Catholic Cemetery, Tariffville, Simsbury, Bushy Hill And Tariffville Cemeteries" (1932 manuscript at NEHGS);
- Jennifer Soltis' *Sense of place: survey of Old Tariffville Cemetery, Simsbury, Connecticut 1838–1960* (Simsbury: Simsbury Historical Society, c2006).

OTHER NOTEWORTHY SOURCES:

- Noah Amherst Phelps' *History of Simsbury, Granby and Canton from 1642 to 1845* (Hartford: Press of Case, Tiffany and Burnham, 1845) (FHL film 897,329);
- Lucius I. Barber's *Record and documentary history of Simsbury: 1643–1888* (Simsbury: DAR. Abigail Phelps Chapter, c1931) (FHL fiche 6,049,695);
- John Edwards Ellsworth's *Simsbury: being a brief historical sketch of ancient and modern Simsbury, 1642–1935* ([Simsbury: Simsbury Committee for the Tercentenary, 1935);
- William M. Vibert's *Three centuries of Simsbury, 1670–1970* (Simsbury: Simsbury Tercentenary Committee, c1970).

---

[857] Charles R. Hale, "Headstone Inscriptions of the Town of Simsbury, Connecticut" (bound manuscript at CSL) (FHL film 3,362). Hale names these Hop Meadow, Bushy Hill, Town Farm, Non. Sec., & St. Bernard's.

[858] Daniel Hearn, "Connecticut gravestones, early to 1800," manuscript (FHL film 1,477,477, item 45).

SOMERS

Barbour's typescript volume for Somers,[859] unlike the GPC edition,[860] begins:

> This volume contains a list alphabetically arranged of all the vital records of the town of Somers from its incorporation to about 1850. This list was taken from a set of cards[861] based on a copy of the Somers Vital Records made in 1912 by James N. Arnold, of Providence, R.I. The entire record of the town prior to 1850 is contained in three volumes. The pagination of Volume 3 begins with page 164. In the Arnold Copy page numbers 180 to 201 have been omitted, so the pagination of the Arnold Copy (11 to 17) has been used.
>
> The Arnold Copy, now in the possession of the Connecticut State Library, has not been compared with the original and doubtless errors exist. It is hoped that as errors or omissions are found notes will be entered in this volume and on the cards which are included in the General Index of Connecticut Vital Records also in the possession of the Connecticut State Library.
>
> Hartford, Conn., May, 1922.[862]

VITAL RECORDS: The Somers volume includes vital records as early as 1734 and as late as 1851. At least two of the three "books" Barbour abstracted appear to be unavailable beyond the Somers Town Hall:

- "1" refers to an unfilmed book covering the years 1734–1826 in at least 180 pages and still in the Somers Town Hall, described by the clerk as "BDM 1729–1826;"[863]
- "2" refers to an unfilmed book covering the years 1819–1832 in alpha order and at least 155 pages long. It is also in Somers, described by the clerk as "BDM 1817–1850;"
- "3" refers to Somers' Records of Births, Marriages, & Deaths, 1827–1929 (contains records of births 1849–1929, marriages 1827–1929, and deaths 1849–1929), Somers Town Hall, (FHL film 1,319,919). It is also in Somers, described by the clerk as "BDM 1827–1929."

In addition, see

- **Somers Vital Records 1830–1915, CSL (CSA RG 072.002, Box 20;**

---

859 See How to Use This Book, note 4, above.

860 Lorraine Cook White, *Barbour Collection of Connecticut Town Vital Records: Somers 1734-1850, Southbury 1787-1830, Southington 1779-1857, South Windsor, 1845-1851*, vol. 40 (Baltimore: GPC, 2000). Digital images at *Ancestry.com*.

861 Now part of the Barbour Index and interfiled with similar slips from other towns in CSL and in FHL films 2,887 *et seq*. See Introduction above, pp. 3–5.

862 Lucius B. Barbour, *Connecticut Vital Records Somers, 1734–1850,* (Hartford: CSL, 1922) page after title page (FHL film 2,979). Digital images at *AmericanAncestors.org* and *FamilySearch.org.*

863 The Somers town clerk reports these five books as containing all the pre-1850 vital records her office possesses: (1) BDM 1727-1850, (2) BDM 1827-1929, (3) BDM 1776-1856, (4) BDM 1817-1850, and (5) BDM 1729-1826. Barbour's "1" should be (5); Barbour's "2" should be (4); and Barbour's "3" is (2).8/7/18 Email from Somers Town clerk Ann Logan.

- **The Somers Town clerk reports possession of two additional vital records books not abstracted by Barbour: "BDM 1727–1850" and "BDM 1776–1856;"**
- **Francis Olcott Allen's *History of Enfield, Connecticut: Compiled From All the Public Records of the Town Known to Exist, Covering From the Beginning to 1850, Together with the [Somers] Graveyard Inscriptions …* vol. 3 (pages 2175 to 2214 transcribe 1730 to 1750 town records from Somers) (Lancaster, PA: Wickersham Printing, 1900) (FHL film 1,321,486.**

CHURCH RECORDS:

- Congregational Church's "Church Records, 1727–1890" (includes baptisms 1769–1787 and marriages 1777–1866) (photocopies at CSL) (FHL film 5,717);
- Somers Methodist Episcopal Church's *Church records, 1838–1885*, originals in Boston University School of Theology Library, (FHL film 1,508,864, item 14).

CEMETERY TRANSCRIPTIONS: The Hale Collection identifies people in order of physical proximity buried at about four named sites in Somers Township.[864] Compare with Daniel Hearn's 1979 copy of 220 pre-1800 gravestones in two Somers cemeteries.[865] See also, James Allen Kibbe's "Graveyard Inscriptions – Enfield," in Allen's 3 volume *History of Enfield*, below, pp. 2310–2453 (FHL film 481,068);

OTHER NOTEWORTHY SOURCES:

- Francis Olcott Allen's *History of Enfield, Connecticut: compiled from all the public records of the town known to exist, covering from the beginning to 1850; together with the graveyard inscriptions and those Hartford, Northampton and Springfield records which refer to the people of Enfield,* vol. 2 (Lancaster, Pa: Wickersham Printing, 1900) (includes 1730–1750 Somers church and town vital records and graveyard inscriptions at pp. 2175–2214 and 2454–2470;
- Fred C. Davis and Richard W. Davis' *Somers: The History of a Connecticut Town* (Somers: Somers Historical Society, c1973);
- James Allen Kibbe's "Church and Town Records of Somers, CT 1727–1750," in Allen's *History of Enfield*, volume 3, 2175–215 (FHL film 481,068).

SOUTH WINDSOR

Barbour's typescript volume for South Windsor,[866] unlike the GPC edition,[867] begins:

> This volume contains a list alphabetically arranged of all the vital records of the town of South Windsor from its incorporation to about 1851. The entire record of this town, prior to 1851, is found in one volume. During the years 1847-1851 entries were recorded with the book re-

---

864 Charles R. Hale, "Headstone Inscriptions of the Town of Somers, Connecticut" (bound manuscript at CSL) (FHL film 3,362). Hale names these West, North, South, & McKinstry.

865 Daniel Hearn, "Connecticut gravestones, early to 1800," manuscript (FHL film 1,477,477, item 46).

866 See How to Use This Book, note 4, above.

867 White, *Barbour Collection: Somers–South Windsor,* vol. 40. Digital images at *Ancestry.com*.

> versed and reference to this part of the book is indicated by the volume number "1-A".
>
> This list was taken from a set of cards[868] based on a copy of the South Windsor Vital Records made in 1927 by Percy Hulbert, of Hockanum, Conn. The Hulbert Copy has not been compared with the original and doubtless errors exist. It is hoped that as errors or omissions are found notes will be entered in this volume and on the cards which are included in the General Index of Connecticut Vital Records also in the possession of the Connecticut State Library.
>
> Hartford, Conn., June, 1928.[869]

VITAL RECORDS: The South Windsor volume includes vital records as early as 1842 and as late as 1852. Barbour abstracted South Windsor's Records of Births, Marriages, & Deaths, 1830–1852, South Windsor Town Hall (FHL film 1,316,429, item 1).

- "1-A" refers to Barbour's label for abstractions from the first 19 sets of facing pages in the book, each having just one page number;
- "1" entries refer to later pages of the book unconsecutively numbered 7 through 247 by Barbour (**who fails to index both parties in some marriages**) while the FHL microfilm numbers them 219 through 459 (in reverse order and not consecutive).

CHURCH RECORDS:

- Wapping Methodist Episcopal Church's "Church Records, 1829–1936" (includes baptisms, marriages) (FHL films 1,012,869 and 1,012,870 or 5,721);
- First Congregational Church's "Church Records, 1694–1898" (includes baptisms 1786–1854, marriages 1786–1835, and deaths 1786–1853) (originals at CSL) (FHL film 5,723);
- Mary Janette Elmore's "Church Records, 1761–1881: Second Congregational Church at Wapping, South Windsor, Connecticut" (includes baptisms and deaths) (typescript at CSL) (FHL film 1,012,869, item 9);
- Second Congregational Church at Wapping's "Church Records, 1830–1936" (includes baptisms 1831–1890 & 1831–1936 and deaths 1837–1890) (originals and manuscripts at CSL) (FHL film 5,722).

CEMETERY TRANSCRIPTIONS: The Hale Collection identifies people in order of physical proximity buried at about eight named sites in South Windsor Township.[870] Compare with Daniel Hearn's 1979 copy of 393 pre-1800 gravestones in two South Windsor cemeteries.[871] See also,

---

[868] Now part of the Barbour Index and interfiled with similar slips from other towns in CSL and in FHL films 2,887 *et seq*. See Introduction above, pp. 3–5.

[869] Lucius B. Barbour, *Connecticut Vital Records: South Windsor; 1845–1851,* (Hartford: CSL, 1928) page after title page (FHL film 2,979). Digital images at *AmericanAncestors.org* and *FamilySearch.org.*

[870] Charles R. Hale, "Headstone Inscriptions of South Windsor, Connecticut" (bound manuscript at CSL) (FHL film 3,363). Hale names these Center, Old South Windsor, East Windsor Hill, Watson lot, Rye Street, Old Wapping, New Wapping, & Single Grave.

[871] Daniel Hearn, "Connecticut gravestones, early to 1800," manuscript (FHL film "1" abstracts 1,477,477, item 49).

- Edith M. Vibert's "Cemeteries of South Windsor, Connecticut" (1976 photocopy at FHL);
- Alice Hubbard Breed Benton's "Cemetery at First Congregational Church, South Windsor, Conn." (1932 typescript) (FHL film 165,997) and (typescript carbon copy at the DAR) (FHL film 850,401);
- Lucius B. Barbour's "Rye Street Cemetery, South Windsor" (manuscript at NEHGS);
- Barney E. Daley's *God's Acre* (S.i.: B.E. Daley, c1984).

OTHER NOTEWORTHY SOURCES: "Henry L. Elmer's Account Book," CSL; see Appendix A.

SOUTHBURY

Barbour's typescript volume for Southbury,[872] unlike the GPC edition,[873] begins:

> This volume contains a list alphabetically arranged of all the vital records of the town of Southbury from its incorporation to about 1830. The entire record of the town prior to 1830 is found in two volumes.
>
> This list was taken from a set of cards[874] based on a copy of the Southbury Vital Records made in 1915 by Mr. James N. Arnold, of Providence, R.I. The Arnold Copy, now in the possession of the Connecticut State Library, has not been compared with the original and doubtless errors exist. It is hoped that as errors or omissions are found notes will be entered in this volume and on the cards which are included in the General Index of Connecticut Vital Records also in the possession of the Connecticut State Library.
>
> Hartford, Conn., January, 1925[875]

VITAL RECORDS: The Southbury volume includes vital records as early as 1748 and as late as 1849. Barbour abstracted two Southbury "books:"

- "1" refers to Southbury's "Town Records, 1752– 1878" (includes records of births 1752–1840, marriages 1769–1817, deaths 1769–1811), Southbury Town Hall) (FHL film 1,420,657, item 1). The Town Clerk refers to this as "Vol 1 Town Journal pages 120 to 150 – Births Marriages & Deaths approximate start & end date is 1774 to 1821;"[876]

---

872 See How to Use This Book, note 4, above.

873 White, *Barbour Collection: Somers–South Windsor,* vol. 40. Digital images at *Ancestry.com*.

874 Now part of the Barbour Index and interfiled with similar slips from other towns in CSL and in FHL films 2,887 *et seq*. See Introduction above, pp. 3–5.

875 Lucius B. Barbour, *Connecticut Vital Records: Southbury, 1787–1830,* (Hartford, CSL, 1925) page after title page (FHL film 2,979). Digital images at *AmericanAncestors.org* and *FmailySearch.org.*

876 Email from Southbury Town Clerk Lynn S. Dwyer, 11 Jun 2018.

- "2" refers to a book the town clerk calls **"**Vital Statistic of the Town of Southbury, Conn –Taken from Early Church Records book."[877] The FHL catalogs this as M.E.N. Lindsay, and G.R. Bourne's "Vital Statistics, the Town of Southbury, Conn.," (1732–1896 records of three South Britain/Southbury churches) (typescript in the Southbury Town Hall) (FHL film 1,420,657, item 2).

See also,

- **A book the town clerk cslls "Vol 2 Town Journal page 108 to 127, Births 1770 to 1835," original at town hall, unfilmed by FHL;[878]**
- **Southbury's "Records of Births, Marriages, and Deaths, 1848–1878" (originals in Town Hall) (FHL film 1,420,657, item 3);**
- **Southbury Vital Records circa 1845–1905, CSL (CSA RG 072.002, Box 22).**

CHURCH RECORDS:

- Methodist Episcopal Church's Records 1832–1896, originals at CSL (FHL film 5,812, item 5);
- "Southbury Church Records, 1731–1808" (includes baptisms 1731–1806, and marriages 1733–1808) (from the manuscript of Ralph D. Smythe) (FHL film 3,054);
- Congregational Church's "Church Records, 1732–1922" (includes burials 1794–1812, baptisms 1813–1870, marriages 1813–1848, and deaths 1813–1851) (originals at CSL) (FHL film 5,813, items 2–4);
- South Britain Congregational Church's "Church Records, 1766–1884" (includes baptisms 1808–1850, deaths 1808–1851, marriages 1808–1836) (originals at CSL) (FHL film 5,812, items 1–4);
- Methodist Episcopal Church's Church records, 1847–1938, photocopies at CSL (FHL film 5,813, item 1);
- Ralph D. Smythe's Southbury church records, 1731–1808, (contains baptisms 1731–1806, and marriages 1733–1808) typescript in NHCHS (FHL film 3,054, item 1)..

CEMETERY TRANSCRIPTIONS: The Hale Collection identifies people in order of physical proximity buried at about nine named sites in what was then Southbury Township.[879] Compare with Daniel Hearn's 1976 copy of 139 pre-1800 gravestones in four Southbury cemeteries.[880] The Hale Collection also identifies people in order of physical proximity buried at one named sites in what was then Middlebury Township.[881] Compare with Daniel Hearn's 1977 copy of 80 pre-1800 gravestones in one Middlebury cemetery.[882] See also, James S. Hedden, SAR's "Roster of Graves of, or Monuments to, Patriots of 1775–1783, and of Soldiers of Colonial Wars in and

---

877 *Ibid.*

878 *Ibid.*

879 Charles R. Hale, "Headstone Inscriptions of the Town of Southbury, Connecticut" (bound manuscript at CSL) (FHL film 3362). Hale names these Pierce Hollow, South Britain, George's Hill, Pine Hill, White Oak (2 different locations), Abandoned Graveyard, French Family Vault, & Old Back or Middle Ground.

880 Daniel Hearn, "Connecticut gravestones, early to 1800," manuscript (FHL film 1,477,477, item 47).

881 Charles R. Hale, "Headstone Inscriptions of the Town of Middlebury, Connecticut" (bound manuscript at CSL) (FHL film 3,345). Hale names this Middlebury Cemetery.

882 Daniel Hearn, "Connecticut gravestones, early to 1800," manuscript (FHL film 1,477,477, item 1).

Adjacent to New Haven County, Connecticut" (typescript photocopy at FHL) (FHL film 1,421,668).

OTHER NOTEWORTHY SOURCES:

- Birth, Marriages and deaths 1847–1878; see Appendix A;
- Marriages by Justus Johnson, J.P., 1791–1812; CSL; see Appendix A;
- William Cothren's *History of Ancient Woodbury, Connecticut, from the first Indian deed in 1659 to 1854: including the present towns of Washington, Southbury, Bethlehem, Roxbury, and a part of Oxford and Middlebury* (vol. 3 contains vital records, including those for ancient Stratford) (Baltimore, MD: Genealogical Pub. Co., 1997) (FHL film 2,055,359 & 6,181);
- William C. Sharpe's *South Britain sketches and records* (Seymour: Record Print, 1898).

SOUTHINGTON

Barbour's typescript volume for Southington,[883] unlike the GPC edition,[884] begins:

> This volume contains a list alphabetically arranged of all the vital records of the town of Southington from its incorporation to about 1857. The entire record of this town prior to 1857 is found scattered through Volumes 1 and 4 of the Land Records and a book of Marriages. Reference to entries found in the Land Records is indicated by the abbreviation "LR" and the number of the volume.
>
> This list was taken from a set of cards[885] based on a copy of the Southington Vital Records made by Mr. Louis H. von Sahler, of Southington, Conn. to about 1820, and from 1820 by Mr. Percy E. Hulbert, of Hockanum, Conn. These copies have not been compared with the original and doubtless errors exist. It is hoped that as errors or omissions are found notes will be entered in this volume and on the cards which are included in the General Index of Connecticut Vital Records also in the possession of the Connecticut State Library.
>
> Hartford, Conn., March, 1928[886]

VITAL RECORDS: The Southington volume includes vital records as early as 1755 and as late as 1854. Barbour abstracted three Southington "books:"

---

883 See How to Use This Book, note 4, above.

884 White, *Barbour Collection: Somers–South Windsor,* vol. 40. Digital images at *Ancestry.com*.

885 Now part of the Barbour Index and interfiled with similar slips from other towns in CSL and in FHL films 2,887 *et seq*. See Introduction above, pp. 3–5.

886 Lucius B. Barbour, *Connecticut Vital Records Southington, 1779–1857*, (Hartford: CSL, 1928) page before p.1 of volume. FHL film 2,979. Digital images at *AmericanAncestors.org.and FamilySearch.org.*

- "LR1" refers to **most of** Southington's Land Records, vol. 1 1779–1789, vol. 2–3 1784–1793, (Volume 1 contains some records of births, marriages, deaths) Southington Town Hall, (FHL film 5,650);
- "LR4" refers to Southington's Land Records, vol. 4–5 1793–1801 (volume 4 contains some records of births, marriages, deaths), Southington Town Hall, (FHL film 5,652).
- "1" refers to Southington's Certificates of Marriage, 1820–1856, Southington Town Hall, (FHL film 1,316,016, item 2);

Barbour did not abstract **Southington's "Records of Births, Marriages, and Deaths, 1847–1900," Southington Town Hall (FHL film 1,316,016, items 3–4).**

CHURCH RECORDS:

- St, Matthew's Episcopal Church's Baptist Church, and Guilford Episcopal Church, "Miscellaneous Church Records" (baptismal record of St. Matthew's and inscriptions from the Baptist Church ground, 1747–1800) (typescript in the NHCHS) (FHL film 3,054, item 4);
- Baptist Church (Southington)'s Miscellaneous church records (contains Southington, Conn., Baptist Church records; 1746–1791; index.) FHL film 3,054, item 4;
- First Congregational Church's Church records, 1728–1876, originals at CSL (FHL film 5,662);
- William Robinson's Copy of the records kept by the Reverend William Robinson, 1780–1834, typescript at CSL (FHL film 1,012,869, item 8).
- St. Paul's Church's Church records, 1876–1941, originals at CSL (FHL film 5,663);

CEMETERY TRANSCRIPTIONS: The Hale Collection identifies people in order of physical proximity buried at about 13 named sites in Southington Township.[887] Compare with Daniel Hearn's 1978 copy of 76 pre-1800 gravestones in four Southington cemeteries.[888] See also, Mrs. Walter D. Wallace, Mrs. Samuel G. Tuell, Mrs. James W. Upson, DAR Hannah Woodruff Chapter's South End Cemetery, Southington, Connecticut, 1773–1952, Typescript with St. Peters Episcopal Church Records (FHL film 924,067, item 1).

OTHER NOTEWORTHY SOURCES:

- Heman Rowlee Timlow, *Ecclesiastical and other sketches of Southington, Connecticut* (Hartford: Case, Lockwood & Brainard, 1875);
- Francis Atwater, *History of Southington, Conn.* (Meriden: Journal Press, 1924);
- Mrs. Walter D. Wallace, Mrs. Samuel G. Tuell, and Mrs. James W. Upson, "South End Cemetery, Southington, Connecticut, 1773–1952" (typescript photocopy) (FHL film 924,067);
- *Genealogical Data from Connecticut Cemeteries : Southington* (originally published: 1932) (Salem, MA: Higginson Book Co., 1997).

---

887 Charles R. Hale, "Headstone Inscriptions of the Town of Southington, Connecticut" (bound manuscript at CSL) (FHL film 3,362-3). Hale names these South End, Oak Hill, St. Thomas, Quinnipiac, Mount Vernon, Wonx Springs, Merriam, Independent Polish, Bradley Graveyard, Dunham, Barnabas Power's yard, Bunce yard, & Old St. Mary's.

888 Daniel Hearn, "Connecticut gravestones, early to 1800," manuscript (FHL film 1,477,477, item 48).

STAFFORD

Barbour's typescript volume for Stafford,[889] unlike the GPC edition,[890] begins:

> This volume contains a list alphabetically arranged of all the vital records of the town of Stafford from its incorporation to about 1850. This list was taken from a set of cards[891] based on a copy of the Stafford Vital Records made in 1912 by James N. Arnold, of Providence, R.I. The entire record for the town prior to 1850 is contained in three volumes. The third volume, entitled "Book of Marriages", appears to have been known as "Book 2". To distinguish it from Book 2 of the series known as "Book 2, Births, Marriages and Deaths", reference to it is indicated by "2-M" in this alphabetical list.
>
> The Arnold Copy, now in the possession of the Connecticut State Library, have not been compared with the original and doubtless errors exist. It is hoped that as errors or omissions are found notes will be entered in this volume and on the cards which are included in the General Index of Connecticut Vital Records also in the possession of the Connecticut State Library.
>
> Hartford, Conn., October, 1921[892]

VITAL RECORDS: The Stafford volume includes vital records as early as 1708 and as late as 1852. Barbour abstracted three Stafford "books" which remain in Stafford, unfilmed by FHL:[893]

- "1" covers the years 1708 to 1753 on pages 14–45;
- "2" covers the years 1744 to 1838 on pages 2–169;
- "2-M" covers the years 1820 to 1852 on pages 1–127.

FHL catalogs a single volume of vital records covering this period: **Stafford's Records of Births, Marriages, Deaths, Freemen and Electors, Stafford, Connecticut: taken from land records vol. 1 and 2, and from vol. A (contains records of births 1709–1852, marriages 1722–1840, deaths 1752–1854, freemen and electors 1757–1856), Stafford Springs Town Hall, (FHL film 1,319,712}**. It would appear that this is a later compilation and that **the town clerk may also possess**

---

[889] See How to Use This Book, note 4, above.

[890] Jan Tilton, *Barbour Collection of Connecticut Town Vital Records: Stafford 1719-1850, Tolland 1715-1850*, vol. 44, (Baltimore: GPC, 2002). Digital images at *Ancestry.com*.

[891] Now part of the Barbour Index and interfiled with similar slips from other towns in CSL and in FHL films 2,887 *et seq*. See Introduction above, pp. 3–5.

[892] Lucius B. Barbour, *Connecticut Vital Records: Stafford, 1719–1850,* (Hartford, CSL,1923) page after title page (FHL film 2,979). Digital images at *AmericanAncestors.org* and *FamilySearch.org*.

[893] In 1935 Stafford reported possession of "12 volumes of Vital Records," presumably including the books Barbour abstracted *Biennial Report*, (1936) p.58.

an 1847–1852 book of detailed vital records by school district, neither abstracted by Barbour nor microfilmed by FHL.[894]

CHURCH RECORDS:

- First Congregational Church of Stafford Springs's, "Church Records, 1797–1892" (includes baptisms 1840–1863, deaths 1840–1869, & marriages 1840–1860) (originals at CSL) (FHL film 5,823;
- Stafford Springs Congregational Church's "Church Records, 1850–1936" (includes baptisms 1850–1870) (originals at CSL) (FHL film 5,822);
- Second Congregational Church, West Stafford, "Church Records, 1780–1895" (includes deaths, marriages, and baptisms) (originals at CSL) (FHL film 5,751 or 1,013,276, items 1–6);
- L. Belle Gorton's "Records of the First Congregational Church, Stafford, Connecticut, 1757–1817" (includes baptisms, marriages, and deaths) (photocopy in CSL) (FHL film 1,013,276, item 10);
- First Universalist Church's Church records, 1814–1917, originals at CSL (FHL film 5,756);
- Stafford Springs Methodist Episcopal Church's Church records, 1830–1949, originals at CSL (FHL film 5,755);
- Baptist Ecclesiastical Society of Stafford's Records, 1832–1909, originals at CSL (FHL film 1,013,276, item 9);
- Baptist Church's Church records, 1809–1913. original at CSL (FHL film 1,013,276).

CEMETERY TRANSCRIPTIONS: The Hale Collection identifies people in order of physical proximity buried at about 14 named sites in Stafford Township.[895] Compare with Daniel Hearn's 1979 copy of 58 pre-1800 gravestones in five Stafford cemeteries.[896] See also,

- Grace Olive Chapman's "West Stafford, Connecticut Cemetery Inscriptions: West Stafford Center; Woodworth, Davis-Blodgett Family Plots, Genealogical Notes" (1940 typescript at NEHGS);
- Grace Olive Chapman, "Cemetery Inscriptions. Hillside Cemetery, Stafford, Tolland County, Connecticut [With Genealogical Notes]" (1939 typescript at NEHGS);
- Grace Olive Chapman's "Inscriptions, Old Cemetery, West Stafford, Tolland County, Connecticut [with Genealogical Notes]" (1939 typescript at NEHGS);
- Grace Olive Chapman's "Inscriptions. West Cemetery, Village Hill, Stafford, Tolland County, Connecticut" (typescript at NEHGS);
- Grace Olive Chapman's "Cemetery inscriptions: Hall District, Staffordville, Tolland County, Connecticut" (1938 typescript at NEHGS);
- Grace Olive Chapman's "Cemetery Inscriptions. West Stafford, Tolland County, Connecticut – the Newer Cemetery on the Myron Kemp Road [With Genealogical

---

894 See note 36 above'

895 Charles R. Hale, "Headstone Inscriptions of the Town of Stafford, Connecticut" (bound manuscript at CSL) (FHL film 3,363). Hale names these Springs, St. Edward's Center, Old, (4 different locations), Belcher, Hillside, Staffordville, West, New (2 different locations), & Old Springs.

896 Daniel Hearn, "Connecticut gravestones, early to 1800," manuscript (FHL film 1,477,477, item 51).

Notes]" (1938 typescript at NEHGS);
- Grace Olive Chapman's "Cemetery inscriptions: Stafford Street, Stafford, Tolland County, Connecticut" (1938 typescript at NEHGS);
- Grace Olive Chapman's "Staffordville, Connecticut cemetery inscriptions" (1937 typescript at NEHGS);
- Walter E. Corbin's "Gravestone inscriptions, Leonard District Cemetery, Stafford, Connecticut" (1933 typescript at NEHGS);
- "Inscriptions in an Old Cemetery, Stafford, Connecticut" (typescript at NEHGS);
- Stafford Springs, Connecticut, Civil War veterans burial records, 1862–1913, originals at CSL (FHL film 1,029,520, item 3).

OTHER NOTEWORTHY SOURCES:
- Eleazer W. Phelps, "J.P. Marriages, 1798–1897;" CSL; see Appendix A;
- Walter E Corbin and Robert J. Dunkle's *Corbin manuscript collection* (vol. 2. Records of Connecticut towns including Gilead, Norwalk, Stafford, Stamford, West Stafford, and Willington,), 3 CD-ROMs (Boston: NEHGS, c2003–c2005).

STAMFORD

Barbour's typescript volume for Stamford,[897] unlike the GPC edition,[898] begins:

> The vital records of Stamford prior to 1852, are found in two volumes. Volume 1 is in two parts and is said to have been taken from two volumes of Town Meetings. Duplication of the page numbers 18-20, 55, 64, 72, 74, 76, 84, 94, 96, 98 and 100-152 of Part 1 appears in Part 2, but if the date of the desired entry is prior to 1723 it may be generally assumed that it is in Part 1.
>
> This alphabetical list, was taken from a set of cards[899] based on a manuscript copy of the records made in 1915 by Mr. James N. Arnold, of Providence, R.I., The Arnold Copy, now in the possession of the Connecticut State Library, has not been compared with the original and doubtless errors exist.
>
> In 1874 the Rev. E.B. Huntington, a.m., published "Registration of Births, Marriages and Deaths of Stamford Families", which contains many of the records prior to 1825, and although the Arnold Copy has not been compared in its entirety with this publication, a few marked differences in names have been noted here-

---

[897] See How to Use This Book, note 4, above.

[898] GOGS, *Barbour Collection of Connecticut Town Vital Records: Stamford 1641-1852*, vol. 42, (Baltimore: GPC, 2000). Digitized at *Ancestry.com*.

[899] Now part of the Barbour Index and interfiled with similar slips from other towns in CSL and in FHL films 2,887 *et seq*. See Introduction above, pp. 3–5.

```
in. It is hoped that as errors or omissions
are found notes will be entered in this volume
and on the cards which are included in the Gen-
eral Index of Connecticut Vital Records also in
the possession of the Connecticut State Library.
          Hartford, Conn., January, 1926.[900]
```

VITAL RECORDS: The Stamford volume includes vital records as early as 1652 and as late as 1862. Stamford's Town Meetings and Vital Records, 1630–1852 have all been independently microfilmed by CSL, which also possesses the original of "Town Meetings & Vital Records, vol. 1, 1630–1723" (CSL film #4240.6), "Stamford Birth, Marriages, Deaths and Earmarks, 1719–1779" (CSL film #4240.7), and "Stamford Birth, Marriages, Deaths and Earmarks, 1779–1852" (CSL film #4240.8)."[901] None are cataloged by FHL.

Barbour abstracted two of Stamford's "books:"

- "1" refers (with **some inaccuracies**) to CSL films #4240.6 and 4240.7;
- "2" refers to the 1779 to 1852 volume of this set (CSL 4240.8).

An unknown number of the records Barbour abstracted are adjusted to match E.B. Huntington's *Stamford Registration of Births, Marriages and Deaths: including every name, relationship, and date now found in the Stamford registers, from the first record down to the year 1825*, (Stamford: Wm. W. Gillespie, 1874) (FHL film 5,592) (images at *AmericanAncestors.org*).

In 1886 Stamford authorized that a copy be made of all that was then still legible in Books A, B, and C of its land records and Books 1 and 2 of its town records.[902] FHL has microfilmed what it calls volumes 1 and 2 of that copy. FHL's volume 1 generally includes the vital records in Barbour's Book 1, including references to Barbour's page numbers. FHL's volume 2 contains no vital records, just town meetings, etc.

Thus Barbour's abstractions exclude all or part of

- **Stamford's "Records of Births, Marriages, and Deaths, 1847–1890" (originals in Stamford Town Hall) (FHL film 1,434,311 or 1848–1906 (FHL film 1,434,312);**
- **Stamford's Town Meeting & Vital Records, 1630–1852 (a more legible but differently paginated transcription of vol. 1) (CSL film # 4240.5);**
- **Paul Finch, *Stamford Town Records, Volume I 1641–1723* (Boston: NEHGS, 2011);**
- **Charles T. Gritman's *Marriage Records, Oyster Bay, Long Island, New York: Register of Marriages Performed by the Rev. Marmaduke Earle, 1793–1855: at Stamford, Connecticut, 1793–1801, at Oyster Bay Long Island, 1802–1855, at New York City, in 1811* (New York,: s.n., 1926) (images online thru *FamilySearch.org*);**

---

900 Lucius B. Barbour, *Connecticut Vital Records: Stamford, 1641–1852*,, (Hartford,: CSL, 1926) page after title pagr (FHL film 2,979). Digital images at *AmericanAncestors.org and FamilySearch.org.*

901 See Jeannie Sherman, Connecticut Town Guides Compiled from Collections at the CT State Library, (History & Genealogy Unit, CSL, 2015) https;//cdm15019.contentdm.oclc.org/digital/api/single/item/image/pdf/p128501coll2/458896/default.png.

902 See Stamford Town Clerk, Town Records, 1630-1806 (a copy of vols. 1 and 2 of an 1882 transcript of town records, containing records of births, marriages, deaths) 1882 transcript in the Stamford Town Hall, FHL film 5,570, pp. 1-2

- **Aaron Fancher and Lester L. Card's Marriage records of Aaron Fancher, Justice of the Peace, Poundridge [sic], N.Y., 1838–1871 (Includes records of persons residing in Ridgefield, Wilton, Norwalk, and Stamford) typescript at NYGBS (FHL film 17,860, item 2);**
- **The Ferguson Library's Local Historical and Genealogical Collection in Stamford (genealogical manuscripts including vital statistics located in its Stamford Room are indexed by surname at *https://fergusonlibrary.org/wp-content/uploads/2016/05/Manuscripts1.pdf*).**

CHURCH RECORDS:

- First Congregational Church's "Church records, 1747–1907" (includes baptisms 1747–1843, 1760–1791 & 1843–1884, marriages 1747–1846, and deaths 1850, 1788–1842 & 1844–1884) (originals at CSL) (FHL film 5,589);
- North Stamford Congregational Church's "Church Records, 1782–1928" (includes deaths 1811–1857 and baptisms 1787–1852) (originals at CSL) (FHL film 5,591);
- Methodist Episcopal Church's "Church Records, 1849*1896" (originals at CSL) (FHL film 5,590, items 3–4);
- Church of England's "Church Records, 1742–1746" (baptisms 1742–1746) (originals at the CSL) (FHL film 5,815);
- William A. Eardeley's *Church Records, 1747–1843* (Stamford: [s.n., 19--]) (FHL film 899,936 or 926,469);
- Methodist Episcopal Church's "Church Records, 1823–1919" (includes baptisms and marriages) (originals at CSL) (FHL film 1,013,279, items 1–10);
- Methodist Episcopal Church's Stamford Circuit, "Church Records, 1788–1849–1896" (includes baptisms, marriages, and deaths 1788–1846) (originals at CSL) (FHL film 5,590, items 1–2);
- Methodist Episcopal Church's "Stamford Circuit, Steward's book, 1813–1848" (includes baptisms, marriages and deaths) (originals at CSL) (FHL film 1,013,279, item 11);
- Lester Card and Aaron Fancher's "Marriage Records of Aaron Fancher, Justice of the Peace, Poundridge [sic], N.Y., 1838–1871" (1931 typescript at NYGBS) (FHL film 17,860);
- Jay Harris' *Records of the Methodist Episcopal/Community Church, Pound Ridge New York* (High Ridge and Hunting Ridge death records 1833–1983) (Pound Ridge NY: Community Church, 1984) (FHL film 1,750,737 or 1,697,927);
- Spencer P. Mead's "Abstract of Church Records of the Town of Stamford, County of Fairfield and State of Connecticut: From the Earliest Records Extant to 1850" (typescript at the CSL, NEHGS, and NYGBS) (FHL film 1,013,277 or 5,561);
- Jay Harris's *Index to Records of the Methodist Episcopal/Community Church, Pound Ridge, New York 1833–1983* (Pound Ridge NY: Community Church, 1991) (FHL film 1,750,737).

CEMETERY TRANSCRIPTIONS: The Hale Collection identifies people in order of physical proximity buried at about 31 named sites in Stamford Township.[903] Compare with

[903] Charles R. Hale, "Headstone Inscriptions of the Town of Stamford, Connecticut" (bound manuscript at CSL) (FHL film 3,363). Hales names these Woodland, Simsbury, Old, Jewish, Roxbury, Westover,

Daniel Hearn's 1977 copy of 51 pre-1800 gravestones in six Stamford cemeteries.[904] See also,

- Jeanne Majdalany and Jean Mulkerin's *Poems on Stone in Stamford, Connecticut* (Bowie MD: Heritage Books, 1998);
- William Applebie and Daniel Eardeley's *Connecticut Cemeteries, 1673–1911* (Stamford: Stamford Genealogical Society, [19--]) (FHL film 899,935, 926,468 or 929,231);
- Charles R. Hale's *Headstone Inscriptions, Town of Stamford, Connecticut* (Stamford: Stamford Genealogical Society, [19-]) (FHL film 899,935, 926,468 or 929,231);
- Francis F. Spies' *"Inscriptions from St. Bridget Catholic Cemetery in Cornwall, Conn., 1817–2001"* (manuscript at NEHGS).
- Francis F. Spies' *Connecticut Epitaphs* (4 vols.: East Lyme CT, Waterford CT, Sound Beach (Potomac Ave, 1st Congregational Churchyard, near Adams Corners), Stamford (St. Andrew's Churchyard, North Street, Mill River yard, Richmond Hill Ave), Noroton in Darien Township, Mianus (Lyon Farm, Bonnell farm), Cos Cob, Montville, Chesterfield (near church, Martenus Farm, by Congregational meeting house, on Warren farm & Great Hill Burial Ground); and Yonkers NY, New Canaan CT, East Port Chester, CT, Greenwich CT, Port Chester, NY; and Rye, NY (manuscript at NEHGS);

OTHER NOTEWORTHY SOURCES:

- Edward R. Lambert's *History of the Colony of New Haven: Before and After the Union with Connecticut: Containing a Particular Description of the Towns Which Composed that Government, viz., New Haven, Milford, Guilford, Branford, Stamford, & Southold, L.I "* (New Haven: Hitchcock & Stafford, 1838).
- Walter E Corbin and Robert J. Dunkle's *Corbin manuscript collection* (vol. 2. Records of Connecticut towns including Gilead, Norwalk, Stafford, Stamford, West Stafford, and Willington,), 3 CD-ROMs (Boston: NEHGS, c2003–c2005);

STERLING

Barbour's typescript volume for Sterling,[905] unlike the GPC edition,[906] begins:

> This volume contains a list alphabetically arranged of all the vital records of the town of Sterling from its incorporation to about 1850. This list was taken from a set of cards[907] based on

---

Palmer Hill, Stillwater Road #1, Stillwater Road #2, North Street, St. Andrew's St. John's West Stamford, Long Ridge, North Stamford, Scofieldtown, Turn of River, Newfield, Belltown, Scofield (2 different locations), Emanuel Chapel, Hoyt (2 different locations), Brush, Bundle, Green, New Jewish, New Woodland, & Smith.

904 Daniel Hearn, "Connecticut gravestones, early to 1800," manuscript (FHL film 1,477,477, item 52).

905 See How to Use This Book, note 4, above.

906 Lorraine Cook White, *Barbour Collection of Connecticut Town Vital Records: Sterling 1794-1850, Stratford 1639-1840*, vol. 41, (Baltimore: GPC, 2000). Digitized at *Ancestry.com*.

907 Now part of the Barbour Index and interfiled with similar slips from other towns in CSL and in FHL films 2,887 *et seq*. See Introduction above, pp. 3–5.

> a copy of the Southington Vital Records made in 1909 by James N. Arnold, of Providence, R.I. The records here indexed are taken from the first two volumes of vital records. Every entry in the first volume has been indexed and in Volume 2 all births prior to December 31 1850, all marriages prior to December 31, 1850 and all of the deaths. The record of deaths ends with an entry bearing the date of September 23, 1867. The Arnold Copy, now in the possession of the Connecticut State Library, has not been compared with the original and doubtless errors exist. It is hoped that as errors or omissions are found notes will be entered in this volume and on the cards which are included in the General Index of Connecticut Vital Records also in the possession of the Connecticut State Library.
> Hartford, Conn., April, 1920.[908]

VITAL RECORDS: The Sterling volume includes vital records as early as 1768 and as late as 1866. Barbour abstracted two Sterling "books:"

- Sterling's Records of Births, Marriages, & Deaths, vol. 1, 1777–1850, Sterling Town Hall, (FHL film 1,378,196, item 1);
- Sterling's Records of Births, Marriages, & Deaths, vol. 2, 1848–1867, Sterling Town Hall, (FHL film 1,378,196, item 2).

CHURCH RECORDS:

- Emma Finney Welch's First book records of the First Presbyterian Church of Voluntown, 1723 to 1764 (FHL film 441,390, item 3);
- Voluntown and Sterling Congregational Church's "Church Records, 1727–1914" (Includes baptisms and marriages) (originals at CSL) (FHL films 5,888 and 5,887 or 5.889);
- Emma Finney Welch's "Abstracts From the Records of the Voluntown and Sterling Congregational Church (The Line Church), 1779–1910" (manuscript in Historical Society of Pennsylvania) (FHL film 441,390, item 4).

CEMETERY TRANSCRIPTIONS: The Hale Collection identifies people in order of physical proximity buried at about 21 named sites in Sterling Township.[909] Compare with Daniel Hearn's 1979 copy of 125 pre-1800 gravestones in two Sterling cemeteries.[910] See also, Emma Finney Welch's "Dorrance Inscriptions, Old Sterling Township Burying Ground, Oneco, Connecticut" (1909. original) (FHL fiche 6,048,969

OTHER NOTEWORTHY SOURCES: See state and county resources above, pages 17 to 21.

---

908 Lucius B. Barbour, *Connecticut Vital Records: Sterling, 1794–1850,* (Hartford: CSL, 1920) page after title page (FHL film 2,979). Digital images at *AmericanAncestors.org* and *FamilySearch,org.*.

909 Charles R. Hale, "Headstone Inscriptions of the Town of Sterling, Connecticut" (bound manuscript at CSL) (FHL film 3,363). Hale names these Parker-Hill, Card-Clark, Ames, Field stones, Bennett, Card-Hill, Hall-Fuller, Young, Arnold, French, Griffiths, Williams, Potter, Dixon, ____, Sheldon, Riverside, Hunt, Gallup, Cedar Swamp, & Benadam Gallup.

910 Daniel Hearn, "Connecticut gravestones, early to 1800," manuscript (FHL film 1,477,477, item 53).

STONINGTON

Barbour's typescript volume for Stonington,[911] unlike the GPC edition,[912] begins:

> The early vital records of Stonington are scattered through the land records, town votes, books of cattle marks, and other volumes of records of the town. In 1859 these scattered items were collected and transcribed in semi-alphabetical arrangement by John D. Noyes, then Town Clerk.[913] The Noyes' Copy preserved the original pagination of the entries which has been followed in this copy.
>
> This volume contains a list alphabetically arranged of all the Vital Records of the Town of Stonington from the earliest records to about 1854. This list was taken from a set of cards[914] based on a copy of the Stonington Vital Records made in 1912 by James N. Arnold, of Providence, R.I. The Noyes' Copy was used by Mr. Arnold as a basis of copy for the early records. The Arnold Copy, now in the possession of the Connecticut State Library, has not been compared with the original and doubtless errors exist. It is hoped that as errors or omissions are found notes will be entered in this volume and on the cards which form the basis of the General Index of Connecticut Vital Records also in the possession of the Connecticut State Library.
>
> **Hartford, Conn., February, 1918.**[915]

VITAL RECORDS: The Stonington volume includes vital records as early as 1656 and as late as 1854. Barbour abstracted six Stonington "books:"

- "1" refers to Stonington's Town Records (1664–1688), vol. 1 (FHL film 1,309,871, item 1);
- "2" refers to Stonington's Town Records (1693–1725), vol. 2 (FHL film 1,309,871, item 2);
- "3" abstracts Stonington's Town Records, (1703–1791) vol. 3 (FHL film 1,309,872, item 2) ;

---

911 See How to Use This Book, note 4, above.

912 Nancy E. Schott, *Barbour Collection of Connecticut Town Vital Records: Stonington 1658-1854,* vol. 43, (Baltimore: GPC, 2000). Digital images at *Ancestry.com*.

913 Probably Stonington Town Clerk, Town Records: 1664 through 1831 (Births, marriages, deaths 1664-1765 & marriages, births, deaths ca.1714-1831) (original records in the Stonington Town Hall), (FHL films 1,309,871 & 1,309,872 items 1-3).

914 Now part of the Barbour Index and interfiled with similar slips from other towns in CSL and in FHL films 2,887 *et seq*. See Introduction above, pp. 3–5.

915 Lucius B. Barbour, *Connecticut Vital Records: Stonington, 1658–1854*, (Hartford: CSL, 1918) page after title page (FHL film 2,980). Digital images at *AmericanAncestors.org* and *FamilySearch.org/*

- "4" refers to an original "Book 4" (1773–1831) not microfilmed by FHL. However, a very legible 1896 transcription of Books 3 and 4, citing the original Books' page numbers is cataloged by FHL as FHL film 1,309,872, item 3;
- "5" refers to Stonington's Certificates of marriage, birth, and death, 1811–1849, Stonington Town Hall (FHL film 1,309,872, item 4);
- "6" refers to Stonington's Certificates of marriage, birth, and death, 1844–1854,
- (includes reports of births, marriages and deaths from the school districts, returns and birth certificates, registration of births, marriages, and deaths, declarations of intent to marry, death certificates, some delayed birth certificates and affidavits, marriage licenses and certificates) Stonington Town Hall (FHL film 1,309,873, item 1).

FHL also catalogs under vital records:

- **Stonington's Land Records, vol. 1–2, 1664–1714; vol. 3–4, 1709–1737; vol. 5–6, 1737–1755 (volumes 1–4 include births, marriages, deaths; contains some records caught by *FamilySearch* indexers but not by Noyes) Stonington Town Hall, (FHL films 5,593 to 5,595);**
- **Stonington's Certificates of Marriage, Birth, and Death, 1811–1846, Stonington Town Hall), (FHL films 1,309,872, item 4 and 1,309,873, item 1;**
- **Stonington's Records of Births, Marriages, Deaths 1847–1869 (includes reports of births, marriages and deaths from the school districts, returns and certificates of birth, registration of births, marriages, and deaths, declarations of intent to marry, death certificates, some delayed birth certificates and affidavits, marriage licenses and certificates), Stonington Town Hall, (FHL film 1,309,873, items 2–4);**
- **Henrietta Mello Mayer's *1846 to 1948 marriages of Portuguese people in Stonington, Ct.* (S.I.: H.M. Mayer, [200-?]);**
- **"Swan family burials, [1743–1876]." *Genealogy* – vol. 7, no. 1 (Jan. 1917).**

CHURCH RECORDS:

- Richard A. Wheeler's *History of the First Congregational Church, Stonington, Conn., 1674–1874 with the Report of the Bi-centennial Proceedings, June 3, 1874.* Norwich: T. A. David and Co., 1875) (images online at *AmericanAncestors.org).*;
- *Index to the Records of the First Church of Stonington, 1674–1879,* Manuscript. RSASCs, NEHGS, Boston, MA (database at AmericanAncestors.org);
- First Congregational Church's "Church Records, 1674–1929" (includes baptisms and marriages) (originals at CSL) (FHL films 5,614);
- First Congregational Church and Ecclesiastical Society's "Church Records, 1731–1892" (originals at CSL) (FHL films 5,615);
- First and Second Congregational Churches' Records 1674–1833, originals at CSL (FHL film 5,616);
- Second Congregational Church, Records 1809–1929, originals at CSL (FHL film 5,617);
- Calvary Church's "Church Records, 1847–1922" (includes baptisms, marriages, and burials) (originals at CSL) (FHL film 1,013,280, items 1–7);
- First Church of Christ's Church records, 1720–1869, Photostats at CSL (FHL film 1,013,280, items 8–9);
- John VOL. Hinshaw's *Stonington Baptist Records, 1772–1848* (Stonington: Stonington Historical Society, c1992);

- Baptisms (1847–64), marriages (1847–64) & burials (1847–64) at Calvary Church (ED Film 1,013,280).

CEMETERY TRANSCRIPTIONS: The Hale Collection identifies people in order of physical proximity buried at about 61 named sites in Stonington Township.[916] Compare with Daniel Hearn's 1978 copy of 253 pre-1800 gravestones in seven Stonington cemeteries.[917] See also,

- Charles R. Hale and Mary H. Babin, "Headstone Inscriptions, Town of Stonington, New London County, Connecticut" (typescript photocopy) (Hartford: February, 1934);
- Frederick E. Burdick, *Wequetequock Burial Ground, Stonington Founder's Cemetery,* CD-ROM, (Stonington: F.E. Burdick, 2002);
- Grace Denison Wheeler, *Old Homes in Stonington, With Additional Chapters & Graveyard Inscriptions* (1930/1993 copy at NEHGS);
- *Stonington graveyards: a guide* (Stonington: Stonington Historical Society, c1980)

OTHER NOTEWORTHY SOURCES:

- "Nathaniel Ingraham Account Book," CSL; see Appendix A;
- Richard Anson Wheeler's *History of the Town of Stonington, County of New London, Connecticut, From Its First Settlement in 1649 to 1900, With a Genealogical Register of Stonington Families* (New London: Press of the Day Publishing Co., 1900) (FHL film 900,000 or 847,758);
- Katharine B. Crandall's *The fine old town of Stonington : a historical tribute to the founders and their descendants* (Watch Hill, RI: Book & Tackle Shop, c1975);
- Thomas Minor and Manasseh Minor's *The Minor diaries, Stonington, Connecticut: Thomas, 1653 to 1684; Manasseh, 1696 to 1720* (Ann Arbor, MI: J.A. Miner, 1976).

STRATFORD

Barbour's typescript volume for Stratford,[918] unlike the GPC edition,[919] begins:

> The vital records of Stratford, prior to 1850, are found scattered through Volumes 1, 2 and 5 of Land Records, and a volume known as "Book A - Marriages". This alphabetical list was taken from a set of

---

916 Charles R. Hale, "Headstone Inscriptions of the Town of Stonington, Connecticut" (bound manuscript at CSL) (FHL film 3,364). Hale names these Wheeler-Bentley, Sherry, Old St. Michael's New St. Michael's Stanton, Davis, Burdick-Culver, Old Wequetequock, Slack, Robinson (2 different locations), Noyes, Rhodes, Stonington Boro, Richmond, St. Mary's Thomas miner, Industrial, Denison, Elm Grove, White Hall, Williams, Hillard, Jonathan Wheeler, Old Tangwank, Breed, Brown or Cogswell, Finks or Williams, Wheeler, Babcock, Helome, Hallam, Hempstead, Bennett (2 different locations), Cranston, Whittlesey, John Wheeler, Bentley, Paul Wheeler's Stanton Hill, Town farm, Pendleton, Warren Palmer, Chesebrough, Richardson, Family, Oliver Denison, William Miner, Miner (2 different locations), Baker, Family, Joseph Denison, Beebe-Davis, Hinckley Hill, Quaker, Burdick-Frink, William Unison, Shaw, & States.

917 Daniel Hearn, "Connecticut gravestones, early to 1800," manuscript (FHL film 1,477,477, item 54).

918 See How to Use This Book, note 3, above.

919 White, *Barbour Collection: Sterling–Stratford*, vol. 41. Digitized at *Ancestry.com*.

cards[920] based on a manuscript copy, part of which was made in 1914 by James N. Arnold, of Providence, R.I. and part in 1924 by Mrs. Kate Hammond Fogarty, of Bridgeport, Conn. Reference to the entries found in the Land Records is indicated by the abbreviation "LR' and the number of the volume, and to the Book of Marriages by "A".

"A History of the Old Town of Stratford and the City of Bridgeport, Connecticut", published in 1886 by Rev. Samuel Orcutt, contained many of the early vital records of Stratford, and although the manuscript copy has not been checked in its entirety with the printed history, a few marked differences have been noted herein.

The manuscript copy, now in the possession of the Connecticut State Library, has not been compared with the original and doubtless errors exist. It is hoped that as errors or omissions are found notes will be entered in this volume and on the cards which are included in the General Index of Connecticut Vital Records also in the possession of the Connecticut State Library.

Hartford, Conn., September, 1925.[921]

VITAL RECORDS: The Stratford volume includes vital records as early as 1640 and as late as 1851. Barbour abstracted four Stratford "books:"

- "A" refers to Stratford's Records of Births, Marriages, and Deaths, vol. A–C, 1820–1914." Stratford Town Hall, FHL film 1,428,083, item 4;
- "LR1" refers to Stratford's Land Records, vol. 1, 1640–1684 (Volumes 1, 2 & 5 include births, marriages and deaths) Stratford Town Hall, (FHL film 5,770, ítem 1);
- "LR2" refers to Stratford's Land Records, vol. 2, 1680–1723 (Volumes 1, 2 & 5 include births, marriages and deaths) (FHL film 5,770, ítem 2 *et seq.*);
- "LR5" refers to Stratford's Land Records, vol. 5 1710–1753 (Volumes 1, 2 & 5 include births, marriages and deaths) Stratford Town Hall, (FHL film 5,771).

See also,

- **Stratford's Records of Births, Marriages, and Deaths, vol. B, 1848–1851." Stratford Town Hall, FHL film 1,428,083, item 5.**
- **William John Slayton's "Stratford, Ct., Vital Records: Births, Marriages, Deaths (1649–1729" (manuscript) (FHL fiche 6,008,143);**
- **Harlan R. Jessup's "Births, Marriages, and Deaths for Stratford, CT, 1848–1852,' *CA*, Vol. 54, No. 4 (May 2012);**
- **Samuel Orcutt's *History of the Old Town of Stratford and the City of Bridgeport, Connecticut*, 2 vols. [New Haven, Conn.]: [Press of Tuttle, Morehouse & Taylor],1886) (images thru FanilySearch,org);**

---

920 Now part of the Barbour Index and interfiled with similar slips from other towns in CSL and in FHL films 2,887 *et seq*. See Introduction above, pp. 3–5.

921 Lucius B. Barbour, *Connecticut Vital Records: Stratford, 1639–1840,* (Hartford, CSL, 1923) page after title page (FHL film 2,980). Digital images at *AmericanAncestors.org* and *FamilySearch.org*

- **Harlan R. Jessup's "More Births and Deaths for Stratford, CT, 1847–1848,"** ***CA*****, Vol. 55, No. 3 (Feb 2013).**

CHURCH RECORDS:

- First Congregational Church's "Church Records, 1688–1927" (includes baptisms 1689–1758, 1832–1872, 1722–1806, marriages 1733–1735 and 1753– 1806, 1832–1872; and burials 1832–1873) (photocopies at CSL) (FHL film 5,800, items 2–7);
- Christ Church and Episcopal Society's "Church Records, 1722–1932" (includes baptisms (1722–1792, 1829–1842 & 1842–1873), marriages (1723–1828, 1829–1842 & 1842–1873), burials (1723–1792, 1842–1843 & 1842–1874), and funerals 1830–1842) (photocopies at CSL) (FHL film 5,799);
- First Ecclesiastical Society's Church records, 1847–1914, photocopies at CSL (FHL film 5,801);
- First Methodist Episcopal Church's "Church Records, 1848–1931" (includes baptisms 1816–1830) (photocopies at CSL) (FHL film 5,802);
- Mary Chaffee Hart's "Congregational Church Records 1814–1849" (Hartford: Connecticut State Library, 1944) (FHL film 5,800, item 1);
- Baptisms (1754–57, 1758–92, 1829–39, 1842–62), marriages (1723–57, 1758–1828, 1829–42, 1842–73), burials (1723–57, 1758–92, 1842–43, 1842–74) & funerals (1830–39, 1839–42) at Christ Church (ED film 5,799);
- Episcopal Church*'s*" Index to Baptisms, Marriages and Deaths 1692–1820" (photocopy at CSL) (FHL film 5,798);
- Baptisms (1829–84), marriages (1832–85), burials (1829–84) & transcription of births & marriages of Church of Christ in Unity & North Stratford, 1731–1808 (ED Film 1,014,187).
- Index to baptisms, marriages & deaths from the Early Records of the Congregational & Episcopal Churches of Stratford, 1692–1820 (ED Film 5,790).

CEMETERY TRANSCRIPTIONS: The Hale Collection identifies people in order of physical proximity buried at about seven named sites in Stratford Township.[922] Compare with Daniel Hearn's 1975 copy of 308 pre-1800 gravestones in two Stratford cemeteries.[923]

OTHER NOTEWORTHY SOURCES:

- William Howard Wilcoxson's *History of Stratford, Connecticut: 1639–1939* (Stratford: Stratford Tercentenary Commission, 1939) ;
- Benjamin Lincoln Swan's *Genealogies of the town of Stratford, Connecticut* (S.i.: s.n., n.d);
- Lewis G. Knapp's *In pursuit of paradise: history of the town of Stratford, Connecticut* (West Kennebunk, ME: Phoenix Pub., c1989).
- Samuel Orcutt's *History of the old town of Stratford and the city of Bridgeport, Connecticut* [New Haven: Press of Tuttle, Morehouse & Taylor, 1886);
- William Cothren's *History of Ancient Woodbury, Connecticut, from the first Indian deed in 1659 to 1854: including the present towns of Washington, Southbury,*

---

[922] Charles R. Hale, "Headstone Inscriptions of the Town of Stratford, Connecticut" (bound manuscript at CSL) (FHL film 3,364). Hale names these Union, St. Michael's Congregational, Episcopal, St. John's (Greek Catholic), Putney, & St. Joseph's (Polish).

[923] Daniel Hearn, "Connecticut gravestones, early to 1800," manuscript (FHL film 1,477,477, item 55).

Bethlehem, Roxbury, and a part of Oxford and Middlebury (vol. 3 contains vital records, including those for ancient Stratford) (Baltimore, MD: Genealogical Pub. Co., 1997) (FHL film 2,055,359 & 6,181).

SUFFIELD

Barbour's typescript volume for Suffield,[924] unlike the GPC edition,[925] begins:

> This volume contains a list alphabetically arranged of all the vital records of the town of Suffield from its incorporation to about 1850. The entire record of this town, prior to 1850, is found in two volumes, one of which is known as "The New Book Vol. 1", Reference to this is indicated herein by the abbreviation "NB1".
>
> In this alphabetical list the vital records on file in the Town Clerk's office have been supplemented by entries found in a book now in the possession of the Kent Library in Suffield. The appearance of this book and the duplication in part of many entries found in "The New Book" indicate that it is the original volume of town records. Reference to this is in dicated by the abbreviation "KL'.
>
> This list was taken from a set of cards[926] based on a copy of the two volumes in the Town Clerk's office made in 1913 by James N. Arnold, of Providence, R.I. and on the original volume belonging to the Kent Library. These copies have not been compared with the original and doubtless errors exist. It is hoped that as errors or omissions are found notes will be entered in this volume and on the cards which are included in the General Index of Connecticut Vital Records also in the possession of the Connecticut State Library.
>
> Hartford, Conn., September, 1928.[927]

VITAL RECORDS: The Suffield volume includes vital records as early as 1668 and as late as 1872. Barbour abstracted three Suffield "books:"

- "1" refers to Suffield's Records of Births, Marriages, & Deaths, vol. 1, 1662–1717, Suffield Town Hall, (FHL film 1,317,067, item 1) (film appears to exclude pages A and B;
- "NB1" refers to Suffield's "Suffield Record – Births – Marriages – and – Deaths – Vol. 1," ("This volume (to page 276) is chiefly a collection and transcription of the

---

924 See How to Use This Book, note 3, above.

925 Nancy E. Schott, *Barbour Collection of Connecticut Town Vital Records. Suffield 1674-1850*, vol. 45, (Baltimore: GPC, 2002).

926 Now part of the Barbour Index and interfiled with similar slips from other towns in CSL and in FHL films 2,887 *et seq*. See Introduction above, pp. 1-3.

927 Lucius B. Barbour, *Connecticut Vital Records: Suffield, 1674–1850*, (Hartford: CSL, 1928) page after title page (FHL film 2,980). Digital image at *AmericanAncestors.org* and *FamilySearch.org*..

original records, from the old Books" in about 1780, but disregard incomplete male only index.) Suffield Town Hall, (FHL film 1,317,067, item 2);

- "KL" refers to *Suffield, Connecticut: town book of vital records 1714–1872, Kent Library copy,* (Hartford: CSL, 1928).

The Barbour Index also abstracts 1760–1897 Private record from Kent Library; CSL; see Appendix A. See also,

- **Suffield's " Births – Marriages – and – Deaths – Vol. 2," (1847–1873) Suffield Town Hall, (FHL film 1,317,067, item 3);**
- **Suffield's Land Records vol. 12 1747–1793 (Vol. 1 includes records of births, marriages, deaths, marriage intentions not abstracted by Barbour and many on different pages in Barbour's "NB1"),** Suffield Town Hall, **(FHL film 5,694);**
- **Connecticut town records: births—marriages—deaths Suffield 1674–1850, Kent Library copy (Hartford: CSL, 1928);**
- **William & John Pynchon's "Vital Records, Massachusetts and Connecticut" (contains births, marriages, and deaths (1638–1696) of towns including Suffield and Enfield) original at Pynchon Memorial Building, Springfield, MA (FHL film 14,766).**

CHURCH RECORDS:

- First Congregational Church and Ebenezer Gay's Church records, 1741–1917 (FHL film 1,014,183–4);
- First Congregational Church, Society Committee book 1776–1812 (FHL film 5,709, item 4);
- First Congregational Church,, *Records of the Congregational Church in Suffield, Conn. (Except Church Votes), 1710–1836* (Hartford: CHS, 1941) (FHL film 928,515) (images online at *AmericanAncestors.org);*
- Second Congregational Ecclesiastical Church, "Church Records, 1792–1858" (includes deaths, baptisms, and marriages) (photocopies at CSL) (FHL film 5,709);
- "Records of the Congregational Church in Suffield, CT 1710–1836," (Hartford: CHS, 1941) (images at *AmericanAncestors.org*).

CEMETERY TRANSCRIPTIONS: The Hale Collection identifies people in order of physical proximity buried at about six named sites in Suffield Township. [928] Compare with Daniel Hearn's 1978 copy of 186 pre-1800 gravestones in three Suffield cemeteries.[929] See also,

- Samuel Lathrop's *Records of the Old Cemetery Suffield, Connecticut* ([S.l: s.n.], 1948);
- Samuel Lathrop's *West Suffield cemetery et cetera (records)*, Kent Library copy (Suffield : The compiler, 1950);
- Patricia Noble's *Gravestone Inscriptions at Zion's Hill Cemetery, Suffield* (West Suffield: P. Noble, 2004);
- Lucius B. Barbour's "Suffield, Conn. Epitaphs" (Mss A 2788), RSASC, NEHGS).

---

[928] Charles R. Hale, "Headstone Inscriptions of the Town of Suffield, Connecticut" (bound manuscript at CSL) (FHL film 3,365). Hale names these Old Center, Woodlawn, We4st Suffield, Phelps-Warner, Hastings Hill, & Graveyard.

[929] Daniel Hearn, "Connecticut gravestones, early to 1800," manuscript (FHL film 1,477,477, item 56).

OTHER NOTEWORTHY SOURCES: Hezekiah Spencer Sheldon, *Documentary History of Suffield in the Colony & Province of Massachusetts Bay in New England, 1660–1749* (Springfield, 1879).

THOMPSON

Barbour's typescript volume for Thompson,[930] unlike the GPC edition,[931] begins:

> This volume contains a list alphabetically arranged of all the vital records of the town of Thompson from its incorporation to about 1850. This list was taken from a set of cards[932] based on a copy of the Thompson Vital Records made in 1909 by James N. Arnold, of Providence, R.I.
>
> The entire record for this town prior to 1850 is contained in three volumes. After page 158 in the first volume, where a record of marriages begins the pagination repeats beginning with the number 43. To distinguish the duplicate numbers in this alphabetical list the letter "m" follows the page numbers of the last half of the book. Every entry in the first two volumes has been indexed and in Volume 3 all births prior to December 31, 1850, all marriages prior to December 31, 1850 and all of the deaths. The record of deaths ends with an entry bearing the date of December 30, 1854.
>
> The Arnold Copy, now in the possession of the Connecticut State Library, has not been compared with the original and doubtless errors exist. It is hoped that as errors or omissions are found notes will be entered in this volume and on the cards which are included in the General Index of Connecticut Vital Records also in the possession of the Connecticut State Library.
>
> Hartford, Conn., July, 1921.[933]

VITAL RECORDS: The Thompson volume includes vital records as early as 1733 and as late as 1854. Barbour abstracted three Thompson "books:"

- "1" refers to "Vital Records kept by the Town Clerk, Volume 1, Births (1733–1877), Marriages, (1746–1884) & Deaths (1760–1904)," Thompson Town Hall, Photostat at CSL (FHL film 1,376,374, item 1);
- "2" refers to "Marriages Volume 2, 1840–1853)," Thompson Town Hall, (FHL film 1,376,374, item 2);

---

930 See How to Use This Book, note 3, above.

931 Carole E. Magnuson, *Barbour Collection of Connecticut Town Vital Records: Thompson 1785-1850*, vol. 46, (Baltimore: GPC, 2002). Digital images at *Ancestry.com*.

932 Now part of the Barbour Index and interfiled with similar slips from other towns in CSL and n FHL films 2,887 *et seq*. See Introduction above, pp. 1-3.

933 Lucius B. Barbour, *Connecticut Vital Records: Thompson, 1785–1850,* (Hartford: CSL 1921) page after title page (FHL film 2,980). Digital images at *AmericanAncestors.org* and *FamilySearch.org*.

- "3" refers to Records of Births, Marriages, & Deaths, vol. 4, 1848–1850 (1854 for deaths), Thompson Town Hall, (FHL film 1,376,374, item 3).

See also, **Helen Schatvet Ullmann and Katherine Smith Black's "Some Marriages from Records of the First Congregational Church in Thompson, Connecticut, 1796–1850, Including Some Corrections to the Barbour Collection of Connecticut Vital Records," *NEHGR*, 155:295–317 (July 2001).**

CHURCH RECORDS:

- Congregational Church, "Church Records, 1728–1930" (includes baptisms, marriages, and deaths) (FHL films 1,003,072–3);
- East Putnam Congregational Church, "Church Records, 1715–1904" (includes baptisms 1839–1876, deaths 1839–1904, marriages 1838–1866) (originals at CSL) (FHL film 5,465);
- Ellen D. Larned's "Transcript of the Baptisms, Marriages and Deaths for 1711–1829 of the Putnam First or Putnam Heights Congregational Church" (typescript in CSL) (FHL film 5,466);
- "Thompson Church Records' 1730–1795" (records of marriages and baptisms in newspaper clippings in NYGBS) (FHL film 5,825 or 1,405,478);
- "Thompson Church Records' 1730–1795: Published in Putnam Patriot, Putnam, Conn." (photocopy of newspaper clippings) (FHL film 1,321,387);
- Congregational Church of Putnam, "Church Records, 1848–1933" (includes baptisms 1848–1850, baptisms, marriages, deaths 1848–1918 & 1848–1928) (photocopies at CSL) (FHL film 5,464);
- Mary B. Bishop and Mrs. William H. Mansfield, "Thompson, Connecticut, Congregational Church's Baptisms 1730–1795" (typescript in CSL) (FHL film 1,014,185);
- Ecclesiastical Society's Minutes of meetings, 1728–1856 (FHL film 1014,185, item 3).

CEMETERY TRANSCRIPTIONS: The Hale Collection identifies people in order of physical proximity buried in about 21 named sites in what was then Thompson Township.[934] Compare with Daniel Hearn's 1979 copy of 156 pre-1800 gravestones in two Thompson cemeteries.[935] The Hale Collection also identifies people in order of physical proximity buried in at least 11 named sites in what was then Putnam Township.[936] Compare with Daniel Hearn's 1979 copy of 86 pre-1800 gravestones in one Putnam cemetery.[937]

---

[934] Charles R. Hale, "Headstone Inscriptions of the Town of Thompson, Connecticut" (bound manuscript at CSL) (FHL film 3,365). Hale names these New Boston, Wilsonville, Tourtellot, Bates, Carpenter, Joslin, Porter, Jacob, Old East Thompson, New East Thompson, Dike, Quaddick, Ross, West Thompson, Whittemore, Swedish, Catholic, North Grosvenor, Cortiss, Winter, & Aldrich.

[935] Daniel Hearn, "Connecticut gravestones, early to 1800," manuscript (FHL film 1,477,477, item 58).

[936] Charles R. Hale, "Headstone Inscriptions of the Town of Putnam, Connecticut" (bound manuscript at CSL) (FHL film 3,359). Hale names these Grove Street, Putnam Heights, Munyan, Wheelock, Mallbone (colored family), Carpenter-Dresser, Day, Babbitt, Aspinwall, St. Mary's & Malbone.

[937] Daniel Hearn, "Connecticut gravestones, early to 1800," manuscript (FHL film 1,477,477, item 33).

OTHER NOTEWORTHY SOURCES:

- "Pomfret Manufacturing Company death records 1814–1851;" CSL; see Appendix A;
- Ellen D. Larned's *Thompson first families (*clippings and typescript Concord, NH State Library (FHL film 15,585, item 1).

TOLLAND

Barbour's typescript volume for Tolland,[938] unlike the GPC edition,[939] begins:

> This volume contains a list alphabetically arranged of all the vital records of the town of Tolland from its incorporation to about 1850. This list was taken from a set of cards[940] based on a copy of the Tolland Vital Records made in 1913 by James N. Arnold, of Providence, R.I. The entire record for the town prior to 1850 is contained in three volumes. In Volume 3 the pagination of the last half of the book duplicates that of the first half. In this alphabetical list an asterisk has been placed after all the duplicate page references.
>
> The Arnold Copy, now in the possession of the Connecticut State Library, has not been compared with the original and doubtless errors exist. It is hoped that as errors or omissions are found notes will be entered in this volume and on the cards which are included in the General Index of Connecticut Vital Records also in the possession of the Connecticut State Library.
>
> Hartford, Conn., February, 1922[941]

VITAL RECORDS: The Tolland volume includes vital records as early as 1706 and as late as 1851. Barbour abstracted three Tolland "books:"

- "1" refers to Tolland's Records of Births, Marriages, & Deaths, 1665–1833 (contains birth, marriage & death arranged in family groups) Tolland Town Hall (FHL film 1,376,026, item 1);
- "2" refers to Tolland's Records of Births, Marriages, & Deaths, 1754–1843 (contains birth, marriage & death arranged in family groups) Tolland Town Hall (FHL film 1,376,026, item 2) – probably largely a copy of #1);
- "3" refers to Tolland's Records of Births, Marriages, & Deaths, 1792–1853 (contains birth, marriage & death arranged in family groups and also a record of marriages, 1820–1853), Tolland Town Hall (FHL film 1,376,026, item 3).

---

938 See How to Use This Book, note 3, above.

939 Tilton, *Barbour Collection:Stafford–Tolland*, vol. 44. Digitized at *Ancestry.com*.

940 Now part of the Barbour Index and interfiled with similar slips from other towns in CSL and in FHL films 2,887 *et seq*. See Introduction above, pp. 1-3.

941 Lucius B. Barbour, *Connecticut Vital Records: Tolland, 1715–1850*, (Hartford: CSL,1922):page after title page.(FHL film 2,981). Digital images at *AmericanAncestors.org.*and *FamilySearch,org.*

FHL also catalogs as Tolland vital records:

- **Tolland's Records of Births, Marriages, and Deaths, 1848–1867, originals in Tolland Town Hall (FHL film 376,026, item 4).**
- **Records of Births, Marriages, and Deaths, Tolland, Connecticut, 1665–1868 (transcript of records of births, marriages, and deaths, from town vital records books, town meeting books, and other sources), Tolland Town Hall, (FHL film 376,026, Item 5);**
- **Tolland's Records of Births, Marriages, and Deaths, 1848–1926 (originals in Tolland Town Hall (FHL film 1,376,026, item 6);**
- **"Miscellaneous records from Tolland Vol. S.," *The Jewett family of America Quarterly*, vol. 3, no. 1 (Winter 1955). p. 16.**

CHURCH RECORDS:

- Congregational Church's Church records, 1806–1928, Photocopies at CSL 9FHL film 5,864);
- Baptist Church's "Church Records, 1807–1890" (includes baptisms and admissions 1808–1850, deaths 1807–1849) (originals at CSL) (FHL film 5,862);
- Methodist Episcopal Church's "Church Records, 1832–1928" (baptisms 1837–1838 & marriages 1838) (originals at CSL) (FHL film 5,863).

CEMETERY TRANSCRIPTIONS: The Hale Collection identifies people in order of physical proximity buried in about three named sites in Tolland Township.[942] Compare with Daniel Hearn's 1979 copy of 259 pre-1800 gravestones in three Tolland cemeteries.[943] See also, Joel N. Eno's "Connecticut Cemetery Inscriptions ," *NEHGR*, vol. 72: 63 & 73:38 (1918).

OTHER NOTEWORTHY SOURCES:

- J. R.Cole's *History of Tolland County, Connecticut: including its early settlement and progress to the present time; a description of its historic and interesting localities; sketches of its towns and villages: portraits of some of its prominent men, and biographies of many of its representative citizens* (New York: W. W. Preston & Co., 1888);
- Walter E Corbin and Robert J. Dunkle's Corbin manuscript collection (vol. 2. Records of Connecticut towns including Gilead, Norwalk, Stafford, Stamford, West Stafford, and Willington,), 3 CD-ROMs (Boston: NEHGS, c2003–c2005).

TORRINGTON

Barbour's typescript volume for Torrington.[944] unlike the GPC edition[945] begins:

---

942 Charles R. Hale, "Headstone Inscriptions of the Town of Tolland, Connecticut" (bound manuscript at CSL) (FHL film 3,366). Hale names these North yard, East yard, & South yard.

943 Daniel Hearn, "Connecticut gravestones, early to 1800," manuscript (FHL film 1,477,477, item 46).

944 See How to Use This Book, note 3, above..

945 Marsha Wilson Carbaugh, *Barbour Collection of Connecticut Town Vital Records: Torrington 1740-1850, Union 1734-1850, Voluntown 1708-1850*, vol. 47, (Baltimore: GPC, 2002). Digitized at *Ancestry.com*.

> This volume contains a list alphabetically arranged of all the vital records of the town of Torrington from its incorporation to about 1850. This list was taken from a set of cards[946] based on a copy of the Torrington Vital Records made in 1916 by James N. Arnold, of Providence, R.I. The entire record for the town prior to 1850 is found in one volume. The Arnold Copy, now in the possession of the Connecticut State Library, has not been compared with the original and doubtless errors exist. It is hoped that as errors or omissions are found notes will be entered in this volume and on the cards which are included in the General Index of Connecticut Vital Records also in the possession of the Connecticut State Library.
>
> Hartford, Conn., May, 1927.[947]

VITAL RECORDS: The Torrington volume includes vital records as early as 1736 and as late as 1850. Barbour abstracted Torrington's "Births, Marriages, Deaths vol. 1, 1741–1849" Torrington Town Hall, (FHL film 1,450,835, item 1).

Pre-1850 vital records not abstracted by Barbour may be found in Torrington's Volume 2, Births (1847–1866), Marriage certificates, (1850–1855) Marriages by school district (1855–1866), Deaths 1862–1864 (FHL film 1,450,835, item 2).

FHL also catalogs as Torrington vital records:

- **Elizabeth B. Gaylord's "Records of Deaths in Torringford, 1777–1884" (manuscript in CSL) (FHL film 1,014,185, item 6);**
- **Mrs. Roderick Bissell's Records of deaths in Torringford Society, 1855–1884, manuscript at CSL (FHL film 1,014,185, item 5);**
- **William H. Moore's "Record of deaths in Torringford, 1777–1864", manuscript at CSL (FHL film 1,014,185, item 4).**

CHURCH RECORDS:

- First Congregational Church's "Church Records, 1741–1901" (marriages 1743–1775 & 1792–1808; baptisms 1742–1775, 1792–1803 & 1828–1876; and deaths 1792–1809) (originals at CSL) (FHL film 5,848);
- Torringford Congregational Church Ecclesiastical Society's Death Records, 1746–1864 (FHL 1,014,185);
- Torringford Congregational Church Ecclesiastical Society's Records, 1757–1849 (FHL 5,847).

---

946 Now part of the Barbour Index and interfiled with similar slips from other towns in CSL and in FHL films 2,887 *et seq*. See Introduction above, pp. 1-3.

947 Lucius B. Barbour, *Connecticut Vital Records: Torrington, 1740–1850*, (Hartford, CSL, 1927) page after title page.(FHL film 2,981). Digital images at *AmericanAncestors.org* and *FamilySearch.org*.

CEMETERY TRANSCRIPTIONS: The Hale Collection identifies people in order of physical proximity buried in about 11 named sites in Torrington Township.[948] Compare with Daniel Hearn's 1978 copy of 44 pre-1800 gravestones in two Torrington cemeteries.[949] See also, Charles R. Hale and Mary H. Babin's "Headstone inscriptions, Town of Torrington, Connecticut" (typescript photocopy) (Hartford: CSL, 1934);

OTHER NOTEWORTHY SOURCES:

- "Torringford Deaths, 1777–1884;" CSL; see Appendix A;
- Samuel Orcutt's *History of Torrington, Connecticut: From Its First Settlement in 1737, With Biographies and Genealogies* (Albany: J. Munsell, Printer, 1878);
- Bess Bailey and Merrill Bailey's *Formative years, Torrington, 1737 to 1852* (Torrington: Torrington Historical Society, c1975);
- Charles H. Johnson's Memories of Wolcottville (Torrington: Torrington Historical Society, 1947).

TRUMBULL

VITAL RECORDS: Trumbull was founded in October 1797, but commenced keeping vital records in September 1796. [950] Its population was 1291 in the 1800 census[951] and 1,309 in 1850 Census.[952] The records Barbour should have abstracted are:

- **Trumbull's "Town Records, 1796–1848" (originals in Trumbull Town Hall) (includes records of births, marriages, deaths) (FHL film 1,491,334);**
- **Trumbull's "Records of Births, Marriages, and Deaths, vol. 1–2, 1848–1906," Trumbull Town Hall, (FHL film 1,491,335).**

These records have been abstracted by Connecticut journals:

- **Robert A, Locke, Jr.'s Trumbull Vital Records – 1734–1841," *CA*, vol. 49, No. 4 (May 2007) 151–77;**
- **Linda MacLachlan and Jan Taylor's "Trumbull, Connecticut: A Town Barbour Missed," *CN*, vol. 41, p. 136 (Sep 2008);**
- **Harlan R. Jessup's "Births, Marriages, and Deaths for Trumbull, CT, 1848–1851" *CA*, Vol. 54, No. 3 (Feb 2012).**

See also, Harlan R. Jessup's "Sources for Early Trumbull, CT," *CA*, Vol. 49, No. 4 (May 2007).

CHURCH RECORDS:

- Congregational Church's "Church Records, 1730–1937" (baptisms 1731–1744), baptisms at Windham 1740 by Rev. Richardson Miner, baptisms 1747–1798, marriages

---

948 Charles R. Hale, "Headstone Inscriptions of the Town of Torrington, Connecticut" (bound manuscript at CSL) (FHL film 3,366). Hale names these Center, Hillside, Old St. Francis, New St. Francis, West Torriungton, Burrville, Hebrew, Torringford, Newfield, Fyler, & Bissell.

949 Daniel Hearn, "Connecticut gravestones, early to 1800," manuscript (FHL film 1,477,477, item 60).

950 Linda MacLachlan and Jan Taylor, "Trumbull, Connecticut: A Town Barbour Missed," *CN*, vol. 41:136 (Sep 2008)

951 U.S. Census, Trumbull, Fairfield Connecticut, p. 183.

952 U.S. Census, Trumbull, Fairfield Connecticut, p. 670.

1747–1791, deaths 1786–1790, and vital records 1825–1890, (FHL film #5,872) and more baptisms, marriages, deaths on FHL film 1,014,186);

- Christ Church at Tashua's Records 1787–1923 (FHL film 5,871);
- William G. and Ada C. Sterling's *Transcript of Births, Baptisms and Marriages: also Membership in Full Communion and Renewed Covenant of the Church of Christ in Unity and North Stratford, Now Trumbull, Conn., 1731–1808 Inclusive* (Bridgeport, Mary Silliman Chapter, DAR, 1954) (FHL film 1,014,187, item 1);
- Christ Church's "Parish register, 1829–1939" (baptisms 1829–1939, marriages 1830–1937, burials 1829–1939) (originals in the archives of the Episcopal Diocese) (FHL film 1,513,534);
- Grace Church at Long Hill's "Parish Registers, vol. 1–2, 1829–1945" (baptisms 1829–1944, marriages 1832–1945, burials 1829–1945) (originals in CSL) (FHL film 1,014,187, item 2);
- Marriages (1830–1932) & burials (1829–1939) at Christ Church of Trumbull (ED Film 1,513,534);
- Baptisms (1829–84), marriages (1832–85) & burials (1829–84) at Grace Church of Trumbull (ED Film 1,513,534).

CEMETERY TRANSCRIPTIONS: The Hale Collection identifies people in order of physical proximity buried in about nine named sites in Trumbull Township.[953] Compare with Daniel Hearn's 1975 copy of 102 pre-1800 gravestones in four Trumbull cemeteries.[954] See also,

- E. Merrill Beach's *They Face the Rising Sun: a Comprehensive Story with Genealogical Material and Complete Charting of Unity Burial Ground, Oldest Cemetery in Trumbull, Connecticut, 1730–1971* (Chester: Pequot Press, c1971);
- Ellwood Count Curtis' *The Unity Burial Ground: Trumbull, Fairfield County, Connecticut* (Cedar Falls, IA: Galactic Press, 2003).

OTHER NOTEWORTHY SOURCES:

- E. Merrill Beach's *Trumbull, church and town : a history of the colonial town of Trumbull and of its church which was the Church of Christ in Unity, the Church of Christ in North Stratford and is now the Church of Christ in Trumbull, 1730–1955* (Trumbull: Trumbull Historical Society, 1972)
- Samuel Orcutt's *History* of the *Town of Stratford and the City of Bridgeport, Connecticut, Part II.*; (New Haven: Fairfield County Historical Society, 1886),

UNION

Barbour's typescript volume for Union,[955] unlike the GPC edition,[956] begins:

---

953 Charles R. Hale, "Headstone Inscriptions of the Town of Trumbull, Connecticut" (bound manuscript at CSL) (FHL film 3,366). Hale names these Tashua, Long Hill, Booth, Brimsmade, Unity, Graveyard, Nichols, Riverside, & Northwest.

954 Daniel Hearn, "Connecticut gravestones, early to 1800," manuscript (FHL film 1,477,477, item 61).

955 See How to Use This Book, note 3, above.

956 Carbaugh, *Barbour Collection: Torrington–Voluntown*, vol. 47. Digital images at *Ancestry.com*.

> This volume contains a list alphabetically arranged of all the vital records of the town of Union from its incorporation to about 1850. This list was taken from a set of cards[957] based on a copy of the Union Vital Records made in 1911 by James N. Arnold, of Providence, R.I. The early vital statistics are scattered through the Town Meetings and Land Records. In this alphabetical list reference to the entries found among the Town Meetings is indicated by "TM" and the pagination, noted in red, is that of the Arnold manuscript. Reference to entries scattered through the Land Records is indicated by the number of the land record volume and the abbreviation "LR". There are three remaining books, each known as Volume 1, but distinguished by the titles "Birth Book No. 1", "Marriage Book No.1" and "Death Book No.1". In this list they are respectively referred to as "1-B", "1-M" and "1-D".
>
> The Arnold Copy, now in the possession of the Connecticut State Library, has not been compared with the original and doubtless errors exist. It is hoped that as errors or omissions are found notes will be entered in this volume and on the cards which are included in the General Index of Connecticut Vital Records also in the possession of the Connecticut State Library.
>
> Hartford, Conn., October, 1921.[958]

VITAL RECORDS: The Union volume includes vital records as early as 1736 and as late as 1738–1854. Barbour abstracted five Union "books:"

- "TM" refers to Union's Town Records, vol. 2, 1718–1749 (contains 1718–1748 records of births, marriages, deaths), Union Town Hall, FHL film 5,874, item 1 or 1,319,916, item 1 or 1,451,122, item 4;
- "2LR" refers to Union's Land Records, vol. 2, 1745–1756, Union Town Hall, (FHL film 5,874, items 2–3);
- "1-B," "1-M," and "1-D" refer to what remains of the pages of three book now rebound as one: Union's vol. 1-B (births, 1749–1851), vol. 1-D (deaths, 1731–1863), vol. 1-M (marriages, 1731–1863), Union Town Hall, FHL film 1,319,915, item 2.

Barbour did not abstract the vital records in:

- **Union's Land Records, vol. 1, 1733–1744, Union Town Hall, (FHL film 5,874, item 1);**
- **Union's Land Records, vol. 3, 1765–1779, Union Town Hall, (FHL film 5,874, item 3);**

---

957 Now part of the Barbour Index and interfiled with similar slips from other towns in CSL and in FHL films 2,887 *et seq*. See Introduction above, pp. 1-3.

958 Lucius B. Barbour, *Connecticut Vital Records Union, 1734–1850*, (Hartford: CSL, 1921) page after title page (FHL film 2,981). Digital images at *AmericanAncestors.org and FamilySearch.org*

- **Union's Vital Statistics, Military Roll, Tax Roll, and Miscellaneous, 1819–1867 (contains a record of births, marriages, deaths in the town of Union 1848–1851, register of births, marriages, deaths in the town of Union 1852–1867) Union Town Hall (FHL film 1,319,916, item 2);**
- **Scott Andrew Bartley's "Unpublished Vital Records of Union, Connecticut," *NEHGR* vol. 171:154 (Spring and Summer 2017).**

See also,

- **Union Town Records, 1751–1862, 5 vols., CSA (CSL 974.62 Un 32);**
- **Scott Andrew Bartley's "Unpublished Vital Records of Union, Connecticut," *NEHGR*, 171:154–58 & 258–60 (2017).**

CHURCH RECORDS:

- Congregational Church's "Church Records, 1759–1922" (includes vital records 1759–1819) (originals at CSL) (FHL film 5,878);
- Eva M. Thrall Smith's "First Congregational Church Records 1824–*1835"* (typescript at CSL) (FHL film 5,901, item 3).

CEMETERY TRANSCRIPTIONS: The Hale Collection identifies people in order of physical proximity buried at about four named sites in Union Township.[959] Compare with Daniel Hearn's 1979 copy of 48 pre-1800 gravestones in one Union cemetery.[960] See also,

- Lucius B. Barbour's "Genealogical Data from Connecticut Cemeteries: Union, Connecticut. Old, New, North and East Cemeteries" (typescript, NEHGS, 1933);
- "Union, Conn. Cemetery Inscriptions Copied by Lucius B. Barbour, 1933, Typed From His Record And Genealogical Notes Added. Old Cem., New Cem., Armour Cem., East Cem., North Cem., Union, Conn." (1949 manuscript at NEHGS).

OTHER NOTEWORTHY SOURCES:

- Charles Hammond and Harvey M. Lawson's H*istory of Union, Conn.* (New Haven: Price, Lee & Atkins, 1893);
- Jeannine M. Upson's *Union lands: a people's history* (Union: Union Historical Society, c1984).

VERNON

VITAL RECORDS: There is no individual volume[961] for Vernon. Vernon was taken from the town of Bolton in 1808, but its vital records prior to 1852 remain in Bolton.[962] Barbour abstracted the slips in his statewide Index[963] from CHS' *Vital Records of Bolton to 1854 and Vernon to 1852*, (Hartford: CHS, 1909) (images at

959 Charles R. Hale, "Headstone Inscriptions of the Town of Union, Connecticut" (bound manuscript at CSL) (FHL film 3,366). Hale names these Union Center, East, Graveyard, & Old Union Center.

960 Daniel Hearn, "Connecticut gravestones, early to 1800," manuscript (FHL film 1,477,477, item 62).

961 See How to Use This Book, note 3, above..

962 Morrison, *Connecting to Connecticut*, 298.

963 The Barbour Index may be viewed only at CSL and on FHL films 2,887 *et seq*. See Introduction above, pp. 1-3

AmericanAncestors.org), which copies them from Vernon's Town Records, 1758–1876, Vernon Town Hall (FHL film 1,319,931, item 1) in two "books:"

- "1" (pp. 155–178) covers births, marriages and deaths 1799 to 1832 from FHL film 1,319,931, item 1, pp. 184–271;
- "2" (pp. 179–206) covers 1833 to 1853 marriages from FHL film 1,319,931, item 1, later pp. 1–47;
- "2" (pp. 207–144) also covers 1847 to 1851 births, marriages and deaths from FHL film 1,319,931, item 1, later pp. 100–144.

CHURCH RECORDS:

- First Congregational Church's Records 1762–1940 (originals at CSL) (FHL film 5,895);
- Herbert A. Porter's First Congregational Church in Vernon; Second Congregational Church in Vernon; First Congregational Church at Rockville; Second Congregational Church at Rockville's Church records, 1762–1945, transcript at CSL (FHL film 5,899);
- Mary Kingsbury Talbott, "Records of the Church in Vernon, Conn., 1762–1824," *NEHGR*, 58:192–69:268;
- Methodist Episcopal Church of Rockville's Church records, 1834–1937, originals at CSL (FHL film 5,903, item 1);
- Rockville First Baptist Church's Church records, 1842–1939, originals at CSL (FHL film 5,896);
- St. John's Church of Rockville's, "Church records, 1827–1924" (includes births 1827–1879) (originals at CSL and ED) (FHL film 5,903, item 2);
- First Congregational Church at Rockville's, "Church Records, 1837–1888" (includes baptisms 1837–1888) (FHL film 5,897);
- Second Congregational Church at Rockville's *Church Records, 1849–1888* (includes baptisms 1849–1872) (originals at CSL) (FHL film 5,898);
- First Congregational Church's "Church Records, 1762–1940" (includes baptisms 1762–1824, marriages 1762–1822, deaths 1774–1824, baptisms 1824–1939, and deaths 1824–1940) (originals at CSL) (FHL film 5,895);
- Herbert A. Porter's "Church Records, 1762–1945" (includes members, marriages, baptisms, births, deaths, etc.) (transcript at CSL) (FHL film 5,899); Births (1827–79) & burials (1872–78) at St. John's Church at Rockville (ED Film 5,903);
- Allyn S. Kellogg's "First Congregational Church Records 1747–1889" (includes baptisms 1747–1889, marriages 1763–1822, deaths 1774–1848) (photocopies and originals at CSL) (FHL film 5,901, items 1-2, 4–5);
- Eva M. Thrall Smith and DAR. Sabra Trumbull Chapter's First Congregational Church records 1824–1835, typescript at CSL (FHL film 5,901, item 3 & 1,014,187, item 4);
- Tolland County, Connecticut, church papers, 1760–1861, originals at CSL (FHL film 1,014,187, item 3).

CEMETERY TRANSCRIPTIONS: The Hale Collection identifies people in order of physical proximity buried in about six named sites in Vernon Township.[964] Compare with

[964] Charles R. Hale, "Headstone Inscriptions of the Town of Vernon, Connecticut" (bound manuscript at CSL) (FHL film 3,366-7). Hale names these Grove Hill, Elmwood, Mt. Hope, Old (2 different locations), & St. Bernard's.

Daniel Hearn's 1979 copy of 94 pre-1800 gravestones in two Vernon cemeteries.[965] See also,

- *Inscriptions From the Cemeteries of the Towns of Bolton and Vernon* (1905/1997 copy at NEHGS);
- Lucius Barnes Barbour's "Inscriptions from Gravestones at Vernon, Conn.," *NEHGR*, vol. 83:357 (19--)..

OTHER NOTEWORTHY SOURCES: George S Brookes' *Cascades and courage: the history of the town of Vernon and the city of Rockville, Connecticut* (Rockville: T.F. Rady and Co., 1955).

VOLUNTOWN

Barbour's typescript volume for Voluntown,[966] unlike the GPC edition,[967] begins:

> This volume contains a list alphabetically arranged of all the vital records of the town of Voluntown from its incorporation to about 1850. This list was taken from a set of cards[968] based on a copy of the Union Vital Records made in 1911 by James N. Arnold, of Providence, R.I. The records her indexed are taken from the first three volumes of vital records. Every entry in the first two volumes has been indexed and in Volume 3 all birth prior to December 31, 1850, all marriages prior to December 31, 1850 and all of the deaths. The record of deaths ends with an entry bearing the date of December 5, 1867. The Arnold Copy, now in the possession of the Connecticut State Library, has not been compared with the original and doubtless errors exist. It is hoped that as errors or omissions are found notes will be entered in this volume and on the cards which are included in the General Index of Connecticut Vital Records also in the possession of the Connecticut State Library.
>
> Hartford, Conn., February, 1919.[969]

VITAL RECORDS: The Voluntown volume includes vital records as early as 1708 and as late as 1866. Barbour abstracted three Voluntown "books:"

- "Vol. 1" is "Voluntown Vital Records, vol. 1 1710–1862, a book unfilmed by FHL, CSL 974.62 fv 889 vi, Hartford;

---

965 Daniel Hearn, "Connecticut gravestones, early to 1800," manuscript (FHL film 1,477,477, item 63).

966 See How to Use This Book, note 3, above.

967 Carbaugh, *Barbour Collection: Torrington–Voluntown*, vol. 47. Digital images at *Ancestry.com*.

968 Now part of the Barbour Index and interfiled with similar slips from other towns in CSL and in FHL films 2,887 *et seq*. See Introduction above, pp. 1-3.

969 Lucius B. Barbour, *Connecticut Vital Records Voluntown, 1708–1850*, (Hartford; CSL,1919) page after title page (FHL film 2,981). Digital images at *AmericanAncestors.org* and *FamilySearch.org*.

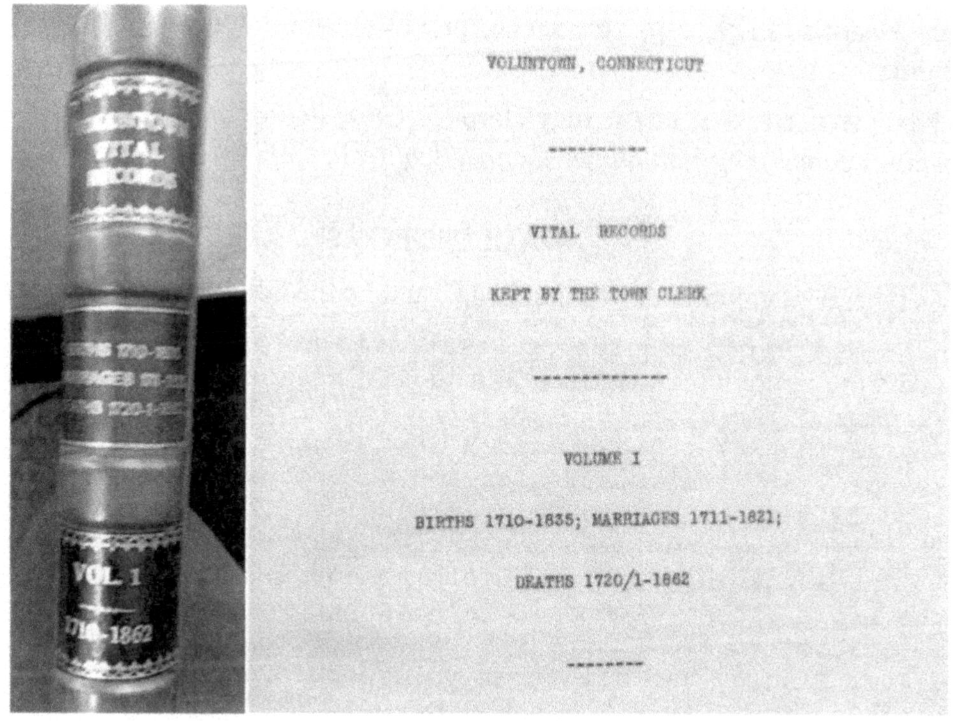

VOLUNTOWN, CONNECTICUT

VITAL RECORDS

KEPT BY THE TOWN CLERK

VOLUME I

BIRTHS 1710-1835; MARRIAGES 1711-1821;

DEATHS 1720/1-1862

Figures 27 & 28: Voluntown Vital Records, Vol. 1

- "Vols. "2" and "3:" are from Voluntown's Records of Births, Marriages, & Deaths, 1808–1943, Voluntown Town Hall (FHL film 1,311,196, items 2–3), **with some omissions**.

CHURCH RECORDS:

- Mrs. J.L. Raymond's "Church Records, 1723–1841" (typescript at CSL) (FHL film 4,307);
- Voluntown Baptist Church's Records 1836–1974, CSA (CSL 974.62 V8891 b);
- Voluntown and Sterling Congregational Church's "Church Records, 1727–1914" (includes baptisms and marriages) (originals at CSL) (FHL films 5,888 and 5,887 or 5,889);
- Emma Finney Welch's "Abstracts From the Records of the Voluntown and Sterling Congregational Church (The Line Church), 1779–1910" (1910 manuscript in Historical Society of Pennsylvania) (FHL film 441,390, item 4);
- Emma Finney Welch's "First Book Records of the First Presbyterian Church of Voluntown, 1723 to 1764" (includes baptisms and marriages) (manuscript in the Historical Society of Pennsylvania) (FHL film 441,390).

CEMETERY TRANSCRIPTIONS: The Hale Collection identifies people in order of physical proximity buried at about 14 named sites in Voluntown Township.[970] Compare with

[970] Charles R. Hale, "Headstone Inscriptions of the Town of Voluntown, Connecticut" (bound manuscript at CSL) (FHL film 3,367). Hale names these Gallup (2 different locations), Robbins, Kennedy, Old (2 different locations), Palmer, ____, Potter, Lewis, Phillips, Bly, Bitgood, & Brown.

Daniel Hearn's 1979 copy of seven pre-1800 gravestones in two Voluntown cemeteries.[971]

OTHER NOTEWORTHY SOURCES: Judy Harpin's *Compilation of facts and not so factual happenings concerning Voluntown, Connecticut* (S.l.: s.n], 1985).

WALLINGFORD

Barbour's typescript volume for Wallingford,[972] unlike the GPC edition[973] begins:

> The vital records of Stratford, prior to 1850 are found scattered through the Proprietors' Records, Volumes 1, 2, 5, 9, 11, 12, 13, 14, 15, 17, 18,19, 21, 22, 23, 24, 27, 28 and 29 of the Land Records,[974] Volume 1 of Vital Statistics and an unpaged book of records kept by Justice Oliver Stanley. The entries in these have been alphabetically arranged and listed.
>
> The abbreviation "PR" refers to entries found in the Proprietors' Records, "V-1" to the volume of Vital Statistics, "O.S." to the private records of Justice Oliver Stanley and all other volume references to the Land Records.
>
> This list was taken from a set of cards[975] based on a copy, of the Wallingford vital Records made in 1914 by Miss Ethel L. Scofield, of New Haven, Conn. The Scofield Copy, now in the possession of the Connecticut State Library, has not been compared with the original and doubtless errors exist. It is hoped that as errors or omissions are found notes will be entered in this volume and on the cards which are included in the General Index of Connecticut Vital Records also in the possession of the Connecticut State Library.
>
> Hartford, Conn., December, 1924.[976]

VITAL RECORDS: The Wallingford volume includes vital records as early as 1671 and as late as 1852. Barbour abstracted 23 Wallingford "books," two of which appear to be uncataloged and unfilmed by FHL:

- "1" and "2" refer to from Wallingford Deeds, vol. 1–2, 1670–1716 (Volumes 1 and 2 include births, marriages and deaths), Wallingford Town Hall, (FHL film 6,018);
- "5" refers to Deeds, vol. 5–6, 1725–1754, Wallingford Town Hall (FHL film 6,019);

---

971 Daniel Hearn, "Connecticut gravestones, early to 1800," manuscript (FHL film 1,477,477, item 64).

972 See How to Use This Book, note 3, above.

973 GOGS, *Barbour Collection of Connecticut Town Vital Records: Wallingford 1670-1850*, vol. 48, (Baltimore: GPC, 2002)..

974 Barbour also abstracts a few vital records from Wallingford Town Clerk, Deeds vol. 7-8 1733-1749, Wallingford Town Hall, FHL Film 6,021.

975 Now part of the Barbour Index and interfiled with similar slips from other towns in CSL and in FHL films 2,887 *et seq*. See Introduction above, pp. 1-3.

976 Lucius B. Barbour, *Connecticut Vital Records: Wallingford, 1670–1850*, (Hartford: CSL,1924) page after title page (FHL film 2,981). Digital images at *AmericanAncestors.org.* and *FamiySearch.org.*

- "7" and "8" refer to Wallingford Deeds vol. 7–8, 1733–1749, (FHL film 6021);
- "9" refers to Wallingford Deeds, vol. 9–10, 1742–1749, (FHL film 6,022);
- "11" refers to Wallingford Deeds, vol. 11, 1746–1751, (FHL film 6,023);
- "12" and "13" refer to Wallingford Deeds, vol. 12–13, 1751–1757, (FHL film 6,024);
- "14" and "15" refer to Wallingford Deeds, vol. 14–15, 1757–1764, (FHL film 6,025);
- "17" refers to Wallingford Deeds, vol. 16–17, 1763–1770, (FHL film 6,026);
- "18" and "19" refer to Wallingford Deeds, vol. 18–19, 1770–1774, (FHL film 6,027);
- "21" refers to Wallingford Deeds vol. 20–21, 1774–1780, (FHL film 6,028);
- "22"and "23" refer to Wallingford Deeds vol. 22–23, 1780–1786, (FHL film 6,029);
- "24" refers to Wallingford Deeds vol. 24–25, 1786–1794, (FHL film 6,030);
- "27" refers to Wallingford Deeds vol. 26–27, 1791–1796, (FHL film 6,031);
- "28" and "29" refer to Wallingford Deeds vol. 28–29, 1796–1801, (FHL film 6,032);
- "PR" is at least 51 pages long and contains records from 1671 to 1679). These records, which remain unfilmed in the town hall,[977] largely replicate those available in Deeds, vol. 1;
- "V-1" refers to Wallingford's Records of Births, marriages, deaths vol. 1–3 (pp.1–344) ca.1762–1888, Wallingford Town Hall, (FHL film 1.405.514);
- "O.S." is an unpaginated book of at least 102 pages containing 1772–1787 records kept by Justice Oliver Stanley. Very few records from the Deed books are repeated in this unfilmed source which may be at the town hall.

See also,

- **Between 420 and 430 abstractions of private records of Billious Avery of Wallingford, in CSL Drawer 380 and not filed in Barbour Index. See Appendix B. They appear to be from "Record of Avery Family in Wallingford, Connecticut: Births, Marriages, and Deaths, 1720–1899." See Appendices A and C.**
- **"Births, Marriages and Deaths of Wallingford, Connecticut: ca. 1670–*1821*" (manuscript in NYGBS) (FHL film 6,052);**
- ***Clippings, Vital Records, From the Norwalk Hour, Beginning With 6 April 1917–1920* (Norwalk: Norwalk Hour, 1917);**
- **The town clerk's office possesses a volume it titles "Church Records."[978]**

CHURCH RECORDS:

- First Congregational Church's "Church Records, 1758–1894" (includes baptisms 1758–1780, 1781–1831, & 1832–1893, marriages 1759–1781, 1781–1822 & 1832–1885, and burials 1760–1780 & 1781–1832) (originals at CSL) (FHL film 6,053);
- Second Baptist Church's Church records, 1790–1822, originals at CSL)FHL film 6,058);
- First Baptist Church's Church records, 1790–1939, originals at CSL (FHL film 6,057);
- St. Paul's Church's "Church Records, 1832–1943" (includes baptisms, marriages, and deaths) (manuscript) (FHL film 1,014,189 or 6,059);

---

977 See, CSL, *First 200 Years.*

978 *Ibid.*

- Baptisms (1832–1900 &1832–1900), marriages (1841–1900 & 1841–1900) & burials (1841–99 & 1841–1900) at St. Paul's Church (ED Films 1,014,189 & 6,059).

CEMETERY TRANSCRIPTIONS: The Hale Collection identifies people in order of physical proximity buried at about six named sites in Wallingford Township.[979] Compare with Daniel Hearn's 1977 copy of 180 pre-1800 gravestones in one Wallingford cemetery.[980] See also,

- Alice Hubbard Breed Benton's "Cemetery Records" (includes Centre Cemetery at Wallingford) (typescript carbon copy at DAR) (FHL film 850,401);
- Alice Hubbard Breed Benton's "Centre Cemetery at Wallingford, Connecticut" (typescript) (FHL film 165,997).

OTHER NOTEWORTHY SOURCES:

- Descendant Committee's *Founders and descendants of Wallingford, Connecticut* (Wallingford: The Descendant Committee, [1970];
- Clara L. Newell, John R. Cottrill, and Clifford Leavenworth, Jr.'s *History of Wallingford, 1669–1935* (Wallingford: [s.n.], 1935);
- C.H.S. Davis' *History of Wallingford, From Its Settlement in 1670 to the Present, Including Meriden & Cheshire* (Meriden: C.H.S. Davis, 1870);
- "Mrs. C.R. Hewitt, a Family Record; CSL; see Appendix A.;
- Charles Henry Stanley's *Early Families of Wallingford, Connecticut* (Baltimore, MD: Genealogical Pub. Co., c1979);
- Josiah Williard's *A census of Newington, Connecticut : taken according to households in 1776* (Hartford: Frederick B. Hartrampf, 1909).

WARREN

Barbour's typescript volume for Warren,[981] unlike the GPC edition,[982] begins:

> This volume contains a list alphabetically arranged of all the vital records of the town of Warren from its incorporation to about 1850. The entire record for this town prior to 1850 is found in two volumes.
>
> This list was taken from a set of cards[983] based on a copy, of the Warren Vital Records made in 1916 by James N. Arnold, of Providence, R.I. The Arnold Copy, now in the possession

---

979 Charles R. Hale, "Headstone Inscriptions of the Town of Wallingford, Connecticut" (bound manuscript at CSL) (FHL film 3,367). Hale names these Center Street, Holy Trinity, St. John's Wallingford Hebrew, In Memoriam, & Polish.

980 Daniel Hearn, "Connecticut gravestones, early to 1800," manuscript (FHL film 1,477,477, item 65).

981 See How to Use This Book, note 3, above.

982 Lillian Bentley Karlstrand, *Barbour Collection of Connecticut Town Vital Records: Warren 1786-1850, Washington 1779-1854, Waterford 1801-1851, Watertown 1780-1850, Westbrook 1840-1851*, vol. 49, (Baltimore: GPC, 2002). Digital images at *Ancestry.com*.

983 Now part of the Barbour Index and interfiled with similar slips from other towns in CSL and in FHL films 2,887 *et seq*. See Introduction above, pp. 1-3.

```
of the Connecticut State Library, has not been
compared with the original and doubtless er-
rors exist. It is hoped that as errors or
omissions are found notes will be entered in
this volume and on the cards which are in-
cluded in the General Index of Connecticut
Vital Records also in the possession of the
Connecticut State Library.
            Hartford, Conn., October, 1926.[984]
```

VITAL RECORDS: The Warren volume includes vital records as early as 1752 and as late as 1849. Barbour abstracted two Warren "books:"

- "1" is from Warren's Records of Births, Marriages, and Deaths, 1765–1835 includes some minutes of meetings, records of delayed registration of births, corrections of birth certificates), Warren Town Hall, (FHL film 1,517,090);
- "2" is from Warren's Records of Births, Marriages, and Deaths, 1833–50. Warren Town Hall, (FHL film 1,517,090).

CHURCH RECORDS: Church of Christ in Warren (formerly East Greenwich Society), "Church Records, 1750–1931" (baptisms 1800–1839, marriages 1801–1839, deaths 1801–1839, baptisms 1859–1930, marriages 1860–1865, and deaths 1774–1931) (originals in CSL) (FHL film 5,949).

CEMETERY TRANSCRIPTIONS: The Hale Collection identifies people in order of physical proximity buried at about three named sites in Warren Township.[985] Compare with Daniel Hearn's 1978 copy of 31 pre-1800 gravestones in one Warren cemetery.[986]

OTHER NOTEWORTHY SOURCES: See state and county resources above, pages 17 to 21.

WASHINGTON

Barbour's typescript volume for Washington,[987] unlike the GPC edition,[988] begins:

```
     The vital records of Washington prior
to 1854 are found in two volumes.
     This alphabetical list was taken from
a set of cards[989] based on a photostat copy of
Volume 1 of the Washington Vital Records and
a manuscript copy of Volume 2 made in 1915
by James N. Arnold, of Providence, R.I.
Both copies are now in the possession of the
```

---

984 Lucius B. Barbour, *Connecticut Vital Records Warren, 1786–1850*, 9Hartford: CSL, 1926) page after title page (FHL film 2,981). Digital images at *AmericanAncestors.org* and *FamilySearch.org.*

985 Charles R. Hale, "Headstone Inscriptions of the Town of Warren, Connecticut" (bound manuscript at CSL) (FHL film 3,367). Hale names these Old, New, & Averill.

986 Daniel Hearn, "Connecticut gravestones, early to 1800," manuscript (FHL film 1,477,477, item 46).

987 See How to Use This Book, note 3, above.

988 Karlstrand, *Barbour Collection: Warren–Westbrook*, vol. 49. Digital images at *Ancestry.com*.

989 Now part of the Barbour Index and interfiled with similar slips from other towns in CSL and in FHL films 2,887 *et seq*. See Introduction above, pp. 1-3.

```
Connecticut State Library. The Arnold Copy,
has not been compared with the original and
doubtless errors exist. It is hoped that as
errors or omissions are found notes will be
entered in this volume and on the cards which
are included in the General Index of Conne-
cticut Vital Records also in the possession
of the Connecticut State Library.
                    Hartford, Conn., August, 1926.[990]
```

VITAL RECORDS: The Washington volume includes vital records as early as 1748 and as late as 1853. Barbour abstracted two Washington "books:"

- "1" is Washington's "Births, Marriages, Deaths: 1764–1851" (FHL film 1,517,000, item 1);
- "2" abstracts an unfilmed book in the town hall with baptisms circa 1748–1775 on pages 1–23, marriages circa 1751–1791 on pages 30–53, and all vital records 1848–1852 on pages 56–98.[991]

Most of Barbour's 1848–1851 records are included with different pagination and more information in **Washington's "Births, Marriages, Deaths: 1847–1851" (FHL film 1,517,000, item 2)," but some records on the film are not in Barbour.**

CHURCH RECORDS:

- First Congregational Church in New Preston's, "Church Records, 1757–1845" (includes deaths 1808–1845) (originals at CSL) (FHL film 6,106);
- First Congregational Church's, "Records, 1741–1919" (originals at CSL) (FHL film 6,106);
- St. Andrew's Church at Marble Dale, "Church Records, 1784–1939" (includes baptisms 1839–1874, marriages 1839–1870; burials 1839–1874) (originals at CSL) (FHL film 6,107);
- St. John's Church's "Church Records, 1794–1933" (includes baptisms, marriages, and burials) (manuscript) (FHL film 1,014,190);
- Baptisms (1839–74), marriages (1839–74) & burials (1839–74) at St. Andrew's Church at Marble Dale (ED Film 6,107);
- Baptisms (1847–71), marriages (1847–70) & burials (1849–71) at St. John's Church (ED Film 1,014,190).

CEMETERY TRANSCRIPTIONS: The Hale Collection identifies people in order of physical proximity buried at about five named sites in Washington Township.[992] Compare with Daniel Hearn's 1977 copy of 103 pre-1800 gravestones in three Washington cemeteries.[993] See also, Helen S. Boyd's Washington: Inscriptions on All Stones Still Standing in the Cemeteries of the Town of Washington (1948/1997 copy at NEHGS).

---

990 Lucius B. Barbour, *Connecticut Vital Records: Washington, 1779–1854,* (Hartford: CSL, 1926) page after title page (FHL film 2,981). Digital images at *AmericanAncestors.org* and *FamilySearch.org.*

991 In 1936 the Washington town clerk possessed "1 vol. of private records of births, marriages, and deaths in the Town Clerk's office." *Biennial Report* (1936)

992 Charles R. Hale, "Headstone Inscriptions of the Town of Washington, Connecticut" (bound manuscript at CSL) (FHL film 3,367). Hale names these New, Old, New Preston, Private, & Davies.

993 Daniel Hearn, "Connecticut gravestones, early to 1800," manuscript (FHL film 1,477,477, item 67).

OTHER NOTEWORTHY SOURCES: William Cothren's *History of ancient Woodbury, Connecticut, from the first Indian deed in 1659 to 1854: including the present towns of Washington, Southbury, Bethlehem, Roxbury, and a part of Oxford and Middlebury* (vol. 3 contains vital records, including those for ancient Stratford) (Baltimore, MD: GPC, 1997) (FHL film 2,055,359 & 6,181).

WATERBURY

Barbour's typescript volume for Waterbury,[994] unlike the GPC edition,[995] begins:

> This volume contains a list alphabetically arranged of all the vital records of the town of Waterbury from its incorporation to about 1853. The entire record for this town prior to 1853 is found in four volumes. Volume 1 refers to vital statistics found in the first volume of Waterbury Land Records, Volume 2 to a book entitled "First Town Meetings and Highways", Volume 3 to a book of "Family Records" and Volume 4 to a "Book of Marriages".
>
> This list was taken from a set of cards[996] based on a copy, of the Waterbury Vital Records made in 1915 by James N. Arnold, of Providence, R.I. The Arnold Copy, now in the possession of the Connecticut State Library, has not been compared with the original and doubtless errors exist. In "The Town and City of Waterbury, Connecticut, from the Aboriginal Period to the Year Eighteen Hundred and Ninety-five", edited by Joseph Anderson, D.D.,[997] the early vital records are alphabetically arranged by families, and although the Arnold Copy has not been compared in its entirety with this publication, a few marked differences have been noted and preference generally given in the indexing to the Anderson Copy. It is hoped that as errors or omissions are found notes will be entered in this volume and on the cards which are included in the General Index of Connecticut Vital Records also in the possession of the Connecticut State Library.
>
> Hartford, Conn., June, 1925.[998]

---

994 See How to Use This Book, note 3, above.

995 Jerri Lynn Burket, *Barbour Collection of Connecticut Town Vital Records: Waterbury 1686-1853*, vol. 50, (Baltimore: GPC, 2002). Digital images at *Ancestry.com*.

996 Now part of the Barbour Index and interfiled with similar slips from other towns in CSL and in FHL films 2,887 *et seq*. See Introduction above, pp. 1-3.

997 Joseph Anderson's *Town and City of Waterbury, Connecticut, From the Aboriginal Period to the Year 1895* (FHL film 1697783 or 1000151).

998 Lucius B. Barbour, *Connecticut Vital Records: Waterbury, 1686–1853*, (Hartford: CSL, 1925) page after title page (FHL film 2,982). Digital images at *AmericanAncestors.org* and *FamilySearch.org*.

VITAL RECORDS: The Waterbury volume includes vital records as early as 1672 and as late as 1854. Barbour abstracted four Waterbury books:"

- "1" refers to Waterbury's Proprietors Records, vol. 1 1672–1721 (includes family records of births (1672–1782), marriages (1682–1763), and deaths (1684–1826)), Waterbury Town Hall, (FHL film 6,111, item 1);
- "2" refers to Waterbury's Town Records vol. 2, 1741–1820 (contains records of birth, marriage, and death organized by family; Waterbury Town Hall, (FHL film 1,412,840, item 1);
- "3" refers to is Waterbury's Town Records vol. 3, (contains records of marriages, 1820–1851), Waterbury Town Hall, (FHL film 1,412,840, item 2);
- "4" refers to Waterbury's Records of Marriages vol., 1851– 1854 (originals in Waterbury Town Hall (FHL film 1,412,885, item 3).

Other Waterbury vital records are:

- **Waterbury's Record of Births, Marriages, and Deaths, 1852–1871 (Record of marriages, births, deaths 1852–1858 Record of births and marriages 1858–1871) (originals in Town Hall, Waterbury) (FHL film 1,412,840, items 3–4);**
- **Waterbury's undated handwritten book of Town Records vol. 1, 1680–1820 (records birth, marriage, and death arranged by family with no page citations to the original volume), Waterbury Town Hall, (FHL film 1,412,886, item 3).**

CHURCH RECORDS:

- St. John's Church's "Church Records, 1761–1927" (baptisms 1830–1877, marriages 1830–1876, and burials 1830–1877) (originals at CSL) (FHL film 6,144);
- First Church of Christ's "Church Records, 1770–1895" (includes marriages, baptisms and deaths) (manuscript) (FHL film 1,014,191 or 6,146);
- Baptisms (1830–77), marriages (1830–76) & burials (1830–77) at St. John's Church (ED Film 6,144).

CEMETERY TRANSCRIPTIONS: The Hale Collection identifies people in order of physical proximity buried at about 18 named sites in what was then Waterbury Township.[999] Compare with Daniel Hearn's 1977 copy of 17 pre-1800 gravestones in two Waterbury cemeteries.[1000] The Hale Collection also identifies people in order of physical proximity buried at about one named sites in what was then Middlebury Township.[1001] Compare with Daniel Hearn's 1976 copy of eight pre-1800 gravestones in one Middlebury cemetery.[1002] See also,

- Charles R. Hale's "WPA Cemetery Records, Waterbury, Connecticut" (1937 transcript at FHL);

---

999 Charles R. Hale, "Headstone Inscriptions of the Town of Waterbury, Connecticut" (bound manuscript at CSL) (FHL film 3,368-9). Hale names these Calvary, New St. Joseph's Old St. Joseph's Riverside, Pine Grove, Russian Orthodox Greek Catholic, Lithuanian Association, Brockett Hill, Waterville, Star Lodge, Waterbury Hebrew Benefit, Brass City Lodge, Workingman's Circle, Melchezidek, Buck's Hill, New pine Grove, East Farms, & City.

1000 Daniel Hearn, "Connecticut gravestones, early to 1800," manuscript (FHL film 1,477,477, item 68).

1001 Charles R. Hale, "Headstone Inscriptions of the Town of Middlebury, Connecticut" (bound manuscript at CSL) (FHL film 3,345). Hale names this Middlebury Cemetery.

1002 Daniel Hearn, "Connecticut gravestones, early to 1800," manuscript (FHL film 1,477,477, item 1).

- Katharine A. Prichard's *Ancient Burying-Grounds of the Town of Waterbury, Connecticut: Together With Other Records of Church and Town* (Higginson reprint of Waterbury: Mattatuck Historical Society, 1917) (FHL film 928,515).

OTHER NOTEWORTHY SOURCES:

- "Elias Ford Account Book," CSL; see Appendix A;
- "John Wells Account Book, 1751–1789," CSL; see Appendix A;
- K. A. Pritchard's *Proprietors' Records of the Town of Waterbury, Connecticut: 1677–1761* (Mattatuck Historical Society, 1911);
- William J. Pape's *History of Waterbury & the Naugatuck* Valley, 2 vols., (1918/1997 copy at NEHGS);
- Sarah J. Prichard's *The Town and City of Waterbury, Connecticut: From the Aboriginal Period to the Year Eighteen Hundred and Ninety-five* (New Haven: Price & Lee, 1896);
- Henry Bronson's *The History of Waterbury, Connecticut: Original Township Embracing Present Watertown and Plymouth, and Parts of Oxford, Wolcott, Middlebury, Prospect and Naugatuck, With an Appendix of Biography, Genealogy and Statistics* (Waterbury: Bronson Bros., 1858);
- Edward R. Lambert's *History of the colony of New Haven : before and after the union with Connecticut: Containing a Particular Description of the Towns Which Composed that Government, viz., New Haven, Milford, Guilford, Branford, Stamford, & Southold, L.I., With a Notice of the Towns Which Have Been Set Off from "the Original Six"* (New Haven: Hitchcock & Stafford, 1838).
- *Town and Miscellaneous Records of Saybrook, Connecticut* (S.I., s.n., 1999).

WATERFORD

Barbour's typescript volume for Waterford,[1003] unlike the GPC edition,[1004] begins:

> The vital records of Waterford prior to 1851 are found in one volume which also contains records of cattlemarks, list of freemen, etc. The "List of the Freemen, 1802–1844" appears in an unpaged section of the volume in semi-alphabetical form. It has been indexed and included with the vital records herein with the date of admission abbreviated "dm.fr." Admission as freemen usually occurred soon after the twenty-first birthday.
>
> This volume contains a list alphabetically arranged of all the Vital Records of the town of Waterford from the earliest records to about 1851. This list was taken from a set of cards[1005] based on a copy of the Waterford Vital Records made in 1911 by James N. Arnold, of Providence, R.I. The Arnold Copy, now in

[1003] See How to Use This Book, note 3, above.

[1004] Karlstrand, *Barbour Collection: Warren–Westbrook*, vol. 49. Digital images at *Ancestry.com*.

[1005] Now part of the Barbour Index and interfiled with similar slips from other towns in CSL and in FHL films 2,887 *et seq*. See Introduction above, pp. 1-3.

> the possession of the Connecticut State Library, has not been compared with the original and doubtless errors exist. It is hoped that as errors or omissions are found, notes will be entered in this volume and on the cards which are included in the General Index of Connecticut Vital Records also in the possession of the Connecticut State Library.
>
> Hartford, Conn., November, 1919.[1006]

VITAL RECORDS: The Waterford volume includes vital records as early as 1741 and as late as 1858 Barbour abstracted Waterford Registrar's Records of Births, Marriages, & Deaths, 1741–1926, Waterford Town Hall, (FHL film 1,376,026. items 1–4).

CHURCH RECORDS:

- Second Baptist Church's "Church Records, 1835–1916" (includes baptisms) (originals at CSL) (FHL film 5,989);
- Mrs. J.L. Raymond's "[First Congregational] Church Records, 1723–1841" (typescript at CSL) (FHL film 4,307);
- First Baptist Church's "Church Records, 1786–1878" (includes baptisms) (originals at CSL) (FHL film 5,988).

CEMETERY TRANSCRIPTIONS: The Hale Collection identifies people in order of physical proximity buried at about 22 named sites in Waterford Township.[1007] Compare with Daniel Hearn's 1982 copy of 16 pre-1800 gravestones in three Waterford cemeteries.[1008] See also,

- Lucius B. Barbour's "Genealogical Data From Connecticut Cemeteries: Waterford, Conn. Headstone Records From East Neck, West Neck, Mullen Hill, Durfey Hill, Quaker Hill And Jordan Cemeteries, And Two Family Yards" (1932 manuscript at NEHGS);
- Benjamin F, Gates' "Graveyard Inscriptions at East Neck, Waterford, Conn.," *NEHGR*, vol.57: 383 (1903).

OTHER NOTEWORTHY SOURCES: See state and county resources above, pages 17 to 21.

WATERTOWN

Barbour's typescript volume for Watertown,[1009] unlike the GPC edition,[1010] begins:

> This volume contains a list alphabetically arranged of all the vital records of the

1006 Lucius B. Barbour, *Connecticut Vital Records: Waterford, 1801–1851*, (Hartford: CSL, 1919) page after title page (FHL film 2982). Digital images at *AmericanAncestors.org* and *FamilySearch.org*.

1007 Charles R. Hale, "Headstone Inscriptions of the Town of Waterford, Connecticut" (bound manuscript at CSL) (FHL film 3,369-70). Hale names these Mullen Hill or Howard, Duffee Hill, Pepper Box Hill, Harkness Estate, Jordan, St. Mary's West Neck, Old Rogers, Gardner, Ames, Graveyard (5 different locations), Old Quaker Hill, New Quaker Hill, Lakes Pond, Sandpit, Brown, Jewish, & Crane Place.

1008 Daniel Hearn, "Connecticut gravestones, early to 1800," manuscript (FHL film 1,477,477, item 69).

1009 See How to Use This Book, note 3, above.

1010 Karlstrand, *Barbour Collection: Warren–Westbrook*, vol. 49. Digital images at *Ancestry.com*..

```
town of Watertown from its incorporation to
about 1850. The entire record prior to 1850
is found in one volume.
     This list was taken from a set of cards[1011]
based on a copy, of the Waterbury Vital Records
made in 1915 by James N. Arnold, of Providence,
R.I. The Arnold Copy, now in the possession
of the Connecticut State Library, has not been
compared with the original and doubtless errors
exist. It is hoped that as errors or omissions
are found notes will be entered in this volume
and on the cards which are included in the
General Index of Connecticut Vital Records also
in the possession of the Connecticut State
Library.
             Hartford, Conn., November, 1926.[1012]
```

VITAL RECORDS: The Watertown volume includes vital records as early as 1745 and as late as 1852. Barbour abstracted the records in Watertown's "Marriages, Births, Deaths, no. O," 1753–1850 Watertown Town Hall, (FHL film 1,521,444 items 1–2). **Barbour does not abstract Watertown's Births, Marriages, Deaths, vol. 1, 1847–1902 (Watertown Town Hall,) (FHL film 1,521,444, item 3).**

FHL also catalogs as Watertown vital records:

- N.S. Richardson's *Historical Sketch of Watertown, From Its Original Settlement: With the Record of its Mortality From 1741 to 1845, Being One Hundred and Four Years* (New Haven: S. Babcock, 1845) (FHL film 908,330);
- N.S. Richardson, Frederick Dayton, M. Grace Dayton, and C.S. Abbott's *Record of the Town of Watertown, Conn: From the Settlement of the Town to the Present Time* (Watertown: Perlee W. Abbott, 1889) (FHL film 1,697,492).

CHURCH RECORDS:

- First Ecclesiastical Society of Watertown's "Church Records, 1785–1887" (includes deaths 1785–1835 & 1835–1874, baptisms 1785–1835 & 1835–1884, and marriages 1835–1875) (originals at CSL) (FHL film 6,091);
- Methodist Episcopal Society's Church records, 1820–1826, originals at CSL (FHL film 6,092);
- Baptisms (1829–38), marriages (1829–39, 1829–45, 1838–45, 1845–50), burials (1829–38 & 1845–49) & Northfield baptisms (1831), marriages (1850–56) at Christ Church (ED Film 6,093);
- Christ Church's "Church Records, vol. 1–6, 8–11, 1784–1913" (includes baptisms, (1829–1838, 1831 & 1838–1845), deaths (1829–1832, 1829–1838; 1838–1845 & 1845–1849), and marriages (1829–1832, 1829–1839, 1838–1845 & 1845–1850)) (originals in CSL) (FHL film 6,093).

[1011] Now part of the Barbour Index and interfiled with similar slips from other towns in CSL and in FHL films 2,887 *et seq*. See Introduction above, pp. 1-3.

[1012] Lucius B. Barbour, *Connecticut Vital Records: Watertown, 1780–1850*, (Hartford: CSL,1926) page after title page (FHL film 2,982). Digital images at *AmericanAncestors.org* and *FamilySearch.org*.

- **CEMETERY TRANSCRIPTIONS:** The Hale Collection identifies people in order of physical proximity buried at about four named sites in Watertown Township.[1013] Compare with Daniel Hearn's 1976 copy of 83 pre-1800 gravestones in one Watertown cemetery.[1014] See also,
  - *Chronological List of Persons Interred in the Old Cemetery at Watertown, Conn: Including Date of Death, Age, and Family Relation* (Woodbury: Woodbury Reporter Print, 1884) (FHL film 928,097);
  - DAR Sarah Whitman Trumbull Chapter's "The Old Burying Ground of Ancient Westbury and Present Watertown" (Watertown: Sarah Whitman Trumbull Chapter, DAR, 1938).

OTHER NOTEWORTHY SOURCES: DAR Sarah Whitman Trumbull Chapter's *History of Ancient Westbury and Present Watertown: From Its Settlement to 1907* (Waterbury: Hemingway Press, 1907), (FHL fiche 6,071,103).

WESTBROOK

Barbour's typescript volume for Westbrook,[1015] unlike the GPC edition,[1016] begins:

> This volume contains a list alphabetically arranged of all the vital records of the town of Westbrook from its incorporation to about 1851. This list was taken from a set of cards[1017] based on a Photostat copy, of the Westbrook Vital Records made in 1924 and now in the possession of the Connecticut State Library. The entire record of the town prior to 1851 is found in one volume.
>
> The cards, from which this list was made and which are now included in the General Index of Connecticut Vital Records also in the possession of the Connecticut State Library, have not been compared with the original and doubtless errors exist. It is hoped that as errors or omissions are found notes will be entered on them and in this volume.
>
> Hartford, Conn., April, 1924.[1018]

VITAL RECORDS: The Westbrook volume includes vital records as early as 1840 and as late as 1851. Barbour abstracted Westbrook's Records of Marriages, Births, & Deaths,

---

1013 Charles R. Hale, "Headstone Inscriptions of the Town of Watertown, Connecticut" (bound manuscript at CSL) (FHL film 3,370). Hale names these Evergreen, Old, Mt. St. James, & New Evergreen.

1014 Daniel Hearn, "Connecticut gravestones, early to 1800," manuscript (FHL film 1,477,477, item 70).

1015 See How to Use This Book, note 3, above.

1016 Karlstrand, *Barbour Collection: Warren–Westbrook*, vol. 49. Digital images at *Ancestry.com*.

1017 Now part of the Barbour Index and interfiled with similar slips from other towns in CSL and in FHL films 2,887 *et seq*. See Introduction above, pp. 1-3.

1018 Lucius B. Barbour, *Connecticut Vital Records: Westbrook, 1840–1851*, (Hartford: CSL, 1924) page after title page (FHL film 2,982). Digital images at *AmericanAncestors.org* and *FamilySearch.org*..

1840–1854 (contains marriage returns, 1840–1854; and reports of births, marriages, and deaths in the school districts, 1848–1851), Westbrook Town Hall, (FHL film 1,398,797 item 1).

CHURCH RECORDS:

- First Congregational Church's "Church Records, 1724–1838" (includes births and deaths 1725–1730) (photocopy at CSL) (FHL film 5,952);
- Jean Rumsey's *First Congregational Church of Westbrook, Connecticut: Baptisms, Marriages, Deaths, Memberships, 1725–1899, From the First Four Volumes of Records, Supplemented by Gravestone Inscriptions From Westbrook Cemeteries* (Dixon IL: Print Shop, 1979).

CEMETERY TRANSCRIPTIONS: The Hale Collection identifies people in order of physical proximity buried at about four named sites in Westbrook Township.[1019] Compare with Daniel Hearn's 1978 copy of 64 pre-1800 gravestones in one Westport cemetery.[1020] See also,

- "Cemetery Inscriptions of Westbrook, Connecticut" (typescript at NYGBS) (FHL film 5,950);
- Saybrook Third Society's "Inscriptions, Town of Westbrook, Conn. *1738–1909* (NEHGS typescript in RSASC) (images at *AmericanAncestors.org*);
- Lucius B. Barbour's "Inscriptions, Town of Westbrook, Conn., Saybrook Third Society" (1907–1910 manuscript at NEHGS).

OTHER NOTEWORTHY SOURCES: "Pond Meadow-Wright" file," CSL; see Appendix A.

WESTON

Barbour's typescript volume for Weston,[1021] unlike the GPC edition.[1022] begins:

> The vital records of Weston prior to 1850 are found scattered through Volumes 1, 11[sic], and 16 of Land Records and a Book of Marriages dated 1835-1852.
>
> In this alphabetical list of the vital records reference to entries found in the Land Records is indicated by the abbreviation "LR" and the number of the volume; reference to the Book of Marriages is indicated by "Vol.1".
>
> This list was taken from a set of cards[1023] based on a copy of the Weston Vital Records

1019 Charles R. Hale, "Headstone Inscriptions of the Town of Westbrook, Connecticut" (bound manuscript at CSL) (FHL film 3,370). Hale names these Old, Lower, Upper, & New Upper.

1020 Daniel Hearn, "Connecticut gravestones, early to 1800," manuscript (FHL film 1,477,477, item 71).

1021 See How to Use This Book, note 3, above.

1022 GOGS, *Barbour Collection of Connecticut Town Vital Records: Weston 1787-1850, West port 1835-1850, Willington 1727-1851*, vol. 51, (Baltimore: GPC, 2002). Digital images at *Ancestry.com*.

> made in 1911 by James N. Arnold, of Providence, R.I. The Arnold Copy, now in the possession of the Connecticut State Library, has not been compared with the original and doubtless errors exist. It is hoped that as errors or omissions are found, notes will be entered in this volume and on the cards which are included in the General Index of Connecticut Vital Records also in the possession of the Connecticut State Library.
>
> Hartford, Conn., March, 1926.[1024]

VITAL RECORDS: The Weston volume includes vital records as early as 1739 and as late as 1852. Barbour abstracted four Weston "books:"

- "1" is from Weston's Town records, 1835–1895 (contains marriage returns, 1835–1852) Weston Town Hall (FHL film 1,735,804, item 2);
- "LR1' refers to Weston's Land Records, vol. 1, 1787–1794, Weston Town Hall (FHL film 6,232);
- "LR11 [sic]" refers to Weston's Weston Town Clerk, Land records, vol. 6, 1799–1834 (FHL film 6,234) *not vol. 10–11 1809–1815, Weston Town Hall (FHL film 6,236)*
- "LR16" refers to Weston's Land Records, vol. 16, 1824–1833, Weston Town Hall, (FHL film 6,239).

Barbour did not review:

- **Weston's "Marriage Records, 1820–1830, 1845–1905" Weston Town Hall (FHL film 1,435,804 item 4);**
- **Weston's "Records of Births, Marriages, and Deaths in Weston, 1847– 1867." Weston Town Hall (FHL film 1,435,804, item 1);**
- **Harlan R. Jessup's "Births, Marriages, and Deaths for Weston, CT, 1847–1850," *CA*, Vol. 54, No. 2 (Nov 2011).**

CHURCH RECORDS:

- Norfield Congregational Church and Society's "Church Records, 1757–1941" (includes baptisms 1757–1878, marriages 1757–1879, deaths 1805 and 1822–1879) (originals at CSL) (FHL film 6,243);
- Emmanuel Church's Church records, 1845–1942, photocopy at CSL (FHL film 6,244);
- Congregational Society's Church records, 1805–1859, originals at CSL (FHL film 1,014,195, item 2);
- Emmanuel Church at Lyons Plain's "Church Records, 1835–1897" (includes baptisms, marriages and funerals) (originals in CSL) (FHL film 1,014,195);
- Baptisms (1835–97), marriages (1849–95) & burials (1836–93) at Emmanuel Church (ED Film 1,014,195);
- Lemuel B. Hull's "Record of Marriages, Baptisms, Admission to the Communion and Funerals, 1822–1835" (manuscript at NEHGS).

1023 Now part of the Barbour Index and interfiled with similar slips from other towns in CSL and in FHL films 2,887 *et seq*. See Introduction above, pp. 1-3.

1024 Lucius B. Barbour, *Connecticut Vital Records: Weston, 1787–1850*, (Hartford: CSL, 1926) page after title page (FHL film 2,982). Digital images at *AmericanAncestors.org* and *FamilySearch.org*

CEMETERY TRANSCRIPTIONS: The Hale Collection identifies people in order of physical proximity buried at about five named sites in Weston Township.[1025] Compare with Daniel Hearn's 1976 copy of 15 pre-1800 gravestones in one Weston cemetery.[1026] See also, Marshall C. Nye's "Easton, Connecticut Cemeteries," (typescript photocopy at FHL);

OTHER NOTEWORTHY SOURCES: See state and county resources above, pages 17 to 21.

WESTPORT

Barbour's typescript volume for Westport,[1027] unlike the GPC edition,[1028] begins:

> **The vital records of Westport from** the formation of the town to about 1850 are found in one volume.
>
> This alphabetical list was taken from a set of cards[1029] based on a manuscript copy made in 1914 by James N. Arnold, of Providence, R.I. The Arnold Copy, now in the possession of the Connecticut State Library, has not been compared with the original and doubtless errors exist. It is hoped that as errors or omissions are found, notes will be entered in this volume and on the cards which are included in the General Index of Connecticut Vital Records also in the possession of the Connecticut State Library.
>
> Hartford, Conn., October, 1925.[1030]

VITAL RECORDS: The Westport Town volume includes vital records as early as 1835 and as late as 1854. Barbour abstracted Westport's Record of Births, Marriages, Deaths, no. 1, 1847–1851, Westport Town Hall, (FHL film 1480168, item 1).
Additional 1852 to 1854 records not abstracted by Barbour may be found in Westport's Births, marriages, and deaths, 1852–1903, Westport Town Hall, (FHL film 1,480,168, items 2–5).

CHURCH RECORDS:

- Saugatuck Congregational Church's "Church Records, 1830–1926" (includes marriages 1833– 1875, baptisms 1833–1879, deaths 1833–1883, and church register

---

[1025] Charles R. Hale, "Headstone Inscriptions of the Town of Weston, Connecticut" (bound manuscript at CSL) (FHL film 3,371). Hale names these Norfield, Lyons Plain, & Graveyard (3 different cemeteries),

[1026] Daniel Hearn, "Connecticut gravestones, early to 1800," manuscript (FHL film 1,477,477, Item 75).

[1027] See How to Use This Book, note 3, above.

[1028] GOGS, *Barbour Collection: Weston–Willington*, vol. 51. Digital images at *Ancestry.com*.

[1029] Now part of the Barbour Index and interfiled with similar slips from other towns in CSL and in FHL films 2,887 *et seq*. See Introduction above, pp. 1-3.

[1030] Lucius B. Barbour, *Connecticut Vital Records: Westport, 1835–1850*, (Hartford: CSL,1925) page after title page (FHL film 2,982). Digital images at *AmericanAncestors.org* and *FamilySearch.org*

1832–1926 with baptisms, marriages and deaths) (photocopies at the CSL) (FHL film 6,259);

- Holy Trinity Church's "Church Records, 1835–1943" (including baptisms 1835–1943) (original records in the archives of the Episcopal Diocese, Hartford) (FHL film 1,513,534, item 9);
- Christ Church's "Parish Registers, 1836–1943" (includes baptisms 1836–1943, marriages 1836–1942, and burials 1836–1943) (original records in the Episcopal Diocese, Hartford) (FHL film 1,513,534 Items 5–8);
- Barbara Dempsey's "Greens Farms Congregational Church, Fairfield/Westport, Records beginning 1715 [through 1822]," *CA*, Vol. 58, No. 4 (August 2015) through Vol. 61, No. 4; (May 2019).

CEMETERY TRANSCRIPTIONS: The Hale Collection identifies people in order of physical proximity buried at about nine named sites in Westport Township.[1031] Compare with Daniel Hearn's 1975 copy of 129 pre-1800 gravestones in three Westport cemeteries.[1032] See also, Harlan R. Jessup's "The Old Burial Ground at Westport from the 1886 Notebook of Rev. James Edward Coley," *CA*, Vol. 51, No. 3 (Feb 2009).

OTHER NOTEWORTHY SOURCES: Edward Coley Birge's *Westport, Connecticut: the making of a Yankee township* (NYC: Writers Publishing Co,, c1926) (FHL fiche 6,089,086).

WETHERSFIELD

Barbour's typescript volume for Wethersfield,[1033] unlike the GPC edition,[1034] begins:

> **This volume contains a list alphabetically arranged of all the vital records of the town of Wethersfield from its incorporation to about 1868. The entire record of the town prior to 1868 is found scattered through Volumes 1, 2, Part 11 of Volume 3 of Land Records and five volumes of Vital Records. Reference to entries found in the Land Records is indicated by the abbreviation "LR" and the volume number. The page numbers of Volume 4 and 5 of Vital Records, given in red, refer to the pagination of the copy as the pages of the original volumes do not appear to have been numbered.**
>
> **This list was taken from a set of cards[1035] based on a copy of Wethersfield Vital Records made in**

1031 Charles R. Hale, "Headstone Inscriptions of the Town of Westport, Connecticut" (bound manuscript at CSL) (FHL film 3,372). Hale names these Willow Brook, Upper Greene Farms, Lower Greene Farms, Christ Church, Catholic, Evergreen, Post Road, King's Highway, & Taylor.

1032 Daniel Hearn, "Connecticut gravestones, early to 1800," manuscript (FHL film 1,477,477, item 76).

1033 See How to Use This Book, note 3, above.

1034 Debra F. Wilmes, *Barbour Collection of Connecticut Town Vital Records: Wethersfield 1634-1868*, vol. 52, (Baltimore: GPC, 2002).

1035 Now part of the Barbour Index and interfiled with similar slips from other towns in CSL and in FHL films 2,887 *et seq*. See Introduction above, pp. 1-3.

> **1917 by James N. Arnold, of Providence, R.I. The Arnold Copy, now in the possession of the Connecticut State Library, has not been compared with the original and doubtless errors exist. It is hoped that as errors or omissions are found, notes will be entered in this volume and on the cards which are included in the General Index of Connecticut Vital Records also in the possession of the Connecticut State Library.**
>
> **Hartford, Conn., February, 1928.**[1036]

VITAL RECORDS: The Wethersfield volume includes vital records as early as **1635** and as late as 1867. Barbour abstracted nine Wethersfield "books:"

- "1" refers to Wethersfield's Records of Births, Marriages, Deaths, vol. 1, 1635–1835, Wethersfield Town Hall, (FHL film 1,315,118, vol.1);
- "2" refers to Wethersfield's Records of Births, Marriages, Deaths, vol. 2, 1726 –1862, Wethersfield Town Hall, (FHL film 1,315,118, vol.2) (index unreliable);
- '3" refers to Wethersfield's Records of Marriages, vol. 3, 1829–1887), Wethersfield Town Hall, (FHL film 1,315,118, vol. 3);
- "4" refers to a paginated copy of Wethersfield's Records of Births, Marriages, Deaths , vol. 4 1847–1868, Wethersfield Town Hall, (FHL film 1,315,118, vol. 4);
- "5" refers to a paginated copy of Wethersfield's Records of Births, Marriages, Deaths, vol. 5 1854–1868, Wethersfield Town Hall, (FHL film 1,315,118, vol. 5);
- "LR1" refers to a 1926 photostat of Wethersfield's Land Records vol. 1 (includes births (1635–1667), marriages (1648–1659), deaths (1649–1660)), Wethersfield Town Hall, (FHL film 5,991, item 2);[1037]
- "LR2" refers to a 1926 photostat of Wethersfield's Land Records vol. 2 (includes birth (1646–1685), marriages (1658–1677), deaths (1711–1757)), Wethersfield Town Hall, (FHL film 5,991, item 4);
- "LR3-B" refers to the second part of a 1926 photostat of Wethersfield's Land Records vol. 3 (1677–1730), Wethersfield Town Hall, (FHL film 5,992, item 1);
- "LR3" refers to an index, Wethersfield's Land Records vol. 3 (1677–1730), Wethersfield Town Hall, (FHL film 5,992, item 2) and duplicate those labeled LR3-B.

See also,

- **Thousands of private records slips in CSL drawer 396 and not interfiled in the Barbour Index. May all be from "Wethersfield Vita; Records, 1887–1904," 9fHl film 3,662, item 12. See Appendix B;**
- **William F.J. Boardman's *An Exact Copy of an Original Manuscript Owned by William F.J. Boardman of A List of Deaths and Burials in The Town of Wethersfield, Connecticut From Jan. 9, 1775 to June 6, 1808* (1910 typescript at NEHGS) (database at *AmericanAncestors.org*);**

[1036] Lucius B. Barbour, *Connecticut Vital Records: Wethersfield, 1634–1868*, (Hartford: CSL, 1928) page after title page (FHL film 2,982). Digital images at *AmericanAncestors.org* and *FamilySearch.org*..

[1037] Filmed letters from CSL dated 26 April 1926 state that the original 3 volumes of Wethersfield Land Records are at CSA.

- **Town of Wethersfield records, 1723–1958. CSL RG 062:159. Administrative, election, court, military, school, tax and vital records for the town of Wethersfield. Archival material;**
- **R. R. Hinman's "Records of Wethersfield, Co.," *NEHGR*, in eight non-consecutive issues in vols. 16, 19, and 20 (Jan, Apr, & Jul 1862; July & Oct 1865; and Jan, Apr & July 1866).**

CHURCH RECORDS:

- First Congregational Church, Roger Welles, Sherman W. Adams, and First Ecclesiastical Society's "Church Records, 1694–1846" (includes marriages and deaths, 1774–1835) (originals and photocopies in CSL) (FHL films 1,014, items 2–5; or 6,015 and 6,016);
- Baptist Church and Society's Church records, 1816–1919, originals at CSL (FHL film 6,017);
- Ecclesiastical Society of Newington's, "Church Records, 1716–1927" (includes baptisms, marriages and intentions, deaths) (originals at CSL) (FHL film 5,352, items 1–3 & 5 or 6,059, item 2);
- Roger Welles' *Early annals of Newington: comprising the first records of the Newington Ecclesiastical Society, and of the Congregational Church connected therewith : with documents and papers relating to the early history of the parish.* (Hartford: Press of the Case, Lockwood & Brainard, 1874);
- Baptist Church's *Articles of faith and covenant of the Baptist Church in Wethersfield, Conn.: with a catalog of its members* (Hartford: Wiley, Waterman & Eaton, 1865).
- Edward Sweetser Tillotson's List of members of the First Congregational Church of Wethersfield, Connecticut, 1694-1908, originals at CSL (FHL film 6,016, item 2);
- Congregational Church's *Manual of the Congregational Church, Wethersfield, Conn : comprising historical and biographical memoranda, chronological catalog, confession of faith, covenant and standing rules, and present list of the church* (Hartford: Charles Montague, 1860 (FHL film 1,598,359, item 21).

CEMETERY TRANSCRIPTIONS: The Hale Collection identifies people in order of physical proximity buried at about four named sites in Wethersfield Township.[1038] Compare with Daniel Hearn's 1978 copy of 384 pre-1800 gravestones in one Wethersfield cemetery.[1039] See also,

- George Wilson Adams and Charles Stoddard Adams's "Wethersfield (Village) Cemetery Records, 1887–1947" (manuscript in CSL) (FHL film 6,014);
- Edward Sweetser Tillotson's *Wethersfield Inscriptions: A Complete Record of the Inscriptions in the Five Burial Places in the Ancient Town of Wethersfield, Including the Towns of Rocky Hill, Newington and Beckley Quarter (in Berlin), Also a Portion of the Inscriptions in the Oldest Cemetery in Glastonbury* (Hartford: William F.J. Boardman, 1899) (FHL film 908,332);

1038 Charles R. Hale, "Headstone Inscriptions of the Town of Wethersfield, Connecticut" (bound manuscript at CSL) (FHL film 3372). Hale names these Village, Emmanuel, Cedar Hill, & States Prison.

1039 Daniel Hearn, "Connecticut gravestones, early to 1800," manuscript (FHL film 1477477, Item 78).

- *Exact Copy of An Original Manuscript Owned by William F. J. Boardman of A List of Deaths and Burials in The Town of Wethersfield, Connecticut From Jan. 9, 1775 to June 6, 1808.*, 1910;" NEHGS typescript, RSASCs, Boston;
- Gladys G. Macdonough's S*tone and the spirit: a walking tour guide to the ancient burying ground in the Wethersfield Village Cemetery* (Wethersfield: Wethersfield Historical Society, c1987).

OTHER NOTEWORTHY SOURCES:

- " Jeremiah Seymour's Account Book, 1790–1878," CSL; see Appendix A;
- Sherman W. Adams' *History of Ancient Wethersfield, Connecticut: Comprising the Present Towns of Wethersfield, Rocky Hill, and Newington: and of Glastonbury Prior to Its Incorporation in 1693, from Date of Earliest Settlement Until the Present Time* (New York: Grafton Press, 1904);
- Frances Wells Fox's *Wethersfield and her daughters: Glastonbury, Rocky Hill, Newington, from 1634 to 1934* (Hartford: The Case, Lockwood & Brainard Co., (c.1934).

WILLINGTON

Barbour's typescript volume for Willington,[1040] unlike the GPC edition,[1041] begins:

> This volume contains a list alphabetically arranged of all the vital records of the town of Willington from its incorporation to about 1851. This list was taken from a set of cards[1042] based on a copy of Wethersfield Vital Records made by James N. Arnold, of Providence, R.I. A few of the early vital statistics are scattered through a volume of Town Meetings and reference to these is herein noted by the abbreviation "TM". The first four volumes of vital records are known as "Book A", "Book B", "Book C" and Book D" and references to entries in these is indicated by the letters "A", "B", "C" and "D".
>
> The Arnold Copy, now in the possession of the Connecticut State Library, has not been compared with the original and doubtless errors exist. t is hoped that as errors or omissions are found notes will be entered in this volume and on the cards which are included in the General Index of Connecticut Vital Records also in the possession of the Connecticut State Library.
>
> Hartford, Conn., November, 1921.[1043]

[1040] See How to Use This Book, note 3, above.

[1041] GOGS, *Barbour Collection: Weston–Willington*, vol. 51. Digital images at *Ancestry.com*.

[1042] Now part of the Barbour Index and interfiled with similar slips from other towns in CSL and in FHL films 2,887 *et seq*. See Introduction above, pp. 1-3.

[1043] Lucius B. Barbour, *Connecticut Vital Records: Willington, 1727–1851,* (Hartford: CSL, 1921) page after title page (FHL film 2,983). Digital images at *AmericanAncestors.org* and *FamilySearch.org*.

VITAL RECORDS: The Willington volume includes vital records as early as 1723 and as late as 1853. Barbour abstracted five Winnington "books:"

- "A" refers to Willington's Records of Births, Marriages, Deaths vol. A 1720–1790, Willington Town Hall, (FHL film 1,376,042, item 1);
- "B" refers to Willington's Records of Births, Marriages, Deaths vol. B 1760–1798, Willington Town Hall, (FHL film 1,376,042, item 1, last part);
- "C" refers to Willington's Records of Births, Marriages, Deaths vol. C 1788–1853, Willington Town Hall, (FHL film 1,376,042, item 2);
- "D" refers to Willington's Records Births, Marriages, Deaths 1819–1854, Willington Town Hall (FHL film 1,376,043, item 1);
- "TM" refers to Willington's Town Records, 1722–1912 (contains some records of birth), Willington Town Hall, (FHL film 1,376,043, item 2).

Barbour did not abstract:

- **Willington's Births, Marriages, and Deaths, 1847–1877, Willington Town Hall (FHL film 1,376,043, item 3);**
- **Willington Vital Records (original marriage certificates) circa 1837–1854, CSL (CSA RG 072.002, Box 18).**

CHURCH RECORDS:

- Baptist Church's "Church Records, 1828–1844" (includes baptisms and deaths) (typescript at American Baptist Historical Society in Chester PA) (FHL film 5,972);
- Congregational Church's "Church Records, 1759–1911" (includes baptisms (1759–1793, 1791–1804 & 1840–1867), marriages (1760–1761, 1791–1793, 1840–1857 & 1872), and deaths 1840–1868) (photocopies at CSL) (FHL film 5,981);
- Ruth A. Powers' List of members of the Methodist Episcopal Church, Willington, Connecticut, typescript (FHL film 1,015,121, item 1).

CEMETERY TRANSCRIPTIONS: The Hale Collection identifies people in order of physical proximity buried at about five named sites in Willington Township.[1044] Compare with Daniel Hearn's 1985 copy of 105 pre-1800 gravestones in two Willington cemeteries.[1045] See also,

- Grace Olive Chapman's "Moose Meadow Cemetery, Willington, Connecticut" (Mss A 2863), RSASC, NEHGS);
- Grace Olive Chapman's "Cemetery inscriptions: Village Hill, Willington, Tolland County, Connecticut" (typescript at NEHGS);
- Joel N. Eno's "Connecticut Cemetery Inscriptions," *NEHGR*, 66:38–42 (Jan 1912), 69:274–80, 334–42 (Jul–Oct 1915), 70:239–45 (Jul 1916).

OTHER NOTEWORTHY SOURCES:

- Walter E Corbin and Robert J. Dunkle's *Corbin manuscript collection* (vol. 2. Records of Connecticut towns including Gilead, Norwalk, Stafford, Stamford, West Stafford, and Willington,), 3 CD-ROMs (Boston: NEHGS, c2003–c2005);

1044 Charles R. Hale, "Headstone Inscriptions of the Town of Willington, Connecticut" (bound manuscript at CSL) (FHL film 3,372). Hale names these Old Willington Hill, New Willington Hill, Morse Meadow, Village Hill, & Stanton.

1045 Daniel Hearn, "Connecticut gravestones, early to 1800," manuscript (FHL film 1,477,477, item 79).

- Willington Historical Society's *Chronology of Willington, Connecticut, 1727–1927 : the first two hundred years* (Willington: Willington Historical Society, c1977).

WILTON

Barbour's typescript volume for Wilton,[1046] unlike the GPC edition,[1047] begins:

> The vital records of Wilton from the formation of the town to about 1850 are found in one volume.
>
> This alphabetical list was taken from a set of cards[1048] based on a manuscript copy made in 1915 by James N. Arnold, of Providence, R.I. The Arnold Copy, now in the possession of the Connecticut State Library, has not been compared with the original and doubtless errors exist. It is hoped that as errors or omissions are found, notes will be entered in this volume and on the cards which are included in the General Index of Connecticut Vital Records also in the possession of the Connecticut State Library.
>
> Hartford, Conn., February, 1926.[1049]

VITAL RECORDS: The Wilton volume includes vital records as early as 1818 and as late as 1852. Barbour abstracted Wilton's Records of Births, Marriages, & Deaths, vol. 1, 1776–1852, Wilton Town Hall, (FHL film 1,435,805, item 1).

CHURCH RECORDS:

- St. Matthew's Church's "Church Records, 1802–1952" (includes baptisms, burials, and marriages) (originals in CSL) (FHL film 1,015,121 or 6,254);
- Aaron Fancher and Lester L. Card's "Marriage Records of Aaron Fancher, Justice of the Peace, Poundridge [sic], N.Y., 1838–1871" (1931 typescript at NYGBS) (FHL film 17,860);
- David H. Van Hoosear's "Wilton Congregational Church Records: Births, Baptisms and Marriages, 1698–1816" (manuscript in CSL) (FHL film 1,015,121 item 2);
- Baptisms (1834–92), marriages (1834–92) & burials (1834–92) at St. Matthew's Church (ED Film 6,254);
- Lester Card's Methodist Church at Bald Hill, Records ca. 1822-1900 (typescript includes deaths) (FHL film 1,015,121);

1046 See How to Use This Book, note 3, above.

1047 Debra F. Wilmes, *Barbour Collection of Connecticut Town Vital Records: Wilton 1802-1850, Winchester 1771-1858, Wolcott 1796-1854, Woodbridge 1784-1832, Woodbury 1674-1850, Woodstock 1848-1866*, vol. 53, (Baltimore: GPC, 2002). Digitized at *Ancestry.com*.

1048 Now part of the Barbour Index and interfiled with similar slips from other towns in CSL and in FHL films 2,887 *et seq*. See Introduction above, pp. 1-3.

1049 Lucius B. Barbour, *Connecticut Vital Records Wilton, 1802–1850*, (Hartford: CSL, 1926) page after title page (FHL film 2,983). Digital images at *AmericanAncestors.org* and *FamilySearch,org*.

- Robert H. Russell's "Wilton, CT Congregational Church Vital Records 1725–1805," *CN*, (September 1991) and in *Ricker Compilation*.

CEMETERY TRANSCRIPTIONS: The Hale Collection identifies people in order of physical proximity buried at about 10 named sites in Wilton Township.[1050] Compare with Daniel Hearn's 1976 copy of 50 pre-1800 gravestones in one Wilton cemetery.[1051] See also, Wilton's Records of Births, Marriages, & Deaths, vol.4, 1852–1880, (includes some transcriptions by David H. Van Hoosear of early cemetery inscriptions and early Congregational church records of the town) Wilton Town Hall (FHL film 1,435,805, item 4).

OTHER NOTEWORTHY SOURCES:

- Mariam Olmstead's "Wilton Parish, 1726–1800: a historical sketch," digital images at *FamilySearch,org*;
- Aaron Fancher and Lester L. Card's Marriage records of Aaron Fancher, Justice of the Peace, Poundridge [sic], N.Y., 1838–1871 (includes records of persons residing in Ridgefield, Wilton, Norwalk, and Stamford) typescript at NYGBS (FHL film 17,860, item 2);
- Robert H., Russell's *Wilton, Connecticut: three centuries of people, places and progress* (Wilton: Wilton Historical Society, c2004).

WINCHESTER

Barbour's typescript volume for Winchester,[1052] unlike the GPC edition,[1053] begins:

> The vital records of Winchester, prior to 1858, are found in two volumes and in a record kept by the Rev. Frederick Marsh.
>
> This alphabetical list was taken from a set of cards[1054] based on a manuscript copy of the Winchester Vital Records made in 1915 by James N. Arnold, of Providence, R.I. Reference to entries found in the Rev. Marsh's book is indicated by the volume number "3" and the pagination of the Arnold Copy.
>
> The Arnold Copy, now in the possession of the Connecticut State Library, has not been compared with the original and doubtless errors exist. It is hoped that as errors or omissions are found, notes will be entered in this volume and on the cards which are included in the General Index of

---

1050 Charles R. Hale, "Headstone Inscriptions of the Town of Wilton, Connecticut" (bound manuscript at CSL) (FHL film 3,372). Hale names these Sharp's Hill, Joe's Hill, Old, Comstock, St. Matthew's. Hillside, Morgan-Davis, Zion Hill, Roscoe, & DeForest.

1051 Daniel Hearn, "Connecticut gravestones, early to 1800," manuscript (FHL film 1,477,477, item 80).

1052 See How to Use This Book, note 3, above.

1053 Wilmes, *Barbour Collection: Wilton–Woodstock*, vol. 53. Digitized at *Ancestry.com*.

1054 Now part of the Barbour Index and interfiled with similar slips from other towns in CSL and in FHL films 2,887 *et seq*. See Introduction above, pp. 1-3.

```
Connecticut Vital Records also in the possession
of the Connecticut State Library.
                    Hartford, Conn., April, 1927.[1055]
```

VITAL RECORDS: The Winchester volume includes vital records as early as 1736 and as late as 1854, but Morrison states that birth, marriage & death records begin in 1750.[1056] Barbour abstracted three Winchester "books:"

- "1" refers to Winchester's "Winchester Town Records, No. 1, 1771–1782" (Includes records of births, marriages, deaths, 1756–1818 Winchester Town Hall (FHL film 1,503,204, item 1;
- "2" refers to Winchester's Births, Marriages, Deaths, 1771–1856 (Records are arranged in family groups) Winchester Town Hall (FHL film 1,503,204 item 2);
- "3" refers to First Congregational Church at Winchester Center's Church Records, 1768–1908 (includes records kept by Rev. Frederick Marsh, 1809–1856, deaths 1809–1858) originals at the CSL, Hartford (FHL film 6,073).

Barbour did not abstract Winchester's "Births, Marriages, and Deaths, 1847–1868" (FHL film 1,503,204, items 3–4).

CHURCH RECORDS:

- First Congregational Church at Winchester Center and First Ecclesiastical Society's "Church Records, 1768–1857" (includes baptisms 1770–1785 & 1790–1857, marriages 1773–1788 & 1791–1803, and deaths 1809–1857 (FHL film 6,072);
- Frederick Marsh's First Congregational Church at Winchester Center, Records 1809–1858, CSA (CSL 974.62 W721c rm);
- First Congregational Church at Winsted's, "Church Records, 1784–1927" (includes baptisms 1801–1843, marriages 1806–1841, and deaths 1806–1842 (originals at CSL) (FHL film 6,070);
- First Ecclesiastical Society's "Church Records, 1768–1908" (includes baptisms 1770–1785 & 1790–1857, marriages 1773–1788 & 1791–1803, and deaths 1809–1857) (originals at CSL) (FHL films 6,072–3);
- Winsted Trinity Church's Records 1835–1923, originals at CSL (FHL film 6,260, item 2);
- St. James Church in Winsted's, "Church Records, 1848–1953" (includes baptisms 1848–1900, marriages 1845–1900, and burials 1848–1900) (originals at CSL) (FHL film 6,074);
- Second Congregational Church at Winsted's, "Church Records, 1853–1952" (includes baptisms 1855–1951 and deaths 1854–1951);
- Mrs. William Allen's "First Congregational Church Records" (includes Winsted baptisms, marriages, deaths) (typescript at CSL) (FHL film 6,260, item 1);
- Baptisms (1848–1900), marriages (1848–1900) & burials (1848–1900) at St. James' Church in Winsted (ED Film 6,076).

[1055] Lucius B. Barbour, *Connecticut Vital Records: Winchester, 1771–1858*, (Hartford: CSL, 1927) page after title page (FHL film 2,983). Digital images at *American Ancestors.org* and *FamilySaerch.org.*

[1056] Morrison, *Connecting with Connecticut*, 150

CEMETERY TRANSCRIPTIONS: The Hale Collection identifies people in order of physical proximity buried at about 10 named sites in Winchester Township.[1057] Compare with Daniel Hearn's 1978 copy of 39 pre-1800 gravestones in two Winchester cemeteries.[1058]

OTHER NOTEWORTHY SOURCES: J. Boyd's *Annals & Family Records of Winchester* (Hartford: Case, Lockwood & Brainard, 1873).

WINDHAM

Barbour's typescript volume for Windham,[1059] unlike the GPC edition,[1060] begins:

> This volume contains a list alphabetically arranged of all the vital records of the town of Windham from its incorporation to about 1850. This list was taken from a set of cards[1061] based on a copy of the Windham Vital Records made in 1911 by James N. Arnold, of Providence, R.I. The records here indexed are taken from the first four volumes of vital records.
>
> Every entry in the first three volumes has been indexed and in Volume 4 all births prior to December 31, 1850, all marriages prior to December 31, 1850, and all of the deaths. The record of deaths ends with an entry bearing the date of September 7, 1860. The Arnold Copy, now in the possession of the Connecticut State Library, has not been compared with the original and doubtless errors exist. It is hoped that as errors or omissions are found notes will be entered in this volume and on the cards which are included in the General Index of Connecticut Vital Records also in the possession of the Connecticut State Library.
>
> Hartford, Conn., September, 1920.[1062]

VITAL RECORDS: The Windham volume includes vital records as early as 1682 and as late as 1860 and as late as 1852. Barbour abstracted five Windham "books:"

- "A" and "1" refer to Windham's "Windham Records A, Births Marriages, Deaths," (1707–1766). Windham Town Hall, (FHL film 1,376,454, item 1) which includes

---

1057 Charles R. Hale, "Headstone Inscriptions of the Town of Winchester, Connecticut" (bound manuscript at CSL) (FHL film 3,372-3). Hale names these Forest View, Winchester Center, Central, St. Joseph's Hemlock, Wallins Hill, Danbury Quarter, Hurlbut, New St. Joseph's & New Winchester Center.

1058 Daniel Hearn, "Connecticut gravestones, early to 1800," manuscript (FHL film 1,477,477, item 81).

1059 See How to Use This Book, note 3, above.

1060 Carole Magnuson, *Barbour Collection of Connecticut Town Vital Records: Windham 1692-1850*, vol. 54, (Baltimore: GPC, 2002). Digital images at *Ancestry.com*.

1061 Now part of the Barbour Index and interfiled with similar slips from other towns in CSL and in FHL films 2,887 *et seq*. See Introduction above, pp. 1-3.

1062 Lucius B. Barbour, *Connecticut Vital Records: Windham, 1692–1850*, (Hartford; CSL, 1920) page after title page (FHL film 2,983). Digital images at *AmericanAncestors.org* and *FamilySearch.org*..

unnumbered pages matching significant portions of Barbour's abstraction of his volume "A," followed by his volume "1." **The filmed pages of "A" appear to have been loose and include many early names and pages not abstracted by Barbour;**

- "2" refers to Windham's Records, Births, Marriages, Deaths, vol. B (1757–1781) Windham Town Hall (FHL film 1,376,454, item 2), matches significant portions of Barbour's abstraction of volume "2." **It also appears to contain loose pages and include many vital records not abstracted by Barbour;**
- "3" refers to Windham's Records, Births, Marriages, Deaths, vol. C (1796–1839) Windham Town Hall (FHL film 1,376,454, item 3);
- "4" refers to the first part of Windham's Births Marriages, & Deaths, D" (1847–1860) Windham Town Hall, (FHL film 1,376,454, item 4).

CHURCH RECORDS:

- Congregational Church of Scotland's, "Church Records, 1732–1915" (includes baptisms 1736–1807 & 1811–1836, marriages 1735/6–1804 & 1811–1816 and baptisms, marriages, and funerals 1844–1869) (originals at CSL) (FHL film 5.819, items 1–5);
- Emma Finney Welch's *Knell, or a Record of the Deaths in the First Society of Windham From 1751 to 1814* (Windham: S. Webb, 1814) (FHL film 441,390 or 1,015,122);
- St. Paul's Episcopal Church's "Church Records, 1832–1925" (includes burials, baptisms, and marriages) (originals at CSL) (FHL film 5,941);
- St. Paul's Episcopal Church's "Church Records, 1833–1950" (photocopy at CSA) (CSL 97462 W742es rb);
- First Congregational Church's "Church Records, 1700–1924" (includes baptisms 1726–1851, marriages 1794–1851, deaths 1801–1851) (originals at CSL) (FHL film 5,942);
- Brunswick (Scotland) Separate Church's Church records, 1746–1846, originals at CSL (FHL film 5,819, item 6);
- CHS and the SMD in CT's "Records of the Congregational Church in Windham, Conn. (Except Church Votes) 1700–1851," Hartford: CHA & SMD, 1943.) (images online at *AmericanAncestors.org*);
- Lillian G. Mattoon's *Parish Records, St. Paul's Church, Windham, Conn., 1835–1967* (Windham: L. G. Mattoon, 1967) (FHL film 824,075);
- CHS's *Records of the Congregational Church in Windham, Conn. (Except Church Votes), 1700–1851* (Hartford: CHS and the State SMD, 1943) (FHL film 1,206,439);
- Baptisms (1832–81 & 1834–1967), marriages (1832–81 & 1833–1967) and burials (1832–81 & 1834–1967) at St. Paul's Church (ED Films 6,254 & 824,075).

CEMETERY TRANSCRIPTIONS: The Hale Collection identifies people in order of physical proximity buried at about six named sites in what was then Windham Township.[1063] Compare with Daniel Hearn's 1979 copy of 339 pre-1850 sites in what was then

[1063] Charles R. Hale, "Headstone Inscriptions of Windham, Connecticut" (bound 1800 gravestones in one Windham cemetery.[1063] The Hale Collection also identifies people in order of physical proximity buried at about four named manuscript at CSL) (FHL film 3,373). Hale names these Ancient, Old, New, St. Joseph's. North Windham, & Windham.

Scotland Township.[1064] Compare with Daniel Hearn's 1979 copy of 265 pre-1800 gravestones in two Scotland cemeteries.[1065] See also, Joel N. Eno's "Connecticut Cemetery Inscriptions," *NEHGR*, vol. 71: 200 (1917).

OTHER NOTEWORTHY SOURCES: "Morse's Justice Court Notes," 1784–1801, CSL; see Appendix A.

WINDSOR

Barbour's typescript volume for Windsor,[1066] unlike the GPC edition,[1067] begins:

> This volume contains a list alphabetically arranged of all the vital records of the town of Windsor from its incorporation to about 1850.
>
> This list was taken from a set of cards[1068] based on a copy of the Old Church Record of Matthew Grant, the Windsor entries found in a book published in 1898 by E. Stanley Welles entitled "Births, Marriages and Deaths---Entered in Volumes 1 and 2 of Land Records and No. D. of Colonial Deeds", a few entries from Vol. 1 of Town Records, and a copy of a book in the Town Clerk's Office in Windsor known as "The Loomis Copy". Reference to entries in the Matthew Grant Record, the pages of which are not numbered, is indicated by the abbreviation "MG"; reference to Mr. Welles' book is indicated by the abbreviation "Col." And the folio number; reference to the volume of Town Records is indicated by the abbreviation TR1" and the manuscript pagination. The copy of the Loomis Record is in three books, the first of which covers Volume 1 and has the original pagination, and the other two cover Volume 2, reference to which is indicated herein by the manuscript pagination.
>
> The copies except the Matthew Grant Record, are now in the possession of the Connecticut State Library. These have not been compared with the original and doubtless errors exist. It is hoped that as errors or omissions are found notes will be entered in this volume and on the cards which form the basis of the General Index of Connecticut Vital Records also in the possession of the Connecticut State Library.

1064 Charles R. Hale, "Headstone Inscriptions of the Town of Scotland, Connecticut" (bound manuscript at CSL) (FHL film 3,361). Hale names these Old Scotland, New Scotland, Palmertown, & Fuller.

1065 Daniel Hearn, "Connecticut gravestones, early to 1800," manuscript (FHL film 1,477,477, item 40).

1066 See How To Use This Book, note 3, above.

1067 Lorraine Cook White, *Barbour Collection of Connecticut Town Vital Records: Windsor 1637-1850*, vol. 55, (Baltimore: GPC, 2002).

1068 Now part of the Barbour Index and interfiled with similar slips from other towns in CSL and in FHL films 2,887 *et seq*. See Introduction above, pp. 1-3.

Hartford, Conn., May, 1929.[1069]

VITAL RECORDS: The Windsor volume includes vital records as early as 1638, but Morrison states that birth, marriage & death records begin in 1633. Barbour abstracted seven Windsor "books:"

- "MG" refers to CHS' *Some early records and documents of and relating to the town of Windsor, Connecticut, 1639–1703*, (Hartford: CHS, 1930);
- "Col. 1", "Col. 2," and "Col. D" refer to Edwin Stanley Welles' *Births, marriages and deaths returned from Hartford, Windsor and Fairfield and entered in the early land records of the colony of Connecticut: volumes I and II of Land records and no. D of Colonial deeds* (Hartford: Case, Lockwood & Brainard, 1898) Barbour copies Welles' citations of the original folios (images at AmericanAncestors.org);
- "TR1" refers to Windsor's Land Records, 1640–1919 (Vol. 1 includes a few records of marriages) Windsor Town Hall, (FHL film 6,188);
- "1" refers to Windsor's Records of Births, marriages, deaths vol. 1, 1638–1703, Windsor Town Hall, (FHL film 1,316,427, item 1);
- "2" refers to Windsor's Records of Births, marriages, deaths vol. 2, 1703–1800, Windsor Town Hall, (FHL film 1,316,427, item 2).

Sources Barbour did not review include:

- **Windsor's Records of Births, marriages, deaths vol. 3, 1847–1852 Windsor Town Hall, (FHL film 1,316,427, item 3);**
- **Windsor Vital Records circa 1845–1905, CSL (CSA RG 072 002, Box 18;**
- **Samuel H. Parsons' 'Record of Marriages and Births," NEHGR vol. 5:63 *et seq.*; "Early Records of Windsor CT," *NEHGR*, vol. 5:359. (1851).**

CHURCH RECORDS:

- First Congregational Church, "Church Records, 1636–1832" (includes deaths, baptisms, marriages 1636–1932 & 1723–1806; persons baptized in infancy 1685–1710) (originals at CSL) (FHL film 6,208);
- First Congregational Church, Certificates of Dessenters, Withdrawals & Members 1781–1865, copy at CSL (FHL film 1,015,123, item 1);
- North Windsor Congregational Church's "Church Records, 1761–1794" (includes baptisms 1761–1794, deaths 1768–1790, marriage 1790) (originals at CSL) (FHL film 6,209, item 1);
- Methodist Episcopal Church's "Church Records, 1835–1923" (includes baptisms and marriages) (originals in CSL) (FHL film 1,015,123, item 4);
- Second Congregational Church at Poquonock's "Church Records, 1771–1782" (includes baptisms 1771–1781, marriages 1773–1782, and deaths 1771–1782) (originals at CSL) (FHL film 6,209, item 2);
- Trinity Methodist Episcopal Church's Church records, 1840–1912, originals at CSL (FHL film 6,209, items 3–40);
- Poquonock Congregational Church's "Church Records, 1842–1927" (includes baptisms and deaths) (originals in CSL) (FHL film 1,015,123, items 2–3).

[1069] Lucius B. Barbour, *Connecticut Vital Records Windsor, 1637–1850,* (Hartford: CSL, 1929) page after title page (FHL film 2,983). Digital images at *AmericanAncestors.org* and *FamilySearch.org*..

CEMETERY TRANSCRIPTIONS: The Hale Collection identifies people in order of physical proximity buried at about six named sites in what was then Windsor Township.[1070] Compare with Daniel Hearn's 1978 copy of 325 pre-1800 gravestones in three Windsor cemeteries.[1071] The Hale Collection also identifies people in order of physical proximity buried at about three named sites in what was then Windsor Locks Township.[1072] See also,

- Lucius B. Barbour's "Genealogical Data from Connecticut Cemeteries: Windsor Locks, Grove Cemetery" (1932 manuscript at NEHGS).
- DAR Abigail Wolcott Ellsworth Chapter's *Cemetery Inscriptions in Windsor, Connecticut: Appendix Containing Filley Records* (Windsor: The Chapter, 1929) (FHL film 874,289);

OTHER NOTEWORTHY SOURCES:

- Kent C. L. Avery and Donna Holt Siemiatkoski's *Settlement of Windsor, Connecticut* (S.i.: s.n., 1983) (FHL film 1,440,334, item 5);
- Donna Holt Siemiatkoski's *Surnames in seventeenth century Windsor [Connecticut] and their earliest occurrence: a portion of the work in progress on "The Foundations of Windsor, volume I"* (Windsor: Connecticut Heritage Press, 1994);
- Henry Stiles' *History of Ancient Windsor, Connecticut: Including East Windsor, South Windsor, and Ellington Prior to 1788, the Date of Their Separation from the Old Town; and Windsor, Bloomfield, and Windsor Locks to the Present Time; also the Genealogies and Genealogical Notes of Those Families Which Settled Within the Limits of Ancient Windsor, Connecticut Prior to 1800*, vol. 2 (Albany, NY: J. Munsell, 1863) (FHL film 417,935;
- Samuel H. Parsons' "Record of Marriages and Births, in Windsor, CT," *NEHGR*, 5:63 *et seq*., (January 1851);
- Lloyd Wright Fowles and William Joseph Uricchio's *Fowles History of Windsor, Connecticut, 1633–1900: an original work* ([Windsor: Loomis Institute, c1976);
- Daniel Howard's *New History of Old Windsor, Connecticut* (Windsor Locks: Journal Press, 1935);
- Charles M. Andrews' *River Towns of Connecticut: a study of Wethersfield, Hartford and Windsor* (Salem, MA: Higginson Book Co., [1994];
- R. S. Pitkin's *Descendants of the founders of ancient Windsor* (S.i., S.n., 2005).

WOLCOTT

Barbour's typescript volume for Wolcott,[1073] unlike the GPC edition,[1074] begins:

1070 Charles R. Hale, "Headstone Inscriptions of the Town of Windsor, Connecticut" (bound manuscript at CSL) (FHL film 3,374). Hale names these Palisado, Riverside, Elm Grove, Old Poquonock, St. Joseph's & Northfield.

1071 Daniel Hearn, "Connecticut gravestones, early to 1800," manuscript (FHL film 1,477,477, item 82).

1072 Charles R. Hale, "Headstone Inscriptions of Windsor Locks, Connecticut" (bound manuscript at CSL) (FHL film 3,374). Hale names these Grove, St. Mary's & Dunslow.

1073 See How to Use This Book, note 3, above.

1074 Wilmes, *Barbour Collection: Wilton–Woodstock*, vol. 53 (GPC ed.) Digitized at *Ancestry.com*.

```
This volume contains a list alphabetical-
ly arranged of all the vital records of the
town of Wolcott from its incorporation to about
1854. The entire record of the town prior to
1854 is found in one volume of three parts. Re-
ference to the pagination of the second and third
parts is distinguished from that of the first
part by "D" and "M", respectively, following the
page number.
     This list was taken from a set of cards[1075]
based on a copy of Wolcott Vital Records
made in 1912. This copy, now in the possession
of the Connecticut State Library, has not been
compared with the original and doubtless errors
exist. It is hoped that as errors or omissions
are found notes will be entered in this volume
and on the cards which are included in the
General Index of Connecticut Vital Records also
in the possession of the Connecticut State Li-
brary.
                    Hartford, Conn., January, 1925.[1076]
```

VITAL RECORDS: The Wolcott volume includes vital records as early as 1779 and as late as 1854. Barbour abstracted Wolcott's Town Records, 1779–1854 (contains records of births 1779–1848, marriages 1821–1854, deaths 1802–1843, arranged alphabetically by first letter of surname), Wolcott Town Hall, (FHL film 1,412,960, item 1). But see also,

- **Wolcott's "Land Records, 1796–1818" (volume 1 includes births, marriages and deaths beginning on p. 516.) (originals in Town Hall, Wolcott) (FHL film 6,211);**
- **Wolcott's "Records of Births, Marriages, and Deaths, 1847–1949" (originals in Town Hall) (FHL film 1,412,960, item 2).**

CHURCH RECORDS:

- Congregational Church's "Church Records, 1773–1922" (includes baptisms 1774–1831 & 1834–1874, marriages 1774–1822 & 1838–1859, and deaths 1774–1825 & 1838–1874) (originals at CSL) (FHL film 6,216);
- All Saints Church's "Church Records, 1811–1867" (includes baptisms and marriages, 1840–1849 and 1850–1867) (originals at CSL) (FHL film 6,215);
- Baptisms (1840–47 & 1850–66), marriages (1840–43 & 1851–55) and burials (1840–44, 1849 & 1851–55) at All Saints Church (ED Film 6,215).

[1075] Now part of the Barbour Index and interfiled with similar slips from other towns in CSL and in FHL films 2,887 *et seq*. See Introduction above, pp. 1-3.

[1076] Lucius B. Barbour, *Connecticut Vital Records: Wolcott, 1796–1854*, (Hartford CSL, 1925) page after title page (FHL film 2,983). Digital images at *AmericanAncestors.org* and *FamilySearch.org*.

CEMETERY TRANSCRIPTIONS: The Hale Collection identifies people in order of physical proximity buried at about four named sites in Wolcott Township.[1077] Compare with Daniel Hearn's 1978 copy of 13 pre-1800 gravestones in one Wolcott cemetery.[1078]

OTHER NOTEWORTHY SOURCES:

- S. Orcutt's *History of the Town of Wolcott, From 1731 to 1874: with.... the genealogies of the families of the town* (Waterbury: American Printing Co., 1874);
- Henry Bronson's *The History of Waterbury, Connecticut: Original Township Embracing Present Watertown and Plymouth, and Parts of Oxford, Wolcott, Middlebury, Prospect and Naugatuck, With an Appendix of Biography, Genealogy and Statistics* (Waterbury: Bronson Bros., 1858).

WOODBRIDGE

Barbour's typescript volume for Woodbridge,[1079] unlike the GPC edition,[1080] begins:

> This volume contains a list alphabetically arranged of all the vital records of the town of Woodbridge from its incorporation to about 1832. The entire record of the town prior to 1832 is found in one volume.
>
> This list was taken from a set of cards[1081] based on a copy of Woodbridge Vital Records made in 1915 by Miss Ethel L. Scofield, of New Haven, Conn. The Scofield Copy, now in the possession of the Connecticut State Library, has not been compared with the original and doubtless errors exist. It is hoped that as errors or omissions re found notes will be entered in this volume and on the cards which are included in the General Index of Connecticut Vital Records also in the possession of the Connecticut State Library.
>
> Hartford, Conn., December, 1924.[1082]

VITAL RECORDS: The Woodbridge volume includes vital records as early as 1769 and as late as 1832. Barbour abstracted "Woodbridge Vital Records 1746–1844" (CSL 974.62f w84vs), a book rebound and archived by CSL and not microfilmed by FHL.

1077 Charles R. Hale, "Headstone Inscriptions of the Town of Wolcott, Connecticut" (bound manuscript at CSL) (FHL film 3,374). Hale names these Center, Woodtick, North East, & South.

1078 Daniel Hearn, "Connecticut gravestones, early to 1800," manuscript (FHL film 1,477,477, item 84).

1079 See How to Use This Book, note 3, above.

1080 Wilmes, *Barbour Collection: Wilton–Woodstock*, vol. 53 (GPC ed.) Digitized at *Ancestry.com*.

1081 Now part of the Barbour Index and interfiled with similar slips from other towns in CSL and in FHL films 2,887 *et seq*. See Introduction above, pp. 1–3.

1082 Wilmes, *Barbour Collection: Wilton–Woodstock*, vol. 53 (GPC ed.) Digitized at *Ancestry.com*.

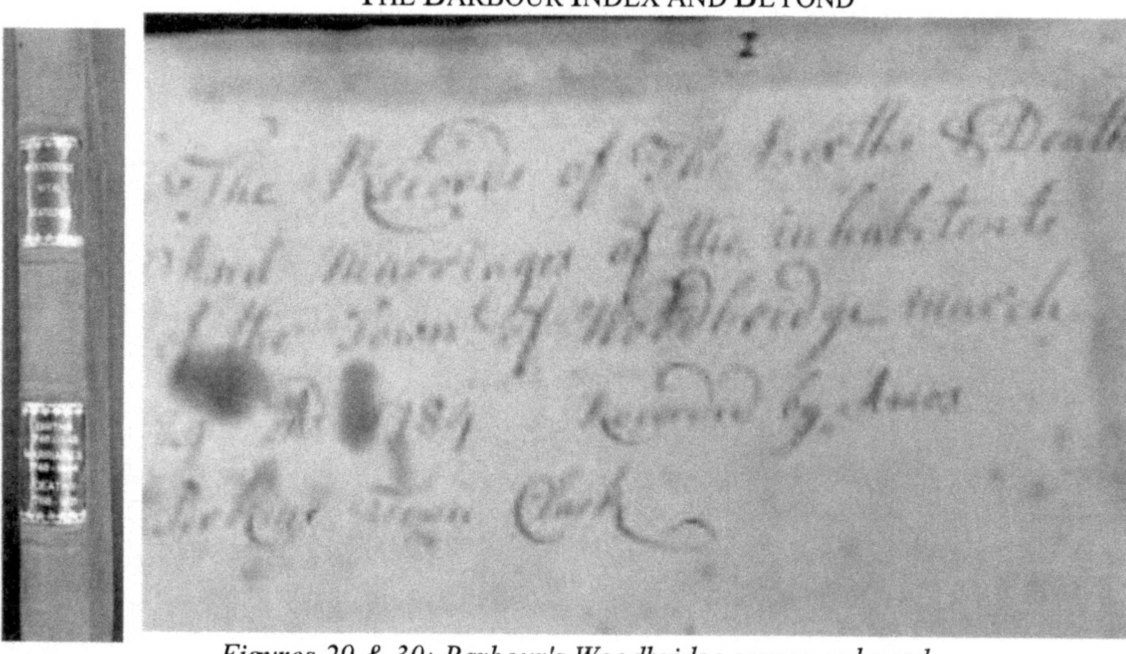

Figures 29 & 30: Barbour's Woodbridge source, rebound

CHURCH RECORDS:

- Silas J. Peck's "Records of the First Church of Christ in Woodbridge, 1738–1889," including baptisms, marriages and deaths.(typescript) (FHL film 1,015,124);
- Louise Tracy's *Records of the Parish of Amity (now Woodbridge) Connecticut, pt. I–II, A–N* (Hartford [s.n.], 1906) (FHL film 1,033,650).

CEMETERY TRANSCRIPTIONS: The Hale Collection identifies people in order of physical proximity buried at about three named sites in Woodbridge Township.[1083] Compare with Daniel Hearn's 1976 copy of 116 pre-1800 gravestones in three Woodbridge cemeteries.[1084] See also,

- T.H. McKeon's James Fitzgerald, and Burton S. Brockett's "East Side Burying Ground, Woodbridge, Connecticut," (1934 typescript at FHL);
- Andrew Barfuss' "Listing of Burials in Northwest Side Cemetery, Woodbridge, Connecticut," (1975 typescript at FHL);
- Richard Asprelli's "The Northwest Side Cemetery, Woodbridge, Connecticut" (1984 copy at: FHL).

OTHER NOTEWORTHY SOURCES: *Woodbridge, Connecticut, a town of one of the original thirteen colonies* ([S.I.]: Woodbridge Bicentennial Commission, 1976).

WOODBURY

Barbour's typescript volume for Woodbury,[1085] unlike the GPC edition,[1086] begins:

1083 Charles R. Hale, "Headstone Inscriptions of the Town of Woodbridge, Connecticut" (bound manuscript at CSL) (FHL film 3,374). Hale names these East Side, Milford, & North West.

1084 Daniel Hearn, "Connecticut gravestones, early to 1800," manuscript (FHL film 1,477,477, item 85).

1085 See How to Use This Book, note 3, above.

1086 Wilmes, *Barbour Collection: Wilton–Woodstock*, vol. 53 (GPC ed.) Digitized at *Ancestry.com*.

> The vital records of Woodbury, prior to 1850, are found scattered through Volumes 2, 3, 4, 5, 6, 7, 8, and 9 of Land Records and Volumes 1 and 2 of Vital Records.
>
> This alphabetical list was taken from a set of cards[1087] based on a manuscript copy of the Woodbury Vital Records made in 1918 by James N. Arnold, of Providence, R.I. Reference to the entries found in the Land Records is indicated by the abbreviation "LR" and the number of the volume.
>
> In "History of Ancient Woodbury", published in 1879 by William Cothren there are many of the vital records of Woodbury, and although the Arnold Copy has not been checked in its entirety with the printed history, a few marked differences have been noted herein.
>
> The Arnold Copy, now in the possession of the Connecticut State Library, has not been compared with the original and doubtless errors exist. It is hoped that as errors or omissions are found, notes will be entered in this volume and on the cards which are included in the General Index of Connecticut Vital Records also in the possession of the Connecticut State Library.
>
> Hartford, Conn., August, 1926.[1088]

VITAL RECORDS: The Woodbury volume includes vital records as early as 1683 and as late as 1854. Barbour abstracted seven Woodbury "books," but not always accurately:

- "1" refers to Woodbury's Births, Marriages, & Deaths, 1718–1819, Woodbury Town Hall, (FHL film 1,491,338 item 2);
- "2" refers to Woodbury's Births, Marriages, & Deaths, 1776–1854, Woodbury Town Hall, (FHL film 1,491,338, item 3);
- "LR2" refers to Woodbury's Land Records, vols. 1–3, 1659–1810, Woodbury Town Hall (FHL film 6,149);
- "LR4" and "LR5" refer to Woodbury's Land Records, vol. 4–5, 1719–1739, Woodbury Town Hall (FHL film 6,150);
- "LR7" refers to Woodbury's Land Records, vol.7, 1743–1748, Woodbury Town Hall (FHL film 6,151, item 2);
- "LR8" refers to Woodbury's Land Records, vol. 8, 1748–1751, Woodbury Town Hall (FHL film 6,152, item 1).

These sources are not abstracted by Barbour:

- **William Cothren's *History of Ancient Woodbury, Connecticut : From the First Indian Deed in 1659, Including the Present Towns of Washington, Southbury, Bethlehem, Roxbury, and a Part of Oxford and Middlebury* (Woodbury: W.**

1087 Now part of the Barbour Index and interfiled with similar slips from other towns in CSL and in FHL films 2,887 *et seq*. See Introduction above, pp. 1–3.

1088 Lucius B. Barbour, *Connecticut Vital Records Woodbury, 1674–1850,* (Hartford: CSL, 1926) page after title page (FHL film 2,983). Digital images at *AmericanAncestors.org* and *FamilySearch.org*.

Cothren, 1872–1879) (FHL films 2,055,359 & 6,181), but "a few" unspecified entries in this book were used by Barbour to "correct" his abstraction of the official records;

- **Woodbury's Births, Marriages, & Deaths, 1683–1868, Woodbury Town Hall, (FHL film 1,491,338, item 1);**
- **Woodbury's Births, Marriages, Attachments, Dog Registry, 1754–1884 (includes marriage records 1776–1854 & also a few records of birth and death 1754–1846) (Woodbury Town Hall) (FHL film 1.491.338, item 3);**
- **Judith Plummer's "Unrecorded Woodbury, CT. Marriages, 1820–1825," *CN*, 31:566–575 (March 1999);**
- **William Cothren's "List of the First Settlers of Woodbury, Conn." and "A List of Marriages in Woodbury, Conn. from 1684 to 1784," NEHGS manuscripts, (digital images online at *AmericanAncestors.org*);**
- **Leon M Barnes' *Mortality record of the town of Woodbury: from the settlement of the town of Woodbury in 1672 to the present day* (Woodbury: L.M. Barnes, 1898) (images online at *AmericanAncestors.org*).**

CHURCH RECORDS:

- First Congregational Church's "Records of the First Congregational Church in Woodbury, Connecticut, vol. 1–4, 1670–1920" (includes marriages 1817–1829 and baptisms) (originals in CSL) (FHL film 6,182);
- Methodist Episcopal Church's Records 1838–1941, originals at CSL (FHL film 6,183);
- St. Paul's Church's "Church Records, 1765–1923" (includes baptisms 1765–1858 & 1765–1923, marriages 1765–1859 & 1765–1915, and burials 1837–1859 & 1788–1915) (originals at CSL) (FHL film 6,184);
- Baptisms (1765–1858 & 1765–1923), marriages (1765–1859 & 1765–1915) and burials (1837–59 & 1788–1915) at St. Paul's Church (ED Film 6,184).

CEMETERY TRANSCRIPTIONS: The Hale Collection identifies people in order of physical proximity buried at about three named sites in what was then Woodbury Township.[1089] Compare with Daniel Hearn's 1976 copy of 77 pre-1800 gravestones in one Woodbridge cemetery.[1090] The Hale Collection also identifies people in order of physical proximity buried at least one named sites in what was then Middlebury Township.[1091] Compare with Daniel Hearn's 1976 copy of eight pre-1800 gravestones in one Middlebury cemetery.[1092]

OTHER NOTEWORTHY SOURCES: See state and county resources above, pages 17 to 21.

[1089] Charles R. Hale, "Headstone Inscriptions of the Town of Woodbury, Connecticut" (bound manuscript at CSL) (FHL film 3,374). Hale names these as South, North, & New North.

[1090] Daniel Hearn, "Connecticut gravestones, early to 1800," manuscript (FHL film 1,477,477, item 86).

[1091] Charles R. Hale, "Headstone Inscriptions of the Town of Middlebury, Connecticut" (bound manuscript at CSL) (FHL film 3,345). Hale names this Middlebury Cemetery.

[1092] Daniel Hearn, "Connecticut gravestones, early to 1800," manuscript (FHL film 1,477,477, item 1).

WOODSTOCK

Barbour's typescript volume for Woodstock,[1093] unlike the GPC edition,[1094] begins:

> The early vital records of Woodstock, covering the period from 1690 to about 1848, were printed and published in 1914 by The Case, Lockwood & Brainard Company of Hartford, Connecticut.
>
> The records herewith are taken from what is known as Volume 3 [sic]. As far as page 242[1095] the entries in Volume 3 [sic] are arranged in Semi-alphabetical order. In many cases they duplicate those found in the printed records and have, therefore, been omitted from this list. Beyond page 242 only marriages and births prior to December 31, 1850, have been indexed, but all the deaths have been listed, the date of the last death being December 27, 1865.
>
> The following alphabetically arranged list was taken from a set of cards[1096] based on a copy made in 1908 by James N. Arnold, of Providence, R.I. The Arnold Copy, now in the possession of the Connecticut State Library, has not been compared with the original and doubtless errors exist. It is hoped that as errors or omissions are found, notes will be entered in this volume and on the cards which are included in the General Index of Connecticut Vital Records also in the possession of the Connecticut State Library.
>
> Hartford, Conn., September, 1921.[1097]

VITAL RECORDS: The Woodstock typescript volume includes only vital records between1846 and 1866, because earlier records were already published in Woodstock's *Vital Records of Woodstock, 1686–1854* (Hartford: Case, Lockwood & Brainard, 1914) (images at *AmericanAncestors.org*). Both volumes are abstracted, however, in the Barbour Index. Barbour's volume abstracts "Woodstock Vital Records, Vol. 4" (FHL film 1,376,372, item 4, p. 242 *et seq*.), rather than volume 3 as his introduction claims. The 1914 book abstracts records from Woodstock's Vital Records, Vols. 1–4, Woodstock Town Hall (FHL film 1,376,372, items 1–4) through page 237 (rather than 242 as claimed) subdivided as follows:

- "Vital Statistics No. 1" (1686–1749) abstractions are **mostly**[1098] in FHL item 1;

1093 See How to Use This Book, note 3, above.

1094 Wilmes, *Barbour Collection: Wilton–Woodstock*, vol. 53, (GPC ed.) Digitized at *Ancestry.com*.

1095 Actually page 237. Unnumbered pages between 237 and 242 index the records after p. 242.

1096 Now part of the Barbour Index and interfiled with similar slips from other towns in CSL and in FHL films 2,887 *et seq*. See Introduction above, pp. 1–3.

1097 Lucius B. Barbour, *Connecticut Vital Records: Woodstock 1848–1866, Part II*, (Hartford: CSL, 1921) pge after title page (FHL film 2,983). Digital images at *AmericanAncestors.org* and *FamilySearch.org*.

1098 Barbour selects additional records in italics from **a later transcription of the volume by town clerk Ezra Childs** who give no source for the additional information. See *Vital Records of Woodstock*, p. 1. The present whereabouts of this Child transcription is unknown.

- "Vital Statistics No. 2" (1743–1830) abstractions are found in FHL item 2;
- "First Book of Records" (1783–1867) abstractions are found in FHL item 3;
- "Book of Births" (1782–1843) abstractions are found in FHL item 4.

See also,

- **Woodstock's "Records of Births, Marriages and Deaths, 1686–1867," volume 3 and the first 243 pages of volume 4 (FHL film 1,376,372, items 3–4) (contains a variety of vital records 18th and 19th century Woodstock vital records not in the Barbour collection at all);**
- **Miscellaneous records of West Woodstock, Connecticut, 1747–1788, typescript at NYGBS (FHL film 4,431, item 3).**

The Barbour Index also interfiles records from the Diary of William C. Brown: Woodstock, 1777–1900, CSL vital records; (FHL film 5,971, item 2).

CHURCH RECORDS:

- North Woodstock Congregational Church's "Church Records, 1727–1900" (includes vital records, 1727–1826) (originals in CSL) (FHL film 5,355);
- First Congregational Church's Records (include baptisms 1763–1827, births 1779, confessions 1764–1778, marriages 1763–1827, deaths 1779–1827. marriages 1827–1844, baptisms 1827–1842, deaths 1827–1846, deaths 1846–1883, baptisms 1846–1894, marriages 1846–1882) originals at CSL (FHL films 5,967 & 5,968, items 1–3);
- First Congregational Church at West Woodstock's "Church Records, 1743/4–1937," originals at CSL (FHL film 5,970);
- East Woodstock Methodist Church's "Church Records, 1827–1920" (includes church register 1827–1920) (originals at CSL) (FHL film 5,969);
- "Woodstock Baptisms, 1727–1799" (manuscript in NYGBS) (FHL film 5,953 or 1,419,455).

CEMETERY TRANSCRIPTIONS: The Hale Collection identifies people in order of physical proximity buried at about 18 named sites in Woodstock Township.[1099] Compare with Daniel Hearn's 1979 copy of 449 pre-1800 gravestones in three Woodstock cemeteries.[1100] See also, Lucius B. Barbour's "Genealogical Data From Connecticut Cemeteries: Woodstock, Conn. Inscriptions: Woodstock Hill; West Woodstock, Bungee Hill, East Woodstock; West Woodstock, New Cemetery; and Central Cemetery, Woodstock" (1908–1911 manuscript at NEHGS).

OTHER NOTEWORTHY SOURCES:

- "Morse's Justice Court Notes," CSL; see Appendix A;
- "Marriage intentions 1811–1819," CSL; see Appendix A;
- "John Call note book, 1762–1808," CSL; see Appendix A;

1099 Charles R. Hale, "Headstone Inscriptions of the Town of Woodstock, Connecticut" (bound manuscript at CSL) (FHL film 3374) He names these cemeteries East Woodstock, North Woodstock, Bradford Marcy, Bungay, Barlow, Center, Graveyard, Hammond, Swedish, Indian (7 different cemeteries with this name), Quasset, & Woodstock Hill.

1100 Daniel Hearn, "Connecticut gravestones, early to 1800," manuscript (FHL film 1477477, Item 87).

- Clarence W. Bowen, Donald L. Jacobus, & William H. Wood's *History of Woodstock & Genealogies of Woodstock Families*, 8 vols., (1926/1997 copy at NEHGS);
- Holmes Ammidown's *Historical Collections: Containing I. The Reformation in France, the Rise, Progress and Destruction of the Huguenot Church: II. The Histories of .... the Town of Woodstock, Now in Connecticut, but Originally Granted and Settled by People From the Province of Massachusetts, and Regarded as Belonging to Her for About Sixty Years* (New York: the author, 1877);
- Clarence Winthrop Bowen's *Woodstock, an historical sketch* (New York: G. P. Putnam's Sons, c1886) (FHL fiche 6,071,099).

FINDING EARLY CONNECTICUT VITAL RECORDS ONLINE

This guide has succeeded in identifying and locating 98 to 99% of Barbour's sources, over 82% of which are found on FHL microfilm and about 90% of which can be seen in some form at CSL. Almost all of the rest are viewable only through the office of the town clerk which generally created them.[1101] Until 100% of his primary sources are rediscovered the Barbour Index is not completely verifiable as both Barbour himself and contemporary genealogical proof standards demand. But his vital statistics can often be verified from alternative sources listed in this book.

This guide is intended to remain a complete bibliography of sources for pre-1850 Connecticut vital statistics by reissuance as an e-book after addenda have been submitted by readers. Search for a website called *ConnecticutGenealogists.com* and a Facebook page called *Barbour Index* for the submission and collection of additions and corrections to these sources for pre-Civil War birth, deaths, and marriages in Connecticut.

When posting additions or corrections, please cite your sources, but also indicate whether or not you wish to be personally credited with the contribution in the e-book. You may contact the author directly at *BarbourIndex143@gmail.com.*

[1101] Towns with yet unlocatable sources for any of Barbour's abstractions are: Ashford (2), Berlin, Bethany, Bozrah (2), Branford (2), Brooklyn (JP), Cheshire (JP), Darien, Fairfield (LR-B), Groton (loose pages), Milford (loose pages), Wallingford (JP).

APPENDIX A

Typed Abstracts of Vital Information from Private Records[1102]

Typed abstracts of vital information, alphabetically arranged, taken from private records such as diaries, letters, or family records. A series of volumes similar to the Barbour Collection was planned, covering especially the period 1850–1897.

Almanacs
The Churchman's Almanac, 1836
Daboll's Almanac, 1881
Methodist Almanac, 1827. "Meth Almanac 1827" refers to personal record inserted in almanac –appears to relate to Colchester area. (8/04 CG).
Middlebrook's Almanac, 1836
Prindle's Almanac, 1828
Transcripts in "Indexes to some CT Private Records" above Barbour volumes. Originals may be in Special Collections Cage. (CMP 10/22/97)

Austin Diary. See SUFFIELD.

Avery Family. See WALLINGFORD.

BLOOMFIELD
Record of Burial Permits kept by George R. Warner, Sexton, 1875–1909
(Note on Card: Not found-card found in Manuscript Accession slips)
Typed abstract (1930) in RG 72, Box 23
2nd carbon of typed abstract (1930) in RG 72, Box 23

Brown Diary. See WOODSTOCK.

Burlesson, E. See HARTFORD.

BOWMAN COLLECTION
John Elliot Bowman Index to Interstate Deaths.
Deaths, mostly in Massachusetts, of natives of Connecticut, ca. 1792–1833 compiled by the Rev. John Elliot Bowman from newspapers such as the Norwich Courier, Connecticut Observer (Hartford), Columbian Centinel (Boston), Massachusetts Spy, Hartford Gazette, New Hampshire and Vermont Journal, and other publications.

CT Vital Records in MA—In Genealogical Source Catalog in hall

Buel, John. See SAYBROOK.

Burgis, Thomas. See GUILFORD.

Button, Mrs. Charles C. See HAMPTON

Cable, E.J. and A. See FAIRFIELD AND LITCHFIELD COUNTIES.

Call, John
Notebook, 1762–1808
No entry under "Call" in Manuscripts and Archives Catalog.

[1102] Working document created by CSL staff and reprinted with their permission.

CANTON
Sexton's Returns, 1915
Typed abstract (1946) shelved above Barbour

Carpenter Family. See COVENTRY.

Cheshire Private Records
See: History of Cheshire D. P. Beach, (note on card: missing 3/'81)
974.62 C423b, disregard PF, PH etc, use page #
Library also has mss. notes, 974.62 C423b ms.

COLCHESTER AND EAST HAMPTON
Notes Taken from the Diary of Elisha Niles, Colchester & East Hampton, 1764–1850.
Original diary in Main Vault q920 N592
Typed abstract (1946) GR 974.62 C67n index shelved above Barbour

COLUMBIA
Deaths—Columbia, Conn. Bill of Mortality, 1814–1869, manuscript
974.62 C72b vault 6

Connecticut & Commercial Gazette & The Intelligencer. Jan 5, 1803

Connecticut Historical Society Bulletin Vols. 1–8
974.6 C765b
Note on card: Barbour Index in 554–555

CONNECTICUT
Connecticut Deaths, 1860 in Connecticut Newspaper Clipping
Typed abstract (1936) in RG 72, Box 23
1st carbon of typed abstract (1936) in RG 72, Box 23
2nd carbon of typed abstract (1929) in RG 72, Box 23

CORNWALL
E.S. Millard's Account Book, 1811–53
Cornwall
974.62 C81mi probate

COVENTRY
Genealogical Notes on the Carpenter & Gurley Families of Coventry, Connecticut.
Original volume: Main Vault 929.2 C22ge

COVENTRY
Record of deaths, North Coventry, 1826–1869, found by G.W.F. Blanchfield in a small paper covered book of 31 pages.
974.62 fC83:Nr
Typed abstract (1929) in RG 72, Box 24
1st carbon of typed abstract (1929) in RG 72, Box 24
Photostat use copy of typed abstract (1929) shelved above Barbour

Cushman Polley's Dictionary

Thomas Danforth's Journal, 1783–1843
975.52 R41d

Davies, Rev. Thomas. See LITCHFIELD COUNTY

Davis, Humphrey
Pension Record. W. C. 473, 226
Shelved above Barbour

Durham Deaths, 1746–1908, 1791–1805
974.62 D93re main vault
Shelved Above Barbour with Durham and Guilford Deaths?

East Granby
Bate's Turkey Hill 1852–3
Special Genealogy File Bates

East Hartford
Rev. Samuel Woodbridge, 1723–1794
Shelved Above Barbour
974.62 Ea751c v main vault
On Search? copy and original Oct. 28, 2004

EAST WINDSOR
Eight births of the Allen Family between 1771 and 1811 found in the Henry W. Allen Collection in the State Library
974.62 Ea 785a, 974.62 fEa78aL Index is lost
Typed abstract (1930) in RG 72, Box 23
2nd carbon of typed abstract (1930) in RG 72, Box 23

Henry L. Elmer's Account Book.
So. Windsor
974.62 So 83e probate

Elias Ford Account Book
Waterbury
974.62 W29fo probate

FAIRFIELD AND LITCHFIELD COUNTIES
Cable, E. J. Accounts of Cemetery Monument Inscriptions of E. J. and A. Cable for Cemeteries in Fairfield and Litchfield Counties, 1836–63.
Original volume: Main Vault 974.6 C112a
Type abstract:
Slips:

Joseph B. Ayer's School Rec.
Franklin
974.62 F83 ay probate pam.

Geer, Ellen, copy. 1773–1814 Private Records North Groton
Gere, Robert
Marriages performed in North Groton, CT, now the town of Ledyard by Robert & Amos Gere, J.P.'s 1773–1814 copied by Ms. Ellen Geer of Norwich
974.62 L51ger, carded main vault, see also 974.62 L51ger 2. SL index to the above

GLASTONBURY
Letters, 1798–1816, of Gideon Hale, Jr.
2nd carbon of typed abstract (1934) in RG 72, Box 23
2nd carbon of typed abstract (1934) in RG 72, Box 23

Goshen
Private Records

GRANBY
Francis Case Account Book –May 1799–June 1845; Contains births 1739–1823; deaths 1833–1887 and weather reports, 1832–1835.
974.62 G76c probate
Typed abstract (1934) in RG 72, Box 23
2nd carbon of typed abstract (1934) in RG 72, Box 23

GRANBY
Marriage, 1821–1828 by James Dibble, J.P. Found in an account book kept by George Thompson and James Dibble, J.P.
974.62 fG76dm case
Typed abstract (1929) in RG 72, Box 23
2nd carbon of typed abstract (1929) in RG 72, Box 23

GRANBY
Oren Lee Diary. Births, Marriages Deaths, made from a diary and journal covering the yrs. 1809–1841 kept by Oren Lee, 1760–1841 a blacksmith from Berlin and later No. Granby
974.62 fG76:NL vault 6
Typed abstract (1934) in RG 72, Box 23
2nd carbon of typed abstract (1934) in RG 72, Box 23

GRANBY
Mortality list from 1874 to 1887 found in an Account book in possession of Mrs. A. C. Green, of Granby
974.62 fG76gr
Typed abstract (1929) in RG 72, Box 24
2nd carbon of typed abstract (1929) in RG 72, Box 24
Photostat use copy of typed abstract (1929) shelved above Barbour

Green, Mrs. A. C. See GRANBY.

GREENWICH
Marriages, 1785–94; By Dr. Amos Mead, Justice of Peace of Greenwich, Conn.
Special Genealogy File
Typed abstract (1936) in RG 72, Box 23
1st carbon of typed abstract (1936) in RG 72, Box 23
2nd carbon of typed abstract (1936) in RG 72, Box 23

Griswold, Andrew, J.P. See LYME

GUILFORD
Burgis, Thomas. Letters written by Thomas Burgis at Guilford, Connecticut….
Original letters: Main Vault 920 B915
Typed abstract in "Indexes to Some CT Private records", filed above Barbour

Guilford
Thomas Fitch's Book, 1815–1874
974.62 G94vi main vault

Guilford Private Records
Deaths, 1735–1783
=Robinson notebook, 974.62 G94d r pam. main vault
Shelved above Barbour with Durham & Guilford?

Gurley Family. See COVENTRY.

James Brainerd Account Book.
Haddam
974.62 H11br probate

Hampshire County Mass. Records of Births, Marriages and Deaths, 1638–1696.
Private records of William & John Pynchon
974.41 fH189p main vault. Copy 2 in stacks F72 .H3 P96 1696a

HAMPTON
Button, Mrs. Charles C. [Death Records, Hampton, Conn., 1867–1877.
Original volume: Main Vault 974.62 H18bu

HARTFORD
Burlesson, E. A Lamentation in Memory of the Distressing Sickness in Hartford....
Photostat of broadside in Broadsides PS 721 .B4 L36 1725

Hartford
Talcott Memorandum Book [photostat of original MV 920 fT1392]
Shelved above Barbour

HARTLAND
Records 1846–1867 kept by Lester K. Gaines, Undertaker, Hartland & East Hartland.
Typed abstract (1935) in RG 72, Box 23
1st carbon of typed abstract (1935) in RG 72, Box 23
2nd carbon of typed abstract (1935) in RG 72, Box 23

Hebron
A.R. Bailey purchase
Shelved above Barbour

Hebron
Burial permits issued from 1875–1909 to George R. Warner, son of Rev. Ransom Warner and Sexton of the Burying Ground in Bloomfield. Private Records loaned to State Library

HEBRON
Baptisms, Marriages, Deaths, 1752–1876 and a few historical facts of Hebron kept by William J. Warner from 1752–1876.
974.62 H35 (1, v, or 4) w. main vault.
Photostat of ms. and typescript index
2nd carbon of typed abstract (1931) in RG 72, Box 24

Hewitt, C.R

Mrs. a Family Record, particularly on the Avery family kept by an ancestor of Mrs. Hewitt's. 929.2 fav 361 av
Special Genealogy File under Avery
Shelved Above Barbour

Miss M. Hine Book, 1827
Middlebury Flyleaf 540 C73c

Hubbell, Ephraim Jr., J.P.. See NEW FAIRFIELD.

M.A. Huntington JO.
Norwich
974.62 N84hu vault 6

Independent Chronicle & Boston Patriot
Mar. 21, 1829

Jarvis, Rev. S. F. See MIDDLETOWN.

LEBANON
Sexton's Records, 1733–1927, of Goshen Cemetery. Lebanon, Connecticut
Photostat. 974.62 fL49Dli
Typed abstract (1934) in RG 72, Box 24
2nd carbon of typed abstract (1934) in RG 72, Box 24

Ledyard. Ellen Geer copy. 1773–1814
Gere, Robert
Marriages performed in North Groton, CT, now the town of Ledyard by Robert & Amos Gere, J.P.'s 1773–1814 copied by Ms. Ellen Geer of Norwich
974.62 L51ger, carded main vault, see also 974.62 L51ger 2, State Library index to the above.

LITCHFIELD COUNTY
Rev. Thomas Davies Record, 1761–1766, Litchfield County
920 D284 920 D284a Index
Typed abstract (no date) shelved above Barbour Collection

Litchfield Co.
Deaths 1820–78
Special Genealogy File

Simon Lyman's Book, 1812–1815
NY Flyleaf
In James Thompson The Seasons 811 T374 1811

LYME
Marriage records of Andrew Griswold, J.P., 1784–1810
974 .62 fL89gr probate
Typed abstract (1929) in RG 72, Box 24
1st carbon of typed abstract (1929) in RG 72, Box 24
Photostat use copy of typed abstract shelved above Barbour

LYME
Lyme, Connecticut (Hamburg) Marriage Certificates, 1834–1853

Typed abstract (1936) in RG 72, Box 23
Tof typed abstract (1929) in RG 72, Box 24
1st carbon of typed abstract (1936) in RG 72, Box 23
2nd carbon of typed abstract (1936) in RG 72, Box 23
Note: Listed as "Connecticut Private Records" but may duplicate entries in Barbour Coll.??

MANSFIELD
Entries found in an old account book kept by Martin Phillips, Sexton, 1819–1866. Photo 974 .62 M33phi vault 16 (or M35?)
Typed abstract (1930) in RG 72, Box 23
2nd carbon of typed abstract (1930) in RG 72, Box 23

MANSFIELD
Private Record. Marriages found in a record kept by Zalman Storrs from 1817 to 1818. 974.62 M35s vault 1
Typed abstract (1930) in RG 72, Box 23
2nd carbon of typed abstract (1930) in RG 72, Box 23

Barrow Account Book, 1807–1825
Mansfield
974 .62 M35bar probate

MIDDLETOWN
Vital Records from Rev. Samuel. F. Jarvis' Manuscript Christ Church Records, 1836–1839
Typed abstract (1929) in RG 72, Box 23
2nd carbon of typed abstract (1929) in RG 72, Box 23
Photostat use copy of typed abstract (1929) shelved above Barbour. Includes additions 1925–1938.

MILFORD
Milford Deaths, 1833–1869

Milford Deaths, 1849–1869
Special Genealogy File??
Typed abstract (1962) shelved above Barbour?

Millard, E. S. See CORNWALL.

NEW FAIRFIELD
Marriages, 1741–1791 kept by Ephraim Hubbell, Jr., J.P., New Fairfield, Connecticut
Typed abstract (1962) shelved above Barbour

NEW HAVEN
Record of Deaths, New Haven, 1793-1859, based on cemetery stones in the Old Burying Ground.
Typed abstract (1929) in RG 72, Box 24
2nd carbon of typed abstract (1929) in RG 72, Box 24

NEW HAVEN COUNTY

Deaths and Marriages, 1824–1883 taken from a volume purchased from Mr. Samuel Tanenbaum.
Typed abstract (no date) shelved above Barbour

New London County
Ralph Hurlbutt, Justice of Peace, 1807–1837
974 .61 N44hu main vault
Shelved above Barbour

NEW LONDON COUNTY
Records of Nehemiah Waterman, J.P., New London County, 1712–1801.
974.62 B719 w d. Note on card: In main vault with Bozrah Ch. Recd.s
Typed abstract (no date) shelved above Barbour.

NEWINGTON
A list of Teachers and Scholars in the Congregational Sunday School, Newington, Conn, May 17, 1840, prepared by Dea. Origen Wells, Superintendant, 1839–1843.
Typed abstract (1936) in RG 72, Box 23
1st carbon of typed abstract (1936) in RG 72, Box 23
2nd carbon of typed abstract (1936) in RG 72, Box 23

Niles, Elisha. See COLCHESTER AND EAST HAMPTON.

Norfolk, Conn
Account Book of Heman Swift
974.62 N76sw main vault
Shelved above Barbour

North Coventry. See COVENTRY.

North Groton.
Ellen Geer copy. 1773–1814
Gere, Robert
Marriages performed in North Groton, CT, now the town of Ledyard by Robert & Amos Gere, J.P.'s 1773–1814 copied by Ms. Ellen Geer of Norwich
974.62 L51ger, carded main vault, see also 974.62 L51ger 2. SL index to the above

North Hampton Gazette
Newspaper Clipping, 1830
Shelved above Barbour

Norwich
Cemetery Inscriptions in Christ Church, 1762–1835

J. Seymour Pardee
Orange
974.62 Or11p vault 6

Payne, Philemon Account Bk.
974.62 P94pa main vault
Shelved Above Barbour

Peck Account Book
Bristol

974.62 B77pc main vault

PLYMOUTH
Record of Two Hundred Nineteen Burials in St. Matthew's Cemetery, East Plymouth, Conn. Kept by Junius Preston, Sexton, 1846-1886.
Two photostatic copies made from a typed copy prepared by James Shepard of New Britain in Stacks, 974.62 p74pm
Typed abstract (1935) in RG 72, Box 23
1st carbon of typed abstract (1935) in RG 72, Box 23
2nd carbon of typed abstract (1935) in RG 72, Box 23

Pomfret Mfg. Company
Deaths (Pomfret & Thompson). 1814–1851
Shelved above Barbour

SAYBROOK
John Buel Account Book Part 1.
974.62 Sa9bu probate?? Main Vault??
Typed abstract (no date) shelved above Barbour volumes

Solomon Purdy
Special Genealogy File

Salisbury, 1812
Rev. Crossman
Special Genealogy File

Daniel Sanford Account Book.
Fairfield Co.
974.62 R2472s vault 6

Seymour, Jeremiah. See WETHERSFIELD.
Sherman Family Papers
920 Sh 57 (sup) Mezz.

Sherman Land Records
Vol. 1 pg 536 (Northrop's Private Records)

Family Register of Lydia Smith
1761–1855
Shelved above Barbour

Stafford
Eleazer W. Phelps, J.P.
Marriages, 1798–1807
RG 3, Justice of the Peace Courts, Stafford, Eleazer Phelps and Jesse Cady

Darius Stone, Sexton 1859
Windsor
Special Genealogy File

Stonington

Nathaniel Ingraham Account Book
974.62 St 7i probate

SOUTHBURY
Births, marriages and deaths, 1847–1878. Note: This should be part of "Barbour II", not Connecticut Private Records.
1st carbon of typed abstract (1933) in RG 72, Box 24

SOUTHBURY
Marriages in Record of Cases, 1791–1812, kept by Justus Johnson, J.P.
Typed abstract (1934) in RG 72, Box 23
2nd carbon of typed abstract (1934) in RG 72, Box 23

SUFFIELD
Family records from a diary, 1860–1872, 1874–1888.
Binders' title: Suffield Vital Records, Austin, 1860–1888.
"Found in interleaved copies of MIddlebrook's New England Almanacs."
Original records: Main Vault 929.1 qSu2a

Suffield
Private Record of Births, Marriages, Deaths, 1760–1807 in possession of the Kent Library
974.62 (g, c, or q?) Su 2v main vault

TORRINGTON
Record of Deaths in Torringford, 1777–1884, compiled from records kept by Fitch Loomis, 1777–1826; Rev. Epaphrus Goodman, 1826–1836; Mrs. Polly Loomis, 1836–1837; Church Records, 1837–1864; and Mrs. Roderick (Fanny Gaylord) Bissell, 1855–1884.
Typed abstract (1962) shelved above Barbour

WALLINGFORD
Record of Avery Family in Wallingford, Connecticut: Births, Marriages, and Deaths, 1720–1899.
Typed abstract (1954) bound with Photostat of original record and shelved above Barbour.
2nd carbon of typed abstract (1931) in RG 72, Box 24

Warner Memorandum
974.62 H35 vw MV
Also typescript copy ("on oversize shelves" crossed out) same call number, also main vault

Waterman, Nehemiah, J.P. See NEW LONDON COUNTY

WATROUS FAMILY
Record of Deaths, Watrous Family, 1818–1838. A record of the Watrous family in possession of Mrs. Bentley Watrous Morse, Providence, RI
929.2 fW329r stack
Typed abstract (1931) shelved above Barbour
2nd carbon of typed abstract (1931) in RG 72, Box 24

John Wells
Account Book, 1751–1789
974.62 H25we vault 6

Westbrook
Pond Meadow-Wright
Special Genealogy File

WETHERSFIELD (NEWINGTON PARISH)
Account Book 1790–1878 of Jeremiah Seymour
Typed abstract (1934) in RG 72, Box 23
2nd carbon of typed abstract (1934) in RG 72, Box 23

WINDHAM AND WOODSTOCK
Notes from Morse's Account of Justice Court Cases, 1784–1801
Typed abstract (1936) in RG 72, Box 23
1st carbon of typed abstract (1936) in RG 72, Box 23
2nd carbon of typed abstract (1936) in RG 72, Box 23

Windsor

Amasa Woodford's Account Book
Farmington
974.62 F22 wo probate

WOODSTOCK
Vital Records from Brown Diary, Woodstock, 1777–1900
974.62 W86br (in stacks??)
Photostat of original diary in RG 72, Box 24
Typed abstract (1929) in RG 72, Box 24
Photostat copy of typed abstract (1929) shelved above Barbour
Photostat copy of original diary and carbon of typed abstract (1929) shelved above Barbour
974.62 W86br index

Last card:
----A marriage and death 1841; place unknown, found in an Almanac for May 1841

APPENDIX B

Vital Records and Private Records not yet interfiled in Barbour Index

Just beyond the Barbour Index in CSL's file room are seven file drawers of record slips abstracted in Barbour's format but never interfiled in the Barbour Index, transcribed into one of Barbour's typescript volumes in or since the 1920's, or filmed by FHL when it filmed the rest of the Barbour Collection at CSL in 1949. These slips may be viewed only by CSL patrons in their file room. The Montville abstractions are most noteworthy.

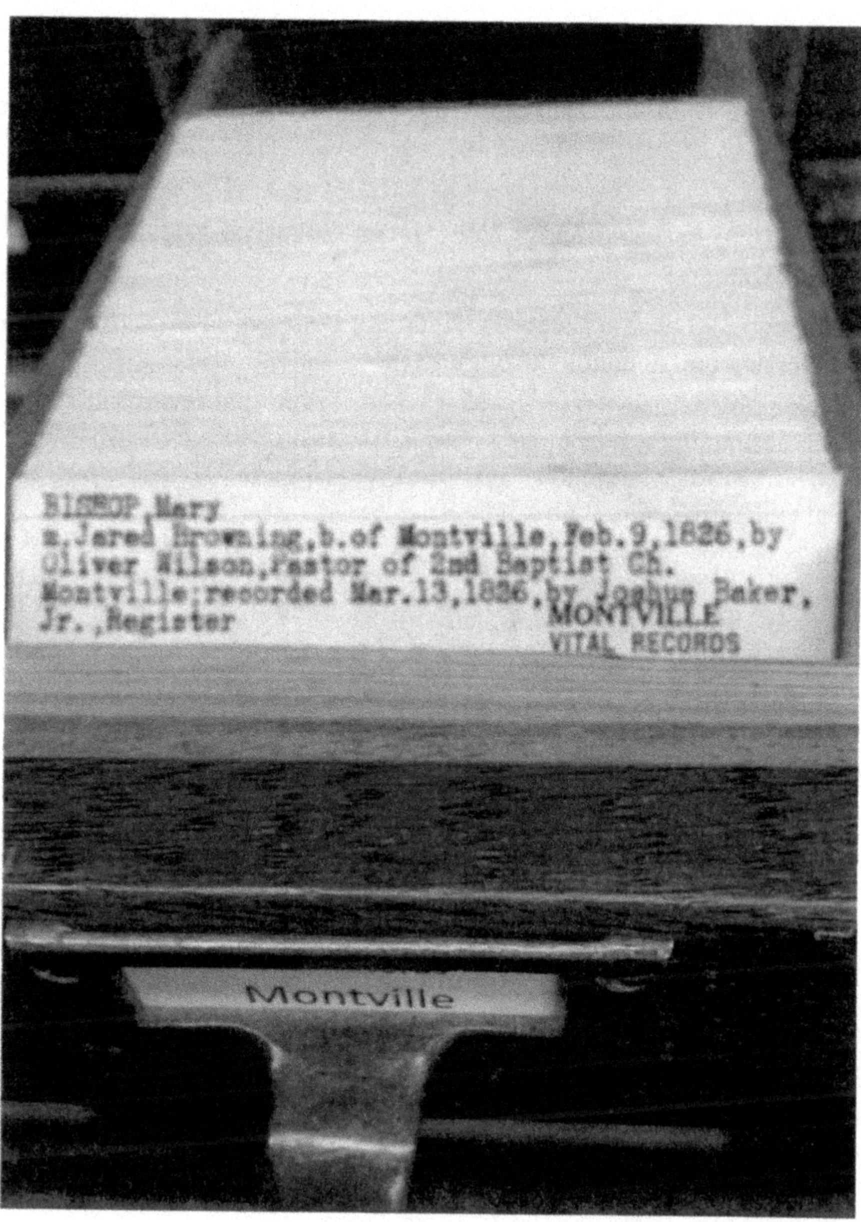

Figure 31 Vital Records of Montville in Drawer 392 at CSL

Drawer 392 is labeled Vital Records: Montville. It contains about 850–900 slips, all apparently abstracted from a 178 page book recording the marriage certificates of Montville, 1820–1855, pursuant to the statute requiring this of Connecticut town clerks at that time. The book was purchased by CSL from a bookstore shortly after Barbour's death and rebound with an explanation of its origin. See Figure 20, at page 185 above. Montville's copy of the rebound book was microfilmed by FHL in 1953 and cataloged as Montville's Marriage Records, 1920–1855 (original at CSL. "This volume was kept [in town] separate from other vital records found in the town of Montville, Connecticut.") (FHL film 4,863, item 1)

Drawer 391 is labeled Vital Records: Madison. It contains about. 1,800–1,850 slips. They appear to all be from Madison's Records of births, marriages, and deaths, 1852 to circa 1863, Madison Town Hall (FHL film 1,420,981, item 3). Barbour may have omitted these records from the Barbour Collection because they cover a later time period.

Drawer 393 abstracts roughly 2,650 New Haven County Marriages and Deaths, 1824-1883. Its source at CSL is listed under New Haven County records on page 20 and in Appendices A and C.

Drawers 394 through 396 abstract records which are both beyond the period covered by the Barbour Collection and available through FHL:

- Drawer 394 is labeled Vital Records: North Stonington vital records It contains about 215–225 slips abstracting deaths circa 1890-1920. It is probably from what FHL catalogs as C.R. Hale's "North Stonington Vital Records 1880–1905: from the town clerk," (typescript at CSL) (FHL film 3,662, item 9).
- Drawer 395 is labeled Vital Records: Rocky Hill. It contains about 1,575–1,625 slips abstracting births, marriages, and deaths circa 1860–1880.They appear to be from what FHL catalogs as "Rocky Hill Vital Records, 1865–1879 (typescript at CSL) (FHL film 3,662, item 10)
- Drawer 396 is labeled Vital Records: Wethersfield. It contains about 2,950–3,000 slips abstracting births, marriages, burials, and deaths circa 1890-1920. It seems to be from what FHL calls "Wethersfield Vital Records 1887–1904" (typescript at CSL) (FHL film 3,662, item 12)

Drawer 380 is labeled "Private Records — Miscellaneous." contains slips of private records from five different Connecticut towns:

- 2 slips from Hebron: marked "Jones St. Cemetery;"
- 4 slips labeled Bridgewater, an 1856 offshoot of New Milford;
- Circa 65–70 slips labeled "East Guilford Parish Deaths." These may be taken from what Appendix A refers to as "Guilford Private Records: Deaths 1735-1783."
- Circa 420–430 slips marked "Billious Avery" of Wallingford. These seem to be taken from what CSL calls "Record of the Avery Family in Wallingford, Connecticut: Births, Marriages, and Deaths, 1720–1899)" in Appendix A and "Avery Family Vital Records, 1720-1899" in Appendix C.

- Circa 560–570 slips labeled Brooklyn Private Records, citing only page numbers and not their source. They may abstract the CSL volume "Brooklyn Vital Records, 1782–1867" (mainly deaths) (CSL 974.62 B 794 vi).

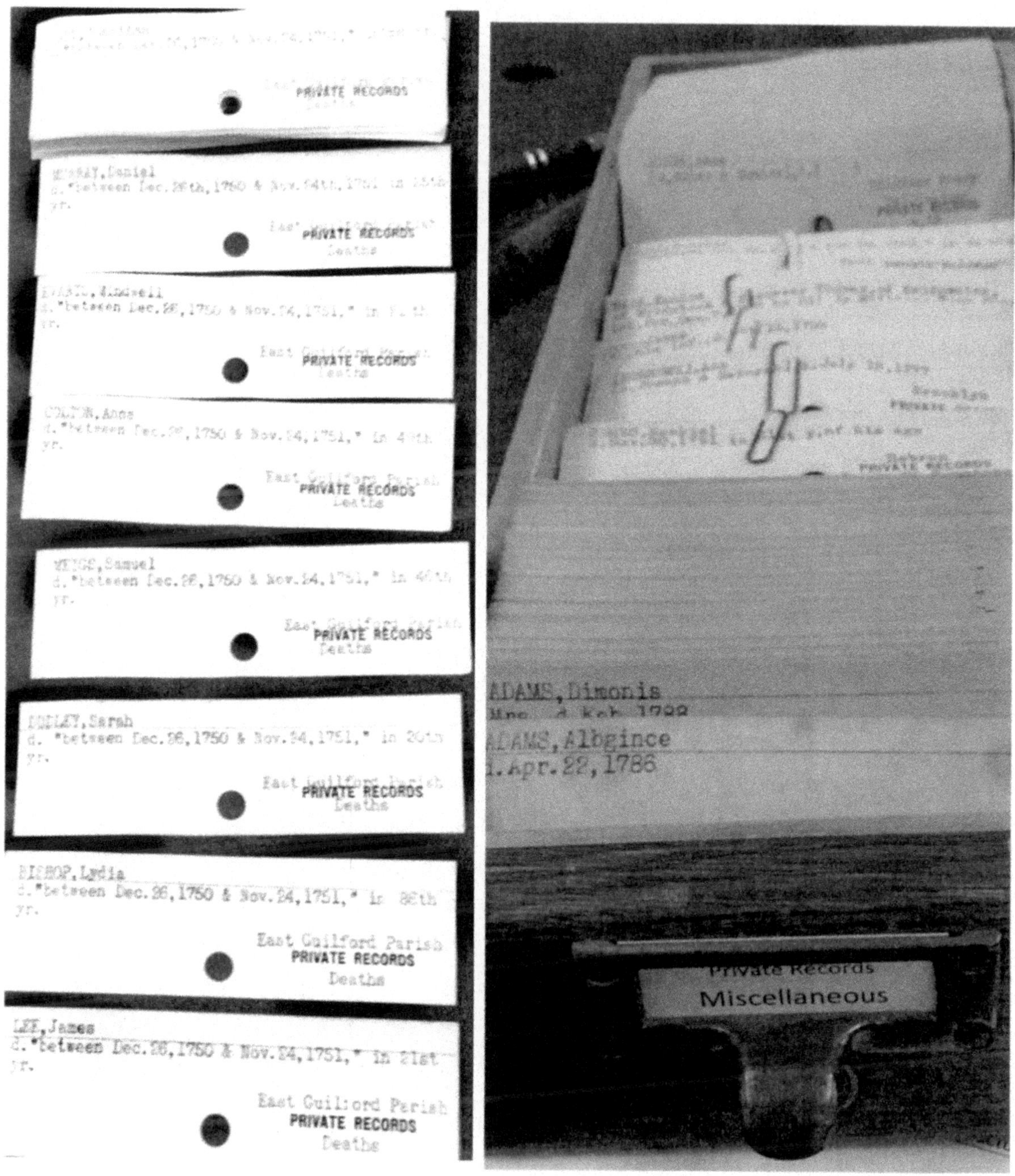

Figures 25 & 26: Private Records in Drawer 380 at CSL

APPENDIX C

Private Records Shelved Above the Barbour Collection:[1103]

Avery Family
Vital Records, 1720–1899
Canton
Sexton's Returns for 1915 [bound with Guilford Thomas Fitch's book]
Colchester and East Haddam
Elisha Niles Diary, 1764–1850
Durham & Guilford
Deaths
East Hartford
Rev. Samuel Woodbridge Records, 1723–1855
Granby
A.C. Green Diary, 1874–1887
Guilford
Thomas Fitch's book, 1815–1874 [bound with Canton Sexton's returns]
Litchfield County
Rev. T. Davies Record, 1761–1766
Lyme
Andrew Griswold, J.P. 1784–1810
Middletown
Rev. S.F. Jarvis, Christ Church Records, 1886–1888
Milford
Deaths, 1849–1869
New Fairfield
Marriages, 1746–1791
New Haven County
Marriages and Deaths, 1824–1883
New London County
Nehemiah Waterman, J.P. , 1712–1801
North Coventry
Death Records, 1826–1869
Saybrook
John Buel Account Book
Torrington
Deaths in Torringford, 1777–1884
Watrous Family
Death Records, 1818–1838
Wethersfield
Vital Records, 1830–1904
Woodstock
Brown Diary Vital Records, 1777–1900

1103 List prepared by the staff of CSL and published with their permission.

Miscellaneous Private Records in One Volume
(Listed in the order they appear in the volume):

Churchman's Almanac, 1836–1837

Daboll's Almanac, 1802–1887

Methodist Almanac, 1827

Middlebrook's Almanac, 1835–1836

Prindle's Almanac, 1828–1860

John Call Notebook, 1762–1808

Humphrey Davis Pension Records

Thomas Burgis Letters

A. R. Bailey Purchase Hebron

Talcott Memorandum Hartford

C.R. Hewitt

Ralph Hurlburt J.P. New London County, 1807–1827

Account Book of Heman Swift, Norfolk,

Northampton Gazette Newspaper Clippings, 1830

Deaths Pomfret & Thompson

Philemon Payne's Account Book

Diary Rev. John Robinson

Family Reg. Lydia Smith, 1756–1871

GLOSSARY, CITATION FORMS, AND ABBREVIATIONS

Publications of the similar material are grouped in a single citation only where it is clear that the material provided is intended to be identical. If some citations appear incomplete, it is because elements were lacking in the citation's source, which is always provided. It is hoped that other Connecticut researchers will communicate bibliographic additions and/or corrections to this book as they use it.

Virtually all out-of-copyright printed matter is available as an image reprint in one or more online locations. The Online Computer Library Center's *WorldCat.org* website tries to index and hyperlink all image reprints.

When two or more FHL film numbers are connected by a dash or the symbol "&," it indicates that the source, as described, may be viewed in its entirety only by viewing all of the films cited. When, however, the film numbers are connected by the word "or," it is meant that the FHL regards the two filmings as duplicative.

Except for the use of postal abbreviation for state names in footnotes, terms which are abbreviated repeatedly in the guide below are all noted here for the reader's convenience. All footnoted towns not described as within some other state are in Connecticut, except for unique cities like Baltimore (MD), Boston (MA), Chicago (IL), New York (NY), and Philadelphia (PA).

The FHL catalog is relied upon for citing most of the Barbour Index's sources. The author, title, repository, and repository location are presented as cataloged, with any detailed catalog description of the birth, marriages, and/or death contained on that microfilm or item. Quotation marks surround a manuscript title only when the document itself includes a title.

For sources that are presented in the main text rather than in footnotes, the citation form is informal. Their citation form is abbreviated to reflect the facts that (1) virtually all cited jurisdictions are in Connecticut, (2) all town vital records were in the possession of town clerks before 1852, (3) virtually all reported microfilms are by and in the FHL, and (4) DAR chapter names are frequently abridged or omitted, especially when an individual author is also named in by the GRC

When a publication date below includes a dash or a question mark, it represents the repository's best estimate for an undated book. Other abbreviations used throughout the bibliography below are:

Abbreviation	For:
137 Connecticut towns	Number of towns with typed volumes in Barbour Collection.
143 Connecticut towns	Number of towns abstracted in the Barbour Index.
149 Connecticut towns	Number of instate towns with vital records by 1850.
AmericanAncestors.org	*https://www.AmericanAncestors.org* (the NEHGS website)
Ancestry.com	*https://www.Ancestry.com*
Arnold copy/records/book	How many town clerks refer to their copies of Barbour's abstraction of their town records

Barbour	Lucius B. Barbour and/or the abstractors he engaged to abstract the Barbour Collection.
Barbour Index	Barbour's statewide index, available only at CSL or on FHL microfilm
Barbour Collection	Barbour statewide Index plus his individual volumes.
BUSTL	Boston University School of Theology Library
Biennial Report (1936)	Connecticut State Examiner, *Biennial Report of the Examiner of Public Records for the Period Ending June 30, 1936* (Hartford: State of CT, 1936)
CA	*Connecticut Ancestry*
CHS	Connecticut Historical Society
CN	*Connecticut Nutmegger*
CSA	Connecticut State Library, State Archives, Hartford
CSG	Connecticut Society of Genealogists
CSL	Connecticut State Library, Hartford
CSL 974….	State Archives, CSL call no. Main Vault 974….
CSL, First 200 Years	CSL, *Connecticut Town Records of the First Two Hundred Years 1620–1820* (Hartford: CSL Reference Desk, 1975) (photocopy of responses to CSL survey by town bound in alpha order, unpaginated)
CT Vital Records	*CSL's CT Vital Records — Additions, Comments, Corrections, Questions on Originals — Not All Towns* Included (Hartford, CSL Reference Desk, various dates) unpaginated in alpha order by town)
DAR	Daughters of the American Revolution
Digital film #	Recent digitization of FHL microfilm, with image numbers
ED	Episcopal Diocese (see note 69)
FamilySearch.org	*https://www.FamilySearch.org* (Website of the Church of Jesus Christ of Latter-day Saints)
FHC	Family History Center
FHL film[s]	Family History Library microfilm number[s]
FHL fiche	Family History Library microfiche number
GOGS	Greater Omaha Genealogical Society
GPC	Genealogical Publishing Company, Baltimore, MD
GPC edition	GPC's republication of Barbour's individual volumes
GRC	Genealogical Records Committee (Reports of DAR Chapters][1104]
Hale Collection	*Charles R. Hale Collection of Headstone Inscriptions* (see notes 71–2)
item[s]	Cataloged section of a FHL microfilm

[1104] Thousands of bound volumes titled "[State of Chapter] *DAR GRC Report*," are detailed in the DAR online catalog. They are digitized and now available only for viewing online at DAR headquarters in Electronic Form, unless they were previously microfilmed by FHL, in which case every effort has been made to cite the particular film, since the FHL does not catalog most of these records specifically as GRC reports.

KHGS	Killingly Historical and Genealogical Society, Inc.
Leclerc	Leclerc, Michael J., *Genealogist's Handbook for New England Research.* 5th ed. (Boston: New England Historic Genealogical Society, 2012)
LoC	Library of Congress, Washington, DC
Morrison	Betty Jean Morrison, *Connecting to Connecticut* (East Hartford, Connecticut Society of Genealogists, 1995)
n.d.	no date for publication
Mss.	Manuscript
NEHGR	New England Historical and Genealogical Register
NEHGS	New England Historic Genealogical Society
NHCHS	New Haven Colony Historical Society
NYGBS	New York Genealogical & Biographical Society
OFPA	Order of the Founders and Patriots of America
Orig. Pub.	Originally Published
p./pp.	page/pages
Registrar	Registrar of Vital Statistics for a Connecticut Town
repr.	reprinted
RG	Record Group in CSA
Ricker or *Ricker Compilation*	Jacquelyn Ladd Ricker, *Ricker Compilation of Vital Records of Early Connecticut,* CD–ROM (Baltimore: Genealogical Publishing Co., 2006)
RSASP	R. Stanton Avery Special Collections
SCWC	Society of Colonial Wars in the State of Connecticut
ser.	series
SLC	Salt Lake City, Utah
S.I.	unknown place of publication
SMD	Society of Mayflower Descendants
TAG	*The American Genealogist*
town	A CT "town" is distinct geographical area which may contain incorporated cities or boroughs, as well as villages, post offices, and railroad depots without a distinct government, equating with the modern concept of township.
Town Clerk	Town Clerk of the subject Connecticut Town
vol.	volume

INDEX OF LOCATIONS

CPSIA information can be obtained
at www.ICGtesting.com
Printed in the USA
FFHW010707221219
56849775-62493FF

9 780806 358956